Lecture Notes in Computer Science   6452

Commenced Publication in 1973
Founding and Former Series Editors:
Gerhard Goos, Juris Hartmanis, and Jan van Leeuwen

Editorial Board

David Hutchison
  Lancaster University, UK
Takeo Kanade
  Carnegie Mellon University, Pittsburgh, PA, USA
Josef Kittler
  University of Surrey, Guildford, UK
Jon M. Kleinberg
  Cornell University, Ithaca, NY, USA
Alfred Kobsa
  University of California, Irvine, CA, USA
Friedemann Mattern
  ETH Zurich, Switzerland
John C. Mitchell
  Stanford University, CA, USA
Moni Naor
  Weizmann Institute of Science, Rehovot, Israel
Oscar Nierstrasz
  University of Bern, Switzerland
C. Pandu Rangan
  Indian Institute of Technology, Madras, India
Bernhard Steffen
  TU Dortmund University, Germany
Madhu Sudan
  Microsoft Research, Cambridge, MA, USA
Demetri Terzopoulos
  University of California, Los Angeles, CA, USA
Doug Tygar
  University of California, Berkeley, CA, USA
Gerhard Weikum
  Max Planck Institute for Informatics, Saarbruecken, Germany

Indranil Gupta Cecilia Mascolo (Eds.)

Middleware 2010

ACM/IFIP/USENIX
11th International Middleware Conference
Bangalore, India, November 29 - December 3, 2010
Proceedings

Volume Editors

Indranil Gupta
University of Illinois at Urbana-Champaign, Center for Computer Science
201 North Goodwin Avenue, Urbana IL 61801-2302, USA
E-mail: indy@illinois.edu

Cecilia Mascolo
Computer Laboratory, University of Cambridge
15 JJ Thomson Avenue, Cambridge, CB3 0FD, UK
E-mail: cecilia.mascolo@cl.cam.ac.uk

Library of Congress Control Number: 2010938797

CR Subject Classification (1998): C.2, H.4, D.2, H.3, H.5, K.6.5

LNCS Sublibrary: SL 2 – Programming and Software Engineering

ISSN   0302-9743
ISBN-10   3-642-16954-6 Springer Berlin Heidelberg New York
ISBN-13   978-3-642-16954-0 Springer Berlin Heidelberg New York

This work is subject to copyright. All rights are reserved, whether the whole or part of the material is concerned, specifically the rights of translation, reprinting, re-use of illustrations, recitation, broadcasting, reproduction on microfilms or in any other way, and storage in data banks. Duplication of this publication or parts thereof is permitted only under the provisions of the German Copyright Law of September 9, 1965, in its current version, and permission for use must always be obtained from Springer. Violations are liable to prosecution under the German Copyright Law.

springer.com

© IFIP International Federation for Information Processing 2010
Printed in Germany

Typesetting: Camera-ready by author, data conversion by Scientific Publishing Services, Chennai, India
Printed on acid-free paper   06/3180

Preface

We are pleased to welcome you to the eleventh edition of the Middleware conference. The program this year is a sign of the robustness, activity, and continued growth of the Middleware community. As computing technology around us has evolved rapidly over the past decade, our notions of middleware have also adapted so that we stay focused on the most challenging and relevant problems for the present and future.

As a result, this year's program features papers that belong to both traditional areas as well as new directions. Cloud computing, social middleware, and transactional memory are some of the vanguard areas that you will find in this year's selection of papers. In addition, topics that have always been central to the community are also prominent this year, including publish-subscribe, multicast, reliability, legacy, location-awareness, trust, and security. The community's wise evolution reflects the dynamic role that middleware continues to play in the development of current software systems.

The program underscores the competitive selection process applied by us and the technical program committee: out of 116 papers submitted this year, we accepted 18 for regular publication. In addition Middleware 2010 also includes a new category of "Big Ideas Papers," which are bold white papers with the potential to drive longer-term innovation in the field. We selected one "big ideas" paper this year. Our industrial track once again brings forth papers that explore middleware foundations in the context of industrial practice. Finally, multiple workshops and a doctoral symposium round off Middleware this year, making it an attractive conference for students, faculty, researchers, and practitioners.

We are very deeply grateful to everyone who has contributed to the conference this year. The technical program committee worked incredibly hard to provide high quality reviews and continued to be highly engaged in discussing the papers after all reviews were submitted. We acknowledge the work of the shepherds who helped some of the authors in improving the papers. We thank all our external reviewers. We owe our gratitude to the organizing committee, the steering committee, and chairs of previous conferences, who have all provided valuable advice and a needed continuity from previous years. Finally, we thank all the authors who have submitted to this conference for their work, support and willingness to share their results.

September 2010

Indranil Gupta
Cecilia Mascolo

Organization

Middleware 2010 was organized under the joint sponsorship of the Association for Computing Machinery (ACM), the International Federation for Information Processing (IFIP), and USENIX.

Organizing Committee

Conference Chair	Guruduth Banavar (IBM)
Deputy General Chair	Koustuv Dasgupta (Xerox India Innovation Hub)
Program Committee Chair	Indranil Gupta (University of Illinios at Urbana-Champain, USA)
	Cecilia Mascolo (University of Cambridge, UK)
Industrial Track Chairs	Lucy Cherkasova (HP Labs, USA)
	Rajeev Rastogi (Bell Labs, USA)
Publicity Chairs	Ningfang Mi (College of William and Mary, USA)
	Pushpendra Singh (Indraprashtha Institute of Information Technology, India)
Information Officer	Amel Bennaceur (INRIA, France)
Tutorials Chair	Oriana Riva (ETH, Switzerland)
Workshops Chair	Fabio Kon (University of Sao Paulo, Brazil)
Local Arrangements Chair	Malolan Chetlur (IBM Research, India)
Poster and Demonstrations Chair	Akshat Verma (IBM Research, India)
Steering Committee Chair	Gordon Blair (University of Lancaster, UK)
Proceedings Chair	Paul Grace (University of Lancaster, UK)
Doctoral Symposium Chair	Bettina Kemme (McGill University, Canada)

Steering Committee

Gordon Blair (Chair)	Lancaster University, UK
Jan De Meer	SmartSpaceLab, Germany
Hans-Arno Jacobsen	University of Toronto, Canada
Elie Najm	ENST, France
Renato Cerqueira	PUC-RIO, Brazil
Nalini Venkatasubramanian	UC Irvine, USA
Wouter Joosen	KUL-DistriNet, Belgium
Valrie ISSARNY	INRIA, France

Roy Campbell — University of Illinois at Urbana-Champaign, USA
Brian F. Cooper — Google, USA
Jean Bacon — University of Cambridge Computer Laboratory, UK
Fred Douglis — IBM Research, USA

Program Committee

Karl Aberer — EPFL, Switzerland
Katerina Argyraki — EPFL, Switzerland
Jean Bacon — University of Cambridge, UK
Christian Becker — University of Mannheim, Germany
Yolande Berbers — KUL-DistriNet, Belgium
Ranjita Bhagwan — Microsoft Research, India
Bharat Bhargava — Purdue University, USA
Gordon Blair — University of Lancaster, UK
Raj Kumar Buyya — University of Melbourne, Australia
Renato Cerqueira — PUC-Rio, Brazil
Roy Campbell — University of Illinois at Urbana-Champaign, USA
Brian F. Cooper — Google, USA
Geoff Coulson — University of Lancaster, UK
Anwitaman Datta — NTU, Singapore
Jan De Meer — SmartSpaceLab, Germany
Fred Douglis — EMC Data Domain, USA
Frank Eliasson — University of Oslo, Norway
Markus Endler — PUC-Rio, Brazil
Paulo Ferreira — Technical University of Lisbon, Portugal
Sathish Gopalakrishnan — University of British Columbia, Canada
Paul Grace — University of Lancaster, UK
Jeff Hammerbacher — Cloudera, USA
Qi Han — Colorado School of Mines, USA
Steven Hand — University of Cambridge, UK
Gang Huang — Peking University, China
Valerie Issarny — INRIA, France
Hans-Arno Jacobsen — University of Toronto, Canada
Wouter Joosen — KUL-DistriNet, Belgium
Bettina Kemme — McGill University, Canada
Anne-Marie Kermarrec — INRIA, France
Fabio Kon — University of Sao Paulo, Brazil
Dejan Milojicic — HP Labs, USA

Ramses Morales   Xerox, USA
David O'Hallaron   CMU/Intel, USA
Gian Pietro Picco   University of Trento, Italy
Peter Pietzuch   Imperial College, UK
Oriana Riva   ETH, Switzerland
Antony Rowstron   Microsoft Research Cambridge, UK
Francois Taiani   Lancaster University, UK
Peter Triantafillou   University of Patras, Greece
Rick Schantz   BBN Technologies, USA
Nalini Venkatasubramanian UCI, USA
Akshat Verma   IBM Research, India
Zheng Zhang   Microsoft Research Asia, China
Ben Zhao   UC Santa Barbara, USA

External Referees

Mourad Alia
Juliana F. Aquino
Gustavo L.B. Baptista
Nicolas Bonvin
Raphael Y. Camargo
Michele Catasta
Alex Cheung
Sand Luz Correa
Fabio Costa
Gregory Farnum
Joo Eduardo Ferreira
Jos Viterbo Filho
Marco Aurlio Gerosa
Daniel Gmach
Stefan Guna
Lin Guo
Vinay Gupta
Laura Itzel
Gholam Abbas Angouti Kolouche
Patrick Lee
Shen Lin
Nebil Ben Mabrouk
Verena Majuntke
Marcelo Malcher

Bala Maniymaran
Alan Marchiori
Giuliano Mega
Arif Merchant
Rammohan Narendula
Partha Pal
Kurt Rohloff
Romain Rouvoy
Françoise Sailhan
Gregor Schiele
Fred Schneider
Reza Sherafat
Francisco J. Silva e Silva
Richard Süselbeck
Amir Taherkordi
Naweed Tajuddin
Alessandra Toninelli
Liu Xin
Chunyang Ye
Surender Reddy Yerva
Young Yoon
Na Yu
Narasimha Raghavan Veeraragavan
Le Hung Vu

Table of Contents

Cloud Computing

FLEX: A Slot Allocation Scheduling Optimizer for MapReduce
Workloads 1
    Joel Wolf, Deepak Rajan, Kirsten Hildrum, Rohit Khandekar,
    Vibhore Kumar, Sujay Parekh, Kun-Lung Wu, and Andrey Balmin

Adapting Distributed Real-Time and Embedded Pub/Sub Middleware
for Cloud Computing Environments 21
    Joe Hoffert, Douglas C. Schmidt, and Aniruddha Gokhale

BrownMap: Enforcing Power Budget in Shared Data Centers 42
    Akshat Verma, Pradipta De, Vijay Mann, Tapan Nayak,
    Amit Purohit, Gargi Dasgupta, and Ravi Kothari

Data Management

A Dynamic Data Middleware Cache for Rapidly-Growing Scientific
Repositories 64
    Tanu Malik, Xiaodan Wang, Philip Little, Amitabh Chaudhary, and
    Ani Thakar

Anonygator: Privacy and Integrity Preserving Data Aggregation 85
    Krishna P.N. Puttaswamy, Ranjita Bhagwan, and
    Venkata N. Padmanabhan

Middleware for a Re-configurable Distributed Archival Store Based on
Secret Sharing 107
    Shiva Chaitanya, Dharani Vijayakumar, Bhuvan Urgaonkar, and
    Anand Sivasubramaniam

Publish-Subscribe and Multicast Systems

Parametric Subscriptions for Content-Based Publish/Subscribe
Networks 128
    K.R. Jayaram, Chamikara Jayalath, and Patrick Eugster

KEVLAR: A Flexible Infrastructure for Wide-Area Collaborative
Applications 148
    Qi Huang, Daniel A. Freedman, Ymir Vigfusson, Ken Birman, and
    Bo Peng

FaReCast: Fast, Reliable Application Layer Multicast for Flash
Dissemination 169
    Kyungbaek Kim, Sharad Mehrotra, and Nalini Venkatasubramanian

Social and Location-Aware Middleware

The Gossple Anonymous Social Network 191
    Marin Bertier, Davide Frey, Rachid Guerraoui,
    Anne-Marie Kermarrec, and Vincent Leroy

Prometheus: User-Controlled P2P Social Data Management for
Socially-Aware Applications 212
    Nicolas Kourtellis, Joshua Finnis, Paul Anderson,
    Jeremy Blackburn, Cristian Borcea, and Adriana Iamnitchi

PerPos: A Translucent Positioning Middleware Supporting Adaptation
of Internal Positioning Processes 232
    Jakob Langdal, Kari R. Schougaard, Mikkel B. Kjærgaard, and
    Thomas Toftkjær

Reliability and Legacy

dFault: Fault Localization in Large-Scale Peer-to-Peer Systems 252
    Pawan Prakash, Ramana Rao Kompella,
    Venugopalan Ramasubramanian, and Ranveer Chandra

Bridging the Gap between Legacy Services and Web Services 273
    Tegawendé F. Bissyandé, Laurent Réveillère,
    Yérom-David Bromberg, Julia L. Lawall, and Gilles Muller

Trust and Security

Enforcing End-to-End Application Security in the Cloud
(Big Ideas Paper) 293
    Jean Bacon, David Evans, David M. Eyers, Matteo Migliavacca,
    Peter Pietzuch, and Brian Shand

LiFTinG: Lightweight Freerider-Tracking in Gossip.................... 313
    Rachid Guerraoui, Kévin Huguenin, Anne-Marie Kermarrec,
    Maxime Monod, and Swagatika Prusty

Distributed Middleware Enforcement of Event Flow Security Policy 334
    Matteo Migliavacca, Ioannis Papagiannis, David M. Eyers,
    Brian Shand, Jean Bacon, and Peter Pietzuch

Transactional Memory

Automatically Generating Symbolic Prefetches for Distributed
Transactional Memories.. 355
   Alokika Dash and Brian Demsky

Asynchronous Lease-Based Replication of Software Transactional
Memory 376
   Nuno Carvalho, Paolo Romano, and Luís Rodrigues

Author Index.. 397

FLEX: A Slot Allocation Scheduling Optimizer for MapReduce Workloads

Joel Wolf[1], Deepak Rajan[1], Kirsten Hildrum[1], Rohit Khandekar[1],
Vibhore Kumar[1], Sujay Parekh[1], Kun-Lung Wu[1], and Andrey Balmin[2]

[1] IBM Watson Research Center, Hawthorne NY 10532, USA
{jlwolf,drajan,hildrum,rohitk,vibhorek,sujay,klwu}@us.ibm.com
[2] IBM Almaden Research Center, San Jose CA 95120, USA
abalmin@us.ibm.com

Abstract. Originally, MapReduce implementations such as *Hadoop* employed *First In First Out* (FIFO) scheduling, but such simple schemes cause job starvation. The *Hadoop Fair Scheduler* (HFS) is a slot-based MapReduce scheme designed to ensure a degree of fairness among the jobs, by guaranteeing each job at least some minimum number of allocated slots. Our prime contribution in this paper is a different, *flexible* scheduling allocation scheme, known as FLEX. Our goal is to optimize any of a variety of standard scheduling theory metrics (response time, stretch, makespan and *Service Level Agreements* (SLAs), among others) while ensuring the same minimum job slot guarantees as in HFS, and maximum job slot guarantees as well. The FLEX allocation scheduler can be regarded as an add-on module that works synergistically with HFS. We describe the mathematical basis for FLEX, and compare it with FIFO and HFS in a variety of experiments.

Keywords: MapReduce, Scheduling, Allocation, Optimization.

1 Introduction

The MapReduce programming model [1] has been growing dramatically in popularity for a number of years now. There are many good reasons for this success. Most are related to MapReduce's inherent simplicity of use, even when applied to large applications and installations. For example, MapReduce work is designed to be parallelized automatically. It can be implemented on large clusters of commodity hosts, and it inherently scales well. Scheduling, fault tolerance and necessary communications are all handled automatically, without direct user assistance. Finally, and perhaps most importantly, the programming of MapReduce applications is relatively straight-forward, and thus appropriate for less sophisticated programmers. These benefits, in turn, result in lower costs.

Originally MapReduce was aimed at large (generally periodic) production batch jobs. As such, the natural goal would be to decrease the length of time required for a batch window. (A dual goal might be to maximize the number of jobs which could be accommodated within a fixed batch window, effectively maximizing throughput.) For such scenarios, a simple job scheduling scheme such as *First In, First Out* (FIFO) works very well. FIFO was, in fact, the first scheduler implemented in Google's MapReduce environment and in Hadoop [2], an opensource MapReduce implementation. Over time, however, the use of MapReduce has evolved in the natural and standard manner, towards more user interaction. There are now many more *ad-hoc* query MapReduce jobs, and these share cluster resources with the batch production work. For users who submit these queries, expecting quick results, schemes like FIFO do not work well. That is because a large job can "starve" a small, user-submitted job which arrives even a little later. Worse, if the large job was a batch submission, the exact completion time of that job might not even be regarded as particularly important.

This basic unfairness associated with FIFO scheduling motivated Zaharia et. al. to build the *Hadoop Fair Scheduler* HFS [3],[5]. (See [4] for the Hadoop implementation.) It is the top layer of HFS that is most closely aligned with our current paper. To understand this, we briefly describe MapReduce in more detail, and then the goal and design of HFS itself.

MapReduce jobs, consist, as the name implies, of two processing phases. Each phase is broken into multiple independent *tasks*, the nature of which depends on the phase. In the *Map* phase the tasks consist of the steps of scanning and processing (extracting information) from equal-sized *blocks* of input data. Each block is typically replicated on disks in three separate racks of hosts (in Hadoop, for example, using the HDFS file system). The output of the Map phase is a set of key-value pairs. These intermediate results are also stored on disk. Each of the Reduce phase tasks corresponds to a partitioned subset of the keys of the intermediate results. There is a shuffle step in which all relevant data from all Map phase output is transmitted across the network, a sort step, and finally a processing step (which may consist of transformation, aggregation, filtering and/or summarization).

HFS can be said to consist of two hierarchical algorithmic layers, which in our terminology will be called the *allocation* layer and the *assignment* layer.

Allocation Layer. Each host is assumed to be capable of simultaneously handling some maximum number of Map phase tasks and some maximum number of Reduce phase tasks. These are the number of *Map slots* and *Reduce slots*, respectively. Aggregating these slots over all the hosts in the cluster, we compute the total number of Map slots, and similarly the total number of Reduce slots. The role of the allocation layer scheme is to partition the Map slots among the active Map jobs in some intelligent manner, and similarly the number of Reduce slots among the active Reduce jobs. In [3] and [5], the node that produces these allocations is known as the *master*. We will call the HFS allocation layer FAIR.

Assignment Layer. It is this layer that makes the actual job task assignment decisions, attempting to honor the allocation decisions made at the allocation level to the extent possible. Host *slaves* report any task completions at *heartbeat* epochs (on the order of a few seconds). Such completions free up slots, and also incrementally affect the number of slots currently assigned to the various jobs. The current slot assignment numbers for jobs are then subtracted from the job allocation goals. This yields an effective ordering of the jobs, from most relatively underallocated to most relatively overallocated. For each currently unassigned slot, the HFS assignment model then finds an "appropriate" task from the most relatively underallocated job that has one, assigns it to the slot, and performs bookkeeping. It may not find an appropriate task for a job, for example, because of host and/or rack affinity issues. That is why HFS *relaxes* fidelity to the precise dictates of the master allocation goals for a time. This is known as *delay scheduling*, and described in [3] and [5].

Let S denote the total number of Map slots. Then the FAIR allocation scheme is *fair* in the following sense: It computes, for each of J Map phase jobs j, a minimum number m_j of Map slots. This minimum number is chosen so that the sum $\sum_{j=1}^{J} m_j \leq S$. (The minima are simply normalized if necessary.) This minimum number m_j acts as a fairness guarantee, because FAIR will always allocate a number of Map slots $s_j \geq m_j$, thereby preventing job starvation. Slack (the difference $S - \sum_{j=1}^{J} m_j$) is allocated in FAIR according to a very simple waterline-based scheme (which also emphasizes fairness). Analogous statements hold for the Reduce phase.

While HFS [3] mentions standard scheduling metrics such as throughput or average response time as a goal of the scheduler, and compares its scheduler to others in terms of these, FAIR makes no direct attempt to optimize such metrics. It is worth noting that schedules designed to optimize one metric will generally be quite different from those designed to optimize another.

1.1 Our Contributions

Our prime contribution in this paper is a different, *flexible* allocation scheme, known as FLEX. The goal of our FLEX algorithm is to optimize any of a variety of standard scheduling theory metrics while ensuring the same minimum job slot guarantees as in FAIR. Thus FLEX will also be fair in the sense of [3]: It avoids job starvation just as FAIR does. The metrics can be chosen by the system administrator on a cluster-wide basis, or by individual users on a job-by-job basis. And these metrics can be chosen from a menu that includes response time, makespan (dual to throughput), and any of several metrics which (reward or) penalize job completion times compared to possible deadlines. More generally, one could imagine negotiating *Service Level Agreements* (SLAs) with MapReduce users for which the penalty depends on the level of service achieved. (Formally, this can be described by a step function, each step corresponding to the penalty that would be incurred by missing the previous pseudo-deadline but making the next one.) FLEX can work towards optimizing any combination of these metrics while simultaneously ensuring fairness. It can minimize either the sum (and, equivalently, the average) of all the individual job penalty functions or the maximum of all of them. While we expect most system administrators to make a single choice of metric, there are natural examples of job-by-job choices. For example, one might employ different metrics for batch jobs and ad-hoc queries.

Note that the FLEX allocation scheduler can be regarded as either a standalone replacement to FAIR *or* as an add-on module that simply works synergistically with FAIR: To understand this point imagine HFS handing FLEX the Map phase minimum slots $m_1, ..., m_J$. After optimizing the appropriate scheduling metrics, FLEX would hand back slot allocations $s_1, ..., s_J$ such that $s_j \geq m_j$ for all jobs j, and there is no slack: $\sum_{j=1}^{J} s_j = S$. These values s_j can then serve as *revised* minima to be handed to FAIR. Because there is no slack, the waterline component of FAIR will be neutralized. Thus FAIR will produce the properly optimized solution $s_1, ..., s_J$. A similar statement holds for the Reduce phase.

Additionally, our FLEX allocation scheme can handle maximum slots M_j for a given job j as well as minima, and they are implicitly dealt with in FAIR as well. For example, at the very end of the Map phase the number of remaining tasks for a particular job might be less than the total number of Map slots S. There is clearly no reason to allocate more slots than the current demand.

The remainder of this paper is organized as follows. An overview of the mathematical concepts behind our FLEX scheduler is given in Section 2. The algorithmic details of FLEX are given in Section 3. Simulation and cluster experiments designed to show the effectiveness of FLEX are described in Section 4. Related MapReduce scheduling work is described in Section 5. Finally, conclusions and future work are given in Section 6.

2 Scheduling Theory Concepts

We give an overview of the fundamental mathematical concepts behind multi-processor task scheduling, focusing on how they apply to MapReduce scheduling in general, and to FLEX in particular. We begin by describing five broad categories of penalty functions, including multiple variants of each. Then, we describe epoch-based scheduling. Finally, we define the notion of a *speedup* function, and how it pertains to the notions of *moldable* and *malleable* scheduling. The algorithmic details of FLEX (a penalty-function-specific, malleable, epoch-based scheduler) will be covered in the next section.

2.1 Penalty Functions

Think of each job as having a penalty function which measures the cost of completing that job at a particular time. Thus each of the five subfigures in Fig. 1 describes the form of a particular per job penalty function. The X-axis represents the completion time of that job, while the Y-axis represents the penalty. We point out that there can still be many potential problem variants for most of them. These combinatorial alternatives involve, for example, whether or not to incorporate non-unit weights into the penalty functions. (In some cases specific weight choices will have special meanings. In other cases they are used basically to define the relative importance of each job.) Also, it generally makes sense either to minimize the sum of all the per job penalty functions, or to minimize the maximum of all the per job penalty functions. The former case is referred to as a *minisum* problem, and the latter case as a *minimax* problem. The five penalty function categories are as follows.

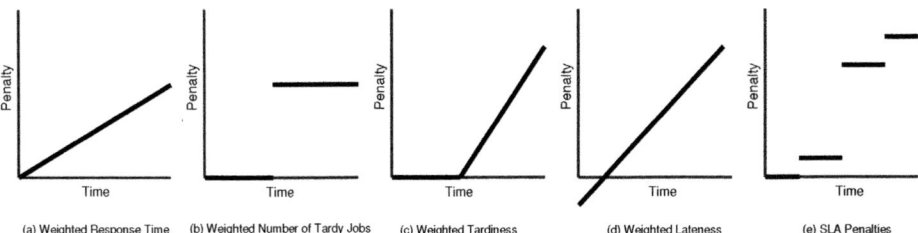

Fig. 1. Per Job Metrics

Response Time. The metric illustrated in Fig. 1(a) is probably the most commonly employed in computer science. (The weight is the slope of the linear function.) Three natural examples come to mind. Solving the minisum problem would minimize either the average response time or the weighted average response time of all the jobs. In the unweighted case, the minimax problem would be used to minimize the *makespan* of the jobs. This is the completion time of the last job to finish and is appropriate for optimizing batch work. Suppose the *work* (or time required to perform job j in isolation) is W_j. Then the completion time of a job divided by W_j is known as the *stretch* of the job, a measure of how delayed the job will be by having to share the system resources with other jobs. Thus, solving a minisum problem while employing weights $1/W_j$ will minimize the average stretch of the jobs. Similarly, solving a minimax problem while employing weights $1/W_j$ will minimize the maximum stretch. Either of these are excellent *fairness* measures, and are in fact precisely the two metrics used in [6]. (They are not, however, formally considered in [3] and [5].)

Number of Tardy Jobs. In this case each job j has a *deadline*, say d_j. In this case only the minisum problem is appropriate. The weight is the height of the "step" in Fig. 1(b). The unweighted case counts the number of jobs that miss their deadlines. But the weighted case makes sense as well.

Tardiness. Again, each job j has a deadline d_j. The tardiness metric generalizes the response time metric, which can be said to employ deadlines at time 0. Only tardy jobs are "charged", and the slope of the non-flat line segment in Fig. 1(c) is the weight. It makes sense to speak of either minisum or minimax tardiness problems, both either weighted or unweighted.

Lateness. Again, each job j has a deadline d_j. The lateness metric generalizes response time also, with the same explanation as that of tardiness above. As before, the weight is the slope of the line. Note that "early" jobs are actually rewarded rather than penalized, making this the only potentially negative metric. The minisum variant differs from the response time metric by an additive constant, and thus can be solved in exactly the same manner as that problem. But the minimax problem is legitimately interesting in its own right. See Fig. 1(d).

SLA Costs. In this metric each job j has potentially multiple pseudo-deadlines $d_{i,j}$ which increase with i. And the penalties $w_{i,j}$ increase with i also. This yields the metric of Fig. 1(e), consisting of a step function for each job, clearly a generalization of the weighted number of tardy jobs metric. As in that case, only the minisum problem is appropriate. One can think of this metric as the total cost charged to the provider based on a pre-negotiated SLA contract.

All of these metrics (except, perhaps, the last) has been studied extensively in the scheduling theory literature. See [7], [8] and [9]. We will borrow and adapt some of these techniques for use in our FLEX scheduling algorithm.

2.2 Epoch-Based Scheduling

FLEX is an example of an *epoch*-based allocation scheduler. This means that it partitions time into epochs of some fixed length T. So if time starts at $t = 0$ the epochs will start at times 0, T, $2T$, $3T$ and so on. Label these accordingly. The scheduler will produce allocations that will be in effect for one epoch, so that the eth epoch allocations will be honored from time eT to time $(e+1)T$. Obviously the work of FLEX for the eth epoch must be completed by the start time eT of that epoch. If T is relatively small it follows that FLEX must be comparably fast.

There will actually be two instances of FLEX running at any given time, one for the active Map phase jobs and one for the active Reduce phase jobs. We will describe the Map instance below, but the Reduce instance is comparable.

The Map instance of FLEX receives input describing the total number of Map slots in the system, the number of active Map jobs, the minimum and maximum number of slots per active Map job, and estimates of the remaining execution times required for each of the active Map jobs. Then the algorithm outputs high quality allocations of slots to these jobs. These allocations may be time-dependent in the sense that there may be several consecutive *intervals*, say I, of different allocation levels. In more detail, consider the eth epoch. The output will take the form $(s_{1,1}, \ldots, s_{1,J}, T_0, T_1), \ldots, (s_{I,1}, \ldots, s_{I,J}, T_{I-1}, T_I)$, where $T_0 = eT$, the ith interval is the time between T_{i-1} and T_i, and $s_{i,j}$ represents the number of slots allocated to job j in interval i. Allocations for the eth epoch will likely extend beyond the start time of the $(e+1)$st epoch. That is, we expect that $T_I > (e+1)T$. But any of these allocation decisions will be superseded by the decisions of newer epochs. In fact, it is expected that the completion time of even the *first* of the consecutive intervals in the eth epoch will typically exceed the length of an epoch, so that $T_1 > (e+1)T$. This means that generally only the first interval in the FLEX output will actually be enforced by the assignment model during each epoch.

An advantage of an epoch-based scheme is its resilience to inaccuracies in input data that might arise from a heterogeneous cluster environment. Epoch by epoch, FLEX automatically corrects its solution in light of better estimates and system state changes.

2.3 Speedup Functions

From a scheduling perspective a key feature of either the Map or Reduce phase of a MapReduce job is that it is *parallelizable*. Roughly speaking, it is composed of

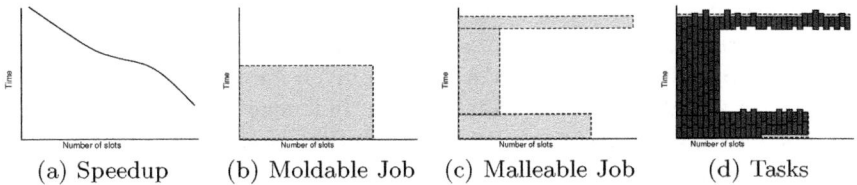

Fig. 2. Moldable and Malleable Scheduling

many atomic tasks which are effectively independent of each other and therefore can be performed on a relatively arbitrary number of (multiple slots in) multiple hosts simultaneously. If a given job is allocated more of these slots it will complete in less time. In the case of the Map phase these atomic tasks correspond to the blocks. In the case of the Reduce phase the atomic tasks are created on the fly, based on keys. The FLEX scheme takes advantage of this additional structure inherent in the MapReduce paradigm.

We now describe the relevant scheduling theory concepts formally. See, for example, [9]. Consider a total of S homogeneous hosts. (In our scenario the hosts will actually be the Map or Reduce slots in the cluster.) A job is said to be *parallel* if it can be performed using some number of hosts $1 \leq s \leq S$ simultaneously, with an execution time E. (One can think geometrically of this job as a rectangle with width equal to the number of hosts s, and height equal to the execution time E.) A job is said to be *parallelizable* if it can be performed variously on an arbitrary number $1 \leq s \leq S$ of hosts simultaneously, with an execution time $F(s)$ that depends on the number of hosts allocated. The execution time function F is known as the *speedup* function. It can be assumed without loss of generality to be non-increasing, because if $F(s) < F(s+1)$ it would be better to simply leave one host idle. This would result in a new (replacement) speedup function $\bar{F}$ for which $\bar{F}(s+1) = \bar{F}(s) = F(s)$. One can think, also without loss of generality, of a job which can be performed on a subset $P \subseteq \{1, ..., S\}$ of possible allocations of hosts as being parallelizable: simply define $F(s) = \min_{\{p \in P | p \leq s\}} F(p)$, where, as per the usual convention, the empty set has minimum ∞. In this sense parallelizable is a generalization of parallel.

As we shall describe below, to a good approximation both the Map and Reduce phases of a MapReduce job have such speedup functions. Fig. 2(a) illustrates a possible speedup function in a MapReduce context. (Note that the X-axis is described in terms of allocated slots.)

2.4 Moldable and Malleable Scheduling

The problem of scheduling multiple parallel jobs in order to minimize some given metric can be visualized as a problem of packing rectangles, with job start times as the decision variables. Parallel scheduling has been studied extensively in the scheduling literature [9]. Problems for most of the natural metrics are NP-hard. See, for example, [10] for the makespan metric, and [11] for the weighted and unweighted response time metrics.

Parallelizable scheduling is a generalization of parallel scheduling. The simplest such variant is known as *moldable* scheduling. Here the problem is to schedule multiple parallelizable jobs to optimize a given metric. The number of hosts is treated as an additional decision variable, but once this allocation is chosen it cannot be changed during the entire execution of the job. The name comes because the rectangles themselves can be thought of as moldable: Pulling a rectangle wider (that is, giving a job more hosts) has the effect of making the rectangle less high (that is, executing the job faster). Fig. 2(b) illustrates a potential choice of host (slot) allocations for a moldable job in a MapReduce context. The top-right vertex in the rectangle corresponds to a point on the speedup function of Fig. 2(a). Moldable scheduling problems can sometimes be solved by using the parallel scheduling problem algorithm as a subroutine. See, for example, [12] for makespan, and [11] for weighted and unweighted response time. In each of these cases, the approximation factor of the parallel algorithm is retained.

Finally, one can generalize moldable scheduling as well, to so-called *malleable* scheduling. Here the problem is to schedule multiple parallelizable jobs to optimize a given metric, as before. But instead of making a permanent decision as to the host allocations each job can proceed in multiple intervals. Different intervals can involve different allocations. Each interval contributes a portion of the total work required to perform the job. Fig. 2(c) illustrates a potential three interval choice of host (slot) allocations for a malleable job in a MapReduce context. See, for example, [13] for makespan.

The optimal malleable schedule for a particular scheduling problem instance will have a cost less than or equal to that of the optimal moldable schedule for the same problem instance, since moldable schedules are also malleable. In this paper we are attempting to find an optimal malleable scheduling solution for each of the relevant objective functions. But we will first solve the moldable scheduling problem. The solution there will then help us to solve the more general malleable problem.

2.5 Malleable Scheduling and the Model

Now we explore how well the MapReduce model fits the malleable scheduling framework. There are several aspects to the answer.

To begin with, the parallel job structure in MapReduce is a direct consequence of the decomposition into small, independent atomic tasks. Consider the assignment layer. Its role is to approximate at any given time the decisions of the allocation layer by assigning job tasks. Consider Fig. 2(d). Over time, the assignment layer will nearly replicate the malleable allocation decisions given in Fig. 2(c) by a set of job task to slot decisions. The approximation is not perfect, for several reasons: First, slots may not free up at precisely the time predicted by the allocation layer. So new task slots won't be assigned perfectly: at the bottom of each interval the rectangle may be slightly jagged. Likewise, slots may not end at precisely the time predicted by the allocation layer. Thus at the top of each interval the rectangle may also be slightly jagged. Finally, the assignment layer may relax adherence to the exact allocation goals for the various jobs, for example, in order to ensure host or rack locality [3],[5].

FLEX: A Slot Allocation Scheduling Optimizer for MapReduce Workloads   9

But the first two are modest approximations *because* individual task times are small relative to the total time required for the job. And discrepancies between the allocation layer goals and the assignment layer are modest by definition. In summary, as illustrated in Figures 2(c-d), the malleable scheduling model fits the reality of the MapReduce paradigm closely.

Moreover, because the tasks are independent, the total amount of work involved in a job is essentially the sum of the work of the individual tasks. Therefore, in conjunction with the statements above, we can actually assume a speedup function of a very special kind: The speedup should be close to *linear*, meaning a speedup function of the form $F(s) = C/s$ between its minimum and maximum numbers of slots. (Here C is a constant for a job proportional to the amount of work required to perform that job.) Note that this is not a statement particularly affected by the factors such as locality. Such factors would affect the constant, not the shape of the speedup function.

Speedup functions for individual jobs must be estimated in order for FLEX to do its job. Fortunately, by assuming relative uniformity among the job task times, we can repeatedly extrapolate the times for the remaining tasks from the times of those tasks already completed. The refined estimates should naturally become more accurate as the job progresses, epoch by epoch. Periodic jobs can also be seeded with speedup functions obtained from past job instances.

3   FLEX Algorithmic Details

With these preliminaries we are ready to describe FLEX. As already noted, FLEX works identically for either the Map or the Reduce phase, so we describe it in a phase-agnostic manner. The FLEX algorithm depends on two key ideas:

1. Given any ordering of the jobs we will devise a *Malleable Packing Scheme* (MPS) to compute a high quality schedule. In fact, it turns out that for any of our possible metrics, there will exist a job ordering for which the MPS schedule will actually be optimal. (The job ordering is strictly input to the packing scheme. There is no guarantee, for example, that the jobs will complete in that order in the MPS schedule.)
2. Unfortunately, finding the job ordering that yields an optimal MPS solution is difficult. We instead find a high quality ordering for any of our possible metrics in one of two ways: One approach is to employ an essentially *generic* algorithm to solve a so-called *Resource Allocation Problem* (RAP). The solution to this RAP will actually be optimal in the context of moldable scheduling, assuming positive minima for each job. In terms of malleable schedules the solution will not be optimal. This leads to the second approach. We create better schemes which are *specific* to selected metrics. (We must omit these details due to lack of space.)

Combining all of this into a single algorithm, FLEX creates a generic ordering and at most a modest number of specific orderings, feeding each of them to MPS. The final output is the best solution MPS found. Now we give the details.

3.1 Malleable Packing Scheme

Fig. 3 contains the pseudocode for the malleable packing scheme. Given a priority ordering, the scheme proceeds iteratively. At any iteration a *current* list $\mathcal{L}$ of jobs is maintained, ordered by priority. Time is initialized to $T_0 = 0$. The current list $\mathcal{L}$ is initialized to be all of the jobs, and one job is removed from $\mathcal{L}$ at the completion time T_i of each iteration i. Call the time interval during iteration i (from time T_{i-1} to T_i) an *interval*. The number of slots allocated to a given job may vary from interval to interval, thus producing a malleable schedule.

```
 1: Set time T₀ = 0
 2: Create list ℒ = {1,...,J} of jobs, ordered by priority
 3: for i = 1 to J do
 4:     Allocate mⱼ slots to each job j ∈ ℒ
 5:     Set L = ℒ, with implied ordering
 6:     Compute slack s = S - ∑ⱼ∈L mⱼ
 7:     while s > 0 do
 8:         Allocate min(s, Mⱼ - mⱼ) additional slots to highest priority job j ∈ L
 9:         Set L = L \ {j}
10:         Set s = s - min(s, Mⱼ - mⱼ)
11:     end while
12:     Find first job j ∈ ℒ to complete under given allocations
13:     Set Tᵢ to be the completion time of job j
14:     Set ℒ = ℒ \ {j}
15:     Compute remaining work for jobs in ℒ after time Tᵢ
16: end for
```

Fig. 3. Malleable Packing Scheme Pseudocode

The ith iteration of the algorithm involves the following steps: First, the scheme allocates the minimum number m_j of slots to each job $j \in \mathcal{L}$. This is feasible, since the minima have been normalized, if necessary, during a precomputation step. (This idea is employed by the FAIR scheduler [4] in addition to our scheme.) After allocating these minima, some slack may remain. This slack can be computed as $s = S - \sum_{j \in L} m_j$. The idea is to allocate the remaining allowable slots $M_j - m_j$ to the jobs j in priority order. The first several may get their full allocations, and those jobs will be allocated their maximum number of slots, namely $M_j = m_j + (M_j - m_j)$. But ultimately all S slots may get allocated in this manner, leaving at most one job with a "partial" remaining allocation of slots, and all jobs having lower priority with only their original, minimum number of slots. (The formal details of these steps are given in the pseudocode.) Given this set of job allocations, one of the jobs j will complete first, at time T_i. (Ties among jobs may be adjudicated in priority order.) Now job j is removed from $\mathcal{L}$, and the necessary bookkeeping is performed to compute the remaining work past time T_i for those jobs remaining in $\mathcal{L}$. After J iterations (and J intervals) the list $\mathcal{L}$ will be depleted and the malleable schedule created.

FLEX: A Slot Allocation Scheduling Optimizer for MapReduce Workloads 11

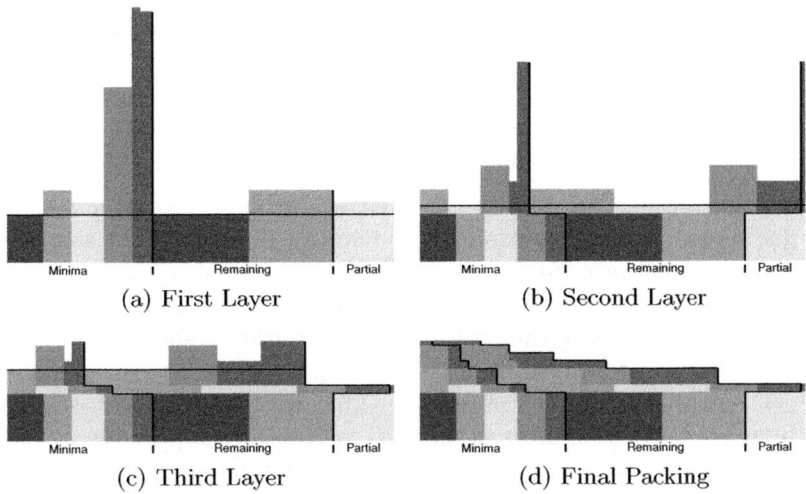

Fig. 4. Malleable Packing Scheme

Fig. 4(a-c) show the first three "intervals" in the malleable packing iterative process for a 6-job example. The priority ordering is given as a rainbow coloring (red, orange, yellow, green, blue and violet). Note the jobs getting their minimum number of slots, the jobs which get their remaining number of slots (up to their maximum), and the single job getting a partial number of slots between its minimum and its maximum. At each of these intervals the completion time T_i is shown as a horizontal line. (The interval extends from the previous time T_{i-1} to the current time T_i, as noted, and the portion of the schedule beyond this time is discarded.) Note that each new iteration involves one fewer job – this job may or may *not* be the next job in the priority ordering. The final malleable packing is shown in Fig. 4(d). In this example there are 6 intervals.

The following lemma states that under linear speedup assumption, for any of the metrics considered here, there exists an ordering of jobs such that the MPS schedule is optimum. The proof of this lemma is omitted due to lack of space.

Lemma 1. *Assume that each job satisfies linear speedup, i.e., the speedup function of job j has the form $F_j(s) = C_j/s$ where C_j is a constant depending on j. Fix any minisum or minimax aggregate objective function of non-decreasing per job penalty functions of the completion time of the jobs. There exists an ordering $\mathcal{L}^*$ of the jobs such that the MPS algorithm in Fig. 3 with $\mathcal{L} = \mathcal{L}^*$ outputs an optimum schedule for the given objective function.*

3.2 Finding a High-Quality Priority Ordering

Considering Lemma 1, we would like to find an ordering $\mathcal{L}$ on jobs for which the MPS algorithm performs well. Unfortunately, finding optimum such an ordering is NP-hard for many of our metrics.

We will therefore determine the priority ordering of jobs to use in the MPS by solving a simplified variant of the overall scheduling problem. Specifically, the completion time ordering of the jobs for this algorithm will become the input priority ordering to MPS. In the case of the generic scheme the simplified problem will be a moldable version of the original problem. (In the case of the metric-specific schemes a closer, malleable version of the problem is considered.)

Generic Scheme. The good news is that regardless of the specific metric chosen, finding the optimal moldable schedule can be formulated as a separable resource allocation problem (RAP). In the first category (*minisum*), we wish to minimize $\sum_{j=1}^{J} F_j(s_j)$. In the second category (*minimax*), we wish to minimize $\max_{1 \leq j \leq J} F_j(s_j)$. In both categories the minimization is subject to the two constraints $\sum_{j=1}^{J} s_j \leq S$ and $m_j \leq s_j \leq M_j$ for all $1 \leq j \leq J$. (See [14] for details on RAPs, including all of the schemes listed below.) Separability here means that each summand $F_j(s_j)$ is a function of a single decision variable s_j, and such resource allocation problems are relatively straightforward to solve exactly.

Minisum. Minisum separable RAPs can be solved by one of several means, the key being whether or not the functions involved are *convex*. In fact, if the individual functions happen to be convex the problem can be solved by one of three standard algorithms: These are the schemes by Fox [15], Galil and Megiddo (*GM*) [16], and Frederickson and Johnson (*FJ*) [17], which can be regarded as fast, faster and (theoretically) fastest, respectively. The *FJ* scheme, which we employ, has complexity $O(\max(J, J \log(S/J))$. If the individual functions, on the other hand, are not convex, the problem may still be solved by a simple dynamic programming (*DP*) algorithm. This scheme has complexity $O(JS^2)$.

Checking for convexity of the underlying summands is easy for the various metrics we consider. Specifically, only the (weighted) number of tardy jobs and the (weighted) total tardiness require the more expensive *DP*. All others minisum metrics can use *FJ*.

Minimax. For minimax separable RAPs the situation is cleaner. As long as the functions F_j are non-decreasing, as all of our metrics are, the minimax problem can be reduced naturally to a minisum convex separable RAP: The transformation is via the functions $G_j(s_j) = \sum_{i}^{s_j} F_j(i)$. Note that this function is convex *because* the original function $F_j(s_j)$ is non-decreasing. Also note that the first differences of G_j correspond to F_j. An easy telescoping argument then shows that the solution to the separable convex RAP of minimizing $\sum_j G_j(s_j)$ subject to the constraints $\sum_j s_j \leq S$ and $m_j \leq s_j \leq M_j$ corresponds precisely to the solution to the minimax RAP for $F_j(s_j)$.

This means that one can apply any of the fast schemes, such as *FJ*, to each of the minimax problems.

4 Experiments

In this section we will describe the performance of our FLEX scheduler by means of a number of experiments. These include both simulation and actual experiments on a cluster of hosts.

We should note that our experiments are in some sense *unfair* to FAIR. That is because FAIR was not designed to behave well with respect to any of the possible metrics on which we are evaluating it. It is merely trying to be fair to the smaller jobs, by incorporating minimum constraints. On the other hand, we are being *more* than fair to FIFO. First, let us be precise by what we will mean by FIFO here. One can imagine three FIFO variants of various levels of freedom and intelligence. We choose the variant which does not obey the minimum constraints but does take advantage of the maximum constraints. This seems to be in the spirit of FIFO, and also at least modestly intelligent. So we are being very fair to FIFO because we are comparing it with two schemes (FAIR and FLEX) which must obey the fairness constraints imposed by the minima. By the way, notice that the FIFO scheme we use can be regarded as an MPS schedule with priority orderings determined by job arrival times, where the minima are set to 0.

4.1 Simulation Experiments

First we will describe the experimental methodology employed. Each experiment represents multiple jobs, in either the Map or Reduce phase.

The amount of work for each job is chosen according to a bimodal distribution that is the sum of two (left) truncated normal distributions. The first simulates "small" jobs and the second simulates "large" jobs. The second mean is chosen 10 times larger than the first, and the standard deviations are each one third of the means. The ratio of small to total jobs is controlled by a parameter which is allowed to vary between 0 and 100%. Once work values are chosen for each job the values are normalized so that the total amount of work across all jobs in any experiment is a fixed constant. Assuming an average amount of work associated with each task in a job the total work for that job can then be translated into a number of slots. If the slot demand for a job is less than the total number of slots available the maximum constraint is adjusted accordingly. Otherwise it is set to the total number of slots. The minimum number of slots, on the other hand, is chosen according to a parameter which controls the total fraction of slack available. This slack parameter can essentially vary between 0 and 100%, though for fairness we insist on a non-zero minimum per job. The actual minimum for each job is chosen from another truncated normal distribution, with a mean chosen based on the slack parameter and a standard deviation one third of that. If the job minimum computed in this manner exceeds the maximum it is discarded and resampled.

As we have noted, there are many possible metrics which can be employed by FLEX, even assuming that all jobs use the same type. The natural minisum problems include average response time, number of tardy jobs, average tardiness, average lateness, and total SLA costs. Each but the last of these can be weighted or unweighted, and the special weight associated with stretch adds yet another metric. The natural minimax problems include maximum response time, tardiness and lateness. And again, each can be weighted or unweighted, and maximum stretch involves a special weight. All job weights except for the stretch-related weights are chosen from a uniform distribution between 0 and 1. Deadlines, pseudo-deadlines and step heights are chosen from similar uniform distributions, with the obvious constraints on multiple steps for SLAs. (The pseudo-deadlines and step heights are simply reordered into monotone sequences.)

A few of our metrics can produce solutions which are zero or even negative (for lateness). In fact, this is one reason why approximation algorithms for these metrics cannot be found. Taking the ratio of a FLEX, FAIR or FIFO solution to the optimal solution (or any other one) may produce a meaningless result. There is actually no "nice" way to deal with this, and for that reason we choose to simply ignore such experiments when they occur, reporting on the others.

We start with simulation experiments involving 10 jobs and 100 Map or Reduce slots. We choose a modest number of jobs so that we can compare each of the three solutions to the optimal solution, which we compute by a brute force exhaustive search. However, by comparing FAIR and FIFO to FLEX directly in much larger experiments we have shown that our conclusions remain intact.

The base case for our experiments is the average response time metric, a small job parameter of 80% and a slack parameter of 75%. Average response time is the most commonly used metric, and the small job and slack parameters should be common cases. Then we vary along each of the three axes, first slack, then small jobs and finally on the choice of metric itself. Each of the experiments shown in the three figures result in 6 data points, namely the average and worst case ratios of FAIR, FIFO and FLEX to the optimum solutions in 100 simulations.

For our base case FIFO exhibits average case performance which is 207% of optimal, and worst case performance which is 324% of optimal. For FAIR the numbers are 154% and 161%, respectively. FLEX is virtually indistinguishable from optimal, with a worst case performance less than .1% higher.

Fig. 5(a) compares the average response time performance as we vary slack percentage on the X-axis. We hold the small job parameter to 80%. The Y-axis on this and the other figures is the ratio of each scheme to the value of the optimal solution, so that 1.0 is a lower bound. Larger percentages give FAIR, FLEX and the optimal solution greater flexibility, but FIFO is agnostic with respect to slack. The FIFO curves increase with slack *because* the optimal solution in the denominator decreases. Note that FIFO is not robust: The worst case performance differs significantly from the average case performance because it is highly dependent on the arrival order of the large jobs. Early large job arrivals destroy the response times of the small jobs. Both FAIR and FLEX, on the other hand, are able to deal with job arrivals robustly, and their average and worst case performance are therefore close to each other. The FAIR curves increase monotonically with greater slack, primarily because the optimal solution improves faster than the FAIR solution does. But FLEX finds a solution very close to the optimal in all cases, so both the average and worst case curves overlay the line at 1.0.

Fig. 5(b) compares the average response time performance as we vary the number of small jobs. We hold the slack parameter to 75%. We do not plot the case with 10 small jobs because the jobs would be picked in this case from a homogeneous distribution. So once normalized by the total amount of work these data points would be comparable to the case with 0 small jobs. Once again FIFO is not robust, exhibiting worst case performance significantly worse than

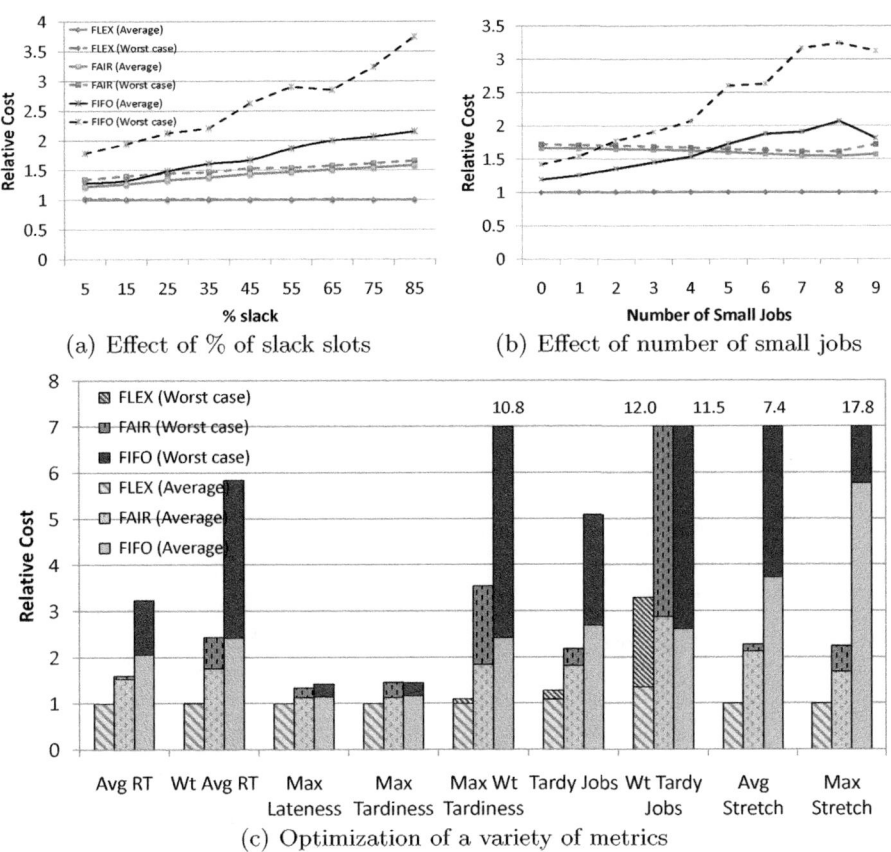

Fig. 5. Comparison of FLEX, FAIR, and FIFO

its average case performance. It performs poorest at about 80% small jobs, and is at its best at the two homogeneous end points. On the other hand, the FAIR and FLEX curves are basically flat, and have individually similar average and worst case performance. The FAIR solutions are, however, uniformly about 50% higher than the virtually optimal FLEX solutions.

Finally, Fig. 5(c) compares the performance of a representative sample of the other metrics, with a small job parameter of 80% and a slack parameter of 75%. In this figure we have overlaid the average and worst case ratios for each metric and scheme. Note that the worst case ratio is by definition at least as large as the average case ratio. If the former is not visible it means that the two coincide. The worst case ratios for some FIFO (and one FAIR) runs are so high that we have truncated the values for readability. From the figure we see that the average response time is a relatively *easy* metric for FLEX to optimize. Both FIFO and FAIR are unaware of these metrics, so their solutions do not vary. On the other hand, the optimal solution in the denominator does change. FLEX does very well compared to the others on weighted average response time, maximum weighted tardiness, weighted and unweighted number of tardy jobs, and both important stretch metrics.

4.2 Cluster Experiments

In these experiments, we compare FLEX to the implementation of FAIR in HFS, and present results for the average response time metric. In addition to being the most commonly used metric, it needs no additional synthetically created input data (weights, deadlines, etc.). We do not present results for FIFO since it ignores the minimum number of slots for each job, and since the simulation experiments show its performance is not competitive anyway.

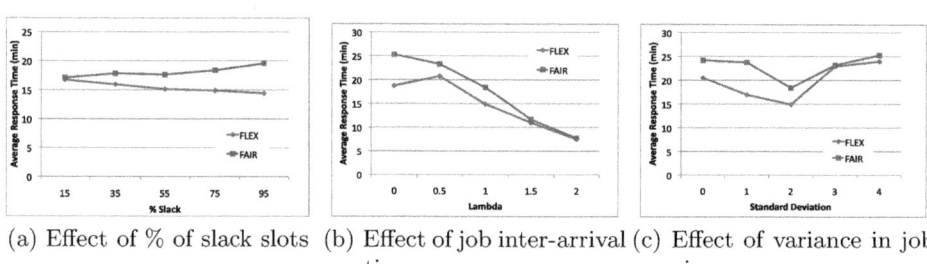

(a) Effect of % of slack slots (b) Effect of job inter-arrival times (c) Effect of variance in job sizes

Fig. 6. Comparison of FLEX and FAIR in real runs

From a code standpoint, we have currently built FLEX as an extension of FAIR allocation layer of HFS (Hadoop version 20.0), overriding its calculation of minimum slot allocations to each job. We use FAIR's infrastructure for calculating minimum slots and deficits to be used in the assignment layer to schedule tasks. Since FLEX requires estimates of total work for a job, whenever a new phase for a job is ready to be executed, we ensure that its number of minimum slots is at least 1. By doing so, at least one task is executed as soon a slot is available (to estimate the total work for that phase). At the completion of each task, we log its processing time, and re-estimate the remaining work for each phase (extrapolating based on the average seen so far, and the number of tasks left). We do not modify FAIR in any other way.

Our experiments are run on a cluster of 26 hosts with 3GHz Intel Xeon processors. This configuration is heterogeneous - 13 4-core blades on a rack and 13 8-core blades directly connected to the network switch. We pre-generate 1.8 TB of synthetic data, to be used as input by our synthetic workload which consists of a job written in Jaql [18]. This job is completely parametrizable. (Both the size of the Maps and Reduces can be modified independently). To simulate jobs of a variety of sizes, we use different versions of this job. For each experiment, we picked a subset of 10 jobs that can be completed on our cluster in about 45 minutes. In all the figures presented, the Y-axis is the average response time in minutes, and the X-axis is the parameter being modified.

Minimum slots are assigned to the jobs by allocating all jobs to the same pool, and configuring the pool's minimum number of slots. We set the same minimum for Map slots and Reduce slots. Observe that the minimum slots given to each job at any time depends on the number of running jobs, since jobs in a pool share the minimum slots. We present experiments with slack of 15%, 35%, 55%, 75%, 95% in Fig. 6(a). When slack is small, FLEX does not do much better than FAIR because the optimization problem is more constrained. However, FLEX does significantly better better as slack is increased, outperforming FAIR by almost 50% when slack is large.

We simulate an on-line problem (where jobs are submitted at various times) by modifying the inter-arrival times based on an exponential distribution. The time between submission of job i and job $i+1$ is chosen from an independently drawn exponential distribution of mean λ minutes. We present results for $\lambda = 0, 0.5, 1, 1.5, 2$ in Fig. 6(b). When $\lambda = 0$, all jobs are submitted at time 0. Observe that both FLEX and FAIR perform better as the inter-arrival time is increased, since jobs are competing less for resources. Values of $\lambda > 3$ result in very little difference between the performance of FAIR and FLEX, since there is not much overlap between the jobs. For smaller λ, FLEX outperforms FAIR significantly, almost 50% when $\lambda = 0$.

We measure the heterogeneity of job sizes in each experiment using the standard deviation (σ) of the estimated work of the jobs in the sample. We present experiments with $\sigma = 0, 1, 2, 3, 4$ in Fig. 6(c). When $\sigma = 0$, all jobs are identical, and when $\sigma = 4$, the smallest job is roughly one-tenth the size of the largest job. As before, FLEX results in lower average response time than FAIR, as low as 50% better in some cases ($\sigma = 1$).

For larger values of σ ($\sigma > 3$), the performance of both FAIR and FLEX degrades, and FLEX is not much better than FAIR in terms of response time. Initially this puzzled us, but looking at the experiments carefully, we realized this was an artifact of the fact that FAIR and FLEX calculate allocations for Maps and Reduces separately, and that Reduces are usually started before Maps finish in an attempt to save shuffle time. This is counter-productive in the following scenario: Suppose a large job is running its Map tasks. When Reduce slots become available Hadoop starts scheduling its Reduce tasks. However, if this job is sufficiently large (more Reduce tasks than slots), then it eventually takes over all the Reduce slots. Now, when other (potentially smaller) jobs arrive, both FAIR and FLEX will start scheduling their Map tasks (FLEX more aggressively than FAIR), but their Reduce slots cannot be scheduled until the large job can finish its Reduces, which will only happen after all its Maps are completed. As the ratio between the size of large and small jobs increases, this is more and more likely to happen. One easy way of solving this problem is by separating the shuffle part of the Reduce phase from the computation part (*copy-compute splitting* [3],[5]), but this is not currently implemented in FAIR, and is, in any case, outside the scope of this paper. Nevertheless, we do no worse that FAIR even in these cases, and significantly better in all other scenarios.

We also compared FLEX with FAIR in experiments involving 20 and 40 jobs, respectively. We observed that FLEX continues to outperform FAIR by almost 20%. We also repeated our experiments using GridMix2 (a standard Hadoop benchmark with 172 jobs in each workload), with an average 30% improvement in response time over FAIR. Even in the largest experiments, we observed that FLEX takes less than 10 milliseconds per run, compared to an epoch interval of about 500 milliseconds. This illustrates that our algorithms and implementations scale as the problem size increases.

5 Related Work

While MapReduce scheduling is relatively new, there have already been a number of interesting papers written. We have room to outline just a few key papers. We have already discussed [3] and [5], which are most related to our current work. The latter paper focuses more on the delay scheduling idea for the assignment level scheme. In our terminology the delay scheduling technique slightly *relaxes* the allocation level decisions in order to achieve better host and/or rack locality. It does so by delaying, within time limits, slot assignments in jobs where there are no currently local tasks available.

Zaharia et al. [19] propose a revised speculative execution scheme for MapReduce systems. The concept of dealing with straggler tasks by occasionally launching speculative copies (restarts) of that task is fundamental to the MapReduce paradigm, but the LATE scheme introduced here is shown to have better performance than that of the default Hadoop scheme.

As noted earlier, Agrawal et al. [6] cleverly amortize the costs of multiple jobs sharing the same input data. Since this is a potentially very large fraction of the total time needed to perform MapReduce jobs, the technique could yield significant benefits. The shared scan scheme introduced attempts to optimize either the average or maximum stretch, two metrics described in this paper.

Isrand et al. [20] propose the *Quincy* scheduler to achieve data locality and fairness for concurrent distributed jobs. They map the scheduling problem to a graph data-structure, where edge weights and capacities encode the competing demands of data locality and fairness; and use a min-cost flow algorithm to compute a schedule. They evaluate the performance based on several metrics like makespan, system normalized performance, slowdown norm, etc.

Saldholm and Lai [21] propose a resource allocation scheme for MapReduce workflows in order to improve the system efficiency metric – the average ratio of actual application performance in a shared system to the application performance in a dedicated system. Their scheme prioritizes MapReduce jobs in order to remove bottlenecks in different stages of the workflows.

6 Conclusions and Future Work

In this paper we have described FLEX, a flexible and intelligent allocation scheme for MapReduce workloads. It is flexible in the sense that it can optimize towards any of a variety of standard scheduling metrics, such as average response time, makespan, stretch, deadline-based penalty functions, and even SLAs. It is intelligent in the sense that it can achieve performance close to the theoretical optimal, and this performance is robust with respect to the underlying workloads, even in a heterogeneous environment. The FLEX allocation scheduler can be regarded as either a standalone plug-in replacement to the FAIR allocation scheme in HFS or as an add-on module that works synergistically with it. We have compared the performance of FLEX with that of FAIR and FIFO in a wide variety of experiments.

There are a number of future work items which we are currently pursuing.

- While we have designed a very generic FLEX scheme capable of optimizing any minisum or minimax scheduling objective, we are continuing to improve the quality of some of the specific schemes. Such schemes are very metric-dependent and they can be notoriously difficult. Results in this area should be of both practical and theoretical importance.
- As with any algorithm, the output quality depends on the quality of the input. For best FLEX performance we need to improve the extrapolation techniques for estimating the remaining work in a job. The estimation routine needs to be accurate, dynamic, and more aware of past history.
- We have only begun to tackle the assignment level scheduling for MapReduce workloads. The assignment level should modestly relax the decisions made at the allocation level in the hopes of achieving better locality, memory usage, threading and multicore utilization. This is a very challenging problem from the system design perspective.
- The shared scan idea described in [6] is an exciting new direction for MapReduce. We have some possibly novel ideas for shared scans.
- We are interested in providing schedulers for flowgraphs consisting of multiple MapReduce jobs. Similar metric choices would apply to these problems, so it could be a natural and ultimate extension of our current work.

References

1. Dean, J., Ghemawat, S.: Mapreduce: Simplified Data Processing on Large Clusters. ACM Transactions on Computer Systems 51(1), 107–113 (2008)
2. Hadoop, http://hadoop.apache.org
3. Zaharia, M., Borthakur, D., Sarma, J., Elmeleegy, K., Schenker, S., Stoica, I.: Job Scheduling for Multi-user Mapreduce Clusters. Technical Report EECS-2009-55, UC Berkeley Technical Report (2009)
4. Hadoop Fair Scheduler Design Document, http://svn.apache.org/repos/asf/hadoop/mapreduce/trunk/src/contrib/fairscheduler/designdoc/fair_scheduler_design_doc.pdf
5. Zaharia, M., Borthakur, D., Sarma, J., Elmeleegy, K., Shenker, S., Stoica, I.: Delay Scheduling: A Simple Technique for Achieving Locality and Fairness in Cluster Scheduling. In: EuroSys 2010: Proceedings of the 5th European Conference on Computer Systems, pp. 265–278. ACM, New York (2010)

6. Agrawal, P., Kifer, D., Olston, C.: Scheduling Shared Scans of Large Data Files. Proceedings of the VLDB Endowment 1(1), 958–969 (2008)
7. Pinedo, M.: Scheduling: Theory, Algorithms and Systems. Prentice Hall, Englewood Cliffs (1995)
8. Blazewicz, J., Ecker, K., Schmidt, G., Weglarz, J.: Scheduling in Computer and Manufacturing Systems. Springer, Secaucus (1993)
9. Leung, J.E.: Handbook of Scheduling: Algorithms, Models, and Performance Analysis. CRC, Boca Raton (2004)
10. Coffman, E., Garey, M., Johnson, D., Tarjan, R.: Performance Bounds for Level-oriented Two-dimensional Packing Problems. SIAM Journal on Computing 9(4), 808–826 (1980)
11. Schwiegelshohn, U., Ludwig, W., Wolf, J., Turek, J., Yu, P.: Smart SMART Bounds for Weighted Response Time Scheduling. SIAM Journal on Computing 28, 237–253 (1999)
12. Turek, J., Wolf, J., Yu, P.: Approximate Algorithms for Scheduling Parallelizable Tasks. In: SPAA 1992: Proceedings of the Fourth Annual ACM Symposium on Parallel Algorithms and Architectures, pp. 323–332. ACM, New York (1992)
13. Blazewicz, J., Kovalyov, M., Machowiak, M., Trystram, D., Weglarz, J.: Malleable Task Scheduling to Minimize the Makespan. Annals of Operations Research 129, 65–80 (2004)
14. Ibaraki, T., Katoh, N.: Resource Allocation Problems: Algorithmic Approaches. MIT Press, Cambridge (1988)
15. Fox, B.: Discrete Optimization via Marginal Analysis. Management Science 13, 210–216 (1966)
16. Galil, Z., Megiddo, N.: A Fast Selection Algorithm and the Problem of Optimum Distribution of Effort. Journal of the ACM 26(1), 58–64 (1979)
17. Frederickson, G., Johnson, D.: Generalized Selection and Ranking. In: STOC 1980: Proceedings of the Twelfth Annual ACM Symposium on Theory of Computing, pp. 420–428. ACM, New York (1980)
18. Jaql Query Language for JavaScript Object Notation, http://code.google.com/p/jaql
19. Zaharia, M., Konwinski, A., Joseph, A., Katz, R., Stoica, I.: Improving Mapreduce Performance in Heterogeneous Environments. In: 8th USENIX Symposium on Operating Systems Design and Implementation, pp. 29–42. USENIX Association (2008)
20. Isard, M., Prabhakaran, V., Curry, J., Wieder, U., Talwar, K., Goldberg, A.: Quincy: Fair Scheduling for Distributed Computing Clusters. In: SOSP 2009: Proceedings of the ACM SIGOPS 22nd Symposium on Operating Systems Principles, pp. 261–276. ACM, New York (2009)
21. Sandholm, T., Lai, K.: Mapreduce Optimization using Regulated Dynamic Prioritization. In: SIGMETRICS 2009: Proceedings of the Eleventh International Joint Conference on Measurement and Modeling of Computer Systems, pp. 299–310. ACM, New York (2009)

Adapting Distributed Real-Time and Embedded Pub/Sub Middleware for Cloud Computing Environments*

Joe Hoffert**, Douglas C. Schmidt, and Aniruddha Gokhale

Vanderbilt University, VU Station B #1829, 2015 Terrace Place, Nashville, TN 37203
jhoffert@dre.vanderbilt.edu

Abstract. Enterprise distributed real-time and embedded (DRE) publish/ subscribe (pub/sub) systems manage resources and data that are vital to users. Cloud computing—where computing resources are provisioned elastically and leased as a service—is an increasingly popular deployment paradigm. Enterprise DRE pub/sub systems can leverage cloud computing provisioning services to execute needed functionality when on-site computing resources are not available. Although cloud computing provides flexible on-demand computing and networking resources, enterprise DRE pub/sub systems often cannot accurately characterize their behavior *a priori* for the variety of resource configurations cloud computing supplies (*e.g.*, CPU and network bandwidth), which makes it hard for DRE systems to leverage conventional cloud computing platforms.

This paper provides two contributions to the study of how autonomic configuration of DRE pub/sub middleware can provision and use on-demand cloud resources effectively. We first describe how supervised machine learning can configure DRE pub/sub middleware services and transport protocols autonomically to support end-to-end quality-of-service (QoS) requirements based on cloud computing resources. We then present results that empirically validate how computing and networking resources affect enterprise DRE pub/sub system QoS. These results show how supervised machine learning can configure DRE pub/sub middleware adaptively in < 10 μsec with bounded time complexity to support key QoS reliability and latency requirements.

Keywords: Autonomic configuration, pub/sub middleware, DRE systems, cloud computing.

1 Introduction

Emerging trends and challenges. Enterprise distributed real-time and embedded (DRE) publish/subscribe (pub/sub) systems manage data and resources that are critical to the ongoing system operations. Examples include testing and training of experimental aircraft across a large geographic area, air traffic management systems, and disaster recovery operations. These types of enterprise DRE systems must be configured correctly to leverage available resources and respond to the system deployment

---

* This work is sponsored by NSF TRUST and AFRL.
** Corresponding author.

environment. For example, search and rescue missions in disaster recovery operations need to configure the image resolution used to detect and track survivors depending on the available resources (*e.g.*, computing power and network bandwidth) [20].

Many enterprise DRE systems are implemented and developed for a specific computing/networking platform and deployed with the expectation of specific computing and networking resources being available at runtime. This approach simplifies development complexity since system developers need only focus on how the system behaves in one operating environment. Thus considerations of multiple infrastructure platforms are ameliorated with respect to system quality-of-service (QoS) properties (*e.g.*, responsiveness of computing platform, latency and reliability of networked data, etc.). Focusing on only a single operating environment, however, decreases the flexibility of the system and makes it hard to integrate into different operating environments, *e.g.*, porting to new computing and networking hardware.

Cloud computing [6, 17] is an increasingly popular infrastructure paradigm where computing and networking resources are provided to a system or application as a service —typically for a "pay-as-you-go" usage fee. Provisioning services in cloud environments relieve enterprise operators of many tedious tasks associated with managing hardware and software resources used by systems and applications. Cloud computing also provides enterprise application developers and operators with additional flexibility by virtualizing resources, such as providing virtual machines that can differ from the actual hardware machines used.

Several pub/sub middleware platforms (such as the Java Message Service [16], and Web Services Brokered Notification [14]) can (1) leverage cloud environments, (2) support large-scale data-centric distributed systems, and (3) ease development and deployment of these systems. These pub/sub platforms, however, do not support fine-grained and robust QoS that are needed for enterprise DRE systems. Some large-scale distributed system platforms, such as the Global Information Grid [1] and Network-centric Enterprise Services [2], require rapid response, reliability, bandwidth guarantees, scalability, and fault-tolerance.

Conversely, conventional cloud environments are problematic for enterprise DRE systems since applications within these systems often cannot characterize the utilization of their specific resources (*e.g.*, CPU speeds and memory) accurately *a priori*. Consequently, applications in DRE systems may need to adjust to the available resources supplied by the cloud environment (*e.g.*, using compression algorithms optimized for given CPU power and memory) since the presence/absence of these resources affect timeliness and other QoS properties crucial to proper operation. If these adjustments take too long the mission that the DRE system supports could be jeopardized.

Configuring an enterprise DRE pub/sub system in a cloud environment is hard because the DRE system must understand how the computing and networking resources affect end-to-end QoS. For example, transport protocols provide different types of QoS (*e.g.*, reliability and latency) that must be configured in conjunction with the pub/sub middleware. To work properly, however, QoS-enabled pub/sub middleware must understand how these protocols behave with different cloud infrastructures. Likewise, the middleware must be configured with appropriate transport protocols to support the required end-to-end QoS. Manual or *ad hoc* configuration of the transport and middleware can be tedious, error-prone, and time consuming.

Solution approach → **Supervised Machine Learning for Autonomous Configuration of DRE Pub/Sub Middleware in Cloud Computing Environments.** This paper describes how we are (1) evaluating multiple QoS concerns (*i.e.*, reliability and latency) based on differences in computing and networking resources and (2) configuring QoS-enabled pub/sub middleware autonomically for cloud environments based on these evaluations. We have prototyped this approach in the *ADAptive Middleware And Network Transports* (ADAMANT) platform, which addresses the problem of configuring QoS-enabled DRE pub/sub middleware for cloud environments. Our approach provides the following contributions to research on autonomic configuration of DRE pub/sub middleware in cloud environments:

- **Supervised machine learning as a knowledge base to provide fast and predictable resource management in cloud environments.** *Artificial Neural Network* (ANN) tools determine in a timely manner the appropriate transport protocol for the QoS-enabled pub/sub middleware platform given the computing resources available in the cloud environment. ANN tools are trained on particular computing and networking configurations to provide the best QoS support for those configurations. Moreover, they provide predictable response times needed for DRE systems.

- **Configuration of DRE pub/sub middleware based on guidance from supervised machine learning.** Our ADAMANT middleware uses the *Adaptive Network Transports* (ANT) [10] to select the transport protocol(s) that best address multiple QoS concerns for given computing resources. ANT provides infrastructure for composing and configuring transport protocols using the scalable reliable multicast-based Ricochet transport protocol [3]. Supported protocols such as Ricochet enable trade-offs between latency and reliability to support middleware for enterprise DRE pub/sub systems in cloud environments.

We have implemented ADAMANT using multiple open-source pub/sub middleware implementations (*i.e.*, OpenDDS(www.opendds.org) and OpenSplice(www.openslice.org)) of the OMG Data Distribution Service (DDS) [18] specification. DDS defines a QoS-enabled DRE pub/sub middleware standard that enables applications to communicate by publishing information they have and subscribing to information they need in a timely manner. The OpenDDS and OpenSplice implementations of DDS provide pluggable protocol frameworks that can support standard transport protocols (such as TCP, UDP, and IP multicast), as well as custom transport protocols (such as Ricochet and reliable multicast).

Our prior work [10,11] developed composite metrics to evaluate pub/sub middleware with various ANT-based transport protocols based on differences in application parameters (*e.g.*, number of data receivers and data sending rate). We also evaluated multiple approaches for adapting to application parameter changes in a dedicated (*i.e.*, non-cloud) operating environment without regard to changes in computing or networking resources. This paper extends our prior work by (1) evaluating pub/sub middleware in a cloud environment to take into account differences in computing and networking resources and

(2) conducting empirical evaluations of an artificial neural network machine learning tool with respect to timeliness and configuration accuracy.

We validated ADAMANT by configuring Emulab (www.emulab.net) to emulate a cloud environment that allows test programs to request and configure several types of computing and networking resources on-demand. We then applied several composite metrics developed to ascertain how ADAMANT supports relevant QoS concerns for various Emulab-based cloud configurations. These metrics quantitatively measure multiple interrelated QoS concerns (*i.e.*, latency and reliability) to evaluate QoS mechanisms (such as transport protocols) used in QoS-enabled pub/sub DRE systems. Our supervised machine learning tools use the results of these composite metrics to determine the most appropriate transport protocol to apply in the Emulab cloud environment.

Paper organization. The remainder of this paper is organized as follows: Section 2 describes a representative search and rescue application to motivate the challenges that ADAMANT addresses; Section 3 examines the structure and functionality of ADAMANT and the supervised machine learning technique it uses to guide the configuration process; Section 4 analyzes the results of experiments conducted to validate ADAMANT in a cloud environment; Section 5 compares ADAMANT with related work; and Section 6 presents concluding remarks.

2 Motivating Example - Search and Rescue Operations in the Aftermath of a Regional Disaster

This section describes a representative enterprise DRE pub/sub application in a cloud computing environment to motivate the challenges that ADAMANT addresses.

2.1 Search and Rescue Operations for Disaster Recovery

To highlight the challenges of configuring enterprise DRE pub/sub systems for cloud environments in a timely manner, our work is motivated in the context of supporting search and rescue (SAR) operations that leverage cloud infrastructure. These operations help locate and extract survivors in a large metropolitan area after a regional disaster, such as a hurricane or tornado. SAR operations can use unmanned aerial vehicles (UAVs), existing operational monitoring infrastructure (*e.g.*, building or traffic light mounted cameras intended for security or traffic monitoring), and (temporary) datacenters to receive, process, and transmit data from various sensors and monitors to emergency vehicles that can be dispatched to areas where survivors are identified.

These datacenters can be mobile (*e.g.*, in truck trailers or large command-and-control aircraft if roads are damaged) and brought into the disaster area as needed. Moreover, these datacenters can be connected to cloud infrastructure via high-speed satellite links [12] since ground-based wired connectivity may not be available due to the disaster. In particular, our work focuses on configuring the QoS-enabled pub/sub middleware used by the temporary *ad hoc* datacenter for data dissemination.

Figure 1 shows an example SAR scenario where infrared scans along with GPS coordinates are provided by UAVs and video feeds are provided by existing infrastructure

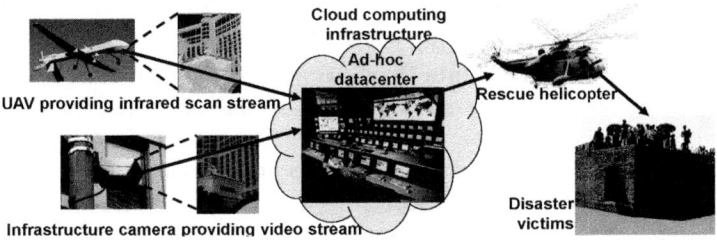

Fig. 1. Search and Rescue Motivating Example

cameras. These infrared scans and video feeds are then sent to a datacenter facilitated by cloud infrastructure where the data are disseminated, received by fusion applications, and processed to detect survivors. Once survivors are detected, the SAR system will develop a three dimensional view and highly accurate position information so that rescue operations can commence.

A key requirement of data fusion applications within the datacenter is the tight timing bounds on correlated event streams such as the infrared scans coming from UAVs and video coming from cameras mounted atop traffic lights. The event streams need to match up closely so the survivor detection application can produce accurate results. If an infrared data stream is out of sync with a video data stream, the survivor detection application can generate a false negative and fail to initiate needed rescue operations. Likewise, without timely data coordination the survivor detection software can generate a false positive thereby expending scarce resources such as rescue workers, rescue vehicles, and data center coordinators unnecessarily. The timeliness and reliability properties of the data are affected by the underlying hardware infrastructure, *e.g.*, faster processors and networks can decrease latency and allow more error correcting data to be transmitted to improve reliability.

SAR operations in the aftermath of a disaster can be impeded by the lack of computing and networking resources needed for an *ad hoc* datacenter. The same disaster that caused missing or stranded people also can diminish or completely eliminate local computing resources. Cloud infrastructure located off-site can provide the needed resources to carry out the SAR operations. Applications using cloud resources can be preempted to support emergency systems such as SAR operations during national crises much as emergency vehicles preempt normal traffic and commandeer the use of traffic lights and roadways. The resources that the cloud provides, however, are not known *a priori*. Thus, the effective QoS for the SAR operations are dependent on the computing resources provided.

2.2 Key Challenges in Supporting Search and Rescue Operations in Cloud Computing Environments

Meeting the requirements of SAR operations outlined in Section 2.1 is hard due to the inherent complexity of configuring enterprise DRE pub/sub middleware based on the computing resources the cloud provides. These resources are not known *a priori* and yet the QoS of the system is affected by the specific resources provided. The remainder of this section describes four challenges that ADAMANT addresses to support the communication requirements of the SAR operations presented above.

Challenge 1: Configuring for data timeliness and reliability. SAR operations must receive sufficient data reliability and timeliness so that multiple data streams can be fused appropriately. For instance, the SAR operation example described above shows how data streams (such as infrared scan and video streams) can be exploited by multiple applications simultaneously in a datacenter. The top half of Figure 2 shows how security monitoring and structural damage applications can use video stream data to detect looting and unsafe buildings, respectively. The bottom half of Figure 2 shows how fire detection applications and power grid assessment applications can use infrared scans to detect fires and working HVAC systems, respectively.

Likewise, the SAR systems must be configured to best use the computing and networking resources from the cloud to address data timeliness and reliability. These systems must therefore (1) use transport protocols that provide both reliability and timeliness and (2) know how these protocols behave in different computing and networking environments. Sections 3.1 and 4.1 describe how ADAMANT addresses this challenge by utilizing composite QoS metrics to measure both timeliness and reliability and incorporating transport protocols that configure the datacenter's pub/sub middleware to balance reliability and low latency.

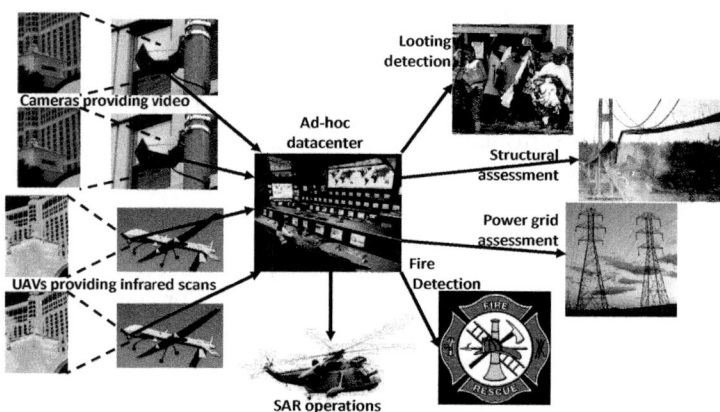

Fig. 2. Uses of Infrared Scans and Video Streams during Disaster Recovery

Challenge 2: Timely configuration. Due to timeliness concerns of DRE systems such as SAR systems, the *ad hoc* datacenter used for SAR operations must be configured in a timely manner based on the computing and networking resources provided by the cloud. If the datacenter cannot be configured quickly, invaluable time will be lost leading to survivors not being saved and critical infrastructure (such as dams and power plants) not being safeguarded from further damage. During a regional or national emergency any wasted time can mean the difference between life and death for survivors and the salvaging or destruction of key regional utilities.

Moreover, applications and systems used during one disaster can be leveraged for other disasters. Available computing and networking resources differ from one set of disaster recovery operations to another. Depending on the available cloud resources, therefore, the configuration times of *ad hoc* datacenters for SAR operations, for example, must be bounded and fast to ensure appropriate responsiveness. Determining appropriate configurations must also provide predictable response to ensure rapid and dependable response times across different computing and networking resources. Sections 3.2 and 4.4 describe how ADAMANT addresses this challenge by utilizing an artificial neural network machine learning tool to autonomically configure the datacenter's pub/sub middleware quickly and predictably.

Challenge 3: Accuracy of configurations. Since data timeliness and reliability is related to the computing resources available and the configuration of the datacenter supporting the SAR operations in a cloud as noted in Challenge 1, configuring the datacenter must be done in an accurate manner. If the datacenter is incorrectly configured then the timeliness and reliability of the data (*e.g.*, the UAV scans and camera video used to detect survivors) will not be optimal for the given computing resources. For critical operations during disasters, such as rescuing survivors, the supporting SAR system must utilize the available resources to their fullest extent. Sections 3.2 and 4.4 describe how ADAMANT addresses this challenge by using the artificial neural network machine learning tool to configure the datacenter's pub/sub middleware accurately.

Challenge 4: Reducing development complexity. Regional and local disasters occur in many places and at many different times. The functionality of applications used during one disaster may also be needed for other disasters. A system that is developed for one particular disaster in a particular operating environment, however, might not work well for a different disaster in a different operating environment. SAR operations could unexpectedly fail at a time when they are needed most due to differences in computing and networking resources available. Systems therefore must be developed and configured readily between the different operating environments presented by cloud computing to leverage the systems across a wide range of disaster scenarios. Section 3.2 describes how ADAMANT addresses this challenge by using an artificial neural network machine learning tool to manage mapping the computing and network resources and application parameters (*e.g.*, data sending rate, number of data receivers) to the appropriate transport protocol to use.

3 Overview of ADAMANT

This section presents an overview of the *ADAptive Middleware And Network Transports* (ADAMANT) platform, which is QoS-enabled pub/sub middleware that integrates and enhances the *Adaptive Network Transports* (ANT) framework to support multiple transport protocols and the *Artificial Neural Network* (ANN) machine learning technology to select appropriate transport protocols in a timely and reliable manner. ADAMANT extends our prior work [10, 11] by empirically evaluating (1) the QoS delivered by DDS pub/sub middleware with respect to differences in computing and networking resources provided by cloud environments and (2) the accuracy and timeliness of ANN-based machine learning tools in determining appropriate middleware configurations.

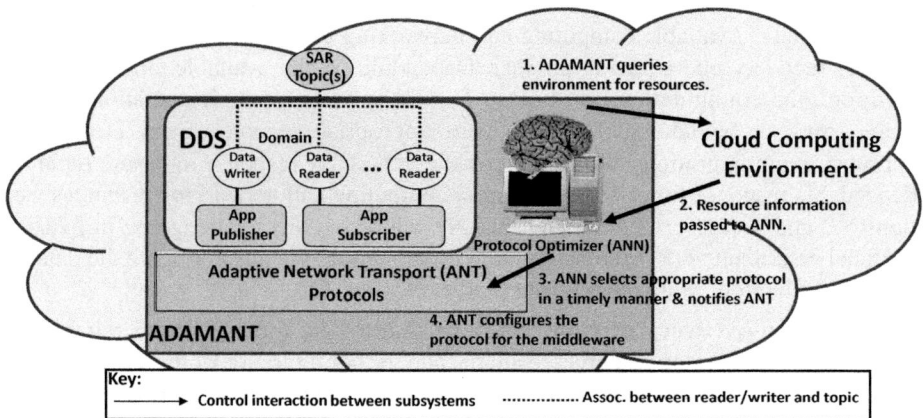

Fig. 3. ADAMANT Architecture and Control Flow

Figure 3 shows how ADAMANT works in a cloud environment (*e.g.*, the *ad-hoc* SAR datacenter) to deploy cloud resources. Since ADAMANT configures itself based on the resources in a cloud, it must determine those resources autonomically when the cloud environment makes them available. ADAMANT queries the environment for hardware and networking resources using OS utilities.

For example, on Linux ADAMANT accesses the /proc/cpuinfo file to gather CPU information and executes the ethtool program to query network characteristics. ADAMANT combines this hardware information with other relevant application properties (*e.g.*, number of receivers and data sending rate) and sends it as input to the ANN, which determines the appropriate protocol in a timely manner and passes this information to ANT. ANT then configures the DDS middleware to use the appropriate transport protocol. The remainder of this section describes the structure and functionality of ADAMANT.

3.1 Adaptive Network Transports (ANT) Framework

The ANT framework supports various transport protocol properties, including multicast, packet tracking, NAK-based reliability, ACK-based reliability, flow control, group membership, and membership fault detection. These properties can be configured at startup to achieve greater flexibility and support configuration adaptation.

The ANT framework originally was derived from the Ricochet [3] transport protocol, which uses a bi-modal multicast protocol and a novel type of forward error correction (FEC) called lateral error correction (LEC) to provide QoS and scalability properties. Ricochet supports (1) time-critical multicast for high data rates with strong probabilistic delivery guarantees and (2) low-latency error detection along with low-latency error recovery. We included ANT's Ricochet protocol and ANT's NAKcast protocol, which is a NAK-based multicast protocol supporting a timeout parameter for when to send NAKs to the sender, with the evaluations done in this paper. These protocols have been selected due to their support for balancing reliability and low latency [10].

The Ricochet protocol has two tunable parameters. The R parameter determines the number of packets a receiver should receive before it sends out a repair packet to other receivers. The C parameter determines the number of receivers that will be sent a repair packet from any single receiver. These two parameters affect the timeliness, reliability, and jitter of the data received as shown in Section 4.3. ANT helps address Challenge 1 in Section 2.2 by supporting transport protocols that balance reliability and low latency.

3.2 Artificial Neural Network Tools to Determine Middleware Configurations

Several machine learning approaches can be used to configure middleware autonomically in a cloud computing environment. We selected ANN technology [11] due to its (1) fast and predictable performance, (2) accuracy for environments known *a priori* (*i.e.*, used for ANN training) *and* unknown until runtime (*i.e.*, not used for ANN training), and (3) low accidental development complexity. In particular, we chose the *Fast Artificial Neural Network* (FANN)(leenissen.dk/fann) implementation due to its configurability, documentation, ease of use, and open-source code. Section 4.4 shows the accuracy and timeliness of a neural network trained and tested using the data collected from the experiments described in Section 4.3. In particular, neural networks provide 100% accuracy for environments known *a priori*, high accuracy for environments unknown until runtime, and the low latency, constant time-complexity required for DRE systems such as SAR operations.

The use of an ANN helps address Challenges 2 and 3 in Section 2.2 by providing accurate, fast, and predictable guidance for determining an appropriate ADAMANT configuration for a given cloud computing environment. An ANN also helps address Challenge 4 in Section 2.2 by autonomously managing the mappings from the computing and network resources available and the application parameters (*e.g.*, data sending rate, number of data receivers) to the appropriate transport protocols. An ANN thus reduces the development complexity for configuring the pub/sub middleware appropriately as compared to manual adaptation approaches (*e.g.*, implementing switch statements), which are tedious and error-prone [13].

4 Experimental Results

The section presents the results of experiments we conducted to empirically evaluate (1) the effect of computing and networking resources on the QoS provided by ADAMANT as measured by the composite QoS metrics defined in Section 4.1 and (2) the timeliness and accuracy of an ANN in determining an appropriate ADAMANT configuration given a particular cloud computing environment. The experiments include ADAMANT with multiple aspects of the operating environment varied, (*e.g.*, CPU speed, network bandwidth, DDS implementation, percent data loss in the network) along with multiple aspects of the application being varied as would be expected with SAR operations (*e.g.*, number of receivers, sending rate of the data).

4.1 Composite QoS Metrics for Reliability and Timeliness

Our prior work [10, 11] on QoS-enabled pub/sub middleware performance for non-cloud environments indicated that some transport protocols provide better reliability (as measured by the number of network packets received divided by the number sent) and latency for certain environments while other protocols are better for other environments. We therefore developed several *composite QoS metrics* to evaluate multiple QoS aspects simultaneously, thereby providing a uniform and objective evaluation of ADAMANT in cloud computing environments. Our composite QoS metrics focus on reliability and average latency, including the QoS aspects of (1) *jitter* (*i.e.*, standard deviation of the latency of network packets), (2) *burstiness* (*i.e.*, the standard deviation of average bandwidth usage per second of time), and (3) network bandwidth usage.

Two of the composite QoS metrics we defined are *ReLate2* and *ReLate2Jit*. ReLate2 is the product of the average data packet latency and the percent loss + 1 (to account for 0% loss) which implies an order of magnitude increase for 9% loss. This adjustment is relevant for multimedia data in our SAR example based on previous research, *e.g.*, if average packet latency is 1,000 μs and the percent loss is 0 (*i.e.*, no packets lost) then the ReLate2 value is 1,000. Having 9% and 19% loss with the same average latency produces the ReLate2 values of 10,000 and 20,000 respectively. ReLate2Jit is a product of the ReLate2 value and the jitter of the data packets to quantify reliability, average latency, and jitter.

We apply these metrics below to QoS-enabled DDS pub/sub middleware using various transport protocols supported by ANT to train the ANN. The ANN is trained with an understanding of how integration of middleware with each protocol affects the QoS properties of reliability and latency given the variability of computing and networking resources of a cloud environment.

4.2 Experimental Setup

We conducted our experiments using the Emulab network testbed, which provides on-demand computing platforms and network resources that can be easily configured with the desired OS, network topology, and network traffic shaping. We used Emulab due to its (1) support for multiple types of computing platforms, (2) numbers of computing platforms, and (3) support for multiple network bandwidths. The flexibility of Emulab presents a representative testbed to train and test ADAMANT's configurability support for cloud computing environments.

As described in Section 2, we are concerned with the distribution of data for SAR datacenters, where network packets are typically dropped at end hosts [4]. The ADAMANT software for the receiving data readers supports programmatically dropping random data packets. We modified ADAMANT to drop packets based on the loss percentage specified for the experiment.

Our experiments were configured with the following traffic generation models using version 1.2.1 of OpenDDS and version 3.4.2 of OpenSplice. One DDS data writer sent out data, a variable number of DDS data readers received the data. The data writer and each data reader ran on its own computing platform and the data writer sent 12 bytes of data 20,000 times at a specified sending rate. To account for experiment variations we ran 5 experiments for each configuration, *e.g.*, 3 receiving data writers, 50 Hz sending rate, 2% end host packet loss, pc3000 computing platform, and 1Gb network bandwidth.

We configured ADAMANT with Ricochet and NAKcast to determine how well it performs using these protocols. We modified NAKcast's timeout value as well as

Table 1. Environment Variables

Point of Variability	Values
Machine type	pc850, pc3000
Network bandwidth	1Gb, 100Mb, 10Mb
DDS Implementation	OpenDDS, OpenSplice
Percent end-host network loss	1 to 5 %

Table 2. Application Variables

Point of Variability	Values
Number of receiving data readers	3 - 15
Frequency of sending data	10 Hz, 25 Hz, 50 Hz, 100 Hz

Ricochet's R and C parameters as described in Section 3.1. Table 1 outlines the points of variability provided by the cloud computing environment. We include the DDS implementation in this table since some cloud computing environments provide hardware and software resources. We include network loss in the table since the network characteristics in cloud computing can be specified in an end-user license agreement, which identifies the services that the cloud computing environment will provide and that consumers accept. The middleware for the SAR operations can then be configured appropriately using this information.

Table 2 outlines the points of variability due to the SAR operations. In particular, we varied the number of data receivers since only a few SAR applications might be interested in one data stream (*e.g.*, for a localized area with fine-grained searching) while many applications might be interested in a different data stream (*e.g.*, for a broader area with coarse-grained searching). Likewise, the sending rate might be high for SAR operations that need high-resolution imaging for detailed searching while a lower sending rate is sufficient for SAR operations where lower resolution imaging is sufficient for more generalized searching.

For computing resources we used Emulab's pc850 and pc3000 hardware platforms. The pc850 platform includes an 850 MHz 32-bit Pentium III processor with 256 MB of RAM. The pc3000 platform includes a 3 GHz 64-bit Xeon processor with 2 GB of RAM. We used the Fedora Core 6 operating system with real-time extensions on these hardware platforms to collect high resolution timings. The nodes were all configured in a LAN configuration indicative of a datacenter.

4.3 Evaluating How Cloud Computing Resources Affect QoS

Below we analyze the results from experiments involving different cloud computing environments. We show experimental data where the selection of ADAMANT's transport protocol to support QoS differs based on the cloud computing environment. Information in this section addresses Challenge 1 in Section 2.2 by characterizing the performance of the transport protocols for various cloud computing environments.

Figures 4 and 5 show the results of experiments where we held constant the number of receivers (3), the percent loss (5%), and the DDS middleware (OpenSplice). We varied the computing platform and the network bandwidth using the pc850 and pc3000 platforms, and 100Mb and 1Gb LANs, respectively. We ran the experiments using NAKcast with a NAK timeout setting of 50ms, 25ms, 10ms, and 1ms, and Ricochet with R=4, C=3 and R=8, C=3. We only include NAKcast with a timeout of 1ms and Ricochet R=4 C=3 since these were the only protocols that produced the best (*i.e.*, lowest) ReLate2 values for these operating environments. Likewise, we ran the ADAMANT experiments with sending rates of 10Hz, 25Hz, 50Hz, and 100Hz but only show results for 10Hz and 25Hz since these highlight different protocols that produce the lowest ReLate2 value.

Figure 4 shows two cases where the Ricochet protocol with R = 4 and C = 3 produces the best (*i.e.*, lowest) ReLate2 values for sending rates of both 10Hz and 25Hz when using the pc3000 computing platform and the 1Gb network. Conversely, Figure 5 shows how the NAKcast protocol with a NAK timeout set to 1 ms produces the best (*i.e.*, lowest) ReLate2 values for the same sending rates of 10Hz and 25Hz when using the pc850 computing platform and the 100Mb network. These figures show that by changing only the CPU speed, amount of RAM, and network bandwidth, different protocols produce a better ReLate2 value and therefore better support the QoS properties of reliability and average latency. The SAR datacenter pub/sub middleware should therefore be configured differently depending on the computing and networking resources that a cloud computing environment provides. No single protocol performs best in all cases based on the computing and networking resources.

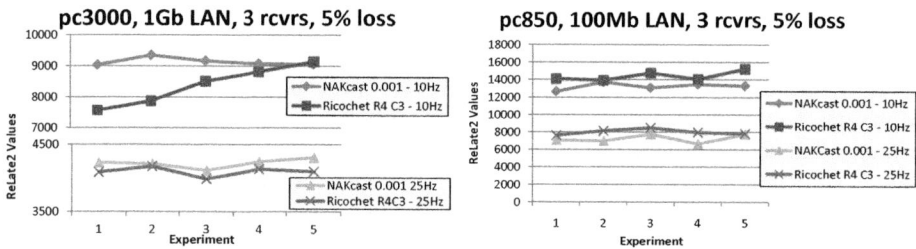

Fig. 4. ReLate2: pc3000, 1Gb LAN, 3 receivers, 5% loss, 10 & 25Hz

Fig. 5. ReLate2: pc850, 100Mb LAN, 3 receivers, 5% loss, 10 & 25Hz

We decompose the ReLate2 metric into its constituent parts of reliability and average packet latency to gain a better understanding of how changes in hardware can affect the QoS properties relevant to the ReLate2 metric. Figures 6 and 7 show the reliability of the NAKcast 0.001 and Ricochet R4 C3 protocols. The reliability of the protocols is relatively unaffected by differences in hardware and network resources as would be expected. The percent network loss is held constant for these experiments and the differences in hardware are not expected to affect how many packets are delivered reliably.

Figures 8 and 9, show that differences in computing speed and networking bandwidth have an effect on the average latency of packet arrival. In particular, there is a wider gap in the average latency times between the NAKcast and the Ricochet protocol when faster computing and networking resources are used.

Since protocol reliability in these experiments is virtually constant, the difference in NAKcast performing better in one environment and Ricochet performing better in another stems from differences in average latency. With faster hardware and networks, Ricochet's average latency can overcome its lower reliability to perform better when reliability and average latency are both considered. Note that the graphs for the individual

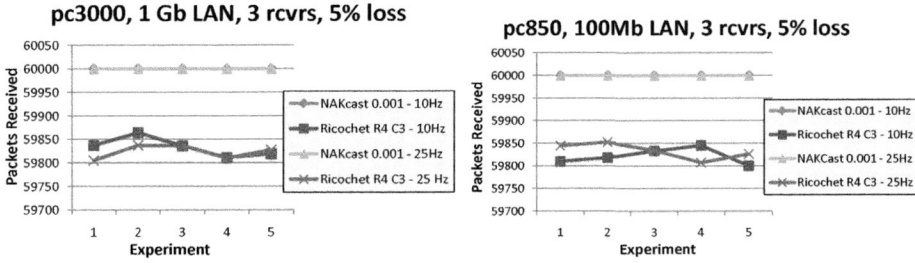

Fig. 6. Reliability: pc3000, 1Gb LAN, 3 receivers, 5% loss, 10 & 25Hz

Fig. 7. Reliability: pc850, 100Mb LAN, 3 receivers, 5% loss, 10 & 25Hz

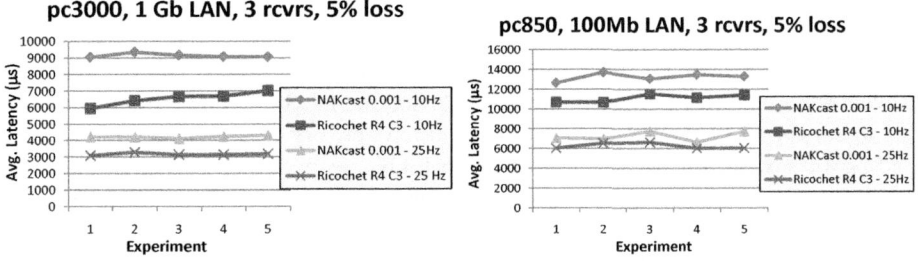

Fig. 8. Latency: pc3000, 1Gb LAN, 3 receivers, 5% loss, 10 & 25Hz

Fig. 9. Latency: pc850, 100Mb LAN, 3 receivers, 5% loss, 10 & 25Hz

QoS property of average latency consistently show Ricochet performing better, while the graphs consistently show NAKcast performing better for reliability. Only when the QoS properties are combined in the ReLate2 metric is there a distinction between the appropriate protocol based on the hardware resources.

Figures 10 and 11 show that the differences in hardware resources affect the protocol to choose based on the ReLate2Jit metric which measures reliability, average packet

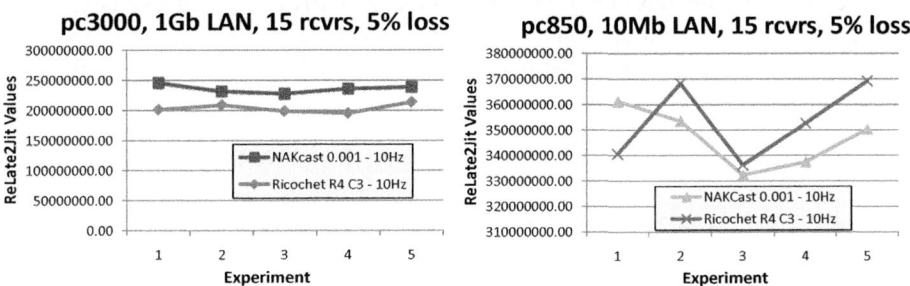

Fig. 10. ReLate2Jit: pc3000, 1Gb LAN, 15 receivers, 5% loss, 10Hz

Fig. 11. ReLate2Jit: pc850, 100Mb LAN, 15 receivers, 5% loss, 10Hz

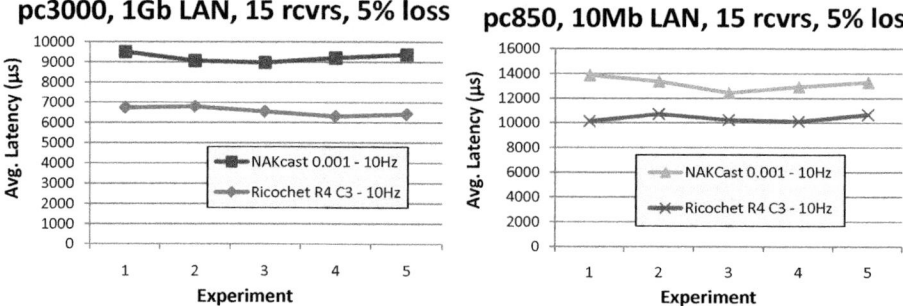

Fig. 12. Latency: pc3000, 1Gb LAN, 15 receivers, 5% loss, 10Hz

Fig. 13. Latency: pc850, 100Mb LAN, 15 receivers, 5% loss, 10Hz

latency, and the standard deviation of packet latency (*i.e.*, jitter). The number of receivers is 15, the network percent loss is 5%, and the DDS middleware is OpenSplice. We again varied the computing platform and the network bandwidth using the pc850 and pc3000 platforms and 100Mb and 1Gb LANs, respectively. The figures only include data for NAKcast with a 1 ms timeout and Ricochet R=4 C=3 both with a 10Hz sending rate since, with this rate, the environment has triggered the selection of different protocols based on the ReLate2Jit values.

Figure 10 shows Ricochet R=4 C=3 to consistently have the best (*i.e.*, lowest) ReLate2Jit values when using pc3000 computers and a 1Gb network. Figure 11 shows NAKcast with a timeout of 1 ms as most of the time (4 out of 5 experiment runs) having the better ReLate2Jit value. We decompose the ReLate2Jit values to have a better understanding of the differences.

Figures 12 and 13 show the average latency broken out from the ReLate2Jit values above. These figures show that Ricochet R=4 C=3 consistently has the lowest average latencies regardless of the computing and network resources. Likewise, Figures 14 and 15 show that Ricochet R=4 C=3 consistently has lower jitter values across the different hardware. Figures 16 and 17 again show that NAKcast provides high reliability, while Ricochet provides less reliability.

All figures for individual QoS properties (*i.e.*, Figures 12 through 17) related to the ReLate2Jit measurements in Figures 10 and 11 show fairly consistent results across differing hardware. When these QoS properties are combined into a single, objective value, however, we are better able to distinguish one protocol from another thus highlighting the advantages to using composite metrics.

4.4 Determining Appropriate Protocol with Artificial Neural Networks

Evaluating the Accuracy of Artificial Neural Networks. The first step to using an ANN is to train it on a set of data. We provided the ANN with 394 inputs where an input consists of data values outlined in Tables 1 and 2 plus the composite metric of interest (*i.e.*, ReLate2 or ReLate2Jit). We also provided the expected output, *i.e.*, the transport protocol that provided the best composite QoS value for ReLate2 or ReLate2Jit.

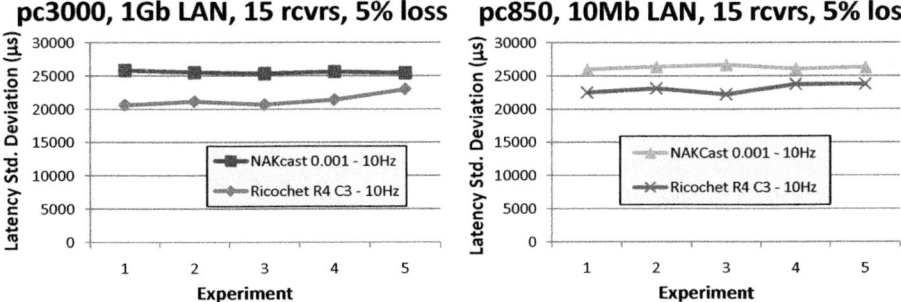

Fig. 14. Jitter: pc3000, 1Gb LAN, 15 receivers, 5% loss, 10Hz

Fig. 15. Jitter: pc850, 100Mb LAN, 15 receivers, 5% loss, 10Hz

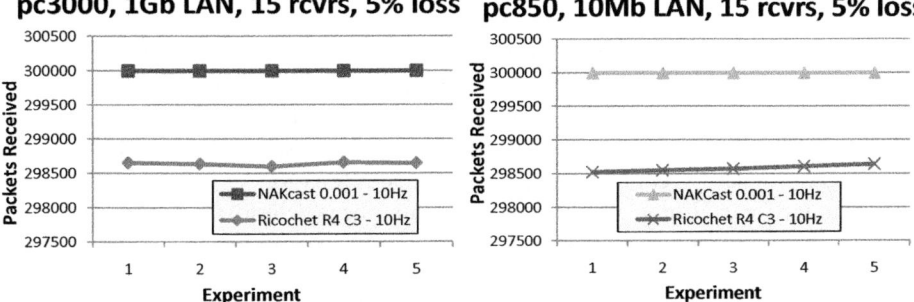

Fig. 16. Reliability: pc3000, 1Gb LAN, 15 receivers, 5% loss, 10Hz

Fig. 17. Reliability: pc850, 100Mb LAN, 15 receivers, 5% loss, 10Hz

An example of one of the 394 inputs is the following: 3 data receivers, 1% network loss, 25Hz sending rate, pc3000 computers, 1Gb network, OpenSplice DDS implementation, and ReLate2Jit as the metric of interest. Based on our experiments, the corresponding output would be the NAKcast protocol with a NAK timeout of 1 ms. All the 394 inputs are taken from experiments that we ran as outlined in Section 4.

FANN offers extensive configurability for the neural network, including the number of *hidden nodes* that connect inputs with outputs. We ran training experiments with the ANN using different numbers of hidden nodes to determine the most accurate ANN. For a given number of hidden nodes we trained the ANN five times. The weights of the ANN determine how strong connections are between nodes. The weights are initialized randomly and the initial values effect how well the ANN learns.

Figures 18 and 19 show the ANN accuracies for environment configurations that were known *a priori* and environments that were unknown until runtime respectively. The ANN was configured with different numbers of hidden nodes and a stopping error of 0.0001 (*i.e.*, an indication to the ANN that it should keep iterating over the data until the error between what the ANN generates and the correct response is 0.0001). Additional experiments were conducted with higher stopping errors (*e.g.*, 0.01), but lower stopping errors consistently produced more accurate classifications as expected.

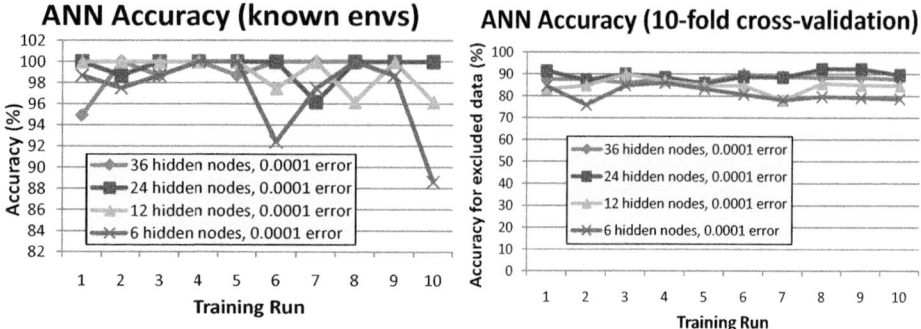

Fig. 18. ANN Accuracy for environments known *a priori*

Fig. 19. ANN Accuracy for environments unknown until runtime

Accuracy for environments known *a priori* was determined by querying the ANN with the data on which it was trained. Since we know the answer we gave to the ANN when it was trained we check to make sure the answer matches the ANN's response. Over the 10 training runs shown in Figure 18 the highest number of 100% accurate classifications was generated using 24 hidden nodes (*i.e.*, 8).

Accuracy for environments unknown until runtime is determined by splitting out the 394 environment configurations into mutually exclusive training and testing data sets. This approach is referred to as n-fold cross-validation where n is the number of mutually exclusive training and testing data sets [15]. The value of n also determines the amount of data excluded from training and used only for testing.

We used 10-fold cross-validation which indicates 10 sets of training and testing data where for each fold the training and testing data are mutually exclusive and the training data excludes 1/10 of the total data. As shown in Figure 19 the ANN with 24 hidden nodes and a stopping error of 0.0001 produced the highest average accuracy of 89.49%. We conducted our timings tests using this ANN since it provided the highest number of 100% accurate classifications for environments known *a priori* and the highest accuracy for environments unknown until runtime.

Evaluating the Timeliness of Artificial Neural Networks. As described in Challenge 2 in Section 2.2, the datacenter for the SAR operations needs to have timely configuration adjustments. We now provide timing information based on the ANN's responsiveness when queried for an optimal transport protocol. Timeliness was determined by querying the ANN with all 394 inputs on which it was trained. A high resolution timestamp was taken right before and right after each call made to the ANN.

Figures 20 and 21 show the average response times and standard deviation of the response times, respectively, for 5 separate experiments where for each experiment we query the ANN for each of the 394 inputs. The figures show that the ANN provides timely and consistent responses. As expected, the response times on the pc850 platform are slower than for the pc3000.

Inspection of the ANN source code confirmed experimental results that the ANN provides fast and predictable responses for both environments known *a priori* and

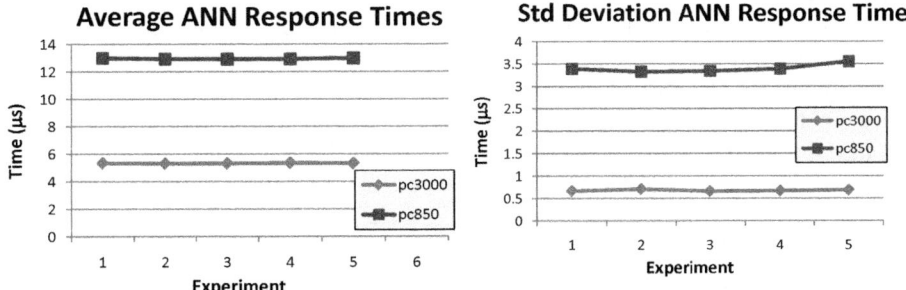

Fig. 20. ANN average response times

Fig. 21. Standard deviation for ANN response times

unknown until runtime. When queried for a response with a given set of input values, the ANN loops through all connections between input nodes, hidden nodes, and output nodes. The number of nodes and number of connections between them were determined previously when the ANN was trained. With a high level of accuracy, predictability, and minimal development complexity, ANNs provide a suitable technique for determining ADAMANT configurations.

5 Related Work

This section compares our work on ADAMANT with related R&D efforts.

Support for adaptive middleware. Ostermann et al. [19] present the ASKALON middleware for cloud environments that is based on middleware for grid workflow application development but enhanced to leverage clouds. ASKALON provides an infrastructure that allows the execution of workflows on conventional grid resources but that can adapt on-demand to supplement these resources with additional cloud resources as needed. In contrast to ADAMANT, however, ASKALON does not address the adaptive configurability needs of enterprise DRE systems in elastic clouds.

Gridkit [8] is a middleware framework that supports reconfigurability of applications dependent upon the condition of the environment and the functionality of registered components. Gridkit focuses on grid applications which are highly heterogeneous in nature. In contrast to ADAMANT, however, Gridkit does not address timely adaptation, nor does it focus on discovering and leveraging the elastic provisioning of cloud resources.

David and Ledoux have developed SAFRAN [7] to enable applications to become context-aware themselves so that they can adapt to their contexts. SAFRAN provides reactive adaptation policy infrastructure for components using an aspect-oriented approach. The SAFRAN component framework, however, provides only development support for maintaining specified QoS. The adaptive policies and component implementation are the responsibility of the application developer. Moreover, SAFRAN does not address timely configuration of components across the elastic resources of cloud computing. In contrast, ADAMANT provides a middleware implementation that adapts to the cloud resources presented to it.

Machine learning in support of autonomic adaptation. Vienne and Sourrouille [23] present the Dynamic Control of Behavior based on Learning (DCBL) middleware that incorporates reinforcement machine learning in support of autonomic control for QoS management. Reinforcement machine learning not only allows DCBL to handle unexpected changes but also reduces the overall system knowledge required by the system developers. In contrast to ADAMANT, however, DCBL focuses only on a single computer, rather than scalable DRE pub/sub systems. Moreover, reinforcement learning used by DCBL can have non-constant and even unbounded time complexities unlike ADAMANT which provides fast and predictable decision making.

RAC [5] uses reinforcement learning for the configuration of Web services. RAC autonomically configures services via performance parameter settings to change the services' workload and also to change the virtual machine configurations. Due to RAC's use of reinforcement learning, its determination of an appropriate response is unbounded due to online exploration of the solution space and modification of decisions while the system is running. In contrast, ADAMANT uses ANN machine learning to provide fast, predictable complexity decision making.

Tock *et al* [21] utilize machine learning for data dissemination in their work on Multicast Mapping (MCM). MCM hierarchically clusters data flows so that multiple topics map to a single session and multiple sessions are mapped to a single reliable multicast group. MCM manages the scarce availability of multicast addresses in large-scale systems and uses machine learning for adaptation as user interest and message rates change during the day. MCM is designed only to address the scarce resource of IP multicast addresses in large-scale systems, however, rather than timely adaptation based on available resources as done with ADAMANT.

Infrastructure for autonomic computing. Grace *et al.* [9] describe an architecture metamodel for adapting components that implement coordination for reflective middleware distributed across peer devices. This work also investigates supporting reconfiguration types in various environmental conditions. The proposed architecture metamodel, however, only provides proposed infrastructure for autonomic adaptation and reconfiguration and does not directly provide an adaptation implementation as ADAMANT does.

Valetto *et al.* [22] have developed network features in support of service awareness to enable autonomic behavior. Their work targets communication services within a Session Initiation Protocol (SIP) enabled network to communicate monitoring, deployment, and advertising information. As an autonomic computing infrastructure, however, this work does not directly provide an implementation unlike ADAMANT.

6 Concluding Remarks

Developers of systems which use DRE pub/sub middleware face several configuration challenges for cloud computing environments. To address these challenges, this paper presented the structure, functionality, and performance of *ADAptive Middleware And Network Transports* (ADAMANT). ADAMANT is pub/sub middleware that uses supervised machine learning to autonomously configure cloud environments with transport protocols that enhance the predictability of enterprise DRE systems.

The results in this paper empirically showed how computing hardware environments affect QoS for these systems and how ADAMANT configures the system based on the computing resources provided at startup in a fast and accurate manner while reducing development complexity over manual adaptation approaches. We selected ANNs to determine appropriate configurations since they provide (1) the highest level of accuracy possible for known environments, (2) better than random or default guidance for environments not known until runtime, and (3) the timing complexity required for DRE systems. The following is a summary of lessons learned from our experience evaluating ADAMANT's configuration performance in various cloud environments:

• **Computing resources affect which QoS mechanism provides the best support**
Differences in CPU speed and network bandwidth affect the choice of the most appropriate QoS mechanism. For certain computing environments, one transport protocol provided the best QoS; for other environments a different transport protocol was best. We leveraged this information to select the appropriate protocol for given computing resources. We are investigating other machine learning techniques that provide timeliness and high accuracy to compare with ANNs.

• **Fast, predictable configuration for DRE pub/sub systems can support dynamic autonomic adaptation.** ADAMANT can accurately and quickly configure a DRE pub/sub system at startup in cloud environments. Some systems, however, run in operating environments that change during system operation. The ADAMANT results have motivated future work on autonomic adaptation of middleware and transport protocols to support QoS in turbulent environments. Fast, predictable configuration can be used to adapt transport protocols to support QoS while the system is monitoring the environment. When the system detects environmental changes (*e.g.*, increase in number of receivers or increase in sending rate), supervised machine learning can provide guidance to support QoS for the new configuration.

• **Composite QoS metrics should be decomposed to better understand behavior of the system.** A change in the values from composite QoS metrics can be caused by changes in any of the individual QoS concerns or any combination of the concerns. The composite QoS metrics provide a higher level of abstraction for evaluating QoS and, as with any abstraction, details which might be important can be obfuscated. The composite QoS metrics we use are fairly easy to decompose as shown by Figures 4–9 in Section 4.3, although the more QoS properties that are composed the more decomposition is needed, which is hard, tedious, and time-consuming.

• **Exploring a configuration space for trade-offs requires a disciplined approach with analysis to guide the exploration.** Depending on the number of dimensions involved in the search space there can be many configurations to explore. In this paper we had multiple variables, *e.g.*, CPU speed, RAM, network bandwidth, update rate, % packet loss, number of data readers, NAKcast's timeout value, and Ricochet's R value. Since the number of potential experiments was large, we found it helpful to make coarse-grained adjustments for initial experiments. We would then analyze the results to guide areas of refinement to find trade-offs between transport protocols.

All ADAMANT source code and documentation and its supporting ANN tools is available as open-source at www.dre.vanderbilt.edu/~jhoffert/ADAMANT.

References

1. Global Information Grid. The National Security Agency, www.nsa.gov/ia/industry/gig.cfm?MenuID=10.3.2.2
2. Net-Centric Enterprise Services. Defense Information Systems Agency, http://www.disa.mil/nces/
3. Balakrishnan, M., Birman, K., Phanishayee, A., Pleisch, S.: Ricochet: Lateral Error Correction for Time-Critical Multicast. In: NSDI 2007: Fourth Usenix Symposium on Networked Systems Design and Implementation, Boston, MA (2007)
4. Balakrishnan, M., Pleisch, S., Birman, K.: Slingshot: Time-Critical Multicast for Clustered Applications. In: The IEEE Conference on Network Computing and Applications (2005)
5. Bu, X., Rao, J., Xu, C.Z.: A Reinforcement Learning Approach to Online Web Systems Auto-configuration. In: The 29th IEEE International Conference on Distributed Computing Systems., pp. 2–11. IEEE Computer Society, Washington (2009)
6. Buyya, R., Yeo, C.S., Venugopal, S., Broberg, J., Brandic, I.: Cloud Computing and Emerging IT platforms: Vision, Hype, and Reality for Delivering Computing as the 5th Utility. Future Generation Computer Systems 25(6), 599–616 (2009)
7. David, P.C., Ledoux, T.: An Aspect-Oriented Approach for Developing Self-Adaptive Fractal Components. In: Löwe, W., Südholt, M. (eds.) SC 2006. LNCS, vol. 4089, pp. 82–97. Springer, Heidelberg (2006)
8. Grace, P., Coulson, G., Blair, G.S., Porter, B.: Deep Middleware for the Divergent Grid. In: Alonso, G. (ed.) Middleware 2005. LNCS, vol. 3790, pp. 334–353. Springer, Heidelberg (2005)
9. Grace, P., Coulson, G., Blair, G.S., Porter, B.: A Distributed Architecture Meta-model for Self-managed Middleware. In: Proceedings of the 5th Workshop on Adaptive and Reflective Middleware (ARM 2006), p. 3. ACM, New York (2006)
10. Hoffert, J., Gokhale, A., Schmidt, D.: Evaluating Transport Protocols for Real-time Event Stream Processing Middleware and Applications. In: Proceedings of the 11th International Symposium on Distributed Objects, Middleware, and Applications (DOA 2009), Vilamoura, Algarve-Portugal (November 2009)
11. Hoffert, J., Schmidt, D.C., Gokhale, A.: Adapting and Evaluating Distributed Real-time and Embedded Systems in Dynamic Environments. In: Proceedings of the 1st International Workshop on Data Dissemination for Large scale Complex Critical Infrastructures (DD4LCCI 2010), Valencia, Spain (April 2010)
12. Ibnkahla, M., Rahman, Q., Sulyman, A., Al-Asady, H., Yuan, J., Safwat, A.: High-speed Satellite Mobile Communications: Technologies and Challenges. Proceedings of the IEEE 92(2), 312–339 (2004)
13. Kavimandan, A., Narayanan, A., Gokhale, A., Karsai, G.: Evaluating the Correctness and Effectiveness of a Middleware QoS Configuration Process in Distributed Real-time and Embedded Systems. In: Proceedings of the 11th IEEE International Symposium on Object-oriented Real-time distributed Computing (ISORC 2008), Orlando, FL, USA, pp. 100–107 (May 2008)
14. Lin, Q., Neo, H.K., Zhang, L., Huang, G., Gay, R.: Grid-based Large-scale Web3D Collaborative Virtual Environment. In: Web3D 2007: Proceedings of the Twelfth International Conference on 3D Web Technology, pp. 123–132. ACM, New York (2007)

15. Liu, Y.: Create Stable Neural Networks by Cross-Validation. In: IJCNN 2006: Proceedings of the International Joint Conference on Neural Networks, pp. 3925–3928 (2006)
16. Menth, M., Henjes, R.: Analysis of the Message Waiting Time for the FioranoMQ JMS Server. Distributed Computing Systems. In: 26th IEEE International Conference on ICDCS 2006, pp. 1–1 (2006)
17. Nathuji, R., Kansal, A., Ghaffarkhah, A.: Q-Clouds: Managing Performance Interference Effects for QoS-Aware Clouds. In: Proceedings of EuroSys 2010, Paris, France, pp. 237–250 (April 2010)
18. Object Management Group: Data Distribution Service for Real-time Systems Specification, 1.2 edn. (January 2007)
19. Ostermann, S., Prodan, R., Fahringer, T.: Extending Grids with Cloud Resource Management for Scientific Computing. In: 10th IEEE/ACM International Conference on Grid Computing, pp. 42–49 (13-15, 2009)
20. Shankaran, N., Koutsoukos, X., Lu, C., Schmidt, D.C., Xue, Y.: Hierarchical Control of Multiple Resources in Distributed Real-time and Embedded Systems. Real-Time Systems 1(3), 237–282 (2008)
21. Tock, Y., Naaman, N., Harpaz, A., Gershinsky, G.: Hierarchical Clustering of Message Flows in a Multicast Data Dissemination System. In: Proceedings of Parallel and Distributed Computing and Systems, PDCS 2005 (November 2005)
22. Valetto, G., Goix, L.W., Delaire, G.: Towards Service Awareness and Autonomic Features in a SIP-Enabled Network. In: Autonomic Communication, pp. 202–213. Springer, Heidelberg (2006)
23. Vienne, P., Sourrouille, J.L.: A Middleware for Autonomic QoS Management Based on Learning. In: Proceedings of the 5th International Workshop on Software Engineering and Middleware, pp. 1–8. ACM, New York (2005)

BrownMap: Enforcing Power Budget in Shared Data Centers

Akshat Verma, Pradipta De, Vijay Mann, Tapan Nayak, Amit Purohit, Gargi Dasgupta, and Ravi Kothari

IBM Research-India

Abstract. In this work, we investigate mechanisms to ensure that a shared data center can operate within a power budget, while optimizing a global objective function(e.g., maximize the overall revenue earned by the provider). We present the *BrownMap* methodology that is able to ensure that data centers can deal both with outages that reduce the available power or with surges in workload. *BrownMap* uses automatic VM resizing and Live Migration technologies to ensure that overall revenue of the provider is maximized, while meeting the budget. We implement *BrownMap* on an IBM Power6 cluster and study its effectiveness using a trace-driven evaluation of a real workload. Both theoretical and experimental evidence are presented that establish the efficacy of *BrownMap* to optimize a global objective, while meeting a power budget for shared data centers.

1 Introduction

The inevitability of power outages in a power grid due to the complex nature of the grid is slowly being realized [2]. Overloads on the electrical system or natural calamities like storms etc. can disrupt the distribution grid, triggering a failure. In the year 2007, more than 100 significant outages had been reported in North America [19]. The gap between the creation of new power generation units and the increasing growth-driven demand in emerging economies make the problem even more acute in developing countries. A 2008 report by Stratfor [15] indicates that the growth in GDP outpaces growth in power production in China by a factor of 5 and in India by a factor of 2. As a result of the power shortages, enterprises depend on back-up generators to deal with outages. However, the backup power available is typically much smaller than the demand leading to another electrical condition called power *brown-outs*, i.e., reduction in the power available to a data center.

A brownout is a temporary interruption of power service in which the electric power is reduced, rather than being cut, as is the case with a blackout. Brownouts may happen due to the reduced power available in the back-up generators as well as grid failures. A brownout may exhibit itself as lower available power (in watts) as well as voltage reduction, for example, the voltage may drop from 120V to 98V or less. Among the 100 power outages in North America in 2007, 33 of them led to brownouts [19]. These brownouts can last anywhere between minutes to few hours depending on their severity and enterprises have to deal with them. In this work, we investigate the problem of handling brownouts for virtualized data centers that host multiple customers (e.g., clouds) with minimal loss in revenue.

1.1 Triggers for Brownout

The increased focus on energy awareness necessitates demand response planning for handling brownouts in data centers. Brownouts may be triggered in a data center due to : (i) blackouts handled by back-up generators with reduced power supply (ii) unplanned grid failures due to natural calamities leading to reduced power(iii) deliberate brownouts undertaken by the grid authority when it is sensed that grid frequency is falling below safe limits (iv) Planned Demand Response by the data center. Planned Demand Response is emerging as a monetary tool to operate data centers in a cost effective fashion. Power grids have started differential pricing to deal with low frequency problems. For example, the KSE grid in India charges Rs 570 per KiloWattHour (KwH) for any additional unit consumed over the allocated quota if the supply frequency dips below 49 Hz, whereas the regular charges at 50 Hz are Rs $4/KwH$ [24]. In developed countries, multiple demand response initiatives are available to large data centers that may lead to significant cost benefits for the data center [8]. The Pacific Gas and Electric (PG&E) company offers multiple demand response alternatives with financial incentives to large customers during periods of peak load [18]. The *PeakChoice* program allows a customer to decide the power reduction the company is comfortable contributing and advance notice it needs. The Critical Peak Pricing (CPP) program gives an option of lower energy rates on non-peak days (up to a factor of 3) in exchange for higher rates on peak load days with a prior day notice. The Demand Bidding Program (DBP) provides an incentive to reduce a customer's electric load according to a bid. For each peak load event, the datacenter may elect to submit or not submit a bid via PG&E's Internet-based energy management system. Hence, demand response or brownout planning is emerging as an important tool for low cost datacenters.

1.2 Brownout and Clouds: Challenges

Virtualization and cloud computing have emerged as the enabling technologies for driving significant cost reductions in large data centers. One of the main drivers of the rapid adoption of shared data centers or clouds is the utility computing model where customers can scale up or down their resource usage on demand. To support this notion of utility computing, while keeping the costs down, the cloud infrastructure needs to ensure that resources could be moved from one customer to another in response to the customers' changes in demand. Hence, dynamic resource allocation to different customers on a shared infrastructure is the key to operating a cloud at low cost. Dynamic resource allocation has the additional challenge of providing customers the abstraction of an infinite resource pool. Further, the presence of differentiated applications (e.g., customers with different SLAs) on the shared resource pool, adds additional complexity to the resource allocation task.

Brownout management adds another layer of complexity to the resource allocation problem. To manage a brownout, power needs to be viewed as a separate resource and allocated to individual applications in the data center in a way such that the overall power budget is met, while maximizing the revenue of the provider. Existing resource management techniques (e.g., CPU allocation) can not be directly applied for allocating powers to applications as (i) different servers in a data center may have different power efficiency (ratio of compute capacity per unit Watt) and hence power allocation of an application depends on the type of the server hosting it, (ii) power consumed by one server may differ widely depending on the placed applications (iii) servers have a large static power that needs to be accounted to hosted applications, and hence the power accounted to an application depends on other applications hosted on the same physical server. Hence, existing CPU/memory allocation techniques can not be used to allocate power to applications in clouds.

Creating a power budget for an ensemble of blade [20] or rack servers [12] has been addressed earlier. The goal in these cases is to find the aggregate peak power consumption and use it as a budget. If the actual power exceeds the estimated budget, a throttling mechanism is used at each server. The presence of virtualization and differentiated applications make application-unaware server throttling of limited use in shared data centers and clouds. Multiple virtual machines running the cloud applications with different SLAs (and utility) may be co-located on a common server and a server-based power management mechanism is unable to differentiate between these applications. Further, due to the limited dynamic power range of a server [26,25], the power reduction due to throttling may even fail to meet the power budget.

1.3 Contribution

In this work, we present *BrownMap*, a fine-grained resource allocation mechanism, which can dynamically expand or shrink resource allocations of individual applications in a shared data center. *BrownMap* is designed to deal with brownouts, where a substantially lower power budget may be available due to a power outage. It can also help a cloud provider to deal with power surges that arise due to workload variability. The contribution of our work is two-fold:
(i) We present the design and implementation of the runtime *BrownMap* power manager. The power manager uses a distributed monitoring and reconfiguration framework. Our design has minimal monitoring overheads and reconfigures the server cluster to meet the power budget in a very short duration. The *BrownMap* architecture is robust enough to deal with noise in monitored data and scales well with the size of the server cluster.
(ii) We present the *BrownMap* placement methodology to find the configuration that maximizes the utility earned by the applications, while meeting the power budget. The methodology uses a novel divide and conquer methodology to break the hard power budgeting problem into *Server Selection*, VM Resizing and *VM Placement* sub-problems. We use an iterative procedure that leverages the nature of the power and utility curves to find a configuration that is close

to the optimal for most practical scenarios. On a real testbed using production traces, we show that *BrownMap* meets the reduced power budget in the order of minutes and can bring the power down by close to 50% for a 10% drop in utility.

2 Model and Preliminaries

We now formally define the brownout problem addressed in this paper. Consider a virtualized data center (cloud or traditional) with upto M servers S_j hosting N applications A_k. Each application may either be single component or multi-tiered. Each application component is run in a dedicated virtual machine (VM) or logical partition (LPAR). We use the terms VM and LPAR interchangeably in this work. The data center experiences a brownout for the next T hours with the available power reduced to P_B. The goal of the *Power Manager* is to re-allocate resources to each application component, migrate virtual machines between servers, and switch servers to low power active states (e.g., using DVFS) or lower power idle states (e.g, nap mode) or inactive (i.e., switched off) states in order to meet the power budget. Further, we need to ensure that the utility is maximized while meeting the budget. Formally, we need to find an allocation (or VM Size) x_i for each application component i and a mapping y_i^j on each server S_j s.t.

$$\arg\max_{\mathbf{x},\mathbf{y}} \sum Utility(x_i) \quad (1)$$

$$\sum_{j=1}^{M} Power_j(\mathbf{x},\mathbf{y}) < P_B; \quad \sum_i y_i^j {x_i}^i \le C_j, \ \forall \ S_j; \quad \sum_{j=1}^{M} y_i^j = 1, \ \forall \ VM_i \quad (2)$$

where $Utility(x_i)$ is the utility earned by VM i if it is assigned x_i resources, $Power_j(\mathbf{x},\mathbf{y})$ is the power drawn by server S_j for the given resource assignment and placement, and C_j is the capacity of the server S_j.

2.1 Deriving VM Utility

We have used a utility maximization framework to capture the importance of each application to the shared data center. The utility would usually be computed based on the revenue earned by the data center for the application. A utility based framework is general enough to capture various other objectives like strict priority and fairness. Application SLAs for clouds that provide platform as a service (PaaS) can be expressed as a 'revenue versus resource' curve. SLAs for clouds that provide application or software as a service (AaaS) are captured as a 'revenue versus application SLA metric' curve, where the application SLA metric could be throughput. In this work, we use 'revenue versus throughput' as the SLA since it captures both PaaS and AaaS. Our framework requires a utility function (utility versus resource curve) to be associated with individual virtual machines, which needs to be derived from application SLAs.

For single component applications, the utility of a VM could be derived in a straightforward manner. For each application, the provider can use a few experimental runs to derive a 'resource versus throughput' curve and combine it with the SLA (revenue versus throughput curve) to obtain a 'revenue versus resource' curve for the application. This curve may be used as the utility for

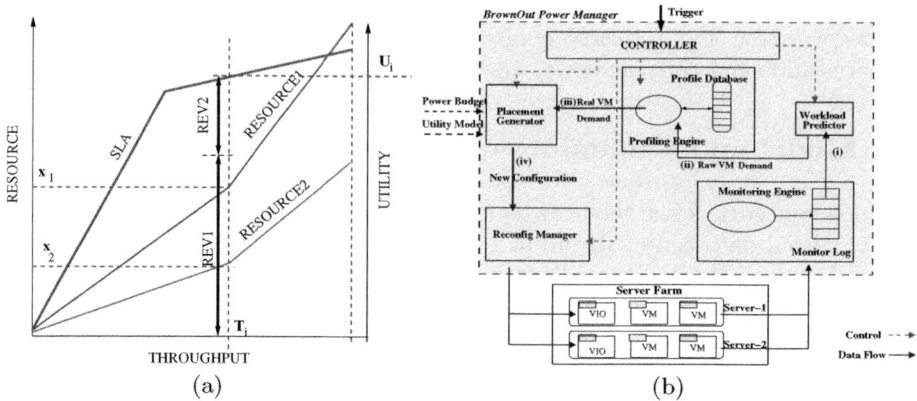

Fig. 1. (a) Utility Computation in BrownMap and (b) BrownMap Architecture

the VM as it accurately captures the revenue obtained by the provider for each unit of resource allocated to the application. The provider may then use these utility curves to determine the applications that provide the least loss in revenue if resources are taken away from them.

Traditional data centers as well as clouds also host many multi-tier applications, where each tier is hosted in a separate VM. Consider an example scenario with a 2-tiered application in Fig. 1(a). The *SLA* function captures the revenue derived by the composite application for a given throughput. The *RESOURCE* function captures the resource consumption of each tier (or VM) for a certain application throughput. Resource functions for each tier can be obtained using monitored data that map resource utilization in each component VM to the application throughput. In cases where an application may have multiple types of requests, the functions are based on average estimates. In order to apply our framework, we need to derive the utility functions for each component from these *SLA* and *RESOURCE* functions.

The chosen utility function for each VM should satisfy the following properties:

1. Proportional Allocation: Resource allocation to each component (VM) of an application should be in a manner such that no component becomes a bottleneck. To understand the need for Proportional Allocation, consider the example in Fig. 1(a). If LPAR1 has x_1 resource assigned and LPAR2 has resource assigned greater than x_2, any additional resource assigned to LPAR2 above x_2 does not lead to an increase in the throughput of the application. This is because, unless, the resources assigned to all the VMs hosting the multiple components of a multi-tier application are increased proportionately, the overall application throughput will remain unchanged and any additional resources assigned to only a few VMs (in this case LPAR2) will get wasted.

2. Utility Preservation: The total utility obtained by all the VMs hosting a multi-component application for aggregate resource usage x_i should equal the utility of the composite application for a resource allocation of x_i. This is required to ensure that the utility attached to the components of an application reflect the SLA of the composite application.

In order to achieve these goals, we have designed a proportional utility assignment method. We divide the utility derived by the application amongst its components in proportion to the resource used by each component. Hence, in Fig. 1(a), we set the revenue $REV1$ of $Component1$ at throughput T_i as $\frac{x_1}{x_1+x_2} * U_i$. Futher, the utility function (revenue versus resource) attached to VM of $Component1$ has utility $REV1$ at resource x_1. The above assignment ensures Utility Preservation, i.e., sum of the utility of all components of an application for a given resource usage equals the actual utility of the application at the resource usage. Further, the utility per unit resource consumed for each component is equal ($=\frac{U_i}{x_1+x_2}$ in the example). We later show (Sec. 4) that our optimization methodology uses the above insight to meet the proportional allocation property as well.

3 BrownMap Architecture

We now describe the overall architecture of the *BrownMap Power Manager*.

BrownMap Power Manager computes a new sizing and placement for the Virtual Machines (VMs) for a fixed duration termed as the consolidation interval (e.g., 2 hours). The key modules in the BrownMap Power Manager, as shown in Fig. 1(b), are (i) *Monitoring Engine*, (ii) *Workload Predictor*, (iii) *Profiling Engine*, (iv) *Placement Generator*, and (v) *Reconfig Manager*. The *Monitoring Engine* periodically collects (a) system parameter values from each logical partition (LPAR) as well as the management partition present on each physical server in the shared cloud infrastructure and (b) Application usage statistics, and stores them in the Monitor Log. The *power management* flow is orchestrated by a *Controller*. The *Controller* executes a new flow on an event trigger, which could be either a change in the power budget or the end of the previous consolidation interval. On receiving an event trigger, it invokes the *Workload Predictor, Profiling Engine, Placement Generator*, and *Reconfig Manager* in the given order to coordinate the computation of the new configuration and its execution. The main steps in the flow are (i) estimation of the resource demand for each VM in the next consolidation interval by the *Workload Predictor*. (ii) update of the VM resource demands to account for VIO resource usage based on the profiles of each application by the *Profiling Engine*, (iii) re-sizing and placement of VMs based on their utility models and a power budget by the *Placement Generator*, (iv) execution of the new configuration by the *Reconfig Manager*. We now describe each component of our architecture separately.

3.1 Monitoring Engine

The monitoring engine collects resource usage statistics for all partitions, including the management partition, on a physical node. For IBM's Power Hypervisor (pHyp) the management partition is called the Virtual I/O (VIO) Server. The monitor agent on each partition collects utilization data for CPU, active memory, network traffic, and I/O traffic, and feeds it back to the monitoring engine. The data is sampled every 30 seconds, and periodically the aggregated log files are pushed to a *Monitor Log*, implemented as a relational database. The script based monitor agent on each partition consumes less than 0.1% of the resource allocated to a partition.

The resource dedicated to a partition can change dynamically under different settings. For example, the number of CPUs allocated to a partition can vary over time. The task of monitor agent is to accurately track the changing resource consumption of the partition, also called "entitlement of the partition". The actual resource usage, for CPU and memory, is percentage utilization with respect to the entitlement. Note that the CPU entitlement for each LPAR in a Power6 virtual environment can be a fraction of the total CPU pool available on the physical server. Many of the modern processors are also capable of scaling the voltage and frequency in order to optimize power consumption, which is known as Dynamic Voltage and Frequency Scaling (DVFS). If DVFS is enabled, the reported entitlement takes into account the scaled CPU frequency. The resource usage statistics of the VIO are similarly monitored and logged. It is important to note that the VIO performs work on behalf of individual LPARs, which should be accounted back to the LPAR. The profiling engine, discussed later ensures that the LPAR resource usage captures the work done by VIO on its behalf.

3.2 Workload Predictor

The goal of the *Workload Predictor* is to estimate the raw resource (CPU, memory, network, disk) demand for each VM in the next consolidation interval. It has been observed in data centers that some workloads exhibit nice periodic behavior and some do not follow any particular pattern [27]. Periodic workloads can be predicted in longer horizons with significant reliability using a long term forecast. However, the prediction error increases rapidly for non-periodic workloads as the horizon increases. We use a two-pronged strategy in the design of our *Predictor* to handle both periodic and non-periodic workloads. We make a short-term as well as a long term prediction and use both to estimate the resource usage.

A popular method for deciding periodicity is the auto-correlation function and the peaks in the magnitude spectrum [1]. Once the periodicity for a workload is determined, we use it to make a long term forecast. The short-term prediction is based on polynomial approximation to minimize the least-square error. We then use a weight parameter to give weightage to the long term and short term forecasts. Let us divide the usage history into a sequence of time periods and we consider the last P periods for estimation. Our goal is to forecast the next K usage values based on last n samples of the usage history, where $n = P*p$ (p is the number of samples in each period). The resource demand at $(n+k)$-th interval is predicted as

$$\hat{D}_{n+k} = (1-\alpha) * \frac{1}{P} \sum_{i=1}^{P} y_{i*p+k} + \alpha * f_p(y_n, y_{n-1}, \ldots, y_{n-N_s-1}), \quad k=1,\ldots,K$$

where y_{i*p+k} are the corresponding usage values at the kth sample of the i-th cycle, f_p is the short term prediction based on last N_s samples and α is the weight parameter. Note that $\frac{1}{P}\sum_{i=1}^{P} y_i$ and $f_p(y_{n-1}, y_{n-2}, \ldots, y_{n-N_s})$ represent the long and short-term components of the forecasted value, respectively. We set α as 1 for workloads without periodicity and 0.5 otherwise. For the resource usage histories we considered, we found that second order is sufficient for reasonable approximation, and the error increases as K increases. Finally, the default value of P is set such that the number of periods cover a week, which has been observed to be sufficient to determine periodicity in data centers [27].

3.3 Profiling Engine

I/O processing for virtual I/O adapters are performed by the Virtualization layer (Virtual I/O Server(VIO) in pHyp and dom0 on Xen) on behalf of individual LPARs. This redirection leads to a CPU overhead for I/O processing [6] that must be accounted back to the LPAR requesting the I/O. As an example, the CPU overhead in VIO due to an LPAR having a network activity of $600KBps$ on an IBM JS-22 BladeCenter is around 4% of 1 $4.0GHz$ Power6 core (Fig 2(b)). The *Profiling Engine* provides an estimate of such VIO CPU overhead and accounts it to the LPAR in order to create the real resource demand for each LPAR.

The *Profiling Engine* uses a *Profile Database* that captures the relationship between hypervisor CPU overhead and the disk and network activity in an LPAR for each physical server type (Fig 2(a) and Fig 2(b)). This profile is created using calibration runs on each server model in the datacenter. During the *power management* flow, the *Profiling Engine* uses the *Profile Database* along with the network and disk activity demand provided by the *Workload Predictor* to estimate the VIO overhead due to each LPAR. The VIO overhead is then added to the raw CPU demand of the LPAR to estimate the real resource demand for each LPAR in the consolidation interval. The real demand is used by the *Placement Engine* for VM sizing and placement.

The *Profiling Engine* also provides an estimate of power consumption for a configuration that the *Placement Generator* comes up with. The power drawn by

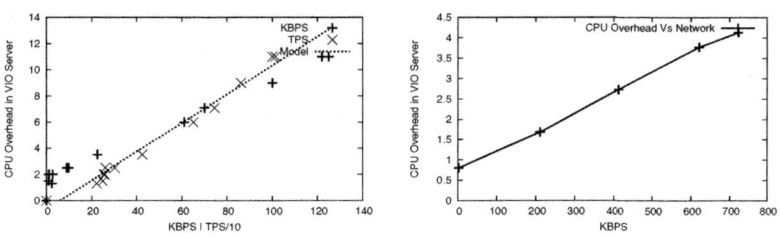

(a) VIO Overhead with LPAR Disk Activity (b) VIO Overhead with LPAR network activity

Fig. 2.

a server can not be accurately estimated only from the expected CPU utilization of the server for heterogeneous applications, as it also depends on the nature of the application [25]. The *Profiling Engine* uses WattApp, a power meter that has been designed for heterogeneous applications [16]. WattApp uses power profiles for each application on a server, which is then used to estimate the power drawn by a server for running a mix of applications. The individual power profile for each application is also stored in the *Profile Database*.

3.4 Placement Generator

The *Placement Generator* takes as input the predicted real resource demand (CPU, Memory, I/O) and the application profiles from the *Profiling Engine*, utility models for the workloads, the previous allocation and the user specified power budget. Based on resource demands and the utility accrued from each application, it computes a a new placement map, which specifies which applications reside on which servers and occupy what capacity (i.e. size) of the host server. Further, based on the application and server profiles, the *VIO* layer is also resized. The power consumed by this new placement map is now within the power budget and maximizes the overall utility. Details of the methodology implemented by the *Placement Generator* are presented in Sec. 4.

3.5 Reconfiguration Manager

The *Reconfiguration Manager* takes as input the new LPAR entitlements and placement provided by the *Placement Engine* and moves the data center to this new configuration in the most efficient manner possible. LPAR migration is an expensive operation (1 to 2 minutes for active LPARs) and it is important to minimize the time taken to reconfigure the data center. Further, since LPARs may both move in or out of a server, it is possible that there may not be available resources for an LPAR moving in till some LPARs are moved out. This may create temporary resource capacity issues leading to failures during reconfiguration. The goal of the *Reconfiguration Manager* is to (a) minimize the total time taken to reconfigure and (b) avoid any temporary capacity failures due to migration. The *Reconfiguration Manager* spawns a new process for each server that has at least one LPAR being migrated from it. This allows the reconfiguration to scale with the number of servers involved in the reconfiguration. In order to overcome any capacity issues during migration, we reduce the reservation of an LPAR being migrated, before migration. This ensures that there is no resource allocation failure when an LPAR is migrating to a target server. The LPAR is resized back to its correct resource allocation, as soon as the target server has finished migrating any LPARs that are moving out of it. If a server has no LPARs running on it, the *Reconfiguration Manager* either switches it off or moves it to *Nap* mode [11], if available. For active servers that are underutilized, an appropriate power-state is selected using DVFS.

4 BrownMap Sizing and Placement Methodology

We now present the *BrownMap* sizing and placement methodology implemented by the *Placement Engine*. There are three sub-problems which are tackled to reach the overall goal of revenue maximization under limited power budget. These are: (i) Selection of active servers that meet the power budget, (ii) Resource Allocation for each VM (x_i) on the available capacity of the servers and (iii) Placement of VMs on active physical servers (y_i^j). The resulting problem is an NP-hard problem, as bin packing becomes a simple case of this problem.

In order to understand the problem, observe that the optimization problem evaluates two functions, namely *Power* and *Utility* as a function of VM sizes (x_i) and their placement (y_i^j). As noted in [25], power consumption by a server is not determined solely by the server's utilization but is also dependent on the nature of applications running on the server. Hence, estimating the power drawn by a heterogeneous mix of applications in a shared cloud is a challenging problem. Since a closed form for an objective function, viz. power, does not exist, off-the-shelf solvers can not be used. The Utility function is again a derived measure and is dependent on the SLA parameter of the application. Typical utility functions would satisfy the law of diminishing marginal returns and may be approximated by a concave curve. The value of the SLA parameter depends on the resource assigned to the application and is typically a convex function (e.g., Fig. 4(b)). Hence, the nature of the utility curve with the resource is a function with potential points of inflection making it a difficult problem to solve.

We now present an outline of our *BrownMap* methodology that solves this problem using an iterative procedure.

4.1 Outline of BrownMap

The *BrownMap* methodology is based on a 'divide and conquer' philosophy. We divide this hard problem into three sub-problems, namely Server Selection, VM

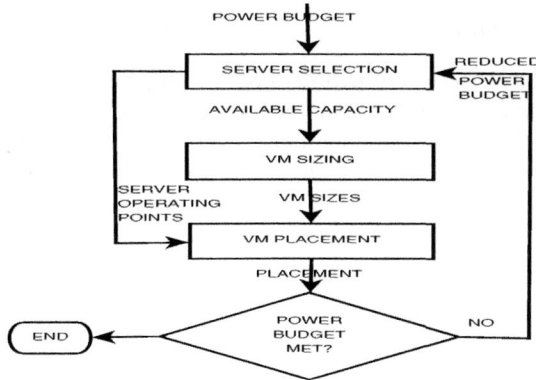

Fig. 3. BrownMap Placement Algorithm Flow

Sizing and VM Placement. One may note that the feasible space for each sub-problem depends on the solution of other sub-problems. For example, the *Server Selection* problem can predict whether the power budget can be met, only if the placement and sizing of the applications are known. To address this problem, we assume a fixed solution for the other two sub-problems, while finding the best solution for each sub-problem. We then iterate over the solution till we can find a placement and sizing that meets the power budget. Our methodology leverages a recent power modeling work Wattapp [16], which is able to predict the power drawn by a heterogeneous mix of applications running on a shared cloud, for convergence. The overall iterative flow of *BrownMap*, as shown in Fig. 3, consists of the following steps.

- Server Selection: In this step, we use the available power budget to pick the most power efficient servers within the power budget for an average application. We leverage the Order Preservation property from an earlier work [25] that allows us to rank servers with respect to power efficiency in an application oblivious manner. Once we identify the active servers, we compute the aggregate server capacity available to the applications.
- VM Sizing: This step takes the available capacity as input and computes the best VM size (x_i) for each application that maximizes the utility earned within the available capacity.
- VM Placement: In this step, we use the servers and their operating points and VM sizes to compute the best placement (y_i^j) of VMs on servers. We use the history-aware iDFF placement method presented in an earlier work [25]. $iDFF$ is a refinement of the First Fit Decreasing bin packing algorithm that also minimizes the number of migrations. For further details of this step, the reader is referred to [25]
- Iterate: If the Placement method is able to place all the applications, we use WattApp [16] to estimate the power drawn. If the estimated power exceeds the budget or the applications can not be placed in the previous step, we iterate from the server selection step with a reduced set of servers.

4.2 Server Selection

We define the *Server Selection* problem as finding a subset of servers and their operating points such that the power drawn by the servers is within a power budget. Further, the total server capacity available for hosting VMs is the maximum possible within the power budget. Note that the power drawn by a server is not determined solely by the CPU utilization but also on the application mix running on the server [9], [25], [26], [16]. Hence, the power drawn by a set of servers can not be represented as a closed function of the capacity used, as it depends on factors other than server capacity. However, we have noted in [25] that an ordering can be established between different servers based on their power efficiency for any fixed application and this ordering holds across applications.

We use the *Ordering property* to order servers and create a power vs capacity curve in Fig. 4(a). We replace the original curve with a convex approximation and find the server capacity that meets the power budget. The convex approximation

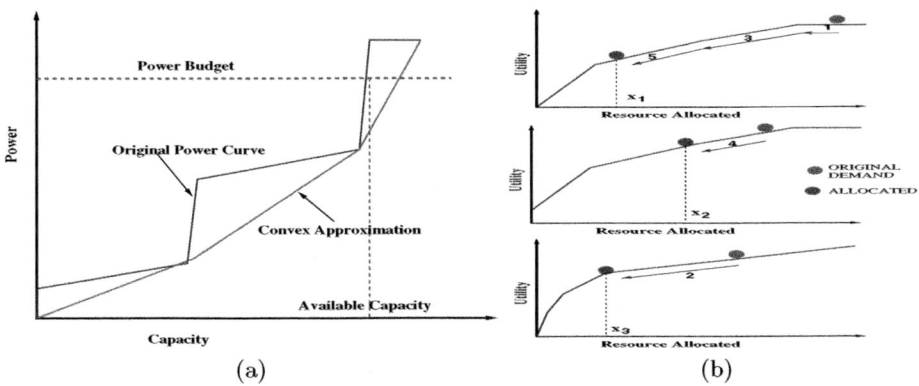

Fig. 4. (a) Server Selection and (b) VM Sizing Method

is employed for the iterative convergence. We use this selection of servers and operating points for VM sizing and placement. Once we get an allocation of VMs to servers and their sizes, we estimate the actual power consumed by the servers using the WattApp meter [16]. If the estimated power drawn exceeds the power budget, we move down on the convex power curve and iterate again.

4.3 VM Sizing

The *VM Sizing* problem takes as input an aggregate server capacity available to host a set of VMs. Further, for each VM, a model of utility as a function of the SLA parameter of the VM and a model of SLA parameter versus resource assigned to the VM is taken from the Pre-Processing step. We use the utility and resource models to create a model of utility versus resource allocated for each server. We start *VM Sizing* by allocating to each VM the maximum resource required by it in the next consolidation interval. We then iteratively take away resources from the VM with the least slope of the Utility-Resource curve (or the VM which has the least drop in utility for a unit decrease in resources allocated). To take the example in Fig. 4(b), we first take away resources from the first VM (with the least slope). In the next step, the third VM has the least slope and we reduce its resource allocation. The *VM sizing* method terminates when (a) the total capacity used by the VMs equals the capacity given by the server selection process and (b) the selected point on each curve is either a corner point or the slope of all the non-corner points are equal (Fig. 4(b)). The first property ensures that we meet the power budget assuming the *Server Selection* process is accurate. The second property ensures that the overall utility drawn by the VMs within the power budget can not be increased by making small changes. It is easy to see (proof omitted due to lack of space) that the resultant solution has the following optimality property.

Theorem 1. *The VM Sizing Method finds a resource allocation that is locally optimal. Further, if the utility versus capacity models for all VMs are concave, then the resource allocation is globally optimal.*

We note that the VM sizing for one VM is independent of other VMs. Hence, if an application has multiple components, with each component hosted in a separate VM, the sizing may lead to resource wastage. A desirable property is that each component of an application should be sized to achieve the same throughput. In order to achieve this, we add another condition to the convergence. If two VMs compete for a resource and have the same slope on the utility-capacity curve, we assign the resource to the VM with a lower achieved SLA value. This property coupled with the utility breakup for multi-tier applications (Sec. 2.1) leads to the following proportional assignment property between VMs belonging to a multi-VM application.

Property 1. Proportional Allocation Property: For a multi-tier application, the VM sizing allocates resources to all the components of an application in a way that they lead to the same application throughput.

4.4 Iterative Procedure

The *Iterative procedure* takes the computed placement and uses the *WattApp* power meter to estimate the power consumed by the placement. If the estimated power meets the power budget, the *Reconfiguration Manager* is triggered to reconfigure the VM placement in the cloud. If the estimated power is more than the budget, we iterate from *Server Selection* with a lower budget.

The *Brownout* problem has two optimization objectives: (i) power minimization and (ii) utility maximization. Minimization problems that have a convex objective function and maximization problems with a concave objective function lead to a fractional optimal solution easily. Hence, we have converted the power curve in the *Server Selection* problem to a convex approximation. In case the utility-capacity curve for all the applications is concave, this implies that the iterative procedure would converge to a solution that minimizes power and maximizes utility for a fixed server capacity. Further, the solution is also within the power budget and is close to the fractional optimal solution. We have formalized the above proof sketch to obtain the following result. The detailed proof is omitted for lack of space.

Theorem 2. *For any instance I of the brownout problem (Eqn. 1), consider the modified problem I′, which replaces the power function by its convex approximation. The BrownMap sizing and placement methodology leads to an integral approximation of the LP-relaxation of I′ for concave utility functions.*

5 Experimental Evaluation

5.1 Prototype Implementation

We have implemented *BrownMap* to manage a cloud consisting of 8 IBM Power6 JS-22 blade servers hosted on an IBM Bladecenter H chassis. Each blade has 4

IBM Power6 4.0 GHz cores with 8GB of RAM installed and is connected to a Cisco Network Switch for network access. The blades use 2 Gbps Qlogic Fiber Channel ports to connect with a SAN consisting of an IBM DS 4800 storage controller with 146 SCSI disks. The *BrownMap* power manager is deployed on a dedicated management server. The management server is an IBM Power5 1.5 GHz machine with 1 GB of RAM running Linux kernel 2.6. In order to completely automate the management, the management server has password-less ssh enabled with all the LPARs and VIOs. Monitoring agents are deployed on all the LPARs and VIOs. The management server uses the BladeCenter Advanced Management Module to get power data about the managed blades.

5.2 Experimental Setup

We now describe the experimental setup used to evaluate *BrownMap*.

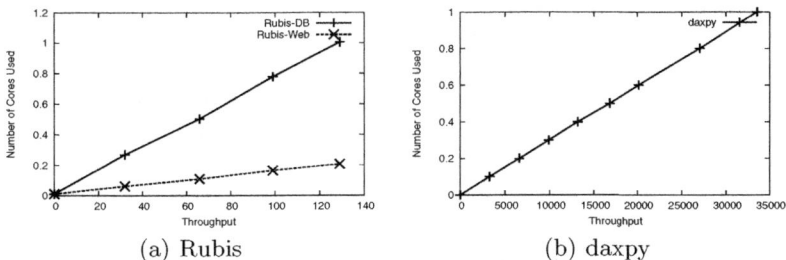

Fig. 5. Resource Vs SLA Models

Applications and Traces Used. We have deployed 2 different applications on our cloud testbed. The first application deployed in our testbed is *Rubis* [21] that simulates an auction site like ebay. *Rubis* is a two-tiered application with a web front end and a backend database server. We denote the web tier as *Rubis-Web* and the database tier as *Rubis-DB*. *Rubis* executes the standard browse and buy mix that is supplied with the application. Our second application is *daxpy*, a BLAS-1 HPC application [7]. *daxpy* takes batch jobs as input and executes them. We run two variants of *daxpy*; namely *daxpyH* as a high priority application and *daxpyL* as a low priority application.

We have instrumented both the applications and created models for throughput versus consumed CPU resource. The CPU resource is expressed in terms of the number of Power6 4.0 GHz cores for normalization across all LPARs (refer Figure 5). We use three different utility models for the applications. *daxpyH* is given a utility function that makes it the highest priority application in the testbed. *daxpyL* has a utility function with the least utility per unit amount of resource consumed. We attach a utility function for *Rubis* that is intermediate between *daxpyH* and *daxpyL*. The exact utility functions for the three applications for a given throughput (ρ) are (i) *daxpyH*: $\text{Util}(\rho) = \frac{5\rho}{33600}$, (ii) *daxpyL*: $\text{Util}(\rho) = \frac{\rho}{33600}$, (iii) *Rubis*:

Util$(\rho) = \frac{3\rho}{129}$. A natural interpretation of the utility functions is that for the same resource used, $daxpyH$, $daxpyL$ and $Rubis$ get utility in the ratio of 5 : 1 : 3. Note that 33600 is the throughput for $daxpy$ and 129 is the throughput of $Rubis$ at 1 core resource usage. We created drivers for each application that takes a trace as input and creates workload for the application in a way that simulates the utilization given by the traces. We used utilization traces collected from the production data center of a large enterprise for our study. More details about the traces are available in an earlier work of ours [27].

Competing Methodologies. We compared $BrownMap$ against a few other methodologies that an administrator can use to deal with brownouts.
Baseline: The first methodology termed as $Baseline$ mimics the scenario where a $Brownout\ Manager$ does not exist. The methodology is useful as it achieves the maximum utility without any resource restriction and can be used to compare with the utility achieved by other methodologies.
Server Throttling: This methodology throttles all the servers in the shared infrastructure to enforce the power budget. However, this approach was unable to bring the power down significantly in order to meet the budget in most cases.
Proportional Switchoff: This methodology switches off enough number of servers to meet the power budget. Further, it reduces the resources allocated to the VMs in a proportional manner. Finally, it migrates LPARs from inactive bladeservers to active blade servers.

We compare all the methodologies with respect to their ability to meet the power budget and the utility achieved, while meeting the power budget. Further, we also study their throughput and migration overheads.

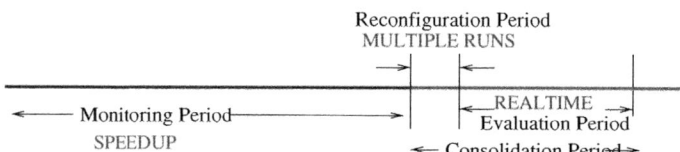

Fig. 6. Experimental Timeline

Experimental Timeline. Each experimental run in our study has three different phases, as shown in Figure-6. In the *Monitoring Period*, we collect monitoring data for the applications and the servers. Once sufficient historical data is available, we periodically run the $BrownMap$ methodology and reconfigure the data center. Each consolidation interval can thus be broken down into *Reconfiguration Period* during which we transition to the new configuration. This is followed by the *Evaluation Period* during which the configuration is allowed to run. Once the evaluation period is over, a new consolidation period starts.

The traces evaluated had weekly periodicity requiring the *Monitoring Period* to be 7 days or more. The reconfiguration activity (VM resizing and migration) depends on a large number of factors and should be repeated multiple times for the results to be meaningful. As a result, each experimental run takes an inordinately large time. In order to speed up the experiments, we divided each run into different parts. The *Monitoring Period* was speeded up using the already available trace data. The *Reconfiguration Period* was repeated multiple times in real time and each measure is a statistical average. The *Evaluation Period* was run in real-time and the throughput obtained by each application was measured.

5.3 Experimental Results

We performed a large number of experiments to evaluate *BrownMap* under a wide variety of settings. We now report some of our important observations.

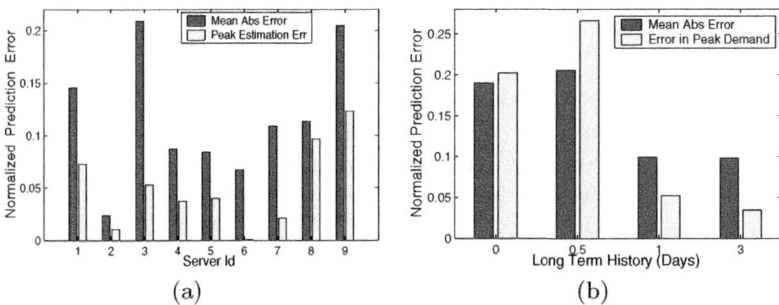

Fig. 7. (a) Error in Prediction of Demand and Peak Demand (b) Impact of Monitoring period on Prediction Accuracy ($\alpha = 0.3$, $N_s = 2.5 Hrs$)

Prediction Accuracy: *BrownMap* uses the prediction made by the *Workload Predictor* to determine the expected load in the next consolidation interval. The *Workload Predictor* makes an estimate of the workload intensity for the entire consolidation interval and the maximum workload intensity during the period is taken as the demand of the LPAR. Hence, we study the accuracy of the complete prediction as well as peak demand prediction in Fig. 7(a). An interesting observation is that the peak workload (max) during the evaluation period is a more stable metric and can be predicted to a greater accuracy than predicting the complete workload for the evaluation period. We observe that the error in predicting max is bounded by 10%, which is quite acceptable. We also observe that the prediction accuracy for both the time-varying workload during the evaluation period and the maximum workload improves with increase in monitoring data available, exceeding 95% for a history of 3 days (Fig. 7(b)). An interesting observation we make is that using a very low history for periodic traces may introduce more errors in long term prediction than not using any history at all (0.5 days history has higher error than 0 history).

Comparative Evaluation: The first scenario we evaluated was on a 2-blade cluster. We created 6 LPARs on the blades and deployed two instances of *daxpyH*

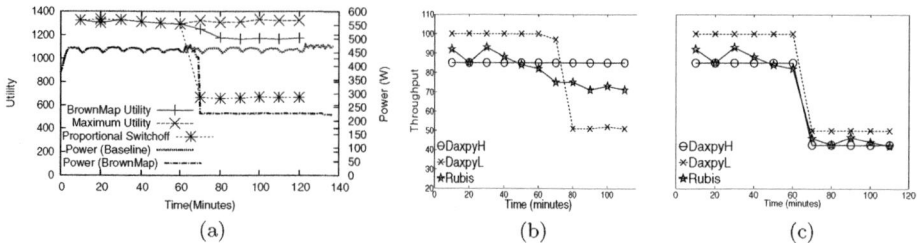

Fig. 8. Consolidating 2 blades with a power budget of 250W: (a) Comparative Power Consumption and Utility Earned. The Power drawn by Proportional SwitchOff is omitted as it closely follows BrownMap. (b) Normalized Throughput achieved by BrownMap (c) Normalized Throughput achieved by Proportional SwitchOff.

and *daxpyL* each. On the remaining two LPARs, we installed the *Rubis*-DB and *Rubis*-Web applications. The cluster during normal operation was consuming 500 watts. We simulate a brownout situation and send a trigger to the *Controller* that the budget had changed to 250 watts.

We study the new configuration executed by *Power Manager* in Fig. 8(a). The *Power Manager* resizes the LPARs and moves them to *blade*1, resulting in a drop in power. We observe the power drawn and utility obtained using (i) BrownMap, (ii) Baseline and (iii) Proportional SwitchOff. The utility drawn by *Baseline* indicates the maximum utility that can be earned if no power management actions are taken. We observe that *BrownMap* is able to meet the power budget without any significant drop in utility (about 10% drop from maximum). On the other hand, *Proportional SwitchOff* incurs a 45% drop in utility from the maximum to meet the power budget.

To understand how *BrownMap* is able to reduce power significantly without incurring a significant drop in utility, we observe the throughput achieved by each application in Fig. 8(b). We note that *BrownMap* is able to keep the throughput of *daxpyH* at the same level as the one before the brownout happened. On the other hand, it takes a lot of resources from *daxpyL* leading to a significant drop in throughput. The *BrownMap* methodology does not take any resources away from *Rubis*. However, since the overall system utilization is now higher, it leads to a marginal drop in the throughput of *Rubis*. In contrast, as seen from Fig. 8(c), *Proportional SwitchOff* drops the throughput of all the applications by 50%. Hence, *BrownMap* carefully uses the utility function to assign more resources to applications with higher utility per unit resource consumed (Fig. 8(a)). This allows *BrownMap* to meet the power budget with minimal drop in utility.

We next investigate a 4 server cluster to investigate how *BrownMap* deals with larger number of servers. We create 12 LPARs with 4 instances of *daxpyH* and *daxpyL* each. On the remaining 4 LPARs, we install 2 instances of Rubis, i.e. 2 LPARs with *Rubis-DB* and 2 LPARs with *Rubis-Web*. We again observe that *BrownMap* adapts to the reduced power budget quickly without a significant drop in utility (Fig. 9(a)). *Proportional SwitchOff* again has to sacrifice a

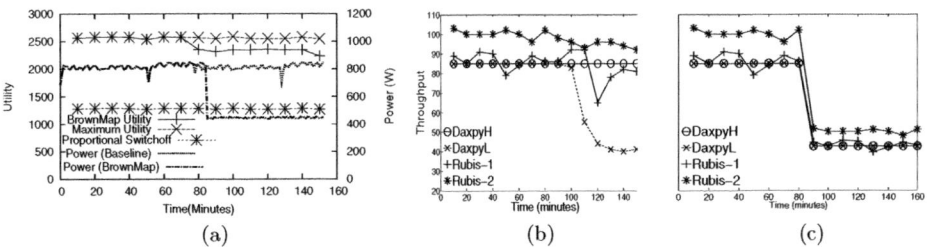

Fig. 9. Consolidating 4 blades with a power budget of 500W: (a) Comparative Power Consumption and Utility Earned. The Power drawn by Proportional SwitchOff is omitted as it closely follows BrownMap. (b) Normalized Throughput achieved by BrownMap (c) Normalized Throughput achieved by Proportional SwitchOff.

significant amount (close to 50%) of utility to achieve the power budget. The brownout is handled by carefully taking away resources from the low priority application, thus meeting the power budget with no more than 10% drop in utility. We also evaluated *BrownMap* with a 6 node cluster that conformed to the above observations. For lack of space, we do not report those results.

Drop in Utility with Change in Power Budget. In real data centers, the reduction in available power due to a brownout varies widely. Brownouts that happen because of increased demand may reduce the available power by 10% or 20% whereas a major outage may reduce available power by as much as 75%. Hence, we next vary the power budget and study the ability of *BrownMap* to deal with brownouts of differing magnitude in Fig. 10(a).

We observe that *BrownMap* is able to meet the budget for upto 50% drop in power with less than 10% drop in utility. This is a direct consequence of the fact the *BrownMap* first takes resources away from the lowest priority applications. These applications do not contribute much to the overall data center utility and

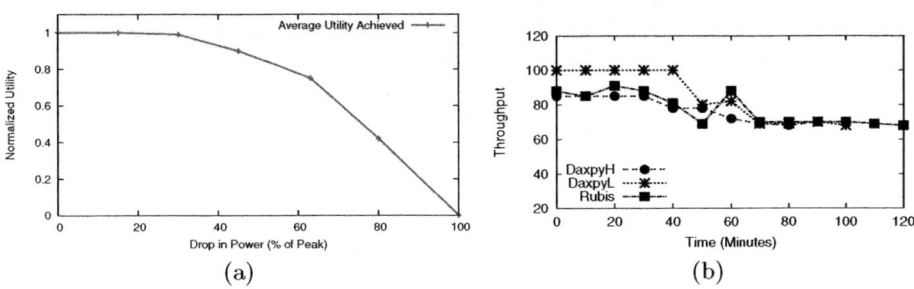

Fig. 10. (a) Utility earned by BrownMap with change in Available Power. Both Power and Utility are normalized. (b) Fairness Scenario: Normalized Throughput Achieved by all applications.

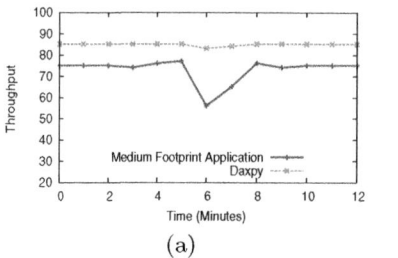
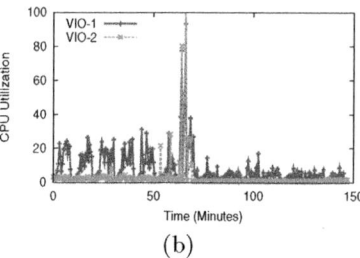

Fig. 11. Impact of migration on (a) application throughput and (b) VIO CPU Utilization

hence, we are able to reduce the power without a proportional drop in utility. It is clear in Fig. 10(a) that a proportional throttling mechanism will not be able to meet the power budget without sacrificing significantly on utility.

Using Utility for Fairness. The *BrownMap* power manager is able to deal with reduced power budgets by taking away resources from the lowest priority applications. This may lead to an unfair situation, which may not be acceptable to all data center administrators. We next show that utility maximization is a flexible tool that can capture diverse requirements including fairness.

In order to investigate if *BrownMap* can meet a power budget, while ensuring fairness, we change the original utility values to a more fair utility functions, namely (i) *daxpyH*: Util(ρ) = $\frac{5\rho}{33600}$, (ii) *daxpyL*: Util(ρ) = $\frac{5\rho}{33600}$, (iii) *Rubis*: Util(ρ) = $\frac{5\rho}{129}$. This ensures that for the same resource used, all applications get the same utility. We study the throughput achieved by each application in Fig. 10(b) and observe that all applications achieve the same normalized throughput in such a scenario after the reconfiguration. This study clearly establishes the flexibility of *BrownMap* to deal with diverse optimization scenarios from strict priority to fairness.

Characterization of Reconfiguration Overheads. The *BrownMap* power manager performs reconfiguration actions to meet a power budget. We next investigate the impact of this reconfiguration.

Cache Contention: Earlier work has observed a drop in throughput due to hardware cache flushes during migration [25]. Initially, we observed minimal throughput drop during migration for both our applications. We conjectured that this minimal drop in throughput during migration may be because our *daxpy* application executes small jobs whereas *Rubis* has a very large memory footprint and does not use cache much. We then used a medium memory footprint version of *daxpy*, which consequently showed a throughput drop of 20% during migration (Fig. 11(a)). Our observations thus confirm that cache contention between applications with medium memory footprint can deteriorate performance.

VIO Overhead: During our experimental study, we also observed that the migration leads to an increase in CPU utilization for the VIO (Figure-11(b)). This was true for all the applications studied. This increase in VIO CPU is because of the fact that VIO has to maintain the list of dirty memory pages used by an LPAR during live migration. The increase in CPU utilization can potentially lead to an impact on performance for the LPARs during migration. However, we capture the potential virtualization overhead due to an application during the profiling step and ensure that the resource demand for a LPAR captures any CPU overhead incurred by the VIO to serve I/O requests for the LPAR. Hence, reconfiguration does not lead to a significant drop in throughput even for I/O intensive applications like Rubis.

Reconfiguration Duration: We also observed that the reconfiguration always completed in an average of 4 minutes. Further, no reconfiguration took longer than 7 minutes. The scalability of the reconfiguration is a direct consequence of the fact that we parallelize the configuration with one thread per server in the data center. This distributed reconfiguration leads to a small reconfiguration period ensuring minimal impact on applications as well as enabling *BrownMap* to scale to large shared data centers. In a large data center with thousands of servers, it may not be possible to run thousands of threads on a single node. In such a scenario, the *Reconfig Manager* can be implemented in a distributed manner on multiple nodes, where each instance of *Reconfig Manager* handles the reconfiguration for a server pool. The separation of the reconfiguration module from the placement intelligence thus allows our design to scale to cloud-sized data centers.

6 Related Work and Conclusion

Brownout is a scenario where there is a temporary reduction in power, as opposed to a complete blackout. Brownouts affect data center operations by forcing them to bring down services and applications which may seriously impact its revenue. The related work in the field of brownout management includes power minimization, virtual machine placement and power budgeting.

Power Minimization: There is a large body of work in the area of energy management for server clusters. Chen et al. [5] combine CPU scaling with application provisioning to come up with a power-aware resource allocation on servers. Chase et al. post a very general resource allocation in [4] that incorporates energy in the optimization framework. However, most of the power minimization work is in a non-virtualized setting, where short-term decisions in response to workload variations or power shortages can not be made. Other approaches to minimize energy consumption include energy-aware request redistribution in web server and usage of independent or cooperative DVFS [3,10,13,14,22].

Virtual Machine Placement: The placement of virtual machines on a server cluster has been studied in [23,17]. The focus in [23] is on load balancing as opposed to power budgeting. In [17], the authors advocate presenting guest virtual machines with a set of soft power states such that application-specific power requirements can be integrated as inputs to the system policies, without application specificity at the virtualization-level.

Power Budgeting: There are other efforts in reducing peak power requirements at server and rack level by doing dynamic budget allocation among sub-systems [12] or blades by leveraging usage trends across collections of systems rather than a single isolated system [20]. However, the goal of this work is not to operate within a power budget but to find a peak aggregate power. In cases where the operating power exceeds the predicted peak, each server is throttled leading to a performance drop. Moreover, these techniques do not leverage virtual machine migration that allows a server to be freed up and put to a standby state. Finally, the presence of multiple virtual machines with possibly different SLAs on a single server make resource actions at server-level impractical.

In an earlier work [25,26], we have proposed power minimization mechanisms that use virtual machine migration to minimize power. However, the work deals with power minimization as opposed to a power budgeting problem. Also, loss in utility of virtual machines is not considered. One may note that the power budgeting problem involves power minimization as a component and is a much more general problem. In this work, we address the problem of handling a brownout with minimum loss in utility and present the design and implementation of *BrownMap*, a power manager that quickly adapts to a brownout scenario by reducing the power consumption within the budget. We present both theoretical and experimental evidence to establish the efficacy of *BrownMap* in dealing with brownouts. Our evaluation on a real cluster of IBM Power6 JS-22 Blades using real production traces indicates that *BrownMap* meets power budget with a drop of 10% in overall utility for a power reduction of 50% for realistic utility models. The reconfiguration operation in *BrownMap* is completely distributed, allowing it to scale with increase in the size of data center.

References

1. Bobroff, N., Kochut, A., Beaty, K.: Dynamic placement of virtual machines for managing sla violations. In: IEEE IM (2007)
2. Carreras, B., Newman, D., Dobson, I., Poole, A.: Initial evidence for self-organized criticality in electric power system blackouts. In: HICSS (2000)
3. Chase, J., Doyle. R.: Balance of Power: Energy Management for Server Clusters. In: Proc. HotOS (2001)
4. Chase, J.S., Anderson, D.C., Thakar, P.N., Vahdat, A.M., Doyle, R.P.: Managing energy and server resources in hosting centers. In: Proc. SOSP (2001)
5. Chen, Y., Das, A., Qin, W., Sivasubramaniam, A., Wang, Q., Gautam, N.: Managing server energy and operational costs in hosting centers. In: Sigmetrics (2005)
6. Cherkasova, L., Gardner, R.: Measuring cpu overhead for i/o processing in the xen virtual machine monitor. In: Usenix ATC (2005)
7. DAXPY, http://www.netlib.org/blas/daxpy.f
8. Dixon, G.: Demand response for today's datacenters. Focus Magazine (2008)
9. Economou, D., Rivoire, S., Kozyrakis, C., Ranganathan, P.: In: WMBS (2006)

10. Elnozahy, M., Kistler, M., Rajamony, R.: Energy conservation policies for web servers. In: Proc. USITS (2003)
11. McCreary, H.-Y., et al.: Energyscale for ibm power6 microprocessor-based systems. IBM Journal for Research and Development (2007)
12. Felter, W., Rajamani, K., Keller, T., Rusu, C.: A performance-conserving approach for reducing peak power consumption in server systems. In: SC 2005 (2005)
13. Heath, T., Diniz, B., Carrera, E.V., Meira Jr., W., Bianchini, R.: Energy conservation in heterogeneous server clusters. In: Proc. PPoPP (2005)
14. Horvath, T., Abdelzaher, T., Skadron, K., Liu, X.: Dynamic voltage scaling in multitier web servers with end-to-end delay control. IEEE Trans. Comput. (2007)
15. Stratfor Global Intelligence (2008), http://www.stratfor.com/analysis/global_market_brief_emerging_markets_power_shortages/
16. Koller, R., Verma, A., Neogi, A.: Wattapp: An application-aware power meter for shared clouds. In: Proc. ICAC (2010)
17. Nathuji, R., Schwan, K.: Virtualpower: coordinated power management in virtualized enterprise systems. In: Proc. SOSP (2007)
18. Pacific Gas and Electric Company. Peak Choice, http://www.pge.com/mybusiness/energysavings/rebates/demandresponse/peakchoice/
19. North American Energy Reliability Corporation, Disturbance Index Public (2007), http://www.nerc.com/ (last accessed April 2009)
20. Ranganathan, P., Leech, P., Irwin, D., Chase, J.: Ensemble-level power management for dense blade servers. In: Proc. ISCA (2006)
21. Rice Univerity Bidding System, http://rubis.ow2.org/
22. Rusu, C., Ferreira, A., Scordino, C., Watson, A.: Energy-efficient real-time heterogeneous server clusters. In: Proc. IEEE RTAS (2006)
23. Singh, A., Korupolu, M., Mohapatra, D.: Server-storage virtualization: integration and load balancing in data centers. In: SC 2008 (2008)
24. KSEBoard. Availability Based Tariff, http://www.kseboard.com/availability_based_tariff.pdf
25. Verma, A., Ahuja, P., Neogi, A.: pmapper: Power and migration cost aware application placement in virtualized systems. In: Issarny, V., Schantz, R. (eds.) Middleware 2008. LNCS, vol. 5346, pp. 243–264. Springer, Heidelberg (2008)
26. Verma, A., Ahuja, P., Neogi, A.: Power-aware dynamic placement of hpc applications. In: ICS (2008)
27. Verma, A., Dasgupta, G., Nayak, T., De, P., Kothari, R.: Server workload analysis for power minimization using consolidation. In: Usenix ATC (2009)

A Dynamic Data Middleware Cache for Rapidly-Growing Scientific Repositories

Tanu Malik[1], Xiaodan Wang[2], Philip Little[4],
Amitabh Chaudhary[4], and Ani Thakar[3]

[1] Cyber Center, Purdue University
tmalik@cs.purdue.edu
[2] Dept. of Computer Science, [3] Dept. of Physics and Astronomy,
Johns Hopkins University
xwang@cs.jhu.edu, thakar@pha.jhu.edu
[4] Dept. of Computer Science and Engg.,
University of Notre Dame
{achaudha,plittle}@cse.nd.edu

Abstract. Modern scientific repositories are growing rapidly in size. Scientists are increasingly interested in viewing the latest data as part of query results. Current scientific middleware cache systems, however, assume repositories are static. Thus, they cannot answer scientific queries with the latest data. The queries, instead, are routed to the repository until data at the cache is refreshed. In data-intensive scientific disciplines, such as astronomy, indiscriminate query routing or data refreshing often results in runaway network costs. This severely affects the performance and scalability of the repositories and makes poor use of the cache system. We present Delta a dynamic data middleware cache system for rapidly-growing scientific repositories. Delta's key component is a decision framework that adaptively *decouples* data objects—choosing to keep some data object at the cache, when they are heavily queried, and keeping some data objects at the repository, when they are heavily updated. Our algorithm profiles incoming workload to search for optimal data decoupling that reduces network costs. It leverages formal concepts from the network flow problem, and is robust to evolving scientific workloads. We evaluate the efficacy of Delta, through a prototype implementation, by running query traces collected from a real astronomy survey.

Keywords: dynamic data, middleware cache, network traffic, vertex cover, robust algorithms.

1 Introduction

Data collection in science repositories is undergoing a transformation. This is remarkably seen in astronomy. Earlier surveys, such as the Sloan Digital Sky Survey (SDSS) [33,40] collected data at an average rate of 5GB/day. The collected data was added to a database repository through an off-line process; the new repository was periodically released to users. However, recent surveys such as the Panoramic Survey Telescope & Rapid Response System (Pan-STARRS) [30] and the Large Synoptic Survey Telescope (LSST) [23] will add new data at an average rate considerably more than 100 GB/day! Consequently, data collection pipelines have been revised to facilitate continuous addition of data to the repository [18]. Such a transformation in data collection impacts how data is made available to users when remote data middleware systems are employed.

Organizations deploy data middleware systems to improve data availability by reducing access times and network traffic [3, 34]. A critical component of middlewares systems are database caches that store subsets of repository data in close proximity to users and answer most user queries on behalf of the remote repositories. Such caches worked well with the old, batch method of data collection and release. But when data is continuously added to the repositories, cached copies of the data rapidly become stale. Serving stale data is unacceptable in sciences such as astronomy where users are increasingly interested in the latest observations. Latest observations of existing and new astronomical bodies play a fundamental role in time-domain studies and light-curve analysis [17, 32]. To keep the cached copies of the data fresh, the repository could continuously propagate updates to the cache. But this results in runaway network costs in data-intensive applications.

Indeed, transforming data middlewares to cache dynamic subsets of data for rapidly growing scientific repositories is a challenge. Scientific applications have dominant characteristics that render dynamic data caches proposed for other applications untenable. Firstly, scientific applications are data intensive. In PAN-STARRS for instance, astronomers expect daily data additions of atleast 100GB and a query traffic of 10TB each day. Consequently a primary concern is minimizing network traffic. Previously proposed dynamic data caches for commercial applications such as retail on the Web and stock market data dissemination have a primary goal of minimizing response time and minimizing network traffic is orthogonal. Such caches incorporate latest changes by either (a) invalidating subsets of cached data and then propagating updates or shipping queries, or (b) by proactively propagating updates at a fixed rate. Such mechanisms are blind to actual queries received and thus generate unacceptable amounts of network traffic.

Secondly, scientific query workloads exhibit a constant evolution in the queried data objects and the query specification; a phenomenon characteristic of the serendipitous nature of science [25,35,42]. The evolution often results in entirely different sets of data objects being queried in a short time period. In addition, there is no single query template that dominates the workload. Thus, it is often hard to extract a representative query workload. For an evolving workload, the challenge is in making robust decisions—that save network costs and remain profitable over a long workload sequence. Previously proposed dynamic data caches often assume a representative workload of point or range queries [5,9,10].

In this paper, we present Delta a dynamic data middleware cache system for rapidly growing scientific repositories. Delta addresses these challenges by incorporating two crucial design choices:

(A) Unless a query demands, no new data addition to the repository is propagated to the cache system, If a query demands the latest change, Delta first invalidates the currently available stale data at the cache. The invalidation, unlike previous systems [6,34], is not followed by indiscriminate shipping of queries or updates; Delta incorporates a decision framework that continually compares the cost of propagating new data additions to the cache with the cost of shipping the query to the server, and adaptively decides whether it is profitable to ship queries or to ship updates.

(B) In Delta, decisions are not made based on assuming some degree of workload stability. Often frameworks assume prior workload to be an indicator of future accesses. Such assumptions of making statistical correlation on workload patterns lead to inefficient decisions, especially in the case of scientific workloads that exhibit constant evolution.

To effectively implement the design choices, the decision framework in Delta decouples data objects; it chooses to host data objects for which it is cheaper to propagate updates, and not host data objects for which it is cheaper to ship queries. The decoupling approach naturally minimizes network traffic. If each query and update accesses a single object, the decoupling problem requires simple computation: if the cost of querying an object from the server exceeds the cost of keeping it updated at the cache, then cache it at the middleware, otherwise not. However, scientific workloads consist of SQL queries that reference multiple data objects. A general decoupling problem consists of updates and queries on multiple data objects. We show how the general decoupling problem is a combinatorial optimization problem that is NP-hard.

We develop a novel algorithm, VCover, for solving the general decoupling problem. VCover is an incremental algorithm developed over an offline algorithm for the network flow problem. VCover minimizes network traffic by profiling costs of incoming workload; it makes the best network cost optimal decisions as are available in hindsight. It is robust to changes in workload patterns as its decision making is grounded in online analysis. The algorithm also adapts well to a space constrained cache. It tracks an object's usage and makes load and eviction decisions such that at any given time the set of objects in cache satisfy the maximum number of queries from the cache. We demonstrate the advantage of VCover for the data decoupling framework in Delta by presenting Benefit, a heuristics based greedy algorithm that can also decouple data objects. Algorithms similar to Benefit are commonly employed in commercial dynamic data caches [21].

We perform a detailed experimental analysis to test the validity of the decoupling framework in real astronomy surveys. We have implemented both VCover and Benefit and experimentally evaluated their performance using more than 3 Terabyte of astronomy workload collected from the Sloan Digital Sky Survey. We also compare them against three yardsticks: NoCache, Replica and SOptimal. Our experimental results show that Delta (using VCover) reduces the traffic by nearly half even with a cache that is one-fifth the size of the server repository. Further, VCover outperforms Benefit by a factor that varies between 2-5 under different conditions. It's adaptability helps it maintain a steady performance in the scientific real-world, where queries do not follow any clear patterns.

RoadMap: We discuss related works in Section 2. The science application, *i.e.*, the definition of data objects, and the specification of queries and updates is described in Section 3. In this Section, we also describe the problem of decoupling data objects between the repository and the cache. An offline approach to the data decoupling problem is described in Section 3.1. In Section 4, we describe an online approach, VCover, to the data decoupling problem. This approach does not make any assumptions about workload stability. An alternative approach, Benefit, which is based on workload stability is described in Section 5. We demonstrate the effectiveness of VCover over Benefit in Section 6. Finally, in Section 7 we present our conclusions and future work.

2 Related Work

The decoupling framework proposed in Delta to minimize network traffic and improve access latency is similar to the hybrid shipping model of Mariposa [38,39]. In Mariposa, processing sites either ship data to the client or ship query to the server for processing. This paradigm has also been explored in OODBMSs [11,22] More recently, applications use content distribution networks for efficiently delivering data over the Internet [31]. However, none of these systems consider propagating updates on the data [28]. In Delta the decoupling framework includes all aspects of data mobility, which include query shipping, update propagation and data object loading.

Deolasee et al. [10] consider a proxy cache for stock market data in which, adaptively, either updates to a data object are pushed by the server or are pulled by the client. Their method is limited primarily to single valued objects, such as stock prices and point queries. The tradeoff between query shipping and update propagation are explored in online view materialization systems [20, 21]. The primary focus is on minimizing response time to satisfy currency of queries. In most systems an unlimited cache size is assumed. To compare, in Benefit we have developed an algorithm that uses workload heuristics similar to the algorithm developed in [21]. The algorithm minimizes network traffic instead of response time. Experiments show that such algorithms perform poorly on scientific workloads.

More recent work [16] has focused on minimizing the network traffic. However the problem is focused on communicating just the current value of a single object. As a result the proposed algorithms do not scale for scientific repositories in which objects have multiple values. Alternatively, Olston et al. [27,29] consider the precision-based approach to reduce network costs. In their approach, users specify precision requirements for each query, instead of currency requirements or tolerance for staleness. In scientific applications such as the SDSS, users have zero tolerance for approximate or incorrect values for real attributes as an imprecise result directly impacts scientific accuracy.

Finally, there are several dynamic data caches that maintain currency of cached data. These include DBProxy [1], DBCache [3], MTCache [14] and TimesTen [41] and the more recent [13]. These systems provide a comprehensive dynamic data caching infrastructure that includes mechanisms for shipping queries and updates, defining data object granularity and specifying currency constraints. However, they lack a decision framework that adaptively chooses between query shipping and update propagation and data loading; any of the data communication method is deemed sufficient for query currency.

3 Delta: A Dynamic Data Middleware Cache

We describe the architectural components in Delta and how data is exchanged between the server repository and the cache (See Figure 1). Data of a scientific repository is stored in a relational database system. While the database provides a natural partition of the data in the form of tables and columns, often spatial indices are available that further partition the data into "objects" of different sizes. A rapidly-growing repository receives updates on these data objects from a data pipeline . The updates, predominantly, insert data into, and in some cases, modify existing data objects. Data is never deleted due to archival reasons. We model a repository as a set of data objects $S = o_1, \ldots, o_N$. Each incoming update u affects just one object $o(u)$, as is common in scientific repositories.

Data objects are stored at the cache of the middleware system to improve data availability and reduce network traffic. The cache is located along with or close to the clients, and thus "far" from the repository. The cache has often much less capacity than the original server repository and is thus space-constrained. We model the cache again as a subset of data objects $C = o_1, \ldots, o_n$. The objects are cached in entirety or no part of it is cached. This simplifies loading of objects. Objects at the cache are invalidated when updates arrive for them at the server. Each user query, q, is a read-only SQL-like query that accesses data from a set of data objects $B(q)$. The cache answers some queries on the repository's behalf. Queries that cannot be answered by the cache are routed to the repository and answered directly from there. To quantify its need for latest data, queries may include user or system specified currency requirements in form of a *tolerance for staleness* $t(q)$, defined as follows: Given $t(q)$, an answer to q must incorporate all updates received on each object in $B(q)$ except those that arrived within the last $t(q)$ time units. This is similar to the syntax for specifying $t(q)$ as described in [14]. The lower the tolerance, the stricter is the user's need for current data.

To satisfy queries as per their tolerance for staleness, the cache chooses between the three available communication mechanisms: (a) *update shipping*, (b)

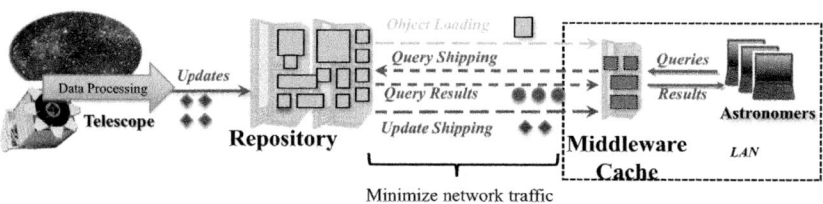

Fig. 1. The Delta architecture

query shipping, and (c) *object loading*. To ship updates, the system sends an update specification including any data for insertion and modification to be applied on the cached data objects. In shipping queries, the system redirects the query to the repository. The up-to-date result is then sent directly to the client. Through the object loading mechanism, the cache loads objects not previously in the cache, provided there is available space to load. The three mechanisms differ from each other in terms of semantics and the cost of using them. For instance, in update shipping only the newly inserted tuples to an object are shipped whereas in object loading the entire data object (including the updates) is shipped.

The system records the the cost of using each of the data communication mechanism. In Delta, we have currently focused on the network traffic costs due to the use of these mechanisms. Latency costs are discussed in Section 4. Network traffic costs are assumed proportional to the size of the data being communicated. Thus when an object o is loaded, a load cost, $\nu(o)$, proportional to the object's size is added to the total network traffic cost. For each query q or update u shipped a network cost $\nu(q)$ or $\nu(u)$ proportional to the size of q's result or the size of data content in u is added respectively. The proportional assumption relies on networks exhibiting linear cost scaling with object size, which is true for TCP networks when the transfer size is substantially larger than the frame size [37]. The quantitative difference in costs between the three mechanisms is described through an example in Section 3.1.

In Delta the difference, in terms of cost, of using each communication mechanism leads to the formulation of the data decoupling problem. We first describe the problem in words and then for ease of presentation also provide a graph-based formulation.

The data decoupling problem: In the data decoupling problem we are given the set of objects on the repository, the online sequence of user queries at the cache, and the online sequence of updates at the repository. The problem is to decide which objects to load into the cache from the repository, which objects to evict from the cache, which queries to ship to the repository from the cache, and which updates to ship from the repository to the cache such that (a) the objects in cache never exceed the cache size, (b) each query is answered as per its currency requirement, and (c) the total costs, described next, are minimized. The total costs are the sum of the load costs for each object loaded, the shipping costs for each query shipped, and the shipping costs for each update shipped.

Graph-based formulation: The decoupling problem given a set of objects in the cache, can be visualized through a graph $G(V, E)$ in which the vertices of the graph are queries, updates and data objects. Data object vertices are of two kinds: one that are in cache, and ones that are not in cache. In the graph, an edge is drawn between (a) a query vertex and an update vertex, if the update affects the query, and (b) a query vertex and a data object vertex, if the object is not in cache and is accessed by the query. In the graph, for presentation, edges between an update vertex and an object not in cache and query vertex and an object in cache are not drawn. Such a graph construction helps to capture the relationships between queries, updates and objects. We term such a graph as an *interaction* graph as the edges involve a mutual decision as to which data communication mechanism be used. The decoupling problem then corresponds to determining which data communication to use since the right combination minimizes network traffic costs.

The interaction graph is fundamental to the data decoupling problem as algorithms can determine an optimal decoupling or the right combination of data communication mechanisms to use. The algorithms must also be robust to incoming query and update workloads since slight changes in the workload lead to entirely different data communication mechanisms becoming optimal (See design choices 1 and 1 in Section 1). This is demonstrated in the next subsection through an example. The example demonstrates that different choices become optimal when the entire sequence of queries, updates and their accompanying costs are known in advance, and there are no cache size constraints.

3.1 Determining Off-Line, Optimal Choices

The objective of an algorithm for a data decoupling problem is to make decisions about which queries to ship, which updates to ship, and which objects to load such that the cost of incurred network traffic is minimized. This is based on an incoming workload pattern. The difficulty in determining the optimal combination of decision choices arises because a slight variation in the workload, *i.e.*, change in cost of shipping queries or shipping updates or the query currency threshold, results in an entirely different combination being optimal. This is best illustrated through an example.

In the Figure2, among the four data objects o_1, o_2, o_3, o_4, objects o_1, o_2, o_3 have been loaded into the cache (broken lines) and object o_4 is currently not in cache (solid lines), and will be available for loading if there is space. Consider a sequence of updates and queries over the next eight seconds. Based on the graph formulation of the decoupling problem, we draw edges between queries, updates and the objects. Query q_3 accesses the set o_1, o_2, o_4 and has edges with $o_4, u_1,$ and u_2. since either q_3 is shipped or the use of other data communication mechanism is necessary, namely o_4 is loaded, and u_1 and u_2 are shipped. For q_7, since object o_2 is in cache, the dependence is only on updates u_1 and u_6 both of which are necessary to satisfy q_7's currency constraints. q_8 accesses set o_1, o_4 and so has edges with o_4 and u_2. Note, it does not have edges with u_4 because shipping u_4 is not necessary till object o_4 is loaded into the cache. If o_4 was loaded before u_4 arrives, then an edge between u_4 and q_8 will be added. There is no edge with u_5 since the tolerance for staleness of q_8 permits an answer from the cached copy of o_1 that need not be updated with u_5.

In the above example, the right choice of actions is to evict o_3 and load o_4 at the very beginning. Then at appropriate steps ship updates u_1, u_2, and u_4, and the query q_7. This will satisfy all currency requirements, and incur a network traffic cost of $26GB$. Crucial to this being the best decision is that q_8's tolerance for staleness allows us to omit shipping u_5. If that were not the case, then an entirely different set of choices become optimal which include not loading o_4,

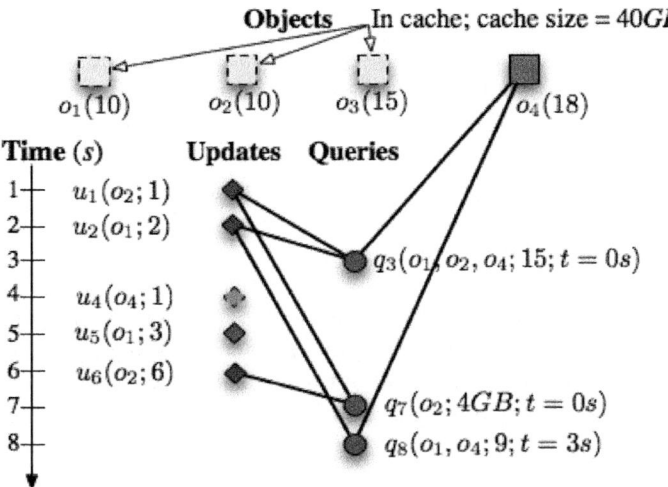

Fig. 2. An decoupling graph for a sample sequence. The notation: $o_1(10)$ implies size of object o_1 is 10 GB, which is also its network traffic load cost. $u_1(o_2, 1)$ implies update u_1 is for object o_2 and has a network traffic shipping cost of $1GB$. $q_3(o_1, o_2, o_4; 15; t = 0s)$ implies query q_3 accesses objects o_1, o_2, and o_4; has a network traffic shipping cost of $15GB$; and has no tolerance for staleness.

and just shipping queries q_3, q_7, and q_8 for a network cost of $28GB$. Such a combination minimizes network traffic.

In the above example, if we focus only on the internal interaction graph of cached objects, which is formed with nodes u_1, u_6 and q_7, we observe that determining an optimal decision choice corresponds to finding the minimum-weight vertex cover [8, 43] on this subgraph. For lack of space, we omit a description on minimum-weight vertex cover and directly state the correspondence through the following theorem:

Theorem 1 (Min Weight Vertex Cover). *Let the entire incoming sequence of queries and updates in the internal interaction graph G be known in advance. Let VC be the minimum-weight vertex cover for G. The optimal choice is to ship the queries and the updates whose corresponding nodes are in VC.*

Proof Sketch. If the entire incoming sequence of queries and updates is known we claim the optimal choice is: (1) choose such that every query q is either shipped or all updates interacting with q are shipped, and (2) make a choice such that the total weights of nodes chosen for shipping is minimized. This is true since the sum of the weights of nodes chosen is equal to the actual network traffic cost incurred for the choice. This corresponds to the minimum-weight vertex cover problem (see definition in [12]). □

The minimum-weight vertex cover is NP-hard problem in general [36]. However, for our specific case the sub-graph is a bi-partite graph in that no edges exist amongst the set of query nodes and the set of update nodes, but only between query and update nodes. Thus we can still solve the minimum-weight vertex cover problem by reducing it to the *maximum network flow* problem [15]. A polynomial time algorithm for the maximum network flow problem is the Edmonds-Karp algorithm [8]. This algorithm is based on the fact that a flow is maximum if and only if there is no augmenting path. The algorithm repeatedly finds an augmenting path and augments it with more flow, until no augmenting path exists.

A primary challenges in employing an algorithm for the maximum network flow problem to Delta is in (a) knowing the sequence of events in advance, and (b) extending it a limited size cache. The computation of the max-cover (or equivalently determining the max flow) changes as different knowledge of the future becomes available. In the example, if we just did not know what would happen at time $8s$, but knew everything before, we would not load o_4, and instead ship q_3 and q_7. Then when q_8 arrives, we would ship it too. Thus, different partial knowledge of the future can lead to very different decisions and costs. The decisions obtained by the computation of the max-cover applies only to the objects in cache. We still need a mechanism for profitably loading objects in the cache.

4 VCover

VCover is an online algorithm for the data decoupling problem. It determines objects for which queries must be shipped and object for which updates must be shipped. The algorithm makes decisions in an "online" fashion, using minimal information about the incoming workload. In VCover we also address the second challenge of a space-constrained cache. The overall algorithm is shown in Figure 3.

The algorithm relies on two internal modules UpdateManager and LoadManager to make two decisions: When a query arrives, VCover first determines if the all objects accessed by the query are in cache. If all objects are in

---

1 VCover
2 **Invocation:** By arriving query q, accessing objects $B(q)$, with network traffic cost $\nu(q)$.
3 **Objective:** To choose between invoking UpdateManager, or shipping q and invoking LoadManager.
4 **if** *all objects in $B(q)$ are in cache* **then**
5   UpdateManager with query q
6 **else**
7   Ship q to server. Forward result to client
8   In background: LoadManager with query q

Fig. 3. The main function in VCover

9 UpdateManager **on** cache
10 **Invocation:** By VCover with query q accessing objects $B(q)$, with network traffic cost $\nu(q)$.
11 **Objective:** To choose between shipping q or shipping all its outstanding interacting updates, and to update the interaction graph.
12 **if** *each update interacting with q has been shipped* **then**
13   Execute q in cache. Send result to client
14 Add query vertex q with weight $(\nu(q))$ to existing internal interaction graph G' to get G
15 **foreach** *object $o \in B(q)$ marked* stale **do**
16   **foreach** *outstanding update u for o* **do**
17   Add update vertex u to G, with weight its shipping cost, if not already present
18 **foreach** *update vertex u interacting with q* **do**
19   Add edge (u, q) to G
20 Compute minimum-weight vertex cover VC of G using incremental network-flow algorithm
21 **if** $q \in VC$ **then**
22   **if** *q not already executed on cache* **then**
23   Ship q to server. Forward result to client

Fig. 4. UpdateManager on cache

cache, this query is presented to the UpdateManager which chooses between shipping the outstanding updates required by the query, or shipping the query itself. If, instead, a query arrives that accesses at least one object not in cache, then VCover ships the query to the server, and also presents it to the LoadManager which decides, in background, whether to load the missing object(s) or not. We now describe the algorithms behind the UpdateManager and the LoadManager.

UpdateManager. The UpdateManager builds upon the offline framework presented in Section 3.1 to make "online" decisions as queries and updates arrive. The UpdateManager incorporates the new query into an existing internal interaction graph G' by adding nodes for it and the updates it interacts with and establishes the corresponding edges. To compute the minimum-weight vertex cover it uses the the Edmonds-Karp algorithm, which finds the maximum network flow in a graph. However, instead of running a network flow algorithm each time a query is serviced, it uses an incremental algorithm that finds just the change in flow since the previous computation (Figure 4). If the result of the vertex cover computation is that the query should be shipped, then the UpdateManager does accordingly (Lines 21–23). If not, then some updates are shipped.

The key observation in computing the incremental max-flow is that as vertices and edges are added and deleted from the graph there is no change in the

1. Let G' be the previous internal interaction graph and H' the corresponding network constructed in previous iteration.
2. Let G be the current internal interaction graph.
3. Add source and sink vertices to G and corresponding capacitated edges as described in [15] to construct network H.
4. Find maximum flow in H, based on the known maximum flow for H'.
5. Determine minimum-weight vertex for G from maximum flow values of H, again as described in [15].

Fig. 5. Single iteration of the incremental network flow algorithm

previous flow computation. Thus previous flow remains a valid flow though it may not be maximum any more. The algorithm therefore begins with a previous flow and searches for augmenting paths that would lead to the maximum flow. As a result, for any sequence of queries and updates, the total time spent in flow computation is not more than that for a single flow computation for the network corresponding to the entire sequence. If this network has n nodes and m edges, this time is $O(nm^2)$ [8]—much less than the $O(n^2m^2)$-time the non-incremental version takes.

The UpdateManager does not record the entire sequence of queries and updates to make decisions. The algorithm always works on a *remainder* subgraph instead of the subgraph made over all the queries and updates seen so far. This remainder subgraph is formed from an existing subgraph by excluding all update nodes picked in a vertex cover at any point, and all query nodes not picked in the vertex cover. The exclusion can be safely done because in selecting the cover at any point the shipping of an update is justified based only on the past queries it interacts with, and not with any future queries or updates and therefore will never be part of future cover selection. This makes computing the cover robust to changes in workload. This technique also drastically reduces the size of the working subgraph making the algorithm very efficient in practice.

Managing Loads. VCover invokes the LoadManager to determine if it is useful to load objects in the cache and save on network costs or ship the corresponding queries. The decision is only made for those incoming queries which access one or more objects not in cache. The difficulty in making this decision is due to queries accessing multiple objects, each of which contributes a varying fraction to the query's total cost, $\nu(q)$. The objective is still to find, in an online fashion, the right combination of objects that should reside in cache such that the total network costs are minimized for these queries.

The algorithm in LoadManager builds upon the popular Greedy-Dual-Size (GDS) algorithm [7] for Web-style proxy caching. GDS is an object caching algorithm that calculates an object's usage in the cache based on its frequency of usage, the cost of downloading it and its size. If the object is not being heavily used, GDS evicts the object. In GDS an object is loaded as soon it is requested. Such a loading policy can cause too much network traffic. In [24], it is shown that to minimize network traffic, it is important to ship queries on an object to the server until shipping costs equal to the object load costs have been incurred. After that any request to the object must load the object into the cache. The object's usage in the cache is measured from frequency and recency of use and thus eviction decisions can be made similar to GDS, based on object's usage in cache.

In VCover queries access multiple objects and the LoadManager uses a simple twist on the algorithm in [24] that still ensures finding the right combination of choices. The LoadManager (a) randomly assigns query shipping costs among objects that a query accesses, and (b) defers to GDS to calculate object's usage in the cache. The random assignment ensures that in expectation, objects are made *candidates* for load only when cost attributed equals the load cost. A candidate for load is considered by considering in random sequence the set of objects accessed by the query (Line 29 in Figure 6). At this point, the shipping cost could be attributed to the object.

The load manager employs two techniques that makes its use of Greedy-Dual-Size more efficient. We explain the need for the techniques:

- Explicit tracking of the total cost (due to all queries) of each object is inefficient. The load manager eliminates explicit tracking of the total cost by using randomized loading (Lines 27-35). This leads to a more space-efficient implementation of the algorithm in which counters on each object are not maintained. When the shipping cost from a single query covers the entire load cost of an object, the object is immediately made a candidate to be loaded. Else, it is made so with probability equal to the ratio of the cost attributed from the query and the object's load cost.
- In a given subsequence of load requests generated by q, say $o_1, o_2, \ldots, o_m$, it is possible that the given $\mathcal{A}_{\text{obj}}$ loads an o_i only to evict it to accommodate some later o_j in the *same* subsequence. Clearly, loading o_i is not useful for the LoadManager. To iron out such inefficiencies we use a lazy version of $\mathcal{A}_{\text{obj}}$, in our case Greedy-Dual-Size.

In the LoadManager once the object is loaded, the system ensures that all updates that came while the object was being loaded are applied and the object is marked fresh by both cache and server.

Discussion: There are several aspects of VCover that we would like to highlight. First, in Delta we have focused on reducing network traffic. Consequently, in presenting VCover we have included only those decisions that reduce network traffic. These decisions naturally decrease response times of queries that access objects in cache. But queries for which updates need to be applied may be delayed. In some applications, such as weather prediction, which have similar rapidly-growing repositories, minimizing overall response time is equally important. To improve the response time performance of delayed queries, some updates can be *preshipped, i.e.,* proactively sent by the server. For lack of space we have omitted how preshipping in VCover can further improve overall response times of all queries. We direct the reader to the accompanying technical report [26] for this.

```
24  LoadManager on cache
25  Invocation: By VCover with query q, accessing objects B(q), with network
    traffic cost ν(q).
26  Objective: To load useful objects
27  c ← ν(q)
28  while B(q) has objects not in cache and c > 0 do
29  │   o ← some object in B(q) not in cache
30  │   if c ≥ l(o) then                      /* l(o) is load cost of o */
31  │   │   A_obj_lazy with input o
32  │   └   c ← c − l(o)
33  │   else                                  /* randomized loading */
34  │   │   With probability c/l(o): A_obj_lazy with input o
35  │   └   c ← 0
36  │   Load and evict objects according to A_obj_lazy
37  │   if A_obj_lazy loads o then
38  └   └   Both server and cache mark o fresh
```

Fig. 6. LoadManager on cache given an object caching algorithm $\mathcal{A}_{obj}$

In the Delta architecture data updates correspond predominantly to data inserts (Section 3). This is true of scientific repositories. However the decision making in VCover is independent of an update specification and can imply any of the data modification statements *viz.* insert, delete or modify. Thus we have chosen the use of the term update.

LoadManager adopts a randomized mechanism for loading objects. This is space-efficient as it obviates maintaining counters on each object. This efficiency is motivated by meta-data issues in large-scale remote data access middlewares that cache data from several sites [26].

Finally, an implementation of VCover requires a semantic framework that determines the mapping between the query, q, and the data objects, $B(q)$, it accesses. The complexity of such a framework depends upon the granularity at which data objects are defined. If the objects are tables or columns, such a mapping can be determined by the specification of the query itself. If the objects are tuples, finding such a mapping a-priori is difficult. However for most applications such a mapping can be found by exploiting the semantics. For instance, in astronomy, queries specify a spatial region and objects are also spatially partitioned. Thus finding a mapping can be done by some pre-processing as described in Section 6.

5 Benefit: An Alternative Approach to the Decoupling Problem

In VCover we have presented an algorithm that exploits the combinatorial structure (computing the cover) within the data decoupling problem and makes adaptive decisions using ideas borrowed from online algorithms [4]. An alternative approach to solving the data decoupling problem is an exponential smoothing-based algorithm that makes decisions based on heuristics. We term such an algorithm Benefit as it is inherently greedy in its decision making.

In Benefit we divide the sequence of queries and updates into windows of size δ. At the beginning of each new window i, for each object currently in the cache, we compute the "benefit" b_{i-1} accrued from keeping it in the cache during the past window $(i-1)$. b_{i-1} is defined as the network cost the object saves by answering queries at the cache, less the amount of traffic it causes by having updates shipped for it from the server. Since a query answered at the cache may access multiple objects, the cost of its shipping (which is saved) is divided among the objects the query accesses in proportion to their sizes. This form of dividing the cost has been found useful in other caches as well [2, 24].

For each object currently not in cache, we compute similarly the benefit it would have accrued if it *had been* in the cache during window $(i-1)$. But here, we further reduce the benefit by the cost to load the object.

A forecast μ_i of the benefit an object will accrue during the next window i is then computed using exponential smoothing: $\mu_i = (1-\alpha)\mu_{i-1} + \alpha b_{i-1}$, in which μ_{i-1} was the forecast for the previous window, and α, which is $0 \leq \alpha \leq 1$, is a learning parameter.

We next consider only objects with positive μ_i values and rank them in decreasing order. For window i, we greedily load objects in this order, until the cache is full. Objects which were already present in cache in window $(i-1)$ don't have to be reloaded. For lack of space, pseudo-code of Benefit is not presented in this paper, but is included in the accompanying technical report.

Benefit reliance on heuristics is similar to previously proposed algorithms for online view materialization [21, 20]. It, however, suffers from some weaknesses. The foremost is that Benefit ignores the combinatorial structure within the problem by dividing the cost of shipping a query among the objects the query accesses in proportion to their sizes. This difference is significant in that Benefit's performance can be proved analytically. However, in VCover the combinatorial structure leads to a mathematical bound on its performance. For details on the proof of performance, the reader is directed to the technical report [26]. Further, Benefit's decision making is heavily dependent on the size of window chosen. It also needs to maintain state for each object (the μ_i values, the queries which access it, etc.) in the database irrespective of whether it is in the cache or not.

6 Empirical Evaluation

In this section, we present an empirical evaluation of Delta on real astronomy query workloads and data. The experiments validate using a data decoupling framework for minimizing network traffic. Our experimental results show that Delta (using VCover) reduces the traffic by nearly half even with a cache that is one-fifth the size of the server. VCover outperforms Benefit by a factor that varies between 2-5 under different conditions.

6.1 Experimental Setup

Choice of Survey: Data from rapidly growing repositories, such as those of the Pan-STARRS and the LSST, is currently unavailable for public use. Thus we used the data and query traces from the SDSS for experimentation. SDSS periodically publishes updates via new data release. To build a rapidly growing SDSS repository, we simulated an update trace for SDSS in consultation with astronomers. The use of SDSS data in validating Delta is a reasonable choice as the Pan-STARRS and the LSST databases have a star-schema similar to the SDSS. When open to public use, it is estimated that the Pan-STARRS and the LSST repositories will be queried similar to the SDSS.

Setup: Our prototype system consists of a server database and a middleware cache database, both implemented on an IBM workstation with 1.3GHz Pentium III processor and 1GB of memory, running Microsoft Windows, each running a MS SQL Server 2000 database. A sequence of data updates are applied to a server database Queries, each with a currency specification criteria, arrive concurrently at a cache database. To satisfy queries with the latest data, the server and cache database uses MS SQL Server's replica management system to ship queries and updates, and, when necessary, it uses bulk copying for object loading. The decisions of when to use each of the data communication mechanism is dictated by the optimization framework of Delta, implemented as stored procedures on the server and cache databases.

Server Data: The server is an SDSS database partitioned in spatial data objects. To build spatial data objects, we use the primary table in SDSS, called the PhotoObj table, which stores data about each astronomical body including its spatial location and about 700 other physical attributes. The size of the table is roughly 1TB. The table is partitioned using a recursively-defined quad tree-like index, called the *hierarchical triangular mesh* [19]. The HTM index conceptually divides the sky into partitions; in the database these partitions translate into roughly equi-area data objects. A partitioning of the sky and therefore the data depends upon the level of the HTM index chosen. For most experiments we used a level that consisted of 68 partitions (ignoring some which weren't queried at all), containing about 800 GB of data. These partitions were given object-IDs from 1 to 68. Our choice of 68 objects is based on a cache granularity experiment explained in Section 6.2. The The data in each object varies from as low as 50 MB to as high as 90 GB.

Growth in Data: Updates are in the form of new data inserts and are applied to a spatially defined data object. We simulated the expected update patterns of the newer astronomy surveys under consultation with astronomers. Telescopes collect data by scanning specific regions of the sky, along great circles, in a coordinated and systematic fashion [40]. Updates are thus clustered by regions on the sky. Based on this pattern, we created a workload of 250,000 updates. The size of an update is proportional to the density of the data object.

Queries: We extracted a query workload of about 250,000 queries received from January to February, 2009. The workload trace consists of several kinds of

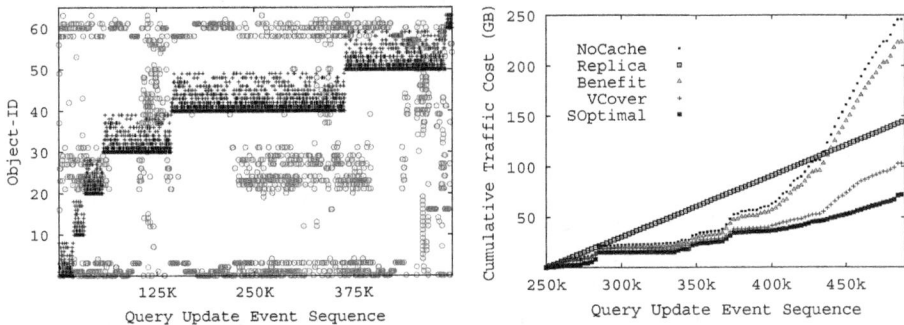

Fig. 7. (a) Object-IDs corresponding to each query (red ring) or update (blue cross) event. Queries evolve and cluster around different objects over time. (b) Cumulative traffic cost. VCover, almost as good as SOptimal, outperforms others.

queries, including range queries, spatial self-join queries, simple selection queries, as well as aggregation queries. Preprocessing on the traces involves removing queries that query the logs themselves. In this trace, 98% of the queries and 99% of the network traffic due to the queries is due to the PhotoObj table or views defined on PhotoObj. Any query which does not query the PhotoObj is bypassed and shipped to the server.

Costs: The traffic cost of shipping a query is the actual number of bytes in its results on the current SDSS database. The traffic cost of shipping an update was chosen to match the expected 100 GB of update traffic each day in the newer databases.

A sample of the query and update event sequence is shown in Figure 7. The sequence is along the x-axis, and for each event, if it is an update, we put a blue diamond next to the object-ID affected by the update. If the event is a query, we put a yellow dot next to *all* object-IDs accessed by the query. Even though this rough figure only shows a sample of the updates and queries, and does not include the corresponding costs of shipping, it supports what we discovered in our experiments: object-IDs 22, 23, 24, 62, 63, 64 are some of the query hotspots, while object-IDs 11, 12, 13, 30, 31, 32 are some of the update hotspots. The figure also indicates that real-world queries do not follow any clear patterns.

Two Algorithms, Three Yardsticks: We compare the performances of VCover, the core algorithm in Delta with Benefit, the heuristic algorithm that forecasts using exponential smoothing. We also compare the performance of these two algorithms with three other policies. These policies act as yardsticks in that the algorithm can be considered poor or excellent if it performs better or worse than these policies. The policies are:
- **NoCache:** Do not use a cache. Ship all queries to the server. Any algorithm (in our case VCover and Benefit), which has a performance worse than NoCache is clearly of no use.

- **Replica:** Let the cache be as large as the server and contain all the server data. To satisfy queries with the most current data, ship all updates to the cache as soon as they arrive at server. If VCover and Benefit, both of which respect a cache size limitation, perform better than Replica they are clearly good.
- **SOptimal:** Decide on the best *static set of objects* to cache *after* seeing the entire query and update sequence. Conceptually, its decision is equivalent to the single decision of Benefit using a window-size as large as the entire sequence, but in an offline manner. To implement the algorithm we loads all objects it needs at the beginning and do not ever evict any object. As updates arrive for objects in cache they are shipped. Any online algorithm, which cannot see the queries and updates in advance, but with performance close to the SOptimal is outstanding.

Default parameter values, warmup period: Unless specified otherwise, in the following experiments we set the cache size to 30% of server size,and the window size δ in Benefit to 1000. The choice are obtained by varying the parameters in the experiment to obtain the optimal value. The cache undergoes an initial warm-up period of about 250,000 events for both VCover and Benefit. A large warm-up period is a characteristic of this particular workload trace in which queries with small query cost occur earlier in trace. As a result objects have very low probability of load. In this warm-up period the cache remains nearly empty and almost all queries are shipped. In general, our experience with other workload traces of similar size have shown that a range of a warm period can be anywhere from 150,000 events to 300,000 events. To focus on the more interesting post warm-up period we do not show the events and the costs incurred during the warmup period.

6.2 Results

Minimizing traffic cost: The cumulative network traffic cost along the query-update event sequence for the two algorithms and three yardsticks is in Figure 7(a). VCover is clearly superior to NoCache and Benefit: as more query and update events arrive it continues to perform better than them and at the end of the trace has an improvement by a factor of at least 2 with Benefit, and to Replica by a factor about 1.5. (For replica load costs and cache size constraints are ignored.) Further, as more data intensive queries arrive, Benefit is barely better than NoCache. VCover closely follows SOptimal until about Event 430K, when it diverges, leading to a final cost about 40% (35 GB) higher. On closer examination of the choices made by the algorithm, we discovered that, with hindsight, SOptimal determines that Object-ID 39 of 38 GB and Object-ID 29 of 4 GB would be useful to cache and loads them at the beginning. But VCover discovers it only after some high-shipping cost queries that arrive for these objects, and loads them around Event 430K, thus paying both the query shipping cost and load cost.

Varying number of updates: A general-purpose caching algorithm for dynamic data should maintain its performance in the face of different rates of

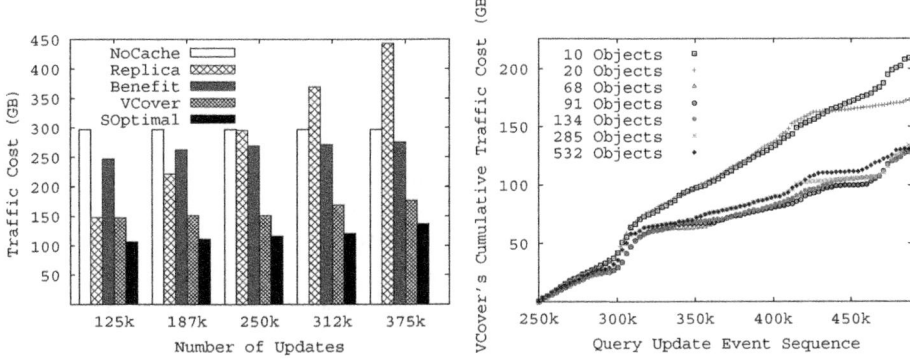

Fig. 8. (a) Traffic cost for varying number of updates. (b) VCover's cumulative traffic cost for different choices of object sets.

updates and queries. In Figure 8(b) we plot the final traffic cost for each algorithm for different workloads, each workload with the same 250,000 queries but with a different number of updates. The simplistic yardstick algorithms NoCache and Replica do not take into account the relative number of updates and queries. Since the queries remain the same, the cost of NoCache is steady at 300 GB. But as the number of updates increase the cost of Replica goes up: the three-fold increase in number of updates results in a three-fold increase in Replica's cost. The other three algorithms, in contrast, show only a slight increase in their cost as the number of updates increase. They work by choosing the appropriate objects to cache for each workload, and when the updates are more, they compensate by keeping fewer objects in the cache. The slight increase in cost is due to query shipping cost paid for objects which are no longer viable to cache. This experiment illustrates well the benefits of Delta irrespective of the relative number of queries and updates.

Choice of objects: In Figure 8(a) we plot VCover's cumulative traffic cost, along the event sequence, for different choices of data objects. Each choice corresponds to a different level in the quad tree structure in SDSS, from a set of 10 objects corresponding to large-area upper-level regions, to a set of 532 objects corresponding to small-area lower-level regions. Each set covers the entire sky and contains the entire data. The performance of VCover improves dramatically as number of number of objects increase (sizes reduce) until it reaches 91 and then begins to slightly worsen again. The initial improvement is because as objects become smaller in size, less space in the cache is wasted, the hotspot decoupling is at a finer grain, and thus more effective. But this trend reverses as the objects become too small since the likelihood that future queries are entirely contained in the objects in cache reduces, as explained next. It has been observed in scientific databases that it is more likely that future queries access data which is "close to" or "related to," rather than the exact same as, the data accessed by current queries [24]. In astronomy, e.g., this is partly because of several tasks that scan the entire sky through consecutive queries.

7 Conclusion

Repositories in data-intensive science are growing rapidly in size. Scientists are also increasingly interested in the time dimension and thus demand latest data to be part of query results. Current caches provide minimal support for incorporating the latest data at the repository; many of them assume repositories are static. This often results in runaway network costs.

In this paper we presented Delta a dynamic data middleware cache system for rapidly growing repositories. Delta is based on a data decoupling framework—it separates objects that are rapidly growing from objects that are heavily queried. By effective decoupling the framework naturally minimizes network costs. Delta relies on VCover, a robust, adaptive algorithm that decouples data objects by examining the cost of usage and currency requirements. VCover's decoupling is based on sound graph theoretical principles making the solution nearly optimal over evolving scientific workloads. We compare the performance of VCover with Benefit, a greedy heuristic, which is commonly employed in dynamic data caches for commercial applications. Experiments show that Benefit scales poorly than VCover on scientific workloads in all respects.

A real-world deployment of Delta would need to also consider several other issues such as reliability, failure-recovery, and communication protocols. The future of applications, such as the Pan-STARRS and the LSST depends on scalable network-aware solutions that facilitate access to data to a large number of users in the presence of overloaded networks. Delta is a step towards meeting that challenge.

Acknowledgments. The authors sincerely thank Alex Szalay for motivating this problem to us, and Jim Heasley for describing network management issues in designing database repositories for the Pan-STARRS survey. Ani Thakar acknowledges support from the Pan-STARRS project.

References

1. Amiri, K., Park, S., Tewari, R., Padmanabhan, S.: DBProxy: a dynamic data cache for web applications. In: Proc. Int'l. Conf. on Data Engineering (2003)
2. Bagchi, A., Chaudhary, A., Goodrich, M.T., Li, C., Shmueli-Scheuer, M.: Achieving communication efficiency through push-pull partitioning of semantic spaces to disseminate dynamic information. Transactions on Knowledge and Data Engineering 18(10) (2006)
3. Bornhövd, C., Altinel, M., Krishnamurthy, S., Mohan, C., Pirahesh, H., Reinwald, B.: DBCache: middle-tier database caching for highly scalable e-business architectures. In: Proc. ACM SIGMOD Int'l Conf. on Management of Data (2003)
4. Borodin, A., El-Yaniv, R.: Online computation and competitive analysis. Cambridge University Press, Cambridge (1998)
5. Candan, K.S., Li, W.S., Luo, Q., Hsiung, W.P., Agrawal, D.: Enabling dynamic content caching for database-driven web sites. In: Proc. ACM SIGMOD Int'l Conf. on Management of Data (2001)

6. Candan, K.S., Li, W.-S., Luo, Q., Hsiung, W.-P., Agrawal, D.: Enabling dynamic content caching for database-driven web sites. SIGMOD Record 30(2), 532–543 (2001)
7. Cao, P., Irani, S.: Cost-aware www proxy caching algorithms. In: Proc. of the USENIX Symposium on Internet Technologies and Systems (1997)
8. Corman, T., Leiserson, C., Rivest, R., Stein, C.: Introduction to algorithms. MIT Press, Cambridge (1990)
9. Dar, S., Franklin, M.J., Jonsson, B.T., Srivastava, D., Tan, M.: Semantic data caching and replacement. In: Proc. Int'l. Conf. on Very Large Databases (1996)
10. Deolasee, P., Katkar, A., Panchbudhe, A., Ramamritham, K., Shenoy, P.: Adaptive push-pull: disseminating dynamic web data. In: Proc. 10th Int'l. World Wide Web Conf. (2001)
11. Deux, O., et al.: The story of O2. Trans. on Knowledge and Data Engineering 2(1) (1990)
12. Garey, M., Johnson, D.: Computers and intractability: a guide to NP-completeness. WH Freeman and Company, San Francisco (1979)
13. Garrod, C., Manjhi, A., Ailamaki, A., Maggs, B., Mowry, T., Olston, C., Tomasic, A.: Scalable query result caching for web applications. In: Proc. Int'l Conf. on Very Large Databases (2008)
14. Guo, H., Larson, P., Ramakrishnan, R., Goldstein, J.: Support for relaxed currency and consistency constraints in mtcache. In: Proc. ACM SIGMOD Int'l. Conf. on Management of Data (2004)
15. Hochbaum, D. (ed.): Approximation Algorithms for NP-hard Problems. PWS Publishing Company (1997)
16. Huang, Y., Sloan, R., Wolfson, O.: Divergence Caching in Client Server Architectures. In: Proc. 3rd International Conference on Parallel and Distributed Information Systems (1994)
17. Kaiser, N.: Pan-starrs: a wide-field optical survey telescope array. Ground-based Telescopes 5489(1), 11–22 (2004)
18. Kaiser, N.: Pan-STARRS: a large synoptic survey telescope array. In: Proc. SPIE, pp. 154–164 (2002)
19. Kunszt, P., Szalay, A., Thakar, A.: The hierarchical triangular mesh. In: Mining the Sky: Proc. MPA/ESO/MPE Workshop (2001)
20. Labrinidis, A., Roussopoulos, N.: Webview materialization. SIGMOD Record 29(2) (2000)
21. Labrinidis, A., Roussopoulos, N.: Exploring the tradeoff between performance and data freshness in database-driven web servers. The VLDB Journal 13(3) (2004)
22. Lecluse, C., Richard, P., Velez, F.: O2, an object-oriented data model. SIGMOD Record 17(3), 424–433 (1988)
23. Large Synoptic Survey Telescope, http://www.lsst.org
24. Malik, T., Burns, R., Chaudhary, A.: Bypass caching: Making scientific databases good network citizens. In: Proc. Int'l. Conf. on Data Engineering (2005)
25. Malik, T., Burns, R., Chawla, N.: A black-box approach to query cardinality estimation. In: Proc. 3rd Conf. on Innovative Data Systems Research (2007)
26. Malik, T., Wang, X., Little, P., Chaudhary, A., Thakar, A.R.: Robust caching for rapidly-growing scientific repositories (2010), http://www.cs.purdue.edu/~tmalik/Delta-Full.pdf
27. Olston, C., Loo, B.T., Widom, J.: Adaptive precision setting for cached approximate values. ACM SIGMOD Record 30 (2001)
28. Olston, C., Manjhi, A., Garrod, C., Ailamaki, A., Maggs, B.M., Mowry, T.C.: A scalability service for dynamic web applications. In: CIDR (2005)

29. Olston, C., Widom, J.: Best-effort cache synchronization with source cooperation. In: Proc. ACM SIGMOD Int'l. Conf. on Management of Data (2002)
30. Pan-STARRS—Panoramic Survey Telescope and Rapid Response System, http://www.pan-starrs.ifa.hawaii.edu
31. Peng, G.: CDN: Content distribution network. Arxiv preprint cs.NI/0411069 (2004)
32. Protopapas, P., Jimenez, R., Alcock, C.: Fast identification of transits from lightcurves. Journal reference: Mon. Not. Roy. Astron. Soc. 362, 460–468 (2005)
33. Sloan Digital Sky Survey, http://www.sdss.org
34. Shoshani, A., Sim, A., Gu, J.: Storage Resource Managers: Essential Components for the Grid. Kluwer Academic Publishers, Dordrecht (2004)
35. Singh, V., Gray, J., Thakar, A.R., Szalay, A.S., Raddick, J., Boroski, B., Lebedeva, S., Yanny, B.: SkyServer Traffic Report: The First Five Years, MSR-TR-2006-190. Technical report, Microsoft Technical Report, Redmond, WA (2006)
36. Skiena, S.: The algorithm design manual. Springer, Heidelberg (1998)
37. Stevens, W.: TCP/IP illustrated. The Protocols, vol. 1. Addison-Wesley Longman Publishing Co., Inc., Boston (1993)
38. Stonebraker, M., Aoki, P.M., Devine, R., Litwin, W., Olson, M.: Mariposa: A new architecture for distributed data. In: Proc. of the Internationall Conference on Data Engineering (1994)
39. Stonebraker, M., Aoki, P.M., Litwin, W., Pfeffer, A., Sah, A., Sidell, J., Staelin, C., Yu, A.: Mariposa: A wide-area distributed database system. The VLDB Journal 5(1) (1996)
40. Szalay, A.S., Gray, J., Thakar, A.R., Kunszt, P.Z., Malik, T., Raddick, J., Stoughton, C., van den Berg, J.: The SDSS skyserver: public access to the Sloan Digital Sky Server data. In: Proc. ACM SIGMOD Int'l Conf. on Management of Data (2002)
41. The Times Ten Team. In-memory data management in the application tier. In: Proc. of the International Conference on Data Engineering (2000)
42. Wang, X., Malik, T., Burns, R., Papadomanolakis, S., Ailamaki, A.: A workload-driven unit of cache replacement for mid-tier database caching. In: Kotagiri, R., Radha Krishna, P., Mohania, M., Nantajeewarawat, E. (eds.) DASFAA 2007. LNCS, vol. 4443, pp. 374–385. Springer, Heidelberg (2007)
43. Weisstein, E.W.: Vertex cover. from mathworld–a wolfram web resource, http://mathworld.wolfram.com/VertexCover.html

Anonygator: Privacy and Integrity Preserving Data Aggregation

Krishna P.N. Puttaswamy[1], Ranjita Bhagwan[2], and Venkata N. Padmanabhan[2]

[1] Computer Science Department, UCSB
[2] Microsoft Research, India

Abstract. Data aggregation is a key aspect of many distributed applications, such as distributed sensing, performance monitoring, and distributed diagnostics. In such settings, user anonymity is a key concern of the participants. In the absence of an assurance of anonymity, users may be reluctant to contribute data such as their location or configuration settings on their computer.

In this paper, we present the design, analysis, implementation, and evaluation of Anonygator, an anonymity-preserving data aggregation service for large-scale distributed applications. Anonygator uses anonymous routing to provide user anonymity by disassociating messages from the hosts that generated them. It prevents malicious users from uploading disproportionate amounts of spurious data by using a light-weight accounting scheme. Finally, Anonygator maintains overall system scalability by employing a novel distributed tree-based data aggregation procedure that is robust to pollution attacks. All of these components are tuned by a customization tool, with a view to achieve specific anonymity, pollution resistance, and efficiency goals. We have implemented Anonygator as a service and have used it to prototype three applications, one of which we have evaluated on PlanetLab. The other two have been evaluated on a local testbed.

Keywords: distributed aggregation, anonymity, integrity, pollution, tokens, scalability.

1 Introduction

Data aggregation is a key aspect of many distributed applications. Examples include aggregation of mobile sensor data for traffic monitoring in a city [20,23], network performance statistics from home PCs for a network weather service [32], and machine configuration information for a distributed diagnosis system [37].

In such settings, user anonymity is a key concern of the participants. In some cases, this concern is driven by privacy considerations. For example, a user may be willing to have their GPS-enabled phone report traffic speed information from a particular street so long as the system is not in a position to identify and tie them to that location. Likewise, a user may be willing to have their home PC report the performance of a download from www.badstuff.com so long as the network weather service they are contributing to is unable to identify and tie them to accesses to possibly disreputable content. In other cases, the desire for anonymity may be driven by security considerations. For example, a host may reveal local misconfigurations (e.g., improperly set registry keys on a Windows machine) while contributing to a distributed diagnostics system such as PeerPressure [37]. Some of these misconfigurations may have security implications, which would leave the host vulnerable to attacks if its identity were also revealed. Given such security and privacy concerns, an absence of an assurance of anonymity would make users reluctant to participate, thereby impeding the operation of community-based systems mentioned above.

To address this problem, we present Anonygator, an anonymity-preserving data aggregation service for large-scale distributed applications in the Internet setting. The model is that the participating hosts contribute data, which is aggregated at a designated aggregation root node. The data contributed by each node is in the form of a histogram on the metric(s) of interest. For example, a node might construct a histogram of the download speeds it has seen in the past hour over one-minute buckets. All of the histograms are aggregated to construct the probability mass function, or PMF, (which we refer to loosely as the "aggregated histogram") at the server.

Prior aggregation systems such as Astrolabe [33] and SDIMS [38] have focused on achieving scalability and performance by leveraging the participating nodes (i.e., peers) to perform aggregation. While Anonygator also leverages P2P aggregation, it makes several novel contributions arising from a different focus complementary to prior work. First, Anonygator focuses on the issue of providing *anonymity* to the participating nodes while at the same time ensuring that anonymity does not undermine the *data integrity* of the aggregation process. We believe that these are important considerations in the context of distributed aggregation of potentially privacy-sensitive data over nodes that are not all trustworthy. To the best of our knowledge, prior work on P2P aggregation has not considered these issues. Second, Anonygator augments prior work on tree-based aggregation with a novel construct, which we term as a *multi-tree*, that introduces a controlled amount of redundancy to achieve the desired degree of robustness to data pollution attacks. Third, to be flexible in accommodating a range of data aggregation applications, Anonygator includes a *customization tool* to help tune the system to achieve the desired anonymity and data integrity properties while staying within the specified bounds on network communication load.

We present the design of Anonygator, including an analysis of the assurances it provides in terms of anonymity and pollution resistance. We also present experimental results derived from running our implementation on a laboratory testbed as well as on PlanetLab, in the context of a few aggregation-based applications, including resource monitoring, distributed diagnostics and voting.

2 Preliminaries

2.1 Assumptions and Problem Context

We assume a setting where a population of nodes is contributing data, which is then aggregated at a designated aggregation root. The designated root node could be a server that is well-provisioned in terms of bandwidth or could be an end host that has much more limited bandwidth resources. Even in the former case, the bandwidth demands of aggregation could exceed what the server is able to spare for aggregation. For example, a million nodes, each uploading 1 KB of data every 10 minutes, would impose a bandwidth load of over 13 Mbps on the server for aggregation alone. This means that Anonygator should be able to scale while respecting bandwidth constraints at both the root node and the other participating nodes. In the remainder of this paper, we use the term "(aggregation) server" interchangeably with "(aggregation) root".

We consider the Internet context rather than the sensor network setting that has been the focus of recent work on data aggregation [28,26,34]. This means that the typical participating node would belong to a user, who cares about privacy, a consideration largely absent in sensor networks. On the other hand, energy cost, a key consideration in sensor networks, is absent in our context.

We assume that there is an identity infrastructure that grants each participant a public key certificate. This PKI is assumed to exist and operate independently of Anonygator, and grant certificates in a manner that mitigates against Sybil attacks [14] (e.g., by requiring users to provide a credit card number or solve a CAPTCHA when they first obtain a certificate). While Anonygator could choose to use these certified identities as part of the protocol, we assume that the data being aggregated itself does not give away the identity of the source.

We also assume the availability of a trusted entity, which we term as the *bank*, with well-known public key. As we elaborate on in §5.1, the bank issues signed tokens to the participating nodes after verifying their identities. The bank might be the root of the PKI's trust chain or be a separate entity. Regardless, we assume that the bank does *not* collude with the participants in the data aggregation process, including the aggregation root.

While a majority of the participating nodes are honest and cooperate in the operation of Anonygator, up to a fraction, p, of the nodes could be malicious. The malicious nodes, acting individually or in collusion, could try to break anonymity. They could also try to compromise the aggregation process and the final result (i.e., cause "pollution") by injecting large amounts of bogus data themselves or tampering with the data uploaded by other nodes. Note that *we cannot prevent nodes from injecting bogus data* (indeed, determining that the data is bogus may require application-specific knowledge and even then may not be foolproof), *so there would be some pollution even in a centralized aggregation system*, where each node uploads its data directly to the aggregation server, disregarding anonymity. However, the impact of such pollution on the aggregate would be limited unless a relatively large amount of bogus data were injected.

The designated aggregation root, however, is assumed to be honest in terms of performing aggregation; after all, the aggregated result is computed and stored at the root, so a dishonest root node would render the aggregation process meaningless. Nevertheless, the root node, whether it is a server or just an end host, may be curious to learn the identities of the sources, so we need to preserve anonymity with respect to the root as well as the other participating nodes.

The assurance that Anonygator seeks to provide with regard to anonymity and data integrity is probabilistic, under the assumption that the malicious nodes are distributed randomly rather than being specifically picked by the adversary. If the adversary could selectively target and compromise specific nodes, it would not be meaningful to limit the adversary's power to only compromise a fraction p of the nodes. In other words, we would have to assume that such a powerful adversary could target and compromise *all* the nodes, rendering the aggregation process meaningless.

Finally, in the present paper, we do not consider the issue of incentives for user participation in a community-based aggregation system. This is undoubtedly an important issue, but we defer it to future work. Also, given space constraints, we focus our presentation here on the novel aspects of Anonygator's design that have a direct bearing on its security properties. Hence we do not discuss details such as onion route formation [13], random peer selection [24] and decentralized tree construction [38].

2.2 Design Goals

The goals of Anonygator are listed below. Although we state these goals as absolute requirements, we seek to achieve these properties with a high probability.

- **Source Anonymity:** No node in the network, barring the source itself, (i.e., neither the root nor any other participating node) should be able to discover the source of a message.
- **Unlinkability:** Given two messages A and B, no node in the network, barring the source itself, should be able to tell whether they originated from the same source.
- **Pollution Control:** The amount of pollution possible should be close to that in a centralized system.
- **Scalability and Efficiency:** The CPU and bandwidth overhead on the participating nodes and on the aggregation root should be minimized. The system should also respect the bandwidth limits that are explicitly set on the participating nodes, including the root.

2.3 Aggregation via Histograms

As noted in §1, the data to be aggregated is in the form of histograms. For instance, in an application where latency measurements are being aggregated, a host may upload data of the form {50ms: 2, 100ms: 6}, representing 2 samples of 50ms and 6 samples of 100ms.

When performing aggregation, we normalize the individual histograms as probability mass functions (PMFs), before combining the PMFs contributed by all nodes. Normalization ensures that each node receives the same weightage, preventing any one node from unduly skewing the aggregate. So, for example, the histogram in the above example would be normalized to {50ms: 0.25, 100ms: 0.75}. When combined with another normalized histogram, say {75ms:

0.5, 100ms: 0.5}, the aggregate would be {50ms: 0.125, 75ms: 0.25, 100ms: 0.625}. In the rest of the paper, we use the terms PMF and histogram interchangeably.

We believe that the histogram (or PMF) representation of data is quite general and would fit the needs of many applications (e.g., enabling PeerPressure [37] to find the distributions of various registry key settings across a population of hosts). Being an approximation of the probability distribution of a random variable of interest, the aggregated histogram would, for eg., allow us to compute the median value and, in general, the xth percentile, for any value of x.

Histogram-based aggregation does have its limitations. Specifically, it makes it challenging to discover correlations across random variables. For instance, an application may seek to correlate the network failures observed (and reported through Anonygator) by end hosts with the OS being run on the host. Doing so would require computing a histogram with as many buckets as the product of the number of buckets for each variable, leading to a combinatorial explosion in the size of the histogram.

There are also other limitations that arise from our model rather than from our choice of histograms as the basis for aggregation. First, normalizing the histogram would mean we may not be computing the true distribution of a variable. For example, when aggregating download time information for a webpage, a host that downloads the page at a 100 different times (i.e., has 100 samples to offer) would be given the same weight as one that downloads the page just once. However, it is difficult to tell a node that has legitimately performed 100 downloads from one that is merely pretending with a view to polluting the aggregate. Given this difficulty, in Anonygator we choose to normalize, thereby erring on the side of protecting against data pollution, despite the limitation arising from the equal weightage given to all nodes. Second, certain metrics such as the sum, mean, max, and min are not amenable to aggregation in our setting, since a single malicious node can skew the result to an arbitrary extent. Again, this is a problem independent of our choice of histograms as the basis of aggregation.

3 Anonygator Design Overview

Anonygator comprises of three components: (a) *anonymous routing*, to preserve source anonymity, and also ensure unlinkability to a large extent, (b) *light-weight accounting*, to prevent data pollution, and (c) *multi-tree-based aggregation*, to achieve scalability while avoiding the risk of large-scale pollution. The first two components use well-studied techniques, but are essential to the complete anonymity-preserving aggregation system. The third component, the multi-tree, is a novel contribution of our work.

Figure 1 provides an overview of how Anonygator operates. When a source node needs to upload a message (i.e., a histogram) for aggregation, it first obtains tokens from the Bank (1). Then, it attaches a token to the message (2). The token mechanism helps prevent pollution. The source then envelopes the message and the token in multiple layers of encryption to build an *onion* [30], and routes the onion to a tail node, via multiple intermediate nodes (3). The source creates

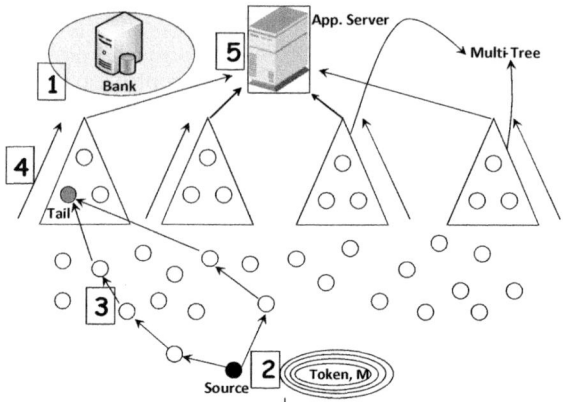

Fig. 1. Design overview of Anonygator

and uses a different onion route for each message to improve the unlinkability of messages. Upon receiving the message, the tail node first validates the token sent with the message, and then passes the message on for aggregation (4). The tail node is part of a distributed structure that we call a *multi-tree*, which performs distributed aggregation on the data. The key idea in a multi-tree, as we will elaborate on later, is to have a many-to-many relationship between parents and children, to help detect any attempts at corrupting the aggregated data. The root of the multi-tree sends the aggregated histograms to the server, which then combines such aggregates from across several multi-trees, if any (5).

Note that the figure shows a *logical* view of our system, for clarity. In reality, any host in the system can be a source, be a tail node for other sources, and also be part of a multi-tree. Also, the tail node that a message is injected into could be in any position in the multi-tree, not just at the leaf. Finally, if we only need anonymity and pollution control, and are willing to sacrifice scalability, the tail node could bypass the multi-tree and upload directly to the server.

4 Anonymous Routing in Anonygator

As described in the overview in §3, a source uses onion routing to convey its message anonymously to a randomly-chosen tail node, which then injects the message into the aggregation tree. To set up an onion path to the chosen tail node, the source uses Tor [13], with the nodes participating in Anonygator serving as the onion routers. §8 discusses how the customization tool chooses the onion route length to achieve specific anonymity and unlinkability goals.

Ideally, we would want to set up a fresh onion path for each message that the source contributes for aggregation. Doing so would minimize the ability of the tail node(s) that receive messages from a source from linking them, even if the same tail node receives multiple messages but over different onion paths.

However, setting up an onion path is expensive, since it involves as many public key operations as the length of the onion path. So the overhead of setting up a fresh onion path for each message would be prohibitive.

To resolve this dilemma, we define the notion of an *unlinkability interval*, which is the period during which we wish to avoid reusing any onion paths, making linking messages difficult. However, an onion path can be reused outside of this interval. While such reuse allows tail nodes to link messages, the linked messages would be spaced apart in time, mitigating the impact on unlinkability.

An onion path enables bidirectional communication. Anonygator takes advantage of this to have acknowledgments sent back from the tail node to the source node, which allows the source node to detect events like a message being dropped by an intermediate onion router or a tail node departing the system.

5 Accountability in Anonygator

The drawback of providing anonymity is the loss of accountability. Malicious nodes can "pollute" the data aggregates at the server by uploading large amounts of spurious data without the risk of being black-listed. To prevent this, we introduce accountability in the service via *tokens* and *hash chains*, ideas we borrow from the literature on e-cash, and broadcast authentication [9,22,25].

5.1 Anonygator Bank

The *Anonygator Bank* is responsible for maintaining accountability for all data sources in the service. The bank performs two important functions: it supplies the source nodes with a suitable number of token/hash chain combinations and it ensures that the source nodes use these tokens at most once, thus preventing double-spending [9].

Upon joining the network, a node directly contacts the bank and proves its identity in a Sybil-attack resistant manner [14,6,15]. The bank then generates a fixed number of signed tokens, based on the node's credentials, and assigns them to the node. When sourcing a message, the node must attach a previously-unused token (or a hash-chain derivative of it, as explained in §5.2) to the message. The limited supply of tokens curtails a node's ability to pollute. The bank also makes sure that source nodes do not double-spend tokens. We explain this procedure in the §5.2 following the explanation of how source nodes use their tokens.

As stated in §2.1 and consistent with previous work [21,17], we assume that the bank is trusted and that it does not collude with the aggregation server or any other node in the aggregation system. Given this assumption, we believe it is safe for the nodes to divulge their identities to the bank. While the bank knows the identity of the sources, their capabilities, and their token usage, it does not know anything about the data and messages that the sources generate. The aggregation server, on the other hand, has access to the data, but it does not know the identity of the sources. This helps us achieve our anonymity goals.

5.2 Using Tokens and Hash Chains

A source node with a data item to be aggregated includes a token, signed by the bank, along with the data item to generate a message, M. It routes this message to tail node T, as explained in §4. T first verifies that the bank has indeed signed the token (one asymmetric cryptography operation) and then contacts the bank to ensure that the token has not already been used. The bank performs this check by treating the token (or its ID) as an opaque blob of bits that is looked up in a local data structure. If the bank informs T that the token was not previously used, T deems the corresponding data item as valid and forwards it on for aggregation. Otherwise, T discards the data item.

Although the verification mechanism described above does provide anonymous accountability, it involves an asymmetric operation and communication with the bank per message, which can be quite expensive, especially if the message generation rate is high. Anonygator uses *hash chains* along with tokens to reduce this overhead. A hash chain [22] is a chain of hash values obtained by recursively hashing a random *seed* using a unidirectional hash function like SHA1. The final hash after y hashes is called the *head* of the hash chain. The contents of a token augmented with hash chain information are: $Token_i = \{ID_i, head_i, sign(hash(ID_i \cdot head_i))\}$ where ID_i is the token ID, $head_i$ is the head of the hash chain generated for this token, and both token ID and the head are signed by the bank.

With this token construction, the modified algorithm to upload messages by a source S via a tail T is as follows: The first time source S sends a data item to tail T, it includes a token with id ID_T with the data. T performs the verification of the token as mentioned earlier. In all subsequent messages that S sends to T, S includes only the tuple (ID_T, H_x) in decreasing order of x. T just needs to verify that for token ID_T, it receives a message with the hash value H_x *only after* it has received a message with hash value H_{x+1}. It can do so simply by applying the hash function to H_x and verifying that the value matches H_{x+1}.

As a result, of all messages that S sends to T, only the first message involves an asymmetric cryptographic operation and direct communication with the bank. Note that, as explained in §4, the source uses the same onion path to communicate with T, thereby allowing messages to be linked. So there is *no* additional diminution of unlinkability because of using the same token.

5.3 Token Management under Churn

Once a source uses a token with a certain tail node, Anonygator does not allow the source to use that token with another tail node. The token is, therefore, "tied" to the tail node on which the source first used it. So if this tail node leaves the system, say due to churn, the source cannot use even the unused portion of the hash chain associated with this token, with any other tail node.

To avoid this problem, we introduce the notion of an *epoch* (T_e). Each source node obtains a set of tokens from the bank at the start of an epoch. At the end of each epoch, all tail nodes report to the bank the last hash value they received (i.e., the last value that was expended by another node) for every token ID. So the bank knows the extent to which each token was used. For example, if the length of a token's hash chain is 100 and the last value reported by a tail node is the 30th one in the chain (counting from the head), the bank can deduce 30 values have been used and 70 values remain unused.

After two epochs, the bank tallies how many hash chain values have been used for each token, and provides a "refund" to source hosts for the remainder. A refund is nothing but appropriate accounting at the bank to reflect the partial- or non-use of a token, so that the source can get a fresh token issued to it while remaining within any quotas imposed by the bank. Since accounting at the bank depends on the tail nodes reporting usage of tokens, there is the risk of a *spurious refund attack*, where a tail node, in collusion with the source node, fails to report the usage of a token. To address this issue, Anonygator introduces redundancy, including at the level of tail nodes, as we elaborate on next.

6 Distributed Aggregation Using Multi-trees

In this section, we address the issue of scalability of data aggregation in Anonygator. Using tree-based aggregation is a natural way to improve scalability of aggregation: as data flows from the leaves to the root, the data gets aggregated, and the root receives aggregated data while processing incoming traffic only from a small set of nodes. However, using a regular trees for aggregation raises several security concerns. For example, a *single* malicious node near the root in the tree can completely change the aggregate histogram from the entire sub-tree below it. This can cause unbounded amount of pollution.

In order to be robust against such attacks, we propose a distributed aggregation mechanism using a structure that we call a *multi-tree*, as in Figure 2. The idea in a multi-tree is to group together the nodes into *supernodes*, each containing a mutually-exclusive set of k nodes. These supernodes are organized as a regular tree. A parent-child relationship between two supernodes is translated into a parent-child relationship between every member of the parent supernode and every member of the child supernode.

The system supports a set of such multi-trees, as shown in Figure 1. The exact number of multi-trees depends on the bandwidth of the aggregation server, as

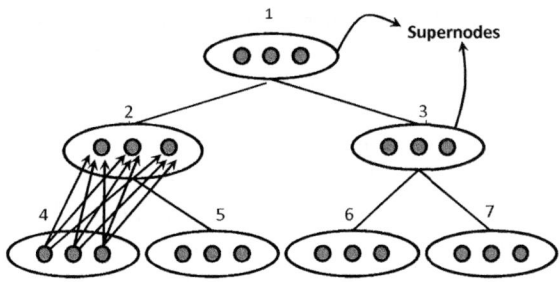

Fig. 2. The structure of a multi-tree

we analyze in §8.2. The node membership of each multi-tree is non-overlapping with respect to the membership of the other multi-trees.

6.1 Data Injection

Every node that serves as a tail node for the purposes of anonymous routing (§4) is a member of a supernode in the tree. Even though new data to be aggregated (i.e., a histogram) is introduced into the multi-tree at a tail node, the supernode that the tail node is a member of can be at any level of the multi-tree, not necessarily at the leaf level.

The source node sends the tail node the new data to be aggregated, along with k tokens, one for the tail node itself and one each for the $k-1$ other nodes in the tail node's supernode. The tail node then forwards the histogram along with one token to each of the other $k-1$ nodes in its supernode. If the membership of the super node changes (say because of node churn), the tree node informs the source through the onion route, so that the source can send fresh tokens, rather than just new hash values, for each new node in the supernode.

The above procedure mitigates against the spurious refund attack noted in §5.3, as we discuss in detail in §7.3. Also, an alternative to routing its message via a single tail node would be for the source to send separate messages, along with their respective tokens, directly to each node in the tail node's supernode. This *k-redundant algorithm* increases messaging cost by a factor of k but reduces the risk of pollution, as we discuss in detail in §7.2.

6.2 Data Aggregation

The objective of having k nodes within each supernode is to be able to compute the correct aggregate histogram with high probability, even in the presence of malicious nodes. Figure 2 shows a sample multi-tree with $k=3$. In this example, each host in supernode 4 (on the bottom left) uploads its histogram to each host in supernode 2. Each node in supernode 2 therefore receives $k=3$ histograms from supernode 4. If all nodes in supernode 4 were honest, the $k=3$ histograms received by each node in supernode 2 would be identical. However, in the presence of malicious nodes, these histograms would diverge, as we discuss next.

At the end of a time period that we call an *aggregation interval*, each node in supernode 2 picks the histogram that is repeated at least $\lfloor \frac{k}{2} \rfloor + 1$ times (2 times, in this example). Histograms that do not meet this minimum count are discarded. Therefore, for a supernode to accept a bogus histogram, more than half the nodes in its child supernode would have to be malicious and colluding. Every parent supernode determines such "majority" histograms for each of its child supernodes and then combines these to compute an aggregate histogram representing data received from all of its child supernodes. For example, supernode 2 in Figure 2 combines the majority histograms from supernodes 4 and 5 to compute an aggregate histogram. Each node in supernode 2 then uploads this aggregate histogram to all k members in its parent supernode (supernode 1, here), and the process repeats. Having the parent do the voting is necessary.

Putting the onus of voting on the parent avoids the complexity and obviates the need for distributed voting.

If each supernode in the multi-tree has a majority of non-malicious nodes, then the multi-tree is said to be "correct", since the correct overall aggregate histogram is produced, despite the presence of malicious nodes. Given the probability of aggregate correctness P_c, which is the probability that the aggregate the multi-trees produce are correct, Anonygator's customization tool determines the best multi-tree configuration that will satisfy this requirement (§8.2).

7 Attacks and Defenses

In this section we discuss several attacks on Anonygator, their impact, and potential defenses against them. We consider the possibility of attacks by source nodes, relay nodes (i.e., onion routers), tail nodes, and nodes in the aggregation tree. These attacks could be aimed at compromising either security (in terms of anonymity or unlinkability) or data integrity (in terms of pollution control). Our focus here is on attacks that are specific to the various mechanisms in Anonygator. For attacks on the underlying Tor system, we refer the reader to [13].

7.1 Attacks by Malicious Source Nodes

Direct Data Injection Attack [8]. This occurs when a source node directly injects erroneous data in the legitimate messages it generates. As explained in §2.1, the server cannot, in general, tell that the data is erroneous. However, the token mechanism in Anonygator (§5.2) limits the amount of data that a node can contribute for aggregation. Hence the *pollution bound* for this attack, i.e., the fraction of data injected that could be spurious, is the same as the fraction, p, of the nodes that are malicious.

Interpreting this pollution bound for histograms, we can say that the histogram will be at most p percentile off from the ground truth. For example, if $p = 0.01 = 1\%$, then the median value in the aggregate histogram would give us a value that lies somewhere in the range of the 49th to the 51st percentiles in the true, pollution-free histogram.

Fake Token Attack. A malicious source could send a flood of messages, each tagged with a fake token, to one or more tail nodes. The tokens and the associated messages are eventually rejected, so data pollution does not occur. However, the attacker intends to tie down computational and network resources at the tail nodes in checking these fake tokens, i.e., attempt resource exhaustion. Existing techniques such as client puzzles [12] could be used by tail nodes as defense when the rate of message receipt is very high.

7.2 Attacks by Malicious Tail Nodes

Message Replacement Attack. A malicious tail node can take the data that a source node sends them and replace it with spurious data. Since a source picks a malicious tail node with probability p, the fraction of data items potentially affected by message replacement attacks is p. Since this is in addition to the pollution of p possible with the direct data injection attack discussed above, the total pollution bound is $2p$.

However, the source could send copies of its message independently to each node in the tail node's supernode (the k-redundant algorithm from §6.1), thereby denying the tail node the ability to subvert aggregation by doing message replacement. This would mean that the overall pollution bound would remain p (rather than $2p$), but this would come at the cost of increased messaging cost.

Finally, note that the message replacement attack subsumes other attacks where a malicious tail node drops the received messages, forwards the tokens in these messages to a colluder, who later uses the tokens to cause pollution.

Spurious Churn Attack. As noted in §6.1, whenever there is churn in the tail node's supernode, the source has to obtain and send fresh tokens, one for each "new" node in the supernode. A malicious tail node can try to exhaust the source node's quota of tokens by pretending that there is churn when there is none. To defend against such an attack, a source node can determine that a particular tail node is reporting much higher churn than is the norm and hence decide to switch to using a different tail node.

7.3 Attack by Colluding Source and Tail

Spurious Refund Attack. The attack involves a source node contributing data for aggregation but, in collusion with a tail node, avoiding expenditure of tokens (or, equivalently, obtaining a refund of the tokens spent, as noted in §5.3). However, as noted in §6.1, Anonygator requires a majority of (honest) nodes in the chosen tail node's supernode to receive and forward a source's data up the tree, for it to be included in the aggregation process. Hence the source will have to expend at least $\lfloor \frac{k}{2} \rfloor + 1$ tokens, even if not the full complement of k tokens, which means less than a 2x savings in terms of token expenditure. Also, note that by expending just $\lfloor \frac{k}{2} \rfloor + 1$ tokens, the source would run the risk of having its data be discarded in the aggregation process if any of the $\lfloor \frac{k}{2} \rfloor + 1$ nodes that it sent the token to turns out to be dishonest.

7.4 Attack by Malicious Relay Nodes

Message Dropping Attack. A relay node, i.e., an onion router, could drop a message that it is supposed to forward on a path leading to a tail node. However, as noted in §4, the bidirectionality of onion paths allows the source node to detect such drops by looking for an acknowledgment from the tail node. Even if such an acknowledgment mechanism were not in place, the worst that the malicious relay node could so is to drop messages randomly, without knowledge of either the source or the contents. Such dropping would, therefore, be no worse than random network packet drops.

7.5 Attack by Malicious Tree Nodes

A malicious tree node could attempt a data injection attack or a message replacement attack with a view to subverting the aggregation result. However, such an attack would not be successful unless a majority of nodes in supernode were malicious and colluding. As we explain in §8.2, Anonygator's customization tool ensures that the likelihood of such an occurrence is below the bounds specified by the application designer.

8 Configurability in Anonygator

This section describes how an application designer can configure Anonygator to best suit the application's needs of anonymity, unlinkability and correctness. Anonygator's customization tool (CT) can configure anonymous routing, token usage and multi-trees to meet the application's requirements while not exceeding the amount of computing and network resources that participating hosts in the system are willing to contribute. We describe how the CT works in this section.

8.1 Customization Tool Overview

Figure 3 shows part of the functionality of the customization tool of Anonygator. The first-class properties that an application needs to specify to Anonygator are *anonymity (A)*, *unlinkability* (P_U) and the *probability of correctness* (P_C). The metric for probability of correctness, as mentioned in §6, is the probability that the distributed aggregation generates the correct aggregate histogram.

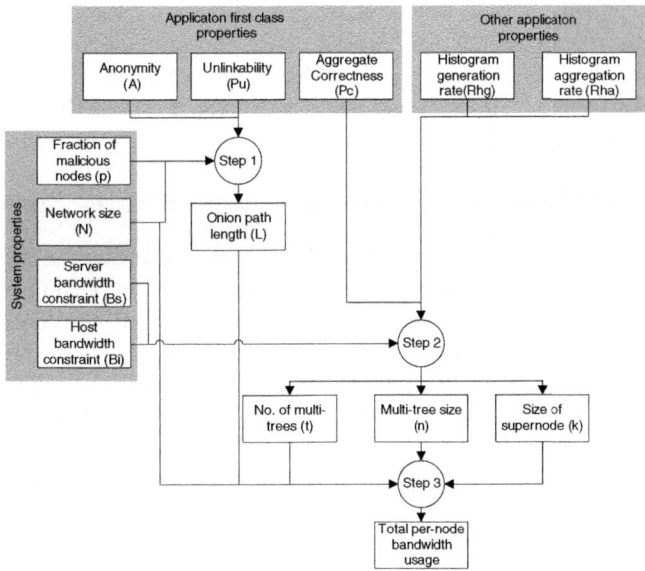

Fig. 3. Procedure used by the CT to determine the total per-node bandwidth overhead

Apart from these, the application has other properties that the designer inputs to the tool. The *histogram generation rate* (R_{hg}), specified in histograms per second, provides the average rate at which sources generate messages or histograms. The *histogram aggregation rate* (R_{ha}), also specified in histograms per second, is the rate at which hosts upload aggregate histograms to their parent supernodes in the multi-tree. For simplicity, we assume that all histograms are of the same size, though in reality, there would be variations based on applications.

The *unlinkability interval* (T_l) is the time interval after which a source node can reuse a previously used onion path or use the next value of an already-used hash-chain. The *epoch length* (T_e) is the duration of time for which tokens are valid and it dictates the periodicity with which the bank assigns fresh tokens.

The designer also inputs several host characterization parameters that define the system's properties. As shown on the left of Figure 3, these parameters include the fraction of malicious nodes (p), the size of the Anonygator network or the number of nodes participating in the network (N), the maximum incoming server bandwidth dedicated to aggregation (B_s) specified in histograms per second, and the maximum incoming host bandwidth (B_h) also specified in histograms per second. Given the application's requirements and system specification, the CT informs the designer of the anonymous route length and multi-tree structure through Steps 1 and 2 in Figure 3.

The churn rate (R_c) is a measure of the number of hosts that leave the system per second (as estimated by the system designer). The key setup rate (R_{ks}) is the rate at which a source node can perform asymmetric cryptographic operations to perform onion path setup discussed in §4. Step 3 of the CT calculates the number of tokens required per epoch and hash chain length per token using churn rate, key setup rate, unlinkability interval, histogram generation rate and epoch length. In this section however, we concentrate on the details of just Step 2. We refer the reader to [29] for the details of the analysis of Step 1, and Step 3. Since this analysis is similar to the analysis in prior work on anonymous communication, and due to space constraints, we leave it out of this paper. Finally, Table 1 has a summary of the symbols we use in the following subsections.

8.2 Step 2: Probability of Correctness to Multi-tree Structure

In this section, we summarize how the CT calculates multi-tree structure. The CT calculates a feasible region for the the number of supernodes in a multi-tree (n) based on three constraints. First, the number of supernodes has to be small enough to satisfy the probability of correctness: the more the number of supernodes, the higher the probability of a "bad" supernode with more than $\lfloor \frac{k}{2} \rfloor + 1$ malicious nodes. Second, the number of supernodes is limited by the number of hosts participating in the system. Third, the number of supernodes needs to be large enough such that nodes in a supernode use less than their maximum specified incoming bandwidth (B_h). These three bounds are expressed in Eq. 1, Eq. 2, and Eq. 3 respectively.

Table 1. Variables used by the customization tool

Symbol	Definition	Type
A	Anonymity (Entropy Ratio)	input
P_U	Unlinkability (Probability)	input
P_c	Aggregation correctness probability from multi-tree	input
N	Total number of hosts	input
p	Fraction of malicious nodes	input
B_s	Maximum incoming server bandwidth (Histograms/Sec)	input
B_h	Maximum incoming host bandwidth (Histograms/Sec)	input
f	Fanout of the multi-tree	input
R_c	Churn rate in system (Nodes/Second)	input
R_{hg}	Histogram generation rate (Histograms/Sec)	input
R_{ha}	Histogram aggregation rate (Histograms/Sec)	input
T_l	Unlinkability interval (Seconds)	input
T_e	The Epoch length (Seconds)	input
R_{ks}	Max. rate of key setup for a node (Numbers/Sec)	input
L	Length of the onion path	output
k	No. of nodes in a supernode	output
n	No. of supernodes per multi-tree	output
t	No. of multi-trees	output
N_t	No. of tokens	output
L_H	Hash chain size	output

$$n \leq \frac{logP_c}{t.logP_{sn}}, P_{sn} = \sum_{i=\lfloor \frac{k}{2} \rfloor + 1}^{k} \binom{k}{i}(1-p)^i p^{k-i} \quad (1)$$

$$n \leq \frac{N}{kt} \quad (2)$$

$$n \geq \frac{NR_{hg}}{t(B_h - R_{hg}L + fkR_{ha})} \quad (3)$$

The CT determines a relation between k and t given the incoming bandwidth capacity B_s set apart by the server for aggregation. The CT calculates the maximum multi-trees that can directly upload data to the server as

$$t = \left\lfloor \frac{B_s}{k.R_{ha}} \right\rfloor \quad (4)$$

This is because each multi-tree's root supernode (with k nodes within) uploads $k.R_{ha}$ aggregate histograms to the server per second. Therefore, the server can dedicate at most $\frac{B_s}{k.R_{ha}}$ bandwidth to each multi-tree.

Figure 4 shows the feasible region for n for different values of k plotted using Equations 1, 2 and 3. The input parameters set are: $p = 0.01$, $N = 1$ million, $P_c = 0.90$, $B_s = 100,000$ histograms/sec, R_{ha} is 10 histograms/sec, R_{hg} is 100 histograms/sec, and $B_h = 5000$ histograms/sec. Note that f is fixed at 3. Based

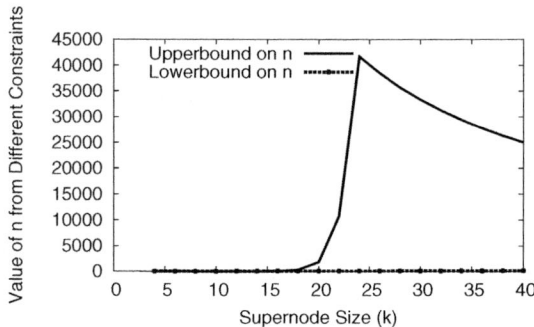

Fig. 4. Visual depiction of the multi-tree constraints

on these constraints, the CT chooses the minimum value of k that makes n fall in the feasible region. In this example, this value is around 16, translating to a value of 45 for n, and 625 for t.

It is possible, though, that for some input values, there are no feasible values of n, k, and t. In such cases, the CT alerts the application designer that their system requirements are too high to be met, and that they need to revise their application or system properties.

9 Implementation

Implementation Status: We have implemented Anonygator on two platforms: our first implementation, built for a Linux testbed, consists of roughly 1400 lines of Python code and uses the pycrypto library for the base cryptographic functions. Our second implementation, built on the .Net framework, consists of 2400 lines of C# code and uses the BouncyCastle [5] cryptographic library. We use RSA (1024 bits keys) as the asymmetric cipher and Rijndael as the symmetric cipher.

The Anonygator implementations provide a library that supports all three components of Anonygator: anonymous routing, data pollution prevention, and multi-tree based aggregation. Currently, in our prototypes, all node discovery and multi-tree construction operation is centralized: a directory service informs nodes of hosts that they could use as tail nodes. The directory service also determines the membership of the multi-tree by assigning hosts to the different supernodes in the multi-tree. However, both node discovery and multi-tree construction could be decentralized using techniques such as DHTs [31] and distributed tree construction algorithms [7,38].

Anonygator API: Table 2 lists the APIs that Anonygator provides: the first two API calls are for the client side, and the last two for the server side. Note that the Anonygator API enables an application's client only to *send* messages anonymously, and the aggregation server to *receive* and *aggregate* these messages. Separately, the application designer uses the customization tool to tune Anonygator's parameters (§8).

Table 2. APIs of the Anonygator library. Client and Server side calls are marked

API	Purpose
initAnonygatorClient() (Client)	Buys tokens, installs keys.
sendData() (Client)	Sends app. data to tree.
initAnonygatorServer() (Server)	Inits agg. server
pushdownConfiguration() (Server)	Sends multi-tree configuration to the clients.

10 Evaluation

To evaluate Anonygator, we have implemented three applications on two separate testbeds. The first application, inspired by systems that measure resource usage on distributed hosts [1], aggregates CPU usage on various hosts over time. The second application, inspired by FTN [19,37], involves aggregating machine configuration parameter settings across a population of hosts. The third is a voting application motivated by Credence [36], a distributed object reputation system. We implemented and evaluated the CPU Aggregation on PlanetLab, while the other two are evaluated on a Windows Vista cluster testbed.

10.1 Aggregation of CPU Utilization

Using our Linux implementation, we have built an application to aggregate percent CPU utilization on a distributed set of Planetlab hosts. The purpose is to understand how the distribution of percent CPU utilization on PlanetLab varies over time. The histograms that the application generates and aggregates consist of buckets at 10% increments, i.e. the first bar represents the fraction of hosts with 0-10% CPU usage, the second bar represents the fraction with 10-20%, etc.

Algorithm 1 shows the pseudo-code for the client side of this application. After initialization, the client periodically uploads its CPU utilization using the sendData call. Our purpose in presenting the algorithm is to show that the code required for implementing this application atop the Anonygator API is fairly simple since the anonymity preservation, and token accounting is done entirely by the Anonygator library.

Since the application itself provides similar functionality as other monitoring systems such as CoMon [1], we refrain from delving into the actual measurements that the application gathers. Instead, we concentrate on evaluating the scalability and bandwidth usage of the components of the Anonygator system itself.

Bank Scalability: Our first experiment evaluated the scalability of the Anonygator bank – the rate at which the bank generates tokens. We found this to be the most resource-intensive function for the bank since each token generation involves one asymmetric crypto operation and generating the head of the hash chain by performing L_H hashes (token verification is more than 20 times faster than generation). In our experiment, we set L_H, the hash chain length, to 1000.

The Anonygator bank was running on a cluster of machines at the University of California, Santa Barbara. Each machine has a 2.3 GHz Intel Xeon processor

Algorithm 1. The Algorithm for Aggregation of CPU Utilization on the Client.

Contribute_Data()
1: initAnonygatorClient() /* Initialize Anonygator */
2:
3: **while** 1 **do**
4:    readCPUUsage() /* Read CPU Usage */
5:    sendData(data) /* Send out data via Anonygator */
6:    sleep(uploadInterval)
7: **end while**

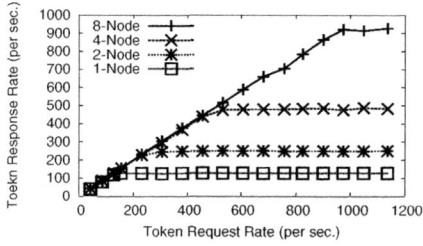
Fig. 5. Bank's scalability in terms of token generation rate

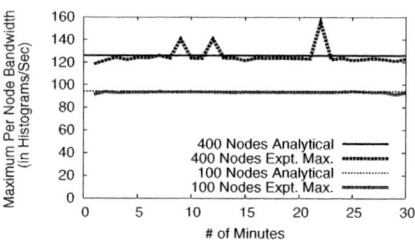
Fig. 6. Maximum incoming bandwidth usage over all hosts in the interior supernodes of the multi-tree

and 2GB memory. All machines ran 32-bit RedHat CentOS and were interconnected through a Gigabit Ethernet switch. We varied the number of machines that constituted the Anonygator bank between 1 and 8. The clients ran on 100 PlanetLab nodes, which periodically contacted and received tokens from the bank. We varied the rate at which the clients requested tokens from the bank.

Figure 5 shows that the rate at which the bank generates tokens varies linearly with the number of machines in the cluster. With 1 machine, the peak rate is 125 tokens/sec, with 2, it is 248 tokens/sec, with 4 it is 486 tokens/sec and with 8, it is 919 tokens/sec. These results follow from the fact that creating a hash-chain of size 1000 takes 3.75 ms and signing the token takes 4.25 ms, for a total of 8ms to generate one token. This implies that with 1,000,000 hosts in the system, the 8-machine bank can support a histogram generation rate of 0.919 histograms per second, or 55 histograms per minute. For many aggregation systems [2,4], this is a fairly high rate of data generation. The capacity of the bank can be further improved by increasing the hash chain length or the cluster size.

Host Bandwidth Usage: Next, we evaluated whether the maximum incoming host bandwidth on each PlanetLab machine was indeed capped by the value input to the customization tool. We created two deployments of the application on PlanetLab, one with 100 hosts and the other with 400 hosts, and ran the application on each of these two host sets for 30 minutes. The value of B_h was set to 94 for the 100 node deployment and 126 for the 400 node deployment.

Table 3. Outputs from the CT for PlanetLab deployment

Total number of nodes	L	k	n	t
100 nodes	3	4	25	1
400 nodes	3	6	66	1

We set the required anonymity A to 0.99, the unlinkability P_U to 0.99, and probability of correctness P_c to 0.7. The number of hosts, N, was set to 100 or 400 depending on the experiment, and the fraction of malicious hosts, p, was 0.05. We set the histogram generation rate to 10 per minute, and the histogram aggregation rate to 2 per minute. The histogram size is approximately 40 bytes, since each histogram has 10 bars and the size of each bar is 4 bytes (int).

In the onion routing phase, the message size due to the onion encapsulation is roughly 400 bytes. While this may seem high, we believe that the overhead is manageable since the histogram generation rate from source to tail node is set to only 10 per minute. At extremely high rates of histogram generation, however, this overhead could significantly affect performance. However in our experience, aggregation-based systems [4,11,2] do not have extremely high data generation rates *per-source* (though the bandwidth usage at the server, with a large number of sources could be significant). The maximum incoming server bandwidth, B_s, was set to 8 histograms per minute for the 100 node experiment and to 12 histograms per minute for the 400 node case. Table 3 shows the value of the various output parameters the CT calculated with these inputs.

Some of these parameters (such as low values of server bandwidth, low correctness probability, and low histogram generation and aggregation rates) are not representative of what one may expect in a real deployment. However, since the experiment's objective was to evaluate the bandwidth usage on a host, we needed to set parameters that created multi-level trees with just hundreds of hosts at our disposal. With our choice of parameters, the 100-node deployment had a multi-tree with 4 levels and the 400-node deployment had 5 levels.

Figure 6 shows a time-series of the *maximum* instantaneous bandwidth (calculated over 1 minute buckets) on a node, calculated over all nodes in the system. Hence each data point comes from the node whose bandwidth usage is maximum in that minute. The figure shows that our implementation of the Anonygator system does conform to the bandwidth constraint specified in both experiments thereby confirming the effectiveness of the customization tool. The three spikes correspond to short-term variability in bandwidth usage on certain nodes: the nodes with maximum bandwidth usage were significantly under-utilized in the minute just prior to the spike.

We performed a similar study to evaluate usage of server bandwidth B_s which yielded similar results. We leave out the experiment details due to lack of space.

10.2 Distributed Diagnostics and Voting Application

We implemented two more applications – a distributed diagnostic application, inspired by FTN [19] and a voting application inspired by Credence [36]. We also deployed them on a lab cluster of 25 machines. We leave out the details due to space limitations, but refer the reader to our technical report at [29].

11 Related Work

Several mobile data collection systems such as CarTel [20], Mobiscopes [3], and Nericell [23] involve sensors uploading data periodically to a central repository. Protecting the privacy of the contributors would be important but has not received much attention in most of these systems.

A notable exception is AnonySense [11], which provides privacy while assigning tasks to mobile sensor nodes and retrieving reports from them. However, AnonySense does not perform data aggregation. SmartSiren [10] collects reports at a server and uses them to detect viruses using certain thresholds. It attempts to provide anonymity to clients, and also describes the problem of pollution control during anonymous report submissions. SmartSiren however assumes that submitting reports via the IP network provides sufficient anonymity. Also, it uses random ticket exchange between clients to avoid the server from tracking smartphones based on tickets.

Several recent systems have used tokens to achieve accountability [35,27,16]. The tokens used in these systems are always involved in the critical paths. Thus, the clients need to contact the bank (and verify the token) for every application-level operation (exchange a block [27], accept a mail [35,16], etc.). However, Anonygator clients need to contact the bank once to verify a token and all subsequent messages are authenticated offline using hash chains, making the bank in Anonygator much more scalable.

A recent work [39] proposed mechanisms to provide anonymity and accountability in P2P systems. However the computational and bandwidth cost of this approach is significantly higher than Anonygator due to its reliance on heavyweight cryptographic constructs.

Several systems explore the problem of performing secure data aggregation in sensor networks [26,18,28,8]. But the mechanisms used in sensor network do not provide anonymity to the contributing sensor nodes. The base station either receives the data from the nodes directly, or shares a unique key with the nodes and hence can easily link the data to nodes.

12 Conclusion

In this paper, we have presented Anonygator, a system for anonymous data aggregation. Anonygator uses anonymous routing, token and hash-chain based pollution control, and a multi-tree based distributed aggregation scheme, to build a scalable, anonymous aggregation system. Anonygator's customization tool allows the designer to meet the desired anonymity and unlinkability goals, while honoring the specified pollution bounds and bandwidth limits. We have built three applications on Anonygator and have tested them on PlanetLab and a local cluster of machines.

References

1. CoMon webpage, http://comon.cs.princeton.edu
2. Microsoft Online Crash Analysis, http://oca.microsoft.com/en/dcp20.asp
3. Abdelzaher, T., et al.: Mobiscopes for human spaces. IEEE pervasive computing (2007)
4. Aggarwal, B., Bhagwan, R., Das, T., Eswaran, S., Padmanabhan, V., Voelker, G.: NetPrints: Diagnosing Home Network Misconfigurations using Shared Knowledge. In: Proc. of NSDI (2009)
5. Bouncycastle: The legion of the bouncy castle, http://www.bouncycastle.org
6. Castro, M., et al.: Security for structured peer-to-peer overlay networks. In: OSDI (December 2002)
7. Castro, M., et al: Splitstream: high-bandwidth multicast in cooperative environments. In: SOSP (2003)
8. Chan, H., Perrig, A., Song, D.: Secure hierarchical in-network aggregation in sensor networks. In: Proc. of CCS (2006)
9. Chaum, D.: Blind signatures for untraceable payments. In: Proceedings of Crypto, vol. 82, pp. 23–25 (1982)
10. Cheng, J., Wong, S., Yang, H., and Lu, S. Smartsiren: Virus detection and alert for smartphones. In: MobiSys (2007)
11. Cornelius, C., et al.: AnonySense: Privacy-aware people-centric sensing. In: MobiSys (2008)
12. Dean, D., Stubblefield, A.: Using client puzzles to protect TLS. In: Proceedings of the 10th USENIX Security Symposium (2001)
13. Dingledine, R., Mathewson, N., Syverson, P.: Tor: The second-generation onion router. In: USENIX Security Symposium (August 2004)
14. Douceur, J.R.: The sybil attack. In: Druschel, P., Kaashoek, M.F., Rowstron, A. (eds.) IPTPS 2002. LNCS, vol. 2429, p. 251. Springer, Heidelberg (2002)
15. Dwork, C., Naor, M.: Pricing via processing or combatting junk mail. In: Brickell, E.F. (ed.) CRYPTO 1992. LNCS, vol. 740, pp. 139–147. Springer, Heidelberg (1993)
16. Gummadi, R., et al.: Not-a-bot (nab): Improving service availability in the face of botnet attacks. In: Proc. of NSDI (2009)
17. Hoh, B., et al.: Virtual trip lines for distributed privacy-preserving traffic monitoring. In: MobiSys (2008)
18. Hu, L., Evans, D.: Secure aggregation for wireless networks. In: Workshop on Security and Assurance in Ad hoc Networks (2003)
19. Huang, Q., Wang, H., Borisov, N.: Privacy-Preserving Friends Troubleshooting Network. In: ISOC NDSS (2005)
20. Hull, B., et al.: Cartel: a distributed mobile sensor computing system. In: SenSys (2006)
21. Johnson, P.C., et al.: Nymble: Anonymous IP-address blocking. In: Borisov, N., Golle, P. (eds.) PET 2007. LNCS, vol. 4776, pp. 113–133. Springer, Heidelberg (2007)
22. Lamport, L.: Password authentication with insecure communication. Communications of the ACM (1981)
23. Mohan, P., Padmanabhan, V., Ramjee, R.: Nericell: Rich monitoring of road and traffic conditions using mobile smartphones. In: SenSys (2008)
24. Nambiar, A., Wright, M.: Salsa: A structured approach to large-scale anonymity. In: Proc. of CCS (November 2006)

25. Perrig, A.: The biba one-time signature and broadcast authentication protocol. In: Proc. of CCS (2001)
26. Perrig, A., et al.: Spins: Security protocols for sensor networks. Wireless Networks (2002)
27. Peterson, R.S., Sirer, E.G.: Antfarm: Efficient content distribution with managed swarms. In: Proc. of NSDI (2009)
28. Przydatek, B., Song, D., Perrig, A.S.: Secure information aggregation in sensor networks (2003)
29. Puttaswamy, K., Bhagwan, R., Padmanabhan, V.: Anonymity Preserving Data Aggregation using Anonygator. Tech. Rep. MSR-TR-2009-162, Microsoft Research (2009)
30. Reed, M.G., Syverson, P.F., Goldschlag, D.M.: Anonymous connections and onion routing. IEEE JSAC 16, 4 (1998)
31. Rowstron, A., Druschel, P.: Pastry: Scalable, distributed object location and routing for large-scale peer-to-peer systems. In: Guerraoui, R. (ed.) Middleware 2001. LNCS, vol. 2218, p. 329. Springer, Heidelberg (2001)
32. Simpson Jr., C.R., Riley, G.F.: NETI@home: A distributed approach to collecting end-to-end network performance measurements. In: Barakat, C., Pratt, I. (eds.) PAM 2004. LNCS, vol. 3015, pp. 168–174. Springer, Heidelberg (2004)
33. van Renesse, R., Birman, K., Vogels, W.: Astrolabe: A robust and scalable technology for distributed system monitoring, management and data mining. ACM Transactions on Computer Systems (2003)
34. Wagner, D.: Resilient aggregation in sensor networks. In: ACM workshop on security of ad hoc and sensor networks (2004)
35. Walfish, M., et al.: Distributed quota enforcement for spam control. In: Proc. of NSDI (2006)
36. Walsh, K., Sirer, E.G.: Experience With A Distributed Object Reputation System for Peer-to-Peer Filesharing. In: Proc. of NSDI (2006)
37. Wang, H., Platt, J., Chen, Y., Zhang, R., Wang, Y.: Automatic Misconfiguration Troubleshooting with PeerPressure. In: Proc. of OSDI (2004)
38. Yalagandula, P., Dahlin, M.: A scalable distributed information management system. In: SIGCOMM (August 2004)
39. Zhu, B., Setia, S., Jajodia, S.: Providing witness anonymity in peer-to-peer systems. In: Proc. of CCS. ACM, New York (2006)

Middleware for a Re-configurable Distributed Archival Store Based on Secret Sharing

Shiva Chaitanya[1], Dharani Vijayakumar[2], Bhuvan Urgaonkar[3], and Anand Sivasubramaniam[3]

[1] Netapp Inc.
[2] VMware Inc.
[3] The Pennsylvania State University

Abstract. Modern storage systems are often faced with complex trade-offs between the confidentiality, availability, and performance they offer their users. Secret sharing is a data encoding technique that provides information-theoretically provable guarantees on confidentiality unlike conventional encryption. Additionally, secret sharing provides quantifiable guarantees on the availability of the encoded data. We argue that these properties make secret sharing-based encoding of data particularly suitable for the design of increasingly popular and important distributed archival data stores. These guarantees, however, come at the cost of increased resource consumption during reads/writes. Consequently, it is desirable that such a storage system employ techniques that could dynamically transform data representation to operate the store within required confidentiality, availability, and performance regimes (or budgets) despite changes to the operating environment. Since state-of-the-art transformation techniques suffer from prohibitive data transfer overheads, we develop a middleware for dynamic data transformation. Using this, we propose the design and operation of a secure, available, and tunable distributed archival store called FlexArchive. Using a combination of analysis and empirical evaluation, we demonstrate the feasibility of our archival store. In particular, we demonstrate that FlexArchive can achieve dynamic data re-configurations in significantly lower times (factor of 50 or more) without any sacrifice in confidentiality and with a negligible loss in availability (less than 1%).

Keywords: Secret sharing, archival storage, confidentiality, performance, availability.

1 Introduction

The last decade has witnessed a deluge of digital data that need to be safely archived for future generations [9]. Rapid increase in sensitive online data such as health-care, customer, and financial records has contributed to this unprecedented growth. The challenges facing such archival data stem from the need to ensure their long-term confidentiality and availability. Many factors mandate these requirements, ranging from preservation, retrieval, and security properties demanded by legislation to long lifetimes expected for cultural and family heritage data. To address data confidentiality, modern storage systems typically employ encryption-based techniques (see survey paper [20]). The use of data encryption for archival lifetimes, however, introduces problems that have been well-documented [22,21]. The primary drawback is that data secured using keyed cryptography are only *computationally secure*—they are decipherable via cryptanalysis given sufficient computing power/time.

Secret sharing is a data encoding technique that offers the promise of overcoming these shortcomings of an encryption-based archival storage. Secret sharing with parameters (m, n) breaks a data block into n fragments (each of the same size as the original data block) in such a manner that at least m fragments must be obtained to re-construct the original block. These fragments are stored in n different storage nodes and an adversary has to obtain access to at least m fragments to decipher the original data - any set of fewer than m fragments provides no information about the original block. This property provides a quantitative notion of data confidentiality. Additionally, the original data item is resilient to the loss of fragments in the following manner: it can be re-constructed even when $(n - m)$ fragments are lost. This provides a quantitative measure of the availability properties of encoded data.

In this paper, we address the important problem of dynamically re-configuring the secret sharing parameters (m, n) used to encode data in a distributed archival store. The need to re-configure could arise as a result of one or more of the following scenarios. First, a subset of the storage nodes comprising the archival store might become unavailable or unreliable due to some form of security compromise or component failure. The data fragments at affected nodes must be considered lost and the archival system must be reverted back to its original settings. Second, there could be infrastructural changes to the storage network (e.g., addition of new nodes) which are likely to happen quite frequently relative to the lifetime of the archival data. Finally, the secrecy, availability, or performance needs of an archival store might change with time (e.g., due to changes in regulations or societal changes resulting in the stored data becoming more sensitive). Existing archival systems that have incorporated secret sharing to achieve the goals of secure long-term preservation of data have either (i) neglected this problem of re-configuration (e.g., Potshards [22]), or (ii) proposed inefficient techniques (e.g., PASIS [24]). Whereas some key aspects of the problem of dynamically re-configuring secret sharing parameters have been studied [4,6,2,3], the approaches emerging out of this body of work have severe drawbacks when used to build a practical archival storage system. In particular, they suffer from the following two main drawbacks:

- **High data access overhead.** Existing re-configuration techniques require access to m fragments for every data object stored using a (m, n) configuration. Many archival storage systems store data across wide-area networks (often with components that need to be accessed via congested or inherently slow links) and use cheap storage media technologies wherein reads to the original data can be quite slow. As we will observe later in this paper, for archival storage, it is desirable for the value of m to be close to n. Thus, the data traffic resulting from a re-configuration can become a limiting factor.
- **High computational overhead.** Existing re-configuration techniques suffer from high computational overheads. These overheads could be prohibitive in the context of archival systems that deal with very large volumes of data. It is desired that a re-configuration technique complete fast enough so the archival system spends a small amount of time in an unstable (and hence, potentially vulnerable) configuration.

1.1 Research Contributions

Our contribution is twofold.

- We propose a re-configuration technique called Multi-share Split that is both lightweight in terms of (i) the computational and I/O overheads it imposes on the archival storage system as well as (ii) tunable in terms of the trade-offs it offers between confidentiality, availability, and performance. We expect that Multi-share Split would enable administrators of archival stores to make appropriate choices to best satisfy the requirements (e.g, completion time targets, network resource constraints) of their systems.
- Using our re-configuration technique, we design and implement a middleware that is used by nodes comprising a distributed archival storage system called FlexArchive. We analyze the security and availability properties offered by FlexArchive and conduct an empirical evaluation of the feasibility and efficacy of FlexArchive using a prototype networked storage system.

1.2 Road-Map

The rest of this paper is organized as follows. We discuss some background material in Section 2. We introduce the proposed FlexArchive system in Section 3 and describe the re-configuration algorithm employed by FlexArchive in Section 4. We develop analytical techniques for characterizing the availability offered by FlexArchive in Section 5. We conduct an empirical evaluation of the efficacy of FlexArchive in Section 6. Finally, we present concluding remarks in Section 7.

2 Background and Related Work

In this section, we provide basic background on secret sharing and its appropriateness for archival storage.

2.1 Basics of Secret Sharing

An (m, n) secret sharing scheme, where $m \leq n, m > 0$, creates n fragments from a data item with the following properties: given any m fragments, one can re-construct the data item; however, fewer than m fragments provide no information about the original data item. Such classes of secret sharing techniques are "perfectly secure" in the sense that they exhibit information-theoretic security. The size of each fragment for secret sharing schemes is provably the same as that of the original data item. Hence, the storage needs are n times the size of the original data.

A number of secret sharing techniques have been proposed that differ very slightly in their computational complexity. We use a secret sharing scheme due to Shamir (often called "Shamir's threshold scheme") [19]). The key idea behind Shamir's threshold scheme is that m points are needed to define a polynomial of degree $(m - 1)$ (e.g., two points for a line, three points for a hyperbola, four points for a third-degree polynomial, and so forth). Shamir's threshold scheme, for representing a data item S with secret sharing parameters (m, n), chooses uniformly random $(m - 1)$ coefficients

$a_1, \cdots, a_{m-1}$, and lets $a_0 = S$. It then builds the polynomial $f(x) = a_0 + a_1x + a_2x^2 + a_3x^3 + \cdots + a_{m-1}x^{m-1}$. Finally, it computes the values taken by this polynomial for n distinct values of x comprising the set $\{x_1, \cdots, x_n\}$. The n shares of the secret S are now given by the pairs $(x_i, f(x_i))$. Given any m of these pairs, one can find the coefficients of the polynomial $f(.)$ by interpolation, and then evaluate the secret $S = a_0$. Geometrically, on a $X - Y$ plane, one can think of the secret S as being the Y-intercept of the curve defined by the polynomial $f(.)$; the shares are the Y-values at $x_1, \cdots, x_n$. Note that since we are dealing with finite values (the secret and the shares are data values and represented by say, q bits), the $X - Y$ plane is a finite field with the range of values 0 to $2^q - 1$. Since the participants holding the shares could implicitly define the n indices for which the shares are computed (e.g., based on their unique names/identities), each share is simply the value $f(x_i)$ and hence can be represented using q bits, same as those needed for the secret S.

2.2 Long Term Data Confidentiality

Two fundamental classes of mechanisms for enforcing data secrecy are those based on encryption and secret sharing, respectively. Many systems such as OceanStore [17], FARSITE [5], SNAD [14], Plutus [11], and e-Vault [10] address file secrecy, but rely on the explicit use of keyed encryption. Keyed encryption may work reasonably well for short-term secrecy needs but it is less than ideal for the long-term security problem that the current work addresses. Keyed cryptography is only computationally secure, so compromise of an archive of encrypted data is a potential problem regardless of the encryption algorithm used. An adversary who compromises an encrypted archive need only wait for cryptanalysis techniques to catch up with the encryption used at the time of the compromise. If an insider at a given archive gains access to all of its data, he can decrypt any desired information even if the data is subsequently re-encrypted by the archive, since the insider will have access to the new key by virtue of his internal access. Encrypted data can be deciphered by anyone, given sufficient CPU cycles and advances in cryptanalysis. Furthermore, future advances in quantum computing have the potential to make many modern cryptographic algorithms obsolete. For long-lasting applications, encryption also introduces the problems of lost keys, compromised keys, and even compromised crypto-systems. Additionally, the management of keys becomes difficult because data might experience many key rotations and crypto-system migrations over the course of several decades. This must all be done without user intervention because the user who stored the data may be unavailable.

Moving away from encryption to secret sharing enables an archival storage system to rely on the more flexible and secure authentication realm. Unlike encryption, authentication need not be done by a computer and authentication schemes can be easily changed in response to new vulnerabilities. Secret sharing improves the security guarantees by forcing an adversary to breach *multiple* archival sites to obtain meaningful information about the data. Several recently proposed archival systems such as POTSHARDS [22], PASIS [25,7], and GridSharing [23] employ secret sharing schemes for this reason.

2.3 Long Term Data Availability

Recovering from disk failures to large-scale site disasters has long been a concern for storage systems. The long lifetimes of archival data make them prone to latter type of scenarious. Keeton et al. [12] highlighted the importance of efficient storage system design for disaster recovery by providing automated tools that combine solutions such as tape backup, remote mirroring, site fail-over, etc. These tools strive to select designs that meet the financial and recovery objectives under specified disaster scenarios. Totalrecall [1], Glacier [8] and Oceanstore [17] are examples of distributed storage systems where high availability is an explicit requirement. These systems use RAID-style algorithms or more general erasure coded redundancy techniques along with data distribution to guard against node failures. Erasure coded techniques could be thought of as similar to secret sharing minus the "secrecy" gauntrates, in the following sense: similar to secret sharing, an (m, n) erasure coding divides a data block into n fragments such that at least m fragments are needed to re-construct the original block. However, unlike secret sharing, access to less than m data fragments might reveal partial information about the data block.

3 FlexArchive: A Re-configurable Secret Sharing-Based Archival Store

We assume a distributed archival system called *FlexArchive* consisting of multiple storage nodes that are spread across various sites. Each site in FlexArchive could be professionally managed with internal redundancy mechanisms to protect data against component failures. In Figure 1 an "archival site" refers to an SSP-managed (SSP stands for Storage Service Provider) or an internal-to-enterprise storage site. A representative example of the system we assume is Safestore [13], which consists of multiple sites, each owned by a different SSP. Each SSP provides storage services in return for fees based on some agreed-upon contract. The contract might also include penalties for losing data. We assume these penalties to be such that it is in the best interests of the SSPs to provide internal redundancy mechanisms. However, large-scale component failures like disasters and correlated site failures [12,15] are harder to protect against. Considering the increased probability of such events during the lifetime of archival data, the secret distribution algorithm employed by FlexArchive must provide for inter-site redundancy as well. FlexArchive employs a secret distribution scheme where each fragment encoding a data unit goes to a different storage node. Assuming secret sharing parameters (m, n) for a data item under discussion, the value $(n - m)$ captures the archival system's resilience against node failures. Even though SSPs can be employed to safely store and retrieve data, they cannot be trusted to preserve data privacy—e.g., multiple sites can collude to obtain the original data. The parameter m captures the difficulty of accessing data in FlexArchive.

For digital data that must last for decades or even centuries, the original writer of a data item must be assumed to be unavailable when it is read. We assume that sites comprising FlexArchive implement access control policies to identify and verify the permissions of the reader/writer. Another important security property is data integrity,

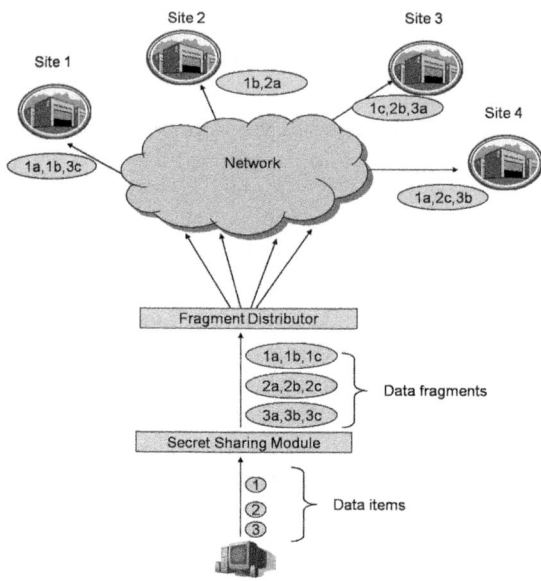

Fig. 1. FlexArchive system model. We show the middleware at a client that facilitates data encoding and placement on servers part of the FlexArchive archival store as well as re-configuration. We show an illustrative system with $N = 4$ storage sites and data being encoded using a configuration confirming to $(m \leq 3, n = 3)$.

which refers to the ability of the system to identify modifications to the data while at rest or in transit. In short-lived storage systems, data integrity is ensured by storing secure hashes along with the data using one-way hash functions such as MD5, SHA1. We assume the problems of user authorization/authentication and data integrity beyond the scope of our current work and focus only on data confidentiality.

We assume that FlexArchive provides an interface to its clients to create data in the form of archival "objects." An object could be a file in a server file system or it could be a smaller granularity unit like a disk block or an extent of blocks. As shown in Figure 1, we assume that each client employs a middleware that implements two units: (i) the secret sharing module and (ii) the fragment distributor. The secret sharing module is responsible for encoding/decoding data and is completely local to the client system. The fragment distributor is responsible for determining the placement of fragments encoded by the secret sharing unit on FlexArchive sites (and decoding fragments read from FlexArchive) and relies on certain information about the current state of FlexArchive for its decision-making. The placement strategy employed by the fragment distribution unit could vary depending on the actual storage structure. For example, in WAN-based distributed storage, it is often the case that the storage nodes across sites (or certain subsets of them) are independent of each other in terms of security breaches and failures. Therefore, a desirable way of assigning fragments representing a data object to sites is to store each fragment on a node within a different site. This would render data fragments independent with respect to failures/compromises and utilize well the properties of secret sharing. Typically, the value of n used for secret sharing is in the range

5-20, significantly smaller compared to the number of participating storage sites, N, that could be in the hundreds or even a few thousands spread across a WAN. We assume that the fragment distributor would use some form of load balancing when distributing the fragments across these sites.

3.1 Re-configuration in FlexArchive: Key Concerns

The usage scenario of FlexArchive is write-once, read-maybe, and thus stresses throughput over low-latency performance. Within each FlexArchive site, writes are assumed to be performed as part of a background process in a way that the accompanying latencies do not affect the foreground system performance. The key factors affecting archival I/O performance are (i) CPU computation at the secret sharing and the fragment distribution units, (ii) network latency between the client and FlexArchive nodes, and (iii) storage access latency at FlexArchive nodes. The choice of secret sharing parameters m and n is dictated by the confidentiality and availability guarantees desired by the client. For example, if it is well understood that the simultaneous occurrence of (i) m or more nodes being compromised and (ii) more than k nodes becoming unavailable simultaneously are extremely unlikely scenarios, a good rule-of-thumb would be to employ an $(m, m + k)$ secret sharing scheme. Selecting the number of shares required to re-construct a secret-shared value involves a trade-off between availability and confidentiality—the higher the number of sites that must be compromised to steal the secret, the higher the number of sites that must remain operational to provide it legitimately. Clearly, no single data distribution scheme is right for all systems. The right choice of these parameters depends on several factors, including expected workload, system component characteristics, and the desired levels of availability and security. PASIS [25,7,24] proposes analytic techniques to ascertain the right secret sharing parameters for a given system. FlexArchive builds upon the insights provided by this body of work for determining appropriate values for these parameters.

We use the term *security budget* to denote the minimum number of fragments that need to be compromised to constitute an attack. For an (m, n) configuration, the security budget is equal to m. Similarly, we use the term *availability budget* to denote the maximum number of sites that can fail while still allowing the reconstruction of a stored data item. Since a preserved data item is available under the loss of at most $(n - m)$ fragments, this number represents its availability budget. After the archival objects have been initially written onto n FlexArchive sites, intermediate changes to the configuration are necessitated by one or a combination of the following.

- **Scenario 1: Node Compromise.** If one of the storage nodes suffers a security breach resulting in the potential exposure of all the data it stores, all affected objects would experience a decrease in their security budgets by one. To revert the system to its original security settings, the system administrator would need to initiate a re-configuration of the remaining fragments of the affected objects to restore their security budgets, i.e., a transformation of a set of fragments belonging to an $(m - 1, n - 1)$ configuration to $(m, n - 1)$. In general, a compromise of k nodes would require a re-configuration of an affected object from a rendered $(m - a, n - a)$ to $(m, n - a)$, where $1 \leq a \leq k$. The parameter a is the number of fragments belonging to the affected object that were stored at the k nodes.

- **Scenario 2: Data Loss.** Permanent loss of data at a storage node reduces the configuration of all affected objects to $(m, n - 1)$. To recuperate, the administrator might wish to deploy a spare storage node or alternate storage space at the affected node. In either case, a re-configuration from $(m, n - 1)$ to (m, n) for all affected objects is required. In general, permanent data loss will require reconfigurations of the form $(m, n - a)$ to (m, n).
- **Scenario 3: Infrastructure Changes.** Due to the lengthy periods of time for which the archival data are stored, they will witness plenty of changes to the underlying storage infrastructure. As a result, the objects may need to be moved to a different configuration to accommodate the new infrastructure. This might mean changes to m or n or both.

Since storage systems retire data slowly compared to the rate of their expansion due to the rapidly decreasing costs of storage and increasing storage densities over time, scenario 3 would often require increasing m or n or both. Scenario 1 would always require increasing the value m, whereas scenario 2 would require increasing the value of n. We focus only on re-configuration techniques that perform up-scaling (increasing m or n or both). A "naive" (m, n) to (m', n') re-configuration technique is as follows: (i) reconstruct the secret by accessing and combining any m fragments, (ii) split the secret into n' fragments using an (m', n') configuration, and (iii) delete the original n fragments and replace them with the n' fragments constructed in the last step. The obvious problem with this approach is the reconstruction of the original secret during the reconfiguration process. The node performing the re-configuration becomes a central point of attack as it can expose the secret. The fact that a secret was originally stored as a (m, n) configuration indicates that an adversary must compromise at least m different entities to obtain a secret. This security property needs to be preserved at all times, even during the re-configuration process.

3.2 Re-configuration in FlexArchive: A Baseline Technique

We now briefly describe a technique by Jajodia et al. [4] to perform an (m, n) to (m', n') re-configuration that preserves the above property. We will use this scheme as a *baseline* against which we will compare our techniques. To the best of our knowledge, this is the only significant body of work that re-configures secret sharing-encoded data without exposing the original secret during the process. A threshold subset m original shareholders perform a (m', n') secret splitting on each of their shares to obtain n' sub-shares each. Following this, each of the n' sub-shares from an original shareholder is sent to a target shareholder. The m sub-shares at each target shareholder are combined via the associated secret construction algorithm to obtain a resultant share. The resultant n' shares at the target shareholders are of a (m', n') configuration for the original secret. The baseline technique is illustrated in Figure 2. The main drawbacks of the baseline technique lie in its high resource consumption.

- **Storage I/O Needs.** This reconfiguration technique consumes excessive storage resources. Accessing m original shares to perform the reconfiguration for each object is a significant system bottleneck. Since the archival storage nodes are designed for write once and read rare type of workloads (typically tapes or log structured storage

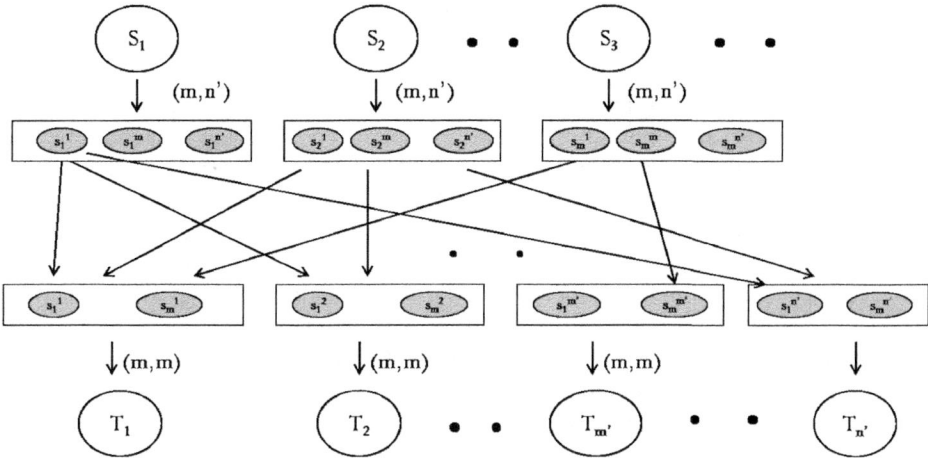

Fig. 2. Baseline re-configuration technique: from starting configuration of (m,n) to (m',n')

on disks [16,18]), the random read access to stored data is quite tedious. Under such conditions, reads to existing data for background tasks such as reconfiguration might bottleneck the actual foreground jobs of archiving. This is further compounded by the fact that re-configurations are typically done as batch jobs for millions of objects at a time. This is because they are triggered by node compromise/failure events causing all objects in the affected nodes to be re-configured. Another important factor is that, at the time of re-configuration, a subset of nodes containing the shares may not be available. In most distributed systems spread over wide geographic sites, nodes experience temporary failures because of various reasons (link failure, remote maintenance etc). There is usually a default churning of nodes, i.e nodes go down temporarily and join the network again at a later time. It is desirable that the re-configuration protocol proceeds with the alive subset of nodes (possibly, with subset of shares $< m$) instead of waiting an indefinite amount of time for m nodes to be available.

- **Network Access.** In addition to the storage access, the baseline technique involves approximately $m * n'$ network messages amongst storage nodes. This can bottleneck a typical archival storage system where all the storage nodes reside in geographically distant locations. The high latency and low bandwidth properties of network links connecting the nodes slows down the completion time of the re-configuration. There is a high possibility that many of the links towards the storage servers would be congested as a result, thereby affecting the foreground archiving jobs.
- **Computational Needs.** The computational requirements of the baseline technique are high: it requires m different instances of (m', n') secret splitting and n' instances of (m, m) secret reconstructions. As we shall observe in the evaluation section, the Shamir secret sharing operations are computationally intensive. These operations are performed in a distributed manner at the various archival sites. Depending on the computing resources available at the various storage sites to perform these operations, the CPU cycles required could become a heavy bottleneck during re-configuration.

4 Re-configuration in FlexArchive

We categorize re-configurations of secret shares as belonging to one of the following three types: (a) Improving only the availability budget (b) Improving only the security budget and (c) Improving both budgets simultaneously. In the remainder of this section, we describe our proposed approach for type (b) reconfiguration - to increase the *security budget* of a set of secret shares. It is desired that the security budget of a data item represented using a (m, n) Shamir encoding be increased by k with access to minimal number (denoted by L) of original shares. The resultant configuration requires an adversary to compromise k more nodes to obtain additional fragments than with the original configuration. It can be seen that any re-configuration technique requires at least $(n - m + 1)$ fragments to be modified. In other words, if m or more original fragments are left unmodified, the security budget remains unchanged. Therefore, $L = n - m + 1$.

4.1 Multi-share Split: FlexArchive Re-configuration Technique

At the heart of our technique, called "Multi-share Split," lies a subroutine called "Multi-transform" that leverages Shamir encoding to create additional (or "secondary") fragments from a subset of the original (or "primary") fragments. In the following discussion, we first describe how Multi-transform works. We then describe the working of the Multi-share Split technique.

How Multi-transform Operates. Multi-transform operates on a set of x primary fragments to produce y secondary fragments ($y > x$, $1 \leq c \leq (y - x)$) with the following property: *to retrieve a subset of size x_1 of the x primary fragments, at least $(x_1 + c)$ of the y secondary fragments must be acquired.* We call this the c-increment property, which has the following implication: access to *any* $(x_1 + c)$ secondary fragments may not result in an exposure of the x_1 primary fragments. Trivially, for $x = 1$, the $(1 + c, y)$ Shamir encoding satisfies the above property. We refer to this special case of Multi-transform as "Uni-transform." Multi-transform is a general technique that works for any values of x, y and c.

We first show the working of Multi-transform(x, y, c) using a couple of examples. In the first example, let $x = 2, y = 3, c = 1$, i.e., we would like to transform two primary fragments p_1, p_2 into three secondary fragments s_1, s_2, s_3 in such a manner that the following holds: (i) at least two secondary fragments must be acquired to obtain any of the primary fragments, and (ii) all three secondary fragments must be acquired to obtain both the primary fragments. Figure 3(a) illustrates how the secondary fragments can be generated. The primary fragments p_1, p_2 are now secrets themselves and represent the Y-intercepts of a finite field. First, Multi-transform randomly generates a secondary fragment s_1 in the finite field at index 1. The points (p_1, s_1) uniquely define a line in the finite field. Next, Multi-transform evaluates the Y-intercept of this line at index 2 to obtain the secondary fragment s_2. Finally, the line defined by the points (p_2, s_2) is used to generate the secondary fragment s_3 at index 3. Clearly, the three secondary fragments satisfy the desired increment property and hence can be used to replace the two primary fragments. Figure 3(b) shows another example for $x = 3, y = 6, c = 2$. Instead of lines,

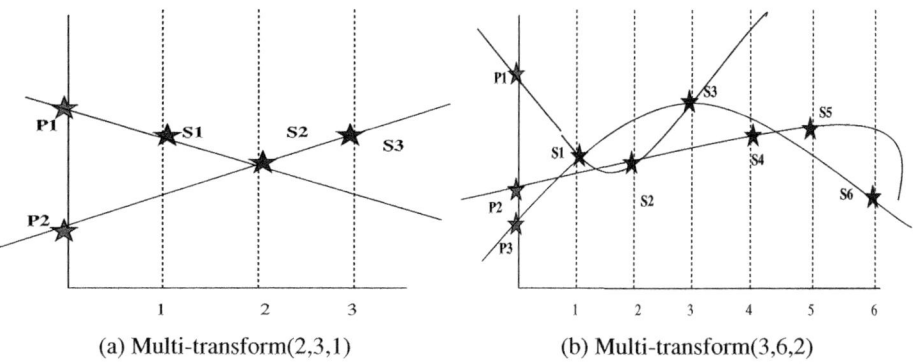

(a) Multi-transform(2,3,1) (b) Multi-transform(3,6,2)

Fig. 3. Graphical illustration of the Multi-transform(x,y,c) technique for small values of x, y, and c

we now have three second-degree polynomials in the finite field. In the general transformation of x primary fragments to y secondary fragments, there are x polynomials of cth degree. Multi-transform(x, y, c) is described formally in Algorithm 1.

The operation of Multi-transform(x, y, c) comprises several phases. In the first phase, using the first primary fragment, $(c + 1)$ secondary fragments are created by constructing a random polynomial of cth degree. This, in fact, amounts to a $(c+1, c+1)$ Shamir splitting of the first primary fragment. Note that this ensures the c-increment property for the first primary fragment. In the second phase, using the second primary fragment and a portion of the $c + 1$ secondary fragments generated so far, additional secondary fragments are created. Similarly, for the third primary fragment and so on till the xth primary fragment. After the first phase, since at each additional phase, at least one new secondary fragment is created ($y \geq x + c$), the c-increment property is preserved in an inductive fashion. The algorithm strives to balance the dependence of primary fragments on the secondary fragments by doing a couple of things. The number of new secondary s at each additional phase after the first phase is determined as $\left(\dfrac{y - (c+1)}{x - 1}\right)$. Also, the subset of already generated secondary fragments chosen at each phase (for constructing the random polynomial) is the one with those secondary fragments that have been least utilized so far in the generation of random polynomials. These two heuristics are crucial to ensuring that the y secondary fragments are equally loaded in the sense that the number of primary fragments affected by a loss of a set of secondary fragments depends solely on the cardinality of the set and not on the actual members within the set.

How Multi-share Split Employs Multi-transform. Let us now turn our attention back to the re-configuration problem of improving the security budget of a (m, n) Shamir encoding by k with access to L original shares. Multi-share Split groups a set of L primary fragments into v sets of x primary fragments and applies Multi-transform(x, y, c) on each of these v sets. We set the input parameters for the Multi-transform as follows. For the security budget to be increased by k, we set $c = k$. To reduce the ratio of secondary fragments as compared to Uni-share Split, the values must satisfy $x \geq a$

Input: x primary fragments at Y-intercepts $p_1, \cdots, p_x$
Output: y secondary fragments $s_1, \cdots, s_y$
Let $Rank(s)$ represent a data value stored for each secondary fragment s. Initialize all $Rank(s_i)$ to zero.
Let $S_{ordered}$ be an ordered set (ascending in rank) of all secondary fragments generated so far.
Let $S_{ordered}^k$ be the first k fragments from $S_{ordered}$.
foreach $i = 1$ *to* c **do**
 | Randomly generate a secondary fragment s_i at index i
end
Points $\{p_1, s_1, ..s_c\}$ define a cth degree polynomial, evaluate the polynomial at index $c+1$ to obtain s_{c+1}
Insert each fragment from set $\{s_1, ..s_{c+1}\}$ in $S_{ordered}$.
Increment $Rank(.)$ of each fragment from set $\{s_1, ..s_{c+1}\}$ by one and update $S_{ordered}$
$r_1 = \frac{y-(c+1)}{x-1}$;
$r_2 = (y-(c+1)) \bmod (x-1)$;
$j = c+2$;
$l = 1$;
if $r_2 > 0$ **then**
 | **foreach** $i = 2$ *to* $r_2 + 1$ **do**
 | | **foreach** $k = 1$ *to* r_1 **do**
 | | | Randomly generate a secondary fragment s_j at index l
 | | | $j = j+1$;
 | | | $l = l+1$;
 | | **end**
 | | Points $\{p_i, s_{j-r_1}, s_{j-r_1+1}...s_{j-2}, s_{j-1}\} \cup S_{ordered}^{c-r_1}$ define a cth degree polynomial,
 | | Evaluate the polynomial at index l to obtain s_j
 | | Insert each fragment from set $\{s_{j-r_1}, ..s_j\}$ in $S_{ordered}$.
 | | Increment $Rank(.)$ of each fragment from set $\{s_{j-r_1}, ..s_j\} \cup S_{ordered}^{c-r_1}$ by one and update $S_{ordered}$
 | | $j = j+1$;
 | | $l = l+1$;
 | **end**
end
foreach $i = r_2 + 2$ *to* x **do**
 | **foreach** $k = 1$ *to* $r_1 - 1$ **do**
 | | Randomly generate a secondary fragment s_j at index l
 | | $j = j+1$;
 | | $l = l+1$;
 | **end**
 | Points $\{p_i, s_{j-r_1-1}, s_{j-r_1}...s_{j-2}, s_{j-1}\} \cup S_{ordered}^{c-r_1+1}$ define a cth degree polynomial, Evaluate the polynomial at index l to obtain s_j
 | Insert each fragment from set $\{s_{j-r_1-1}, ..s_j\}$ in $S_{ordered}$.
 | Increment $Rank(.)$ of each fragment from set $\{s_{j-r_1-1}, ..s_j\} \cup S_{ordered}^{c-r_1+1}$ by one and update $S_{ordered}$
 | $j = j+1$;
 | $l = l+1$;
end

Algorithm 1. The Multi-transform(x,y,c) Algorithm

and $y = x + c$. Therefore, there are different ways of employing the Multi-share Split for a given input, each differing in the choice of x. It can be seen that the encoding offered by Multi-share Split improves the security budget by k. The proof is easily derived from the aforementioned increment property of Multi-transform. We formally describe Multi-share Split in Algorithm 2. The secondary fragments obtained from the v applications of Multi-transform are used to replace the L primary fragments.

Input: (m, n) Shamir encoding, $L, k, x : x \geq a$
Output: $(m + k, n)^{M(L,k,x)}$
$y = x + k$;
$v = \frac{L}{y}$;
if $L \bmod y == 0$ **then**
    foreach *group of x primary fragments out of some v groups* **do**
        Apply Multi-transform(x,y,k) to generate y secondary fragments
    end
end
else
    $r_1 = (L \bmod y) / v$;
    $r_2 = (L \bmod y) \bmod v$;
    foreach *group of x primary fragments out of some r_2 groups* **do**
        Apply Multi-transform$(x, y + r_1 + 1, k)$ to generate secondary fragments
    end
    foreach *group of x primary fragments out of some $v - r_2$ groups* **do**
        Apply Multi-transform$(x, y + r_1, k)$ to generate secondary fragments
    end
end
Replace the L primary fragments with the secondary fragments

Algorithm 2. The Multi-share Split Algorithm

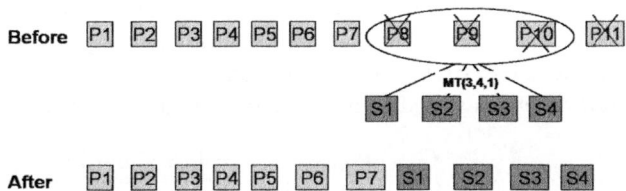

Fig. 4. Increasing the security budget of a data item represented using a $(8, 11)$ Shamir encoding from 8 to 9 using Multi-share Split. We use Multi-transform(3,4,1).

Figure 4 shows an example invocation of Multi-share Split. It is instructive to compare this with the special case corresponding to $x = 1$ that we call "Uni-share Split." With Uni-share Split, two primary fragments would be permanently erased and two of them would be used for the generation of secondary fragments. On the other hand, the Multi-share Split shown in Figure 4 involves three primary fragments in generating secondary fragments and permanently erases only one of them. We denote the configuration resulting from Multi-share Split by $(m+k,n)^{M(L,k,x)}$. Thus, Multi-share Split can results in fewer instances of permanent loss of primary fragments by controlling the number of secondary fragments generated per participating primary fragment. The value of x to be used in a Multi-share Split re-configuration method would be chosen based on the availability properties desired from the resultant configurations. We investigate this issue in the following sections.

5 FlexArchive Availability Characterization

In a regular (m,n) secret sharing configuration (e.g., Shamir's), all the n fragments are equivalent in the following sense: the configuration can tolerate the loss of up to *any* $(n-m)$ fragments to recover the secret. We refer to this as the *fragment-equivalence* property. As seen at the end of last section, Multi-share Split yields configurations that violate this property. This is because the resultant configurations have *a mixture of primary and secondary shares*. A loss of a set of secondary shares could render some other set of secondary shares useless for the secret construction. On the other hand, the loss of a primary share does not affect the reconstruction potency of any of the other shares. We attempt to analytically characterize the availability properties of configurations offered by Multi-share Split.

The heterogeneity in fragments introduced by Multi-share Split renders the estimation of the availability more complex than for configurations with fragment-equivalence. We quantify the availability for a Multi-share Split configuration using a function $CFT(R)$ defined as the (conditional) probability that the data item can be recovered given that R out of the total of N FlexArchive nodes have failed. In the current analysis, we assume that the failures of all nodes are governed by independent and identical stochastic processes. Consequently, any combination of R failed nodes among the total N shares is equally likely. It is easy to enhance this to incorporate different failure behaviors but we omit such analysis here. Furthermore, we assume that each fragment is equally likely to be placed on any of the N nodes. This is likely to correspond closely to a well load-balanced FlexArchive system. For an (m,n) fragment-equivalent configuration of an archival object stored on a system of N nodes, $CFT(.)$ is given by

$$\text{CFT(R)} = \begin{cases} 1 \text{ if } R \leq n-m \\ \sum_{i=m}^{n} \dfrac{\binom{i}{N-R} \times \binom{n-i}{R}}{\binom{n}{N}} \quad \text{otherwise} \end{cases}$$

where $\binom{i}{j}$ is the combinatorial function. For a set of fragments obtained by Multi-share Split, a closed expression for $CFT(.)$ is less straightforward. For the sake of simplicity, we focus on the special case of Uni-Share Split (which offers a lower bound on the availability for Multi-share Split in general). Furthermore, we assume that the number of system nodes $N=n$. Let us denote by $(m,n)^{U(L,k)}$ (same as $(m,n)^{M(L,k,1)}$) the configuration obtained from an $(m-k,n)$ Shamir configuration via Uni-share split by increasing the security budget by k. It consists of v sets of secondary fragments obtained by (t,t) splitting. Without loss of generality, we assume $L \mod t = 0$ and therefore, we ignore the cases where some sets of the secondary fragments are obtained by $(t,t+r)$

splitting. The secondary fragments can be used to reconstruct any of the v original primary fragments belonging to the original $(m - k, n)$ Shamir configuration. Note that $(L-v)$ primary fragments are permanently deleted, i.e., they can never be reconstructed from the secondary fragments. We refer to the deleted (albeit only temporarily) v fragments as *imaginary primary fragments*. The number of primary fragments that were retained, denoted as *retained primary fragments*, is $w = n - L$. Clearly, if the number of lost fragments is greater than $(n - m)$, the data can not be recovered—the resultant configurations from Multi-share Split can not tolerate more fragment failures than the maximum limit allowed by the corresponding Shamir configuration.

We enumerate the possible failure scenarios of $(m, n)^{U(L,k)}$, when the number of lost fragments $i \leq (n - m)$. Suppose the loss of i fragments in the resultant configuration has effectively rendered a loss of z fragments amongst the combined set of retained and imaginary primary fragments. Only if $z \geq (n - m + k)$ does it contribute to the loss of the data. For each such value of z, there are multiple possibilities of the number of fragments lost amongst the retained and imaginary primary fragments. For example, one fragment could be lost from the set of retained primary fragments and $(z - 1)$ from imaginary primary fragments, or 2 from retained primary fragments and $(z - 2)$ from imaginary primary fragments, and so on. In general, j fragments being lost from the set of retained primary fragments could occur in $\binom{w}{j}$ ways. The other $(i - j)$ lost fragments are then secondary which have effectively resulted in the loss of $(z - j)$ imaginary primary fragments (the number of possible combinations of the lost imaginary primary fragments is $\binom{v}{z-j}$). For a fixed set of $(z - j)$ lost imaginary primary fragments, let us denote the possible number of combinations by which $(i - j)$ secondary shares could have resulted it by a function called $c(z-j, t, i-j)$. The function $c(.)$ can be recursively defined as follows:

$$c(A,B,C) = \begin{cases} \binom{B}{C} & \text{if } A = 1 \\ \sum_{i=1}^{B} \binom{B}{i} \times c(A-1, B, C-i) & \text{otherwise} \end{cases}$$

We, therefore, have:

$$1\text{-CFT(R)} = \frac{1}{\binom{n}{i}} \times \sum_{z=n-m+k+1}^{n} \sum_{j=0}^{z} \binom{w}{j} \times \binom{v}{z-j} \times c(z-j, t, i-j).$$

6 Empirical Evaluation of FlexArchive

6.1 Experimental Setup

We implement the baseline technique and Multi-share Split in our prototype LAN-based archival storage system. The LAN consists of 41 machines with little outside contention for computing or network resources. We use a dedicated machine to host a client with the rest serving as archival stores. All machines have dual Hyper-threaded Intel Xeon processors clocked at 3.06 GHz and 1 GB RAM. The operating system running on the machines is Linux v2.6.13-1.1532. For the computations using Shamir's secret sharing algorithm, we use the *ssss* tool. In all our experiments, we use $GF(2^{16})$, i.e., the size of the finite field used for Shamir's polynomial interpolation is 16 bits.

6.2 Performance Evaluation

We consider re-configurations where the security budget of archival objects is increased by 1, 2, or 3 starting from three different configurations (6,10), (12,20) and (15,20). We consider a varying number of objects in a batch job of re-configuration where each object size is assumed to be 1MB. We vary the batch size from 1 up to 500 objects to understand the scalability with job size and processing parallelism of the different re-configuration approaches. We set the value of L, the number of original shares allowed to be accessed for Multi-share Split to its minimum value, i.e., $L = n - m + 1$.

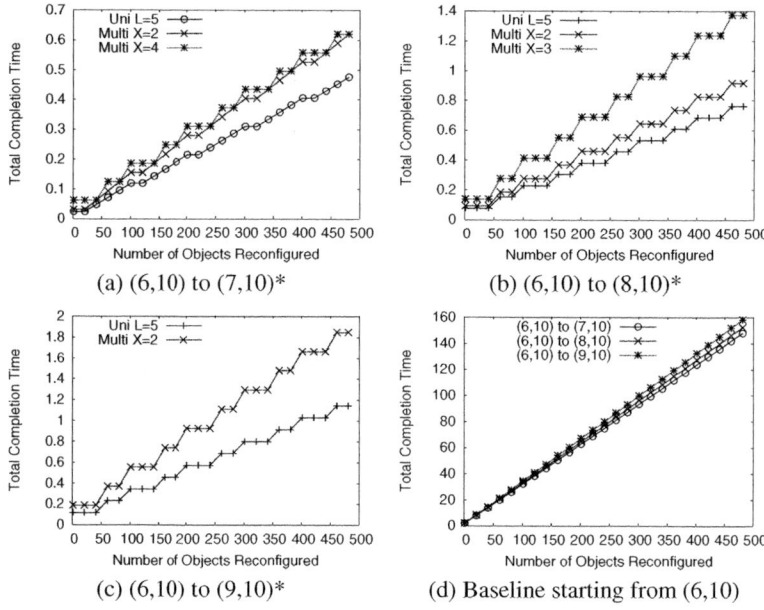

Fig. 5. Comparison of completion time (in minutes) offered by Baseline, Uni-share Split, and Multi-share Split. Recall that Uni-share Split is a special case of Multi-share Split. We use * to denote a non-fragment-equivalent configuration resulting from Multi-share Split. We report the average of several runs with the 95% confidence intervals small enough to be omitted in this figure.

We first consider re-configurations starting from (6,10). We observe that in our LAN setting when the batch size is 100 objects, the completion times of Uni-share Split for moving to (7,10)*, (8,10)*, and (9,10)* are 0.09, 0.15, and 0.22 minutes, respectively. We report these in Figures 5(a)-(d). We use "*" to indicate the non-fragment-equivalent configurations resulting from Multi-share Split. (Recall that these configurations have inferior availability properties than the corresponding fragment-equivalent configuration; we study this degradation in availability in Section 6.3). The corresponding values for Multi-share Split with the aggregation parameter $x = 2$ are 0.12, 0.18, 0.36 minutes. As seen, the completion time increases with the aggregation parameter. Most importantly, we find that Multi-share Split completes by an order of magnitude sooner than the state-of-the-art Baseline technique. The corresponding values for the Baseline technique are 30.5, 31.4, and 32.6 minutes, respectively. As the batch size increases from 100 to 500 objects, the completion times of Uni-share Split for moving from (6,10) to (7,10)*, (8,10)* and (9,10)* increase by 0.38, 0.61, and 0.92 minutes, respectively. For Multi-share Split with $x = 2$, the corresponding increase in values are 0.49, 0.73, and 1.48 minutes, respectively. On the other hand, the completion times for Baseline increase by 122.0, 125.6, and 130.4 minutes, respectively. We observe that Baseline also scales very poorly with the batch size. This supports our proposition that our Multi-share Split can be deployed to achieve significantly faster re-configuration times compared to the Baseline. Multi-share Split exhibits increased parallelism compared to Baseline and is not limited by the additional synchronization phase of fragment reconstruction required by Baseline.

Finally, we conduct measurements of completion time for starting configurations of (12,10) and (15,20) and make similar observations about the significant speedup offered by Multi-share Split. Due to space constraints, we only mention two salient observations here. First, our experiments yield similar observations as above about the significant speedup offered by Multi-share Split. Second, we find that the completion times for the starting configuration of (12,20) are much larger compared to that of (15,20) for Multi-share Split, whereas the opposite is true for Baseline. This is because Multi-share Split operates only on $(n - m + 1)$ original fragments whereas Baseline uses m fragments.

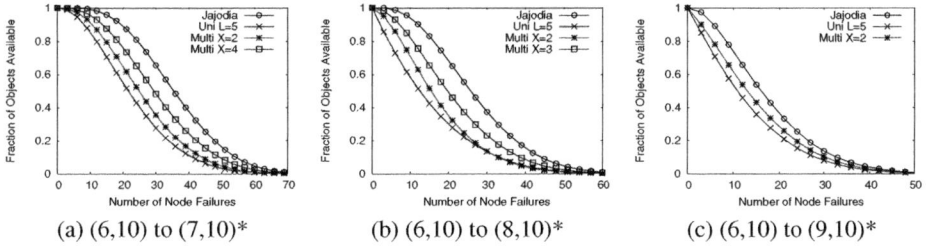

Fig. 6. Comparison of availability of configurations obtained using Baseline, Uni-share Split, and Multi-share Split. We use the $CFT(.)$ as our measure of availability. Recall that Uni-share Split is a special case of Multi-share Split. We use * to denote a non-fragment-equivalent configuration resulting from Multi-share Split.

6.3 Availability Evaluation: Conditional Fault Tolerance

We evaluate the availability resulting after a re-configuration using $CFT(.)$ as definition in Section 5. We measure the $CFT(.)$ of resultant configurations obtained by incrementing the security budget of three fragment-equivalent configurations (6,10), (12,20) and (15,20). As before, due to limited space, we present the results for only (6,10). Figures 6(a)-(c) show $CFT(.)$ for configurations obtained by incrementing the security budget of (6,10) configuration. In all the cases, we assume the stringiest budget in terms of the number of original fragments that are permitted to be accessed during the re-configuration, i.e., $L = n - m + 1$. In Figure 6(a), we compare the $CFT(.)$ of (7,10)* configuration achieved using Uni- and Multi-share Split techniques with

Table 1. Three failure traces used in our study

Trace	Duration	Nature of nodes	No. of nodes	Probe interval
WS	09/2001 to 12/2001	Public Web servers	130	10 mins
PL	03/2003 to 06/2004	PlanetLab nodes	277 on avg	15 to 20 mins
RON	03/2003 to 10/2004	RON testbed	30 on avg	1 to 2 mins

the (7,10) configuration achieved using Baseline when the security budget increment $k = 1$. Figures 6(b),(c) report $CFT(.)$ for final configurations (8,10)* and (9,10)*, respectively.

As expected, we observe that the $CFT(.)$ of configurations using Multi-share Split lag behind those using Baseline. The gap initially increases when the security budget increment k is raised from 1 to 2 but it tends to become smaller for $k \geq 3$. We also observe that $CFT(.)$ using Multi-share Split improves with the aggregation parameter x. In particular, $CFT(.)$ using Multi-share Split with $x > 1$ are superior to those using Uni-share Split. One might argue that a FlexArchive administrator should always prefer Multi-share Split with the largest possible x as it provides the best CFT. However, as already seen this improvement in availability comes with an increased completion time for re-configurations. For example, the completion times for Multi-share Split with $x > 1$ are larger than those for Uni-share Split. In fact, the completion time increases with x in general. This is because of the following reasons. In Uni-share Split, there is inherent parallelism in the sense that the (t, t) splittings are done in parallel on the nodes storing the primary shares. The amount of parallelism is reduced as we move to Multi-share Split with larger values of x. Also, the computation involved in transforming primary fragments to secondary fragments is higher in Multi-share Split than in Uni-share Split.

6.4 Availability Evaluation: Failure Traces

In our availability characterization so far, we have assumed failure independence of nodes. However, the failure correlation between nodes may not be completely absent in real world systems, e.g., due to nodes being managed using common management strategies, system software bugs, DDos attacks, etc. We study three real-world traces with failure information (described in Table 1) to evaluate the impact of realistic failure patterns. WS trace [15] is intended to be representative of public-access machines that are maintained by different administrative domains, while PL and RON traces [15] potentially describe the behavior of a centrally-administered distributed system that is used mainly for research purposes as well as for a few long-running services. A probe interval is a complete round of all pair pings; a node is declared as failed if none of the other nodes can ping it during that interval.

We estimate the "availability of data," for a given configuration as follows. First we assume that the nodes used to store the fragments of an object are chosen uniformly at random from among the nodes associated with the trace. We then determine the probability that the object can be recovered within every probe interval. Availability of data is then expressed using the average of these probability values over the entire trace. With our assumption on placement of fragments, availability of data is given by $\sum_{R=1}^{N}$

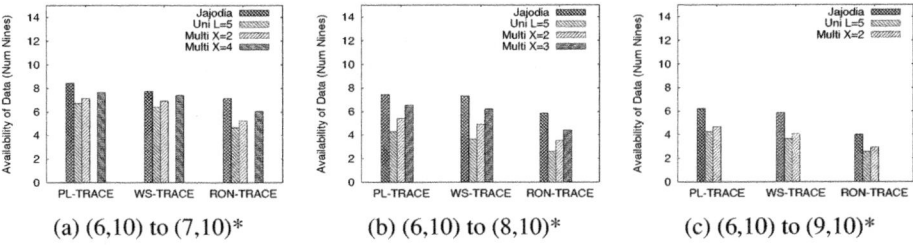

Fig. 7. Availability of configurations resulting from various re-configuration techniques. The initial configuration is fragment-equivalent (6,10). Confidence intervals, found to be very small, have been omitted in the figures.

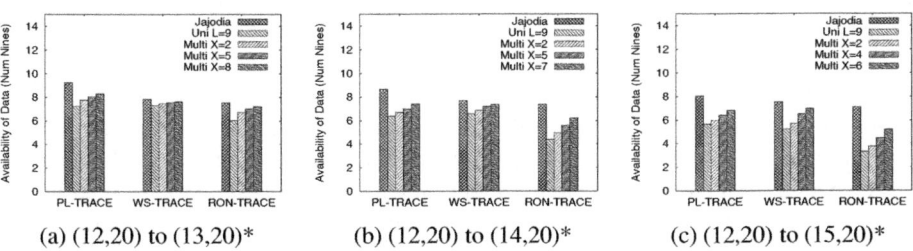

Fig. 8. Availability of configurations resulting from various re-configuration techniques. The initial configuration is fragment-equivalent (12,20). Confidence intervals, found to be very small, have been omitted in the figures.

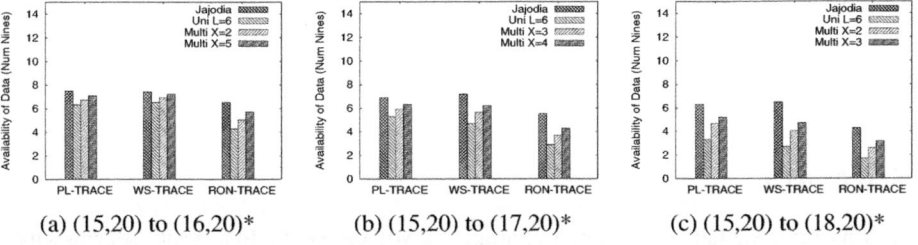

Fig. 9. Availability of configurations resulting from various re-configuration techniques. The initial configuration is fragment-equivalent (15,20). Confidence intervals, found to be very small, have been omitted in the figures.

$(CFT(R) \times FSF(R))$. Here, $CFT(.)$ is the conditional fault tolerance computed for a resultant configuration with the number of system nodes N set to the total number of nodes in a given failure trace. The function $FSF(R)$ represents "failure size frequency" and is the fraction of instances in the trace where exactly R nodes fail. Figures 7- 9 show the availability for different resultant reconfigurations and traces. The "Num Nines" on the y-axes indicate that the availability values are extremely close to one, hence we use the number of leading nines after the decimal point in our presentation. From these figures, we observe results similar to those seen in Section 6.3 where as we move from Uni-share Split to Multi-share Split with higher values of the aggregation parameter, the availability of data increases and approaches that for the corresponding fragment-equivalent configuration.

7 Concluding Remarks

The motivation for this work stems from the complex trade-offs between the confidentiality, availability, and performance that modern storage systems need to address. We argued that secret sharing-based encoding of data offers two desirable properties— (i) information-theoretically provable guarantees on data confidentiality unlike conventional encryption, and (ii) quantifiable guarantees on the availability of encoded data— that make it particularly suitable for the design of increasingly popular and important distributed archival data stores. These guarantees, however, come at the cost of increased resource consumption during reads/writes and hence could degrade the performance offered to clients. Consequently, we argued, it is desirable that such a storage system employ techniques that could dynamically transform data configuration to operate the store within required confidentiality, availability, and performance regimes (or budgets) despite changes to the operating environment. Since state-of-the-art transformation techniques suffer from prohibitive data transfer overheads, we developed a middleware that facilitates dynamic data re-configuration. at significantly lower overheads. Using this, we proposed the design and operation of a secure, available, and tunable distributed archival store, called FlexArchive, spanning a wide-area network. Using a combination of analysis and empirical evaluation, we demonstrated the feasibility of FlexArchive.

Acknowledgements

This research was supported in part by NSF grants CCF-0811670, CNS-0720456 and a gift from Cisco Systems Inc.

References

1. Bhagwan, R., Tati, K., Cheng, Y., Savage, S., Voelker, G.M.: Totalrecall: Systems support for automated availability management. In: Proceedings of the Usenix Symposium on Networked Systems Design and Implementation (2004)
2. Blakley, B., Blakley, G.R., Chan, A.H., Massey, J.L.: Threshold schemes with disenrollment. In: Brickell, E.F. (ed.) CRYPTO 1992. LNCS, vol. 740, pp. 540–548. Springer, Heidelberg (1993)
3. Cachin, C.: On-line secret sharing. In: Boyd, C. (ed.) Cryptography and Coding 1995. LNCS, vol. 1025. Springer, Heidelberg (1995)
4. Desmedt, Y., Jajodia, S.: Redistributing secret shares to new access structures and its applications. Technical Report ISSE TR-97-01, George Mason University, Fairfax, VA (July 1997)
5. Adya, A., et al.: Farsite: Federated, available, and reliable storage for an incompletely trusted environment. In: Proceedings of the 5th Symposium on Operating Systems Design and Implementation, OSDI (2002)

6. Frankel, Y., MacKenzie, P.D., Yung, M.: Adaptive security for the additive-sharing based proactive RSA. In: Kim, K.-c. (ed.) PKC 2001. LNCS, vol. 1992, pp. 240–263. Springer, Heidelberg (2001)
7. Goodson, G.R., Wylie, J.J., Ganger, G.R., Reiter, M.K.: Efficient byzantine-tolerant erasure-coded storage. In: Proceedings of the 2004 International Conference on Dependable Systems and Networking, DSN 2004 (June 2004)
8. Haeberlen, A., Mislove, A., Druschel, P.: Highly durable, decentralized storage despite massive correlated failures. In: Proceedings of the 2nd symposium on Networked Systems Design and Implementation (NSDI) (May 2005)
9. Hey, T., Trefethen, A.: Data deluge - an e-science perspective. In: Grid Computing - Making the Global Infrastructure a Reality (January 2003)
10. Iyengar, A., Cahn, R., Garay, J.A., Jutla, C.: Design and implementation of a secure distributed data repository. In: Proceedings of the 14th IFIP International Information Security Conference (SEC 1998) (September 1998)
11. Kallahala, M., Riedel, E., Swaminathan, R., Wang, Q., Fu, K.: Plutus: Scalable secure file sharing on untrusted storage. In: Proceedings of the Second USENIX Conference on File and Storage Technologies (FAST) (March 2003)
12. Keeton, K., Santos, C., Beyer, D., Chase, J., Wilkes, J.: Designing for disasters. In: Proceedings of the Third USENIX Conference on File and Storage Technologies (FAST) (April 2004)
13. Kotla, R., Alvisi, L., Dahlin, M.: Safestore: A durable and practical storage system. In: Proceedings of the USENIX Annual Technical Conference (2007)
14. Miller, E.L., Long, D.D.E., Freeman, W.E., Reed, B.C.: Strong security for network-attached storage. In: Proceedings of the 2002 conference on File and Storage Technologies, FAST (2002)
15. Nath, S., Yu, H., Gibbons, P.B., Seshan, S.: Subtleties in tolerating correlated failures in wide-area storage systems. In: Proceedings of the 3rd conference on 3rd Symposium on Networked Systems Design and Implementation, NSDI (2006)
16. Quinlan, S., Dorward, S.: A new approach to archival storage. In: Proceedings of the Conference in File and Storage Technologies, FAST (2002)
17. Rhea, S., Eaton, P., Geels, D., Weatherspoon, H., Zhao, B., Kubiatowicz, J.: Pond: the oceanstore prototype. In: Proceedings of the Second USENIX Conference on File and Storage Technologies (FAST) (March 2003)
18. Santry, D.S., Feeley, M.J., Hutchinson, N.C., Veitch, A.C., Carton, R.W., Ofir, J.: Deciding when to forget in the elephant file system. In: Proceedings of the 17th ACM Symposium on Operating Systems Principles, SOSP (1999)
19. Shamir, A.: How to share a secret. Communications of the ACM (November 1979)
20. Stanton, P., Yurcik, W., Brumbaugh, L.: Protecting multimedia data in storage: A survey of techniques emphasizing encryption. In: International Symposium Electronic Imaging/Storage and Retrieval Methods and Applications for Multimedia (2005)
21. Storer, M.W., Greenan, K., Miller, E.L.: Long-term threats to secure archives. In: Proceedings of the Workshop on Storage Security and Survivability (2006)
22. Storer, M.W., Greenan, K.M., Miller, E.L., Voruganti, K.: Potshards: Secure long-term storage without encryption. In: Proceedings of the USENIX Annual Technical Conference (2007)
23. Subbiah, A., Blough, D.M.: An approach for fault tolerance and secure data storage in collaborative work environments. In: Proceedings of the 2005 ACM Workshop on Storage Security and Survivability (November 2005)
24. Wong, T.M., Wang, C., Wing, J.M.: Verifiable secret distribution for threshold sharing schemes. Technical Report. CMU-CS-02-114-R, Carnegie Mellon University (October 2002)
25. Wylie, J.J., Bigrigg, M.W., Strunk, J.D., Ganger, G.R., Kilicotte, H.P.: K Khosla. Survivable storage systems. IEEE Computer (August 2000)

Parametric Subscriptions for Content-Based Publish/Subscribe Networks*

K.R. Jayaram, Chamikara Jayalath, and Patrick Eugster

Department of Computer Science, Purdue University
{jayaram,cjalayat,peugster}@cs.purdue.edu

Abstract. Subscription *adaptations* are becoming increasingly important across many *content-based publish/subscribe* (CPS) applications. In algorithmic high frequency trading, for instance, stock price thresholds that are of interest to a trader change rapidly, and gains directly hinge on the reaction time to relevant fluctuations. The common solution to adapt a subscription consists of a *re-subscription*, where a new subscription is issued and the superseded one canceled. This is ineffective, leading to missed or duplicate events during the transition. In this paper, we introduce the concept of *parametric subscriptions* to support subscription adaptations. We propose novel algorithms for updating routing mechanisms effectively and efficiently in classic CPS broker overlay networks. Compared to re-subscriptions, our algorithms significantly improve the reaction time to subscription updates and can sustain higher throughput in the presence of high update rates. We convey our claims through implementations of our algorithms in two CPS systems, and by evaluating them on two different real-world applications.

1 Introduction

By focusing on the *exchanges* among interacting parties rather than the parties themselves, the *publish/subscribe* interaction paradigm [1] is very attractive for building scalable decentralized applications. This dynamic interaction culminates in *content-based* publish/subscribe (CPS), where subscriptions are based on event *content* rather than on channels or topics.

1.1 Static and Dynamic Subscriptions

Although current CPS systems are dynamic in the way they support the joining and leaving of publishers and subscribers, they fall short in supporting subscription *adaptations*, which are becoming increasingly important to many CPS applications. Consider *high frequency trading* (HFT), which as of 2009, accounts for 73% of all US equity trading volume [2]. A typical subscription to IBM stock

---

* This research is supported, in part, by the National Science Foundation (NSF) under grant #0644013 and #0834529. Any opinions, findings, conclusions, or recommendations in this paper are those of the authors and do not necessarily reflect the views of the NSF.

I. Gupta and C. Mascolo (Eds.): Middleware 2010, LNCS 6452, pp. 128–147, 2010.
© IFIP International Federation for Information Processing 2010

quotes with values below a specific threshold could be expressed through a CPS API as CPS.subscribe("firm =='IBM' and price < 10.0"), and could be used to trigger purchases. But, HFT uses various techniques to determine and update price thresholds continuously during the trading day – from simple linear regression to game theory, neural networks and genetic programming. HFT typically thrives precisely on rapid adaptations in subscriptions such as rectifications of thresholds for issuing buying or selling orders [3,4,2]. Hence, the speed with which a CPS system reacts to subscription adaptations is vital to HFT applications using CPS middleware.

Another emerging family of applications inherently requiring subscription adaptations are mobile location-aware applications (location-specific advertising, location-based social networks like loopt[1], etc.). In such applications, a subscription is a function of the subscriber location such as a perimeter surrounding the subscriber's location (GPS coordinates). Whenever the device moves, the subscription needs to adapt.

Current solutions for subscription adaptations can be categorized as follows:

Ad-hoc solutions: In location-based services, locations are typically handled as "context" separately from event content [5,6]. Corresponding middleware solutions which support updates handle them thus in an ad-hoc manner [7].

Wildcards: The simplest approach from a programmers' perspective to support adaptations on content-based subscriptions is to use wildcard matching for respective event attributes, leading to universal subscriptions reminiscent of topic-based subscriptions. In the HFT example, this simply means subscribing to all stock tickers for IBM or even to all stock tickers if the company of interest may vary. This wastes bandwidth – it may not matter for someone investing only in IBM stock, or even a few tech stocks, but is not an option for portfolio managers dealing with hundreds or even thousands of stocks and commodities.

Re-subscription: The common solution to adapt a subscription involves a *re-subscription*, where a new, parallel, subscription is issued and the superseded one is canceled. This solution has several limitations. First, it is coupled with high overhead which may lead to missing many events in the transition phase. If the frequency of subscription adaptations is high, as in HFT, the bulk of the computational resources of event brokers in a CPS is spent on processing re-subscriptions rather than filtering events and routing them to interested subscribers. This leads to drastic drops in throughput and increased latency overall. Second, in the absence of synchronization of (un-)subscriptions in most CPS engines, the application must cater for duplicates if the old and new subscriptions overlap which is usually the case.

1.2 Parametric Subscriptions

Since these solutions all have clear limitations, we propose the concept of *parametric subscriptions* — subscriptions with dynamically varying parameters — to capture the aforementioned subscription adaptations.

---
[1] http://www.loopt.com

Consider the HFT example. Intuitively, we would like to express subscriptions à-la CPS.subscribe("firm =='IBM' and price < "+ **ref** threshold) where the value of the variable threshold can be updated dynamically by the program and its most current value is considered whenever inspecting a stock quote event for that subscription. This immediately hints to the challenges in implementing parametric subscriptions. Simply passing the reference to threshold throughout the network means that nodes filtering events on behalf of the subscriber would access the variable, introducing failure - and performance dependencies.

1.3 Contributions

This paper tackles the problem of subscription adaptation in CPS broker overlay networks (CPSNs) through the following technical contributions:

- We introduce the concept of parametric subscriptions and discuss feasible and desired properties of corresponding solutions.
- We propose novel algorithms for updating routing mechanisms in CPSNs based on the original concept of *broker variables* to avoid global variable references (between publishers/subscribers) and thus global dependencies.
- To demonstrate the applicability and the efficacy of parametric subscriptions and our algorithms in CPSNs that use different algorithms for matching events to subscriptions, we evaluate two implementations of our algorithms, one in the well-known Siena [8] CPSN, and a second one in our own CPSN which uses the Rete algorithm for event matching. Our evaluation includes two benchmark applications, namely (1) algorithmic trading, and (2) a highway traffic control system, and a scalability analysis. Compared to re-subscriptions, our approach in both systems significantly improves the reaction time to subscription changes (up to 6.05×), reduces the load on subscribers by reducing the number of stale events delivered (up to 6.1×), and allows to sustain higher throughput (up to 7.9×).

Roadmap. Section 2 presents background information and related work. Section 3 introduces parametric subscriptions and feasible properties. Section 4 describes our CPSN algorithms. In Section 5 we introduce two implementations and evaluate them. Section 6 concludes with final remarks.

2 Background and Related Work

Content-based publish/subscribe (CPS) promotes *content-based routing* to deliver events produced by *publishers* to *subscribers* with appropriate *subscriptions*. That is, the routing of an event in CPS is guided exclusively by its content. Most CPS systems employ a network of interconnected *event brokers* to mediate events between *client processes*, i.e., to route events from the publishers to the appropriate subscribers. We refer to such a network as a *content-based publish/-subscribe network* (CPSN). Examples of existing CPS systems based on CPSNs are Siena [8], HERMES [9], REBECA [12], Gryphon [13], or PADRES [14].

2.1 Handling Subscriptions in CPSNs

Siena [8] introduces a covering-based scheme known as *subscription subsumption* – an elementary predicate (*attribute-value constraint*) in a subscription is said to be subsumed by that of another if the attributes are the same and the bound in the latter is more lax. *Subscription summarization* [15] builds on subscription subsumption by propagating only subscription summaries to brokers. New subscriptions are independently merged to their respective summary structures. Several systems use concepts similar to subsumption and summarization. REBECA [12] for instance uses subscription subsumption by *merging* filters in a way yielding a linear execution time irrespective of the number of subscriptions. In merging based routing, a broker merges the filters of existing routing entries and forwards them to a subset of its neighboring brokers. A perfect merging based algorithm generates perfect mergers and additionally ensures that the generated mergers are forwarded in a way such that only interesting notifications are delivered to a broker. Li et al [14] propose subscription covering, merging, and content matching algorithms based on binary decision diagrams (BDDs) in PADRES. HERMES [9] provides content-based filtering on top of type- and attribute-based routing and makes use of a distributed hashtable (DHT) to orchestrate processes. Jafarpour et al. [11] present a new CPS framework that accommodates richer content formats including multimedia publications with image and video content. The work presented in [11] is orthogonal to this paper, though we anticipate future extensions of our approach to handle richer content. Jafarpour et al. [10] present a novel approach based on negative space representation for subsumption checking and provides efficient algorithms for subscription forwarding in CPSNs. The proposed heuristics for approximate subsumption checking greatly enhance the performance without compromising the correct execution of the system and only adding incremental cost in terms of extra computation in brokers.

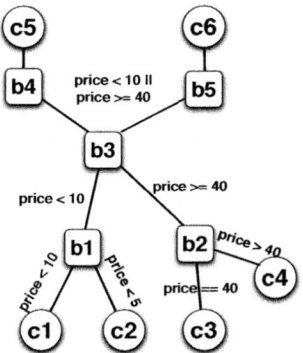

Fig. 1. Example of a CPSN

Subscription summarization can attenuate the overheads of joining and leaving subscribers [15], but for updates the improvements are more a side-effect and insufficient. Our support proposed later-on is amenable to most CPS systems.

2.2 Alternative Implementation Strategies and Models

Astrolabe [16] and PMcast [17] are examples of an alternative category of CPS systems. With an emphasis on fault tolerance, processes periodically exchange membership information with their peers. This information includes interests of processes, which is aggregated based on physical or logical topology constraints. Processes are selected to represent others based on the same criteria, leading to an overlay hierarchy reducing memory complexity on processes. This approach attempts to avoid dedicated brokers, but processes appearing high up in the hierarchy must handle high loads which probably exceed the capacities of regular desktop machines. The proactive gossiping about interests inherently propagates changes, but incurs a substantial overhead if none occur.

Meghdoot [18] is a CPS system that uses a DHT to determine the location of subscriptions and to route events to the subscribers. The partitioning of the DHT across peers allows Meghdoot to eliminate the need of brokers, however, the design is inflexible when the schema is dynamic as it requires the complete cartesian space to be reconstructed.

In *topic-based* publish/subscribe, topics represent the interests of subscribers that receive all events pertaining to the subscribed topic. Each topic corresponds to a logical channel that connects each publisher to all interested subscribers. Examples of topic-based publish/subscribe systems include SCRIBE [19] and Spidercast [20]. The topic-based publish/subscribe model provides less expressiveness than the content-based one.

3 Parametric Subscriptions

This section presents our model of parametric subscriptions as well as desired and feasible properties for corresponding support.

3.1 Model

An event e is of a certain type τ comprising a sequence of named attributes $[a_1, \ldots, a_n]$ which are typically of primitive types. An event e can thus be viewed as a record of values $[v_1, \ldots, v_n]$ for the attributes of its type. We consider subscriptions Φ represented in disjunctive normal form following a BNF grammar:

$$\begin{array}{llll} Subscription & \Phi ::= \Phi \vee \Psi \mid \Psi & Predicate & P ::= a \ op \ v \\ Conjunction & \Psi ::= \Psi \wedge P \mid P & Operator & op ::= \leq \mid < \mid = \mid > \mid \geq \mid \neq \end{array}$$

Intervals or set inclusion can be expressed above by a conjunction of two predicates or a disjunction of equalities respectively.

To decide on the routing of an event $e = [v_1, \ldots, v_n]$, subscriptions Φ are evaluated on e, written $\Phi(e)$. We assume type safety, meaning that a subscription has a type τ and is never evaluated on an event e of type $\tau' \neq \tau$. A predicate $P = a_k \ op \ v$ is evaluated as $P(e) = v_k \ op \ v$. Obviously, satisfying a conjunction $(\Psi = P_1 \wedge \ldots \wedge P_m)$ requires satisfying each of its predicates $(\Psi(e) = \bigwedge_{l=1}^{m} P_l(e))$, and a disjunction $(\Phi = \Psi_1 \vee \ldots \vee \Psi_s)$ is satisfied by any of its conjunctions $(\Phi(e) = \bigvee_{r=1}^{s} P_r(e))$. We say that subscription Φ covers Φ', denoted by $\Phi' \preceq \Phi$, iff $\forall e \ \Phi'(e) \Rightarrow \Phi(e)$.

A *parametric* subscription, in addition, allows predicates to compare event attributes a to *variables* x local to the respective processes. This addition leads to the following extended definition of predicates substituting the one above:

$$Predicate \quad P ::= a \ op \ v \mid \underline{a \ op \ x}$$

As variables x are time-sensitive, the evaluation of a subscription Φ is no longer only parameterized by an event e, but also by a time t: $\Phi(e,t)$. This evaluation takes place on variables at that point in time: $x(t)$.

3.2 Example

The expression and management of variables in parametric subscriptions can be made by the means of an API. Perhaps a more concise way of illustrating the use of variables is through a programming language. In EventJava [21] for instance, events are represented by specific, asynchronously executed, *event methods* preceded by the keyword **event**. Content-based subscriptions are defined by *guards* on these methods, following the **when** keyword. Guards can refer to event method arguments (event attributes a) and specific fields (variables x) of the subscriber object. Events can be published by invoking them like **static** methods on classes or interfaces declaring them. Consider the algorithmic trading scenario below. A stock quote can be published as StockMonitor.stockQuote(...). Now we can trigger a reaction when the stock price of IBM drops below the lowest previous value:

```
class StockMonitor {
    float lastBuy = ...;
    ...
    event stockQuote(String firm, float price)
        when (firm == "IBM" && price < lastBuy) {
            lastBuy = price;
            // e.g. issue purchase order
        }
}
```

Being a field of StockMonitor, lastBuy can be modified in other parts of the class than the body of stockQuote. Tracking such changes requires language support but mostly requires distributed runtime support for propagating them.

3.3 Desired Properties

Just like we represent parametric subscriptions with a temporal dimension, we can characterize events with a time of production. With Φ_i referring to the subscription of a process p_i, we can define the following guarantees on delivery of events in response to parametric subscriptions. Assume a process p_i's subscription does not change after a time t_0, i.e., $\forall e, \forall t \geq t_0 \; \Phi_i(e,t)$ or $\forall t \geq t_0 \; \neg \Phi_i(e,t)$:

STRICTNESS: Process p_i delivers no event e published at time $t' \geq t_s \geq t_0$ if $\neg \Phi_i(e, t_0)$.
COVERAGE: An event e published at time $t' \geq t_c \geq t_0$ is eventually delivered by p_i if $\Phi_i(e, t_0)$.

Intuitively, STRICTNESS captures a possible *narrowing* underlying a subscription update: if the conditions become tighter in one place there is a time t_s after which no more events falling exclusively into the outdated broader criteria will be delivered. COVERAGE captures a *broadening*: after some time t_c no more events of interest are missed. A subscription which "switches", such as an equality '=' for which the target value changes, can be viewed as a combination of a broadening (include the new value) and a narrowing (exclude the old value).

3.4 Practical Considerations

STRICTNESS and COVERAGE represent safety and liveness and may compete which each other. A system which never delivers any event to any process trivially ensures STRICTNESS for $t_s=t_0$ but fails to ensure COVERAGE. Conversely, a system which delivers every event to every process ensures COVERAGE for $t_c=t_0$ but not STRICTNESS. STRICTNESS can be achieved by the means of local filtering mechanisms. In fact, we can get t_s arbitrarily (making use of local synchronization) close to t_0 by fully evaluating a subscription $\Phi_i(e,t)$ locally on a subscriber process p_i at the last instance before possibly delivering any event e to it. Relying *solely* on such a mechanism for filtering leads to many *spurious events* being routed all the way to p_i and thus does not constitute an ideal solution. More interesting are solutions which filter en route, like CPSNs. Yet, in *asynchronous* distributed systems it is impossible for a process to inform another one of new interests in bounded time, so there is no bound on t_c-t_0 in a CPSN. However, we can investigate solutions which *in practice* yield small values for t_c-t_0.

In practice, subscriptions that change over time may of course change more than once. In a sequence of successive changes, intermittent values might get skipped or their effects might not become apparent because no events arrive during their (short) period of validity. This can not be systematically avoided in the absence of lower bounds on transmission delays. A particularly interesting case arises if a variable switches back and forth between two values v_1 and v_2 (or more), e.g., $v_1 \cdot v_2 \cdot v_1 \ldots$. Events *delivered* in response to the second epoch with v_1 might very well have been *published* during the epoch of v_2 but before the first switch to v_2 had successfully propagated throughout the network. An important property which may be masked by such special cases is that any visible effects of changes in subscriptions appear in the order of the changes.

4 Algorithms

This section outlines a simple algorithm based on subscription subsumption/-summarization and then presents our algorithms for parametric subscriptions.

4.1 CPSN Model

We assume in the following a CPSN which uses dedicated broker processes b_i to convey events between client processes c_i. Brokers are interconnected among themselves. Brokers which serve client processes are called *edge* brokers. For simplicity we assume the absence of cycles in the broker network and a single process p_i (broker or client) per network node. Processes communicate via pairwise FIFO reliable communication channels offering primitives SEND (non-blocking) and RECEIVE. We assume failure-free runs; fault tolerance can be achieved by various means which are largely orthogonal to our contributions. Client processes PUBLISH events and DELIVER events corresponding to their subscriptions (SUBSCRIBE, UNSUBSCRIBE). For presentation simplicity, clients issue at most one subscription.

4.2 Static Subscriptions

The client primitives are illustrated in the simple client algorithm for the case of static subscriptions, i.e., without any variables x, in Figure 2. Figure 3 outlines the corresponding broker process algorithm. All primitives (e.g., **upon**) execute atomically and in order of invocation.

Algorithm. A broker stores processes that it perceives as subscribers in *subs*, and those that it acts as subscriber towards in *pubs*. It uses the covering relation ($\preceq$) to construct a *partially ordered set* (poset) $\mathcal{P}[\tau]$ of predicates of type τ received. The algorithm uses two elementary operations:

– INSERT($\mathcal{P}[\tau], \Phi$) is used to insert Φ into the poset $\mathcal{P}[\tau]$, which is ordered with respect to $\preceq$.
– DELETE($\mathcal{P}[\tau], \Phi$) is used to remove Φ from poset $\mathcal{P}[\tau]$.

The *least upper bound* (LUB) of $\mathcal{P}[\tau]$ is the predicate that covers all other predicates. If no LUB exists, this predicate — dubbed LUB($\mathcal{P}[\tau]$) — is computed as a disjunction of all predicates that are not already covered by another predicate. All events of type τ that don't satisfy LUB($\mathcal{P}[\tau]$) are discarded by the broker and events that satisfy individual subscriptions are forwarded to the corresponding subscribers. In practice, it is the poset that is "evaluated" on the event to avoid repetitive evaluation among predicates ordered in the poset.

Unadvertisements, the analogous to unsubscriptions, are omitted for brevity. They are simpler to handle than unsubscriptions as posets remain unchanged.

CPSN client algorithm. Executed by client c_i
1: init
2:     b {*edge broker*}
3: **for all** published type τ **do**
4:     SEND(AD,τ) to b
5: **to** PUBLISH(e) of type τ **do**
6:     SEND(PUB,τ,e) to b
7: **to** UNSUBSCRIBE(Φ) from type τ **do**
8:     SEND(USUB,τ, Φ) to b
9: **to** SUBSCRIBE(Φ) to type τ **do**
10:     SEND(SUB,τ, Φ) to b
11: **upon** RECEIVE(PUB, τ, e) **do**
12:     DELIVER(e)

Fig. 2. Simple client algorithm. The client is instantiated with an edge broker. Updating a subscription goes through unsubscribing the outdated subscription and issuing a new one (or vice versa).

CPSN broker algorithm. Executed by broker b_i	
1: **init**	13: **upon** RECEIVE(SUB, τ, Φ) from p_j **do**
2: $\quad pubs[]$ $\qquad$ {Indexed by event types τ}	14: $\quad subs[\tau][\Phi] \leftarrow subs[\tau][\Phi] \cup \{p_j\}$
3: $\quad \mathcal{P}[]$ $\qquad$ {Indexed by event types τ}	15: $\quad \Phi_{old} \leftarrow \text{LUB}(\mathcal{P}[\tau])$
4: $\quad subs[][]$ $\qquad$ {Indexed by τ and Φ}	16: $\quad \text{INSERT}(\mathcal{P}[\tau], \Phi)$
	17: $\quad$ **if** $\Phi_{old} \neq \text{LUB}(\mathcal{P}[\tau])$ **then**
5: **upon** RECEIVE(AD, τ) from p_j **do**	18: $\quad\quad$ SEND(SUB, LUB($\mathcal{P}[\tau]$)) to all $b_k \in pubs$
6: $\quad pubs[\tau] \leftarrow pubs[\tau] \cup \{p_j\}$	19: $\quad\quad$ SEND(USUB, LUB($\mathcal{P}[\tau]$)) to all $b_k \in pubs$
7: $\quad$ SEND(AD, τ) to	
$\quad\quad$ all $b_k \in \bigcup_\Phi subs[\tau][\Phi] \cup pubs[\tau] \setminus \{p_j\}$	20: **upon** RECEIVE(USUB, τ, Φ) from p_j **do**
	21: $\quad subs[\Phi] \leftarrow subs[\Phi] \setminus \{p_j\}$
8: **upon** RECEIVE(PUB, τ, e) from p_j **do**	22: $\quad \Phi_{old} \leftarrow \text{LUB}(\mathcal{P}[\tau])$
9: $\quad$ **if** $\text{LUB}(\mathcal{P}[\tau])(e)$ **then**	23: $\quad \text{DELETE}(\mathcal{P}[\tau], \Phi)$
10: $\quad\quad$ **for all** $\Phi \in \mathcal{P}[\tau]$ **do**	24: $\quad$ **if** $\Phi_{old} \neq \text{LUB}(\mathcal{P}[\tau])$ **then**
11: $\quad\quad\quad$ **if** $\Phi(e)$ **then**	25: $\quad\quad$ SEND(SUB, LUB($\mathcal{P}[\tau]$)) to all $b_k \in pubs$
12: $\quad\quad\quad\quad$ SEND(PUB, τ, e) to all $p_k \in subs[\Phi]$	26: $\quad\quad$ SEND(USUB, LUB($\mathcal{P}[\tau]$)) to all $b_k \in pubs$

Fig. 3. Algorithm for event processing in a CPSN with subscription summarization. $\mathcal{P}[\tau]$ is the predicate poset ordered by $\preceq$. $pubs[\tau]$ stores the advertising peers. $subs[\tau][\Phi]$ stores peers that subscribe with Φ. $subs[\tau][\Phi]$ avoids the need to duplicate Φ in $\mathcal{P}[\tau]$, if more than one peer subscribes with Φ.

Illustration. Figure 1 shows an example of a CPSN with six clients – four subscribers (c_1, c_2, c_3, c_4), two publishers (c_5, c_6) and five brokers (b_1, b_2, b_3, b_4, b_5). We focus on a single event type StockQuote with two attributes a_1=firm and a_2=price. We assume that all the clients subscribe to StockQuotes of the same firm, e.g. firm =="IBM", which we omit from this illustration for presentation simplicity. Figure 4 shows a part of the CPSN, and how subscriptions propagate. c_1 subscribes to StockQuote with the predicate Φ_1=(price < 10)[2]. b_1 gets the subscription, stores it and propagates it to b_3. Then c_2 subscribes with predicate Φ_2=(price < 5). b_1 gets this subscription, but does not forward it to b_3, because (price < 10) covers (price < 5) (since $\Phi_2 \preceq \Phi_1$). Figure 1 illustrates subscription summarization throughout the overlay. Brokers b_1 and b_2 summarize subscriptions from $\{c_1, c_2\}$ and $\{c_3, c_4\}$ respectively, and b_3 summarizes the "summaries" from b_1 and b_2.

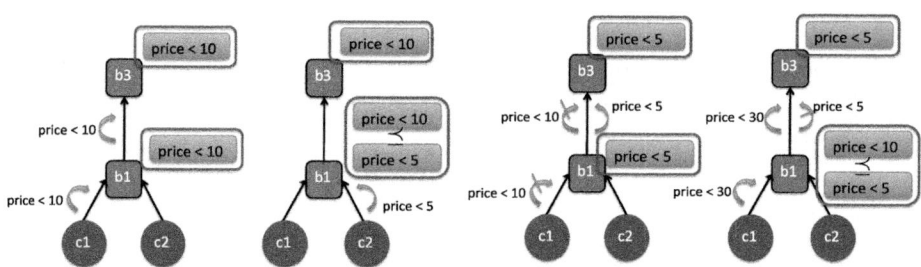

Fig. 4. Update propagation with re-subscriptions

---

[2] Predicates are wrapped in parentheses for clarity.

When c_1 unsubscribes from (price $<$ 10), b_1 forwards (price $<$ 5) to b_3. Then, when c_1 subscribes to (price $<$ 30), b_1 reconstructs the poset. Since the LUB($\mathcal{P}$[StockQuote]) changes to (price $<$ 30), b_1 unsubscribes from (price $<$ 5) and subscribes to (price $<$ 30). Figure 4 shows how the poset of predicates changes at b_1 and b_3. Calculating LUB($\mathcal{P}$[StockQuote]) is shown in Figure 1 through an example. Subscriptions are routed to all brokers that have at least one publisher with a matching advertisement.

Subscription updates. When a subscriber c wants to update its subscription, it unsubscribes and re-subscribes. Unsubscription on a broker involves searching the poset $\mathcal{P}[\tau]$ for Φ, removing Φ from it, and readjusting it with respect to $\preceq$. If the poset is implemented as a $d-ary$ max-heap ordered with respect to $\preceq$, with d the maximum degree of the heap, readjusting is $O(|\mathcal{P}[\tau]|)$ [22]. The worst case occurs when Φ is the root of the poset and all other nodes are its children. Searching $\mathcal{P}$ is $O(|\mathcal{P}[\tau]|)$. Hence processing an unsubscription is $O(|\mathcal{P}|)$. Similarly, subscription (SUBSCRIBE(Φ)) involves searching $\mathcal{P}$ to check whether Φ already exists, in this case, c is simply added to the list of subscribers of Φ. If not, Φ is inserted into the $\mathcal{P}$. Insertion is $O(log_d|\mathcal{P}[\tau]|)$ [22]. If LUB($\mathcal{P}$) changes as a result of subscription/unsubscription, then the broker unsubscribes the old LUB($\mathcal{P}[\tau]$) and issues a fresh subscription with the new LUB($\mathcal{P}[\tau]$).

Note that a client might also want to issue a new subscription first, before unsubscribing, and filter any duplicates in the interim. In common CPSNs, both subscription and unsubscription operations are asynchronous though, providing no information on their penetration into the CPSN. A practical solution consists in canceling the outdated subscription upon reception of the first event which does *not* match the outdated subscription.

4.3 Supporting Parametric Subscriptions

We now outline a solution to supporting variables x in subscriptions.

Algorithm. Figure 5 describes the new client algorithm as extension to that of Figure 2. Besides the addition of a reaction to changes of variables appearing in a subscription Φ, the algorithm performs additional local evaluation of Φ on a client to enforce STRICTNESS, as the view of it's end broker may be lagging.

CPSN client algorithm with parametric subscriptions for c_i. Reuses lines 1-8 of algorithm in Figure 2	
9: **upon** RECEIVE(PUB, τ, e) **do** 10: **if** $\Phi(e,$ current time$) \mid \Phi$ is on τ **then** 11: DELIVER(e)	12: to SUBSCRIBE(Φ) to τ **do** 13: $\overline{x},\overline{v} \leftarrow$ vars in Φ and respective vals 14: SEND(SUB,τ, Φ, $\overline{x},\overline{v}$) to b 15: **upon** change of variable x to v in Φ **do** 16: SEND(UPD,τ, Φ, x, v) to b

Fig. 5. Client algorithm with support for parametric subscriptions

```
CPSN broker algorithm supporting parametric subscriptions. Executed by broker b_i.
 1: init                                                    29: upon RECEIVE(USUB, τ, Φ) from p_j do
 2:    pubs[]         {Indexed by event types τ}            30:    subs[τ][Φ] ← ∅
 3:    P[]            {Indexed by event types τ}            31:    node ← (Φ^V, Φ, (x,v)) ∈ P[τ]
 4:    subs[][]       {Indexed by τ and Φ}                  32:    for all x ∈ x̄ do
 5:    brokervars[]                    {Indexed by τ}       33:       lookup[τ][x] ← ⊥
 6:    lookup[][]     {Indexed by τ and var x}              34:    node_0 = (Φ_0^V, Φ_0, (x^0,v^0)) ← LUB(P[τ])
                                                            35:    DELETE(P[τ], node)
 7: upon RECEIVE(AD, τ) from p_j do                         36:    node_ν = (Φ_ν^V, Φ_ν, (x^ν,v^ν)) ← LUB(P[τ])
 8:    pubs[τ] ← pubs[τ] ∪ {p_j}                            37:    PROPAGATE(node_0, node_ν)
 9:    SEND(AD, τ) to
          all b_k ∈ ⋃_Φ subs[τ][Φ] ∪ pubs[τ]\{p_j}          38: upon RECEIVE(PUB, τ, e) from p_j do
                                                            39:    for all node = (Φ^V, Φ, (x',v')) ∈ P[τ] do
10: upon RECEIVE(SUB, τ, Φ, (x,v)) from p_j do              40:       if Φ^V(e) ∧ subs[τ][Φ^V] ∉ {⊥, p_j} then
11:    Φ^V ← SUBSTITUTE(v̄, x̄, Φ)     {Var subst}          41:          SEND(PUB, τ, e) to subs[τ][Φ^V]
12:    subs[τ][Φ] ← p_j                {At most 1}
13:    node ← (Φ^V, Φ, (x,v))                               42: upon RECEIVE(UPD, τ, x, v) from p_j do
14:    for all (x,v) ∈ (x,v) do                             43:    node_0 = (Φ_0^V, Φ_0, (x^0,v^0)) ← LUB(P[τ])
15:       lookup[τ][x] ← ref node   {Store ref}             44:    node_upd ← deref lookup[τ][x]
16:    node_0 = (Φ_0^V, Φ_0, (x^0,v^0)) ← LUB(P[τ])         45:    UPDATE(P[τ], node_upd, x, v)
17:    INSERT(P[τ], node)                                   46:    node_ν = (Φ_ν^V, Φ_ν, (x^ν,v^ν)) ← LUB(P[τ])
18:    node_ν = (Φ_ν^V, Φ_ν, (x^ν,v^ν)) ← LUB(P[τ])         47:    PROPAGATE(node_0, node_ν)
19:    PROPAGATE(node_0, node_ν)

20: procedure PROPAGATE((Φ_0^V, Φ_0, (x^0,v^0)), (Φ_ν^V, Φ_ν, (x^ν,v^ν)))
21:    if Φ_ν^V ≠ Φ_0^V then                                {Different concrete subscriptions}
22:       if Φ_ν = Φ_0 then                                 {Same structure and variables}
23:          for all v^ν ≠ v^0 do                           {Can be regrouped}
24:             SEND(UPD, τ, brokervars[τ], v^ν) to all b_k ∈ pubs[τ]
25:       else
26:          brokervars[τ] ← fresh x_1...x_n | x̄^ν = x'_1...x'_n
27:          SEND(SUB, τ, SUBSTITUTE(brokervars[τ], x̄^ν, Φ_ν), (x,v^ν)) to all b_k ∈ pubs[τ]
28:       SEND(USUB, τ, Φ_0) to all b_k ∈ pubs[τ]
```

Fig. 6. Broker algorithm for parametric subscriptions. Common handling of poset updates (new subscriptions, unsubscriptions, updates) are regrouped in PROPAGATE.

The broker algorithm shown in Figure 6 follows the same structure as the previous broker algorithm. The main differences are that nodes in the poset are now tuples of the form $(\Phi^V, \Phi, \overline{(x,v)})$ where Φ is the original predicate without values substituted for variables, and Φ^V after substitution (e.g. line 11 of Figure 6). $\overline{(x,v)}$ is a set of mappings of values v_i for variables x_i. Furthermore, poset additions (INSERT) and removals (DELETE) are now parameterized by nodes. These changes lead to two new primitives being used in the algorithm:

- SUBSTITUTE(v, x, Φ) denotes the substitution of v for x in Φ. This primitive is also used by brokers to substitute variables of neighbors against their own.
- UPDATE$(\mathcal{P}[\tau], node, x, v)$ (see line 45) updates *node within* the poset, by adopting v as new value for x in the substitution to v, re-performing the variable substition, storing the updated predicate in the node, and re-ordering the poset if needed. Poset ordering is based on Φ^V; if two predicates need to be disjoined, the corresponding variable mappings are merged.

$lookup[\ldots][x]$ stores identifiers of nodes containing respective variables x for fast lookup and modification upon incoming update messages. Since such variables are always specific to a single predicate, they are introduced by one node. Disjunctions created for summarization will indirectly be modified by updates to such introducing nodes. Similarly, due to variables in subscriptions, there is now never more than one subscriber stored for a given predicate Φ in $subs[\ldots][\Phi]$. This can be overcome in practice by variable substitution.

Procedure PROPAGATE captures the common part of all subscription modifications – new subscriptions, unsubscriptions, updates. It compares the root node of the poset ($node_0$, e.g. line 36) with the root node after modification ($node_\nu$, line 34), and initiates corresponding transitive updates. Hence, subscriptions/unsubscriptions are reduced, and when an update message arrives, a hash table based index can for example be used to guarantee a $O(1)$ bound on updates with $lookup$.

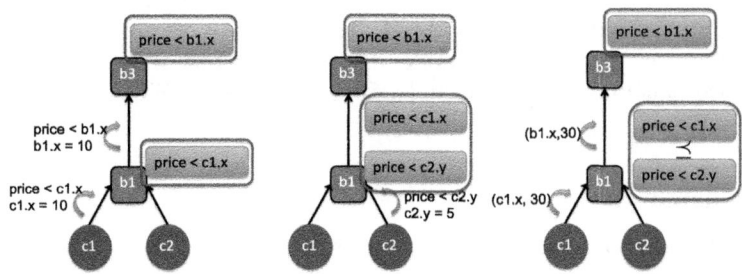

Fig. 7. Update propagation with support for parametric subscriptions

Last but not least, PROPAGATE illustrates the concept of *broker variables* (*brokervars*, see line 24). These limit the scope of variables to a client and its edge broker or to a broker and its immediate neighbors thus avoiding global dependencies. When a new subscription is sent to a neighbor broker, variables in the root predicate Φ of the poset $\mathcal{P}[\ldots]$ are substituted by freshly chosen ones.

Illustration. The main difference to a CPSN without parametric subscriptions is illustrated in Figure 7, which contrasts with Figure 4. In Figure 7, updating a subscription involves unsubscribing the old one (price $<$ 10) and issuing a new subsciption (price $<$ 30). In a CPSN with parametric subscriptions, Φ contains predicates, some of which involve local variables. Each subscription message sent to a broker now must include the values of the variables used in the subscription. However, changing a subscription doesn't necessarily lead to an unsubscription and a re-subscription. The subscriber (c_1 in Figure 7, for example) merely specifies the name of the variable and its new value.

In Figure 7, when client c_1 subscribes to price $< c_1.x$, the variable $c_1.x$ is shared between c_1 and b_1. When b_1 propagates the subscription to b_3, $c_1.x$ is mapped to $b_1.x$, which is shared between b_1 and b_3. Note that, in Figure 7, updating the value of $c_1.x$, doesn't change the structure of the predicate involved. Also, new variables are introduced (by the variable mapping algorithm) only at those predicate containing variables. If a predicate has *sub-predicates* comparing event attributes with constants, a change to a constant will result in an unsubscription and a re-subscription instead of an update. To avoid this, we can go a step further and replace all values in predicates by variables (omitted for simplicity). A single update message can then be used instead of two messages (subscription/unsubscription) in further cases.

5 Evaluation

The goal of our experimental evaluation is to demonstrate improvements in performance due to parametric subscriptions. In this section, we first introduce two implementations of our algorithms, namely as an extension to Siena [8] and in our own CPSN implemented in EventJava based on Rete [23]. While our own CPSN yields much higher throughput than Siena, it requires more resources which is why we compare both implementations against their respective extensions on two benchmarks – highway traffic management (HTM) and algorithmic trading (AT).

5.1 Implementation

For both benchmarks, we compare two "bare" CPSN — making use of re-subscriptions — against respective extensions following our proposal.

EventJava. EventJava is an extension of Java for generic event-based programming which supports the expression of event correlation, multicast, asynchronous event consumption (subscriptions) as well as synchronous consumption (message queuing) in an integrated manner. EventJava is implemented as a framework, with substitutable runtime components for event propagation, filtering, and correlation. Parametric subscriptions are supported naturally in EventJava as expressed in the example in Section 3.2, by allowing fields of subscriber objects to be used in event method guards.

We have extended the EventJava [21] compiler to track changes in the values of variables used in parametric subscriptions. The compiler translates EventJava to standard Java together with calls to the framework components, instrumenting assignments to relevant fields in order to issue UPD messages. It relies on a specialized static analysis, leading to the following steps:

1. Identify all fields used in subscriptions, all assignments to such fields.
2. Inject code to issue an UPD message after the assignment.
3. Protect this assignment together with the sending of the UPD message by a field-specific lock added to the respective class. This ensures that the update occurs in mutual exclusion with respect to other instrumented assignments to the same field, preventing race conditions/lost updates.

To ensure completeness of the static analysis, fields that can be used in guards are currently limited to **protected** and **private** fields of primitive types, e.g. **float**.

UPDSiena. Siena was chosen instead of other systems because it is the only publicly available open source CPSN with acceptable performance. The source code was necessary because we had to implement our algorithms in existing systems to measure the gains in performance due to our proposal. We extended the Java Siena implementation to support a new message type named UPD (update) sent from subscribers to edge brokers and from edge brokers to the their neighboring brokers. When defining a predicate a user can optionally specify a variable for each of his predicates which will be later used to update the predicate in the broker network. This API can be used directly without EventJava. The class HierarchicalSubscriber implementing broker functionality was modified to create a new set of variables once a new predicate gets added to the root of a poset analogously to what is described in Figure 6. These can be used to update the subscription with the parent broker. Other classes modified include Poset, Filter, and ThinClient. Java applications can exploit our parametric subscription in UPDSiena as well as in our EventJava CPSN through APIs, i.e., independently of EventJava.

5.2 Metrics

To assess COVERAGE and STRICTNESS (see Section 3.3) we use three metrics:

Delay: To approximate COVERAGE we measure the *delay* between an update and the reception of the first corresponding event. If a subscriber c_i changes its subscription Φ_i to Φ'_i at time t_0, and the first event matching Φ'_i but not Φ_i is delivered at time t_1, then the delay at subscriber c_i is defined as t_1-t_0.

Throughput: To gauge the load imposed on the system to achieve STRICTNESS by update propagation, we first evaluate *throughput* in the presence of an increasing amount of updates. More precisely we consider is the average number of events *delivered* by a subscriber per second. This throughput depends on the number of publishers, event production rates at each publisher, the selectivity of the subscriptions of the subscribers, and the rate at which each subscriber updates its subscriptions. Selectivity of a subscription is the probability that an event matches a subscription. A selectivity of 1.0 implies that a subscription is satisfied by every published event of the respective type and a selectivity of 0.0 implies that none do.

Spurious events: The effect of inefficient updates might be offset if brokers are powerful dedicated servers or individual clients are only interested in few events to start with. Increased stress might otherwise manifest, especially on resource-constrained clients. To gauge this stress, we measure the amount of spurious events delivered by clients. If a subscriber c_i changes its subscription Φ_i to Φ'_i at time t_0, then spurious events are those matching Φ_i but not Φ'_i

and received by the client *after* t_0 and filtered out locally to it (see line 10 in Figure 5). These capture the overhead imposed on clients.

5.3 Infrastructure

All brokers were executed on dual core Intel Xeon 3.2Ghz machines with 4GB RAM running Linux, with each machine executing exactly one broker. Subscribers were deployed on a 16-node cluster, where each node is an eight core Intel Xeon 1.8Ghz machine with 8GB RAM running Linux, with 8 subscribers deployed on each node (one subscriber per core). Publishers were deployed on dual core Intel Pentium 3Ghz machines with 4GB RAM, with no more than 2 publishers per machine (one publisher per core). Deploying publishers, subscribers and brokers on different nodes ensured that all relevant communication (publisher-broker, broker-broker and subscriber-broker) was over a network, and in many cases across LANs. 10msec delays were added to each network link to simulate wide area network characteristics as is done in EmuLab[3].

5.4 Highway Traffic Management (HTM)

Publish/subscribe systems have been used in several traffic management systems, the best example being the Tokyo highway system [24,25].

Scenario. Such a system consists of a CPSN with several sensors and cameras located at various points along the highway, monitoring road conditions, traffic density, speeds, temperature, rainfall, snow etc. So publishers are the various sensors and the subscribers are vehicles, and traffic monitoring stations. Consider a vehicle equipped with a GPS-based navigation system driving through the highway – many contemporary vehicles have touchscreen navigation systems with nearly real-time traffic information. Typically, the navigation system is interested in traffic density in the geographic area around it – an example being red, yellow and green colored highways in Google Maps[4].

The navigation system uses this information to plot alternate routes — with minimum traveling time — to the destination. Each sensor connects to one broker, and publishes events to the CPSN. While traveling a portion of the road covered by a broker, a car navigation system connects to the broker and subscribes to events of interest, parameterized by current location (GPS coordinates). The location of a moving car changes constantly and thus the navigation system updates its subscriptions periodically, or as initiated by the driver. Brokers in an HTM system are usually interconnected by a wired network.

Setup. We used a traffic management CPSN based on [24] with 20 brokers, and 10 publishers per broker, resulting in a total of 200 publishers. The rate of subscription updates is dependent on the following parameters: (1) the length

---

[3] http://www.emulab.net
[4] http://maps.google.com. Select a U.S. city and click on "Traffic".

of highway controlled by a broker (*Highway-length*), (2) periodicity of subscription updates by the navigation system (*Periodicity*), and (3) average number of appropriately equipped vehicles on the stretch of highway controlled by a broker (*Vehicles*). In an urban setting, if *Highway-length* = 10 miles, *Periodicity* = 1 update/minute, and *Vehicles* = 1000, then the number of subscribers attached to one broker is 1000. During any 1 minute interval, each of the 1000 cars updates its subscription, hence the number of updates/second is 1000/60 = 16.67 updates/second. One thousand subscribers means that the traffic density is 100 cars/mile of highway, which is sparse traffic. Assuming a six lane highway (3 lanes in each direction), traffic densities can easily reach 500 cars/mile (250 cars in either direction) during heavier traffic periods. Thus, frequency of subscription updates easily reaches 500x10/60 = 83.33 updates/second/edge broker. Hence, on this benchmark, we evaluate our algorithms with update frequencies ranging from 10 updates/second to 100 updates/second/edge broker. CPSNs in traffic management are not hierarchical, because highways around major urban cities are not hierarchical. Hence the only assumption on the CPSN used for this benchmark is that it is a connected undirected graph. The distribution of operators in subscriptions was 40% '$\geq$', 40% '$\leq$', and 20% '='.

5.5 Algorithmic Trading (AT)

Algorithmic trading (AT) is the use of computer programs for entering trading orders, with the computer algorithm deciding on aspects of the order such as the timing, price, or quantity of the order, or in many cases initiating the order without human intervention.

Scenario. We consider the monitoring component of an algorithmic commodity trading system. By commodities we mean basic resources and agricultural products like iron ore, crude oil, ethanol, sugar, coffee beans, soybeans, aluminum, copper, rice, wheat, gold, silver, palladium, or platinum. We use a CPSN that disseminates commodity prices with 20 brokers, 5 publishers and 150 subscribers.

Setup. In AT, the number of publishers is small – commodity prices are published by commodity exchanges and stock quotes by stock exchanges. For this benchmark, we assume that a subscriber is a computer at an AT firm. Our benchmark had 200 event types, which includes the price quotes of 100 commodities, analyst predictions, etc. In the experimental setup used for this benchmark, we employed a hierarchical broker overlay network, which is typical in stock and commodity price quote dissemination. Stock and commodity markets publish quotes and information into a market data system, like DOWJONES newswires, Reuters Market Data Systems (RMDS), which are at the top of the hierarchy. At the next level are large clearing houses (e.g., Goldman Sachs, Merrill Lynch, J.P Morgan). The next level contains large brokerages and trading firms, to which small trading firms connect. In the overlay network used for this benchmark, publishers and subscribers are separated by at least 3 brokers. The distribution of operators was 35% '$\leq$', 33% '$\geq$', and 32% '='.

5.6 Results and Analysis

The performance improvements of UPDSiena over Siena, and EventJava (with parametric subscriptions) over EventJava respectively are summarized in Table 1 and detailed in Figure 8. Apart from speedups we observe that:

1. The drastic drop in Siena's throughput in both benchmarks (Figures 8a and 8g) is due to the increase in time spent processing un-subscriptions/re-subscriptions – recall that both operations involve computing the least upper bound and rearranging subscriptions in a poset, the complexity of which is linear in the size of the poset. The same poset is used for event forwarding.
2. The throughput of EventJava degrades more gracefully with an increasing update frequency (Figures 8j and 8d) as opposed to the Siena (Figures 8g, 8a) because Rete constructs a *separate* event flow graph to "remember" events that partially match subscriptions in a poset, representing each subscription as a chain of nodes. Hence, event filtering and forwarding at the brokers is independent of the updates to the poset.
3. The drastic increase in the number of spurious events received per second by a Siena or an EventJava (re-subscriptions) subscriber corresponds to the increase in delay between a variable update and the receipt of the first matching event for both benchmarks.
4. The increase in the number of spurious events received by an EventJava subscriber (> 100 spurious events per second) as opposed to UPDSiena (Figures 8f, 8l vs. Figures 8c, 8i) is due to (1) the high event matching throughput of Rete compared to Siena's algorithm, and (2) the presence of a separate event flow graph. Since a broker using Rete processes more events per second, more spurious events are delivered to subscribers in CPSNs using Rete before an update propagates to the broker.

Table 1. Performance improvements for HTM and AT with parametric subscriptions. EventJava is abbreviated as EJ.

Metric	Incr. in throughput		Decr. in delay		Decr. in spurious events	
Benchmark	HTM	AT	HTM	AT	HTM	AT
UPDSiena vs. Siena	Fig. 8a up to 7.9×	Fig. 8g up to 4.4×	Fig. 8b up to 6.05×	Fig. 8h up to 2.5×	Fig. 8c up to 6.1×	Fig. 8i up to 5.94×
EJ (resub) vs. EJ	Fig. 8d up to 51%	Fig. 8j up to 33%	Fig. 8e up to 1.89×	Fig. 8k up to 4.05×	Fig. 8f up to 2.82×	Fig. 8l up to 4.27×

5.7 Throughput Scalability

Given that the empirical evaluation in Sections 5.4 and 5.5 considers update frequencies between 10 and 100, one obvious issue is the scalability of throughput with increasing number of updates. The original Siena does not scale beyond 100 updates/second/subscriber. Figure 9 shows that EventJava with parametric subscriptions retains a throughput of well above 9000 events/second, even

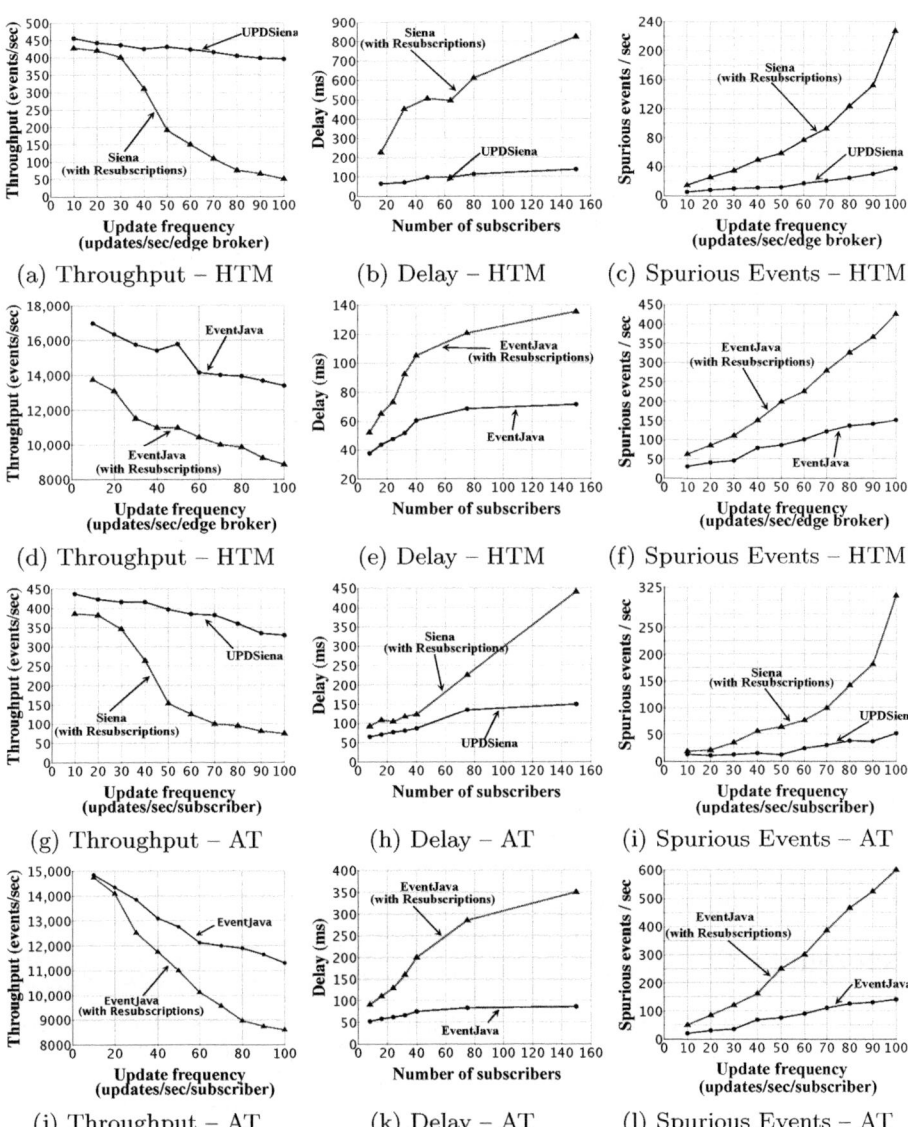

Fig. 8. Comparing re-subscriptions against parametric subscriptions in both algorithmic trading (AT) and highway traffic management (HTM) benchmarks for Siena and EventJava's Rete-based CPSN

when the update frequency per receiver is 1000 updates/second. However, the throughput of EventJava with re-subscriptions degrades faster and drops to 4000 events/second. At 1000 updates/second/subscriber, the throughput of EventJava with parametric subscriptions is 2.27× that of EventJava with re-subscriptions. This experiment is independent of the benchmarks described in Sections 5.4 and 5.5, and used a programmatically generated (artificial) workload with 200 event types, 20 brokers, 100 publishers and 150 subscribers and a broker overlay which was a connected graph and non-hierarchical.

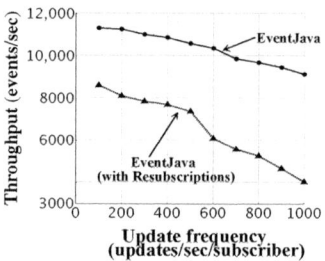

Fig. 9. Throughput scalability

6 Conclusions

The publish/subscribe paradigm supports dynamism by allowing new publishers as well as subscribers to be deployed dynamically. This ability allows applications to adapt online by issuing new subscriptions. The mechanisms used to that end are not geared towards important changes *within* subscriptions. We thus propose parametric subscriptions. Through the novel concept of broker variables our algorithms proposed in this paper and implemented in two CPSNs (and easily adapted to others) retain the scalability properties of common CPSNs.

We are currently investigating several extensions. For instance, we are considering uniformly representing all predicates based on operators '<', '≤', or '=' internally as range queries where the upper and lower bounds are implicitly variables, assuming minimum and maximum values for the respective data-types in the case of wildcards, and over-approximating summaries to normalize subscriptions at all levles. This allows us to easily support *structural* subscription updates, i.e., the *addition* of predicates. Furthermore, we are investigating approximation techniques for oscillating variables and prediction algorithms for high frequency monotonic variable changes.

References

1. Oki, B., Pfluegl, M., Siegel, A., Skeen, D.: The Information Bus - An Architecture for Extensible Distributed Systems. In: SOSP 1993, pp. 58–68 (1993)
2. Lati, R.: The Real Story of Trading Software Espionage. AdvancedTrading.com (2009), http://advancedtrading.com/algorithms/showArticle.jhtml?articleID=21840150
3. The Economist: Moving Markets: Shifts in Trading Patterns are Making Technology Ever More Important (2006), http://www.economist.com/business-finance/displaystory.cfm?story_id=E1_VQSVPRT
4. Aite Group: Algorithmic Trading: Hype or Reality? (2005), http://www.aitegroup.com/reports/20050328.php
5. Cugola, G., Margara, M., Migliavacca, M.: Context-aware Publish-Subscribe: Model, Implementation, and Evaluation. In: ISCC 2009, pp. 875–881 (2009)

6. Schwiderski-Grosche, S., Moody, K.: The SpaTeC Composite Event Language for Spatio-temporal Reasoning in Mobile Systems. In: DEBS 2009, pp.1–12 (2009)
7. Eugster, P.T., Garbinato, B., Holzer, A.: Location-based Publish/Subscribe. In: NCA 2005, pp. 279–282 (2005)
8. Carzaniga, A., Rosenblum, D., Wolf, A.: Design and Evaluation of a Wide Area Event Notification Service. ACM TOCS 19(3), 332–383 (2001)
9. Pietzuch, P., Bacon, J.: Hermes: A Distributed Event-Based Middleware Architecture. In: ICDCS 2002 Workshops (DEBS 2002), pp. 611–618 (2002)
10. Jafarpour, H., Hore, B., Mehrotra, S., Venkatasubramanian, N.: Subscription subsumption evaluation for content-based publish/Subscribe systems. In: Issarny, V., Schantz, R. (eds.) Middleware 2008. LNCS, vol. 5346, pp. 62–81. Springer, Heidelberg (2008)
11. Jafarpour, H., Hore, B., Mehrotra, S., Venkatasubramanian, N.: CCD: Efficient Customized Content Dissemination in Distributed Publish/Subscribe. In: Bacon, J.M., Cooper, B.F. (eds.) Middleware 2009. LNCS, vol. 5896, pp. 62–82. Springer, Heidelberg (2009)
12. Fiege, L., Gärtner, F., Kasten, O., Zeidler, A.: Supporting Mobility in Content-based Publish/Subscribe Middleware. In: Endler, M., Schmidt, D.C. (eds.) Middleware 2003. LNCS, vol. 2672, pp. 103–122. Springer, Heidelberg (2003)
13. Aguilera, M., Strom, R., Sturman, D., Astley, M., Chandra, T.: Matching Events in a Content-Based Subscription System. In: PODC 1998, pp. 53–62 (1998)
14. Li, G., Hou, S., Jacobsen, H.: A Unified Approach to Routing, Covering and Merging in Publish/Subscribe Systems based on Modified Binary Decision Diagrams. In: ICDCS 2005, pp. 447–457 (2005)
15. Triantafillou, P., Economides, A.A.: Subscription Summarization: A New Paradigm for Efficient Publish/Subscribe Systems. In: ICDCS 2004, pp. 562–571 (2004)
16. van Renesse, R., Birman, K.P., Vogels, W.: Astrolabe: A Robust and Scalable Technology For Distributed Systems Monitoring, Management, and Data Mining. ACM TOCS 21(3) (2003)
17. Eugster, P.T., Guerraoui, R.: Probabilistic Multicast. In: DSN 2002, pp. 313–324 (2002)
18. Gupta, A., Sahin, O.D., Agrawal, D., Abbadi, A.: Meghdoot: Content-Based Publish/Subscribe over P2P Networks. In: Jacobsen, H.-A. (ed.) Middleware 2004. LNCS, vol. 3231, pp. 254–273. Springer, Heidelberg (2004)
19. Castro, M., Druschel, P., Kermarrec, A.M., Rowstron, A.: SCRIBE: A Large-Scale and Decentralized Application-level Multicast Infrastructure. IEEE JSAC 20(8), 100–110 (2002)
20. Chockler, G., Melamed, R., Tock, Y., Vitenberg, R.: Spidercast: a Scalable Interest-aware Overlay for Topic-based Pub/Sub Communication. In: DEBS 2007, pp. 14–25 (2007)
21. Eugster, P., Jayaram, K.R.: EventJava: An Extension of Java for Event Correlation. In: Drossopoulou, S. (ed.) ECOOP. LNCS, vol. 5653, pp. 570–594. Springer, Heidelberg (2009)
22. Cormen, T.H., Rivest, R., Leiserson, C., Stein, C.H.: Introduction to Algorithms. MIT Press, Cambridge (2009)
23. Forgy, C.L.: On the Efficient Implementation of Production Systems. PhD Thesis, Carnegie-Mellon University (1979)
24. Schneider, S.: DDS and Distributed Data-centric Embedded Systems. Dr. Dobb's Journal, http://www.drdobbs.com/embedded-systems/196601852
25. Barnett, D.: Publish-Subscribe Model Connects Tokyo Highways. Industrial Embedded Systems, http://www.industrial-embedded.com/articles/barnett/

KEVLAR: A Flexible Infrastructure for Wide-Area Collaborative Applications

Qi Huang[1,2], Daniel A. Freedman[2], Ymir Vigfusson[3], Ken Birman[2], and Bo Peng[2]

[1] SCTS & CGCL, Huazhong University of Science and Technology, Wuhan, China
[2] Cornell University, Ithaca, New York, USA
[3] IBM Research, Haifa, Israel

Abstract. While Web Services ensure interoperability and extensibility for networked applications, they also complicate the deployment of highly collaborative systems, such as virtual reality environments and massively multiplayer online games. Quite simply, such systems often manifest a natural peer-to-peer structure. This conflicts with Web Services' imposition of a client-server communication model, vectoring all events through a data center and emerging as a performance bottleneck. We design and implement the KEVLAR system to alleviate such choke points, using an overarching network-overlay structure to integrate central hosted content with peer-to-peer multicast. KEVLAR leverages the given storage and communication models that best match the respective information: data most naturally retrieved from the cloud is managed using hosted objects, while edge updates are transmitted directly peer-to-peer using multicast. Here, we present the KEVLAR architecture and a series of carefully controlled experiments to evaluate our implementation. We demonstrate KEVLAR's successful and efficient support of deployments across wide-area networks and its adaptivity and resilience to firewalls, constrained network segments, and other peculiarities of local network policy.

Keywords: Distributed systems, Overlay networks, Collaboration.

1 Introduction

The rapid evolution of the Internet has both produced and relied upon standards for interoperability, enabling client systems to easily interact with sophisticated data centers that host data, or create content. To leverage these standards, more and more collaborative applications — virtual reality immersion environments [15], massively multiplayer online games [9], conference systems [10], and other distributed tools — are now designed as Web Services [1], bouncing client-initiated events off central shared data centers for relay to other clients. While such an architecture functions acceptably in most settings, it performs and scales poorly in particular environments: when the link between some set of clients and the data center is congested, the latency on such a link is too high, or the servers in the data center are overloaded.

In prior work, we introduced a new method for combining standard Web Services with peer-to-peer replication protocols. The Live Distributed Objects (LO) platform [5,16] supports a simple drag-and-drop style of application development, similar to that used by non-programmers to design Web pages. The resulting applications have an XML representation suitable for sharing: for example, via e-mail or through a networked file system. Each user who "opens" an LO application activates the objects within some scope (for example, objects visible from some location in a game environment), and each of the resulting object instances function as a replica of what is conceptually a distributed object. We provide more details about our LO approach in Sect. 2, but, for now, note that the design of LO starts to address the issues listed above.

However, LO lacks the type of protocol capable of fully exploiting this flexibility, leaving open the question of whether our LO platform actually includes the full range of needed mechanisms. In particular, although LO is effective in enterprise network settings, the LO replication protocols are stymied by the many barriers that arise in practical Internet deployments across wide-area networks (WANs): performance variability, firewall interference, IP multicast (IPMC) policy non-uniformity, and more [14]. In the public Internet of 2010, point-to-point TCP is often the only option to work reliably (and, even that, at times only in one direction).

In this work, we introduce a substantially more capable wide-area multicast solution embodied by our KEVLAR system. KEVLAR allows applications to create multicast regions ("patches"), sewn together into a single spanning application-layer multicast structure, for content distribution or event-style notifications. KEVLAR is a decentralized and improved re-implementation of our prior work, Quilt [12], restructured into a collection of Live Objects more robust to node failures. Here, we also apply KEVLAR to demonstrate a substantial application: a search-and-rescue command-and-control system, useful in responding to environmental events such as hurricanes or earthquakes. We then undertake a careful evaluation of our solution, accurately emulating potential deployment scenarios and measuring associated event delivery latencies, data rates, and overhead.

KEVLAR addresses a difficulty that arises from the need to construct applications that will run as a network of interconnected components and do so in a way sensitive to their local runtime environments. Here, we focus on the selection of a multicast component from among a set of multicast protocols, each specialized for a different setting, but the potential applicability is broader. While our research community has recognized that applications using component architectures should benefit from such improved structure, the issue of *adapting* such applications to match their runtime environments has received much less attention. Our work shows that this is a solvable problem, and, through our detailed evaluation, that the solutions are truly practical. The key enabler is the KEVLAR platform architecture: it is structured to support plug-in components along with developer-provided rules, used at runtime to decide which component best matches a given runtime environment.

The primary contributions of this work are the following:

- WAN collaboration requires sophisticated management of firewalls, bottleneck links, organizational policy, and performance-driven protocol optimization. KEVLAR automates such tasks and shows that Web Services and peer-to-peer protocols can co-exist in Internet WAN environments, despite the many complexities that arise from network configurations and performance limitations. KEVLAR illustrates a new and interesting form of runtime adaption, in which a distributed application must determine which components to launch on the basis of runtime criteria evaluated on a per-node basis.
- KEVLAR applies the LO component model to replace the centralized features of our Quilt system with a completely decentralized, gossip-based solution, thus eliminating a central point of failure, as well as an additional performance bottleneck.
- We evaluate KEVLAR across a range of experiments within a challenging and complex network environment. In contrast to most popular Web-Service architectures, as well as our prior Quilt system, neither of which deliver acceptable or reliable performance in this scenario, KEVLAR succeeds in its design goals for efficient collaborative applications.

The KEVLAR system is distributed under a FreeBSD license, available for download and deployment from http://kevlar.cs.cornell.edu/. While the current version scales to hundreds of simultaneous users, our ongoing work expands support to configurations with tens of thousands or hundreds of thousands of users. To achieve such scalability, we are extending KEVLAR's multicast-forwarding components to allow for pre-emptive filtering of data during multicast. This capability would align KEVLAR more closely with the needs of distributed virtual worlds and online games and their high-volume, rich data streams: the server need only send all the data once, for each client to receive an optimal, personalized subset of the complete stream. Further discussion of such extensions is outside the scope of this work.

2 Background

In detailing the architecture of KEVLAR, we will first briefly summarize the Live Objects component model [5,16], upon which KEVLAR is built. LO presents a new kind of "live distributed object," replicated at each node in the system. The replicas can communicate among themselves with any choice of protocol, and the ensemble together represents the actual live object. These live objects can be composed as a graph, in which case, the replicas of each distinct live object on a given node interact using a simple, but flexible, event-based interface. Type checking is employed both at design time and at run-time, and the type-checking system itself is highly flexible. For example, an LO representation of an airplane might compose an airplane rendering object with an object that fault-tolerantly captures location data from a GPS source, which in turn is composed with a multicast protocol presented through an LO interface: a "data replication"

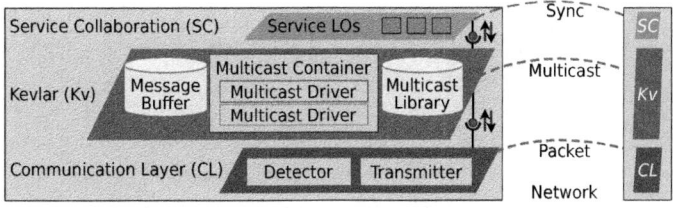

Fig. 1. Architecture of a KEVLAR-enabled LO application. Three major Live Objects compose a demonstration application: Service Collaboration (SC), KEVLAR (KV), and Communication Layer (CL). As the application executes, all replicas of each LO communicate with one another across the network.

object. The airplane might require protocols that support total ordering and real-time delivery, and the type checker would have to verify that the associated protocols offer these properties (though the LO platform does not independently ensure such claims are correct).

As mentioned earlier, LO includes a drag-and-drop application builder. Many applications require little to no programming, simply using existing objects parameterized with URLs pointing to data sources. Additional objects simply implement a standard interface that we provide. This style of development would be familiar to any Java or C# user familiar with graphical interface design. The resulting LO application resides as an easily shared XML representation.

Figure 1 presents the architecture for a prototypical KEVLAR application. Here, Service Collaboration (SC), KEVLAR (KV), and Communication Layer (CL) live objects interface, on a given system node, through their respective event-based interfaces. Inside each live object (such as SC), we find a graph composed by several service objects (e.g., maps, airplanes, weather, etc.). In a distributed environment, the replicas for each service live object communicate with other replicas of their type across the network, sharing content or synchronizing state. Meanwhile, the KV and CL objects provide multicast function and real packet delivery on their own respective levels.

Prior work on the LO approach focused on type checking and event-driven interaction mechanisms [16] and efforts to scale through multicore parallelism [17]. But the actual LO multicast protocols have thus far been simple, rather limited, ones that operate only in enterprise data centers or other local-area networks among groups of computers without intermediate firewalls or performance barriers. As a result, prior to this work, all LO demonstration applications have been unsuitable for WAN deployment.

3 Patchwork Overlay in KEVLAR

While KEVLAR uses the LO component model, it also extends a more recent system of ours: Quilt distributed event-notification [12]. As a free-standing library, Quilt combines independent multicast patches for separate network regions into

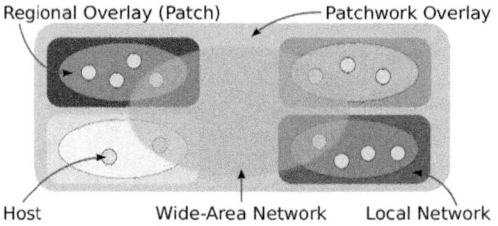

Fig. 2. Patchwork overlay. KEVLAR automates the construction of multicast overlays across complex environments, with hosts in various local and wide-area networks. Here, KEVLAR combines a collection of regional multicast overlays (patches) into a single system-wide patchwork overlay, thus separating the multicast interface for the application from the runtime-driven, performance-optimized implementation of the overlay.

Byte Offset	0	1	2	3	4	5	6	7	8	.....	23	24	25	26	27	28	29	30	31	...	34
EUID Content	Direction (d)	Protocol (p)	List of {d,p} tuples		# of routers		IPMC range			Router Stack (path of routers to local DNS)		Optional flag	Performance type (t)		Min value (l)		Max value (h)			List of {t,l,h} triples	
Type	Connectivity				Local Topology							Measured Performance									

Fig. 3. EUID. Components of KEVLAR'S Environmental Unique IDentifier with accompanying byte offset (bar atop number signifies variable width of particular entry), enumerating metrics for connectivity, local topology, and measured performance.

a single application-layer overlay across complex WAN settings. Figure 2 depicts this process for KEVLAR, with a single overlay including WAN links and connecting four independent local networks, each with its own multicast policies, firewall placement, and congestion profile. As one might expect, there is no single, simple solution that can operate optimally in all such settings.

A KEVLAR application developer creates a set of multicast "drivers," each consisting of a protocol implemented as an LO, and an associated rule describing the conditions under which that protocol can be used. (The API for these driver rules is that of Quilt [12].) As earlier shown in Fig. 1, KEVLAR itself consists of a library into which these drivers are linked. At initialization of a KEVLAR application, the system profiles its local environment through a series of sophisticated measurements and updates the performance measurements continually during runtime. The resulting metrics are aggregated as the "environmental unique identifier" (EUID) in Fig. 3, which is used for assignment of nodes to a particular patch.

During application initialization, KEVLAR nodes send their EUIDs to a bootstrap server and obtain a list of other nodes that appear to be "close" to the node with respect to the topology, latency, bandwidth, and protocol compatibility, as indicated by the EUID. Unlike Quilt, which relies on a central server to

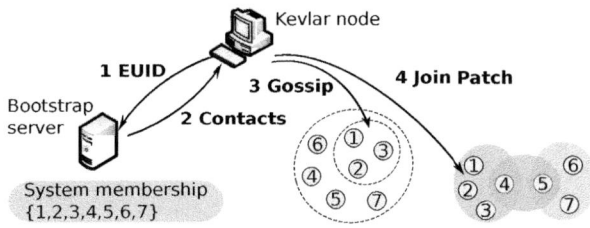

Fig. 4. Patch assignment. Upon initialization, a KEVLAR node tests its local environment to produce an EUID; (1) sends this EUID to a bootstrap server; (2) receives a contact list in return; (3) uses this list to identify other nearby members and patches via gossip; (4) applies these EUID metrics to dynamically select patches to join.

incrementally construct and maintain the patchwork, KEVLAR nodes create and maintain patches in a peer-to-peer fashion. Quilt's single point of failure is thus eliminated, since the bootstrap functionality is trivial. This decentralized scheme also improves security and privacy, as domains have the option of running protocols and networking rules privately with no dependence on an external Quilt server.

In a further departure from Quilt, KEVLAR runs a system-wide anti-entropy gossip protocol [18] to exchange information about membership, EUIDs, and patches that are formed, along with their identifiers and the protocols in use. For our experiments, we set the gossip rate to one exchange per second. The choice of a gossip recipient is biased towards proximate nodes, according to the EUID information. More specifically, we compose a fixed-length portion of the EUID into a number that reflects protocol compatibility, presence on the routing path (shorter routing paths are padded with zeros), average latency, and bandwidth. We then define the approximate *distance* between two nodes to be the absolute difference between these numbers mapped from their EUIDs; thus the above order of composition reveals the priority of each component in determining proximity and compatibility between end-hosts. In each gossip round, we rank the recipients by the distance and select the recipient of rank i with probability proportional to 2^{-i}. This results in membership sets biased toward nearby nodes; hence, updates in the node's surrounding environment are disseminated faster.

KEVLAR seeks to maximize connectivity while relaying multicasts between patches in a fault-tolerant manner. It also avoids duplicate event delivery, even under node churn. Figure 4 illustrates patch formation and assignment logic (details as in Quilt [12]).

The KEVLAR multicast protocols used in this paper include:

1. **IP multicast** (IPMC) [7]. This protocol assigns a distinct IPMC class-D multicast address to each region. The associated rule checks to make sure that IP multicast is permitted by examining all network interfaces used by each application, and testing their IPMC-enabled bit.

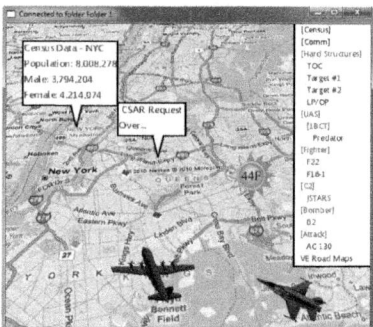

Fig. 5. Example application. This KEVLAR demonstration, showcasing a search-and-rescue application, requires significant communication traffic among cooperating users at the network edge as well as constant query and retrieval of centralized data objects.

2. **DONet** [21]. This protocol implements a mesh-structured application layer multicast that uses TCP for the links. The actual content is disseminated on a random-graph overlay maintained by a gossip protocol. It works in the style of BitTorrent [6]: every node advertises its local content buffer snapshot epidemically with a fixed fanout; then, by the end of each scheduled epoch, it solicits non-received data in a bandwidth-aware manner; once a request is received, the node returns the associated data, also in a bandwidth-aware manner. KEVLAR uses DONet for physically close end-users without IPMC support, since such users have lower latencies between them, varied bandwidth capacities, and more churn than data center servers.
3. **OMNI Tree** [4]. The OMNI tree is a latency-optimized application layer multicast (ALM) overlay, serving both multicast receivers and Multicast Service Nodes (MSN), which are actually local proxies. Assuming MSN nodes have negligible latency, the OMNI Tree optimizes the average root-to-client latency based on the root-to-MSN latency and the number of clients each MSN is serving, but with constrained outdegree between MSNs. KEVLAR uses OMNI Tree as the inter-patch protocol to sew different patches together. For fast and stable forwarding among regional patches, the associated rule prefers nodes with accessible connections and high network performance.

4 Anatomy of a KEVLAR Application

As a canonical demonstration of KEVLAR, we implement a distributed search-and-rescue application which exercises almost all of the functionality described above. Figure 5 depicts a representative user interface, displaying both centrally hosted and edge objects and allowing for user manipulation of the scenario. Such an application could readily be designed and assembled by a non-programmer, using pre-existing Live Objects (stored, for example, in a local or shared file system) that each represent a different piece of data: aircraft, ground vehicles, rescue workers, weather information, maps, etc. The developer simply synthesizes the scenario from pertinent objects and associates them with their data sources. Further changes to the application can be made at runtime, by any of the users sharing the system (provided, of course, that they have appropriate permissions). For instance, commanders may modify the positions of aircraft or adjust the demographic statistics displayed on the interface. Components can also be reused, even simultaneously: those involved in Fig. 5 could separately participate in any other sort of KEVLAR application.

The user accesses this application through its XML representation, which includes references to the "live folders" that hold content added at runtime. Thus, the user interface can be viewed as a visualization of the theoretical "graph" of program composition, expressed in its XML representation. While the overall graph structure is determined by the original application designer, some portions are, by design, extensible by other users at runtime: the live folders just mentioned, for example. The "leaves" of the graph are the airplanes, maps, weather, etc. Some leaf objects extract and display content from cloud repositories, while others use peer-to-peer protocols (for example, to track locations of moving objects). As the graph evolves (either through movement of objects, or their explicit addition or deletion), the interface will automatically update in sync.

Much of the functionality behind this user interface requires communication, using multicast channels established by KEVLAR. These channels retrieve hosted content, share edge updates, or coordinate or synchronize some other action. For example, satellite imagery might be updated via multicast to all users as a satellite over-flies a region of interest. A first responder in the field could, similarly, use a multicast group to share a status report on some disaster victims; his unit commander could multicast orders to a larger rescue unit, and so forth.

The KEVLAR runtime is implicitly launched through the execution of associated applications. As determined by the KEVLAR application developer, a given application includes some set of built-in multicast protocols (for our experiments here, the three defined in Sect. 3). For each node and multicast group, KEVLAR determines the appropriate protocols to launch and helps these protocols form initial peering relationships with other members of a given node's patch. Beyond this, each protocol maintains its own peer structure. Thus, where IPMC is permitted and other peers are also present, KEVLAR will launch the IPMC protocol modules and provide them with class-D multicast addresses as parameters, as well as a few contacts for initialization. Using an OMNI network, KEVLAR will sew this IPMC region together with other remote regions: KEVLAR will launch the OMNI protocol and help the module peer with appropriate remote nodes. On nodes that run both OMNI and IPMC protocols, KEVLAR will help relay multicasts between them, minimizing the risk of network partition through redundant dual-protocol nodes, while simultaneously suppressing the duplicate delivery of updates. If failures occur or nodes quit the overlay, KEVLAR orchestrates the repair of the mesh, all in a fully decentralized manner.

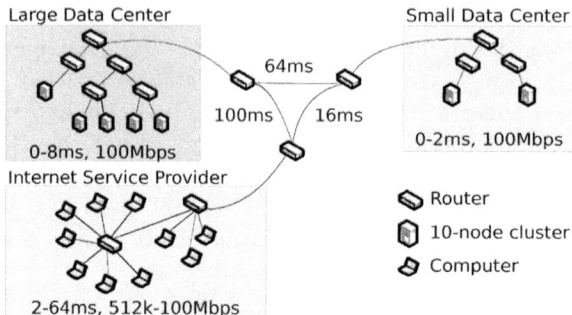

Fig. 6. Network topology. Experimental network topology, as emulated on DETERlab, with data centers and an Internet service provider: node numbers, latencies, and data rates as indicated, with IP multicast internally enabled in data centers.

5 Evaluation

5.1 Experiment Setup

The remainder of this paper presents an experimental evaluation of our KEVLAR system in a number of distinct application scenarios.

We first explore the ability of KEVLAR, compared to other multicast protocols, to establish an efficient overlay topology and minimize latencies from a single given sender to the ensemble of receivers. Further, we investigate the bandwidth utilization in such a topology, comparing KEVLAR to the native OMNI Tree and DONet protocols, as well as to a pure IP multicast (which, of course, might not actually be a legal choice in settings where KEVLAR is launched, but represents something of an ideal when permitted). We explore a number of various simple application scenarios, each characterized by a set of input traffic parameters of fixed message size and data rate; these tests reveal the applications for which KEVLAR's quality of service determination yields improved results. We continue our systematic exploration of KEVLAR's performance for complex real-time collaborative applications by considering the needs of the search-and-rescue application discussed earlier, and illustrated in Fig. 5. Finally, we conclude our evaluation by examining the robustness of KEVLAR to recover from catastrophic failure cases.

We rely upon DETERlab [8], an Emulab [20] environment, to construct our experimental environment and establish a network topology that includes various types of local subnets. In total, we use 80 nodes, distributed among three different regions and connected across an emulated Internet backbone. As shown in Fig. 6, the regions consist of: (1) a large data center whose internal LAN has three layers of depth to its hierarchy; (2) a smaller data center with a 2-layer LAN; and (3) a consumer ISP, remote from big data center but topologically near the small one; the ISP supports consumers via various last-mile access technologies (including cable, DSL, and satellite, each with appropriate latency, jitter, and bandwidth constraints). IP multicast is enabled inside data centers, but unusable for home

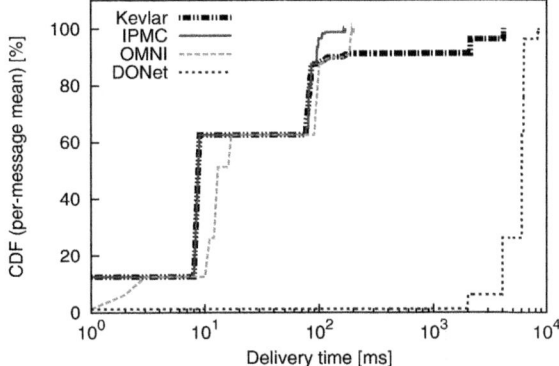

Fig. 7. Delivery latency. Cumulative distribution function (CDF) of the latency for a given data-center sender to contact some percentage of all other nodes (in experimental topology in Fig. 6), for each of four competing protocols: mean computed over ten messages; KEVLAR closely tracks IPMC except for the final 15% of the nodes (which, as part of the ISP, cannot access IPMC), where it instead uses the bandwidth-efficient, but higher-latency, DONet protocol.

users. Bandwidth and latency settings accompany Fig. 6. The object of this topology is to accurately mimic a portion of the real Internet, including some large data centers hosting the primary server farm and working in concert with small data centers distributed around the world to provide low-latency support for nearby users.

Unless otherwise specified, all data points correspond to an average over ten trials. Error bars are calculated as one sample standard deviation but omitted from figures when too small to be clearly visible.

5.2 Examination of Overlay Topology

We first examine the raw performance of KEVLAR along with the various alternative protocols in the overlay topology without the influence of particular traffic patterns of any specific application. We accomplish this measurement by sending a series of small messages (10-Byte payloads) at low data rates (100 messages per second), so that the available bandwidth across the links and data transfer delays do not affect these results.

Finding low-latency paths. First, we evaluate the efficiency of each protocol in matching its overlay to the actual physical network topology. Any efficient multicast service should identify fast delivery pathways to each receiver irrespective of the application traffic input. Figure 7 shows just such a comparison among IPMC, DONet, OMNI Tree, and KEVLAR — the latency for a sender to send data to all the receivers in the experiment environment. Here, and in the ensuing sections, we use the cumulative distribution function (CDF) to display many of our measurements; the structure of many of the dissemination patterns

Table 1. Forwarding load. Comparison of the skew in load among four competing protocols, demonstrating both the average forwarding load per system node, as a percentage of the traffic stream, as well as the number of nodes that forward traffic, among all eighty system nodes. With network hardware support, IPMC requires only a single forwarding node, while OMNI Tree and DONet must rely on many intermediate nodes. KEVLAR nodes generally only forward one-fifth of the packets they receive.

Protocol	Load per node [%]	Forwarding nodes [#]
IPMC	1.3	1
KEVLAR	20.3	12
OMNI Tree	100.0	20
DONet	102.8	66

incorporate bursts of traffic, such that the associated probability density function (PDF) would be filled with spikes that are difficult to interpret visually.

A number of qualitative observations emerge from Fig. 7. First, we note that our KEVLAR multicast protocol is closest to what IPMC offers (recall that IPMC is generally unavailable in a real WAN deployment, hence it represents an ideal, but one that may not be an actual option). Both show a largely stair-stepped CDF that corresponds to (1) low-latency communication in the large data center from which the sending traffic originates; (2) fast transfer to the smaller data center; and (3) final delivery to small, remote ISP. We also note the differentiation between KEVLAR and IPMC for delivery to the final 15% of nodes, located in the remote ISP; this is due to the lack of IPMC among the ISP customers (which therefore receive *no* IPMC traffic), and KEVLAR's reliance there on the underlying DONet protocol (which utilizes bandwidth better than OMNI Tree for such end-host users). To understand the performance of the OMNI Tree protocol, we must recall that it cannot, by design, leverage IPMC even within the data centers where it is available and must instead build its own tree structure to disseminate data. This consumes time and thus accounts for CDF values that are universally lower than (or equal to) that of IPMC (and KEVLAR, again by design). Finally, we see that DONet is the least capable of the protocols in creating an efficient overlay. As explained above in Sect. 3, DONet's protocol uses only "pull" semantics (rather than "push" in the other protocols) and this introduces significant latency to identify the node location that possesses the required data. DONet's use of epochs and timers only exacerbates this problem (though, in general, as we see later, the use of epochs has some benefits in enabling better bandwidth utilization).

Forwarding load on overlay nodes. Recall that some intermediate nodes in an ALM may need to bear the burden of forwarding packets to other receivers. We explore the efficiency of overlay formation for the multicast protocols by examining the average volume of traffic that each node in the overlay needs to transmit to distribute a given stream, as a fraction of the total traffic volume.

Table 1 shows this amount of traffic that must be forwarded by an average overlay node, as well as the number of nodes that forward packets. With IPMC, only a single sender needs to forward packets, so, on average, nodes transmit only a fraction (1/80) of the stream. As expected, the OMNI Tree and DONet protocols do not benefit from network-level multicast and thus the typical node must forward every packet received. KEVLAR is second to IPMC in performance: an average node forwards 20% of packets; this indicates that KEVLAR is able to exploit IPMC where supported and to use an ALM (DONet) otherwise.

5.3 Performance of Simple Applications

This section focuses upon the realized delivery performance among a number of applications with simple, fixed traffic patterns. Specifically, we measure the performance with respect to fifteen different ensembles of traffic streams, each with different fixed values for message size (150, 1500, and 15 000 Bytes) and data rate (100 kbps, 300 kbps, 1 Mbps, 3 Mbps, and 10 Mbps). As mentioned before, these streams represent five different levels of media production: standard-quality audio MP3, network video conferencing, Video CD (VCD), standard-definition (SD) IP Television (IPTV), and high-definition (HD) IPTV [11]. In each scenario, we contrast the four protocols in terms of their CDF, determined by message delivery times averaged across ten measurements.

Figure 8 shows our results, here. We make three primary qualitative observations from this series of measurements: The first point is that all of these subfigures show the same qualitative structure for each protocol, considered independently, as we found in the application-agnostic evaluation from Fig. 7. We would expect as much — the qualitative features of the performance, for a particular application (with a given fixed data rate and message size) using a specific multicast protocol, are largely determined by the corresponding overlay. However, for each particular application, the curves for the individual protocols show various offsets in time as well as dilation or contraction of features in time. Next, for delivery to a large fraction ($\gtrsim 90\%$) of the receivers, KEVLAR shows identical (ideal) performance when compared to IPMC within all application scenarios. For dissemination to the final fraction of nodes (those within the ISP), KEVLAR out-performs DONet in all cases, while it exceeds OMNI Tree only for 15 000-Byte messages at 10 Mbps (see Fig. 8(d)). Lastly, we observe no qualitative distinctions among the measurements conducted at data rates of 100 kbps, 300 kbps (for either message size) and those of 1 Mbps (additional tests at 3 Mbps and for 150 Byte messages gave identical results). Thus, due to space constraints, we do not reproduce the former in Fig. 8.

We now separately examine the behavior of each protocol within the same measurements conducted above, and previously shown in Fig. 8. This allows us to discuss more subtle distinctions in protocol performance at varying data rate and message size parameterization, that are otherwise not apparent above. Figure 9 presents a comparison of the IPMC, OMNI Tree, DONet, and KEVLAR protocols for different application domains (different fixed input parameters).

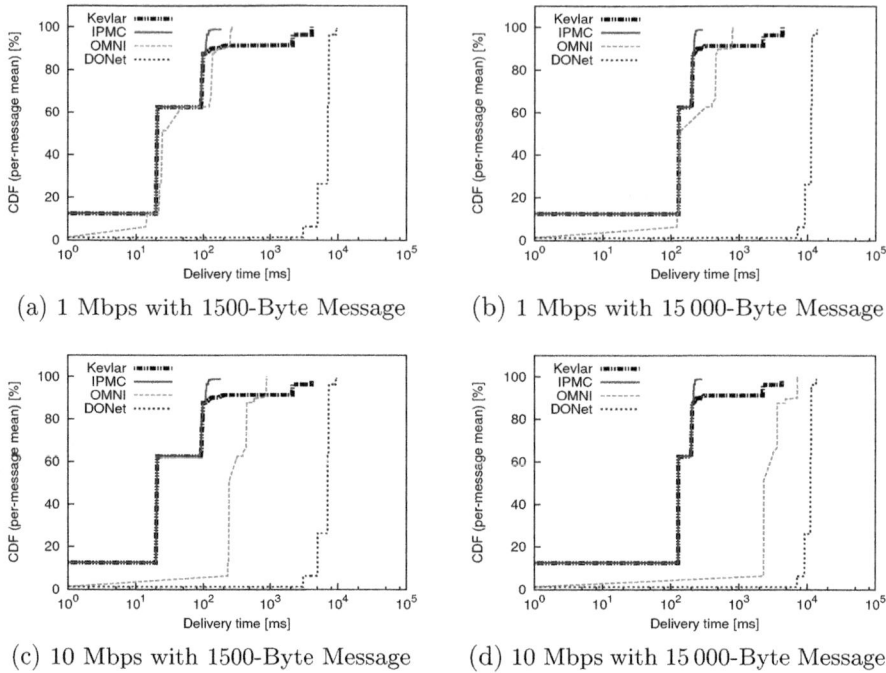

Fig. 8. Performance of simple applications (input traffic dependence). Performance comparison of multicast protocols for input traffic of various message size and data rate: each subfigure, corresponding to a different set of input parameter values, shows the CDF (per-message mean as in Fig. 7) of message delivery time. Space constraints preclude visualization of the remaining eleven experiments (specifically, data rates of 100 kbps, 300 kbps and 3 Mbps, and message size of 150 Bytes), with nearly identical results.

Two quantitative observations emerge: In contrasting data rates of 1 and 10 Mbps (for all message sizes), we note that the curves representing IPMC, KEVLAR, and DONet protocols are completely unaffected by data rate considerations. (In fact, such curves identically overlap each other, to the extent that we remove such extra labels within each subfigure to increase legibility.) Conversely, the OMNI Tree protocol collapses with increasing data rates: the curves for the higher rates are shifted to the right in time by factor of ratio between rates (10 in figure). The impact of data rate on OMNI Tree is suitably severe that its performance for smaller messages at higher data rates (1500 Bytes at 10 Mbps) is worse (or equal, at times) than that for larger messages at lower data rates (15 000 Bytes at 1 Mbps). We conjecture that this effect is due to the inefficiency of bandwidth utilization by the OMNI Tree protocol.

We also contrast message sizes of 150, 1500, and 15 000 Bytes for all data rates and note a key qualitative difference: The curves for IPMC, KEVLAR, and OMNI Tree protocols are all shifted to the right by an order of magnitude in

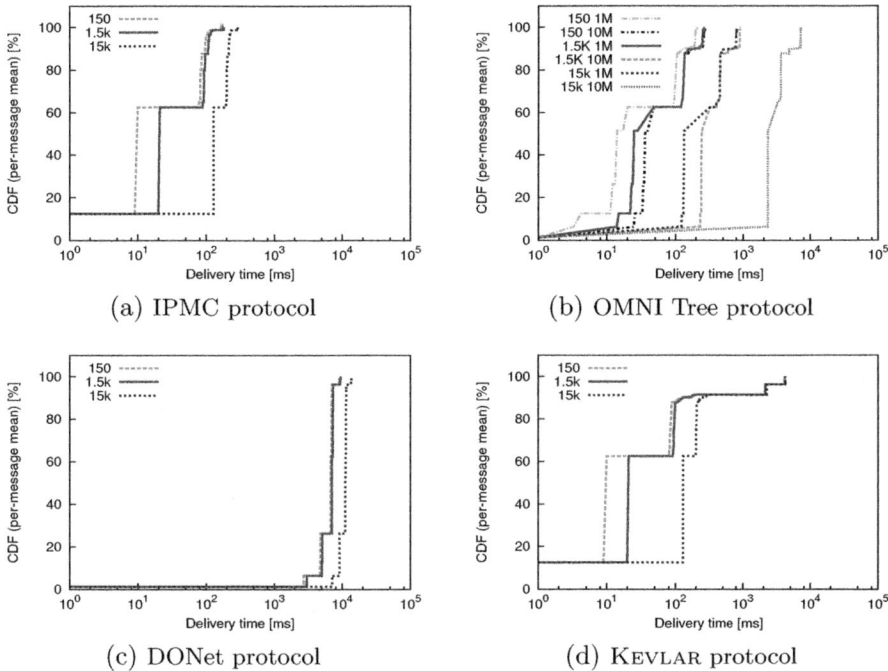

Fig. 9. Performance of simple applications (protocol dependence). Performance comparison of multicast protocols for input traffic of various message size and data rate: each subfigure, corresponding to a different protocol, shows the CDF of delivery time. (Note, for protocols with data-rate independent results, only message size is shown.)

time, while DONet is significantly less affected by this variation in message size parameter. This observation follows trivially due to the need to transfer larger amounts of data to the receivers. The smaller correlation between message size and DONet performance can be explained by DONet's parallelization of data transfers for small portions of each message amongst many nodes (within each epoch that it defines).

Finally, Fig. 10 extracts the performance trends from the raw data presented in Figs. 8 and 9. Now, for each of the four multicast protocols studied, we consider the time required to distribute application traffic to various cumulative subsets of the entire environment. Thus, the family of curves for each protocol is comprised of three separate curves, which represent the delivery to different cumulative values (10%, 50%, and 90%) of the total node population; increasing color saturation of each curve in the family denotes more complete dissemination of traffic.

This figure further confirms many of the trends we discussed above: (1) strong dependence on input traffic data rate for OMNI Tree; (2) correlation between input message size and delivery time for IPMC, KEVLAR, and OMNI Tree (weak for DONet); and (3) for IPMC and KEVLAR protocols, the faster relative increase

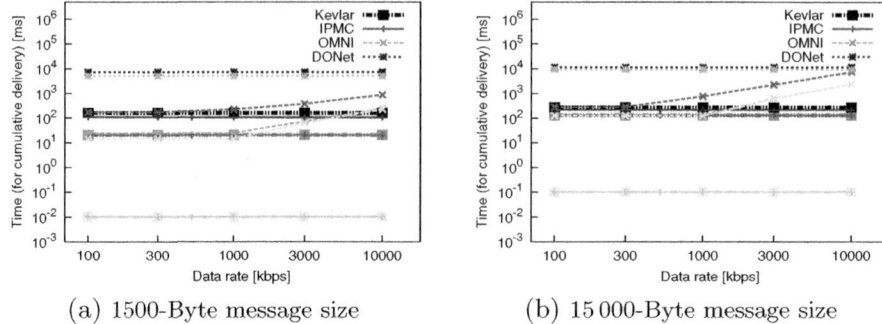

(a) 1500-Byte message size (b) 15 000-Byte message size

Fig. 10. Overall trends for simple application delivery. Performance of multicast protocols for transmission of various traffic streams (each with fixed message size and data rate) associated with different video delivery standards. Subfigures show distinct message sizes (1500 and 15 000 Bytes, respectively), and, as a function of data rate, each plots the time required to distribute messages to cumulative subsets of the entire environment: the three separate curves, in each protocol family, display the time corresponding to different cumulative values (10%, 50%, and 90% delivery in the corresponding CDFs of Fig. 8). Space constraints preclude display of third subfigure with five additional curves, associated with 150-Byte packets at all five possible data rates.

(more vertical CDF) in distribution for 15 000-Bytes messages as compared to 1500-Byte messages; this is seen in the narrower spacing within a given family of curves in Fig. 10(a) as compared to Fig. 10(b).

5.4 Performance of a Complex Application

Above, we have just evaluated the performance for a few simple, model applications that exhibit constant traffic patterns with fixed message size and data rate. Now, we expand upon such an evaluation by discussing the performance implications from diverse traffic patterns of a type associated with more complicated applications, focusing on the search and rescue application discussed in Sect. 2.

In Fig. 11, the inset depicts the input traffic pattern for this scenario. It plots message size as a function of time over the 10 minute period of application execution and communication. (We note that the data rate, here, is a secondary feature based upon the density of messages in time; however, we present the data in this manner, rather than as a 2D histogram, so as to reveal the time correlations of data, which would be absent in the histogram presentation.) This input figure depicts various traffic patterns generated by users' operations: during the start up, the collaborative application requires a checkpoint of existing service objects, generating a burst of messages followed by low traffic during local resource initialization; after a short time, users are able to explore the world map and add or remove new services of their choosing, all resulting in bulk transfers of texture contents from the data center; after fetching all the needed data, communications among users are steady and moderate, primarily at the network edge.

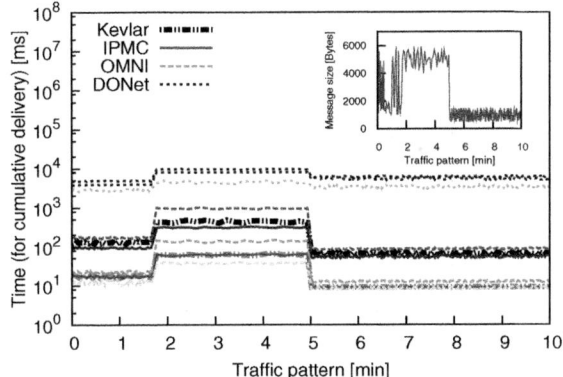

Fig. 11. Performance of a complex collaborative application. Performance for multicast protocols while executing a complex collaborative application: inset shows the varying input traffic pattern of the application, with message size as a function of the position in time in the pattern. For each protocol, the main panel displays a family of curves plotting the time required to distribute messages to cumulative subsets of the entire environment, as a function of position in the input traffic pattern (increasing color saturation corresponds to cumulative delivery as in Fig. 10).

The main panel of Fig. 11 shows the resulting performance for each protocol in this scenario. We first compute CDFs associated with all four protocols, for each of the (dozens of) individual sample points — representing a distinct value of data rate and message size — as seen in the inset of Fig. 11. From each of these CDFs, we then extract the time for the protocols to achieve different cumulative distributions of 10%, 50%, and 90%. Figure 11 thus shows four families of curves, one for each of the protocols, with each family differentiating the behavior associated with various completion levels in the dissemination of data. Here, increasing saturation levels of each curve color denote more completion of traffic distribution.

We make four observations, here: (1) KEVLAR tracks IPMC very closely, for all completion levels up to, but not including 90%. This reflects KEVLAR's underlying usage of IPMC within both data centers, its need for DONet in the non-IPMC-enabled ISP, and its use of a small-sized OMNI Tree for sewing its multicast patches together. (2) Throughout this experiment, across all varying message sizes and data rates, OMNI Tree shows a consistent performance penalty of approximately 400%. (3) DONet is the slowest of the protocols here, requiring seconds for the traffic to arrive at a significant fraction of the receivers. Indeed, its performance is degraded 100-fold, compared to both IPMC and KEVLAR; as discussed above, this primarily results from the its inclusion of a handshake scheme, an epoch-based time line, and a "pull"-based communication pattern. However, in fairness to DONet, we recognize that its performance variance upon varying data rate is significantly lower that that of OMNI Tree; this meets its design goal to optimize for bandwidth utilization instead of latency. (4) Finally,

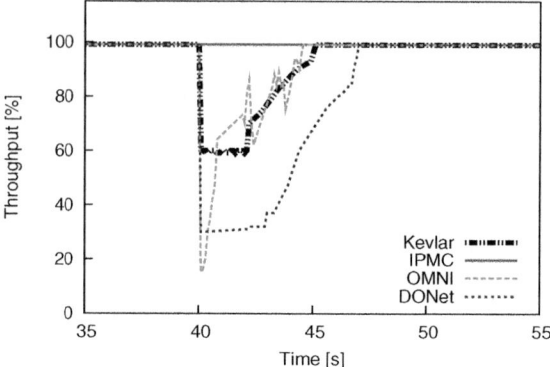

Fig. 12. Robustness under failure. Robustness of the various multicast protocols upon fail-stop (at 40 seconds) of a random 50% of the nodes during transmission of 1500-Byte messages at 1 Mbps data rate: figure plots percentage throughput to remaining live nodes relative to the throughput prior to failures, as a function of time.

we examine the difference in time for each protocol to achieve 50% versus 90% cumulative distribution of traffic: First, we note that DONet shows little difference between these curves; we expect as much from previous measurements (see Fig. 8) in which the DONet curves show very abrupt transitions from negligible completion to almost total distribution of traffic. Conversely, IPMC, OMNI Tree, and KEVLAR all show an approximate 5-fold increase in time required to reach 90% of receivers compared to that needed to deliver to 50% of receivers. Lastly, we note that KEVLAR's relative performance with respect to the ideal of IPMC is not as strong for delivery to 90% of nodes as it is for 50%; this is due to KEVLAR's reliance upon non-IPMC underlying protocols for its ISP transmission as compared to its dissemination within each data center.

5.5 Robustness

We conclude our evaluation by considering the robustness of KEVLAR in contrast to other multicast protocols. To obtain this measurement, we introduce catastrophic failures in a large portion of the nodes within our environment and monitor the resulting recovery for each multicast protocol. Specifically, we select the scenario from Sect. 5.3 with 1500-Byte messages sent at a data rate of 1 Mbps; after steady, non-perturbed communication for 40 seconds, we fail-stop a random selection of 50% of the nodes. (To ensure that each protocol confronts the identical failure scenario, we perform the random selection of nodes only once, and then reuse the same choice of failed nodes for the measurements of all the different protocols.) In quantifying the robustness of each system, we compute the percentage throughput received by the remaining live nodes relative to the amount before onset of node failures.

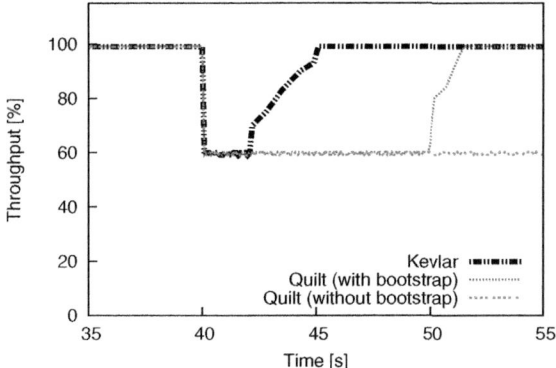

Fig. 13. KEVLAR'S **improvement in robustness over Quilt.** Comparison of robustness of KEVLAR'S distributed patchwork maintenance against Quilt patchwork implementations, both with and without centralized bootstrap servers (same scenario as in Fig. 12). KEVLAR shows a 100% improvement in recovery time versus Quilt with bootstrap servers; without bootstrapping, Quilt never recovers from the failure scenario.

Figure 12 depicts the robustness results for this measurement. We immediately observe that IPMC performs ideally, showing no loss of throughput. All other protocols suffer a dramatic reduction in throughput as their overlays are disturbed by node failures; this is to be expected for ALMs, in contrast to physical IPMC. We observe that the OMNI Tree protocol has the largest loss of throughput; this likely results from the failure of high-level (root) nodes in its tree structure that then disrupt delivery to all the nodes in their sub-hierarchy. Recovery of OMNI Tree is relatively quick, though; its event-driven rejoin procedure reconstructs the tree overlay faster than DONet's epoch-style protocol recovers its overlay. We also observe that OMNI Tree shows fluctuations in its recovery as it is attempting to simultaneously optimize its structure for latency considerations while new nodes are also rejoining the overlay. The DONet ALM is slower to recover than OMNI Tree; however, since traffic load is balanced across its nodes, DONet throughput does not ever decrease as dramatically as that of OMNI Tree. Finally, we consider KEVLAR and observe that it outperforms both OMNI Tree and DONet in terms of robustness: KEVLAR maintains higher throughput than either other ALM, as it can still utilize the underlying IPMC protocol in patches were it is available. Further, KEVLAR recovers as quickly as the OMNI Tree protocol. Finally, during recovery, KEVLAR'S throughput monotonically increases, unlike the fluctuations during OMNI Tree's overlay reconstruction.

We perform one additional measurement to quantify KEVLAR'S enhanced robustness. In Fig. 13, we contrast KEVLAR against two different versions of our Quilt [12] protocol, as introduced in Sect. 1 above. Here, we include Quilt both with and without its use of a bootstrap server. In the centralized Quilt framework, we observe that the bootstrap system assures recovery, at a cost of increased recovery time due to greater load on a few central bootstrap servers. KEVLAR's use of distributed patch maintenance shows at least a 100% improvement in recovery time compared with Quilt.

5.6 Summary of Measurement Evaluation

We now summarize our measurements and observations from this section: we showed that KEVLAR empirically achieves a performance envelope matching our design goals articulated earlier. The KEVLAR system consistently leveraged whichever protocol was most efficient among those available in each topological network patch. Obviously, if IPMC were available in all situations, simply using IPMC might be the best plan. But when IPMC is not available, KEVLAR is a very practical and effective alternative.

6 Related Work

KEVLAR's object-oriented design was inspired by Quality Objects (QuO) [3,19]. The QuO middleware provides quality-of-service information to allow programs to function reasonably well on WANs and LANs. During run-time, QuO applications may alter modes, between "safe," "overloaded," or "graceful shutdown," causing objects to change their behavior accordingly.

We are unaware of technologies, other than KEVLAR and Quilt that use environmentally aware patchwork overlays for multicast. Patchwork overlays for other purposes, however, have been proposed: A large-scale routing system, MONET [2], groups together different kinds of client links into "patches" to allow IP packets to traverse NATs and firewalls and to optimize inefficient application-level routing paths. Similarly, OCALA [13] accommodates legacy applications over modern network architectures by combining different overlays to reach disadvantaged network hosts.

7 Conclusions

KEVLAR delivers a flexible architecture for creating collaborative applications that can be efficiently utilized in the wide-area Internet. The system encourages modular extension and facilitates development of sophisticated applications through composition of distributed objects to form graphs, within which object instances interact by event-passing.

Typical users of collaborative applications, such as virtual reality platforms and massively multiplayer online games, are subject to quite non-uniform Internet environments. Thus, runtime adaptation is required to appropriately configure these deployed applications. Indeed, KEVLAR automates selection and activation of the correct component out of a set of functionally similar options, each optimized for different conditions.

KEVLAR innovates at several levels: through its flexible and modular architecture; through the mechanisms used to select appropriate components; and through the optimization-driven decision layers that create the desired distributed infrastructure. This structure controls what might otherwise be a very complex system. A careful evaluation shows that KEVLAR really does function as designed.

Acknowledgments. We are grateful to the Chinese National Science Foundation (Project No. 60731160630), National Science Foundation, Air Force Research Laboratory, EU IST Project CoMiFin (FP7-ICT-225407/2008), Intel Corporation, and Cisco Systems for their support of this research.

References

1. Alonso, G., Casati, F., Kuno, H., Machiraju, V.: Web Services Concepts, Architectures and Applications. Springer, Heidelberg (2004)
2. Andersen, D.G., Balakrishnan, H., Kaashoek, M.F., Rao, R.N.: Improving Web Availability for Clients with MONET. In: Proc. of NSDI 2005, Boston, MA, USA (2005)
3. Atighetchi, M., Pal, P.P., Jones, C.C., Rubel, P., Schantz, R.E., Loyall, J.P., Zinky, J.A.: Building Auto-Adaptive Distributed Applications: The QuO-APOD Experience. In: Proc. of ICDCSW 2003, Washington, DC, USA (2003)
4. Banerjee, S., Kommareddy, C., Kar, K., Bhattacharjee, B., Khuller, S.: Construction of an efficient overlay multicast infrastructure for real-time applications. In: Proc. of INFOCOM 2003, San Francisco, CA, USA (2003)
5. Birman, K., Cantwell, J., Freedman, D., Huang, Q., Nikolov, P., Ostrowski, K.: Edge Mashups for Service-Oriented Collaboration. IEEE Computer 42(5), 90–94 (2009)
6. Cohen, B.: Incentives Build Robustness in BitTorrent, Tech. Report (2003)
7. Deering, S.E., Cheriton, D.R.: Multicast routing in datagram internetworks and extended LANs. ACM Trans. Comput. Syst. 8(2), 85–110 (1990)
8. DETERlab, http://www.isi.deterlab.net/
9. Feng, W.-c., Brandt, D., Saha, D.: A Long-Term Study of a Popular MMORPG. In: Proc. of NetGames 2007, Melbourne, Australia (2007)
10. Google Voice and Video Chat, http://www.google.com/chat/video/
11. HDV Specification, http://www.avchd-info.org/format/
12. Huang, Q., Vigfusson, Y., Birman, K., Li, H.: Quilt: A Patchwork of Multicast Regions. In: Proc. of DEBS 2010, Cambridge, UK (2010)
13. Joseph, D., Kannan, J., Kubota, A., Lakshminarayanan, K., Stoica, I., Wehrle, K.: OCALA: An Architecture for Supporting Legacy Applications over Overlays. In: Proc. of NSDI 2006, San Jose, CA, USA (2006)
14. Leighton, T.: Improving Performance on the Internet. Commun. ACM 52(2), 44–51 (2009)
15. Miller, F.P., Vandome, A.F., McBrewster, J.: Second Life. Alpha Press (2009)
16. Ostrowski, K., Birman, K., Dolev, D., Ahnn, J.H.: Programming with Live Distributed Objects. In: Vitek, J. (ed.) ECOOP 2008. LNCS, vol. 5142, pp. 463–489. Springer, Heidelberg (2008)

17. Ostrowski, K., Sakoda, C., Birman, K.: Self-Replicating Objects for Multicore Platforms. In: D'Hondt, T. (ed.) Proc. of ECOOP 2010. LNCS, vol. 6183, pp. 452–477. Springer, Heidelberg (2010)
18. van Renesse, R., Minsky, Y., Hayden, M.: A Gossip-Based Failure Detection Service. In: Proc. of Middleware 1998, The Lake District, UK (1998)
19. Vanegas, R., Zinky, J.A., Loyall, J.P., Karr, D., Schantz, R.E., Bakken, D.E.: QuO's runtime support for quality of service in distributed objects. In: Proc. of Middleware 1998, The Lake District, UK (1998)
20. White, B., Lepreau, J., Stoller, L., Ricci, R., Guruprasad, S., Newbold, M., Hibler, M., Barb, C., Joglekar, A.: An Integrated Experimental Environment for Distributed Systems and Networks. In: Proc. of OSDI 2002, Boston, MA, USA (2002)
21. Zhang, X., Liu, J., Li, B., Yum, T.-S.P.: CoolStreaming/DONet: a data-driven overlay network for peer-to-peer live media streaming. In: Proc. of INFOCOM 2005, Miami, FL, USA (2005)

FaReCast: Fast, Reliable Application Layer Multicast for Flash Dissemination

Kyungbaek Kim, Sharad Mehrotra, and Nalini Venkatasubramanian

Dept. of Computer Science
University of California, Irvine, USA
{kyungbak,nalini,sharad}@ics.uci.edu

Abstract. To disseminate messages from a single source to a large number of targeted receivers, a natural approach is the tree-based application layer multicast (ALM). However, in time-constrained *flash dissemination* scenarios, e.g. earthquake early warning, where time is of the essence, the tree-based ALM has a single point of failure; its reliable extensions using ack-based failure recovery protocols cannot support reliable dissemination in the timeframe needed. In this paper, we exploit path diversity, i.e. exploit the use of multiple data paths, to achieve fast and reliable data dissemination. First, we design a forest-based M2M (Multiple parents-To-Multiple children) ALM structure where every node has multiple children and multiple parents. The intuition is to enable lower dissemination latency through multiple children, while enabling higher reliability through multiple parents. Second, we design multidirectional multicasting algorithms that effectively utilize the multiple data paths in the M2M ALM structure. A key aspect of our reliable dissemination mechanism is that nodes, in addition to communicating the data to children, also selectively disseminate the data to parents and siblings. As compared to trees using traditional multicasting algorithm, we observe an 80% improvement in reliability under 20% of failed nodes with no significant increase in latency for over 99% of the nodes.

1 Introduction

Our work is motivated by the need for highly reliable data dissemination that delivers critical information to hundreds of thousands of receivers within a very short period of time. An example is the flash dissemination of disaster (natural or man-made) warning messages that must be rapidly delivered to urban populations in a matter of a few seconds to enable citizens to take self-protective measures (e.g. duck-cover-hold on for earthquakes, shelter underground for tornadoes). The key challenge lies in delivering messages scalably (reaching large populations), reliably (despite network outages and message losses) and efficiently (low operational cost during non-disaster times with quick ramp-up when needed). Given the rarity of these events, it is unlikely that a dedicated infrastructure, such as communication connections between peoples and the source of the messages, that is operational and available 24/7 will be deployed. Our objective, therefore, is to leverage any and all available infrastructure and exploit knowledge of network connectivity to ensure that interested recipients are able to actually receive the messages within a very short period of time.

In this paper, we develop an ALM-based solution for the flash dissemination problem above using a peer-oriented architecture where the peer nodes are formed by those interested in receiving the messages. We argue that the problem lends itself well to a peer-based architecture; an ALM-based solution is attractive due its potential for easy deployment (no changes to lower layer network protocols at the participating nodes)[3] and its ability to deal with a variety of recipients. Challenges arise since (a)end-devices are autonomous and hence unreliable; (b)end-devices are nodes that are executing other tasks and must typically be rapidly repurposed to deal with the rare warning messages when it occurs. Our ALM-based solution must deliver the messages reliably and in time, while handling the node churn as well as minimizing the maintenance overhead.

We view the ALM approach as consisting of two key aspects - (a) the ALM structure and (b)the multicasting algorithm deployed on the structure. Participating nodes in the ALM structure organize themselves into an overlay topology (typically a tree or mesh) for data delivery - each edge in this topology corresponds to a unicast path between two nodes in the underlying Internet. Once the ALM structure is constructed, data from the source node is delivered to all multicast recipients using the implemented multicasting algorithm. Note that all multicast-related functionality is implemented at the nodes (instead of at routers as in network-layer multicast). Typical ALM applications include file sharing and content streaming; specialized protocols have been designed for these applications [4][5][6][7][8][9][10]. Our prior work on flash dissemination focused on fast dissemination of medium to large sized data. We leveraged a dynamic mesh-based overlay network constructed using a random walker protocol, CREW[11] to concurrently disseminate multiple chunks of a large message. The Roulette protocol extended the random walker implementation to enable low dissemination overhead despite catastrophic failures; it was used to implement a P2P webserver, Flashback [12] to deal with flash crowds. However, the cost of metadata propagation and overlay maintenance in CREW/Roulette is unwarranted in the current scenario where (a) the end recipients are known and (b) the message size is small.

Our target scenario consists of a single source and several receivers; A tree-based ALM structure (where every node has a single parent and multiple children) seems appropriate for fast data dissemination[3][4][16][25]. A tree-based structure exploits concurrency in that all nodes that have received data can communicate with their children concurrently. As the *fan-out*,i.e. the number of children per node, of the tree increases, the data delivery time decreases logarithmically with the number of fan-out as the base. Unfortunately, the tree structure is highly vulnerable to failures since every intermediate node in a tree structure is a point of failure[14][15][22] that can block delivery of the message to the entire subtree under it. In fact, this problem is further aggravated as the fan-out of a tree structure increases, since the number of nodes impacted by a failure increases exponentially.

Typical reliable multicast approaches detect such failures during operation and recover from them (usually by reconstructing parts of the tree). Protocols have been designed to recover the tree structure by substituting the failed node with an existing online node[3][4][5][6] - this requires tree reconstruction which is a time-consuming operation; techniques have also been proposed to use backup information to reduce recovery time to some extent[16][20][21][22][23][24]. Many of these approaches rely on TCP retransmission to detect and retransmit lost packets and support reliability at the communication layer. In our flash dissemination scenario, i.e. dissemination of disaster warning messages, delivery times are highly constrained; existing approaches to detect and recover from failures or employ per-packet acknowledgements require interactions and handshakes with other nodes, which makes it difficult to respond within the required time constraints.

In this paper, we present FaReCast, an ALM protocol for fast and reliable data dissemination that exploits the use of multiple data paths between nodes judiciously by (a) designing a new ALM structure and (b) developing a new multicasting algorithm that efficiently exploits the proposed structure. Specifically, we design a forest-based M2M (Multiple parents-to-Multiple children) ALM structure where each participant node has multiple parents as well as multiple children. Care is taken in the construction of the M2M structure to support path diversity (through the choice of unique parent node sets); this supports increased reliability by minimizing the probability that nodes with failed common parents lose data. To complement the M2M ALM structure, we design a multidirectional multicasting algorithm that effectively utilizes the multiple data paths in the M2M ALM structure. In addition to top-down communication characteristic of traditional multicasting, the multidirectional multicasting algorithm deploys bottom-up data flow and horizontal data flow carefully. Since there is prior knowledge of the M2M structure at each node, nodes can trigger communication and send data to parents from which it has failed to receive the expected data. Additionally, in the case of leaf nodes, FaReCast forwards data to the other leaf nodes which it anticipates may have not received the data. A key design issue for FaReCast is addressing the tradeoff between two conflicting factors - higher fan-out (increased speed) vs. higher fan-in (increased reliability).

Multiple fan-in ALM structures are not new; approaches such as [7][9][13][14][15][18][19] all increase the number of data paths to a target node to stream large data concurrently and efficiently. Here, the large data is divided into smaller data chunks that are disseminated through the multiple paths concurrently. The chunking techniques are combined with loss tolerant decoding/encoding [7], e.g. erasure coding[17] to ensure that all recipient nodes get the entire large data correctly. Such expensive coding schemes are unnecessary in our scenario where the information delivered to target nodes is small (order of a few bytes/Kbytes). FaReCast exploits path redundancy to send the same data through multiple paths and thereby improves dissemination reliability. Another aspect of performance is the number of duplicate messages received by a node (any duplicate messages are considered to be unnecessary overhead).

While our primary goals are scalability, speed and reliability, our secondary goal is to reduce maintenance overhead during normal times when there is no event. In FaReCast, we minimize the client-side maintenance overhead by storing the snapshots of current network status at the configuration manager. Each individual user retrieves accurate parent/children information from the configuration manager periodically. The configuration manager detects node failure based on this periodic update request and updates the snapshot asynchronously. Through both simulation and implementation-based evaluations, we show that FaReCast tolerates over 40% random failures while meeting the latency constraints, i.e. FaReCast can endure high user churn as well as a certain level of snapshot inconsistency.

The rest of the paper is organized as follows. In Section 2, we describe the design and management of the M2M ALM structure having multiple fan-in and fan-out. The multidirectional multicasting algorithm achieving high reliability with small data latency is described in Section 3. We conduct a simulation-based performance evaluation of FaReCast in Section 4. In Section 5, we present an implementation of the FaReCast system as well as its evaluation by using a campus cluster platform and a emulated wide area network. Finally, we present concluding remarks in Section 6.

2 The Forest-Based M2M ALM Structure

In this section, we present our forest-based M2M ALM structure. Figure 1 depicts the overall architecture of the envisioned system and illustrates the proposed ALM structure. The system primarily consists of (a) target nodes interested in receiving the dissemination, (b) an originating server where the dissemination is initiated and (c) a configuration manager that maintains and manages the structure and connectivity information (discussed later). We will construct an overlay structure consisting of the originating server and target nodes and effectively use that structure to address our dual needs of reliability and timeliness in information dissemination. To maintain separation of concerns, we distinguish two clear-cut steps in enabling reliable, fast ALM: (a) construction of an overlay structure that enables concurrency and reliability (b) use of the constructed overlay in a multicast protocol that efficiently implements concurrency (aka speed) and reliability tradeoffs in the dissemination process under dynamic conditions.

The process begins with the construction of the forest-based M2M overlay structure which consists of the originating server (or a well-established representative) as the root-node and target nodes (interested recipients) that form the sub-tree rooted at the originating server. The goal is to organize the target nodes into levels and establish overlay connections between them to enable concurrency and reliability for dissemination. The overall design philosophy is as follows: to support fast dissemination, every node in the structure will have multiple children from which concurrent content dissemination can occur. To handle reliability, every node in the structure will have multiple (redundant) parents that it receives content from. Determining the arities and connections of nodes in the M2M (Multiple parents to Multiple children) overlay structure to maximize speed and reliability while minimizing redundant transmissions is the key challenge. Prior to establishing the properties of the M2M structure, we provide some definitions and assumptions that will be used in creating the M2M structure.

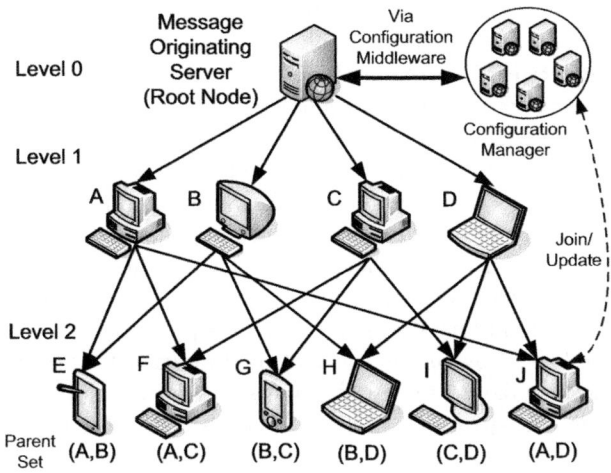

Fig. 1. The forest-based M2M ALM structure ($F_o = 2$, $F_i = 2$)

Level of a node (L) : The level of a node is the length of the path, expressed as number of hops, from the root to this node. The level of the root node is assumed to be 0, children of the root node are at level 1 etc.

Sibling Nodes : Nodes having same level are referred to as sibling nodes. Sibling nodes at a level belong to a *level-group*. N_L is the number of sibling nodes at level L.

Fan-in (F_i) : The fan-in of a node is the number of parents of a node. All participating nodes (except those at levels 0 and 1) have F_i parents.

Fan-out factor (F_o) : The fan-out factor is the ratio of N_{L+1} to N_L, and is a measure of the minimum number of nodes at a level, i.e. $N_L \geq (F_o)^L$.

The **Configuration manager** enables the management of the M2M structure by performing the following tasks: (a) management of information on nodes, level-groups and sibling nodes in a level-group; (b) construction and maintenance of the overlay structure, (c) answering of queries about the M2M structure - for example, it responds to update requests from target nodes with information on their current parents/children. The update requests also serve as periodic heartbeat messages to the configuration manager indicating that a node is alive; in FaReCast, we keep the frequency of such update requests very low - (~ 1 hour) in our experiments. Communications between the configuration manager, target nodes and the originating server occur via a pre-established API.

2.1 Properties of the M2M ALM Structure

- **Root-node Reliability:** The root node (at level 0) is expected to be continuously available.
- **Fan-in constraint:** Each participating node should have F_i distinct parents just one level above. If the level of a node is L, all the parents are picked from the same level, $L - 1$, as illustrated in Figure 1. The only exceptions

are nodes at level 1 that have only one parent since the level-group for level 0 has only one node, the root node.
- **Loop-free nature:** We assume loop-free transmission when data flows from parent nodes to child nodes. In particular, we assume that the assignment of levels in the M2M ALM structure is done in such a way that all paths from the root to a node have the same length. Assuming that the latency of message transmission over any two links is not significantly different[26], the M2M ALM structure can guarantee that data reaching a node from different parents arrive close to each other in time. That is, in the M2M ALM structure with F_i parents, each node should get F_i data items within a short period of time under the failure-free situation. This property is later exploited (and selectively relaxed) by the multidirectional multicasting protocol to improve reliability and make up for missing messages from failed parents.
- **Parent Set Uniqueness:** All nodes in the M2M ALM structure (with $level \geq 2$) have a unique set of parents. That is, there is at least one different parent in the parent-sets of two nodes at the same level. Without this property, concurrent failures of nodes at a level can potentially block out messages to the level below; parent-set uniqueness enforces path diversity in the propagation of the message and consequently improves the chances of reliable delivery.

Achieving the parent-set uniqueness property brings out an interesting relationship between fan-in and fan-out factor as described below. The following equation should be satisfied to guarantee parent-set uniqueness:

$$N_{L+1} \leq C(N_L, F_i) \quad \text{where } F_i > 1, L > 0 \tag{1}$$

In the equation 1, $C(n, k)$ represents the number of k-combinations from a given n elements. That is, the number of distinct subsets with F_i-combinations that represent the parent sets of nodes in level L should be equal or greater than the number of nodes (N_{L+1}) in level $L+1$. If we assume that the number of sibling nodes is $N_L = (F_o)^L$, the equation 1 can only be satisfied when the value of L is large enough or F_o is greater than F_i. With this assumption (i.e. $N_L = (F_o)^L$), when $F_i = 2$, $F_o = 2$, the equation 1 is satisfied only if $L > 2$. In other words, N_L calculated using only the fan-out factor may not be sufficient to guarantee the parent-set uniqueness property at a level - additional nodes may therefore be needed at a level L - we call these nodes *complement nodes*.

To get the proper number of complement nodes, we take into account F_i as well as F_o. Consider the case where a node A at level L attempts to get F_o children with F_i parents each. To come up with a conservative estimate of the number of complement nodes, let us further assume that none of the pre-existing nodes at level L (besides A) are available to meet the fan-in need. In other words, the fan-in requirement must be satisfied by additional complement nodes at level L. Since A is already a parent for its children, we need at least $F_i - 1$ complement nodes for the first child. To guarantee parent-set uniqueness for the remaining $F_o - 1$ children, we need $F_o - 1$ additional complement nodes. Consequently, $(F_o - 1) + (F_i - 1)$ nodes is a sufficient condition for a node having F_o children to assign a unique set of parents to each child node. To satisfy the equation 1, N_L is determined by the following equation.

$$N_L = (F_o)^L + F_o + F_i - 2 \quad \text{where } F_o > 1,\ F_i > 1,\ L > 0 \tag{2}$$

Lemma 1. *Given $F_o > 1$, $F_i > 1$ and $L > 0$, $N_L = (F_o)^L + F_o + F_i - 2$ is enough to satisfy the parent set uniqueness property.*

Proof. When the equation 2 is applied to the equation 1, we get the following expanded equation, $(F_o \cdot (F_o)^L + F_o + F_i - 2) \leq \prod_{x=1}^{F_i}(A/x + 1)$, where $A = (F_o)^L + F_o - 2$. Since A is always greater than zero, and $F_i > 1$, the right hand side of the expanded equation has the minimum value when $F_i = 2$. Also note that the right hand side always increases as F_i increases. Below, we show that the minimum value of the right hand side is always equal to or greater than the left hand side, i.e. the expanded equation is always true.

We apply $F_i = 2$ to the above expanded equation followed by some straightforward algebraic manipulation. This yields

$$((F_o)^L + 1) \cdot F_o \leq ((F_o)^L + F_o) \cdot ((F_o)^L + F_o - 1)/2. \tag{3}$$

Comparing terms on the right hand side and the left hand side, we can see that the equation always holds true for $F_o > 1$ and $L > 0$.

2.2 Node Operations and Structure Maintenance

Given an initial root node (possibly the originating server), the creation of an M2M ALM structure that is compliant with the properties described above proceeds as a series of node joins. Subsequent evolution of the structure consists of a series of node join/leave requests coordinated by the configuration manager. Interspersed with node joins and node leaves, the configuration manager detects node failures (i.e. an unstructured node leave) and reorganizes the M2M ALM structure to recover from the failure. FaReCast employs periodic *update request* messages from participant nodes to the configuration manager to communicate that a participant node is still alive. The CM responds to a nodes *update request* with the current parents/children of the node. As discussed earlier, the frequency of *update messages* is kept low to prevent bottlenecks at the configuration manager and reduce structure maintenance cost. The details of each operation are described below.

Node Join: When a new node, N_{new}, joins the system, it is first given a new nodeID. the node sends a join request to the configuration manager in order to determine (a)its level and (b)its parent/children nodes. In accordance with equation 2, the configuration manager determines current information about each level group and selects the lowest level requiring more nodes as the *level* of the new node in the M2M ALM structure. Parent selection for the node proceeds as follows. If the selected level is $L + 1$, the configuration manager randomly picks F_i different nodes among the level L nodes as the parents of the new node. The configuration manager next determines whether the selected parent set satisfies the *parent set uniqueness property* at level L. The configuration manager maintains a *parents pool* structure managed by each level-group - that contains entries of the form {child, parent-set}. If the newly selected parent-set is not unique, we choose to replace one of the nodes (the one with the maximum number of children) in the current parent set with another distinct randomly selected node at the same level (excluding the most recent selection). This uniqueness checking operation is repeated until a unique set of parents is found. According to Lemma 1, every new node can find a unique set of parents. After finding a unique set of parents, the configuration manager registers the new node with the new nodeID and its selected parent-set in the corresponding parent pool, and each parent of the new parent-set registers the new node as a child using its nodeID. The configuration manager then responds to the join request with the nodeID, the level, and parents/children information.

Node Leave: When a node leaves the M2M ALM structure, it notifies the configuration manager to coalesce the hole caused by it in the ALM structure. All the impacted nodes - parents-sets that include the leaving node, children of the leaving node and parents of the leaving node should be invalidated and updated. Also the number of nodes in the level-group of the leaving node reduces by one. The key idea is to quickly find a replacement node for the leaving node with minimum maintenance overhead including communication and processing cost. To do this, we invalidate the registered node information of the leaving node. The invalidated node information is retained at the configuration manager for a while (this is captured by a *retainment-timer*) with the expectation that a new node will join quickly and it can simply replace the invalidated node. If this happens, the configuration manager validates all the impacted nodes to accommodate the newly arrived node. If there are not enough new nodes to cover the invalidated nodes, the configuration manager must repair these holes with other existing nodes. A retainment-timer is associated with each invalidated node; when the retainment-timer of an invalidated node expires without any replacement, the configuration manager picks a random leaf node to replace the invalidated node and subsequently invalidates the leaf node information. The configuration manager does not notify the updated information to all the impacted nodes right away, but responds with it to their periodic requests for the recent structure information.

Node Failures: Failed nodes are those that leave the M2M ALM structure without any notification. The configuration manager detects the failed nodes by an *update-timer*. Each participant node sends a periodic update request in order to refresh the parents/children information. Once a node joins the system and its information is registered, the configuration manager sets the update-timer of the node and resets the timer whenever it receives an update request from the node. If the update-timer of a node is expired, the node information is invalidated, and the repair of the M2M ALM structure proceeds similar to the case of a leaving node. The nodes in the lower level-groups use shorter update-timers than the nodes in the higher level-groups, because lower level nodes are critical to preserving the reliability of the M2M structure.

Maintenance Overhead and Reliability: In our target scenario, an interesting event occurs rarely and participating nodes join/leave the system far more frequently than the event. It is therefore imperative that the management overhead (e.g. network bandwidth, processing power) incurred by the M2M ALM structure is low, especially during non-event times. In order to reduce the maintenance overheads of the participating nodes, we implement a cooperative solution in which the configuration manager and nodes participate. Firstly, we effectively and efficiently use the configuration manager to maintain the M2M ALM structure and required meta-data; participating nodes send update requests to the configuration manager for current structure information. At the node end, we increase the length of timers (retainment-timer and update-timer) to keep neighborhood information updated. There is an obvious tradeoff between the overhead and reliability since delaying timers implies that the M2M ALM structure from the view of participant nodes is not as updated as desired. In the next section, we propose an effective multidirectional multicasting protocol (when the event occurs) that can tolerate stale information in the M2M ALM structure - allowing us to achieve low maintenance overhead with high reliability.

3 Multidirectional Multicasting Algorithms

In this section, we describe our proposed multidirectional multicasting algorithms. The key idea here is to enable reliable message delivery despite failures with limited increase in latency and messaging overhead. We do this by pushing the multicast message along directions where failures are estimated to have occurred. Recall that when a node in the M2M ALM structure receives a message (the first one) from one parent, it is expected that messages from all the other parents will arrive shortly (due to equal path length and similar delay assumption). When messages do not arrive from parents, we conservatively assume

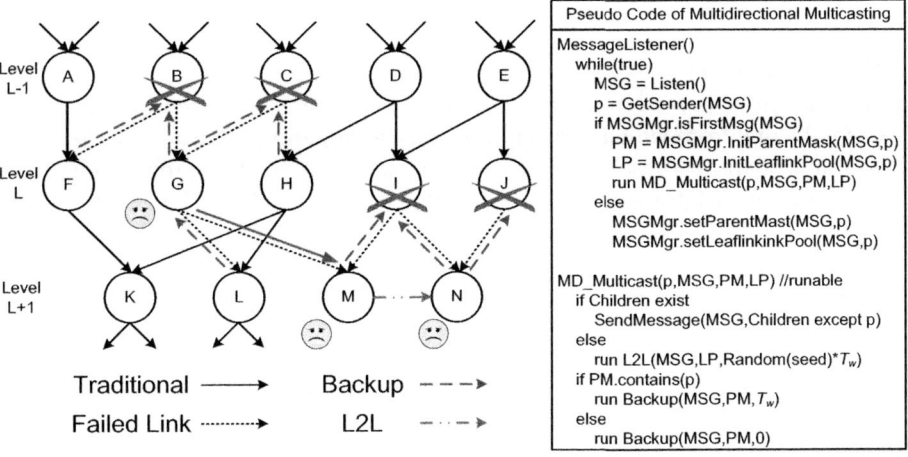

Fig. 2. Example and Pseudo Code of Mutidirectional Multicast

possible failures in the direction of those parents - and enhance the multicasting algorithm to send additional messages in these directions. We propose a protocol that encompasses two forms of multidirectional multicast - *Backup* and *Leaf-to-Leaf (L2L) dissemination*.

3.1 The Bypassing Problem and Backup Dissemination

In our M2M ALM structure, although a node has multiple parents, the message remains undelivered to the node if all parents of a node have failed. Note that if this node is an intermediate node, its children can still receive the message from the other parents and paths. In other words, the message may bypass this node even though the node is operational - we refer to such nodes as *bypassed nodes*. Once a node is bypassed, its children lose one data path and the probability of message loss increases. For example, in Figure 2, node G is the bypassed node and its child, node M does not get the message. One objective of our multicasting protocol design is to reduce the degradation of the reliability caused by the bypassed nodes.

Traditional multicasting protocols propagate messages unidirectionally along the tree from parents to children and cannot address the bypassing problem. If however, bottom-up propagation is permitted, i.e. messages from children to parents, the bypassed nodes can receive a message from one of its children who have received the message from alternate parents. Since this creates possibly redundant messages - careful determination of potential bypassed parent nodes by children is essential.

The selection of bypassed nodes exploits the constant-path-length property maintained by the M2M ALM structure. According to this property, when a node receives the first message from one of its parents, it expects that other $F_i - 1$ parents will send the same message within a short period of time, T_w. When a node fails to receive a message within T_w from a parent, the node assumes that the parent node has been bypassed or has failed - and forwards the message to this parent – we refer to this selective bottom-up dissemination as *backup dissemination*.

If a parent node gets the first message from a child, it recognizes that it is bypassed. The bypassed node (a) forwards the message to the remaining children (except the one from which it received the message) and (b)initializes the backup dissemination immediately to forward the message to its parent nodes. This process is repeated iteratively until the failed node is reached. Note that since the child initiating the backup dissemination has already waited for T_w, parents in the chain do not need to wait to initiate their respective backup disseminations. This selective upward and downward message propagation initiated by backward dissemination handles the reliability degradation caused by the bypassed nodes.

3.2 Missing Leaf Nodes and Leaf-to-Leaf Dissemination

While backup dissemination handles missing messages to bypassed intermediate nodes,it cannot be applied to a leaf node whose parents have all failed – we refer to such a leaf node as a *missing leaf node*. Given the M2M ALM structure (larger number of nodes at higher levels of the tree), a significant number (almost half) of the participating nodes are leaf nodes. Techniques to ensure that messages get to leaf nodes on time is critical to the reliable dissemination process.

We introduce the notion of *leaf links* to address the problem of missing leaf-nodes. Here, each leaf node maintains a *leaf link pool*, i.e. a set of links to leaf nodes sharing the same parents, i.e. *leaf-links*. When a leaf node gets the first message from a parent, the following actions are performed. First, leaf links sharing that parent are masked in the leaf link pool since it is assumed that the other leaf nodes can also receive the message from the shared parent. Second, as in backup dissemination, the node waits for a stipulated period of time T_w, to receive messages from all the other parents. After the waiting time passes, the leaf node sends the message to the other leaf nodes corresponding to the unmasked leaf links. In Figure 2, node M getting the first message from node G recognizes that node I is bypassed or failed, and sends the message to node N which shares node I as a parent. The direction of this dissemination is horizontal (leaf node to leaf node) and we refer to it as *L2L (leaf-to-leaf) dissemination*. Using L2L dissemination, therefore, makes up for reliability degradation due to missing leaf nodes.

Unlike backup dissemination, we argue that having different waiting times for starting the L2L dissemination will help reduce redundant messages. Since every path from the root to leaf nodes at the same level have the same hop-length, transitively every message that originated at the root reaches all sibling nodes within the same bounded time period T_w, assuming no failure. If all sibling leaf-nodes use the same duration of time to wait for the other messages, they start the L2L dissemination at the similar time, resulting in multiple redundant messages. Specifically, if one missing leaf node can be detected by $F_o - 1$ other leaf nodes, the leaf node gets $F_o - 1$ messages from other leaf nodes, in other words, there are $F_o - 2$ redundant messages.

To alleviate these redundant L2L disseminations, we employ differential waiting periods at leaf-nodes, similar to exponential backoff strategies. Leaf nodes that wait for longer periods now receive messages from recovered bypassed parents (due to backup dissemination) and from other leaf nodes (due to L2L dissemination). This causes related leaf links to be masked and redundant messages are avoided. To achieve random waiting time, each leaf node generates a random integer in the range $[1,N]$ and the waiting time is set to $N * T_W$, where T_w is the waiting time for the backup dissemination. As N increases, the variance of random waiting time increases and we more redundant messages are avoided. We set N as 4 in the evaluation.

4 Simulation Based Evaluation of FaReCast

To gain a better understanding of how FaReCast works under massive failures, we evaluated FaReCast along multiple dimensions, primarily in comparison to tree-based multicast, mesh-based multicast and flooding based (epidemic) protocols. These dimensions include: (a)Reliability (the ratio of unfailed nodes that finally receive the message); (b)Latency (the delay of message delivery to unfailed nodes that are able to receive the message); and (c)Efficiency/Overhead (number of duplicated/redundant messages and its impact on system overhead).

We simulated message dissemination over networks with large number of nodes based (in the order of 100,000s) - however, several input parameters for the simulations, e.g. link latency, bandwidth availability, context switch overhead were obtained from network emulators that mirror Internet scale parameters accurately. According to outcomes of this emulation in section 5, we modeled link latency between any two nodes used in the simulation. We obtained inter-node link latencies ranging from 150ms to 200ms, the average latency being 180ms. Moreover, we set bandwidth constraints (from 100Kbps to 500Kbps) and network packet loss rates (from 1% to 5%) for each link. We also measured processing delays for sending a message to multiple children. In the implementation, each node is multithreaded and the management of links incurred context switching overheads - Modelnet[1] emulation yielded processing delays per node that varied from 3ms to 6ms.

The failure models considered accommodate *node failure* and *link failure*. *Node failures* occur primarily due to node churn - i.e. at a certain time, a node cannot communicate with some of its neighbors (children/parents) which have gone offline. Node update messages capture changes in its neighborhood - further node failures may occur while these updates happen. In addition to node failures, network congestion may cause dropped messages, leading to *link failures*. A node that does not receive a message from a parent (either due to node or link failures) classifies that parent as a *failed node*. An offline leaf node is also assumed to be a failed node. We assume that the failure can happen uniformly, that is, any node can fail with same probability. To simulate message dissemination under massive failures, we took snapshots of the multicast structure just before starting the message dissemination. After applying the failure model to this snapshot, the leftover online nodes/links are only used for the dissemination in our experiments. Since we are only interested in the messages received within a short timeframe, we do not assume a structure recovery process during the dissemination. In our typical experimental setup, the network size is 100,000 nodes and the fraction of failed nodes varies from 0% up to 40%. The typical waiting time for nodes to initiate backup/L2L dissemination, T_w is set to 200ms.

4.1 Effectiveness of FaReCast under Failure

In Figure 3, we compare FaReCast with other protocols, specifically, Tree, forest/mesh based dissemination such as SplitStream[7] and MultipleTree[18][19], and flooding-based approaches such as Epidemic[9][11], to disseminate an urgent message. SplitStream categorizes nodes into streams; nodes which belong to each stream form a tree with a *fan-out*, nodes also become leaf nodes of trees for other streams - thereby creating a forest. Eventually, the *given number of streams* is the given fan-in of a node. SplitStream is used to distribute a large volume of data by sending a different chunk to each stream; in our case, the root node sends the same message to all the streams. The MultipleTree protocol generates a given number of trees with a *predetermined fan-out*. A node locates

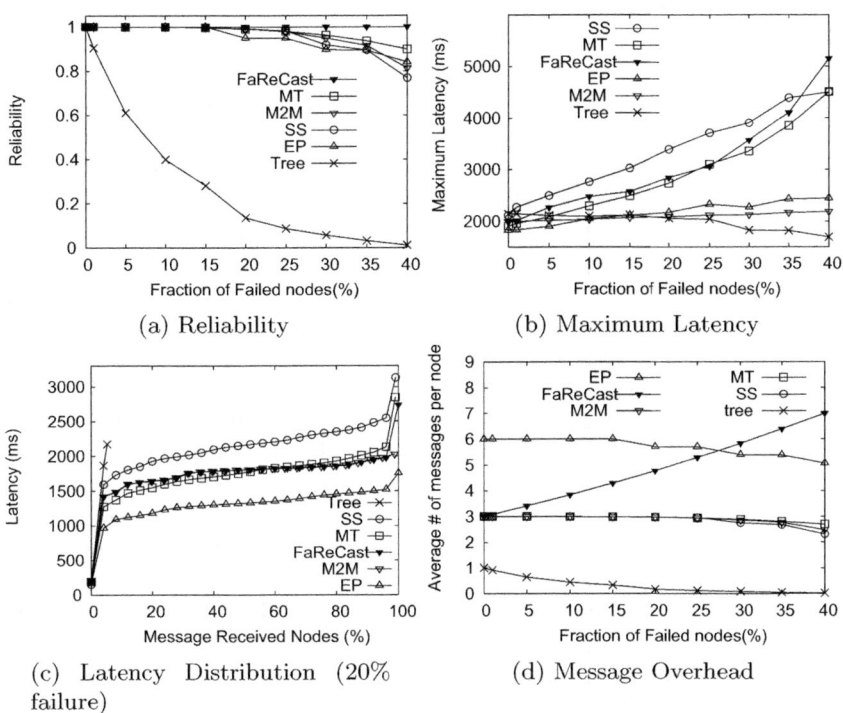

Fig. 3. Performance Comparison of FaReCasts(F_i=3,F_o=3, M2M with Backup/L2L Dissemination) with other protocols under various failures with 100,000 nodes.(SS:SplitStream, MT:MultipleTree, EP:Epidemic)

a different root position for each tree, eventually the *given number of trees* is the given fan-in of a node. The Epidemic protocol uses a flooding based mechanism for dissemination; every node selects a given number of *neighbor nodes* randomly. When a node gets the first message, it sends the message to all other neighbors, otherwise, it simply drops the message. To compare these protocols in a fair manner, we set the number of fan-in and fan-out as 3 and 3 for all protocols, respectively, except Tree which has only one fan-in. Also, we set the number of neighbors in Epidemic to 6, since neighbors can be parents or children.

Figure 3(a) compares the reliability of the various protocols as a function of the fraction of failed nodes. Reliability is measured as the number of nodes receiving the message over the number of online nodes. As expected, the Tree protocol is affected adversely by the failure. Protocols having multiple parents can tolerate up to 15% failures reasonably well. When the number of failures exceed 15%, FaReCast continues to achieve 100% reliability, while others including M2M (which do not use multidirectional multicasting) lose substantial reliability.

We evaluate relative latencies using two metrics - (i) maximum (worst-case) latency, i.e. latency of the last node that receives the message and (ii)latency distribution over the set of nodes that actually receive the data. Figure 3(b) plots the maximum latency as a function of the fraction of failed nodes. The Tree, Epidemic and M2M protocols appear to have lower maximum latencies - a closer look reveals that this comes at the cost of reliability (many nodes do not receive the message at all). SplitStream and MultipleTree lose reliability and exhibit increased latencies as the number of failures increase. The key reason is that the distance between the root and a node increases under failure in SplitStream and MultipleTree. M2M has a slightly reduced latency since its loop-free nature holds under failures. We observe that the maximum latency of FaReCast also increases along with failures. A deeper analysis indicates that this increase is caused by the waiting time to trigger the multidirectional multicasting. To understand general latency behavior, we plot the distribution of latency under 20% failures in Figure 3(c). We observe that FaReCast delivers the message to around 99% of the total nodes with small latencies; higher latencies are incurred by a few bypassed nodes reached by backup/L2L dissemination (more details in section 4.3). Epidemic exhibits good average latency behavior since the number of nodes reached in each dissemination step (in the early stage) is twice that of other protocols.

Figure 3(d) shows the message overhead as a function of the fraction of failed nodes. We define the message overhead as the average number of messages sent by an *online* node. In Tree, the message overhead decreases because most of nodes can not get the message under failures. M2M, SplitStream, and MultipleTree have almost same overhead (around 3); Epidemic sends twice as many message (around 6). Note that many of these protocols lose substantial reliability in spite of the high message overhead. In FaReCast, the message overhead increases along with failures. When more failures occur, more backup/L2L messages are required to rescue the bypassed nodes. For example, notice that under 30% failure the message overhead of FaReCast is similar to Epidemic; however, FaReCast achieves 100% reliability, as compared to 90% reliability of the Epidemic protocol.

In summary, FaReCast achieves 100% reliability under various failure conditions as compared to other protocols that lose reliability; all protocols exhibit comparable latencies and message overheads. In the next section, we show how FaReCast can be tuned to maintain its reliability with lower latencies and overheads.

4.2 Tuning FaReCast by Adjusting Fan-In and Fan-Out Factor

We first explored the possibility of reducing latency and message overhead in FaReCast by adjusting the fan-in(F_i) and fan-out factor(F_o). In order to figure out the trade off between the different settings of F_o and F_i, we plot each aspect of FaReCast performance as a function of the fraction of failed nodes in Figure 4. FaReCast achieves 100% reliability regardless of F_i/F_o and the fraction of failed nodes. Even though we decrease F_i from 3 to 2, FaReCast still provides its 100% reliability. However, the latency is affected by the various F_i and F_o (See Figure 4(a)). As either F_o or F_i increases, the maximum latency decreases. Increasing F_o helps increase the number of nodes reached by each step of dissemination. Also, as F_i increases, the probability that a node detects a bypassed

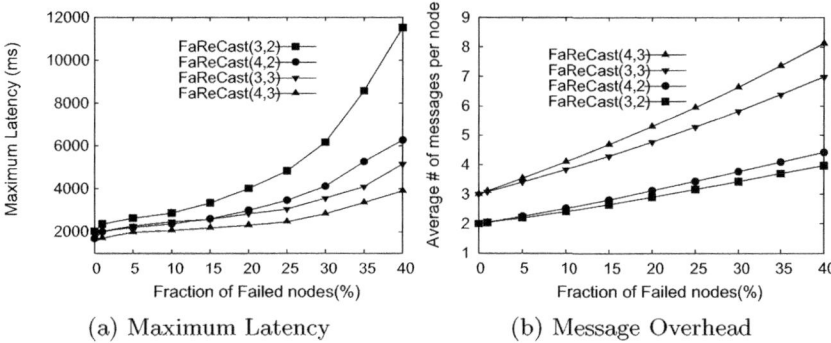

Fig. 4. Performance Comparison between FaReCasts having various fan-in and fan-out with 100,000 nodes (FaReCast(F_o, F_i)=M2M(F_o, F_i)+Backup+L2L)

node with the parent information increases and a node can initiate backup/L2L dissemination faster. However, increasing either F_i or F_o causes higher message overhead (Fig 4(b)). F_i affects the message overhead significantly since each node gets $F_i - 1$ duplicated messages. Moreover, the number of leaf links used by L2L dissemination is approximately $F_o*(F_i - 1)$ – these leaf links are used when failures are detected. That is, as the failure increases, message overhead also increases and the amount of the increment is affected by both of F_i and F_o. However, since the ability to detect bypassed nodes is dependant on F_i, message overhead is more significantly affected by F_i.

What these tradeoffs indicate is that different settings can be used for the specified purposes. With big values of F_o and F_i, FaReCast supports high reliability, low latency, but incurs high overhead. With small F_o and big F_i, FaReCast supports high reliability with acceptable latency and overhead. With the big F_o and small F_i, FaReCast supports acceptable reliability and latency with low overhead - this setting can be comparable with Epidemic in terms of latency and overhead. With small F_o and small F_i, FaReCast incurs low overhead and can support acceptable reliability, but at the cost of high latency.

4.3 Effect of Backup/L2L Dissemination

We now study the impact of the various features of FaReCast on reliability, latency and overhead. We notice that a protocol that uses only the M2M ALM structure (without the multidirectional multicasting components) loses substantial reliability (loses 20% reliability under 40% failures - Figure 5(a)). The addition of backup dissemination increases the reliability to 95.5%, further addition of L2L dissemination brings the reliability to 100% under the same failure conditions. We also notice that nodes that did not receive the message with the backup dissemination were leaf nodes which were then reached by the L2L dissemination. This demonstrates that FaReCast, which includes the M2M ALM structure along with the multidirectional multicasting protocols (backup/L2L dissemination), can guarantee the very high reliability under massive failures.

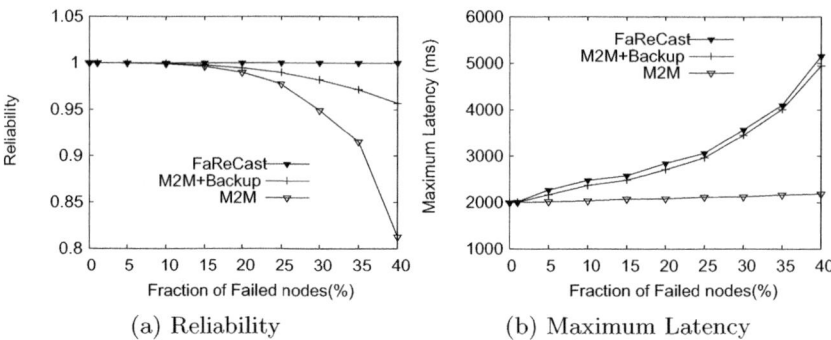

Fig. 5. Performance comparison with backup and L2L dissemination under various failures with 100,000 nodes (FaReCast = M2M+Backup+L2L)

In figure 5(b), the maximum latency of the M2M ALM structure slightly increases along with failures, still at the cost of some loss in reliability. When a node has multiple paths from multiple parents and there is no failure, each node obtains the first message from the fastest path. However, as the fraction of failed nodes increases, the number of multiple paths decrease, and the maximum latency under failures becomes bigger. When backup/L2L disseminations are used, the maximum latency increases rapidly. Much of this is due to the waiting time, T_w (set to 200ms in this experiment) required for initiating backup/L2L disseminations that proceed in the opposite direction to the traditional multicast. This additional latency can be further adjusted by changing the setup parameters in FaReCast such as fan-in and fan-out factor as we discussed in section 4.2.

For FaReCast to achieve 100% reliability, we need additional messages caused by backup/L2L disseminations. The message overheads of FaReCast increase linearly with the fraction of failed nodes like Figure 3(d), while the M2M ALM structure takes almost constant message overhead. The backup/L2L dissemination is triggered by the possibly bypassed nodes. According to this, as the fraction of failed nodes increases, the probability that a node is bypassed increases, and this consequently increases the number of messages FaReCast uses for the backup/L2L dissemination.

4.4 Scalability

Since FaReCast must work under different network sizes (including very large networks), scalability studies are critical. Figure 6(a) plots the maximum latency as a factor of the network size (i.e. total number of nodes) under no failures. We compare latency between the tree-based ALM structures and M2M ALM structures under various fan-out factor (F_o) and fan-in (F_i). In Figure 6(a), we observe that the latency of all structures increases logarithmically with the number of nodes. The reason is that all the ALM structures exploit parallelism in message dissemination. As F_o increases, a node can send the message to more

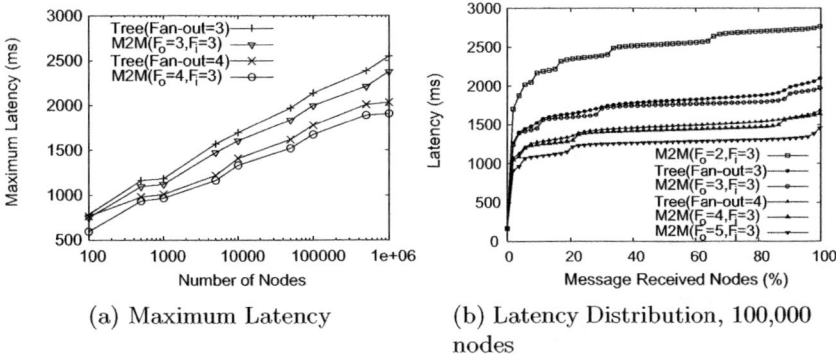

Fig. 6. Latency Comparison without failure

children at the same time, that is, the latency decreases. So, This illustrates that the basic M2M ALM structure is fundamentally scalable with respect to the network size.

Surprisingly, we note that the latencies of the M2M ALM structure are better than tree-based structures (in the absence of failures). Consider the case where the number of nodes is 100,000. The difference in latency between M2M and Tree having same fan-out factor is about 100ms. We argue that this is because in the tree structure, each node has only one message path from its single parent, and if the sole link is very slow, there is no alternative way to get the message faster. But, in the M2M ALM structure each node has multiple message paths since there are multiple parents. To take a closer look, we plot the latency of all the nodes for the network having 100,000 nodes in Figure 6(b). In the M2M ALM structure, each node can get the message from the fastest link among the multiple parents at each level (step), and most of the nodes in the same level have very similar latency to each other unlike the tree structure.

5   FaReCast System Implementation and Evaluation

We implemented the FaReCast protocol in a middleware suite and evaluated it on a campus cluster testbed with nodes connected through a wide-area Internet emulator (ModelNet). Modelnet[1] is a real-time network traffic shaper that allows for customized setup of various network topologies and provides an ideal base to test various systems for wide-area performance without modifying them. The cluster platform consists of multiple nodes that implement the emulator, the end-user nodes and the configuration management platform for FaReCast. The Model emulator node has a dual 2.6Ghz CPU with 2GB RAM and runs a custom FreeBSD Kernel with a system clock at 100HZ (as required by Modelnet). End-user hosts are modeled as virtual nodes on an IBM E-server cluster with multiple (7) 900Mhz CPU with 500MB RAM. The hosts run Linux with a customized 2.6 version kernel which efficiently supports multiple threads. The hosts support Java version 1.5 and Python version 2.3.5. All hosts are

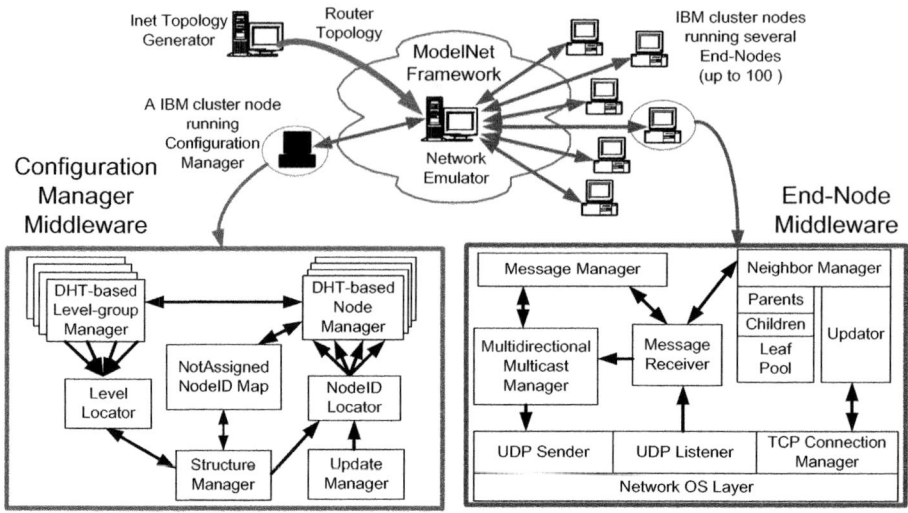

Fig. 7. FaReCast System Architecture Implemented on a ModelNet Cluster

synchronized to with 2msec through NTP (Network Time Protocol). All machines have Gigabit Ethernet connectivity connected by a dedicated Gigabit router.

Figure 7 illustrates the various components of the FaReCast system implementation and more detailed software architecture for two of the key modules - the configuration management module and the end-node middleware. While our initial implementation and measurements were conducted on a centralized configuration manager; we are currently working on a DHT based distributed implementation of the configuration management module.

Configuration Manager Middleware: The primary job of the configuration manager is to (a) generate and maintain the M2M ALM overlay structure given initial and updated connectivity information and (b)communicate with end-nodes to provide and gather configuration information. In the configuration manager, every participant node is mapped to a node object that contains logical information on each node - including a nodeID and node information - this includes contact information such as IP address of the node, its level, and nodeIDs of its parents/children. We are currently working on a distributed DHT-based implementation of the configuration manager where node objects are distributed based on their nodeID and managed by multiple Node Managers. Whenever the configuration manager receives the update request for parents/children information of a specific node, it gathers the nodeIDs of the requested parents/children, extracts the contact information that is mapped to the nodeIDs and supplies them with the updated information. The configuration management functionality also incorporates a Level-group Manager that maintains information on each level-group including number of sibling nodes in the same level and the

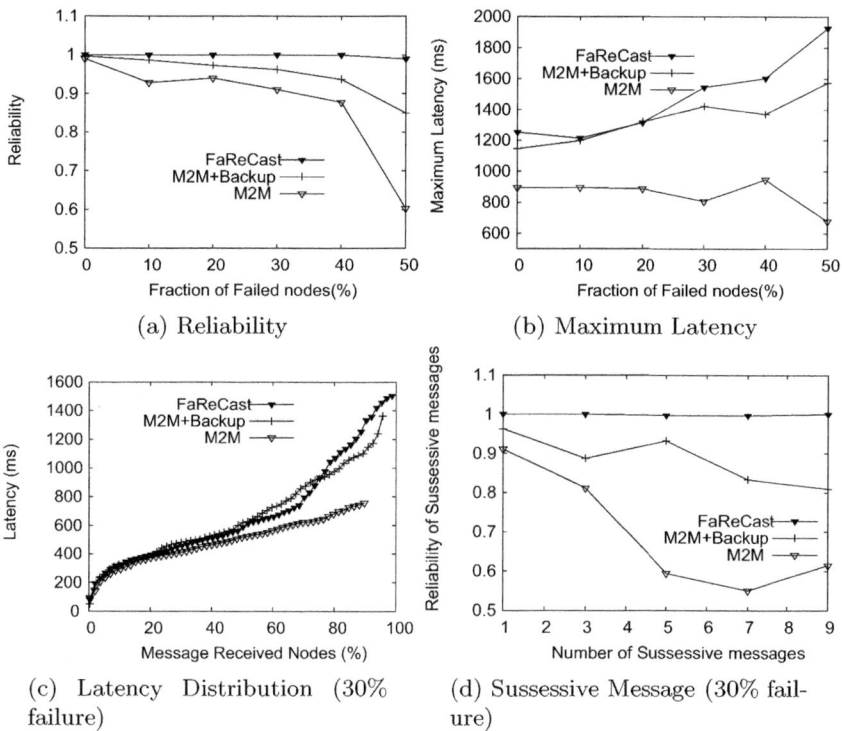

Fig. 8. Performance comparison between FareCast(F_i=3,F_o=3) under various failures with 600 nodes

parent pool. The Level group manager checks for the parent uniqueness condition when requested by a Node Manager. NotAssignedNodeID Map contains the invalidated node information. The Structure Manager and Update Manager are front-end modules that communicate with end nodes.

End-Node Middleware: An end node has two key components (i) a Neighbor Manager, which maintains information of parents, children and leaves (only if the peer has no children) of the node and (ii) a Message Manager that verifies, authenticates and processes incoming messages to the node. Neighbor Manager information is updated periodically (every 1 hour) via requests to the configuration manager, as opposed to probing the parents/children/leaves themselves. Since FaReCast is tolerant to high levels of inconsistency between the current system status and the information of the configuration manager, the frequency of the update can be low. Message Manager is responsible for authorization and authentication of messages to ensure that there are no unintended duplicate messages. When a new message arrives at the Message Manager, it generates a parent mask to sort out the parents who have sent the message. This parent mask is exploited by the Multidirectional Multicast Manager which initiates and executes the Backup and L2L dissemination. While TCP is used for control messages, i.e. monitoring and updates, we use UDP for disseminating the actual message to deliver the messages as fast as possible.

Experimental Results from Implementation: To model the underlying Internet, we used the Inet[2] topology generator to generate Internet router topologies of 5000 routers. Inet generates a topology on a XY plane and Modelnet uses this to generate heterogeneous inter-router (and hence inter-node) latencies. Link properties were specified separately; bandwidth constraints vary from 100Kbps to 500Kbps and network packet loss varies from 1% to 5% for each link. This length of queue of each router is set to 10 (default ModelNet value) and packet losses do not include the dropped packets by queue.

Figure 8 presents some of the experimental results from the real world deployment of FaReCast. On the whole, the implementation based evaluation yielded similar overall results to that of the simulation-based evaluation. As can be observed, reliability of dissemination was close to 100% and latency and overhead increased with an increased number of simultaneous node failures. We also experimented with multiple successive messages to mimic a scenario where a series of messages were sent in succession. In a real deployment, we notice that the pure M2M policy (i.e. M2M ALM structure with traditional multicast) exhibited poor performance - this is primarily related to the UDP-based implementation that was used to disseminate the data.

6 Conclusion

We propose FaReCast, a Fast and Reliable data dissemination system for flash dissemination scenarios such as earthquake early warning where the target network is large and potentially unreliable. FaReCast constructs a forest-based M2M ALM structure where each node has multiple children guaranteeing the fast delivery of the message as well as multiple parents ensuring the reliability of the delivery. The FaReCast M2M ALM structure is accompanied by a multidirectional multicasting algorithm which sends data not only to the children but also to the selected parents or the selected siblings. Unlike ack-based communication, the multidirectional multicasting algorithms proactively figure out the direction of failures and target message resends along the direction. As compared to trees using a traditional multicasting algorithm, we observe an 80% improvement in reliability under 20% failed nodes with no significant increase in latency for over 99% of nodes. Under extreme failures, e.g. more than 30% failed nodes, we observe that existing mesh-based protocols exhibit low reliability, FaReCast achieves 100% reliability with a small increase in latency and overhead.

A natural extension of our work is to adapt the proposed techniques to support rapid, reliable dissemination over wireless mobile devices. Our future plans are to study failure scenarios in this environment more deeply and design mechanisms for addressing timeliness/reliability tradeoffs for information dissemination using mixed wired/wireless networks.

References

1. Modelnet, http://issg.cs.duke.edu/modelnet.html
2. Inet, http://topology.eecs.umich.edu/inet/
3. Chu, Y., Rao, S.G., Seshan, S., Zhang, H.: A Case for End System Multicast. In: Proc. of ACM Sigmetrics (2000)
4. Banerjee, S., Bhattacharjee, B., Kommareddy, C.: Scalable Application Layer Multicast. In: Proc. of SIGCOMM 2002 (2002)
5. Tran, D.A., Hua, K.A., Do, T.T.: ZIGZAG: An Efficient Peer-to-Peer Scheme for Media Streaming. In: Proc. of INFOCOM (2003)
6. Rowstron, A., Kermarrec, A., Castro, M., Druschel, P.: Scribe: The design of a large-scale event notification infrastructure. In: Networked Group Communication, pp. 30–43 (2001)
7. Castro, M., Druschel, P., Kermarrec, A.-M., Nandi, A., Rowstron, A., Singh, A.: SplitStream: High-bandwidth multicast in a cooperative environment. In: Proc. of SOSP 2003 (2003)
8. Kosti, C.D., Rodriguez, A., Albrecht, J., Vahdat, A.: Bullet: High Bandwidth Data Dissemination Using an Overlay Mesh. In: Proc. of SOSP 2003 (2003)
9. Pai, V., Kumar, K., Tamilmani, K., Sambamurthy, V., Mohr, A.E.: Chainsaw: Eliminating Trees from Overlay Multicast. In: Castro, M., van Renesse, R. (eds.) IPTPS 2005. LNCS, vol. 3640, pp. 127–140. Springer, Heidelberg (2005)
10. Cohen, B.: BitTorrent (2001), http://www.bitconjurer.org/BitTorrent/
11. Deshpande, M., Xing, B., Lazardis, I., Hore, B., Venkatasubramanian, N., Mehrotra, S.: CREW: A Gossip-based Flash-Dissemination System. In: Proc. of ICDCS 2006 (2006)
12. Deshpande, M., Amit, A., Chang, M., Venkatasubramanian, N., Mehrotra, S.: Flashback: A Peer-to-Peer Webserver for Handling Flash Crowds. In: Proc. of ICDCS 2007 (2007)
13. Snoeren, A.C., Conley, K., Gifford, D.K.: Mesh-Based Content Routing using XML. In: Proc. of SOSP 2001 (2001)
14. Bansal, M., Zakhor, A.: Path Diversity Based Techniques for Resilient Overlay Multimedia Multicast. In: Proc. of PCS 2004 (2004)
15. Tian, R., Zhang, Q., Xiang, Z., Xiong, Y., Li, X., Zhu, W.: Robust and efficient path diversity in application-layer multicast for video streaming. IEEE Transactions on Circuits and Systems for Video Technology 15(8) (2005)
16. Frey, D., Murphy, A.L.: Failure-Tolerant Overlay Trees for Large-Scale Dynamic Networks. In: Proc. of P2P 2008 (2008)
17. Rodrigues, R., Liskov, B.: High Availability in DHTs: Erasure Coding vs. Replication. In: Castro, M., van Renesse, R. (eds.) IPTPS 2005. LNCS, vol. 3640, pp. 226–239. Springer, Heidelberg (2005)
18. Padmanabhan, V.N., Wang, H.J., Chow, P.A.: Resilient Peer-to-Peer Streaming. In: Proc. of ICNP 2003 (2003)
19. Venkataraman, V., Francisy, P., Calandrinoz, J.: Chunkyspread: Multitree Unstructured PeertoPeer Multicast. In: Proc. of IPTPS 2006 (2006)
20. Yang, M., Yang, Y.: A Peer-to-Peer Tree Based Reliable Multicast Protocol. In: Proc. of Globecom 2006 (2006)
21. Rong, B., Khalil, I., Tari, Z.: Making Application Layer Multicast Reliable is Feasible. In: Proc. of LCN 2006 (2006)
22. Zhang, J., Liu, L., Pu, C., Ammar, M.: Reliable Peer-to-peer End System Multicasting through Replication. In: Proc. of P2P 2004 (2004)

23. Kusumoto, T., Kunichika, Y., Katto, J., Okubo, S.: Tree-Based Application Layer Multicast using Proactive Route Maintenance and its Implementation. In: Proc. of P2PMMS 2005 (2005)
24. Birrer, S., Bustamante, F.: Resilient Peer-to-Peer Multicast without the Cost. In: Proc. of MMCN 2005 (2005)
25. El-Ansary, S., Alima, L.O., Brand, P., Haridi, S.: Efficient Broadcast in Structured P2P Networks. In: Kaashoek, M.F., Stoica, I. (eds.) IPTPS 2003. LNCS, vol. 2735, pp. 304–314. Springer, Heidelberg (2003)
26. Ciavattone, L., Morton, A., Ramachandran, G.: Standardized Active Measurements on a Tier 1 IP Backbone. IEEE Communications (June 2003)

The Gossple Anonymous Social Network[*]

Marin Bertier[1], Davide Frey[2], Rachid Guerraoui[3]
Anne-Marie Kermarrec[2], and Vincent Leroy[1]

[1] INSA de Rennes, Rennes, France
[2] INRIA-Rennes Bretagne Atlantique, Rennes, France
[3] EPFL, Lausanne, Switzerland

Abstract. While social networks provide news from old buddies, you can learn a lot more from people you do not know, but with whom you share many interests. We show in this paper how to build a network of anonymous social acquaintances using a gossip protocol we call GOSSPLE, and how to leverage such a network to enhance navigation within Web 2.0 collaborative applications, à la LastFM and Delicious. GOSSPLE nodes (users) periodically gossip digests of their interest profiles and compute their distances (in terms of interest) with respect to other nodes. This is achieved with little bandwidth and storage, fast convergence, and without revealing which profile is associated with which user. We evaluate GOSSPLE on real traces from various Web 2.0 applications with hundreds of PlanetLab hosts and thousands of simulated nodes.

1 Introduction

Context: The Web 2.0 has radically changed the way people interact with the Internet: this has turned from a read-only infrastructure to a collaborative read-write platform with active players. Content is no longer generated only by experts but pretty much by everyone. Web 2.0 applications, such as LastFM, Flickr, CiteULike and Delicious [1], contain a goldmine of information. Yet, matching a specific query in such a mine might rapidly turn out to be like looking for a needle in a haystack, for the content of the Web is not indexed with a controlled vocabulary, e.g, *ontology*. Instead, freely chosen keywords are typically used to *tag* billions of items, i.e., with a *folksonomy* (folk + taxonomy). In short, the freedom left to the users to express their interests underlies the success of the Web 2.0 but it is also an impediment to navigation.

This paper proposes to improve navigation in such systems through implicit personalization: we associate every user with a network of *anonymous acquaintances* that are interested in similar items, independently of how they expressed their interests, e.g., which keywords they used to tag those items. These acquaintances are then implicitly used to guide and refine users' search operations.

Insight: To illustrate the benefit of *implicit personalization*, consider the following real example. After living for several years in the UK, John is back to Lyon

---

[*] This work is supported by the ERC Starting Grant GOSSPLE number 204742.

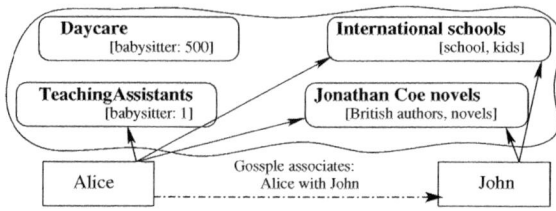

Fig. 1. Associating John to Alice enables John to leverage the unusual association between the keywords teaching assistants and baby-sitter

in France. To maintain his kids' skills in English, he is looking for an English speaking baby-sitter who would be willing to trade baby-sitting hours against accommodation. There is no doubt that such an offer would be of interest to many of the young foreigners living in a big city such as Lyon. Yet, John's Google request *"English baby-sitter Lyon"* does not provide anything interesting for the term *baby-sitter* is mainly associated with *daycare* or local (French) baby-sitting companies.

None of John's Facebook buddies in Lyon or the UK can help either as none has ever looked for an English speaking baby-sitter in Lyon. Yet, Alice living in Bordeaux after several years in the US, and who was looking for a similar deal with her kids, has been lucky enough to discover that teaching assistants in primary schools are a very good match. Clearly, John could leverage Alice's discovery if only he knew about it. Should a system be able to capture the affinity between Alice and John, through their *common interest* in international schools and British novels for example (Figure 1), John could use Alice's information.

Indeed, consider a collaborative tagging system through which Alice has annotated the *teaching assistant* URL with *baby-sitter* (Figure 1). Assume both Alice and John have expressed their interest in international schools and British novels by tagging related URLs. A personalized search could leverage these affinities to return Alice's *teaching assistant* URL first instead of the millions of URLs of standard (non English speaking) baby-sitter related URLs. Likewise, a personalized query expansion could expand John's query appropriately with tags derived from Alice's activities on the Web and make it easy to solve by any reasonable search engine. The crucial aspect here is the unusual (personal) association between baby-sitter and teaching assistant, which is relevant to a niche community (the one gathering Alice and John) while baby-sitter is dominantly associated with (non English speaking) daycare. Discovering such specific affinity is very rewarding for the users, yet challenging to automatically capture.

Challenges: First, capturing associations between tagging profiles is difficult with millions of users, each with a dynamic variety of interests. Meaningful associations that help retrieve appropriate matching results, without drowning these within tons of useless information, should be derived from a large amount of information about proximity between user profiles. Such information grows not only with the number of users, but also with the number of interests per user. To illustrate this, consider our previous example. John, besides being interested in a baby-sitter, does also search for music over the Internet. Despite their proximity as far as kids and English are concerned, Alice and John have opposite tastes music-wise. The fact that Alice and John are identified as acquaintances should not prevent John from benefiting from relevant music information using other acquaintances.

Second, discovering social acquaintances might be hampered by the resistance of users to publicize their tagging behavior. In fact, the apparent eagerness of companies to benefit from user-generated content might already dissuade users from generating new content and making their interests explicit[1]. A decentralized solution is appealing to address both the scalability and *big-brother* issues but poses nontrivial maintenance and efficiency issues, besides the fact that users might still be reluctant to reveal their interests to other unknown users.

Contributions: This paper presents GOSSPLE, a system that takes up these challenges, in a pragmatic way, to *automatically* infer *personalized* connections in Internet-scale systems. GOSSPLE nodes (users) continuously gossip digests of the tagging profiles (of their corresponding users) and locally compute a personalized *view* of the network, which is then leveraged to improve their Web navigation. The view covers *multiple interests* without any explicit support (such as explicit social links or ontology) and without violating *anonymity*: the association between users and profiles is hidden. In the context of the Alice-John example above, GOSSPLE leverages the very fact that John's request can benefit from Alice's tagging profile, without knowing who the profile belongs to. Basically, every GOSSPLE node has a proxy, chosen randomly, gossiping its profile digest *on its behalf;* the node transmits its profile to its proxy in an encrypted manner through an intermediary, which cannot decrypt the profile.

To reduce bandwidth consumption, the gossip exchange procedure is *thrifty*: nodes do not exchange profiles but only Bloom filters of those until similarity computation reveals that the two nodes might indeed benefit from the exchange. To limit the number of profiles maintained by each node, while encompassing the various interests of the user associated with the node, we introduce a new similarity metric, we call the *set cosine similarity*, as a generalization of the classical *cosine similarity* metric [2,3], as well as an effective heuristic to compute this new metric.

While GOSSPLE can serve recommendation and search systems as well, we illustrate the effectiveness of GOSSPLE through a query expansion application for collaborative tagging systems. We believe this application to be interesting in its own right. We compute scores between tags using GOSSPLE and apply ideas from ranking Web pages (PageRank) to leverage the relative centrality of the tags through an algorithm we call *GRank*.[2]

---

[1] See recent events with privacy threats of Facebook.
[2] Classical file sharing applications could also benefit from our approach: our experiments with eDonkey (100, 000 nodes) provided very promising results.

Evaluation: We evaluated GOSSPLE with a wide-range of Web 2.0 application traces, including Delicious, CiteULike, LastFM and eDonkey, up to 100,000 users through simulation and in a real distributed system of 223 PlanetLab nodes.

We first show that our multi-interest similarity metric improves on state-of-the-art ones by up to 70% in the considered datasets. Our gossip exchange procedure effectively builds a GOSSPLE network from scratch in less than 20 cycles, and maintains a baseline bandwidth of 15kbps. This is achieved with good anonymity guarantees through the use of onion-routing-like techniques.

We also evaluate our query expansion application independently and show how we retrieve items that state-of-the-art search systems do not (recall, also called completeness) whilst improving precision (accuracy) at the same time. We show, among other things, how GOSSPLE addresses the Alice-John baby-sitter situation above. For instance, a query expansion of size 20 retrieves 40% of unsuccessful original queries while improving the precision by 58% with respect to the originally successful queries (against resp. 36% and 24% for competitors [4]) on a Delicious trace. This is achieved in a thrifty manner: 10 acquaintances are enough to achieve effective query expansion in a 50,000-user system, while exchanging gossip messages and profile digests of approximately 12.9KBytes and 603Bytes respectively.

In summary: The contributions of this paper are threefold: (i) an *anonymous, thrifty* gossip protocol; (ii) a *set cosine similarity* metric to compute semantic distances; and (iii) a *query expansion* application.

Roadmap: Section 2 details the GOSSPLE protocol. Section 3 reports on its evaluation. Section 4 describes the application of GOSSPLE to query expansion. Section 5 surveys the related work. Section 6 highlights some of the limitations of GOSSPLE.

2 The Gossple Protocol

GOSSPLE is a fully decentralized protocol aimed at building and maintaining dynamic communities of anonymous acquaintances. Such communities differ from networks of *explicitly* declared friends (e.g. Facebook) which are often not the most suited to enhance the search procedure as reported in [5].

2.1 Overview

More specifically, GOSSPLE provides each user with *GNet*, a network of semantically close anonymous interest profiles. Building and maintaining a node's *GNet* goes first through determining a *metric* to identify which profiles exhibit similar interests. This is particularly challenging for the goal is to capture the whole range of a node's interests while limiting the number of profiles in the *GNet*. Another challenge is to devise an *effective* communication procedure for profile exchange while limiting the amount of generated network traffic and hiding the association between nodes and profiles to preserve *anonymity*.

We detail in the following how GOSSPLE addresses these challenges. We assume, for presentation simplicity, a one-to-one mapping between a user and a machine: we refer to a node henceforth. From an abstract perspective, we model the profile of a node as a set of items $I = \{i_1, \ldots, i_n\}$. Each item can be described by a potentially large amount of meta-information, such as tags describing it in the case of a folksonomy. Depending on the target application, this set may represent downloaded files, a summary of published content, etc. In the following, we first present a novel *multi-interest (set item cosine similarity)* metric; then, we describe our *thrifty gossip-based* protocol to establish and maintain connections between nodes (i.e., compute *GNet*) using this metric. For presentation simplicity, we present our protocol in a modular manner: we present first how a node communicates with other nodes to review a large set of profiles, how it encodes a profile, and finally how it preserves its anonymity.

2.2 Selecting Acquaintances

Selecting relevant acquaintances requires nodes to rate each-other's profile.

Rating individuals. One way to build a node's *GNet* is to individually rate other nodes and select the ones that score the highest. Cosine similarity [6] is widely used in the area of data mining. The score between two nodes increases when interests are similar, specific overlapping of interests being favored over large profiles. Our preliminary experiments have shown indeed that cosine similarity outperforms simple measures such as the number of items in common. Thus we implemented cosine similarity as a reference in our experiments. More specifically, let I_{n_i} be the set of items in the profile of node n, the item cosine similarity between two nodes is defined as follows: $ItemCos(n_1, n_2) = \frac{|I_{n_1} \cap I_{n_2}|}{\sqrt{|I_{n_1}| \times |I_{n_2}|}}$.

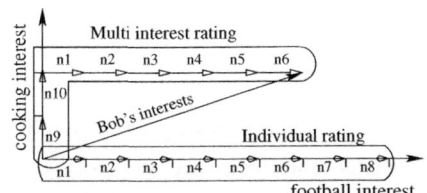

Individual rating, and thus cosine similarity, selects nodes having the most similar profiles. Yet, this may lead to consider only the dominant interest, ignoring minor, potentially important, ones. In a large-scale system where a node can only keep track of a limited number of profiles, individual rating cannot capture emerging interests until they represent an important pro-

Fig. 2. Multi-interest rating *vs.* Individual rating

portion of the profile, which they might never. Consider Bob whose tagging actions reveal that 75% of his interests are in football while 25% are in cooking. Selecting the profiles of the closest nodes might lead to only selecting those interested in football: the cooking topic will not be represented enough to provide interesting information. In Figure 2, the individual rating selects a view of 8 nodes interested only in football (users n_1, n_2, ... n_8).

On the contrary, the *GNet* should preserve the distribution of 75% of football and 25% of cooking. We achieve this by rating a *set of profiles* as a whole rather than each profile independently. This is crucial to achieve scalability and limit the size of the *GNet wrt* the overall size of the network. In the example, *multi-interest* scoring would lead to selecting 2 nodes interested in cooking: n_9 and n_{10} and 6 in football, covering Bob's interest in cooking as well.

Rating sets. Rating a set of profiles as a whole involves a balance between the extent to which nodes in the set share interests with a given node n, and how well the distribution of the interests in the set matches the one in n's profile. This is precisely what the GOSSPLE *item set cosine similarity* metric achieves.

Let $IVect_n$ be the vector that represents the items in the profile of n. If item i is in the profile of node n $IVect_n[i] = 1$, otherwise 0. Following the same principle, $SetIVect_n(s)$ builds an item vector that represents the distribution of items in a set of nodes s with respect to the node n. Each value of this vector is computed as follows: $SetIVect_n(s)[i] = IVect_n[i] \times \sum_{u \in s} \frac{IVect_u[i]}{\|IVect_u\|}$. The rationale behind this metric is to represent the distribution of interests in *GNet* while normalizing the contribution of each node to favor specific interests. The items that are not present in the profile of node n are discarded since their distribution should not impact the score of *GNet*. Following the cosine similarity between nodes, a node n computes a score for a set of nodes as follows:

$$SetScore_n(s) = (IVect_n \cdot SetIVect_n(s)) \times cos(IVect_n, SetIVect_n(s))^b$$

The first part of the formula sums all the values in the vector representing the distribution of items in s, while the second represents how well the distribution of the items in s matches the one in n's profile, i.e. how fair the contribution to all the interests of n is. b is the *balance* between the amount of shared interests and a fair distribution that does not favor any item. The set that scores the highest forms the node's *GNet*. It is important to notice that for $b = 0$ (no cosine impact), the distribution is not considered and the resulting *GNet* is exactly the same as the one obtained from the individual rating.

2.3 Discovering Acquaintances

GOSSPLE's multi-interest metric is key to selecting the best set of profiles to fill a given node's *GNet*. This would however be of little use without an effective mechanism to review a large set of candidate profiles while ensuring rapid convergence to the ideal *GNet*. GOSSPLE achieves this through a *gossip* protocol to establish and maintain connections between nodes. The GOSSPLE protocol relies on two sub-protocols (Figure 3): a *Random Peer Sampling protocol*

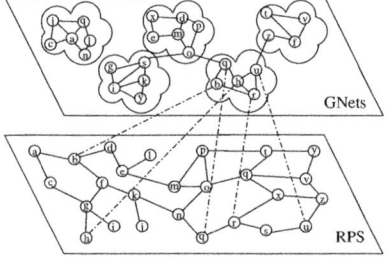

Fig. 3. GOSSPLE network

(RPS) [7] and a multi-interest clustering protocol (*GNet* protocol). Each node maintains two corresponding data structures, *a random view* and the *GNet*.

RPS. In the RPS, each node maintains a *view* of a random subset of network nodes. Periodically, it selects a node from this view and they exchange parts of their views. This provides each node with a random, changing, subset the network used for the bootstrap and the maintenance of the *GNet* protocol. Each entry in the random view contains *(i)* the IP address and the GOSSPLE ID of the node; *(ii)* a digest of its profile in the form of a Bloom filter (discussed in Section 2.4) and, *(iii)* the number of items in the profile (used for normalization). GOSSPLE relies on Brahms [8], a byzantine resilient RPS, which provides the building blocks to build GOSSPLE's anonymity (presented in Section 2.5).

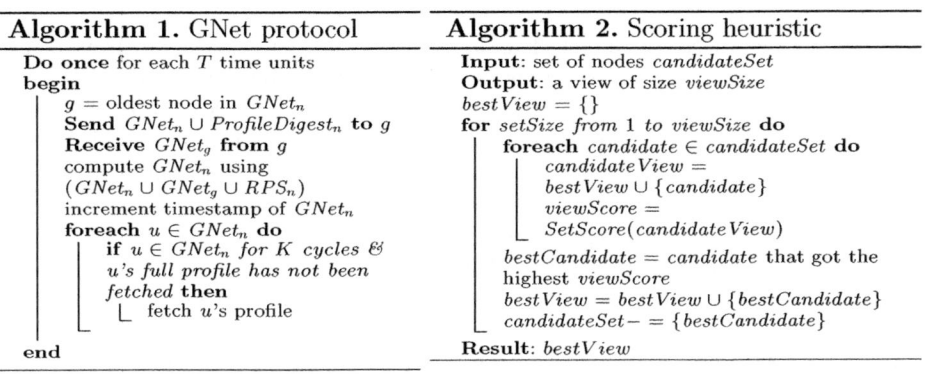

GNet protocol. GNet contains c entries composed of the same fields as the random view entries with the addition of a timestamp representing the last time the entry was updated in the view. c is a parameter of the system that selects the trade-off between the amount of available information and its personalization degree. In addition, each entry also contains the full profile of nodes that have been chosen as acquaintances. We denote by $GNet_n$ the *GNet* of a node n.

The *GNet* protocol (Algorithm 1) is also gossip-based and maintains a list of implicit acquaintances (nodes). Each node n periodically selects the oldest (according to the timestamp) node g in its *GNet*, or a node picked from the RPS view if $GNet_n$ is empty. Then n sends the descriptors of c nodes in $GNet_n$ to g and g does the same. Upon receiving the other node's *GNet*, n and g update their own *GNet* structure. It first computes the union of $GNet_n$, $GNet_g$ and its own RPS view, then it selects the c nodes that maximize the GOSSPLE metric described in Section 2.2. Selecting the best view consists of computing the score of all possible combinations of c nodes out of $3c$ nodes. Because the corresponding running time is exponential in c, our protocol uses a heuristic (Algorithm 2) as an approximation. It incrementally builds a view of size c from an empty view by adding at each step the node that provides the best view score. This heuristic has complexity $O(c^2)$ and turns out to be very appropriate in our evaluations.

2.4 Gossiping Digests

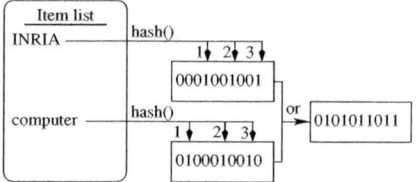

Fig. 4. The Bloom filter of a profile

In order to keep the bandwidth consumption of GOSSPLE within reasonable bounds, nodes do not send their full profiles during gossip. Instead, they exchange a Bloom filter [9]: a compact representation of the set of items in the profile. The Bloom filter provides a reasonably good approximation of a node's profile that can be used to compute GOSSPLE's metric with a negligible error margin (as we discuss in Section 3.3).

The Bloom filter, as depicted in Figure 4, is an array of bits representing a set. When an item is added to the set, h hash functions are used on the item to obtain h positions in the array: these are set to 1. In order to query for the presence of an item in the set, one uses the same hash functions and checks if all the bits at the h indexes are set to 1. In the case of several additions to the Bloom filter, the request can return true even if the item was never added to the set. The rate of false positives depends on the size of the set, h, and the number of items in the system. However, a Bloom filter never returns a false negative.

In GOSSPLE, the Bloom filter is used as a first approximation of a node's profile. If a node remains in the *GNet* for K gossip rounds, it is considered as a good candidate and the entire profile is requested ($K = 5$ in our experiments). Once the full profile of the node has been retrieved, it is used to compute an exact similarity score. This prevents the expensive transfers of useless entire profiles of nodes that will reveal distant according to the GOSSPLE metric. For example, the profile of a Delicious user is on average 12.9KBytes large, while the corresponding Bloom filter is only 603Bytes. This leads to a 20-fold improvement in bandwidth usage.

Since a Bloom filter can return false positive results, some nodes considered as acquaintances through their Bloom filters can be discarded when the exact score is computed with the profile. However, a node that should be in the *GNet* will never be discarded due to a Bloom filter approximation. Hence, an entry for a node in the *GNet* contains either the full profile of the node or a Bloom filter of the profile with a counter incremented at each cycle. When the counter reaches the value of K, it triggers the retrieval of the corresponding full profile. The pseudo-code of the *GNet* protocol is presented in Algorithm 1.

2.5 Preserving Anonymity

The decentralized nature of GOSSPLE somehow inherently preserves some level of anonymity, as compared to a central entity which would control and store all personal data. We go a step further by observing that, while personalized applications may benefit from the profile information contained in *GNets*, they need not know which nodes are associated with which profiles. In the Alice-John example, what matters is that John can leverage the information provided by

Alice: he does not need to know Alice. This observation underlies our *gossip-on-behalf* approach: each node n is associated with a proxy p that gossips on its behalf. Since P2P networks are subject to churn, p periodically sends snapshots of $GNet_n$ to n so that n can resume the gossip protocol on a new proxy without losing any information. This *anonymity by proxy* setup is achieved by an encrypted two-hop communication path *à la* onion routing [10]. Therefore p receives n's profile and its updates but does not know n's identity while the nodes relaying the communication cannot decrypt the profile. GOSSPLE relies on the Byzantine resilience properties of the RPS protocol to prevent colluders from manipulating the selection of the proxy and the relays. Furthermore, we assume that the system is protected against Sybil attacks through a certificate mechanism or a detection algorithm [11]. Finally, we also consider that it is a user's responsibility to avoid adding very sensitive information to her profile. In that case, the profile alone would be sufficient to find the identity of the user as it was the case in the famous anonymized AOL query-log dataset. GOSSPLE ensures anonymity deterministically against single adversary nodes and with high probability against small colluding groups.

3 Gossple Evaluation

We report on the effectiveness and cost of GOSSPLE by means of both simulation (100,000 nodes) and PlanetLab deployment (446 nodes). The former provides insights about GOSSPLE's behavior with a very large number of participants while the latter about the inherent overhead of GOSSPLE in a real distributed setting.

3.1 Setting and Methodology

We evaluated the quality of GOSSPLE's *GNet*, its convergence speed, as well as its bandwidth consumption and behavior under churn. We considered various Web 2.0 datasets: *(i)* a trace crawled from Delicious (social URL bookmarking) in January 2009; *(ii)* a trace from CiteULike (reference management system) available on October 9, 2008; *(iii)* a LastFM (music recommender system) trace crawled in Spring 2008 and composed of the 50 most listened-to artists for each user; and *(iv)* an eDonkey (P2P file-sharing) trace [12]. Table 5 provides the figures for each trace. We configured GOSSPLE's *GNets* size to 10 and the gossip cycle length to 10 seconds. We deliberately select a small *GNet* size in order to stress the system and highlight the impact of the selection of each acquaintance.

In this section, we evaluate the quality of a node's *GNet* through its ability to provide the node with interesting items. This measures the basic usefulness of GOSSPLE's *GNets* in search applications and recommender systems. We remove a subset (10%) of the items in the profile of each node, which we call the *hidden interests* of the node. GOSSPLE uses the remaining part of the profile to build the *GNets*. We express the quality of a *GNet* in terms of *recall*, i.e. the proportion of hidden interests of a node n that are present in the profile of at least one node in n's *GNet*. The better the *GNet*, the more hidden interests it contains. Each hidden interest is present in at least one profile within the full network: the maximum recall is always 1. Recall is enough to evaluate quality here because n contacts a fixed number of nodes. We further evaluate precision in Section 4.

We evaluate the overall quality by computing the recall for the whole system: we divide the sum of the number of hidden interests retrieved by GOSSPLE for each node and divide it by the sum of the number of hidden interests of each node.

3.2 Metric (The Quality of GNets)

Our item set cosine similarity (multi-interest) metric enables GOSSPLE to cover the diversity of user interests in a large scale system by assessing the quality of the whole *GNet* at once, instead of rating profiles individually. Parameter b in the definition of *SetScore* (*cf.* Section 2.2) represents the weight of minor interests *wrt* major ones. We evaluate the impact of b using the hidden-interest test described above. Intuitively, too small a value of b will achieve poor results because the *GNet* will fail to provide items related to minor interests. On the other hand, too high a value of b might select profiles with too little in common with the node to provide relevant items. Figure 6 presents the normalized recall achieved by *GNets* on the datasets with increasing values of b. The score is normalized to take as a reference the case when $b = 0$, equivalent to individual rating. As expected, the performance initially increases with increasing values of b, but it decreases for greater values of b. Multi-interest improves recall from 17% (LastFM) to 69% (Delicious). For all datasets, GOSSPLE significantly improves the quality of *GNets* over traditional clustering algorithms illustrated by the $b = 0$ configurations. The exact recall values are given in Table 5. We also observe that the improvement of multi-interest has more impact when the base recall is low. Further experiments, omitted due to space constraints, revealed that this is because GOSSPLE is particularly good at finding rare items. Finally, we observe that the maximum performance is not obtained for a specific value of b, but for a full range of values, $b \in [2, 6]$, across all datasets. This demonstrates GOSSPLE's effectiveness on a wide variety of datasets without requiring prior fine tuning of parameters.

	Delicious	CiteULike	LastFM	eDonkey
Nb users	$130k$	$34k$	$1,219k$	$187k$
Nb items	$9,107k$	$1,134k$	$964k$	$9,694k$
Nb tags	$2,214k$	$237k$		
Avg profile size	224	39	50	142
Nb nodes	$50k$	$10k$	$100k$	$100k$
Recall $b = 0$	12.7%	33.6%	49.6%	30.9%
Recall GOSSPLE	21.6%	46.3%	57.6%	43.4%

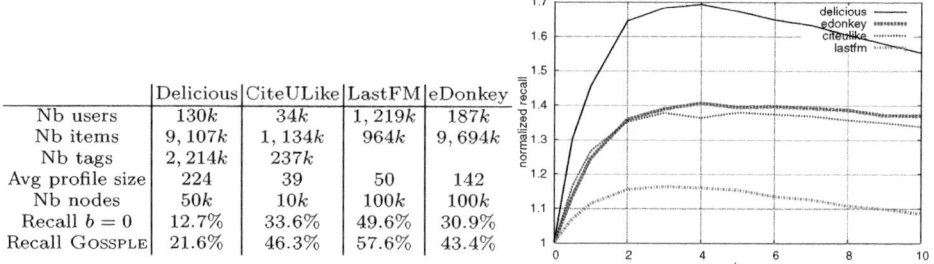

Fig. 5. Dataset properties   **Fig. 6.** Impact of b on normalized recall

3.3 Convergence Time

We evaluate GOSSPLE's ability to build and maintain a useful *GNet* for each node. First, we consider the time required to build a network of GOSSPLE acquaintances from empty *GNets*. Then we consider the maintenance of this network by evaluating convergence in a dynamic scenario where nodes join an existing stable network.

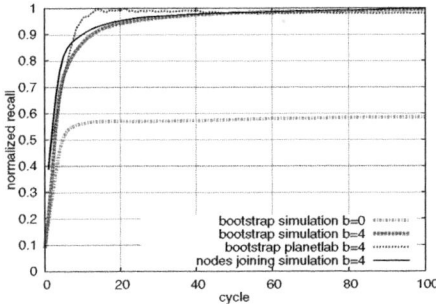 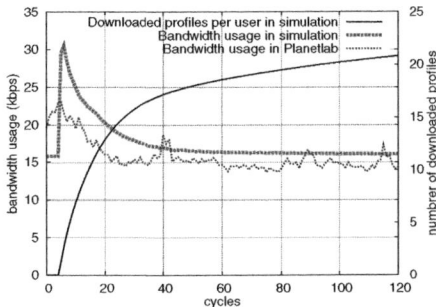

Fig. 7. Recall during churn   **Fig. 8.** Bandwidth usage at cold-start

Bootstrapping. We consider a simulation of 50,000 nodes and a real-world PlanetLab deployment with 446 nodes on 223 machines. Figure 7 plots the hidden-interests' recall (*cf.* Section 3.2) during the construction of the GOSSPLE network. It is normalized by the value obtained by GOSSPLE at a fully converged state.

As expected, the multi-interest clustering ($b = 4$) constantly outperforms the standard one ($b = 0$), although it requires slightly longer to reach a stable state. The difference is minimal, GOSSPLE reaches 90% of its potential after only 14 gossip cycles in simulation in our Delicious traces for instance. This convergence is extremely fast given the size of the network (50,000) and the small size of the *GNet* and RPS (10). The measures conducted on LastFM confirm the scalability of the protocol: for twice as large a network, only 3 more cycles are needed to reach the same convergence state. The PlanetLab deployment confirms the simulation results. The smaller scale of the experiments causes GOSSPLE's *GNets* to reach 90% of their potential after an average of 12 cycles and stabilize after 30. This confirms the scalability of our protocol by demonstrating convergence times that grow very slowly with the size of the network.

Maintenance. Bootstrapping represents a worst-case scenario for the convergence of our protocol. It is, in fact, a one-time event in the life of a GOSSPLE network. During normal operation, the system will instead experience perturbations that cause it to deviate from a stable state in which each node has converged to its best possible *GNet*. Examples of such perturbation include variations in the interests of users, or the presence of nodes that join and leave the network.

To evaluate the impact of these perturbations, we consider a scenario where 1% of new nodes join an existing GOSSPLE network at each gossip cycle. We measure the hidden-interest recall of these new nodes to see how many gossip cycles are needed for them to reach a quality of *GNet* equivalent to the one of the previously converged nodes (i.e. 1 on the normalized score). Joining an existing network is indeed faster than bootstrapping, as 9 cycles are enough to reach a 90%-quality *GNet*. Clearly, this represents an upper bound on the time required for convergence in the presence of dynamic profiles or nodes that leave the network. In both of these cases, nodes that are required to converge only need to partially reconstruct their *GNets* as they already have some good neighbors to rely on. Moreover, the removal of disconnected nodes from the network is automatically handled by the clustering protocol through the selection of the oldest peer from the view during gossip exchanges as discussed in detail in [13].

3.4 Bandwidth

The bandwidth consumption of GOSSPLE when the *GNets* are built from scratch is depicted in Figure 8. This cost is the result of: *(i)* the exchange of profile digests upon gossip; *(ii)* the download of the full profiles of nodes in the *GNet*; *(iii)* the extra communication required to maintain anonymity. Each node gossips through the RPS and the *GNet* protocols every $10s$: each message containing respectively 5 and 10 digests. This results in a maximum bandwidth consumption of 30kbps in the most demanding situation, that is during the burst at the beginning of the experiment. This is because no profile information has yet been downloaded.[3] As soon as the *GNets* start to converge, the rate of exchange of full profiles decreases, as shown by the line depicting the total number of downloaded profiles per user. This causes bandwidth consumption to decrease to the fixed cost of gossiping digests, 15kbps, a clearly irrelevant value for almost any user on the network today.

If GOSSPLE did not use Bloom filters, on the other hand, profile information would be exchanged continuously, thereby increasing bandwidth consumption. In the considered data trace, replacing Bloom filters with full profiles in gossip messages makes the cost 20 times larger. Finally, we observe that, while GOSSPLE's anonymity protocol continuously sends keep-alive messages, the only ones that impact bandwidth are those sent when new profile information needs to be exchanged.

4 Gossple at Work: Query Expansion

A query expansion system seeks to extend a query with additional keywords to improve the results. We now describe how to use GOSSPLE to expand queries within a collaborative tagging system, such as Delicious or CiteULike, where every node is associated with a tagging profile. As we show, GOSSPLE significantly improves the completeness (recall [14]) and accuracy (precision [14]) of the results, *wrt* the state-of-the-art centralized personalized approach, namely Social Ranking [4].

---
[3] The is burst is slightly longer on PlanetLab due to the lack of synchronization between nodes.

4.1 Overview

We use GOSSPLE *GNets* to compute a data structure we call *TagMap* (Figure 9), a personalized view of the relations between all tags in a node's profile and in its *GNet*. This is updated periodically to reflect the changes in the *GNet*. A query from the node is then expanded using the *TagMap* of that node through a *centrality* algorithm we call *GRank*, which we derived from the seminal *PageRank* [14] algorithm. While PageRank computes the relative importance of Web pages (eigenvector centrality [15]), *GRank* computes the relative importance of tags on a given node: we refer to this notion as the *tag centrality* from now on. *GRank* estimates the relevance of each tag in the *TagMap* wrt the query and assigns a score to the tag. We then recursively refine the correlation between tags by computing their distance using random walks, along the lines of [16].

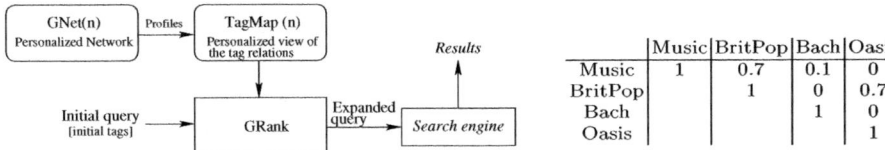

Fig. 9. Expanding queries with GOSSPLE

Fig. 10. Example of a TagMap

	Music	BritPop	Bach	Oasis
Music	1	0.7	0.1	0
BritPop		1	0	0.7
Bach			1	0
Oasis				1

4.2 TagMap

The *GNet* of a node n contains a set of profiles covering its interests. These profiles are used to compute the *TagMap* of a node n, namely a matrix $TagMap_n$, where $TagMap_n[t_i, t_j]$ is a score that reflects the distance between tags t_i and t_j as seen by node n. We denote by IS_n the information space of node n, namely its profile and the profiles in its *GNet*; T_{IS_n} and I_{IS_n} denote the set of all the tags and items in IS_n. The *TagMap* uses item-based cosine similarity to compute a score between the tags. The information needed to fill the *TagMap* is, for each tag in T_{IS_n}, the number of occurrences of the use of that tag per item, i.e., for all $t \in T_{IS_n}$, a vector $V_{n,t}$ of dimension $|I_{IS_n}|$ is maintained such that $V_t[item_i] = v$, where v is the number of times the item $item_i$ has been tagged with t in IS_n. More precisely: $TagMap_n[t_i, t_j] = cos(V_{n,t_i}, V_{n,t_j})$. Table 10 depicts an example of a node's *TagMap*. In this example $TagMap_n[Music, BritPop] = 0.7$.

4.3 GRank

The *TagMap* contains a personalized view of the scores between pairs of tags. This information can be directly used to expand queries as in [4]. In this approach, called *Direct Read (DR)*, the number of tags q added to the initial query is a parameter of the query expansion algorithm. With DR, a query is expanded with the q tags scoring the highest. More precisely: $DRscore_n(t_i) = \sum_{t \in query} TagMap[t, t_i]$. While this approach seems intuitive, it gives bad results when the item sparsity of the system is high. This is very likely to happen for niche content: with a very large number of items, the relationships between tags might not always be directly visible in the *TagMap*. To illustrate the issue, consider the *TagMap* presented in Table 10 and a query on *Music* with $q = 2$. The *TagMap* exhibits a high score between *Music* and *BritPop* (based on a given set of items). In addition, there is a low score between *Music* and *Bach* suggesting that the node is more interested in *BritPop* than in *Bach*. However *BritPop* and *Oasis* have also a high score in the same *TagMap* (gathered from a different set of items), DR will never associate *Music* and *Oasis* whilst this association seems relevant for that node. In fact, DR would instead expand the query with *Bach*, increasing the result set size and reducing the precision of the search (Figure 11).

Our approach is based on the observation that, by iterating on the set of newly added tags, more relevant tags can be selected for the query. We capture this idea through an algorithm inspired by *PageRank* [14], which we call *GRank*[4]. In short, *GRank* runs a personalized PageRank on the tag graph extracted from the *TagMap* and assigns the set of priors to the tags in the query. More specifically, considering the weighted graph provided by the *TagMap*, all the tags in T_{IS_n} are vertices and, for each non-null score in the *TagMap*, we add an edge weighted by the score. These scores affect the transition probabilities when generating the query expansion. As opposed to PageRank, where each link is chosen with equal probability, in *GRank*, the transition probability (TRP) from one tag to another depends on the edge weight provided by the *TagMap*: $TRP_n(t_1, t_2) = \frac{TagMap_n[t_1,t_2]}{\sum_{t \in T_{IS_n}} TagMap_n[t_1,t]}$

To limit the computation time of a score (which can be prohibitive in a large graph), instead of running an instance of *GRank* per query, we divide the computation per tag in the query, forming partial scores. These are approximated through random walks [16] and cached for further use whenever the same tag is used in a new query. Still, a centralized server computing *GRank* for all nodes would not scale. It can only be applied in the context of GOSSPLE where each node provides its processing power to compute its own *GRank*.

Expanding a query using *GRank* then simply consists in adding to the original query the q tags scoring the highest. All tags receive a score which is transmitted to the companion search engine.

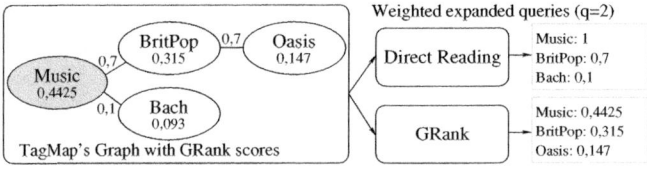

Fig. 11. Example of query expansion

---

[4] PageRank provides information about the importance of vertices in a graph. Personalized PageRank (PageRank with priors) compute centrality *wrt* a set of vertices.

4.4 Evaluation

We evaluated GOSSPLE's ability to achieve a complete and accurate query expansion. We describe our experimental setup, report on the evaluation of the GOSSPLE query expansion mechanisms on Delicious and CiteULike traces, and finally, we consider synthetic traces modeling the baby-sitter example given in the introduction, as well as the behavior of a mad tagger trying to disrupt GOSSPLE's operation.

Evaluation setup. **Workload.** Each node is associated with a user (and her profile) from a real trace (Delicious or CiteULike). The profiles drive the generation of requests: let I_n be the set of items in n's profile, n generates a query for each item $i \in I_n$ such that at least two users have i in their profiles. The initial query consists of the tags used by n to describe item i since they are also likely to be the ones n would use to search for i. We evaluate GOSSPLE's query expansion using the generated queries. Given a query from node n on an item i, we first remove i from n's profile so that n's *GNet* and *TagMap* are not built with it, then we determine if i is indeed an answer to the expanded query.

Search engine. Although any search engine could be used to process a query expanded by *GRank*, for the sake of comparison, we consider the search engine and ranking method used in [4]. The search engine runs on the set of items available in the real trace. An item is in the result set if it has been tagged at least once with one of the tags of the query. To rank the items, the score of an item is the sum, for each tag in the query, of the number of users who made an association between the item and the tag, multiplied by the weight of the tag.

Evaluation criteria. The query expansion mechanism is evaluated along the two classical and complementary metrics: *recall* (completeness) and *precision* (accuracy). Recall expresses the ability of the query expansion mechanism to generate a query that includes the relevant item in the result set. In these experiments, we are interested in the item i for which the query has been generated. A query succeeds when i is in the result set: recall is 1 if i is in the result set, 0 otherwise. Note that the size of the result set increases with the length of the query expansion, potentially reducing the visibility of the relevant item. To balance this effect, we also assess the quality of the query expansion by evaluating *precision*. We consider the absolute rank (based on the score provided by the search engine) of the items in the result set as a metric for precision: namely, the precision is defined as the difference between the rank with query expansion and the rank with the initial query.

Recall is evaluated on the queries that do not succeed without query expansion. This comprises 53% of the queries in the CiteULike trace and 25% in the Delicious one. These results show that a significant proportion of items have been tagged by several users with no tags in common and highlights the importance of query expansion. Precision is evaluated on the queries that are successful even without query expansion since they provide a reference rank for the item.

Impact of GOSSPLE*'s personalization.*
Our first results, in Figure 12, isolate the impact of personalization through a *TagMap* based on a small *GNet* wrt to a global *TagMap* based on all users' profiles. Figure 12 shows the extra recall obtained with query expansion sizes from 0 to 50 on the Delicious[5] traces with *GNet* sizes from 10 to 2,000. We compare these results with those of Social Raking, i.e. the case where *GNet* contains all the other users. The figure presents the proportion of items that

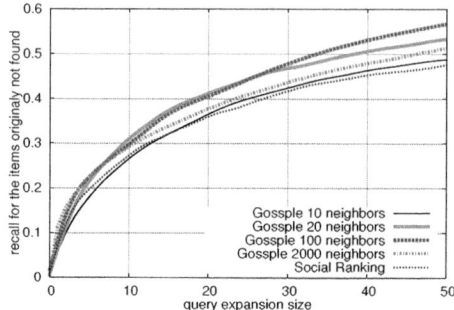

Fig. 12. Extra recall (Delicious)

were found with the query expansion out of the ones that were not found without. For example, the point ($x = 20, y = 0.37$) on the GOSSPLE 10-neighbor curve says that 37% of the requests not satisfied without query expansion are satisfied with a 20-tag expansion based on a *GNet* of 10 nodes.

The figure highlights the benefit of personalization over a *TagMap* that would involve all users such as Social Ranking. Even though increasing the size of the *GNet* up to 100 has a positive impact on recall, larger sizes degrade performance. With a 30-tag query expansion, a 10-node *GNet* has a recall of 43%; recall goes up to 47% in a 100-node network and drops to 42% in the case of Social Ranking. As the number of node profiles integrated in the *TagMap* increases, relevant tags are gradually *swallowed* by less relevant tags or popular ones. This is clearly an illustration of how the baby-sitter/teaching assistant association in the example presented in Section 1 could be diluted if we had considered all users.

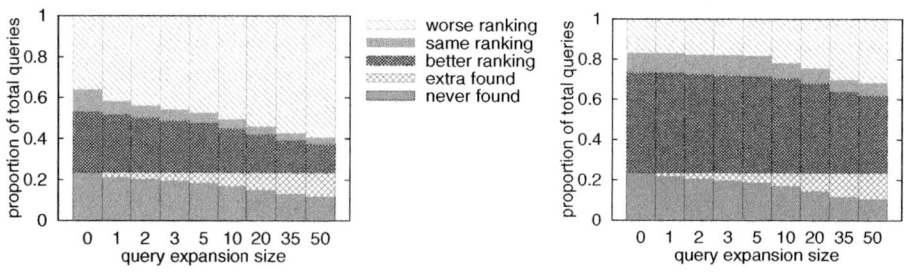

Fig. 13. Overall performance (Delicious) for Social Ranking (left) and GOSSPLE (right)

Impact of GOSSPLE*'s centrality.* We evaluate here the impact of computing the relative importance of tags (*GRank*) over the DR query expansion. As mentioned previously, personalization is mostly responsible for increasing recall. However,

---

[5] Experiments on the CiteULike trace lead to the same conclusions but the results are not presented for space reasons.

computing the relative importance of tags (i.e., tag centrality) significantly improves the precision of the results. This is clearly illustrated in Figure 13, which compares our results against those of the non personalized DR query expansion, i.e. Social Ranking.

On Figure 13(right), as the query expansion size increases, the recall for items which were not found initially, improves. With a 20-tag query expansion, we observe a 37% recall of the items which were not originally found. Yet, this is accompanied by a significant drop in the precision for 71% of the items originally found. *GRank* however with a 20-, resp. 50-tag query expansion, increases the recall of items not found initially up to 40%, resp. 56%, while increasing the ranking of approximately 58, 5% resp. 40% of the items which were returned to the initial query. This is a clear illustration of the impact of *GRank* on the precision. Interestingly enough, GOSSPLE improves the precision for approximately 50% of the items when using a query expansion of 0. This is due to the fact that in GOSSPLE the tags' weights reflect their importance.

To summarize, while the direct use of the *TagMap* improves the recall over existing approaches, mostly through personalization, the precision is significantly improved through the centrality provided by *GRank*. The latter is of utmost importance as the better precision enables us to expand queries with more tags.

Synthetic traces. We also assessed the benefit of GOSSPLE, on specific cases, through two synthetic traces. Due to space limitations, we only give an overview of these experiments. The first trace was generated to demonstrate the ability of GOSSPLE to address the baby-sitter example of the introduction with query expansion. The measures show that the personalized view, provided by GOSSPLE and leveraged in the GOSSPLE query expansion system, efficiently clustered users into interest communities enabling users interested in international schools and English novels to expand babysitter with teaching assistant. The second trace shows that the GOSSPLE personalization of *TagMap* limits the impact of a user trying to force an association between tags. We call this situation a GOSSPLE *bombing*, in reference to *Google bombing*. If an attacker builds a profile with very diverse items, then no node adds the attacker to its *GNet* and the attack fails. If the attacker targets a specific community, then it can have an impact on their query expansion, but the number of users affected is very limited.

5 Related Work

5.1 Semantic Overlays

Explicit approaches. Many user-centric approaches [17,18,5] consider an explicit (predefined) social network, typically derived from systems such as Facebook, LinkedIn, LastFM or MySpace, to improve the search on the Web. The assumption here is that the explicit, declared, relationships between users reflect their shared interests [19] and can help their search. In many cases, however, and as pointed out in [5,20], the information gathered from such networks turns out to be very limited in enhancing the navigation on the Web. A couple of alternative approaches exploit the unknown acquaintances of a user to improve the search further [21]. These require the user to explicitly declare a list of topics of interest and assume a strict topic classification, rendering it impossible to dynamically detect new communities. GOSSPLE goes a step further and automatically assigns acquaintances to users solely based on their common items: GOSSPLE's associations naturally evolve over time.

Implicit approaches. Some approaches form semantic acquaintances by associating users with those that successfully answered their queries in the past [12,22,23,24,25,26]. In file sharing communities, these approaches gradually transform a random overlay into weakly structured communities that improve the success ratio of queries. A major drawback is the need for a warm-up phase to establish the network based on a reasonable sample of queries: the first queries are sent to random users, leading to poor results. Furthermore, because the acquaintances of a user only reflect her last few queries, queries on new topics are inefficient. GOSSPLE actively locates the acquaintances of a user independently of her past queries but based on her (full interest) profile instead. In order to avoid the warm-up phase, some (active) clustering approaches rely on gossip. [13] uses the number of shared files in common as a proximity metric. While this approach improves search, it overloads generous nodes that share many files. [27] considers the cosine similarity of the users as a metric to penalize non-shared interests. This gives better performance than simple overlap and underlies our GOSSPLE metric. These approaches also tend to choose uniform acquaintances that only reflect the primary interest of a user, while GOSSPLE spreads the acquaintances among all the interests of a user. As discussed in [28], a user has usually several areas of interests, typically non-correlated: on average, a node requires three clusters to find 25% of the data it is looking for. [29] uses gossip to select semantic acquaintances for RSS feed transmission. The selection algorithm increases the score of nodes that provide items not covered by other acquaintances. GOSSPLE's multi-interest metric can be considered a generalization of this idea.

In [30], a centralized ontology-based analysis of all the items in the system assigns a type to each one of them and infers users' interests. This procedure is centralized and relies on an external source of knowledge for the classification, while GOSSPLE is fully distributed and only uses the item interest pattern of users as a source of information. In [31], the attributes of the items generate a navigable overlay. This approach is centered on items rather than users, and does not scale with the number of items a user shares. It is also limited to items which carry a lot of metadata, like music or text files. The system proposed in [32] is fully distributed: it clusters items in order to obtain semantic coordinates. The node joins the unstructured community responsible for most of its items and obtains small-world links to other communities. Although the node has to advertise the items which are not part of its main community, this approach scales quite well with the size of the user profile. However, it suffers from the same drawback as [31] and requires items with a lot of metadata for clustering.

5.2 Query Expansion

Personalized systems. Personalized query expansion has so far considered two approaches. The first consists in leveraging information about users' past behavior. In [33], the query is expanded by tags already used in previous queries. In [34], the query is expanded using the information available on the user's local computer. The tags are chosen with a local search engine and completed by user feedback. In both cases, no information is inferred from other users. The second approach [17,18,5] consists in enhancing the queries using an explicit social network of the user. As already discussed, this is not always appropriate.

Global approaches. Centralized Web search engines often rely on handwritten taxonomies (Wordnet, Open Directory Project, Yahoo! Directories) to expand queries. Instead, we only consider knowledge that is automatically extracted from the user's profile. [35] proposes a query-expansion framework that uses social relations to rank results. However, only the scoring model is personalized. The query-expansion mechanism exploits the co-occurrence of tags in the full document collection leading to a non-personalized query-expansion output. Social Ranking [4] is somehow similar but relies on the cosine similarity of tags to infer their proximity. This is, in a sense, the closest to our query expansion technique. We presented our comparison in Section 4.4.

6 Concluding Remarks

We presented GOSSPLE, an Internet-scale protocol that discovers connections between users and leverages them to enhance navigation within the Web 2.0. With little information stored and exchanged, every GOSSPLE node (user) is associated with a relevant network of anonymous acquaintances. Nodes can join and leave the system dynamically and the profile of a node that left the system is eventually automatically removed from all personalized networks. No central authority is involved and there is no single point of failure. Decentralization makes it furthermore possible to effectively perform certain tasks, such as computing the *TagMap* and the *GRank*, which would have been computationally prohibitive in a centralized system. Interestingly, GOSSPLE naturally copes with certain forms of free-riding: nodes do need to participate in the gossiping in order to be visible and receive profile information. As we have also shown, the impact of arbitrary tagging, or even individual malicious tagging, is very limited.

Yet, GOSSPLE has some limitations and many extensions might need to be considered. Our gossip-on-behalf approach is simple and lightweight, but users may require additional security even by enduring a higher network cost. It would be interesting to devise schemes where extra costs are only paid by users that demand more guarantees. It would also be interesting to explore the benefits of a social network of explicit friends. For instance, GOSSPLE could take such links into account as a ground knowledge for establishing the personalized network of a user and automatically add new implicit semantic acquaintances. This would pose non-trivial anonymity challenges.

References

1. Web 2.0, www.citeulike.org, www.delicious.com, www.flickr.com, www.last.fm
2. Yildirim, H., Krishnamoorthy, M.S.: A random walk method for alleviating the sparsity problem in collaborative filtering. In: RecSys, pp. 131–138 (2008)
3. Cattuto, C., Benz, D., Hotho, A., Stumme, G.: Semantic analysis of tag similarity measures in collaborative tagging systems. In: OLP3, pp. 39–43 (2008)
4. Zanardi, V., Capra, L.: Social ranking: uncovering relevant content using tag-based recommender systems. In: RecSys, pp. 51–58 (2008)
5. Bender, M., Crecelius, T., Kacimi, M., Miche, S., Xavier Parreira, J., Weikum, G.: Peer-to-peer information search: Semantic, social, or spiritual? TCDE 30(2), 51–60 (2007)
6. McGill, M., Salton, G.: Introduction to modern information retrieval (1986)
7. Jelasity, M., Voulgaris, S., Guerraoui, R., Kermarrec, A.M., van Steen, M.: Gossip-based peer sampling. TOCS 25(3) (2007)
8. Bortnikov, E., Gurevich, M., Keidar, I., Kliot, G., Shraer, A.: Brahms: byzantine resilient random membership sampling. In: PODC, pp. 145–154 (2008)
9. Bloom, B.H.: Space/time trade-offs in hash coding with allowable errors. CACM 13(7), 422–426 (1970)
10. Syverson, P.F., Goldschlag, D.M., Reed, M.G.: Anonymous connections and onion routing. In: SP, pp. 44–59 (1997)
11. Yu, H., Kaminsky, M., Gibbons, P.B., Flaxman, A.D.: Sybilguard: defending against sybil attacks via social networks. TON 16(3), 576–589 (2008)
12. Handurukande, S.B., Kermarrec, A.M., Le Fessant, F., Massoulie, L., Patarin, S.: Peer Sharing Behaviour in the eDonkey Network, and Implications for the Design of Server-less File Sharing Systems. In: EuroSys, pp. 359–371 (2006)
13. Voulgaris, S., van Steen, M.: Epidemic-style management of semantic overlays for content-based searching. In: Europar, pp. 1143–1152 (2005)
14. Brin, S., Page, L.: The anatomy of a large-scale hypertextual web search engine. Computer Networks and ISDN Systems 30(1-7), 107–117 (1998)
15. Abiteboul, S., Preda, M., Cobena, G.: Adaptive on-line page importance computation. In: WWW, pp. 280–290 (2003)
16. Fogaras, D., Rácz, B., Csalogány, K., Sarlós, T.: Towards scaling fully personalized pagerank: Algorithms, lower bounds, and experiments. Internet Mathematics 2(3), 333–358 (2005)
17. Amer-Yahia, S., Benedikt, M., Lakshmanan, L., Stoyanovich, J.: Efficient network aware search in collaborative tagging sites. In: VLDB, pp. 710–721 (2008)
18. Mislove, A., Gummadi, K.P., Druschel, P.: Exploiting social networks for internet search. In: HotNets (2006)
19. Mislove, A., Marcon, M., Gummadi, K.P., Druschel, P., Bhattacharjee, B.: Measurement and analysis of online social networks. In: IMC, pp. 29–42 (2007)
20. Ahn, Y.Y., Han, S., Kwak, H., Moon, S., Jeong, H.: Analysis of topological characteristics of huge online social networking services. In: WWW, pp. 835–844 (2007)
21. Khambatti, M., Ryu, K.D., Dasgupta, P.: Structuring peer-to-peer networks using interest-based communities. In: DBISP2P, pp. 48–63 (2003)
22. Sripanidkulchai, K., Maggs, B., Zhang, H.: Efficient content location using interest-based locality in peer-to-peer systems. INFOCOM 3, 2166–2176 (2003)
23. Cholvi, V., Felber, P., Biersack, E.: Efficient search in unstructured peer-to-peer networks. In: SPAA, pp. 271–272 (2004)

24. Chen, G., Low, C.P., Yang, Z.: Enhancing search performance in unstructured p2p networks based on users' common interest. TPDS 19(6), 821–836 (2008)
25. Sedmidubsky, J., Barton, S., Dohnal, V., Zezula, P.: Adaptive approximate similarity searching through metric social networks. In: ICDE, pp. 1424–1426 (2008)
26. Eyal, A., Gal, A.: Self organizing semantic topologies in p2p data integration systems. In: ICDE, pp. 1159–1162 (2009)
27. Jin, H., Ning, X., Chen, H.: Efficient search for peer-to-peer information retrieval using semantic small world. In: WWW, pp. 1003–1004 (2006)
28. Le-Blond, S., Guillaume, J.L., Latapy, M.: Clustering in p2p exchanges and consequences on performances. In: Castro, M., van Renesse, R. (eds.) IPTPS 2005. LNCS, vol. 3640, pp. 193–204. Springer, Heidelberg (2005)
29. Patel, J.A., Rivière, Ł., Gupta, I., Kermarrec, A.M.: Rappel: Exploiting interest and network locality to improve fairness in publish-subscribe systems. Computer Networks 53(13), 2304–2320 (2009)
30. Crespo, A., Garcia-Molina, H.: Semantic overlay networks for p2p systems. In: Moro, G., Bergamaschi, S., Aberer, K. (eds.) AP2PC 2004. LNCS (LNAI), vol. 3601, pp. 1–13. Springer, Heidelberg (2005)
31. Banaei-Kashani, F., Shahabi, C.: Swam: a family of access methods for similarity-search in peer-to-peer data networks. In: CIKM, pp. 304–313 (2004)
32. Li, M., Lee, W.C., Sivasubramaniam, A., Zhao, J.: Ssw: A small-world-based overlay for peer-to-peer search. TPDS 19(6), 735–749 (2008)
33. Carman, M., Baillie, M., Crestani, F.: Tag data and personalized information retrieval. In: SSM, pp. 27–34 (2008)
34. Jie, H., Zhang, Y.: Personalized faceted query expansion. In: SIGIR (2006)
35. Bender, M., Crecelius, T., Kacimi, M., Michel, S., Neumann, T., Parreira, J.X., Schenkel, R., Weikum, G.: Exploiting social relations for query expansion and result ranking. In: ICDE Workshops, pp. 501–506 (2008)

Prometheus: User-Controlled P2P Social Data Management for Socially-Aware Applications

Nicolas Kourtellis[1], Joshua Finnis[1], Paul Anderson[1], Jeremy Blackburn[1], Cristian Borcea[2], and Adriana Iamnitchi[1]

[1] Department of Computer Science and Engineering, University of South Florida
{nkourtel,jfinnis,paanders,jhblackb,anda}@cse.usf.edu
[2] Department of Computer Science, New Jersey Institute of Technology
borcea@cs.njit.edu

Abstract. Recent Internet applications, such as online social networks and user-generated content sharing, produce an unprecedented amount of social information, which is further augmented by location or collocation data collected from mobile phones. Unfortunately, this wealth of social information is fragmented across many different proprietary applications. Combined, it could provide a more accurate representation of the social world, and it could enable a whole new set of socially-aware applications.

We introduce Prometheus, a peer-to-peer service that collects and manages social information from multiple sources and implements a set of social inference functions while enforcing user-defined access control policies. Prometheus is socially-aware: it allows users to select peers that manage their social information based on social trust and exploits naturally-formed social groups for improved performance. We tested our Prometheus prototype on PlanetLab and built a mobile social application to test the performance of its social inference functions under real-time constraints. We showed that the social-based mapping of users onto peers improves the service response time and high service availability is achieved with low overhead.

Keywords: social data management, P2P networks, socially-aware applications.

1 Introduction

Recently, we have witnessed the emergence of a wealth of socially-aware applications, which utilize users' social information to provide features such as filtering restaurant recommendations based on reviews by friends (e.g., Yelp), recommending email recipients or filtering spam based on previous email activity [19], and exploiting social incentives for computer resource sharing [37]. Social information is also leveraged in conjunction with location/collocation data to provide novel mobile applications such as Loopt, Brightkite, Foursquare and Google's Latitude.

These applications need to collect, store, and use sensitive social information (including location and collocation). The state of the art is to collect and manage such information within the context of an application (as in the examples above) or to expose this information from platforms that specifically collect it, such as online social networks (OSN). For example, Facebook allows third-party application developers and websites to access the social information of its roughly 500 million users. Similarly, OpenSocial provides a common API for third-party applications to access social information stored on any of the supported social networks.

However, relying on social information exposed by OSNs has two major problems. First, the hidden incentives for users to have as many "friends" as possible lead to declarations of contacts with little connection in terms of trust, common interests, shared objectives, or other such manifestations of (real) social relationships [12]. Thus, an application that tries to provide targeted functionalities must wade through a lot of noise. Second, the business plans of the companies behind the social networks often conflict with the need to respect user privacy. Additionally, some social networks institute particularly draconian policies concerning the ownership of user-contributed information and content. For example, users cannot easily delete their OSN profiles, as in the case of Facebook which owns their data; they cannot export their social data to a service of their choice; and their social information has restricted use.

This paper presents Prometheus, a peer-to-peer service for user-controlled social data management that enables innovative socially-aware applications. Prometheus collects social information from multiple sources (e.g., OSNs, email, mobile phones) by quantifying the actual social interactions between users. Thus, it maintains richer and more nuanced social information, which can lead to more accurate inferences of trust, interests, and context. Prometheus implements and exposes to applications several social inference functions.

The choice of a peer-to-peer (P2P) architecture was motivated by two factors: user privacy and service availability. We considered two alternative architectures. In a centralized architecture (as in current OSNs) there are no incentives or appropriate business models to store social data for free and allow users to control the privacy of their data. Prometheus leverages the P2P infrastructure of Mobius [4] to provide user-controlled social data management and social inferences for services and applications. An alternative architecture stores social information on users' mobile devices, as proposed in [26,27,34,36]. Even though much of the social information is nowadays generated by mobile devices, they are inherently unsuitable for running a complex social service such as Prometheus due to resource constraints: the mobile devices may not be always online or synchronized to provide fast and efficient inference support, and energy and computation power may be scarce.

Prometheus gives users the ultimate control over where their private information is stored in the system, and which applications and users are allowed to access it. We ensure data security and access control on the peers using built-in public-key cryptography primitives and user-defined access control policies.

We prototyped and evaluated Prometheus on a large-scale deployment on PlanetLab and tested its performance with realistic workloads. The results show that the response time for social inferences decreases when user information is mapped onto peers using a social-aware approach. Furthermore, high service availability is achieved with low overhead. To test the Prometheus service under real-time deadlines, we implemented CallCensor, a mobile social application that uses Prometheus to decide whether to filter out incoming calls based on the current social context. The response time for this application running on a Google Android phone meets the real-time deadlines, proving that the Prometheus service overhead is reasonable.

An overview of the Prometheus service is presented in Section 2, and related work is covered in Section 3. Section 4 presents a detailed design of Prometheus, and Section 5 describes the experimental evaluation. We conclude in Section 6.

2 Prometheus Overview

Prometheus is a peer-to-peer service that enables socially-aware applications by collecting information from multiple sources and exposing it through an interface that implements non-trivial social inferences. This is accomplished via decentralized storage and management of a weighted, labeled, directed multi-edge social graph on user-contributed nodes. The access to social data is controlled by user defined policies.

Specifically, users register with Prometheus and allow it to collect social information about them from multiple sources that we refer to as *social sensors*. Social sensors are applications running on behalf of a user which report to Prometheus information such as interactions with other users via email, phone, instant messaging, comments on blogs, ratings on user-generated content, or even face-to-face interactions determined from collocation data. Social sensors can therefore be deployed on the user's devices (e.g., mobile phone) or on the Web (e.g., as a Facebook application reporting wall writing interactions).

The information collected by social sensors is processed by Prometheus to create a decentralized, weighted, directed, and labeled multi-edged graph, where vertices correspond to users and edges correspond to interactions between users as reported by social sensors. The interactions are described with a label (e.g., "work", "hiking") and a weight that specifies the intensity of the interaction. Prometheus uses this decentralized graph to answer various social queries from applications. Both the social information from sensors and the social subgraphs are stored and maintained in a P2P network formed by user PCs. The information from sensors is stored in an encrypted form and can be decrypted only by "trusted" peers, which are selected by users. The subgraph of each user is stored on her trusted peers. The trusted peers also enforce user-defined access control policies for each social query.

Figure 1 presents the Prometheus architecture. Prometheus runs on top of Pastry [31], a distributed hash table (DHT)-based overlay, and uses Past [32] for replicated storage of sensor data. Each user has a group of trusted peers responsible for maintaining replicas of her social subgraph for high service availability. Only trusted peers can decrypt the user's social data. The maintenance of the

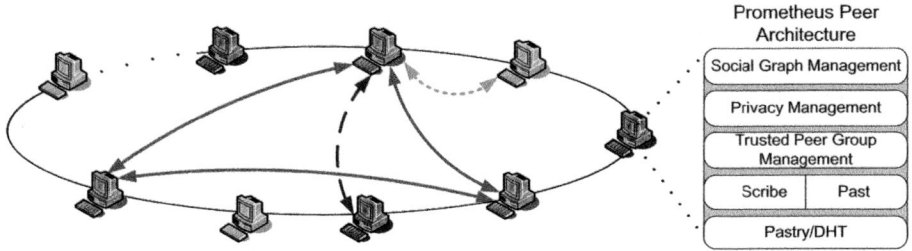

Fig. 1. Prometheus architecture: The service runs on top of Pastry, a DHT-based overlay, Scribe, a DHT multicast infrastructure, and Past, a DHT storage system. The social data from sensors are encrypted and can be stored at any peer. The social subgraphs are stored on groups of trusted peers. Each peer runs three Prometheus components for social graph management, privacy management, and trusted group management. Same color nodes are members of a user's trusted peer group. Continuous (*red*) arrows show group communication for social graph maintenance, while dashed (*blue* and *green*) arrows show social inference queries submitted to other peers.

trusted peer group is done by leveraging Scribe [6], an application-level DHT multicast infrastructure.

Prometheus exposes an interface that enables applications to have access to a rich set of social inference requests computed over the distributed social graph. For example, an application can request on its user's behalf to receive the top relations (a function of a specified label and weight) of its user. Similarly, it can request the social strength between its user and another user not directly connected in the social graph. Prometheus provides the mechanism by which inference requests can access not only a single user's social graph (i.e., directly connected users), but also the social information of users located several hops away in the global social graph.

All inferences are subject to users' access control policies. These policies allow users to have fine-grained control over the access of all or parts of their graph by other users. For example, these policies can specify access control as a function of social labels. Prometheus uses a public-key infrastructure (PKI) to ensure both message confidentiality and user authentication. Each user and group has its own pair of public/private keys. For access control purposes, users are identified by their public keys. Social sensors use the appropriate keys to encrypt the data submitted to Prometheus.

Prometheus not only enables novel socially-aware applications but also specifically takes advantage of social-based incentives. Social awareness is embedded in the design of Prometheus in two ways. First, Prometheus allows users to select trusted peers to maintain their social subgraph based on out-of-band relationships. Socially-incentivized users keep their computers online, thus reducing churn [22] and consequently increasing service availability for their friends' social inference requests. Second, given the characteristics of social graphs, socially-related users will likely select the same trusted peers to store their social subgraphs (i.e., friends have common friends who contribute peers in the system and thus select the same trusted peers). This allows complex social inferences over several social graph hops to be fulfilled locally, without traversing multiple network hops to access all the needed social information.

3 Related Work

Socially-aware applications and services have so far addressed ways to leverage out-of-band social relationships for diverse objectives such as improving security [41], inferring trust [23], providing incentives for resource sharing [37], or building overlays [28] for private communication. Leveraging online social information has been used to rank Internet search results relative to the interests of a user's neighborhood in the social network [13], to favor socially-connected users in a BitTorrent swarm [29], and to reduce unwanted communication [25].

In all of these cases, social knowledge has been mined in the context of a single application and from a single source of information. Our work differs from these systems in four important ways. First, we collect information from multiple sources. The only system we are aware of that considers social information aggregation for enriching information value is SONAR [16]. Unlike our approach, SONAR is limited to improving information flow in an organization by aggregating social network information within the enterprise context, from sources such as email, instant messaging, etc. Second, we extract social knowledge from the social graph by accessing larger portions of the network, not only a user's direct neighborhood. Somewhat similarly, RE [11] uses two hop relationships to automatically populate email whitelists. Third, in Prometheus, social information can cross application boundary contexts, similar to Ramachandran and Feamster's proposal to "export" the social ties formed in social networks for authentication in off-social applications [30]. And finally, our social graph representation offers richer information for fine-grained evaluation of social ties. Kahanda and Neville also represent interactions with a weighted, directed multi-edged graph [17]. Prometheus differs in its generality of the graph—its edges can represent interactions collected from different sources.

APIs for accessing social information has been offered by Facebook through its Open Graph API [1] for access to simple, unprocessed social data. This API does not provide direct "friends of friends" inferences as Prometheus does, but instead an application must explicitly crawl the graph.

Privacy in Online Social Networks (OSNs) through decentralization has been addressed in [7]. Prometheus similarly forwards messages based on social relations while restricting a large scale view of the graph through a P2P mechanism. Prometheus differs dramatically, however, in the exposure of the graph as a first class data object through inference functionality. Persona [3] uses an attribute-based encryption (ABE) to provide privacy in OSNs. Prometheus can leverage this system to provide more flexible access control policies.

Peer-to-peer management of social data is also proposed in PeerSoN [5] and Vis-à-Vis [35]. PeerSoN uses direct data exchange between users' devices.

Prometheus differs from this approach by using trusted peers, which are independent from the users' devices, to store and exchange social data. Vis-à-Vis introduces the concept of a Virtual Individual Server (VIS) where each user's data are stored on a personal virtual machine. While similar to the trusted peer concept in Prometheus, VISs are hosted by a cloud computing provider to counter peer churn, while Prometheus uses social incentives to reduce churn on user-supplied peers.

Our work significantly differs from the previously noted approaches in that it not only collects and stores user social information from multiple sources in a P2P network but also exposes social inference functions useful for novel socially-aware applications. This approach shares ideas with the MobiSoc middleware[15]; however, the MobiSoc middleware is logically centralized leading to "big brother" concerns similar to existing OSNs.

4 Prometheus Design

4.1 User Registration

Users register with Prometheus from a trusted device by contacting any peer in the network and are assigned a unique user id (UID). At registration time, they specify the peer(s) they will contribute to the network (if any). The peer handling the registration creates a mapping between UID and the list of these peers' IP addresses. This mapping is stored in the network as the key-value pair UID={IP_1, ..., IP_n}. When a peer returns from an offline state, it updates the mapping with its current IP address. Users have a pair of public/private keys, and the mappings are signed with their private key.

Users select, deploy, and configure the social sensors they want to use. They may wish to declare particular social relationships, such as family relations, that may prove difficult or impossible to infer by social sensors. Finally, they select an initial set of trusted peers based on out-of-bound trust relations with other Prometheus users. The larger the size of this set, the higher the service availability; but at the same time, the consistency and the overall performance may decrease. Users have also a pair of public/private keys for their trusted peer group. The group keys are transferred to each group peer by encrypting them with the peer's owner public keys. As social information about a new user will be incorporated in the social graph, users may be prompted with different choices for trusted peers (e.g., peers belonging to users with stronger ties).

4.2 Trusted Peer Group Management

We address three issues concerning the trusted peer group management of a user: (a) group membership, (b) search for trusted peers, and (c) group churn.

A user can add peers in the trusted peer group by executing a secure three-way handshake procedure which establishes a two-way trust relationship between her and the peer owner. All the messages in this exchange are signed and verified. If the owner of a candidate peer accepts a peer addition request, the initiator will send the group keys to the new peer as described above. Then, the new peer subscribes to the Scribe *Trusted_Peer_Group_UID* of the user.

If a user decides to remove a peer from the trusted group (e.g., she no longer trusts the peer's owner), the user submits an unsubscribe request to one of the other trusted peers. This request is multicast to all group peers. Then, the peer generates a new pair of public/private keys for the group; this pair is distributed to all other trusted peers except the newly removed one. Additionally, the social sensors must be informed that the public key of the group has been changed. A peer owner may also decide to remove her peer from a trusted group of another user. This request is multicast to all the other group members.

Service requests can be sent to any peer, but only the trusted peers of a user can provide data about that user. Therefore, a random peer can find trusted peers for a user by submitting a multicast request to the user's trusted peer group. The group peers respond with their signed membership which is verified for authenticity with the user's group public key. The random peer is subsequently able to directly communicate with the individual trusted peers.

Past replicates the sensor data, thus maintaining data availability. However, the social graph for a user is unavailable if all her trusted peers leave the network; no service requests involving this user can be answered until a trusted peer rejoins the network. We ensure that generated data (e.g., input from social sensors) are not lost while a user's group is down via replication in the DHT by PAST. If a peer becomes untrusted while offline, a trusted peer from the particular group instructs the returning peer to unsubscribe.

4.3 Geo-social Graph Representation

Prometheus represents the social graph as introduced in [2]: a directed, labeled, and weighted multi-edged graph, maintained and used in a decentralized fashion, as presented in Figure 2.

Multiple edges can connect two users, and each edge is labeled with a type of social interaction and assigned a weight that represents the intensity of that interaction. The labels for interactions and their associated weights are assigned by sensors. From an application point of view, distinguishing between different types of interactions allows for better functionality. Weights are assigned as a function of the number and frequency of interactions. This allows for a more accurate estimation of relationship strengths [40]. The latest known location of a user is also maintained as an attribute of the vertex representing the user in the graph.

We chose to represent the graph as directed because of the well-accepted result in sociology that "ties are usually asymmetrically reciprocal" [38]. Representing edges as directed enhances security by limiting the potential effects of illegitimate graph manipulation. For example, if Alice repeatedly performs interactions with Bob that are not reciprocated, only the edge connecting Alice to Bob will have its weight increased, not the edge from Bob to Alice.

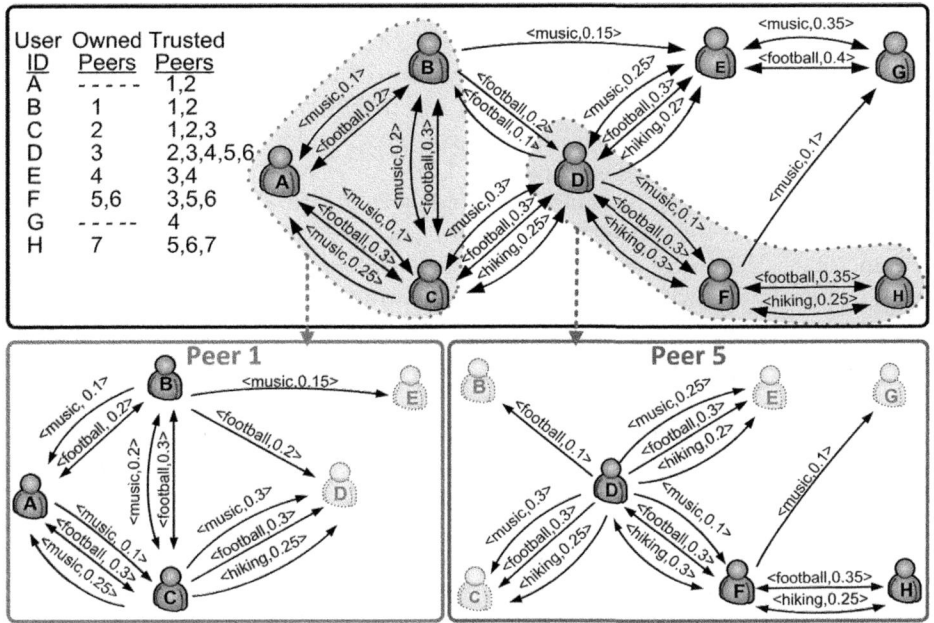

Fig. 2. An example of a social graph for eight users (*A-H*) who own seven peers. The mapping between users, peer owners, and trusted peers is shown in the upper left corner. Each edge is marked with its label and weight. The bottom figures illustrate the subgraphs maintained by peers *1* and *5*. Users shown in dark color (e.g., users *A*, *B* and *C* on peer *1*) trust the peer to manage their social data. Users shown in light shaded color (e.g., users *E and D* on peer *1*) do not trust the peer but are socially connected with users who do.

4.4 Social Sensors

Two types of social ties can typically be inferred from user interactions. The first type, *object-centric* ties, is identified through the use of similar resources or participation in common activities. Examples include tagging the same items in collaborative tagging communities such as Delicious or CiteULike and repeatedly being part of the same BitTorrent swarms. The second type, *people-centric* ties, is determined from declared social relationships (e.g., in online social networks), declared membership to groups (e.g., networks in Facebook or company name in LinkedIn), or collocation information.

Social sensors are applications that are installed on the user's mobile device or PC that aggregate and analyze the history of user's interactions with other users and report to Prometheus labels and weights corresponding to directed edges. These social data are encrypted with the public key of the user's trusted group, signed with the user's private key, and stored in the DHT by Past. Note that if web sensors (such as Facebook applications) are used, the data have to be first sent to one of the user's devices to be signed and encrypted. The data for each user are stored as records in an append-only file, named *Social_Data_UID*. Only the trusted peers can decrypt these records.

We designed Prometheus to be oblivious to the types of social activity reported by social sensors, thus allowing extensibility. For example, many such sensors already exist, although they have been implemented in different contexts; these sensors record and quantify OSNs' user activity [21], co-appearance on web pages [24], or co-presence recorded as collocation via Bluetooth [8]. Sensors can perform relatively sophisticated analysis before sending the data to Prometheus. For instance, collocation social sensors can differentiate between routine encounters with familiar strangers and interactions between friends [8].

4.5 Social State Maintenance

The social data for each user are stored in the file *Social_Data_UID* as encrypted records. To ensure atomic appends, a lock file associated with the data file is created by the sensor trying to append a record. Other sensors trying to append concurrently will receive an error when trying to create this file. Once the append is done, the lock file is deleted. Since the file is append-only, readers can access it at any time: in the worst case, they will miss the latest update.

Social sensors can send updates to create new edges, remove old edges, or modify an edge weight. Each record contains a sequence number and encrypted data with the label and its associated weight. Trusted peers periodically check the file for new records and retrieve all such records: this is easily done based on sequence number comparison starting from the end of the file. The peer decrypts the new records and verifies the digital signature to make sure the updates are authentic. Then, it updates the subgraph of the user with the newly retrieved records. For short periods of time, the trusted peers may have inconsistent data, but this is not a major problem as social graphs do not change often.

Social sensors may specify that certain edges must be "aged" over time if no new updates for those edges are received (i.e., lack of social interactions associated with those labels). The social sensors may also specify the decrement value and the time period for aging (these values are also stored in the *Social_Data_UID* file for each user).

4.6 Service Interface

Prometheus implements in a distributed fashion a set of basic social inference functions, which are exposed to applications through a service interface. We assume that every device running an application that interacts with Prometheus caches a number of peer IP addresses to bootstrap the interaction.

Social Inference Functions: We implemented the following social inference functions; more complex inferences can be built on top of this set.

relation_test(ego, alter, α, x) is a boolean function that checks whether *ego* is directly connected to *alter* in the social subgraph of *ego* by an edge with label α and with a minimum weight of x. A mobile phone application can use this function, for example, to determine whether an incoming call is from a coworker with a strong social tie, and therefore, should be let through even on weekends.

top_relations(ego, α, n) returns the top *n* users in the social subgraph of *ego* (ordered by decreasing weights) who are directly connected to *ego* by an edge with label α. An application can use this function, for example, to invite users highly connected with *ego* to share content related to activity α.

neighborhood(ego, α, x, radius) returns the set of users in *ego*'s social neighborhood of size *radius* who are connected through social ties of a label α and minimum weight of *x*. The *radius* parameter allows for a multiple hop search in the social graph (e.g., setting *radius* to 2 will find friends of friends). Our Call-Censor mobile phone application which silences *ego*'s cell phone during meetings at work (Section 5.3) uses this function to determine if a caller is in *ego*'s work neighborhood in the social graph even if not directly connected.

proximity(ego, α, x, radius, min_distance, timestamp) is an extension of the neighborhood function which filters the results of the social neighborhood inference based on physical distance to *ego*. After the location information is collected for *ego* and the set of users is returned by *neighborhood*, *proximity* returns the set of users who are within *min_distance* from *ego*. A mobile phone application might use this function to infer the list of collocated coworkers within a certain distance of *ego*. Users who do not share the location or have location information older than the *timestamp* will not be returned.

social_strength(ego, alter) returns a real number in the range of [0, 1] that quantifies the social strength between *ego* and *alter* from *ego*'s perspective. The two users can be multiple hops apart in the social graph. The return value is normalized, as shown below, to *ego*'s social ties to ensure that the social strength is less sensitive to the social activity of the users. *NW* is the normalized weight between two directly connected users, *K* is the path length joining two indirect users, N_i is a user in this path, *w* is the weight of an edge, and *strength* is the return value for a multi-hop path:

$$NW(ego, neighbor_i) = \frac{\sum_{all-labels} w(ego, neighbor_i)}{\max_{all-neighbors}\left(\sum_{all-labels} w(ego, neighbor)\right)}. \quad (1)$$

$$strength\bigl(path(N_1, N_2, \ldots, N_K)\bigr) = \max_{all-paths} \frac{\min_{i=1,\ldots,K-1}\bigl(NW(N_i, N_{i+1})\bigr)}{K}. \quad (2)$$

Such a function could be used, for example, to estimate social incentives for resource sharing. We limit the length of the indirect path that connects two users to two, using a well-accepted result in sociology known as the "horizon of observability" [9].

Inference Function Execution: Social inference requests are signed with the private key of the user who submitted them and sent to any Prometheus peer.

The request will then be forwarded to one of the trusted peers of the user, which enforces the access control policies and verifies the submitter's identity through her public key. The peer fulfills the request by traversing the local social subgraph for the information requested by the application, encrypting and signing the result using the requesting user's public key and the trusted group's private key, respectively, and returning the result to the application.

For functions that need to traverse the graph for more than one hop (e.g., social_strength), the peer will forward requests for information about other users to their trusted peers. The requests include the UID of the original submitter (in order to verify her access rights). The peer signs these requests with the group private key and optionally encrypts them with the destination group public key. Each receiving peer authenticates the request and checks the access control policies for the requesting user. If the request is granted, the result is returned to the requesting peer. If the request still needs more information, the peer repeats the same process. Finally, the original requesting peer collects recursively all the replies and submits the final result to the application.

4.7 Access Control Policies

Users can specify access control policies (ACP) upon registration and can update them any time thereafter. These policies are stored on each trusted peer of the user and are applied each time an inference request is handled by these peers. For availability, the policies are also stored encrypted with the group public key in the DHT, thus allowing rejoining trusted peers to recover policies updated while the peer was offline. The same mechanism used for updating the social graph is used to update policies. As future work, we plan to investigate providing strong consistency for policies.

Currently, we consider four different categories of social information for which users can set access control policies: relations, labels, weights, and location. By design, ACPs are whitelists. To specify who is allowed to access these categories of social information, ACPs allow the following elements to appear: individual users, groups of users identified by labels, application name to allow access to certain applications no matter which user runs them, and number of social hops the requesting users must be within. To verify the access rights, Prometheus may call its inference functions. For example, to detect whether the originator of the request is within a certain number of hops, the originator is checked against the result of a two-hop *neighborhood* function. ACPs also allow for blacklisted users to provide convenience in the case that a user wants to provide access to a large set of users and exclude a small number of members of that set.

Relations, labels, and weights allow fine-grained control over access to users' social graphs. Setting the relations field would prevent any user not allowed access from completing an inference that asks whether the user is connected with some other user, which accounts for most social inferences. Social inference functions which make use of labels as a filter provide an increased amount of data about a user; hence, it is likely that users will set this field more restrictively than the relations field. Prometheus allows users to set restrictions for any label

```
               relations: hops-2
               hiking-label: lbl-hiking
               work-label: lbl-work
               general-label:
               weights:
               location: hops-1
               ------------------
               blacklist: user-Eve
```

Fig. 3. Example of an access control policy in Prometheus

in their social graph in their ACP. Upon an inference request, Prometheus will first check to see if the specific label has any restrictions, and if not, check the "general-label" category for restrictions on all labels. Weights provide even more detail about user social graphs. Users can set additional restrictions upon social inferences that request weighted data. Finally, location governs access to any inference function which asks for a user's location.

Figure 3 shows an example ACP for Alice that disallows any social inference that makes use of the social graph (through the relations field) originating from a user outside of two social hops, with an additional restriction that only those connected to her with a "hiking" label can request social inferences for her "hiking" information, excluding the user Eve. Social inferences which use location are restricted to those she is directly connected with. If a "hiking" neighborhood inference is submitted to Alice, Prometheus checks her ACP in the order relations→hiking-label→weights.

5 Experimental Evaluation

We implemented Prometheus on top of the FreePastry Java implementation of Pastry DHT which also provides API support for Scribe and Past. The social graph management is implemented in Python. The Prometheus prototype was deployed and evaluated on PlanetLab.

Our evaluation had three goals: (1) measure Prometheus performance over a large scale worldwide distributed network using realistic workloads with a large number of users, created based on previous studies of social media user behavior; (2) assess the effect of socially-aware trusted peer selection on the system's overall performance; and (3) validate Prometheus with a social application developed on mobile phones and measure the performance of this application. An implicit goal was to identify potential performance optimizations, as we focused so far on building a robust end-to-end system. The two metrics used in this evaluation were *end-to-end response time* to quantify the user-perceived performance and *number of network messages* to quantify the service overhead.

In the first set of experiments, we used 100 peers deployed on PlanetLab, and each peer submitted workload on behalf of 1000 users. The number of users trusting each peer was varied from 10 to 30, i.e., each user trusted 1 and 3 peers respectively. The user distribution across peers was varied using two methods: i) *random* — users randomly trust peers, and ii) *social* – socially connected users trust the same peer. We limit the number of users assigned on a peer to 30, based on sociological studies [10] that claim that, on average, an urban person has meaningful social relationships with about 30 other individuals.

The second set of experiments was designed to assess Prometheus performance when used with a real application and on a real social graph. We implemented a mobile application, CallCensor, that silences the phone ring based on the social context of the callee and the relationship with the caller.

In the experiments, we used a timeout of 15 seconds for every social hop in the graph traversed by Prometheus to fulfill a request. After this timeout, a Prometheus peer handling either the initial request or subsequent secondary requests responded with the results it had at that point. Applications could modify the timeout parameter to trade waiting time for more information returned by social inferences.

5.1 Synthetic Workloads and Social Graph

We evaluated the operation of Prometheus with a large user base. We emulated the workload of two socially-aware applications and one social sensor based on previous system characterizations [39,20,14].

Workload for Social Sensor: We emulated a Facebook social sensor based on a Facebook trace analysis [39]. The workload was characterized by the probability distribution function for users to post comments on walls and photos. Users were ranked into groups based on their social degree and each group was mapped onto a probability class using the cumulative distribution function from Figure 8 in [39]. To emulate a social interaction from *ego* to *alter*, a group was selected based on its associated probability, and a user *ego* from the group (who was not selected yet) was picked as the source of input. *Alter* was randomly selected from the *ego*'s direct social connections. The weight of each input was kept constant to a small value for all users. Since users were picked based on their social degree, the users with higher social degree probabilistically produced more input, leading to higher weights on their corresponding edges in the social graph.

Workload for Neighborhood Inference: We used an analysis of Twitter traces [20] to associate a tweet with a neighborhood request (centered at the leader of the tweet) in Prometheus. Thus, we extracted the probability distribution function of submitted requests. Users were ranked into groups based on their social degree ratio (the number of incoming edges divided by the number of outgoing edges). Based on Figure 4 in [20], each group was mapped onto a particular probability to be selected for a neighborhood request. Once the group was selected, a user from the group (who was not selected yet) was picked to be the source of the request. The number of hops for the request was randomly picked from 1, 2 or 3 hops.

Workload for Social Strength Inference: We used an analysis of BitTorrent traces to emulate the workload of a battery-aware BitTorrent application [18] on

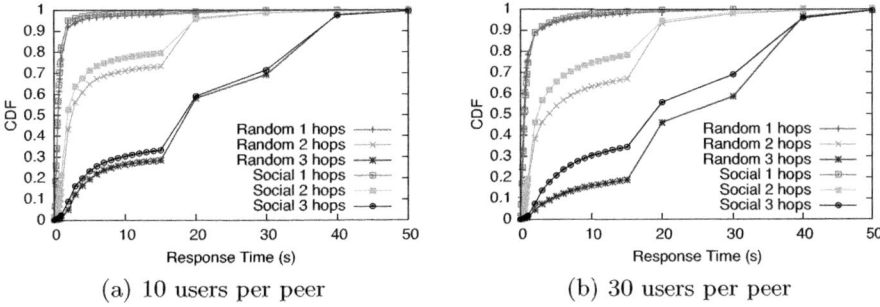

Fig. 4. CDF for the average end-to-end response time of *neighborhood* inference for two types of user-to-peer mapping (*Random* and *Social*) and two numbers of users per peer (*10* or *30*)

mobile devices: a user may rely on social incentives to be allowed to temporarily "free ride" the system when low on battery. Members of the same swarm check their social strength with the needy leecher to see if they want to contribute by uploading on her behalf.

We assumed that users participated at random in swarms. Two users were randomly selected as the source and destination of the social strength inference request. The user selected as the source was associated with a total number of requests she would submit throughout the experiment. This number was extracted from an analysis of BitTorrent traces (Figure 9b in [14]).

Social Graph: We used a graph of 1000 users created with a synthetic social graph generator described in [33]. The generator consistently produces graphs with properties such as degree distribution and clustering coefficient similar to real social graphs. We used this graph as a bidirectional graph and applied a low weight threshold on the inference requests to produce a high-stress load.

5.2 Results from Synthetic Workload Experiments

For every run of the experiments, more than 200,000 social strength and neighborhood requests and more than 32,000 social inputs were submitted from the emulated applications and social sensors. Figure 4 shows the end-to-end average response time for the *neighborhood* inference. We learn four lessons from these experiments.

First, the social-based mapping of users onto peers leads to significant improvements, especially for the 30 users/peer case. For this case, we have as much as 15% of the invocations finishing faster when compared to the random case (some invocations can finish in half the time). Additionally, the benefits compound as the number of hops increases. Of course, the difference is visible only for 2 and 3 hops, as the 1 hop function is computed locally. While we do not plot the number of messages in the system for the sake of brevity, we notice that the social-based mapping reduces the communication overhead by more than an order of magnitude.

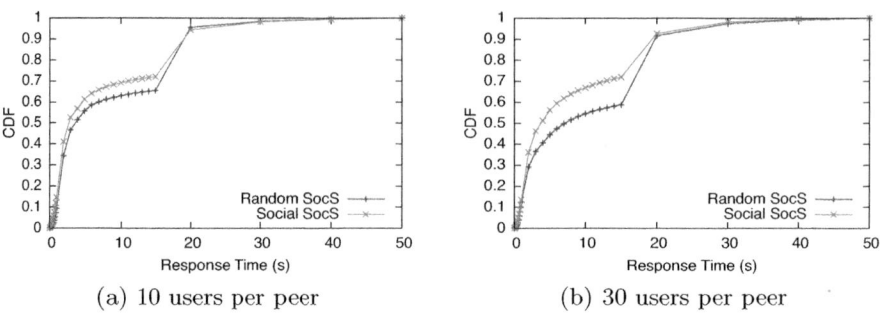

Fig. 5. CDF for the average end-to-end response time of social inference function *social strength (Socs)* for two types of user-to-peer mapping (*Random* and *Social*) and two levels for number of users per peer (*10* and *30* users per peer)

Second, the results show that a three-fold improvement in service availability can be achieved with minimum performance degradation. This is because the graph on the right side has three times more trusted peers per user and its overall response time is only marginally inferior compared with the graph on the left. Therefore, Prometheus design for availability (i.e., replicating the social graph on all trusted peers) is proven to work well in a realistic scenario.

Third, the absolute values of the response time are relatively high, especially for 2 and 3 hops. This is mostly due to the communication delay introduced by the P2P network. In our testbed, the average RTT is 200-300 msec. This value is multiplied by the number of hops traveled by a request/response. For example, for 10 users/peer, an average of 67 peers have to be contacted to collect *neighborhood* data from users located 3 social hops away (the number of users is 350). To improve these results, we plan to implement caching of recently computed results as well as pre-computing results in the background. These methods are expected to work well because the social graph changes rarely. Therefore, the cost associated with maintaining consistency should be low.

Fourth, creating the trusted peer list can be an expensive operation. Let us recall that a request can arrive at a random node, which has to first acquire the list of trusted peers for the user, and then forward the request to one of these trusted peers. This operation involves several lookups in the DHT, which result in multiple peer traversals. To solve this problem, Prometheus caches the list of trusted peers after the first access. The two graphs show the performance using this caching mechanism. The overhead associated with the cold start of creating the trusted peer list is as much as 10 sec for 3 hops.

Figure 5 shows the end-to-end average response time for the *social strength* inference. The performance is almost identical to the one for *neighborhood* for 2 hops because this function has to verify all possible paths between two users, but is limited to users located 2 social hops away.

5.3 CallCensor: A Real-Time Mobile Socially-Aware Application

The CallCensor application leverages social information received from Prometheus to decide whether to allow incoming calls to go through. In addition to the social information from Prometheus, this application uses the phone location to infer whether the user is in a meeting (e.g., in the office). For each incoming call, the application queries Prometheus with a *social strength* or *neighborhood* inference request to assess the type of social connection between the caller and the phone owner. Based on the owner settings (e.g., allow calls from the spouse anytime), the application decides if the phone should ring, vibrate or silence upon receiving the call. The application was written in Java for mobile devices running the Google Android OS and was tested on a Nexus One mobile phone from HTC (1GHz processor, 512MB RAM).

We tested three scenarios in which a caller can be connected to the callee: directly connected within 1 social hop, indirectly connect by 2 social hops, and connected with a high social strength (independent of the number of hops). We tested each of these scenarios 50 times on 3 PlanetLab peers. We measured the end-to-end response time of an inference request submitted to Prometheus. This experiment introduced additional overhead due to the communication between the mobile application and Prometheus.

The social graph used in these experiments was based on data collected at NJIT. The graph has two types of edges, representing Facebook friends and Bluetooth collocation. Mobile phones were distributed to students and collocation data (determined via Bluetooth addresses discovered periodically by each mobile device) were sent to a server. The same set of subjects installed a Facebook application to participate in a survey, and they gave us permission to collect their friend lists. The user set was small (100 users) compared to the size of the student body (9000), therefore resulting in a somewhat sparse graph. About half of the subjects reported less than 24 hours of data over the span of a month. The collocation data have two thresholds of 45 and 90 minutes for users to have spent together; thus, the 90 minute collocations comprise of a subgraph of the 45 minute collocations.

While the edges on the graph were not initially weighted, we applied synthetic weights of 0.1 for "facebook" edges, 0.1 for "collocation" of 45 minutes and 0.2 for "collocation" of 90 minutes. For the experiments, we consider the "collocation" edges to represent a work relationship, while the "facebook" edges represent a personal relationship. The user (*ego*) was assumed to be in a work environment when another user (*alter*) called. Figure 6(a) illustrates this graph and demonstrates one of the features of Prometheus: using multi-edge graphs provides for better social inferences. Neither the "facebook" nor the "collocation" graph is connected, but the graph containing both types of edges is.

The users were assigned to trust 3 PlanetLab peers using a social-based distribution. For each of the scenarios tested, the *ego* and *alter* were randomly chosen, and the inference request was sent to a random peer.

Figure 6(b) presents the end-to-end average response time for the requests sent by CallCensor for the three cases mentioned above. The results also show

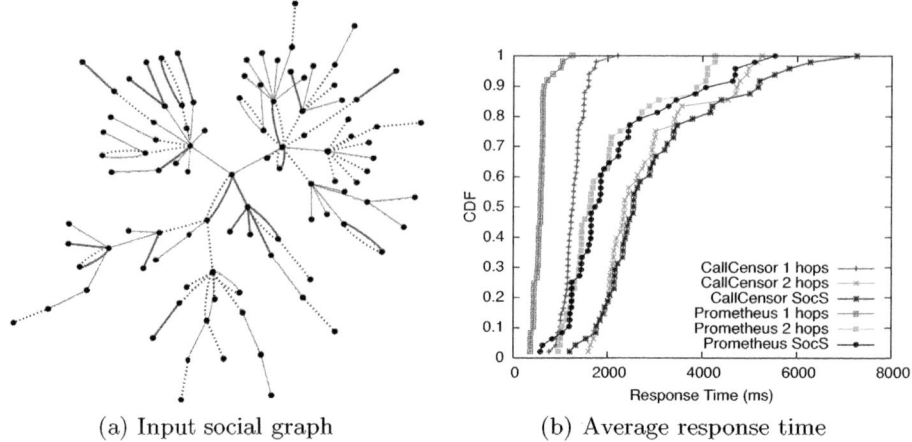

Fig. 6. The input social graph (*a*) has two types of edges: black dashed lines are Facebook edges, and red continuous lines are collocation edges. Line thickness demonstrates the weight of the edge. The results (*b*) show the CDF for the average end-to-end response time of CallCensor on 3 PlanetLab nodes for *neighborhood* for *1* and *2 hops* and *social strength (SocS)*. We show the time needed by Prometheus to produce a response and also the overall time needed by CallCensor to request and handle this response.

the time spent by the requests only in Prometheus. We first observe that the results are acceptable for the real-time constraint of the application: the response must arrive before the call is forwarded to the voice-mail of the callee. Second, we notice that the application itself introduced a significant overhead: for example, 50% in the 2-hop *neighborhood* and *social strength* cases due to both communication overhead and relatively slow execution on the mobile phone. Third, we observe the similarity of the *social strength* results with the *neighborhood* for 2 social hops, as found in the previous experiments.

6 Conclusions and Future Work

This paper presented Prometheus, a P2P service that enables socially-aware applications by providing decentralized, user-controlled social data management. Its decentralized, multi-edged, directed and weighted graph offers a fine-grained representation of the users' social state. Since Prometheus provides good privacy and availability, we expect users to provide a significant amount of social information, well beyond what is available today. We built and evaluated Prometheus using a large scale distributed testbed and a realistic workload. Additionally, we implemented a proof-of-concept mobile social application that utilizes Prometheus functionalities.

The performance results can certainly be optimized as we focused only on functionality so far. As mentioned in the previous section, we plan to cache and pre-compute results benefiting from the slow changes that occur in social graphs. A possible solution for ensuring consistency in such a case is to use the DHT storage to store "dirty bits" for each user. These bits would show if users' information has been updated by social sensors, thereby informing peers that their cached results are stale and that they should rerun the inferences.

We plan to expand the set of social inferences as well as to allow different sensors to provide input for the same label. Additionally, we will explore activity ontologies, provided to social sensors by Prometheus, to support label consistency across multiple sensors.

Prometheus peers have been assumed trusted and cooperative. Due to its distributed nature, Prometheus is harder to be completely compromised than centralized solutions. Similarly, it is more resilient to DoS attacks. Nevertheless, we plan to examine the implications of malicious users and peers in the near future. Of special concern is the case where a (previously) trusted peer becomes malicious. While this newly malicious peer can certainly be removed from a user's trusted peer group, it still retains previously acquired social knowledge, and thus, the ability to subvert the service experienced by the user-owner of the social data. Also, a trusted peer can become faulty and provide inaccurate results. We plan to investigate Byzantine fault-tolerance protocols to guarantee the validity of the results. Finally, while our default access control policies prevent any single user from gaining knowledge of the entire graph, we have yet to ascertain what level of collusion between users would expose the entire graph.

Acknowledgments. This research was supported by the NSF under Grants No. CNS 0952420, CNS 0831785 and CNS 0831753. Any opinions, findings, and conclusions or recommendations expressed in this material are those of the authors and do not necessarily reflect the views of the sponsors. We thank Daniel Boston, Juan Pan, and Steve Mardenfeld from NJIT for collecting the Bluetooth collocation traces.

References

1. Graph api - facebook developers, http://developers.facebook.com/docs/api
2. Anderson, P., Kourtellis, N., Finnis, J., Iamnitchi, A.: On managing social data for enabling socially-aware applications and services. In: 3th Workshop on Social Network Systems (2010)
3. Baden, R., Bender, A., Spring, N., Bhattacharjee, B., Starin, D.: Persona: An online social network with user-defined privacy. ACM Computer Communication Review 39(4), 135–146 (2009)
4. Borcea, C., Iamnitchi, A.: P2P systems meet mobile computing: A community-oriented software infrastructure for mobile social applications. In: 2nd Int. Conf. on Self-Adaptive and Self-Organizing Systems Workshops, pp. 242–247 (2008)
5. Buchegger, S., Schiöberg, D., Vu, L., Datta, A.: PeerSoN: P2P social networking: early experiences and insights. In: 2nd Workshop on Social Network Systems, pp. 46–52 (2009)
6. Castro, M., Druschel, P., Kermarrec, A., Rowstron, A.: Scribe: A large-scale and decentralized application-level multicast infrastructure. IEEE Journal on Selected Areas in Communications 20(8), 1489–1499 (2002)

7. Cutillo, L., Molva, R., Strufe, T.: Privacy preserving social networking through decentralization. In: 6th Int. Conf. on Wireless On-Demand Network Systems and Services, pp. 133–140 (2009)
8. Eagle, N., Pentland, A.S.: Reality mining: sensing complex social systems. Personal and Ubiquitous Computing 10(4), 255–268 (2006)
9. Friedkin, N.E.: Horizons of observability and limits of informal control in organizations. Social Forces 62(1), 57–77 (1983)
10. Friedkin, N.E.: The development of structure in random networks: an analysis of the effects of increasing network density on five measures of structure. Social Networks 3(1), 41–52 (1981)
11. Garriss, S., Kaminsky, M., Freedman, M.J., Karp, B., Mazières, D., Yu, H.: Re: reliable email. In: 3rd Conf. on Networked Systems Design and Implementation (2006)
12. Golder, S.A., Wilkinson, D., Huberman, B.A.: Rhythms of social interaction: Messaging within a massive online network. In: 3rd Int. Conf. on Communities and Technologies (2007)
13. Gummadi, K.P., Mislove, A., Druschel, P.: Exploiting social networks for internet search. In: 5th Workshop on Hot Topics in Networks, pp. 79–84 (2006)
14. Guo, L., Chen, S., Xiao, Z., Tan, E., Ding, X., Zhang, X.: Measurements, analysis, and modeling of bittorrent-like systems. In: 5th Conf. on Internet Measurement (2005)
15. Gupta, A., Kalra, A., Boston, D., Borcea, C.: MobiSoC: a middleware for mobile social computing applications. Mobile Networks and Applications 14(1), 35–52 (2009)
16. Guy, I., Jacovi, M., Shahar, E., Meshulam, N., Soroka, V., Farrell, S.: Harvesting with SONAR: the value of aggregating social network information. In: 26th Conf. on Human Factors in Computing Systems, pp. 1017–1026 (2008)
17. Kahanda, I., Neville, J.: Using transactional information to predict link strength in online social networks. In: 3rd AAAI Int. Conf. on Weblogs and Social Media (2009)
18. King, Z., Blackburn, J., Iamnitchi, A.: BatTorrent: A battery-aware bittorrent for mobile devices. In: 11th Int. Conf. on Ubiquitous Computing, Poster Session (2009)
19. Kong, J.S., Rezaei, B.A., Sarshar, N., Roychowdhury, V.P., Boykin, P.O.: Collaborative spam filtering using e-mail networks. Computer 39(8), 67–73 (2006)
20. Krishnamurthy, B., Gill, P., Arlitt, M.: A few chirps about twitter. In: 1st Workshop on Online Social Networks, pp. 19–24 (2008)
21. Lewis, K., Kaufman, J., Gonzalez, M., Wimmer, A., Christakis, N.: Tastes, ties, and time: A new social network dataset using Facebook.com. Social Networks 30(4), 330–342 (2008)
22. Li, J., Dabek, F.: F2F: reliable storage in open networks. In: 5th Int. Workshop on Peer-to-Peer Systems (2006)
23. Maniatis, P., Roussopoulos, M., Giuli, T.J., Rosenthal, D.S.H., Baker, M.: The LOCKSS peer-to-peer digital preservation system. ACM Trans. Comput. Syst. 23(1), 2–50 (2005)
24. Matsuo, Y., Mori, J., Hamasaki, M., Ishida, K., Nishimura, T., Takeda, H., Hasida, K., Ishizuka, M.: Polyphonet: an advanced social network extraction system from the web. In: 15th Int. Conf. on World Wide Web, pp. 397–406 (2006)
25. Mislove, A., Post, A., Druschel, P., Gummadi, K.P.: Ostra: leveraging trust to thwart unwanted communication. In: 5th Symposium on Networked Systems Design and Implementation, pp. 15–30 (2008)

26. Mokhtar, S.B., McNamara, L., Capra, L.: A middleware service for pervasive social networking. In: 1st Int. Workshop on Middleware for Pervasive Mobile and Embedded Computing, pp. 1–6 (2009)
27. Pietiläinen, A.K., Oliver, E., LeBrun, J., Varghese, G., Diot, C.: MobiClique: Middleware for mobile social networking. In: 2nd Workshop on Online Social Networks, pp. 49–54 (2009)
28. Popescu, B., Crispo, B., Tanenbaum, A.: Safe and private data sharing with Turtle: Friends team-up and beat the system. In: Christianson, B., Crispo, B., Malcolm, J.A., Roe, M. (eds.) Security Protocols 2004. LNCS, vol. 3957, pp. 213–220. Springer, Heidelberg (2006)
29. Pouwelse, J., Garbacki, P., Wang, J., Bakker, A., Yang, J., Iosup, A., Epema, D.H.J., Reinders, M., van Steen, M., Sips, H.: Tribler: A social-based peer-to-peer system. Concurrency and Computation: Practice and Experience 20, 127–138 (2008)
30. Ramachandran, A.V., Feamster, N.: Authenticated out-of-band communication over social links. In: 1st Workshop on Online Social Networks, pp. 61–66 (2008)
31. Rowstron, A., Druschel, P.: Pastry: Scalable, decentralized object location, and routing for large-scale peer-to-peer systems. In: Guerraoui, R. (ed.) Middleware 2001. LNCS, vol. 2218, p. 329. Springer, Heidelberg (2001)
32. Rowstron, A., Druschel, P.: Storage management and caching in PAST, a large-scale, persistent peer-to-peer storage utility. In: 18th Symposium on Operating Systems Principles, pp. 188–201 (2001)
33. Sala, A., Cao, L., Wilson, C., Zablit, R., Zheng, H., Zhao, B.Y.: Measurement-calibrated graph models for social network experiments. In: 19th Int. Conf. on the World Wide Web, pp. 861–870 (2010)
34. Sarigol, E., Riva, O., Alonso, G.: A tuple space for social networking on mobile phones. In: 26th Int. Conf. on Data Engineering (2010)
35. Shakimov, A., Varshavsky, A., Cox, L., Cáceres, R.: Privacy, cost, and availability tradeoffs in decentralized OSNs. In: 2nd Workshop on Online Social Networks, pp. 13–18 (2009)
36. Toninelli, A., Pathak, A., Seyedi, A., Sepicys Cardoso, R., Issarny, V.: Middleware support for mobile social ecosystems. In: 2nd Int. Workshop on Middleware Engineering (2010)
37. Tran, D.N., Chiang, F., Li, J.: Friendstore: cooperative online backup using trusted nodes. In: 1st Workshop on Social Network Systems, pp. 37–42 (2008)
38. Wellman, B.: Structural analysis: From method and metaphor to theory and substance. Social structures: A network approach, 19–61 (1988)
39. Wilson, C., Boe, B., Sala, A., Puttaswamy, K.P.N., Zhao, B.Y.: User interactions in social networks and their implications. In: 4th European Conf. on Computer Systems, pp. 205–218 (2009)
40. Xiang, R., Neville, J., Rogati, M.: Modeling relationship strength in online social networks. In: 19th Int. Conf. on World Wide Web, pp. 981–990 (2010)
41. Yu, H., Kaminsky, M., Gibbons, P.B., Flaxman, A.: Sybilguard: defending against sybil attacks via social networks. In: Conf. on Applications, Technologies, Architectures, and Protocols for Computer Communications, pp. 267–278 (2006)

PerPos: A Translucent Positioning Middleware Supporting Adaptation of Internal Positioning Processes

Jakob Langdal[1], Kari R. Schougaard[2],
Mikkel B. Kjærgaard[2], and Thomas Toftkjær[3]

[1] Alexandra Institute Ltd., Denmark
jakob.langdal@alexandra.dk
[2] Department of Computer Science, Aarhus University, Denmark
{kari,mikkelbk}@cs.au.dk
[3] Systematic A/S, Denmark
ttr@systematic.com

Abstract. A positioning middleware benefits the development of location aware applications. Traditionally, positioning middleware provides position transparency in the sense that it hides low-level details. However, many applications require access to specific details of the usually hidden positioning process. To address this problem this paper proposes a positioning middleware named PerPos that is translucent and adaptable, i.e., it supports both high- and low-level interaction. The PerPos middleware provides translucency with respect to the positioning process and allows programmatic definition of application specific features that can be applied to the internal position processing of the middleware. To evaluate these capabilities we extend the internal position processing of the middleware with functionality supporting probabilistic position tracking and strategies for minimization of the energy consumption. The result of the evaluation is that using only the proposed capabilities we can, in a structured manner, extend the internal positioning processing.

1 Introduction

The development of location aware applications benefit from a positioning middleware. A number of these exist. However, existing positioning middleware has shortcomings in their support for extending the middleware functionality and inspecting the positioning mechanisms. The problem is that although location-aware applications often need a neat position, with all technological details and sensing uncertainties hidden away, often access to these details are needed. For instance, for improving positioning using probabilistic tracking [1], visualizing the positioning infrastructure [2], minimizing energy consumption of location-aware applications [3] or adding high-level reasoning based on machine learning [4]. Therefore, a positioning middleware that gives a structured cross-level access to the positioning mechanisms is needed.

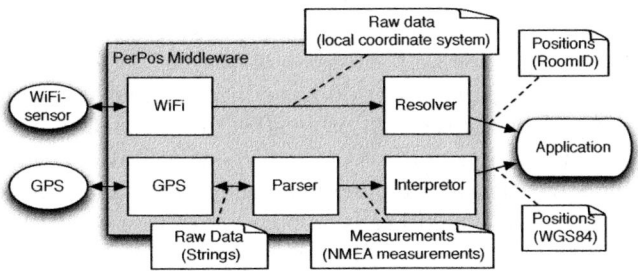

Fig. 1. Concrete positioning processes for the example Room Number Application

Imagine a simple location aware application that shows the current position as a point on a map when outdoor and highlights the currently occupied room when within a building. It may be implemented on a mobile phone, using the internal Global Positioning System (GPS) receiver and WiFi-signal strength measurements, and interfacing with a server containing an indoor WiFi positioning system [3] and a location model service for translation of the position to a room number. A positioning middleware is used to encapsulate the positioning systems, the location model service and the conversion between various coordinate systems. The positioning process for the example is shown in Figure 1. Now, maybe it turns out that the positioning is not accurate enough. The developer wants to improve the positioning by probabilistic tracking implemented as a particle filter [1] that takes into account the likely user movement specific for the application, and location models to impose restrictions on possible movements in the environment. The following requirements for a positioning middleware can be derived from this example.

- Adding a new kind of positioning mechanism and use this in the middleware, without changing the interface, on which the application using the positioning middleware relies.
- Allowing low-level access to the currently employed positioning mechanism and inspection of the process behind.
- Allowing extension of the provided functionality at steps in the process that leads to the production of a position.

Given a middleware that fulfills these requirements a particle filter can be inserted as a new kind of positioning mechanism, without affecting the high-level functionality and Application Programming Interface (API) of the middleware. Necessary functions of the particle filter, e.g., for calculating the likelihood of sensor readings can be implemented by accessing low-level sensor information and exposing it at the correct step in the positioning process. This also enables developers to address many of the timing issues associated with combining multiple sensor readings to one measurement, which is further complicated by sensors with different output frequency.

Particle filters are only one example of applications that require a middleware that fulfills these three requirements. Generally, access to low-level information and the ability of inspection and extension is needed to visualize the positioning infrastructure when authoring location-aware applications [2], manage sensors to minimizing energy consumption [3] or to structure the reasoning process when determining transportation mode of a target by segmentation, feature extraction, decision tree classification and hidden-markov model post processing [4]. When designing a middleware it is virtually impossible to foresee all the features that will be useful in the future. Therefore, it is desirable to be able to extend core middleware functionality.

The first requirement of adding a new kind of positioning mechanism and using this in the middleware, without changing the interface has been fulfilled by existing positioning middleware: MiddleWhere [5], the Location Stack [6], and PoSIM [7]. Although some architectural issues remain, e.g., in the Location Stack the particle filter may be plugged in as a new kind of sensor. However, this positioning middleware use a layered architecture, with sensors in the first layer, adaptation of sensor input to a common representation of measurements in the second, and a fixed reasoning engine for multi-sensor fusion in the third. This means that the new complex sensor, which incorporates sensor fusion, will violate the architecture of the middleware as also argued by Graumann et al. [8].

In connection with the second requirement positioning middleware, such as MiddleWhere [5] and the Location Stack [6], expose a common representation of position information and uncertainty for all kinds of sensors. This means that they do not support accessing information that is not part of the interface or the process behind. PoSIM [7] allows the user to specify control mechanisms and information that the positioning technologies must or may expose. This enables access to low-level information, however, it does not provide the application developer with access to the positioning process.

With regards to the third requirement, the layered architecture of the Location Stack inappropriately restricts possible extension points and has architectural issues as argued for above. MiddleWhere [5] and PoSIM [7] do support that new functionality is specified and implemented in sensor wrappers but not that new features are attached to the position information at a higher level or a later stage in the processing. In order to do this, the process that lies behind the construction of a high-level position must be exposed by the middleware as provided by the PerPos middleware.

The PerPos platform is a middleware for pervasive positioning that can be leveraged when building indoor and outdoor location-aware applications. The services provided by the middleware range from specific utility services to application components that can be deployed in several ways. To provide translucency and adaptation the PerPos middleware is designed around the central idea of representing the steps of the actual positioning process explicitly as a graph based on the flow of information from sensors to application code. This representation constitutes a reflection mechanism [9] that allows application developers to control and extend the positioning process and for the design to fulfill the three requirements stated above. We do not provide the functionality of a generic reflective middleware, and in Section 4 we argue that careful design of what is exposed through reflection decreases the conceptual overhead involved when developers perform adaptations.

1.1 Contributions

In this paper we present our positioning middleware: PerPos. We concentrate on how the middleware fulfills the three requirements stated above, in short, supporting plug-in of complex positioning mechanisms and allowing structured access to and adaptation of the actual internal positioning process.

- We present our multi-level abstraction of the position processing and explain the programming model it provides for location-based application developers (Section 2).
- For three examples: detecting unreliable GPS readings, a particle filter for position improvement, and a power reduction scheme, we explain how we have implemented them by using the adaptation programming model of PerPos (Section 3). These examples are provided as proof of concept for the proposed positioning processing abstractions and programming model.
- In order to compare our solution with others, we analyze what would be needed to implement the examples in existing positioning middleware (Section 3). In comparison with existing middleware designed for transparent use, PerPos allows adaptation of the positioning process without access to the code. In comparison with existing translucent middleware PerPos supports timing information and control of the positioning process itself.
- We introduce the concept of seamful design for developers (Section 4). We explain the needs for a translucent and adaptable middleware for positioning and how the supported programming model make PerPos fulfill these needs. We discuss how this relates to the concept of seamful design, and argue that the seamful metaphor is usefull for developers of translucent sensing middleware.

2 Design of Layered Reification and Adaptation of Position Processes

Generally, positioning middleware encapsulates the processing of sensor measurements that is necessary to obtain a position in a technology independent format. The PerPos middleware is designed around the central idea of representing individual steps of the actual positioning process explicitly as a directed acyclic graph based on the flow of information from sensors to application code. Nodes in this graph represent the implementation of processing steps and are called Processing Components. Edges in the graph represent the data that flows between components. The notion of explicit representation of processing graphs has previously been applied in a number of other domains, e.g., Solar [10] for generic context fusion, PAQ [11] which supports generic queries over temporal-spatial data and PCOM [12] which uses a component graph to compose behavior.

The PerPos positioning middleware uses the graph representation to support inspection and adaptation of the positioning process by exposing the processing graph to developers. The graph is exposed as a tree where data is traveling from leaf nodes toward the root. The root node represents the application that is receiving position data and the leaf nodes represent actual sensors. Internal nodes represent discrete processing steps. Branching (or merging if viewed in the processing direction) in the three occurs when position data from several sources are combined. Usually, combinations of data from several sources take place in special sensor fusion components which often is a part of positioning middlewares [5, 6]. However, it may also take place in other high-level data reasoning components that also take into account other kinds of information, e.g., context information, user input or physical constraints based on building models. In Figure 1 we see an example of two linear trees connected to the same application providing it with WiFi data and GPS positions.

The PerPos API exposes the processing tree to developers through three levels of abstraction providing increasing control of the positioning process. The levels constitute three different views on the positioning process as it is implemented internally in the middleware. The first is the positioning layer providing the abstractions of a traditional positioning middleware. The next two layers provide inspection through reflection on two different levels. The reason for splitting this functionality into two layers is to minimize the complexity involved when using a general reflective programming style. Therefore, the second layer provides access to an abstract structure of the underlying positioning process. In many cases the information in this layer will be sufficient to understand, e.g., the component composition that produced a position, thereby avoiding the added complexity of the more detailed layer. The third layer is responsible for reifying the actual positioning process as a tree structure and maintaining a causal connection between the positioning system and the tree. In Figure 2 we see how a processing graph is represented at the three levels. The configuration shown in the figure is from an application which incorporates a particle filter aggregating measurements from a GPS and a WiFi sensor.

The primary interaction with the PerPos middleware is through a traditional positioning API associated with the top-most layer in Figure 2. It supports both push and pull semantics for retrieving position-based data as derived based on input from connected sensors. The structure of the API resembles the Java Location API for J2ME (JSR-179) [13] where applications can request a location provider which matches a set of criteria. Position-based data can then be obtained through this location provider in a technology transparent way. The API provides operations for specifying functional requirements for the location provider, retrieving position-based data, e.g., a WGS84 position, a room number or the k-nearest targets and setting up location related notifications, e.g., based on proximity to a point or target etc.

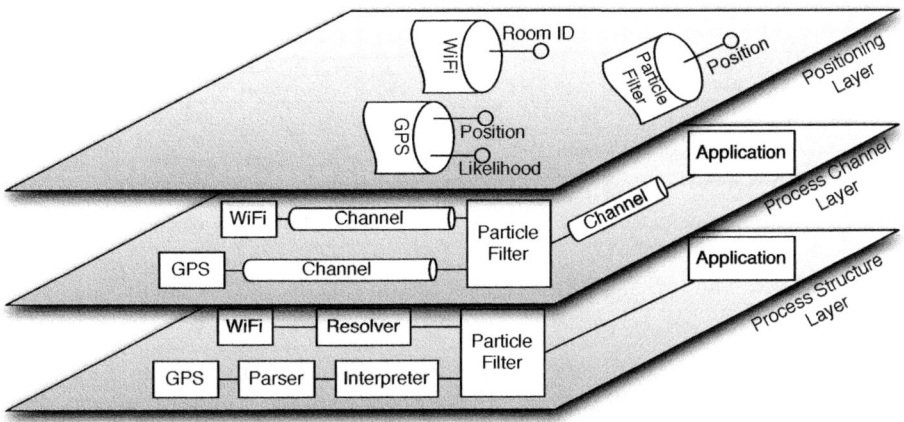

Fig. 2. The three levels of abstraction on the positioning process provided by the PerPos middleware

At the second layer the API provides access to an abstract structure of the underlying positioning process presented as a tree consisting of tree basic node types and the processing channels connecting them. The nodes are either: data sources, components that merges data sources, or the root node representing the application. The API provides operations for inspecting the data flowing through the processing channels as well as handles for changing the functionality of the channels. The data processing channels provide a high-level extension model that allow application developers to implement algorithms that reason about the data delivered to the application.

At the third and most detailed layer the application has access to a detailed processing graph representing each processing step of the positioning system. At this level the API supports fine-grained control of both the structure of the positioning process and its internal behavior.

In the following sections each layer exposed by the PerPos API is presented in more detail. The layers are presented in increasing order of abstraction level of the provided concepts, starting with the most detailed layer.

2.1 Process Structure Layer

The layer exposing the structure of the positioning process, the bottom layer in Figure 2, is called the Process Structure Layer (PSL) and represents the most detailed level of interaction provided by the PerPos middleware. This layer is responsible for reifying the actual positioning process as a tree structure and maintaining a causal connection between the positioning system and the tree. Each node in the tree is a Processing Component that acts as either a producer or a consumer of data contributing to the positioning process, or both.

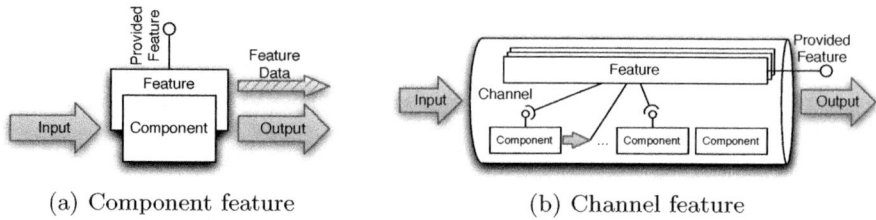

Fig. 3. The two kinds of extension features in the PerPos middleware

Applications can manipulate the composition of components in the tree through the API of the PSL, e.g., `insert`, `delete` and `connect`. Furthermore, the API allows applications to extend the tree with new components and augment existing components with new functionality.

Processing Components consist of three main elements: input ports, output port and implementation of functionality. A Processing Component has a single output port and may have multiple input ports. Input ports are connected to output ports of other components. These connections are established either by direct calls to the graph manipulation API, based on explicitly defined system level configurations or through dynamic resolution of dependencies between components. To make sure that port connections are realizable Processing Components must declare requirements for input ports and define a set of provided capabilities for output ports. When extending a processing tree with new components developers must specifically declare these requirements and capabilities. As custom components are added to the PerPos middleware the dependencies are resolved and when satisfied the components are added to the processing graph appropriately and the classes implementing the Processing Component functionality is instantiated. The PerPos middleware provides the concrete implementation with access to a set of input ports as well as a reference to the output port to which it should deliver data.

The PSL API supports inspection of the reified processing graph including access to all methods available on the implementing classes of the Processing Components. Both the behavior of the Processing Components and the set of available methods can be modified by attaching what we call Component Features to them. Component Features are small code modules that can hook into a component and augment it in three ways. Firstly, data can be manipulated when flowing into or out of the component. Secondly, additional data can be associated with the data flowing out of the component. Thirdly, component state can be read, exposed and manipulated. Figure 3(a) illustrates a Processing Component with a Component Feature attached. The input requirements of Processing Components also include a listing of any Component Feature that the component is dependent upon. In the following we explore the dynamics of each of these augmentation types.

Changing Produced Data. A Component Feature can intercept the flow of data before and after it enters the component to which it is attached. This allows the Component Feature to effectively control the external behavior of the component. Whenever data is sent to a component the middleware calls the consume method on every Component Feature attached to the component which allows the Component Feature to alter the data before it is delivered to the component. The same process is repeated for outgoing data where the produce method of the Component Feature is called allowing for alteration of data. Note that this type of extension cannot change the data type of the data produced.

Adding Data. In addition to altering the data produced by the component, a Component Feature is able to provide new data that may be based on both input and output of the component. A Component Feature can call the method produce(data) on the component to which it is attached. This will result in the data passed to the method being propagated through the processing tree as if it were produced by the component itself. When adding data the capabilities of the output port is changed to include the new type of data. The generated data is only propagated through the processing graph if the next component in the graph explicitly declares that it accepts input from the Component Feature.

Changing Component State. Lastly, a Component Feature can add state manipulation and inspection functionality to individual Processing Components. When doing this, the component will to its surroundings appear to implement the functionality provided by the feature. Examples of this kind of extension are features that expose internal state of a component like various threshold levels used or provide access to changing parameters of component implementations. The application developer can create complex high-level functionality by combining the ability to traverse the nodes of the processing tree with this kind of state manipulation features.

2.2 Process Channel Layer

The middle layer is called the Process Channel Layer (PCL) and it is a view of the position processing where only data sources and merging processing components and the data-flow between them are represented. Thus, the PCL allows inspection of the positioning process in terms of the major processing components. In many cases the information in this layer will be sufficient to understand the component composition that produced the position, thus avoiding the added complexity of the PSL. The process is presented as a tree structure where the application is the root and the nodes are Processing Components representing either the originating data source or components that merge input from two or more data sources, effectively becoming a data source itself. The connection between components in the PSL are called Channels and encapsulates the positioning process taking place between its end points. An example of the channel abstraction is visualized in the middle layer of Figure 2. Channels are dynamically created when the PerPos middleware assembles the Processing Components involved in the positioning process. The PerPos API supports inspection of the Channels and the methods they provide and Channels can be extended through the use of what we call Channel Features similarly to the way that Processing Components are extended through Component Features. Channel Features are used to add functionality to a Channel that requires access to data at different stages in the positioning process, especially, functionality that cannot be achieved by connecting to a single Processing Component. Figure 3(b) shows how a Channel Feature can depend on several internal elements of a Channel. The functionality of a Channel Feature is often partly decomposed into Component Features which the Channel Feature then depends on. A Channel Feature declares its input requirements and output capabilities. Input requirements may include Component Features, Channel Features, and Processing Components. Output capabilities may relate to the data produced by the Channel or to the Channel itself. From the perspective of a Processing Component or from the application a Channel Feature is semantically equivalent to a Component Feature attached to the last Processing Component of the Channel.

To support extension a Channel groups the output of every internal processing step into logically coherent groups. For each data element produced by a Channel it collects all intermediate data elements that logically contributed to that element and places them in a hierarchical data structure. This grouping is achieved by having a notion of logical time that relates to the data process of an entire Channel. Data will always flow from the source through the processing graph until the Channel produces a result. Therefore, it is possible for the Channel to assign a logical time unit to every layer of the processing tree that can be used to identify which processing steps are contributing to the final output of the Channel. For each logical time step the Channels registers all corresponding data produced by the Processing Components in the Channel in a tree structure representing the logical chronology. An example of a data tree for the GPS-channel is presented in Figure 4. In the figure the data is presented as tuples with three elements: the data, the logical time of the current layer, the time range of the data used to generate the element. The example shows data produced by the GPS sensor, the Parser and the Interpretor components respectively. In the example several strings from the GPS sensor is needed to produce one NMEA[1] sentence, and the first NMEA sentence did not contain a valid position, therefore another is needed before the Interpretor produces a WGS84[2] position.

A Channel Feature is required to implement the `apply(dataTree)` method and update its internal state when it is called. The method is called by the middleware every time the Channel delivers a data element. Through this method the Channel Feature has access to the concrete data tree that was used to produce the Channel output. The exact structure of Processing Components in the

---

[1] National Marine Electronics Association is a standard data format for produced by GPS receivers.
[2] World Geodetic System dating from 1984 is the predominant coordinate system for encoding global coordinates.

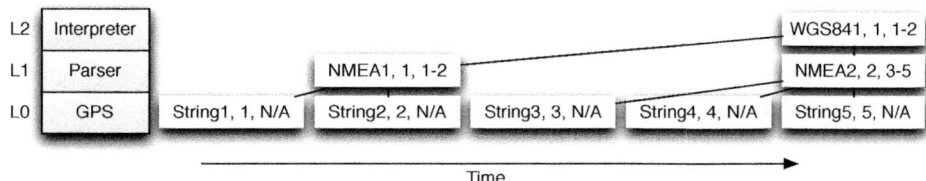

Fig. 4. An example data tree for the GPS Channel

Channel is not known at implementation time. Therefore, the feature must handle the complexity of not knowing for example the number of layers in the data tree or the number of data chunks of each kind. For example, when implementing a Likelihood feature for the GPS Channel, the feature specifies that it depends on a Processing Component that provides the Component Feature which can access Horizontal Dilution of Precision (HDOP) information. Because, the Interpretor is implemented so that it only returns a value when a valid position is produced several National Marine Electronics Association (NMEA) sentences will be available in the data tree related to one output of the Channel. Components that filter according to certain rules may be inserted in the Channel, and the Channel Feature must implement strategies to cope with this fact.

In summary, the PCL contains a representation of the major flow of data in the position data process. The Channel tree exposes how single strained source-to-sink-flows connect the components as well as the features they provide. Furthermore, it supports adaptation of functionality that depends on several steps in the process, by allowing definition of a Channel Feature.

2.3 Positioning Layer

The top layer of the PerPos middleware exposes high-level position data and we call this the Positioning Layer. It presents a view of the position data processing that contains the Channel end-points including their features. All the features originally implemented in the PerPos middleware are visible as well as all available Channel Features. It is especially in the ability to access middleware adaptations in the high-level interaction, where details are abstracted away, that the PerPos middleware distinguishes itself from existing positioning middlewares. We consider the logical timing functionality of the Channels to be an important part of this ability. Even though, interactions with features take place at this abstract level, the middleware takes care of the coupling to the details that were actually a part of the high-level position in question.

At this level the PerPos API exposes the middleware functionality that is also part of a traditional closed positioning middleware. This includes push and pull semantics for retrieving positions from currently available sensors; definition of tracked targets, which may have several sensors attached to them; and a selection of services that can be leveraged for the development of location-aware applications [14]. To summarize, the combined effect of providing the specific extension mechanisms, presented here, is that the high-level API of the PerPos middleware can be effectively extended without requiring changes to the middleware itself.

3 Middleware Adaptations Enable Development of Detail Demanding Applications

In this section we support the utility of our design by explaining a number of concrete use-case examples that exploit the flexible API of the PerPos middleware. The examples are based on our own work with positioning technologies and particle filters. We will flesh out the details of the examples and include code snippets. After each example we will muse over how the example would be implemented in other positioning middleware.

We have for this evaluation realized the PerPos middleware in the Java language and built it on top of the OSGi service platform [15]. The components of the PerPos layers are mapped into the OSGi platform as service components and the dynamic composition mechanisms of OSGi is used for connecting the components.

3.1 Detecting Unreliable Readings by Adding Component Feature

The quality of GPS readings are greatly affected by atmospheric conditions and satellite constellation properties. GPS devices usually continue to produce measurements even if they loose sight of the satellites. Therefore, as argued in [8], filtering positions delivered by a GPS receiver according to the number of satellites available for the measurement can be used as a technique for increasing the reliability of readings. We have implemented this functionality by creating a new filtering Processing Component and inserting it into the processing tree. The Processing Component depends on a Component Feature named `NumberOfSatellites` which provides access to the concrete number of satellites available in each measurement. We insert the filter component after the Parser component. `NumberOfSatellites` is implemented as a Component Feature that is attached to the Parser component and adds a new data element to its output. The filter component extracts the number of satellites and forwards only measurements based on a satisfactory number.

In the Universal Location Framework (ULF), an implementation of The Location Stack [8], the problem is solved by adding the satellite information to the position format used by the middleware. This means that satellite data is part of the position information for other kinds of positioning technologies as well. A resembling solution would be needed for MiddleWhere. Implementation of the extension of the position format requires access to the code for the middleware. In PoSIM [7] an `info` could be specified and implemented in the Sensor Wrapper in order to obtain the number of satellites. However, PoSIM does not focus on filtering and it is unclear how a policy that tested the number of satellites would be used to delete an already obtained position from the system.

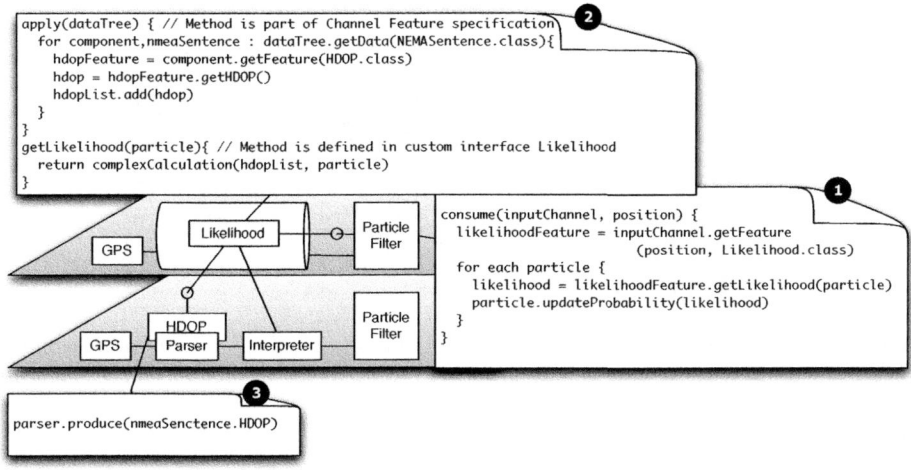

Fig. 5. Code snippets used to provide the particle filter with a likelihood estimate based on HDOP values. The code is shown as pseudo code for clarity, the actual code is Java.

3.2 Integrating a Particle Filter Using Channel Feature

The particle filter we have implemented requires access to a number of low-level properties of the positions used in its calculations. In particular, the implementation of the filter depends on functionality that can provide a value indicating how likely it is that the current sensed position represents the actual true position.

Using the PerPos middleware we have implemented this likelihood functionality as a Channel Feature that calculates the probability based on HDOP values associated with the raw GPS reading. The HDOP values are extracted by a Component Feature from an intermediate parsing components in the positioning tree. This construction is visualized in Figure 5 and involves three different code artifacts, labeled by numbers in the figure. 1) Shows the key input handling parts of the Particle Filter implementation. Upon reception of a new position the Channel Feature called `Likelihood` is retrieved from the current input port and applied to each particle. 2) Shows how the `Likelihood` feature is implemented. The `apply(dataTree)` method is called by the middleware each time the Channel produces data. The method implementation collects the HDOP values from the data tree and uses it to update the internal state of the feature. When the method `getLikelihood(particle)` is called by the Particle Filter it calculates the likelihood estimate based on the collected HDOP values. 3) shows how the HDOP value is extracted and added to the output of the Parser component.

For testing this approach, we used some previously recorded sensor data and fed it into our PerPos middleware implementation of the particle filter. This was done using an emulator component that reads sensor data from a file and presents itself as a sensor. The emulator was plugged into the processing graph,

Fig. 6. Example run of a particle filter implemented using the PerPos middleware. Red dots indicate particle positions, the blue line indicates the evaluated trace, and white lines indicate walls.

taking the place of the sensors. Using this approach we were able to produce a refined trace as shown in Figure 6.

In the Location Stack [6] or MiddleWhere [16] the HDOP information is not available through a public API. The information is, therefore, not accessible to application developers. It may of course be accessed by circumventing the middleware, but then the timing functionality that connects the information to the correct position must be implemented as well. Another possibility is to extend the middleware's representation of a position with the information. This, however, requires access to the source code of the middleware. Furthermore, it would mean that this information is propagated up to highler levels always, even though most middleware uses does not need it. In PoSIM [7] a HDOP `info` may be specified and a wrapper for the GPS that extracts the information and make it available for higher levels may be written. However, when questioned it will always return the latest HDOP value, which may correspond to a new position.

3.3 Power Efficiency

In previous work we have created a power efficient solution for tracking mobile targets called EnTracked [3]. The EnTracked system targets mobile clients that report positions to a server for further processing. In short, the system minimizes the amount of data sampled at the mobile device according to a motion model and thereby reducing the number of power consuming data transmissions made to the server. As part of the validation of the PerPos middleware design we have reimplemented key parts of the EnTracked system using the processing graph abstractions.

The processing graph of the reimplemented version of EnTracked is shown in Figure 7. The actual GPS sensor is located on a mobile device along with an instance of the PerPos middleware. The Processing Component called Sensor Wrapper in the figure is running on the mobile device while the Parser and Interpreter components run on a server. The application is supplied a position provider that delivers positions provided by the Channel with end-point after

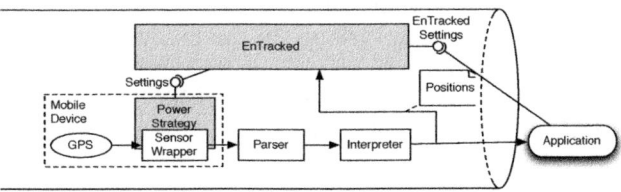

Fig. 7. Processing graph for the implementation of EnTracked using the extensible PerPos API

the Interpreter component. This channel is illustrated as the "tube" wrapping the components.

The original EnTracked system contains a client-side updating scheme that dynamically determines when to activate and deactivate the GPS device. The operation mode of this scheme is controlled by a server-side component. To obtain the same behavior using the graph abstractions we have implemented this updating scheme as a Component Feature, called Power Strategy, attached to the Sensor Wrapper component. The Power Strategy feature provides methods for controlling the operation mode of the updating scheme. In the EnTracked system the server-side component is controlling the updating scheme based on threshold levels for the maximum distance between two consecutive position updates. This behavior is implemented in the Channel Feature labeled EnTracked in the figure. This Channel Feature continuously monitors the output of the Interpreter component and calls the appropriate methods on the Power Strategy feature.

As stated earlier the PerPos middleware is realized in the Java language and built on top of the OSGi service platform [15]. Because, OSGi supports transparent distribution of services through the D-OSGi specification the processing graph can span several hosts with little added configuration overhead.

As MiddleWhere [16] provides a Position middleware containing a World Model, where all available position information is stored, this scenario does not apply to their domain. Configuration of sensors is not discussed. Likewise, The Location Stack [6] places obtained Measurements in a database and does not discuss sensor configuration. How to implement a power consumption scheme using PoSIM is discussed in [7]. They suggest to define a PowerConsumption PoSIM control feature and allow it to be set to for example low and high. Again, a Sensor Wrapper that implements the feature must be defined. A policy of when to invoke the feature can be written. It will then be evaluated along with other policies in order to reason on the dynamic management of the positioning.

3.4 Concluding on the Examples

We have seen that in traditional positioning middleware as The Location Stack [6] and MiddleWhere [16] we need access to the code in order to propagate extra information up by extending the position data format. This solution does not scale well; if there is a large variance in the needed information for different applications and positioning technologies, as we expect, this is problematic.

For translucent positioning middleware as PoSIM [7] extra information may be accessed and devices controlled. Nonetheless, PerPos is superior in its retainment of timing information connecting low-level and high-level information and in the ability to controll the positioning process itself.

4 Translucent Middleware Guided by the Notion of Seamful Design for Developers

In this section we discuss the need for a positioning middleware that provides both transparency and translucency. Moreover, we introduce the notion of seamful design for developers and argue that designing for seamful use is a usefull metaphor for developers of translucent middleware.

In the reflection community it is common to refer to the dichotomy of transparent and translucent middleware. For example in this quote: "A desirable middleware model provides transparency to the applications that want it and translucency and fine-grain control to the applications that need it" [9, p. 37]. Positioning middleware designed for the traditional goal of transparency aims for the widely recognized principle of information hiding [17] and hides all aspects of positioning from the application developer to provide a transparent experience when working with heterogeneous technologies. This means that it abstracts away imperfections in technologies and hides uncertainty for the developer [13, 18]. In some cases, as in the examples presented in Section 3, this leaves the application developers at a loss, because the middleware they employ does not provide adequate support for handling imperfections of the underlying technologies.

The concept of translucency may advocate a generally open middleware with full access to change functionality. However, a designed reification that focus on certain aspects of the middleware may be easier to understand and use than a full and only allowing specific adaptations gives a safer although less powerful development model. In our work we have been inspired by the notion of seamful design for developers, which we will now introduce.

In Weiser's seminal paper: The computer for the 21st century [19], seamless design is presented as a goal for how computers should be integrated into the world. A seamless design will allow computers to disappear from our awareness. This will enable us to focus on the goal for which we use the computer, instead of focusing on the computer itself. Such seamless designed systems should make the computerized infrastructure components they depend on disappear from the focus of the user. In the positioning domain, this means that the concrete positioning systems and their characteristics are hidden for the user who employ the position information.

However, due to the inherent imperfection of sensing technologies, in practice, it is hard to hide the characteristics of positioning in order to provide transparency. For instance, positioning technologies do not provide pervasive coverage because buildings, humans, and walls might block signals used for positioning. The positions delivered can be erroneous due to signal noise, delays, or faulty system calibration. Motivated by the imperfection of sensing technologies used in ubiquitous computing, several authors such as Chalmers and Galani [20], and Benford et al. [21] have argued for contrasting the goal of *seamless* design with one of *seamful* design. They define seams as "[...] the places where [components and technologies] may imperfectly connect to one another or to the physical environment." [21, p.126]. The goal of seamful design is to make the seams available in a designed manner, but not in focus at all times, so "one can selectively focus on and reveal [seams] when the task is to understand or even change the infrastructure." [20, p. 251].

Previously, seamful design has been directed towards the end user. Nonetheless, our focus is on the developer which has to face the same technology imperfections, only they occur during application development. For the developer of position based applications, imperfect connections might both occur within software components and between the positioning technology and the physical environment.

Instead of only focusing on position transparency, a seamful positioning middleware should expose and internalize key aspects of the positioning process in a designed manner. Thus, the developer can access both the imperfections of sensing technology to capture reality and the "imperfections" in the processing of position data, namely the design of the encapsulation and the abstracting away details. The set of seams a developer might be interested in cannot be determined uniquely. Therefore, a seamful middleware must provide means for the developer to extend the set of exposed seams.

To apply seamful design to the domain of positioning developers have to identify that the seamless design of the middleware is problematic under specific circumstances. Furthermore, they must posses some knowledge of the seams of the positioning technologies or in the position calculation process, and they must know how to use information about seams to improve their application. It is clear that seamful use of a positioning middleware requires expert domain knowledge. Therefore, a positioning middleware should be designed for both seamless and seamful use, with concepts for both seamless and seamful positioning. The seamful middleware should not only support one type of developers, but developers with different skills, short and long schedules, and different types of applications.

The PerPos middleware supports both seamless and seamful interaction in that is delivers technology independent positions at a high-level layer while allowing for structured inspection and adaptation of the internal processing that lead to the high-level positions. Thus, to the extend that sensors and processing elements contains information that may be used to deduce for example, current coverage, accuracy, and signal noise, this information, which is usually hidden for the sake of transparency, can be used to expose the seams.

Concretely, in PerPos we reify the actual processing in a graph of processing components and flows of data and allow adaptation of processing components.

Moreover, the processing is reified in a position source view, where the pipeline from one source to either a merge or the application is abstracted to a data channel. Through this view we allow adaptations that depend on data produced at several intermediate steps of the positioning process.

Our experience in developing services for positioning based on the PerPos middleware shows that it is the seams that calls for extra functionality in the middleware. This is concordant with the experience reported by Graumann et al. [8]. The inherent position uncertainty called for the development of a likelihood feature. The poor performance of GPS in indoor environments coupled with the device strategy of continuing to send positions called for the number of satellites feature. The limited battery capacity called for the power conservation feature. The approach of exposing and allowing adaptation of the processing components and the positioning process is especially suited to support the developer to choose when to access and possibly propagate to a higher level the information that is abstracted away in a seamless approach.

The concept of seamful design for developers has inspired the design of PerPos. It is a powerful metaphor when designing middleware for sensing domains, because it focuses the design of how to develop the handles available in a translucent and adaptive middleware to allow representation and improvement of the imperfections.

5 Related Work

In this section we will cover related work with respect to existing positioning middleware and to reflective middleware.

MiddleWhere by Ranganathan et al. [5] is a general purpose middleware for building location based applications. The primary purpose of MiddleWhere is to provide location information to applications in a technology agnostic way. The Location Operating REference model (LORE) [22] focuses on providing high-level location data together with sensor fusion and intelligent notification. Cascadia by Welbourne et al. [23] is a middleware for detecting location events from RFID-based events. The middleware implements probabilistic fusion for detecting location events from raw RFID events. It provides both a declarative approach and an API that facilitates the development of applications which rely on location events. However, in all three systems the functionality (e.g., location models or sensor fusion) are statically implemented into the system and cannot be extended by application developers. Furthermore, there is no support for allowing application developers to extend the systems with functionality for handling cross-cutting concerns.

Location Stack by Hightower et al. [6] is a generic software engineering model for location in ubiquitous computing. The model is intended to be both a conceptual framework as well as a high-level layered architecture for implementing location based systems. However, the only true implementation of the Location Stack, the Unified Location Framework (ULF), has shown that the fundamental principles of the model cannot be followed in practice [8]. According to the report on the ULF, actual location based applications tend to require some level of access to low-level details of the positioning process. In the Location Stack this translates to creating cross-layer functionality which breaks the fundamental assumptions of the model.

PoSIM by Bellavista et al. [7] is a middleware for positioning applications designed to mediate access to heterogeneous positioning systems. The middleware is designed to provide application developers with some level of visibility into the internal workings of the underlying positioning systems. Operations for handling cross-cutting concerns are executed by adding or removing behaviors to the system expressed as declarative policies. The policies are written in a declarative language and the set of operations for conditions consists of simple comparison of data values while actions are limited to passing values to operations of the sensor wrapper.

There also exist more general context provision middlewares. An example is Contory proposed by Riva [24] that based on a query abstraction allow applications to request context information including spatial information.

In comparison, PerPos is a positioning middleware that supports a designed inspection and adaptation of the internal position processing. The middleware facilitates both seamless use of high-level positions and seamful use of details in the form of extraction of low-level information and adaptation of the position data processing, along with exposure of seams in the high-level interaction.

Traditional middleware are not well suited for dealing with dynamic aspects such as device-sizes and network availability. Given information about device types or network infrastructures the handling of such dynamic aspects can be optimized, e.g., by selecting protocols that better fit the underlying network infrastructure. To address this problem, reflective middleware has been proposed, as described by Kon et al. [9], to provide traditional transparency coupled with translucency and fine-grain control. Reflective middleware provides inspection of their internal state using reflective meta interfaces. In a mobile context Carisma is a middleware proposed by Capra et al. [25] that support reflection by allowing programmers using policies to specific how the middleware should handle context changes for the provided services. PCOM proposed by Becker et al. [12] provides adaptation for pervasive component-based systems by contracts that specify dependencies between components and resources. PAQ [11] supports adaptive persistent queries over temporal-spatial data in dynamic networks. The system provides reflective programming abstractions to support the construction of applications that dynamically evaluate the cost of executing a query in the current environment and adjust the query's processing according to the application's needs. In comparison, PerPos is also a reflective middleware but provides a designed inspection and adaptation of the internal positioning process.

6 Conclusion and Future Work

In this paper we presented the design of PerPos a middleware for pervasive positioning that supports a designed inspection and adaptation of the internal position processing. The middleware facilitates both seamless use of high-level positions and seamful use of details in the form of extraction of low-level information and adaptation of the position data processing, along with exposure of seams in the high-level interaction. We have demonstrated the utility of the design by demonstrating how three example applications that all required access to internal details of the positioning process can be implemented using the adaptability of the middleware. Furthermore, we have argued for the potential of an adaptable positioning middleware. Finally, we have introduced the concept of seamful design for developers and discussed how the concept may focus the notion of translucent middleware.

In the future, we plan to research how traditional software qualities can be supported by the model based approach to translucency, e.g., reliability, scalability and performance. Furthermore, we will conduct user studies to validate the concept of translucency provided through seamful design.

Acknowledgements. We thank the rest of the PerPos group for help in implementing the middleware or applications that use the middleware. The authors acknowledge the financial support granted by the Danish National Advanced Technology Foundation under J.nr. 009-2007-2.

References

1. Hightower, J., Borriello, G.: Particle filters for location estimation in ubiquitous computing: A case study. In: Davies, N., Mynatt, E.D., Siio, I. (eds.) UbiComp 2004. LNCS, vol. 3205, pp. 88–106. Springer, Heidelberg (2004)
2. Oppermann, L., Broll, G., Capra, M., Benford, S.: Extending authoring tools for location-aware applications with an infrastructure visualization layer. In: Dourish, P., Friday, A. (eds.) UbiComp 2006. LNCS, vol. 4206, pp. 52–68. Springer, Heidelberg (2006)
3. Kjærgaard, M.B., Langdal, J., Godsk, T., Toftkjær, T.: Entracked: Energy-efficient robust position tracking for mobile devices. In: Proceedings of the 7th International Conference on Mobile Systems, Applications, and Services (2009)
4. Zheng, Y., Liu, L., Wang, L., Xie, X.: Learning transportation mode from raw gps data for geographic applications on the web. In: Proceedings of the 17th International Conference on World Wide Web, WWW 2008, pp. 247–256 (2008)
5. Ranganathan, A., Al-Muhtadi, J., Chetan, S., Campbell, R., Mickunas, M.D.: MiddleWhere: a Middleware for Location Awareness in Pervasive Computing Applications. In: Jacobsen, H.-A. (ed.) Middleware 2004. LNCS, vol. 3231, pp. 397–416. Springer, Heidelberg (2004)
6. Hightower, J., Brumitt, B., Borriello, G.: The location stack: a layered model for location in ubiquitous computing. In: Proceedings of the 4th IEEE Workshop on Mobile Computing Systems and Applications (2002)
7. Bellavista, P., Corradi, A., Giannelli, C.: The PoSIM middleware for translucent and context-aware integrated management of heterogeneous positioning systems. Computer Communications 31(6), 1078–1090 (2008)
8. Graumann, D., Hightower, J., Lara, W., Borriello, G.: Real-world implementation of the location stack: The universal location framework. In: Proceedings of Fifth IEEE Workshop on Mobile Computing Systems and Applications, pp. 122–128. IEEE Computer Society, Los Alamitos (2003)

9. Kon, F., Costa, F., Blair, G., Campbell, R.H.: The case for reflective middleware. Communications of the ACM 45(6), 33–38 (2002)
10. Chen, G., Kotz, D.: Solar: An open platform for context-aware mobile applications. In: Mattern, F., Naghshineh, M. (eds.) PERVASIVE 2002. LNCS, vol. 2414, pp. 41–47. Springer, Heidelberg (2002)
11. Rajamani, V., Julien, C., Payton, J., Roman, G.C.: PAQ: Persistent Adaptive Query Middleware for Dynamic Environments. In: Bacon, J.M., Cooper, B.F. (eds.) Middleware 2009. LNCS, vol. 5896, pp. 226–246. Springer, Heidelberg (2009)
12. Becker, C., Handte, M., Schiele, G., Rothermel, K.: PCOM - A Component System for Pervasive Computing. In: Proceedings of the Second IEEE International Conference on Pervasive Computing and Communications (PerCom 2004), pp. 67–76 (2004)
13. Loytana, K.: JSR 179: Location API for J2ME. Nokia Corporation (2006)
14. Blunck, H., Godsk, T., Grønbæk, K., Kjærgaard, M.B., Jensen, J.L., Scharling, T., Schougaard, K.R., Toftkjær, T.: Perpos: A platform providing cloud services for pervasive positioning. In: COM.Geo 2010, 1st International Conference on Computing for Geospatial Research & Application (2010)
15. Alliance, O.: Open Services Gateway Initiative. Specification download (2009), http://www.osgi.org/Download/Release4V42 (Online, cited February 18, 2010)
16. Ranganathan, A., Al-Muhtadi, J., Chetan, S., Campbell, R.H., Mickunas, M.D.: Middlewhere: A middleware for location awareness in ubiquitous computing applications. In: Jacobsen, H.-A. (ed.) Middleware 2004. LNCS, vol. 3231, pp. 397–416. Springer, Heidelberg (2004)
17. Parnas, D.: On the criteria to be used in decomposing systems into modules. Communications of the ACM 15(12), 1053–1058 (1972)
18. Kupper, A., Treu, G., Linnhoff-Popien, C.: Trax: a device-centric middleware framework for location-based services. IEEE Communications Magazine 44(9), 114–120 (2006)
19. Weiser, M.: The computer for the 21st century. Scientific American 265(3), 94–104 (1991)
20. Chalmers, M., Galani, A.: Seamful interweaving: heterogeneity in the theory and design of interactive systems. In: Proceedings of the Conference on Designing Interactive Systems: Processes, Practices, Methods, and Techniques, pp. 243–252. ACM, New York (2004)
21. Benford, S., Crabtree, A., Flintham, M., Drozd, A., Anastasi, R., Paxton, M., Tandavanitj, N., Adams, M., Row-Farr, J.: Can you see me now? ACM Trans. Comput. 13(1), 100–133 (2006)
22. Chen, Y., Chen, X.Y., Rao, F.Y., Yu, X.L., Li, Y., Liu, D.: Lore: an infrastructure to support location-aware services. IBM J. Res. Dev. 48(5/6), 601–615 (2004)
23. Welbourne, E., Khoussainova, N., Letchner, J., Li, Y., Balazinska, M., Borriello, G., Suciu, D.: Cascadia: a system for specifying, detecting, and managing RFID events. In: Proceedings of the 6th International Conference on Mobile Systems, Applications, and Services, pp. 281–294 (2008)
24. Riva, O.: Contory: A middleware for the provisioning of context information on smart phones. In: van Steen, M., Henning, M. (eds.) Middleware 2006. LNCS, vol. 4290, pp. 219–239. Springer, Heidelberg (2006)
25. Capra, L., Emmerich, W., Mascolo, C.: Carisma: Context-aware reflective middleware system for mobile applications. IEEE Transactions on Software Engineering 29(10), 929–945 (2003)

dFault: Fault Localization in Large-Scale Peer-to-Peer Systems

Pawan Prakash[1], Ramana Rao Kompella[1],
Venugopalan Ramasubramanian[2], and Ranveer Chandra[2]

[1] Purdue University
{pprakash,kompella}@cs.purdue.edu
[2] Microsoft Research
{rama,ranveer}@microsoft.com

Abstract. Distributed hash tables (DHTs) have been adopted as a building block for large-scale distributed systems. The upshot of this success is that their robust operation is even more important as mission-critical applications begin to be layered on them. Even though DHTs can detect and heal around unresponsive hosts and disconnected links, several hidden faults and performance bottlenecks go undetected, resulting in unanswered queries and delayed responses. In this paper, we propose dFault, a system that helps large-scale DHTs to localize such faults. Informed with a log of failed queries called *symptoms* and some available information about the hosts in the DHT, dFault identifies the potential *root causes* (hosts and overlay links) that with high likelihood contributed towards those symptoms. Its design is based on the recently proposed dependency graph modeling and inference approach for fault localization. We describe the design of dFault, and show that it can accurately localize the root causes of faults with modest amount of information collected from individual nodes using a real prototype deployed over PlanetLab.

Keywords: distributed systems, DHTs, fault localization, PlanetLab.

1 Introduction

Distributed Hash Tables (DHTs) have gained widespread acceptance as building blocks of large-scale distributed systems. From the initial success of publicly deployed academic research projects such as CoDoNS [21], CoralCDN [6] and OpenDHT [24] to the more recent enterprise, cloud storage systems such as Amazon's Dynamo [8] and its open-source equivalent Voldemort [28], DHT-based systems are becoming increasingly prevalent. As even more critical services and commercial applications begin to rely on DHTs, their robustness—ability to run free of errors and inefficiencies—would be crucial.

Fortunately, DHTs have high resilience and can "heal" themselves quickly and effectively upon detecting a failure. In fact, they do so well for failures that are visible to their protocols—namely, broken network connections and unresponsive or crashed hosts. However, they are not currently equipped to detect other types of critical but "latent" failures. For example, a fault (*e.g.*, bug or race condition) in a critical application component might keep a host up and responsive to protocol messages while silently dropping application messages. Or, a bad network connection might unpredictably delay the delivery of some messages, without triggering the DHT host to break the connection. These and other subtle faults identified by recent studies on widely deployed DHTs [7,18,23], which go undetected and therefore not recovered from, ultimately affect the performance and availability of the system.

Our goal is to automate the *localization* of such faults. That is, identify components that potentially contain faults, so that the necessary repair actions can then be taken. One approach for fault localization is to instrument the DHT code heavily to individually track messages as they pass between different hosts and components and log them. However, this approach is likely to result in a massive collection of logs to be pored over—an overwhelmingly expensive task for large-scale deployments.

We propose a light-weight probabilistic inference approach for fault localization. We start from the *symptoms* of the faults, namely unanswered queries and unusually delayed responses, visible to the consumers or clients of the DHT. Their *root causes* lie in the failures and performance bottlenecks at some system component. Now, if many of the failed queries are meant for keys that have a common home node (the primary host in a DHT responsible for storing items associated with that key), then we can infer that a fault at that home node likely caused the failure of those queries.

The above simple example highlights the *key intuition* behind our approach. However, probabilistic inference in practice is more complicated. For instance, it is possible in the above example that the queries share another common host through which they all traverse before reaching the home node. In this case, the root cause could be either of the two hosts, or both, or in the network route between them. Additional information from the routing tables at the DHT hosts and failure statistics of other queries is necessary to refine the inference further. Similarly, if there is a cache at an intermediate host in the path taken by a query that happens to contain the response for the query, the cache would mask faults in subsequent hosts in the path. A suitable cache model or some knowledge of cache contents may be necessary to improve the effectiveness of fault localization even further.

In this paper, we present a new system called dFault for localizing faults in DHT-based applications and services. dFault is designed to work on any DHT. It runs as a centralized service that collects a list of query failures from participating DHT clients and a small amount of routing and cache information from individual DHT hosts. (It uses several optimizations to ensure that the system incurs low communication bandwidth and scales well.) It then uses the collected information to diagnose the root causes for a set of query failures, which includes both hard failures (unanswered queries) as well as performance degradations (delayed responses). Internally, dFault builds a dependency graph consisting of the *symptom set* (failed queries) and *root causes* (hosts, overlay links) and uses a new probabilistic inference algorithm that meets the scalability requirements of these systems.

We have evaluated dFault through a Pastry [25] deployment on 100 PlanetLab hosts, as well as scaled simulations. We found that dFault could localize 5 simultaneous failures (nodes injected with faults) with 100% accuracy and no false positives with as low as 110 symptoms. Furthermore, our estimates show that the total communication bandwidth required for accurate fault localization is of the order of about 1.2 Kbps per node (for a system of 100,000 hosts this translates to about 100 Mbps total bandwidth at the diagnosis entity).

Overall, this paper makes the following key contributions: (1) First, it presents a new fault localization framework for DHTs based on the light-weight approach of dependency modeling and inference. It shows how to develop probabilistic dependency graphs connecting queries with the DHT components they depend on, incorporating practical aspects of caching and routing. (2) Second, it presents a novel inference algorithm suitable for the large probabilistic dependency graphs we derive. (3) Finally, it characterizes the tradeoff between the fidelity of information included in the model and the effectiveness of fault localization, showing that accurate and precise localization can be achieved for large scale DHT-based systems with modest overhead.

2 Background

A DHT is a networked system of hosts that collectively provides a *key-value* storage service. The DHT provides a core interface of *put(key,value)* and *get(key)* operations for accessing the storage service. Several DHTs [19,22,25,27] have been designed to provide this abstraction, each with a different topology and routing algorithm; we base our work on principles common to most DHTs.

DHTs assign a *home node* to each key as the host responsible for storing the items associated with the key. Other hosts in a DHT may further replicate the items for failure resilience and performance improvement. The most common approach is *consistent hashing* [14], where both host identifiers and item keys are hashed to the same space, and the host whose identifier falls "closest" to the key in the hashed space is set as its home node.

An application can store or retrieve the items associated with a key by locating the key's home node. This process usually involves a multi-hop routing protocol. First, the application issues a *get* or a *put* operation for a specific key K to the local DHT host A it interacts with. A then forwards the operation to another host B, which it deems to be closer to the home node. Unless, A itself happens to be the home node, in which case, it provides the items to the application. The above step continues until the operation reaches the home node. Each DHT host maintains links to a subset of other hosts in the DHT in a *routing table*, using which given a key K, a host can easily find a next hop that is closer (in the hashed space) to the key than A to forward to. DHTs have protocols for failure-detection and routing-table repair in order to ensure that correct and efficient routing tables are maintained at the hosts and operations complete within asymptotically bounded worst-case latency (often $O(\log N)$ hops, where N is the number of hosts).

However, despite the asymptotic worst-case bounds, DHT operations can incur long delays as the multi-hop routing protocol crisscrosses over many links. So, DHTs often use caching to decrease the average latency of *get* operations. While there are aggressive DHT caching solutions that guarantee high performance through sophisticated algorithms [20], the most commonly used approach is to cache the results of a *get* operation at intermediate hosts through which it was routed through. When a host finds a hit in its cache, it returns the items directly instead of forwarding it to the home node. To manage the cache, hosts may use any well-known cache eviction policies such as least-recently-used (LRU) or least-frequently-used (LFU).

3 dFault System Overview

Our system, dFault, focuses on a class of *latent failures* that have been known to exist in DHTs which the in-built failure detection mechanisms cannot automatically detect and repair. These pathologies and inefficiencies typically lead to failed queries or excessively delayed responses [7,18,23]. Examples of such latent faults include: (1) a failed application or component that stops processing messages at a host (even though the host itself is responsive to protocol messages); (2) a subtle network problem such as the lack of transitivity (*i.e.*, a scenario where a host B can forward a query it received from host A to host C, but host C is unable to send a response back to host A due to a network problem); or, (3) a weak network connection or performance bottleneck at a host that delays a message or slows down its processing.

Our goal is to design a system that can localize the root causes of failures and inefficiencies in DHT-based applications. A system for fault localization in DHTs should ideally possess three primary properties.

- *P1) Accuracy.* Our system should be able to accurately detect a significant fraction if not all the failures. Further, the number of false positives reported should be quite low.
- *P2) Scalability.* We seek to apply dFault in large-scale DHT systems with thousands of nodes and queries per second. Therefore, dFault needs to be lightweight—prudent in the quantity of information it uses and quick in the execution of the inference algorithm. This rules out several Bayesian schemes that have been proposed in the literature [12,2].
- *P3) Non-intrusiveness.* We seek to minimize heavy, intrusive modifications to the DHT system and its applications. Although more accurate localization might be possible by heavily instrumenting the DHT to log more data, such an approach is cumbersome and excludes legacy applications.

3.1 Architecture of dFault

dFault targets applications running on managed DHTs, where it is possible to monitor application performance and collect required information for diagnosis. A *centralized diagnosis server* (CDS) forms the core of dFault where

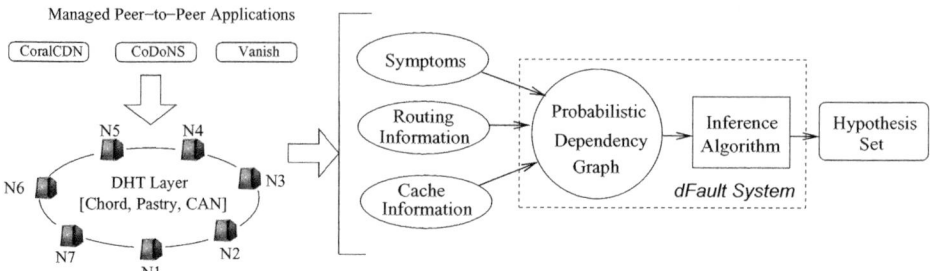

Fig. 1. dFault system overview

appropriate information is collected from individual nodes in a DHT for diagnosis. For redundancy purposes, multiple CDS servers can be used by the management entity. The CDS obtains three types of information from DHT nodes: (1) failure symptoms in the form of failed or delayed queries, (2) routing tables, and (3) relevant caching information in the form of, say, cache contents. It then constructs a probabilistic dependency graph that codifies the dependencies between *root-causes* (nodes and overlay links in the DHT) and the failure symptoms. Finally, the CDS executes an inference algorithm to determine the most likely set of root causes that can help explain the particular set of failed queries. Figure 1 illustrates this architecture of dFault.

In order to scale to large deployments, CDS minimizes the amount of information for diagnosis from each node. For instance, it uses only a sample of failure symptoms for diagnosis (evaluation indicates 100 failed symptoms are sufficient for good accuracy). Routing tables are already quite compact (scale as $O(\log N)$) and the associated overhead can be further reduced by encoding only the changes in routing table entries. We perform similar optimizations for cache details that makes the system overall quite scalable.

Failure symptoms. A query that fails to evoke a response or obtains a response delayed beyond a certain time threshold is considered a *failure symptom*. A failure symptom is detected at the first DHT node encountered by the query, either by the application running on that node or the DHT component that originates the query on behalf of the actual user client. dFault can monitor application failures in several ways. Actively monitoring each node for failed queries is unscalable; therefore, we follow a passive 'reporting' approach, whereby each node alerts the CDS whenever a query fails. In a real operational system, it is impractical to assume all the failure symptoms will be accurately reported in a timely fashion. Further, there could be a large number of spurious and transient symptoms in a large scale distributed environment such as in our setting. Our system therefore does *not* require all the failure symptoms from all the nodes before it can perform diagnosis. Indeed, dFault can generate an inference hypothesis based on whatever subset of the failed queries that are input to the system.

Routing tables. Fault localization in dFault is enabled with the help of a dependency graph that dictates which set of nodes $N_{i1}, N_{i2}, ..., N_{ik}$ in the system a given query q_i that originates at node N_{i1} depends on. One way to achieve this is to allow every node in the system to log every query that passes through them, and subsequently collect all these logs at the CDS. This approach, however, is likely to be extremely intensive in communication going against our scalability goal (*P2*). As discussed in Section 2, nodes in a DHT use a routing table that helps identify the host closest to the query key. Instead of enabling each node to track dependencies directly, therefore, it is prudent to collect the routing tables from each node, that are typically compact consisting of only $O(\log N)$ entries. Once the base routing tables are collected, subsequent runs require only the incremental changes which will be even smaller than the entire routing tables. Thus, in dFault, each node transmits its routing table entries periodically to the CDS which, as we describe later in Section 4.1, constructs the appropriate dependency graph required for fault localization.

Note that our system only depends on the ability to determine the path from a source node to a home node within a given DHT. Thus, it can work with several DHTs such as Pastry, Chord, and others where it is easy to compute such paths just with the knowledge of routing tables from individual nodes. In some environments, keeping track of all the DHT nodes' routing tables at the CDS precisely synchronized can be hard, especially when the number of DHT nodes is really huge. Updates from the DHT nodes may be lost, connections may be terminated or could be extremely slow in transferring the routing tables. Thus, dFault is designed to work with partial and stale routing tables in diagnosing failures. We evaluate the efficacy of dFault under such conditions in Section 5.

Cache information. In the context of dFault, caching in the DHT makes fault localization harder because, the path a query is supposed to take from a source node to a home node may only be *partially* traversed. Thus, while hypothetically, the query depends on all the nodes along the path, it is actually only dependent on a subset of nodes until it hits the first cache along the path that contains the query's response.

We consider three options that explore different tradeoffs in modeling caches.

- 1) *No cache.* The first option is to choose not to model the caching effects at all in our dependency graphs. This simplest of all approaches may yield reasonable results if the localization algorithm itself is resilient to small amounts of errors in modeling dependencies.
- 2) *Modeling query popularity.* The second approach we consider is based on the observation that the popularity of most objects stays stable for reasonable lengths of time. For example, in CoDoNS, which uses a DHT to store DNS records, many extremely popular records continue to remain popular for days and months (same for many unpopular records). Thus, we can estimate object popularity and obtain a probabilistic value that dictates how likely a given object is to be cached at any given node.
- 3) *Polling cache contents.* Finally, we consider collecting cache contents at periodic intervals of time from nodes in the system. Note that nodes need not push all of their cache contents; they can just report the differences from the previous transmission to keep the communication overheads low.

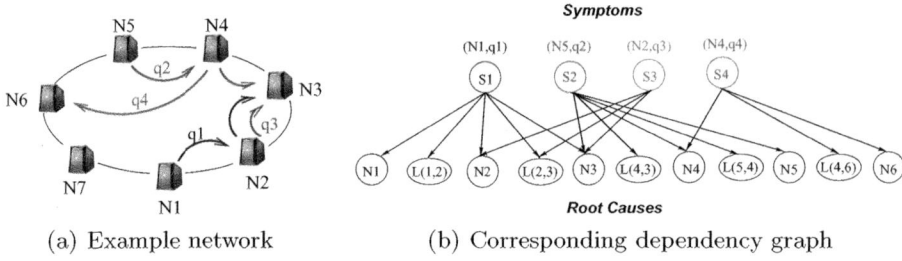

Fig. 2. Constructing dependency graph from routing tables

From the routing table and caching information collected from the network, dFault needs to construct a dependency graph that describes the relationship between possible root causes and the failure symptoms collected from the network. The construction of the dependency graph is dependent on the particular information available; we show this construction for each of these three options next.

4 Probabilistic Inference

dFault uses the failure symptoms, routing table and cache information collected from individual DHT nodes to create a probabilistic dependency graph that models the relationship between the observed failure symptoms and the set of root causes (DHT nodes and overlay links between these nodes). Based on this dependency graph, it outputs a hypothesis set of root causes that explain the observed set of failure symptoms using a new scalable inference algorithm. We explain these individually next.

4.1 Dependency Graph

In dFault, we formulate the dependencies in the form of a bi-partite dependency graph $G(V, E)$. An edge $e_i \in E$, from an observed failure symptom $S_i \in V$ to a root cause $C_i \in V$ implies that the failure S_i depends on the root cause C_i. Note that the root causes C_i that dFault models (as discussed before in Section 3) include application-level failure at a DHT node (henceforth, referred to as *node*) or network-level failure at an overlay link between two DHT nodes (referred to as *link*).

We define the symptoms collected from the network S_j as the tuple (N_k, q_k) where q_k is the query that has failed in the network, and N_k is the first node in the DHT the query is sent to, referred to as source node. Simplistically, given a DHT maps queries and nodes on to consistent hash space and forwards the queries to the home node N_l, the query q_k is dependent on all the nodes, which according to the routing tables, lie along the path between the source node N_k and home node N_l.

We illustrate this using the following example. In Figure 2(a), we show a DHT network with 7 nodes N_1 through N_7 logically laid out on top of a ring. Symptoms $S_1 = (N_1, q_1)$, $S_2 = (N_5, q_2)$, $S_3 = (N_2, q_3)$, and $S_4 = (N_4, q_4)$ are shown in the Figure, with q_1 being a query issued at source node N_1 that is forwarded to the query's home node N_3. The success or failure of the query is dependent on the set of nodes between and including the source and home nodes, which happens to be the set $\{N_1, L(1,2), N_2, L(2,3), N_3\}$ for S_1, where $L(i,j)$ indicates the link between nodes N_i and N_j. Similarly, symptom S_2 depends on the set of nodes $\{N_5, L(5,4), N_4, L(4,3), N_3\}$. These nodes are determined directly using the routing table information obtained at the CDS. The corresponding bipartite dependency graph is shown in Figure 2(b), with edges between symptoms and the corresponding root causes.

Each of the edges in the dependency graph is assigned a weight w_i that reflects the strength of this dependency between the symptom and the root cause. The assignment of this weight is dependent on the amount of information we collect and use in modeling the dependencies (as dictated by the three options in Section 3.1). In the first case of *no cache modeling*, the system does not have any additional information to differentiate different root causes in terms of their edge weights. Hence, all edge weights are the same in this simplest of the cases. We discuss the other two cases next.

Modeling object popularity. dFault incorporates query popularity to model caching in the dependency graph by associating a probability with each dependency. The probability captures the likelihood that the response to the query will be found in the cache of the dependent node. In general, this cache hit probability needs to be specific to each query; a single global cache hit probability would only work if the queried items are uniformly popular—a rarity in practice [4,11]. The probability depends on the relative popularity of the query and the number of items the cache can contain. It is higher for popular queries than unpopular queries, and for a query of given popularity, a larger cache is more likely contain its response than a smaller-sized cache.

We capture the above trade-off using the following heuristic formula.

$$p_i = q_i^{\left(\frac{1}{2c-i}\right)} \text{ if } i < 2c, \text{ and } 0 \text{ otherwise.}$$

In this formula, i denotes the rank in the popularity order of the queried key, (*i.e.*, key i is the ith most popular key in the system), q_i denotes the relative popularity of the key i (*i.e.*, the number of queries to key i over total number of queries), and c denotes the number of responses the cache can hold on average.

This formula is designed for heavy-tailed popularity distributions typically found in DHTs [4,11]. It gives a value very close to 1 for really popular keys, as they are likely to be cached everywhere. Unpopular keys have a negligible likelihood of being cached anywhere. Here, we consider $2c$ as a threshold to define the number of popular keys for which the cache will play a significant role. Finally, for those keys whose popularity falls in the middle, the formula gives a number less than 1 but proportional to the relative popularity. We compute this directly from the query logs at just the source node through random sampling. Each source node forwards periodically (say, daily) its local ordering of queries (along with the number of times a query has been issued) for the top $2c$ queries over a given day. The relatively low frequency of updating this information does

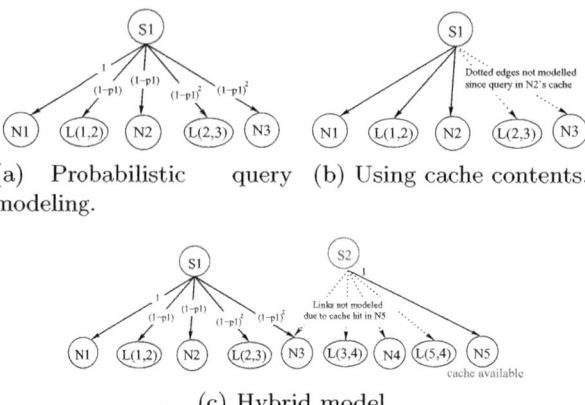

(a) Probabilistic query modeling. (b) Using cache contents.

(c) Hybrid model.

Fig. 3. Dependency graphs depending on query modeling and factoring cache contents

not affect the accuracy since object popularities have been shown to persist for days in many systems (*e.g.*, [21]). The CDS computes a global ordering of the queries by aggregating this per-node information to identify the popularity of a given query, and hence, the probability according to the heuristic formula outlined before.

In Figure 3(a), we show the corresponding dependency graph when we factor in the query popularities. The sequence in which nodes are accessed for the query corresponding to symptom S_1 are N_1, N_2 and N_3. The query is dependent on the first node N_1 with probability 1 since N_1 is the source node for the query. S_1 is dependent on N_2 only when there is no cache hit in the node N_1 which happens with probability $(1-p)$, where p is the probability calculated as above. Generalizing this further, the probability with which a query is dependent on the nth node along the path from the source node to the home node is $(1-p)^{n-1}$.

Using cache content information. This case addresses option (3) discussed in Section 3.1 where cache contents are fetched from individual nodes. Although the routing tables may indicate that a given query is dependent on all the nodes from the source node to the home node, the query may be satisfied much earlier due to a potential hit in the cache at an intermediate node. In that case, all the subsequent nodes should not be considered as part of the dependency graph. For the example in Figure 2(b), suppose that N_2's cache contents indicate the presence of the query corresponding to the symptom S_1. In this case, S_1 will not further depend on the node N_3. Thus, as shown in Figure 3(b), we remove the edge between S_1 and $L(2,3)$, and S_1 and N_3 from the dependency graph.

Hybrid dependency graph. We construct a hybrid dependency graph if we have access to both the popularity model as well as the cache contents at the end of a measurement interval. The hybrid dependency model uses the cache contents to prune out the links that are not required, and assigns probabilities for the other edges just as the dependency graph that only models query popularity would. In this paradigm, we can also model cases where we have cache contents from only a small subset of nodes. We show an example in Figure 3(c) where we have cache contents from N_5, and had a hit in the cache, which allowed pruning out S_2's dependencies with N_3, $L(3,4)$, N_4, and $L(5,4)$. For other nodes, as we can see in the figure, the probabilities are assigned just as we have in Figure 3(a).

4.2 Inference Algorithm

Once the dependency graph has been created, dFault runs an inference algorithm on the graph to output a *hypothesis set* that contains the most likely set of failed nodes that can completely explain the set of observed symptoms. There are two standard approaches for inference that we can use in our setting. First, similar to Sherlock [2] or Shrink [12]), one could apply Bayesian inference on the dependency graph. The problem, however, is that it can take very long (more than 10 minutes) as discussed in Sherlock for large graphs such as what we have in our case. Second, we can model the problem as finding a minimum set cover in a bipartite graph, as systems such as SCORE [16] proposed in the past. Although SCORE is quite scalable, SCORE is designed to operate on a deterministic bipartite graph; our dependency graph, in contrast, is probabilistic in nature. Given the importance of scalability in our setting, we follow the minimum set cover framework of SCORE, while adapting it to our probabilistic setting.

We formulate the problem of identifying the most probable hypotheses that can explain the set of symptoms as finding a minimum *set cover*. Let us denote the set of symptoms dependent on a given node N_i, i.e., the nodes that have an edge incident on N_i, as a set $\Psi_i = \{S_{i1}, S_{i2}, ...\}$, where S_i is an observed symptom. Then, the problem is to find the set $\{\Psi_{j1}, \Psi_{j2}, ...\}$ such that $\bigcup \Psi_{jk} = S$, where S is the set of all observed symptoms. Out of multiple hypotheses that can explain (cover) the set of all observed symptoms (set covers), the inference algorithm typically should favor smallest hypothesis. This is in accordance with the principle of Occam's razor that suggests that out of all explanations for a given observation, the simplest is most likely. Thus, the inference problem is therefore reduced to finding the minimum set cover of the dependency graph, that is known to be NP-hard [15] in general.

dFault uses greedy approximation to the minimum set-cover problem that finds a solution guaranteed to be an $O(\log n)$-approximation to the optimal. Of course, the size of the hypothesis set is not necessarily of great interest, as much as the overlap with the actual failures. Below, we show the pseudo-code for the inference algorithm.

procedure $infer\_hypothesis(R, S, W)$

1: $R \leftarrow$ root_causes, $S \leftarrow$ symptoms
2: Matrix $W[S][R]$ // stores the edge weights
3: unexplained $U = S$, hypothesis $H = \{\}$
4: **while** ($U\ !=$ empty) **do**
5:     $find\_score(U, R)$;
6:     find R_i s.t $\forall j\ score(R_i) > score(R_j)$;

7: $H = H \cup R_i$;
8: $R = R - R_i$;
9: $U = S - S_i$;
10: **end while**

The key idea in the inference algorithm is to iteratively find a candidate root cause that gets the highest score within each iteration, remove the set of symptoms that can be explained by this root cause, and repeat the process until all the symptoms are explained by some root cause or the other.

One key function within the inference algorithm here is the scoring function $find\_score(U, R)$. The scoring function varies depending on the particular type of the dependency graph input to the system in the form of the *edge weight* matrix $W[S][R]$. If all edge-weights are the same, such as when there is no cache model, then the scoring function is just the raw count of number of symptoms explained by each node (each element of $W[S][R]$ is 1).

In case of a global query popularity model, each of the elements in edge weight matrix $W[S][R]$ are the dependency probabilities computed between root causes and symptoms. In this case too, we use the same algorithm that we used for the case when all edge weights are the same. In our inference algorithm, we just add the raw probabilities to assign a score to each node. The intuition is that multiple low probability edges cannot increase the score of a node by so much that the score exceeds that of a few high probability edges. We show later in Section 5 that our simple heuristic is remarkably effective and accurate.

Post-processing the hypothesis. Given a DHT, there could be failures due to inherent churn in network due to nodes getting added, nodes dying and so on. But these are not of our interest as DHT reconverges. We refer to these as spurious failures. Because there is no correlated reason for the spurious failures, the number of candidates in the hypothesis set could be quite large. To address this problem, we perform post-processing of the hypothesis set generated by the inference algorithm to rank the elements and choose the ones that are most important. Our *ranking algorithm* sorts the scores of individual nodes in ascending order and computes a normalized score based on the highest score assigned to any node (*i.e.*, $s_i/Max\{s_i\}$), where s_i is the score of the ith root cause in hypothesis set). We consider only those candidates that exceed a given threshold τ. Choosing high value of τ will only output failures that contribute the most towards failed symptoms but may miss a few genuine failures (higher false negatives), while choosing a low value of τ will include several false positives in the hypothesis. We conduct experiments in Section 5 to identify the right balance between false positives and false negatives.

5 Evaluation

We use a combination of simulations and a real PlanetLab DHT deployment to evaluate the efficacy of dFault in localizing failures. The goals of our experiments are three-fold: First, we wish to compare and contrast the different variants of our system with different kinds of dependency graphs outlined in Section 4.1. Second, we intend to study the effect of *incomplete information* both in terms of the number of symptoms, routing information, and cache information available for diagnosis. For these two experiments, we use a prototype Pastry DHT implementation over PlanetLab. Given we cannot scale beyond few hundreds of nodes in PlanetLab, the third part focuses on simulation results with hundreds of thousands of nodes.

5.1 Prototype Implementation

We use the FreePastry implementation from Rice University [25], further revamped by the Cornell Beehive project as the canonical DHT for our evaluations. There are two configurable parameters in Pastry, the base parameter and the leaf-set size, which we set to 16 and 32 respectively. On top of the Pastry DHT layer, we deploy a simple application wrapper that emulates the basic functionality such as distribution of objects across different nodes in the system, issuing and accepting queries for those objects from the hosts in the network, caching of responses received (we use LRU scheme for cache eviction), and so on. The objects in our system have unique 128-bit identifiers obtained through the SHA-1 hashing algorithm. The home node, the closest node in the identifier space, stores permanent copies of the objects for which it is responsible.

Our implementation also includes a query injection mechanism that allows us to query for objects following a Zipf distribution to simulate realistic caching effects (described before in more detail in Section 3.1). Each node issues a query, waits for the response, caches the response. In case the node does not get the response within a stipulated time interval (5 minutes), it flags the query to have failed and reports it as a symptom. Apart from failure reporting, each node is also responsible for reporting any churn in the DHT network in form of routing updates. We also implement a *suspend/resume* API, that allows us to control the behavior of each node directly and inject realistic faults into the system. Thus, if we wish to simulate a fault, we trigger the suspend routine which will essentially drop (or delay) the forwarding of all application queries, but continues to participate in the DHT itself, in effect simulating the realistic failure modes we have discussed in Section 2. We also include a mechanism to inject network delays between two DHT nodes by delaying selected queries within the sender side of the overlay link.

In addition to the Pastry DHT implementation, we implement a prototype version of our dFault system. Our current implementation polls individual DHT nodes for any failed query messages every 'diagnosis interval', collects routing and cache contents information from (some or all nodes), builds the appropriate dependency graph and generates the most likely set of failed nodes.

In section 3.1, we discussed about different alternatives which can be used to model the effect of caching in the DHT network. Depending on which model we choose to use, we can have possibly 4 different adaptations of dFault: (1) dFault indicates the version that employs no cache model. (2) dFault-C includes a cache snapshot. (3) dFault-Q uses query popularity model. (4) dFault-QC uses both

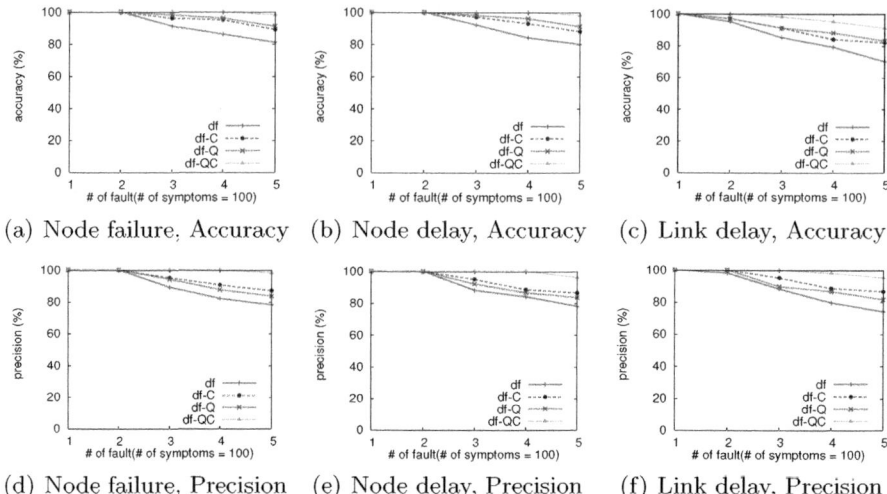

Fig. 4. Comparison of accuracy and precision for inference algorithms df (short for dFault), df-Q, df-C, df-QC for different number of simultaneous failures for node failure, node delay and link delay types of failures

query popularity model and the cache snapshot. We present a comparison of the performance of all these alternatives in this section.

Metrics for evaluation. We measure the goodness of our system using two basic metrics, *accuracy* and *precision*, as used before in the literature [16,17]. Accuracy is defined as the percentage of real faults (ground truth) captured in the hypothesis. Define H to be the hypothesis set, and G as the real ground truth, and $|.|$ denoting the usual cardinality of a set, then, accuracy is computed as $|H \cap G|/|G|$ and precision as $|H \cap G|/|H|$. In our evaluation, we consider accuracy and precision above 80% as a good diagnosis. This effectively means that 4 out of 5 faults have been accurately diagnosed and that, 4 out of 5 faults in the hypothesis set are real failures.

5.2 PlanetLab Experimental Methodology

For our experiments, we have deployed our DHT prototype system on 110 nodes in PlanetLab. We use a total of 100,000 unique objects for the DHT. We choose a relatively small cache size of 50 objects at each server, to ensure that caching alleviates, but does not completely eliminate routing in the DHT network. Queries are injected using a Zipfian distribution with parameter value of 0.9.

We inject faults using the suspend/resume API mentioned before in Section 5.1 for our Pastry implementation. To simulate a scenario, we suspend a given node (or a set of nodes to inject multiple simultaneous failures) until a total of 5,000 queries are injected into the DHT at all the nodes put together. For all our experiments, we choose the averages of 20 different random runs in order to smooth out the results. This ensures, that about 50 queries on an average are issued per node in any given diagnosis interval. Note that while diagnosis interval is typically in units of time, there is one-to-one relation between number of queries issued in the system and diagnosis interval time for a given rate at query injection. Since our query injection rate is somewhat arbitrary, we focus on number of queries instead of absolute time. On average, injecting 5,000 queries into our system takes about 4-5 minutes of time (with mean inter-query interval of about 50ms) . We use a threshold value of 0.5 (τ discussed in Section 4.2) that we found to represent a good trade-off between accuracy and precision.

We simulate three types of faults—node failure, node delay and link delay. For node failure, we use the suspend/resume API to silently drop DHT queries at the node (without affecting DHT layer connectivity itself). Failure symptoms at individual nodes are collected at individual nodes by using a timeout of 1 second (any query not responded to within 1 second is deemed a failure symptom). Node delays simulate adding 1 second latency for each and every query that passes through a given DHT node (at which we inject the failure). For these failures, we use 1 second as a timeout for failure symptoms. For link delays, we add an addition 300 millisecond latency at the sender-side of the failed link. We use 500 millisecond latency as a timeout for nodes to report as a failure. These numbers are somewhat arbitrary and chosen based on our setting; an operator can easily choose which ever timeout values to report the failure symptoms based on their setting.

5.3 Comparing Different dFault Variants

We compare the different variants of dFault across different failure scenarios (by varying the number of simultaneous injected failures). For this experiment, we only select (randomly) a total of 100 symptoms out of potentially many more. Figure 4 compares the accuracy and precision across these different variants for different types of failures injected (node fault, node delay and link delay). The base variant of dFault assumes no cache information or query popularity, and yet, as we can see from the figure, in all types of failures, it achieves almost 100% accuracy and precision for up to 2 faults. However, as the number of faults increases beyond 2, both accuracy and precision reduces to almost 75% at 5 faults (which is still reasonable since 3 out of 4 faults are localized accurately).

The effects of bringing in caching information and query popularity can be observed in df-C and df-Q variants. Somewhat curiously, both these techniques have similar accuracy and precision numbers, although one of them employs a probabilistic dependency model, while the other uses cache information to refine dependencies obtained from the routing table information alone. The query popularity modeling appears to slightly out-perform even obtaining cache contents, although, we believe this is in part because of the reduction in precision (which naturally lifts up the accuracy as more nodes are added), and hence, not significant. Note that, although the significance of these two types of information is comparable, it does not mean both are exactly doing the same thing. This is exemplified by the fact that, when we combine both caching and query popularities, we obtain the "best of both worlds" marked by a dramatic increase in accuracy and precision—almost 100% up to 5 failures in all types of faults.

5.4 Reducing the Volume of Symptoms

We study the effects of lost or delayed symptoms by *randomly sampling* a candidate set of symptoms from the actual set of observed symptoms and feed them into our system for diagnosis.

Figures 5(a) and 5(b) depicts the accuracy of dFault (for the different variants) as a function of the number of symptoms available for fault localization for 3 and 5 faults; we assume full routing information and cache snapshots at the end of every diagnosis interval. We do not show the precision curves since they follow very similar trends to accuracy. Two observations can be made from the figure. First, we observe that the number of symptoms required for achieving 100% accuracy in fault diagnosis is dependent on the number of faults in the system. For a single failure scenario (not shown in Figure), even as low as 20 symptoms is sufficient to achieve 100% accuracy and precision for all algorithms. As the number of faults increases, it requires increasingly more number of symptoms for the same accuracy and precision values. Second, the difference between the various versions of dFault becomes more apparent with more number of failures, with dFault-QC consistently out-performing both the C and Q variants. Note however that, dFault-QC suffers from low accuracy and precision just like others when the number of symptoms is less than 20 since there is not enough evidence collected to clearly identify the root causes. This is fundamental as collecting the cache contents and modeling the query popularities accurately cannot compensate for the lack of sufficient evidence.

5.5 Partial and Stale Routing Information

One of the key ingredients in building the dependency graph is the routing information which CDS collects from the nodes in the DHT network. Once the base routing tables are collected, dFault needs to know only the routing updates representing any churn in the network. As with symptoms, routing updates could be lost, delayed and sometimes be incorrect or stale. To evaluate the efficacy of our system under such conditions, we perform two experiments, one with partial routing information, and the other with stale information.

Partial routing information. Figure 5(c) depicts the performance in cases when it has access to routing tables from only a fraction of nodes in the DHT. Here, we fix the number of available symptoms to 150, which is larger than strictly required. From the figure, we can observe that the dFault does not lose any accuracy even for the five-failure scenario without the availability of routing information from up to 10% of the nodes. The system is more robust to non-availability of routing information when the number of faults is less— for 1 and 2 fault scenarios, accuracy is 100% even without the routing information for about 30% of nodes. This, of course, is expected since the chance that the

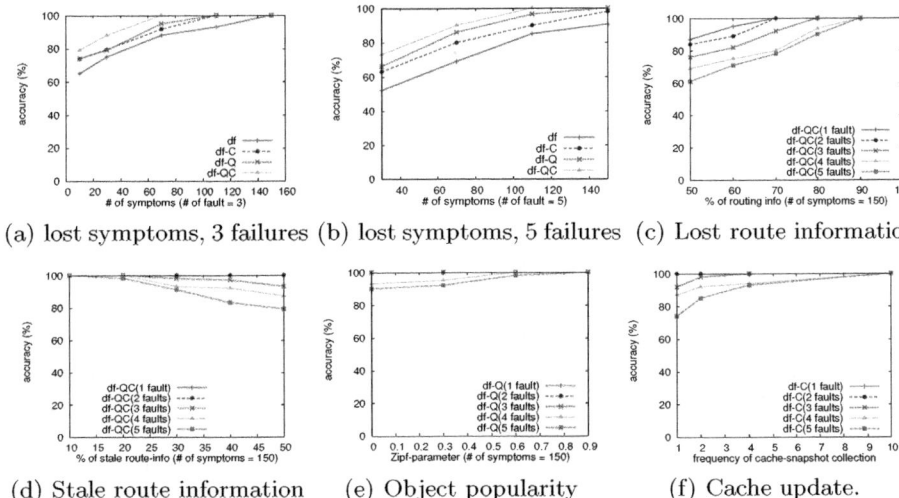

Fig. 5. Robustness to lost symptoms, lost or stale routing tables, and cache effects

routing information necessary for diagnosing the fault is missing is smaller for less number of failures. One thing we observe from our experiments was that the loss of routing information can be somewhat compensated by the number of extra symptoms dFault gets to use in diagnosing compared to previous results in Figure 4. Precision graphs show a similar trend and hence omitted for brevity.

Figure 5(d) depicts the performance when a set of nodes have not been able to report the routing updates to the CDS. We created this scenario by starting the system with 110 PlanetLab nodes, then killing 10 nodes so that the eventual system has only 100 nodes. We collected our failure symptoms from the 100 nodes, but used the routing information from when there were 110 nodes, which means, some of the routing table entries will be stale and inaccurate. We varied the fraction of nodes that used old routing tables from the 110 node scenario on the x-axis in Figure 5(d). We can observe that, while the accuracy of the system goes down as the amount of stale information increases, the accuracy is higher than that of lost routing information. In essence, we observe that loss of routing information affects the performance to a much greater extent compared to the staleness of routing information, *i.e.*, out-dated information, that may be false, is still better than no information. This is because, even though there may be erroneous entries in the routing tables that will confuse the inference algorithm, they are not going to be a whole lot. If there is no information, however, there is no way to create a dependency graph that makes inference harder.

5.6 Impact of Caching

We study the impact of cache model on our system by varying the Zipfian parameter and the frequency of cache snapshot collection.

Variation with Zipf parameter. A lower value of Zipfian parameter results in a more uniform query distribution; indeed a parameter of 0 is exactly the uniform distribution model. It results in more frequent changes to overall cache content. For this experiment, we used dFault-Q since we are mainly interested in modeling the effects of the popularity distribution while isolating the effects of cache, which we consider next. As expected, we can see from Figure 5(e) that the accuracy of dFault-Q in case of uniform query distribution (Zipf parameter = 0) is somewhat lesser than for higher values of Zipf parameter. For a smaller number of failures (< 4), the Zipf-parameter has no direct effect on the accuracy.

Effect of more cache information. As discussed in Section 3.1, given a finite size of the cache at any given node, the cache contents are likely to undergo frequent changes. Since we collect cache contents only at the end of a diagnosis interval, the snapshot of cache collected may not be the true representation of the state of cache viewed by a given failed query. A way to reduce this effect to some extent is to access more number of cache snapshots per diagnosis interval. While this also increases communication bandwidth, we wish to determine the tradeoff in this experiment Indeed, in Figure 5(f), we can clearly observe the increased accuracy as a result of multiple cache updates per diagnosis interval. We experimented with different time interval of collecting cache snapshots. In our setup, dFault-C delivered 100% accuracy when the snapshots were collected every 10 times per diagnosis interval. Although, it may appear that this truly involves sending 10 copies of the cache, we can encode only the differences when transmitting to the CDS which will drastically reduce the communication bandwidth required.

5.7 Scalability Experiments

Our PlanetLab implementation results are all based on around a 100 node deployment; in order to evaluate how dFault performs when deployed on large-scale DHTs consisting of thousands of nodes, we build a custom simulator that abstracts several key features of the DHTs and conduct our experiments in this simulator. In our framework, we simulate a simple $O(\log N)$ routing protocol, with N being the the total number of nodes. We start with 600,000 objects which are distributed among all the nodes, *i.e.*, each object is assigned to a unique *home node*. We also simulate caching with LRU as the cache eviction policy. Every node has a cache of size 5% of the number of objects each node in the DHT is responsible for, i.e. it is a home node for. Similar to the PlanetLab experiments, we set the Zipfian parameter to 0.9. Just as before, we simulate faults by determining how many and which nodes to fail randomly. After a fixed interval of time, we collect these failed queries (symptoms) and perform failure analysis using the same technique as described above. So, our simulator simulates the typically behavior of DHTs, with hooks for fault injection.

Figure 6 shows the performance of dFault (the QC variant with full routing and cache snapshot information) as we inject a variable number of failures into the DHT. The number of failures in the Figure is not absolute, but a percentage of total number of nodes. We varied the percentage from 0.1% to all the way 3.2%

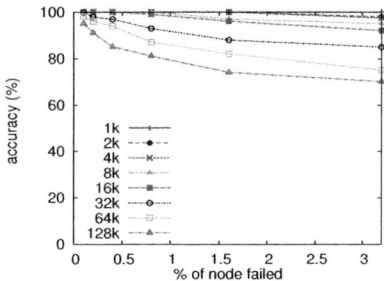

Fig. 6. Accuracy of dFault with size of network

in multiples of 2. Thus, in the worst case scenario, in a network of 128,000 nodes, about 4,096 would have failed, which is quite a large number of failures. As can be observed from Figure 6, dFault can identify with almost $70 - 90\%$ accuracy. For a network experiencing less than 1% node failures, dFault performs with more than 80% accuracy even for a system with $128K$ nodes.

Bandwidth requirements. We now discuss briefly the bandwidth requirements for transfer of information from nodes to the CDS. Assuming nodes and queries are represented by 128-bit hash values, we can calculate the amount of bandwidth required for data communication for smooth functioning of dFault. The maximum number of entries each Pastry node has to maintain is given by the formula $(2^b - 1) \times \log_{2^b} N + l$. In our evaluation, we have used $b = 4$ and $l = 32$, which translates to roughly 100 entries per node at the most; assuming $20 bytes$ per entry, routing tables are not more than $2KBytes$ in size. A cache size of about $2,000 \times 20 Bytes = 40 KBytes$ (assuming a relatively large cache of 2,000 elements) also needs to be transferred for modeling the cache effects. Including another $100 \times 20 = 2Kbytes$ for the network symptoms (assuming 100 symptoms per node), a total of about $44KBytes$ needs to be transferred from every node in the DHT. If we assume that the diagnosis time interval is 5 minutes, then a bandwidth of $44KBytes/300s = 1.2Kbps$ is sufficient per node. Even for a system with 100,000 nodes, this translates to a bandwidth of less than 100 Mbps aggregate at the CDS.

6 Related Work

Fault isolation and diagnosis is a well-researched topic with several systems proposed for fault localization over the past few years. However, there have been very few systems for localizing application-layer faults in DHTs. To the best of our knowledge, dFault is the first attempt to systematically develop a fault localization framework for DHT applications.

Most practically deployed fault localization systems are in the context of enterprise services, where these tools provide invaluable service to IT administrators to pin-point the location of faults. For example, EMC's SMARTS [26], IBM

Tivoli [1], HP OpenView [9], to name a few, provide general management support by pulling together alarms from several components and correlating them to understand where the failures occur. Unfortunately, while they provide general correlation support, these systems operate with SNMP-based [5] measurements, and hence do not localize application layer faults. SMARTS uses a codebook based approach to diagnose faults for some well known applications. The dependency for these applications is known a priori, and the codebook is built by application experts.

Our work is closest to systems that exploit dependency graphs for fault isolation [16,12,2,13] involve the creation of a dependency graph that represents the complex chain of dependencies that exists in services, and a localization algorithm that amasses the set of symptoms from the network and outputs a hypothesis that contains the candidate set of root causes. While our system dFault also follows a similar general approach, there are significant differences as well. Sherlock [2] provides new abstractions such as multi-tier dependency models and uses Bayesian inference for fault diagnosis in enterprise networks. Sherlock is not directly applicable in our framework, because dependencies in our system are not as complex; simple bi-partite modeling suffices. In addition, the inherently large scale of p2p networks makes scalability an important requirement, while the use of Bayesian inference in Sherlock increases the computation time for large p2p networks.

Bi-partite graphs have also been used before for modeling dependencies between root causes and observed symptoms. SCORE [16], for instance, uses bi-partite graphs for modeling 'shared-risks' and diagnosing IP link layer faults and optical components. Similarly, [17] uses bi-partite graph modeling to diagnose MPLS black holes in backbone networks. While dFault shares a similar setup, the presence of caching effects and dynamic routing information from the underlying p2p layer makes our modeling *probabilistic* in nature, and thus, different compared to their deterministic model.

7 Conclusions

Although DHT-based systems began mainly as research prototypes, they have quickly found mainstream adoption. As they make headway into more commercial applications, their robustness requirements increase tremendously. Unfortunately, there exist several latent failure modes in DHTs that can affect application performance significantly. In this paper, we present dFault for accurate localization of these latent failures. dFault collects a sample of failure symptoms from the individual DHT nodes and formulates a bi-partite dependency graph with the help of routing tables and caching information collected from nodes. It runs an inference algorithm over this graph to output a candidate set of faults. In our evaluation of dFault with a real deployment over PlanetLab as well as using simulations, we found dFault to produce accurate and precise hypothesis for multiple failures, even in the presence of erroneous and incomplete fault and dependency data.

References

1. http://www.tivoli.com
2. Bahl, P., Chandra, R., Greenberg, A., Kandula, S., Maltz, D.A., Zhang, M.: Towards highly reliable enterprise network services via inference of multi-level dependencies. In: ACM SIGCOMM (August 2007)
3. Barham, P., Donnelly, A., Isaacs, R., Mortier,R.: Using magpie for request extraction and workload modelling. In: OSDI 2004 (December 2004)
4. Breslau, L., Cao, P., Fan, L., Phillips, G., Shenker, S.: Web Caching and Zipf-like Distributions: Evidence and Implications. In: Proc. of IEEE INFOCOM Conference, New York, NY (March 1999)
5. Case, J., Fedor, M., Schoffstall, M., Davin, J.: A simple network management protocol (SNMP). RFC 1157, IETF (May 1990)
6. Freedman, M.J., Freudenthal, E., Mazières, D.: Democratizing content publication with Coral. In: Proc. of the USENIX Symposium on Networked Systems Design and Implementation (NSDI), San Francisco, CA (March 2004)
7. Freedman, M.J., Lakshminarayanan, K., Rhea, S., Stoica, I.: Non-transitive connectivity and dhts. In: WORLDS, San Francisco, CA (December 2005)
8. Hastorun, D., Jampani, M., Kakulapati, G., Pilchin, A., Sivasubramanian, S., Vosshall, P., Vogels, W.: Dynamo: Amazon's highly available key-value store. In: SOSP, Stevenson, WA (October 2007)
9. HP Technologies, Open View, http://www.openview.hp.com
10. Dunagan, J., et al.: Fuse: Lightweight guaranteed distributed failure notification. In: OSDI 2004 (2004)
11. Jung, J., Sit, E., Balakrishnan, H., Morris, R.: DNS Performance and Effectiveness of Caching. In: Proc. of SIGCOMM Internet Measurement Workshop (IMW), San Francisco, CA (November 2001)
12. Kandula, S., Katabi, D., Vasseur, J.P.: Shrink: A tool for failure diagnosis in IP networks. In: Proc. ACM SIGCOMM MineNet Workshop (August 2005)
13. Kandula, S., Mahajan, R., Verkaik, P., Agarwal, S., Padhye, J., Bahl, V.: Detailed diagnosis in computer networks. In: ACM SIGCOMM (August 2009)
14. Karger, D., Lehman, E., Leighton, T., Levine, M., Lewin, D., Panigraphy, R.: Consistent hashing and random trees: Distributed caching protocols for relieving hot spots on the World Wide Web. In: Proc. of the ACM Symposium on Theory of Computing (STOC), El Paso, TX (April 1997)
15. Karp, R.M.: Reducibility among combinatorial problems. In: Miller, R.E., Thatcher, J.W. (eds.) Complexity of Computer Computations, pp. 85–103.
16. Kompella, R., Yates, J., Greenberg, A., Snoeren, A.C.: IP fault localization via risk modeling. In: NSDI (May 2005)
17. Kompella, R., Yates, J., Greenberg, A., Snoeren, A.C.: Detection and localization of network black holes. In: IEEE Infocom (May 2007)
18. Li, Z., Goyal, A., Chen, Y., Kuzmanovic, A.: P2PDoctor: Measurement and diagnosis of misconfigured peer-to-peer traffic. Technical Report NWU-EECS-07-06, North Western University (2007)
19. Maymounkov, P., Mazières, D.: Kademlia: A peer-to-peer information system based on the xor metric. In: Druschel, P., Kaashoek, M.F., Rowstron, A. (eds.) IPTPS 2002. LNCS, vol. 2429, p. 53. Springer, Heidelberg (2002)
20. Ramasubramanian, V., Sirer, E.G.: Beehive: O(1)lookup performance for power-law query distributions in peer-to-peer overlays. In: NSDI, San Francisco, CA (March 2004)

21. Ramasubramanian, V., Sirer, E.G.: The design and implementation of a next generation name service for the Internet. In: SIGCOMM, Portland, OR (August 2004)
22. Ratnasamy, S., Francis, P., Handley, M., Karp, R., Shenker, S.: A scalable content-addressable network. In: ACM SIGCOMM, San Diego, CA (August 2001)
23. Rhea, S., Chun, B.-G., Kubiatowicz, J., Shenker, S.: Fixing the embarrassing slowness of opendht on planetlab. In: WORLDS, San Francisco, CA (December 2005)
24. Rhea, S., Godfrey, B., Karp, B., Kubiatowicz, J., Ratnasamy, S., Shenker, S., Stoica, I., Yu, H.: OpenDHT: a public DHT service and its uses. In: Proc. of the ACM SIGCOMM Conference, Philadelphia, PA (August 2005)
25. Rowstron, A., Druschel, P.: Pastry: Scalable, decentralized object location, and routing for large-scale peer-to-peer systems. In: Guerraoui, R. (ed.) Middleware 2001. LNCS, vol. 2218, p. 329. Springer, Heidelberg (2001)
26. SMARTS Inc., http://www.smarts.com
27. Stoica, I., Morris, R., Karger, D., Kaashoek, F., Balakrishnan, H.: Chord: A scalable peer-to-peer lookup service for Internet applications. In: ACM SIGCOMM, San Diego, CA (August 2001)
28. Project Voldemort: A distributed database, http://project-voldemort.com

Bridging the Gap between Legacy Services and Web Services

Tegawendé F. Bissyandé[1], Laurent Réveillère[1], Yérom-David Bromberg[1], Julia L. Lawall[2,3], and Gilles Muller[3]

[1] LaBRI, University of Bordeaux, France
[2] DIKU, University of Copenhagen, Denmark
[3] INRIA/Lip6, France

Abstract. Web Services is an increasingly used instantiation of Service-Oriented Architectures (SOA) that relies on standard Internet protocols to produce services that are highly interoperable. Other types of services, relying on legacy application layer protocols, however, cannot be composed directly. A promising solution is to implement wrappers to translate between the application layer protocols and the WS protocol. Doing so manually, however, requires a high level of expertise, in the relevant application layer protocols, in low-level network and system programming, and in the Web Service paradigm itself.

In this paper, we introduce a generative language based approach for constructing wrappers to facilitate the migration of legacy service functionalities to Web Services. To this end, we have designed the Janus domain-specific language, which provides developers with a high-level way to describe the operations that are required to encapsulate legacy service functionalities. We have successfully used Janus to develop a number of wrappers, including wrappers for IMAP and SMTP servers, for a RTSP-compliant media server and for UPnP service discovery. Preliminary experiments show that Janus-based WS wrappers have performance comparable to manually written wrappers.

1 Introduction

The Web Services (WS) instantiation of Service-Oriented Architectures has progressively been adopted as a practical means to implement distributed applications [18]. WS exploit the pervasive infrastructure of the World Wide Web to set up loosely coupled software systems composed of a collection of services. Services rely on a set of standards and specifications[1] to make their functionalities available according to platform-independent interfaces, facilitating the construction of heterogeneous compositions.

Many services, however, continue to rely on legacy application layer protocols (ALPs). Examples of such protocols include IMAP for retrieving mail, SMTP for sending mail, RTSP for controlling media streaming, and UPnP for discovering networked home appliances. These protocols are considered to be reliable and effective, but complicate service composition. While WS can easily and safely be combined using widely used standards, such as WS-BPEL [16] and WS-CDL [23], composing ALP-based services requires integrating a protocol stack for each ALP in the client application.

---
[1] A specification is a potential standard that has not yet been approved.

To provide ALP-based services with a uniform interface, to allow them to be more easily combined to provide rich functionalities, one solution is to use wrappers to convert them to Web Services. A wrapper is essentially a gateway that provides a WS interface to the existing capabilities of an ALP-based service. It makes accessible, through appropriate operations, the independent functionalities that the service provides, without the complexity of reimplementing the service as a WS. Nevertheless, this approach requires translating WS requests into ALP requests and ALP responses into WS responses. Implementing these translations safely and efficiently involves challenging programming at both the network and systems level.

At the network level, the wrapper programmer must take into account the variety of ALP definitions. For example, some ALPs are symmetric, relying on request-response communication, while others are asymmetric, relying on message-based communication. An ALP may also support sessions or reliability, which must then be accounted for at the WS level. WS are normally unicast; wrapping an ALP-based service relying on a multicast ALP requires using UDP rather than HTTP, and a specific set of WS standards. Finally, in practice, to ease the development of a WS client and improve efficiency, it may be desirable to create a single WS operation that corresponds to a series of ALP requests and responses.

At the systems level, expertise in thread, memory and socket management is necessary to efficiently handle simultaneous requests, to dispatch responses to appropriate endpoints and to keep track of established sessions. Furthermore, in order to avoid requiring a wrapper to actively wait for asynchronous responses, the execution of a request handler must be stopped until corresponding responses arrive, then restarted to process results. These processing tasks must not prevent the wrapper from handling other synchronous and asynchronous requests. The complexity of such programming tasks makes manual wrapper construction laborious and error prone. Naive implementations of such code can introduce severe performance bottlenecks.

This Paper. In this paper we propose a generative language-based approach for constructing wrappers to enable the migration of legacy service functionalities to Web Services. This approach involves two domain-specific languages: z2z, which was developed in our previous work [2] for describing ALP message structures and behaviors, and Janus, which is the main contribution of this work and targets the specific needs of WS. Our approach targets programmers who are familiar with an ALP and with basic Java programming. Its main benefit is to allow such developers to quickly and easily develop efficient and safe WS wrappers. Our contributions are:

- We define the Janus domain-specific language that allows describing the interface of a legacy service and its representation as a WS. A Janus description is expressed at a high level that hides the low-level details of the WS paradigm and of the ALPs.
- We describe the translation of a Janus description into a wrapper implementation compatible with a WS environment, and the Janus runtime system that supports the execution of this wrapper. The translation and the runtime system together address various network and systems programming issues, hiding this complexity from the programmer.
- We show that the expressiveness of Janus is sufficient to describe the interface of a number of ALP-based services and to generate the appropriate WS wrappers. Our

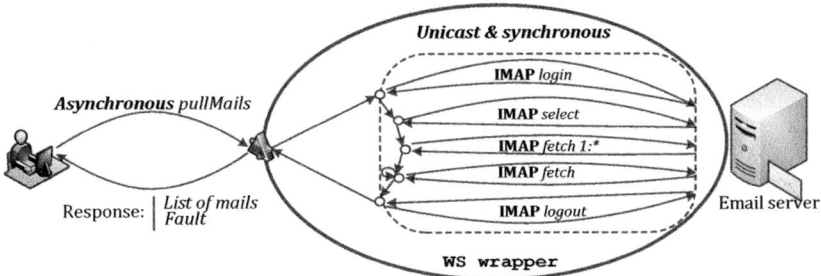

Fig. 1. IMAP service wrapper

case studies include well-known legacy services relying on ALPs such as IMAP, SMTP, RTSP and UPnP.
– The experiments that we have carried out show that our approach produces wrappers that have performance comparable to manually developed wrappers based on existing WS and ALP stacks.

The rest of this paper is organized as follows. Section 2 introduces the case studies that we use to present the details of our approach and the issues that these case studies entail. Section 3 presents the Janus language and Section 4 describes the generated code. Section 5 demonstrates the efficiency of our approach. Section 6 discusses related work. Finally, Section 7 concludes the paper.

2 Case Studies

A developer creating a WS wrapper for an ALP-based service by hand must first select the functionalities that should be made available as WS operations and then describe for each operation the corresponding WS interface and the structure of the operation's parameters and results. We present some of the issues confronting the developer in creating such wrappers, and illustrate these issues using wrappers for IMAP and SMTP mail services, for an RTSP-compliant media service and for UPnP service discovery.

Message granularity. ALPs are generally implemented directly on top of TCP, resulting in lightweight messages, and thus are able to provide fine-grained functionalities. WS, on the other hand, are built on top of SOAP and either HTTP or UDP, resulting in messages that are complex and verbose. Thus, in a WS environment, to reduce the bandwidth consumption and to simplify the client implementation, it is often desirable to provide higher-level operations. As an example of this granularity mismatch, we consider a WS wrapper for an IMAP server, illustrated in Figure 1. The IMAP server shown inside the oval on the right side of the figure allows a client to retrieve mail using a sequence of synchronous exchanges of messages, for authentication, folder selection, message listing, message fetching, etc. The WS wrapper, however, encapsulates this sequence of low-level IMAP requests and responses as a single WS operation, *pullMails*. A WS wrapper for an SMTP server could be constructed similarly.

Message transmission synchrony. In the implementation of our IMAP wrapper, we have chosen to make the WS operation asynchronous, even though the protocol used by the service is synchronous. The management of this asynchrony must be implemented by the wrapper developer.

Message return values. The result of the WS operation is the list of mails retrieved from the server in case of success, or an error message otherwise. The wrapper programmer has to be aware of the specific data types to be used in constructing WS error messages.

Session management. Our second case study involves the construction of a session-based WS wrapper to remotely control a RTSP-compliant media server. Although RTSP requests flow within different TCP streams, some requests need to be associated to the same session. For instance, the *play* and *stop* requests include session information. The wrapper developer must thus translate RTSP session management into WS session management, through the use, for instance, of the WS-reliability specification.

Multiple ALPs. The media server case study also illustrates the case of a wrapper that needs to process messages from several different ALPs. For instance, the media service wrapper may need to process SDP messages describing multimedia session information that are encapsulated in the body of RTSP responses.

Multicast. In a networked environment, UPnP-enabled clients discover the services provided by available UPnP-compliant devices. To successfully discover existing services, clients have to send UPnP search requests to a multicast group address. However, supporting the multicast communication paradigm in the WS realm requires the use of several WS specifications that are not part of the basic WS standards. Our implementation of the WS wrapper for UPnP relies on the specifications SOAP-Over-UDP [17] and WS-Addressing [22]. The development of this wrapper is significantly different from other traditional wrappers because SOAP messages are not encapsulated inside HTTP messages but flow directly over UDP. Therefore, constructing such multicast wrappers significantly raises the level of expertise required by the wrapper developer.

3 Wrapper Development

A WS wrapper converts a WS invocation into a sequence of ALP interactions, and then converts the information collected by these ALP interactions into a WS result. Constructing such a wrapper requires information about the ALP behavior (*e.g.*, whether messages are transmitted by unicast or multicast, synchronously or asynchronously, etc.), the structure of the WS and ALP messages, and the logic for translating between them.

In previous work, we have developed the z2z language for constructing network protocol gateways [2]. A WS wrapper can be seen as a particular kind of gateway, dedicated to the specific needs of WS. Z2z provides facilities for describing network protocol behaviors, message structures, and translation logics, and an optimized run-time system. It is suitable for expressing the behaviors and message structures of protocols that are built directly on the transport protocols TCP and UDP, which is typically the case of ALPs. WS, however, are at a higher level, being built on SOAP [24], which in turn is

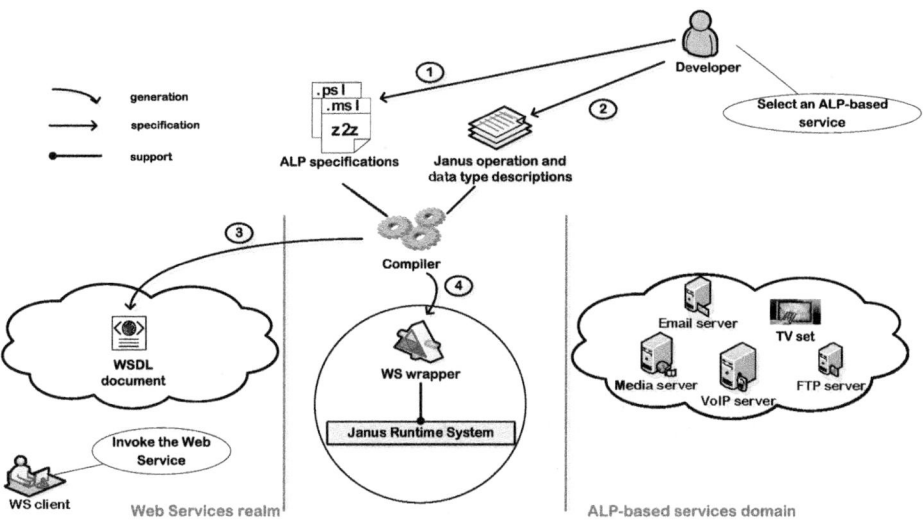

Fig. 2. Scenario for constructing wrappers with z2z and Janus

built on HTTP or directly on top of UDP in the multicast case. Defining WS messages and the WS-ALP translation logic using z2z would require expressing these features in terms of SOAP/HTTP or SOAP/UDP messages, which would be extremely tedious and require a high degree of WS expertise. We have thus developed a new language, Janus, for describing WS messages and the translation between WS and ALP messages directly, and a supporting runtime system that translates WS interactions to the lower level SOAP and HTTP protocols. To fit with the expertise of the expected developer community, Janus uses a Java-like syntax.

Based on z2z and Janus, we propose a generative language-based approach to WS wrapper construction that relies on z2z for describing ALP behaviors and message structures, and Janus for describing WS message structures and the translation between WS messages and ALPs. Fig. 2 gives an overview of this approach. For each ALP relevant to the functionalities that the developer has chosen to expose as WS operations, the developer provides a z2z specification, consisting of a *protocol specification*, describing how the ALP interacts with the network, and a *message specification*, describing the structure of ALP requests and responses.[2] The developer then uses Janus to describe the desired WS interface to these functionalities, including the structure of the WS operation arguments and return values and the translation of each WS operation to the corresponding ALP messages. The Janus compiler translates the z2z and Janus specifications to an executable wrapper and a WSDL document that describes the generated WS. The wrapper is then linked with a runtime system that provides various optimized systems functionalities.

---

[2] As shown in Fig. 2, a protocol specification is provided in a .psl file and a message specification in a .msl file.

```
 1  protocol rtsp {
 2    int cseq_number;
 3    attributes { transport = tcp/554; mode = sync; }
 4    start { cseq_number = 1; }
 5    request req {
 6      response DESCRIBE when req.method == "DESCRIBE";
 7      response PLAY      when req.method == "PLAY";
 8      ...
 9    }
10    sending request req { req.cseq = cseq_number++; }
11    flow = { cseq }
12    tcp { void tcp_connect(); }
13  }
```

a) RTSP protocol specification

```
1  read {
2    mandatory public fragment code;
3    mandatory public fragment line;
4  }
```

b) IMAP request message view

```
1  request template response getMail {
2    magic   = "SEP";
3    newline ="\r\n";
4    public int id;
5    private int tag;
6    --SEP
7    <%tag%> fetch <%id%> body[text]
8    --SEP
9  }
```

c) IMAP request template

Fig. 3. Z2z protocol behavior and message structure descriptions

In the rest of this section, we present the use of z2z for describing ALPs and the Janus language for describing WS messages and operations.

3.1 Z2z Protocol Behavior and Message Structure Descriptions

The first step of our approach uses z2z to describe how the relevant ALPs interact with the network, as illustrated for the RTSP protocol in Fig. 3a. A z2z protocol specification first declares any needed local variables, such as cseq_number in line 2, and then contains a collection of blocks describing various properties of the interaction with the network. The attributes block specifies the transport protocol used, whether requests are sent in unicast or multicast, and whether ALP responses are received synchronously or asynchronously (line 3). The start block initializes the local variables (line 4). The request block specifies how to dispatch a received request to a specific handler for processing (lines 5-9). The sending block specifies some default information for each request or response, such as the cseq_number for an RTSP message (line 10). The flow block indicates the message information that a wrapper must use to match asynchronous requests to their subsequent responses (line 11). A similar session_flow block is used to recognize messages that are associated with a particular session, when the protocol supports sessions. Finally, the tcp block specifies a handler for opening connections on a socket (line 12).

A WS wrapper must also be aware of the structure of ALP messages. These messages are also described using z2z. A z2z *message view* defines the information to be extracted from incoming messages (Fig. 3b). Similarly, z2z *templates* (Fig. 3c) describe the structure of new ALP messages to be created by the wrapper. Both message views and templates may contain fields declared as private that are handled automatically by the runtime system and fields declared as public that must be managed by the Janus message translation logic. For example, the tag field is declared as private in Figure 3c (line 5) because its value is automatically generated for each constructed IMAP request message. This is also the case of the cseq field for RTSP, which, as illustrated in Figure 3a (line 10), is filled in by the sending block of the RTSP protocol specification. Whenever a RTSP request is sent, the value of the `cseq` field is automatically incremented by the runtime system.

3.2 Janus Service Operation Descriptions

The second step of our approach uses the Janus domain-specific language to describe how to invoke the chosen functionalities of the ALP-based service. Janus has been designed according to requirements that we have identified as critical to ease WS development and to enforce good practices in WS design. For instance, Janus follows a *contract-first strategy* in the implementation of a WS. That is, an abstract description of a WS (e.g., WSDL) is made available before the actual production of the WS. By design, Janus *supports stateful Web Services* by enabling side-effects. While presenting a Java-like syntax (see Fig. 4), with which programmers are familiar, Janus *limits the functionalities to what is needed for WS development*. The only objects available are data structures which only have a default constructor, for initializing their different fields, and a default method (`send`), for forwarding them in the network. Finally, Janus enables the creation of robust wrappers by *encapsulating subtle and error-prone code* such as code for network message processing. For example, it provides the `send` operator for sending messages on the network and the structure field notation for easily accessing message fields. These features are provided within a language, rather than in a library as done in Java, allowing the complete code to be checked for various coherence properties. For example, the Janus compiler checks that the code is *type safe*, that all variables are *initialized before they are used*, and that all message fields are *initialized before the message is sent*.

program	::=	*external_import** *service_def*
external_import	::=	`#import` interface_id ;
	|	`#import protocol.` protocol_id ;
service_def	::=	[*qualifier*] `service` (*service_params*) { *datatype_def** *operation*$^+$ }
service_params	::=	*COMMA_LIST* (*primitive_type* datatype_id)
datatype_def	::=	`class` complex_type_id [`extends` complex_type_id] { *nested_data** }
nested_data	::=	*primitive_type COMMA_LIST* (var) ;
operation	::=	*datatype* operation_id ([*operation_params*]) { *statement*$^+$ }
datatype	::=	*primitive_type* | *complex_type*
	|	`List<`*datatype*`>`
operation_params	::=	*COMMA_LIST* (*datatype* datatype_id)
primitive_type	::=	`String` | `int`
complex_type	::=	complex_type_id
qualifier	::=	`multicast`
statement	::=	*decl_stmt* | *affect_stmt* | *if_stmt* | *for_stmt* | *except_stmt* | *return_stmt* | {*statement*$^+$}
decl_stmt	::=	*datatype COMMA_LIST* (var) ;
	|	`request<`protocol_id`>` *COMMA_LIST* (var) ;
	|	`response<`protocol_id`>` *COMMA_LIST* (var) ;
affect_stmt	::=	var `=` *data* ; | *datatype* var `=` *data* ;
data	::=	`new` *complex_type* ([*COMMA_LIST* (primitive_type_id)])
	|	*data* `.` field | *data* `.send()` | function (*data*)
if_stmt	::=	`if` (*boolean_expr*) *statement*$^+$
for_stmt	::=	`for` (*datatype* var `:` list_var) { *statement** }
except_stmt	::=	`throw` *data* ;
return_stmt	::=	`return` *data* ;
boolean_expr	::=	*data* | boolean
COMMA_LIST(*elem*)	::=	*elem* (`,` *elem*)*

Fig. 4. Janus language grammar

```
1   import protocol.rtsp.*;
2
3   service mediaPlayer (String hostname, int port) {
4     /* Data type definitions */
5     class MediaRequest { String resource; }
6     class PlayRequest extends MediaRequest { ... }
7     class PauseRequest extends MediaRequest { ... }
8     class StopRequest extends MediaRequest { ... }
9
10    ...
11    /* Operation descriptions */
12    Media PLAY (PlayRequest req) { ... }
13    ...
14  }
```

Fig. 5. Janus service for RTSP Media service

In Janus, the wrapper functionalities are described in a service definition. As shown in Fig. 5, a Janus service is defined by the keyword `service` (line 3), followed by the name of the service being defined. The service is parametrized by the hostname and port number of the machine that hosts the WS wrapper. These values are set when invoking the Janus compiler. A Janus service defines data types to describe the parameters and return value of a WS operation, and a set of methods to specify the series of ALP messages that need to be exchanged with the service to define each WS operation. The ALP attributes previously defined with z2z are imported through the `#import` directive at the beginning of the file. Other utilities' interfaces can also be referred to using this directive.

Data types. A WS operation typically has some arguments and return values, of various data types. The wrapper must know the structure of these data types so that it can extract information from the arguments in order to construct the corresponding ALP requests, and so that it can construct the return values from the ALP responses. Janus data types are either primitive or complex. Primitive types are strings and integers. A complex type is defined by a Java-like class containing only fields. Such a class also defines an implicit constructor that takes as arguments the initial values of the fields in the order in which they appear in the class definition. Janus provides an inheritance mechanism that enables one data type to be defined as an extension of another. This is useful when data types share a number of fields, as in the case of the invocation parameters of the `PLAY`, `PAUSE`, and `STOP` operations defined by the media service wrapper (Fig. 5). For each of these operations, the parameter includes a `Resource` field that defines the URI of the media being served. Therefore, the corresponding Janus classes extend the `MediaRequest` class that contains this `Resource` field.

Operation descriptions. A WS operation is described in Janus as a method whose arguments and return values correspond to the input and output parameters of the WS operation. The main function of such a method is to translate between WS and ALP messages. Nevertheless, Janus also provides abstractions to support sessions and multicast services. Using the example of the *pullMails* operation defined in Fig. 6 for our IMAP server case study, we illustrate how the interface to a functionality of an ALP-based service is expressed using Janus.

```
1   List<Mail> pullMails(String login, String passwd, String folder) {
2   /* operation pullMails retrieves unread mails from an IMAP server */
3       request<imap> req;
4       response<imap> resp;
5       List<Mail> mails = new List<Mail>();
6       List<int> ids = new List<int>();
7       Mail m;
8
9       req = new Login(login, passwd); resp = req.send();
10      if (resp.code == "error")
11          throw new ServiceFault("[login]", "server failed");
12
13      req = new selectFolder(folder); resp = req.send(); ...
14      req = new listMessage(); resp = req.send(); ...
15
16      ids = List.parse2int (resp.line, " ");
17      for (int id : ids) {
18          req = new getMail(id); resp = req.send(); ...
19          m = new Mail(id, resp.line);
20          List.add (m, mails);
21      }
22
23      req = new Logout(); resp = req.send(); ...
24      return mails;
25  }
```

Fig. 6. IMAP `pullMails` service operation

A Janus method exchanges a sequence of ALP messages with a service in order to provide the requested functionality to the WS client. To create an ALP message, the Janus code uses the constructor implicitly associated with the corresponding z2z template (line 9). This constructor takes as arguments the values for the template's `public` fields in the order in which they appear in the template definition. A template also provides a method `send` for sending a created message into the network (line 9). The Janus compiler translates a use of the `send` method into an invocation of the z2z `send` operator. This operator transparently handles the difference between sends with synchronous and asynchronous responses, freeing the developer from the need to manage this complexity. To extract information from an ALP response, the Janus code uses the standard field access notation (line 10), as in Java. Any field that is qualified as `public` in the corresponding z2z message view is accessible in this manner.

As in Java, the `return` keyword indicates the value returned by a method to its caller (line 24). In Janus, the returned value of a method is represented by a complex data type and must be created by the Janus code using the data type's associated constructor. To send the returned value back to the WS client, the Janus compiler generates code to serialize and encapsulate this value as a WS compliant message.

Janus also supports a mechanism for error management. For example, if the login to the IMAP server fails (line 10), a fault message has to be sent back to the WS client. As in Java, a Janus exception is raised using the keyword `throw` (line 11), aborting the method execution. Unlike in Java, Janus exceptions cannot be caught by the programmer and are only used to report unexpected situations to the WS client. A fault message can be created using the constructor of the default `ServiceFault` data type (line 11) or of a defined data type that extends this one.

When an ALP uses sessions and the requests within a session are associated with different WS operations, then the WS wrapper must manage sessions as well. For

```
 1  import protocol.rtsp.*;
 2
 3  service mediaPlayer (String hostname, int port) {
 4    String SESSION_ID;
 5    ...
 6    Media PLAY (PlayRequest preq) {
 7      ...
 8      req = new Setup(...); resp = req.send(); ...
 9      /* Save the session ID returned by setup */
10      SESSION_ID = resp.sessionId;
11      ...
12    }
13    Media STOP (StopRequest sreq) {
14      ...
15      /* Use the session ID previously saved */
16      req = new Teardown(hostname, sreq.resource,
17                                   SESSION_ID);
18      ...
19    }
20    ...
21  }
```

a) Excerpt of the RTSP PLAY service operation

```
 1  import protocol.ssdp.*;
 2
 3  multicast service controlPoint () {
 4    class UPnPService { ... }
 5    ...
 6    List<UPnPService> SEARCH(SearchRequest sreq){
 7      ...
 8    }
 9    ...
10  }
```

b) Excerpt of the UPnP control point wrapper description

Fig. 7. Janus descriptions

example, as described in Section 2, the media service wrapper needs to manage a session that has been set up by the media service. As shown in the Janus implementation in Fig. 7a, to process a WS STOP operation, an ALP *Teardown* request must be sent with the session information (line 16) that was previously returned by the ALP *Setup* request (line 10). However, these ALP requests are sent within different WS operations. Janus implements sessions using the WS-Reliability [15] specification. The Janus code can then declare global variables that are visible within a session. For example, line 4 of Fig. 7a declares a global variable SESSION_ID that maintains the ALP session identifier across multiple WS requests. Such a variable can be set (line 10) and read (line 16) like a local variable. The Janus compiler automatically generates the code to manage session information in the WS realm.

In the excerpt of Fig. 7b, the Janus description of the wrapper for UPnP service discovery is declared with the keyword *multicast* (line 3), indicating that the implementation must be multicast-compliant. Janus then produces a wrapper that can process SOAP messages carried by UDP instead of HTTP. All information that is carried by HTTP in the unicast case, including the client endpoint reference to which WS responses must be returned, is now encapsulated in the SOAP message using the WS-Addressing specification.

4 Code Generation

Based on the z2z descriptions of ALP behaviors and message structures and the Janus descriptions of WS message structures and the translation between WS messages and ALPs, the Janus compiler generates various documents, specifications and program code, as shown in Fig. 8, to create a complete wrapper implementation. In this section we describe the generation of these artifacts.

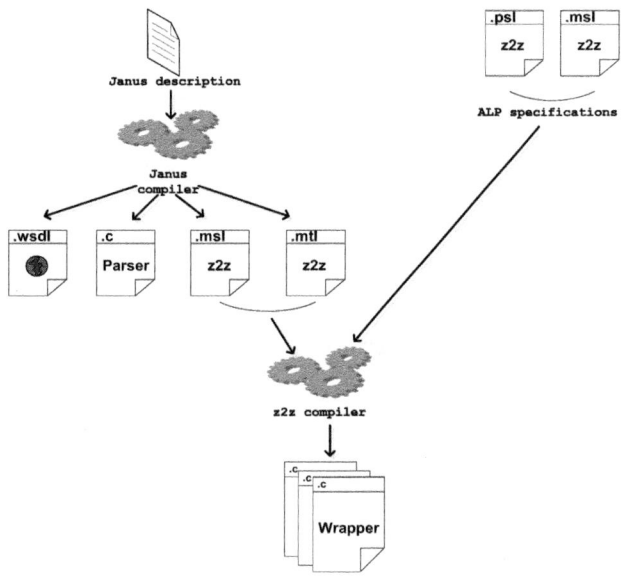

Fig. 8. Overview of the generated code

4.1 WS Framework

From a WS wrapper specification written in Janus, the compiler generates code for publishing the service operations in a WS framework and for processing WS messages.

Publishing the service operations. In the WS framework, a WS is accompanied by a WSDL document that makes information about the operations provided by the WS available in a machine-readable form. A WSDL document also specifies concrete bindings that describe how the abstract service description is mapped to a specific service access protocol. Nevertheless, WSDL, as a machine-readable format, is not well suited to being written by hand, especially for a service that defines multiple operations.

Based on the Janus service operation descriptions and compiler arguments indicating the endpoint where the service is to be deployed, the Janus compiler creates the WSDL description of the wrapper. The generated WSDL document includes *types*, which are data type definitions specified using the XML Schema language, *messages*, which are typed definitions of the data to communicate, and *operations*, which are abstract descriptions of the actions supported by the service. Furthermore, the WSDL document specifies the endpoint address where the service is available as well as the protocol (e.g., SOAP) to be used for invoking the service. The Janus compiler also includes in the WSDL document the WS specifications that are required by the wrapper. Once created, the WSDL document is made available via a web server, thus allowing client programs to call any of the operations that are listed.

WS message structures and processors. Once the wrapper is exposed to potential WS clients, it may begin to receive WS messages. It must parse these messages and may need to construct WS messages to send in response. The structure of these messages is

```
1  message soap {
2    read {
3      mandatory public fragment subject;
4      mandatory public fragment from;
5      ...
6      mandatory public int smtpPort;
7    }
8    ...
9  }
```

a) message view for a SMTP message

```
1   #include "msg_soap.h"
2   ...
3   void xml_data(void * d, const char * data, int l) {
4     struct IGDdatas * datas = (struct IGDdatas *)d;
5     char buf[l];
6     if ( !z2z_strcmp(datas->elt_name, "subject") ){
7       sprintf(buf, "%.*s",l, data);
8       msg_soap_view_set_subject(datas->view,
9                                 make_string(buf));
10    }
11    ...
12  }
```

b) Excerpt of the SOAP parser for SMTP

Fig. 9. Generation of a SOAP message view and the associated parser

```
1   import protocol.imap.*;
2   service ImapServer(String hostname, int port) {
3     ...
4     serverResponse imapCreateFolder(String login,
5              String passwd, String folderName) {
6       response<imap> resp; request<imap> req;
7       ...
8       req = new createFolder(folderName);
9       resp = req.send();
10      ...
11      return new serverResponse(resp.line);
12    }
13  }
```

a) imapCreateFolder operation with Janus

```
1   template createFolderResponse {
2     magic = "SEP"; newline ="\r\n";
3     public fragment serverResponseLine;
4     --SEP
5     <soapenv:Envelope ...>
6     ...
7     <cli:createFolderResponse>
8       <resp><%serverResponseLine%></resp>
9     </cli:createFolderResponse>
10    ...
11    </soapenv:Envelope>
12    --SEP
13  }
```

b) z2z generated template

Fig. 10. Message template generation

determined by the parameter and return type specifications in the signatures of the Janus operation descriptions and the associated Janus data type specifications. To provide support for processing received WS messages, the Janus compiler generates a z2z message view and a dedicated SOAP parser from the data types representing the parameters of each WS operation. The message view contains all the fields of the data type, including those of any data type it inherits. The SOAP parser is a C program that extracts invocation parameter values from an XML document, embedded inside an incoming HTTP message or on top of UDP, and uses these values to initialize the message view fields listed in Fig. 9 (a). Fig. 9 (b) shows an excerpt of a generated parser that recovers the subject to use in a *sendMail* operation from a WS message. For each data type that is used to describe a WS operation return value, as in the example of Fig.10a (line 11), the Janus compiler generates a z2z SOAP template whose public fields correspond to the primitive types that compose the return data type (Fig.10b). This template is used to create a SOAP message that carries the operation result.

4.2 Wrapper Implementation

The wrapper implementation is based on the z2z specifications of protocol behaviors and message structures, and the Janus operation descriptions. These are translated by the Janus compiler into the corresponding lower level z2z message translation logic code, which is then translated into C code by the z2z compiler. Furthermore, the Janus compiler adds into the translation logic of the operation descriptions the code necessary for taking into account any WS specifications that are used to address issues that are supported by Janus, but are not handled by the basic WS standards. Developers need not be aware of the details of these specifications.

To support client sessions, Janus relies on the WS-Reliability [15] specification. Using this specification, a WS message is identified by a message ID, consisting of a group ID and a sequence number. In our design, a WS wrapper recognizes messages from the same session by the shared message group ID. Based on this information, the wrapper code has access to the values of the global variables corresponding to the session, which it can then use to construct ALP messages containing appropriate session identifiers. The Janus compiler automatically detects the use of ALP sessions in the operation descriptions and generates the corresponding code to manage WS sessions.

When a Janus service is declared as `multicast`, the Janus compiler generates code to parse and create SOAP messages directly over UDP. This generated wrapper code uses the SOAP-over-UDP [17] and WS-Addressing [22] specifications. The wrapper listens to a multicast group address and does not include HTTP processing capabilities.

The C code generated by the composition of the Janus and z2z compilers is supported by a dedicated runtime system. Janus relies on a enhanced version of the z2z runtime system that provides a framework for processing SOAP messages and currently supports the WS specifications WS-Reliability, SOAP-over-UDP and WS-Addressing.

5 Assessment

To assess our approach, we have implemented wrappers for the various ALP-based service functionalities described in the case studies of Section 2. For each considered case study, Figure 11 compares how many lines of source code the developer needs to manually write against how many lines of source code are generated by the Janus compiler. Among our examples, only 204 (SMTP) to 582 (RTSP) lines of source code, including ALP specifications (z2z), operation descriptions (Janus) and ALP parsers (C), need to be written by hand to implement the WS wrapper. Using only z2z, but not Janus, the WS wrapper for SMTP requires 642 lines of source code, including SOAP parsers, WSDL documents, and z2z specifications, and the WS wrapper for RTSP requires 882 lines of source code. This comparison of code size furthermore does not fully take into account the amount of WS and network expertise that is required to implement a

		Developer code (lines of code)			Generated code						
		ALP specifications	Janus descriptions	ALP Parsers	z2z specifications (lines of z2z code)	SOAP parsers (lines of C code)	WSDL document (lines of code)	Wrapper source code (lines of C code)	WS wrapper (size in KB)		
									Wrapper	Runtime System	Total
IMAP Server wrapper	IMAP	161	79	102	370	208	102	1861	44	80	124
SMTP Server wrapper	SMTP	129	48	27	216	222	75	918	24	80	104
Media Server wrapper	RTSP SDP	193 41	97	153 98	297	227	122	2488	48	80	128
UPnP service discovery	UPnP	58	13	304	115	312	113	1877	32	80	112

Fig. 11. The size of specifications and the generated WS wrapper

wrapper without using Janus. Compared to the final generated C code, excluding the runtime system, the Janus compiler provides around 77% of the code. Moreover, as illustrated in Figure 11, the size of the wrappers does not exceed 128KB, including 80KB for the runtime system. Thus, Janus wrappers can be embedded in constrained devices.

To fully evaluate the performance of Janus generated wrappers, we have carried out three experiments involving an IMAP and an SMTP service, a UPnP service, and an ALP-based echo protocol. Our experiments were carried out on a 2GHz Intel Core 2 duo with 4GB of RAM. In each case, to reduce the impact of the network latency on the response time, the client, the wrapper, and the service are all collocated on the same machine and interact using the loopback interface.

WS wrappers for IMAP and SMTP services. We evaluate the capacity of wrappers to manage both WS to IMAP and WS to SMTP translations under stress tests. To this end, several WS clients simultaneously invoke either a WS *pullMails* operation on a user folder to retrieve two mails, or a WS *sendMail* operation to send five mails to a remote mailbox. The IMAP wrapper translates WS invocations into IMAP messages, that are sent to a Dovecot IMAP server (*http://www.dovecot.org*) The SMTP wrapper similarly translates WS invocations into SMTP messages that are sent to a POSTFIX SMTP server (*http://www.postfix.org*).

Figures 12 and 13 compare, respectively, the performance of the Janus IMAP wrapper with that of a manually developed IMAP wrapper, and the Janus SMTP wrapper with that of a manually developed SMTP wrapper. The handmade wrappers, using neither Janus nor z2z, are implemented in Java with the JAX-WS Reference implementation and Tomcat. The execution time is measured from the time when the wrapper receives a WS invocation to the time when the corresponding response is sent back to the WS client. The performance is expressed in terms of CPU cycles, to be independent of the CPU frequency.

In our experiments, two parameters may impact the performance: (i) the number of simultaneous clients, and (ii) the number of simultaneous invocations performed by each client. Consequently, our test procedure involves several simultaneous clients and consists of a set of rounds, successively increasing the stress on the wrapper in each round. In the first round each client fetches or sends all mails once, resulting in two or five simultaneous requests per client for the IMAP or SMTP tests respectively. In the second round each client fetches or sends all mails twice, resulting in four or ten simultaneous requests per client. This pattern continues until the thirtieth round where each client fetches or sends all mails 30 times, resulting in 60 or 150 simultaneous requests per client. The test procedure is undertaken 30 times. Figures 12 and 13 show only median values.

As expected, the graphs show that the higher the number of simultaneous clients (*i.e.*, 5 or 15 clients for IMAP and SMTP wrappers), the higher the response times. Janus wrappers perform better than the wrappers developed by hand, because the Janus wrappers can rely on a fine grained runtime support that includes generated code that is dedicated to mapping IMAP and SMTP messages into SOAP messages and vice versa. Specifically, Janus wrappers include a WS stack stripped down to the bare essentials according to the Janus description given to the Janus compiler. In contrast, handmade

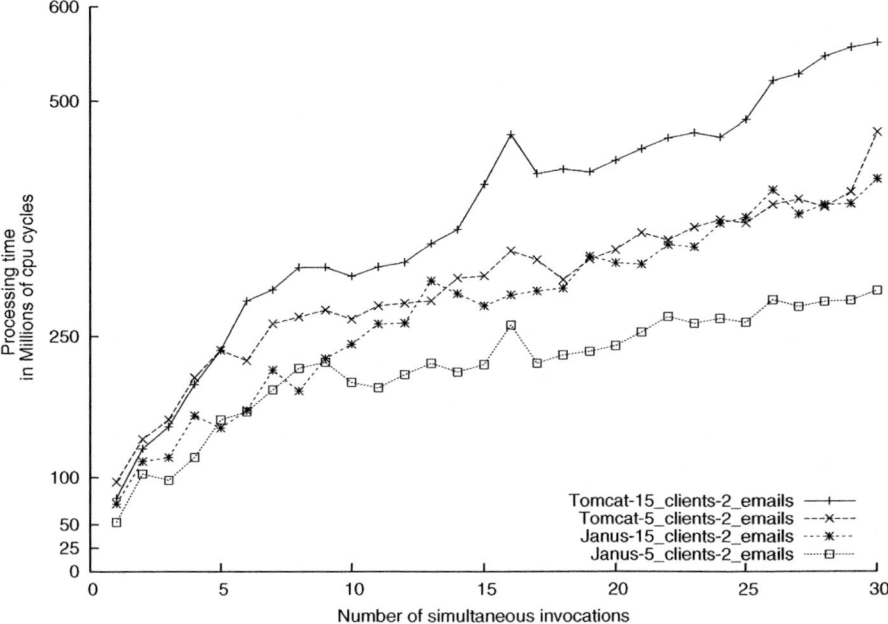

Fig. 12. IMAP server wrapper

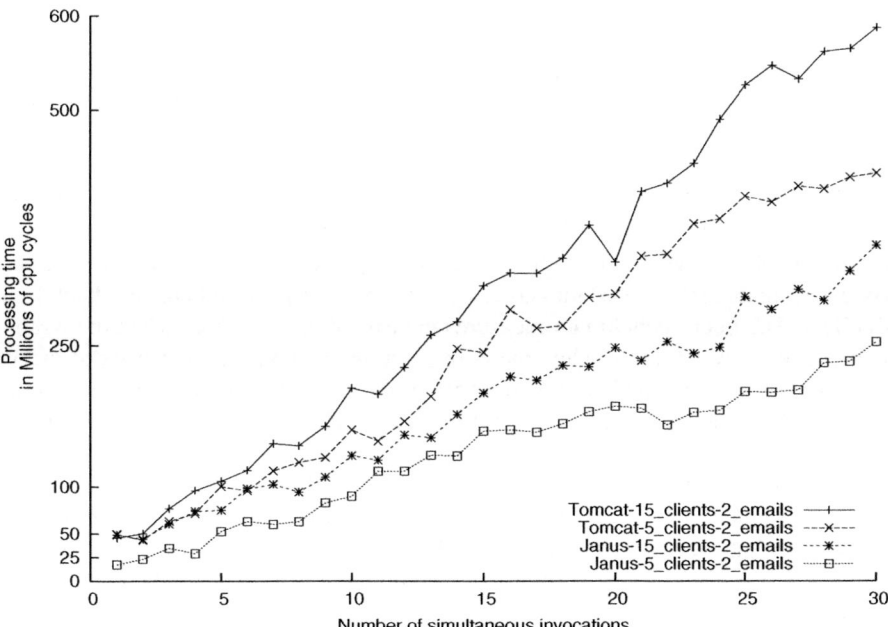

Fig. 13. SMTP server wrapper

wrappers use a general-purpose WS stack and runtime that offer no particular optimizations for wrappers.

WS wrapper for UPnP service. The Janus-generated wrapper for UPnP service relies on multicast addressing both in the WS realm, requiring support of extra WS-* standards, and in the UPnP native domain. We have therefore carried out an experiment to estimate the overhead introduced by the wrapper processing layers. To evaluate the Janus UPnP wrapper, we compare the response time required by a WS client to discover a UPnP service with the time required for a UPnP client to discover a UPnP service. In both cases, we measure, at the client side, the time taken between an initial discovery request and the corresponding successful response. Any standard WS toolkit can be used to generate the WS client from the WSDL Document published by with Janus wrapper. We have chosen the gSOAP[3] toolkit for its efficiency, as it is developed in C. The UPnP client and the service are developed with the C implementation of the CyberLink[4] stack.

In our experiment, the response time of the native UPnP client reaches 1220 million CPU cycles whereas for the WS wrapper client it takes 1805 million CPU cycles, amounting to a slowdown of 50%. This slowdown results from the cost of the various steps of the translation logic. The Janus wrapper needs to: (i) listen on a multicast group address, dedicated to the WS realm, to intercept incoming SOAP-over-UDP requests, (ii) deserialize received SOAP requests to generate the corresponding UPnP requests, (iii) forward the newly generated UPnP requests and listen for potential UPnP responses from the multicast group address dedicated to UPnP, and (iv) transform UPnP responses to SOAP messages to send them back to the WS client. In comparison, the UPnP client interacts directly with the UPnP service, it does not need to listen on two different multicast group addresses, and it does not need to serialize and deserialize SOAP messages.

WS wrapper for an ALP-based echo service. We have implemented a micro benchmark to evaluate the performance of the SOAP serialization/deserialization performed by Janus wrappers. The experiment involves a Janus wrapper for an ALP-based echo service that echoes primitive data types such as integers and strings. In this case, a WS client, generated by the gSOAP compiler from the Janus WSDL document, sends SOAP primitive data types to a Janus wrapper that extracts the data value to forward it, without any XML tags, to an echo service. Messages from the echo service are similarly encapsulated into SOAP messages by the Janus wrapper and are sent back to the WS client. The micro benchmark measures the execution time from when the wrapper receives a WS invocation to when the corresponding response is sent back to the WS client. We consider the median time over 50 executions. We find that with serialization and deserialization, this takes around 1.1 million CPU cycles for an integer value, and around 1.4 million CPU cycles for a string of 50 characters. Without serialization and deserialization, we find that the time is around 0.3 million CPU cycles for an integer value and around 0.5 million CPU cycles for a string of 50 characters. Although these results show that the cost of serialization is high, they represent a worst case due to the simplicity of the echo server. Normally the total treatment time would be dominated by the server computations.

---

[3] http://www.cs.fsu.edu/~engelen/soap.html
[4] http://www.cybergarage.org/cgi-bin/twiki/view/Main/CyberLinkForC

6 Related Work

Alternative forms of Web Services. This paper has focused on the SOAP/WS-* stack for Web Services. In the last decade, RESTful Web Services [8] have been increasingly used. RESTful Web Services are praised for the simplicity of their design and implementation, in comparison with WS-* standards which are increasingly complex and often not implemented. Nevertheless, as extensively discussed by Pautasso *et al* [19], SOAP/WS-* remains the most appropriate choice in many contexts. Our goal is to provide interoperability between existing services. The use of SOAP/WS-* allows these services to remain outside the Web; the web is only used as a message enchange interface. On the other hand, RESTful Web Services exist only within the Web, requiring more reengineering and preventing other kinds of accesses. Furthermore, contrary to REST, SOAP/WS-* technology comes with a fairly robust body of standards for QoS. Thus, when advanced functionalities, such as multicast, are needed, existing WS-* standards can deliver the appropriate capabilities. RESTful WS would have to be extended to support these capabilities in an ad hoc manner [19]. Finally, the variety of formats that can be used to represent a RESTful WS can hinder interoperability, as WS clients may not be able to process all types of payloads. In the rest of this section, WS refers to web services constructed with the SOAP/WS-* stack.

WS implementation. As WS technologies mature, many research projects [5,7,10] have focused on devising methods and tools that help with WS development, testing and deployment. Kelly *et al.* have analysed existing programming languages and development environments used by SOA programmers and have identified a number of limitations [10]. For instance, they point out that since object-oriented and scripting languages were originally designed for standalone environments, the extra functionalities that have been added to them for network and distributed processing fail to provide a simple means for designing and implementing services that are invoked remotely. They stress that a good language for WS development should support static typing, so that WSDL definitions can be automatically generated from function definitions. In addition, all data should be serializable so that it can be sent within SOAP messages. The Janus language meets these requirements.

Kelly *et al.* also propose the GridXSLT execution engine for exposing programs as WS. GridXSLT relies on a language that extends the XSLT programming language for specifying WS operations. GridXSLT only supports functions that are side-effect free, meaning that a service may not maintain state. This constraint makes impossible to implement WS wrappers that involve sessions, such as our RTSP media service wrapper. Janus does not place any restrictions on the type of applications that can be wrapped.

Legacy services migration. Several companies have succeeding in re-packaging their legacy services as WS so as to enable better integration of Web information. For instance, in 2002, Amazon.com released a WS interface (*http://aws.amazon.com*) linked to their existing query engine to provide to computer programs the same service that their primary keyword-based search interface has been offering to humans. Google Web APIs are another example of the migration of human-oriented Web Site interfaces to web services. Lately, many researchers have proposed tools for extracting from web documents information that can then be requested by WS clients [9,13].

The idea of migrating a legacy service to WS has been explored in the literature [3,4,11,21]. Almoanaies et al. have recently published a survey of the various existing approaches [1]. Attempts to move legacy services to the SOA environment have been motivated by issues ranging from software reuse and maintenance to interoperability. Our work is dedicated to migrating services built on top of incompatible ALPs to WS so as to benefit from the many features provided by SOA.

Migration solutions that are close to our work have been proposed by Sneed [20] and by Canfora et al. [3,4]. Sneed has designed a tool for extracting and wrapping individual functions from legacy code. Canfora et al. have devised a method for constructing a wrapper that interprets a Finite State Automaton that models the interaction between the client and the legacy system. In our approach, a wrapper developer is allowed to adjust the characteristics of this interaction so as to fulfill other requirements. For instance, in the case of IMAP server case study, we have designed a WS wrapper with asynchronous operations while messages are sent synchronously in IMAP. Thus the WS client is not required to actively wait while all mail is collected from the server.

Other projects have re-designed and re-implemented ALP-based application functionalities using WS standards. Though such re-engineering solutions can provide flexibility in design and ensure performance, their invasive aspect prevents their wide adoption. WSEmail [14] replaces the existing protocols for email (i.e., SMTP, POP, IMAP, S/MIME) with protocols based on SOAP, WSDL, and other XML-based formats. However, WSEmail does not fully exploit existing email infrastructures and thus fails to recover the logic perfectly [25]. Similarly, Chou et al. [6] have proposed an entirely WS-based protocol, WIP, to replace SIP in their WSIP [12] endpoint for converged multimedia/multimodal communication over IP. All communicating entities, however, must support the new protocol.

A compromise approach to legacy service migration is to provide wrappers that interface different parts of a service. The legacy service is thus broken up to several parts, each implementing one or more functionalities. This approach avoids reimplementing these functionalities in the WS, and thus yields practical and less invasive solutions. Zhang and Yang [25] have presented a service-oriented approach that uses a hierarchical algorithm to understand the legacy code and extract independent services from it. Janus on the other hand lets the developer choose the granularity of the functionalities to expose.

7 Conclusion

In this paper, we have introduced an approach for migrating ALP-based service functionalities to Web Services using wrappers. To this end, we have designed the Janus language, which provides dedicated constructions and operations to hide low-level ALP and WS details from the wrapper programmer. We have also developed a compiler for Janus that automatically generates the corresponding wrapper code in C and the wrapper's associated WSDL service description. Finally, we provide a Janus runtime system that is to be linked with the generated wrappers and that encapsulates the required low-level networking and systems code.

We have successfully used Janus to develop a number of wrappers, including wrappers for IMAP and SMTP servers, for a RTSP-compliant media server and for UPnP service discovery. Our experience in using Janus for wrapper construction shows that our approach drastically reduces the level of expertise required. By freeing the wrapper developer from manually managing both WS details and ALP-based communication issues, Janus bridges the gap between the WS realm and ALP-based services.

Preliminary experiments show that Janus-based WS wrappers have performance comparable to manually written wrappers. Furthermore, the size of the executable code of our Janus-based wrappers, including the runtime system, is small, not exceeding 128KB, which is acceptable in contexts where code size must be minimized, as in some embedded systems. We are currently extending the Janus approach to support WS specifications such as WS-Notification, WS-Eventing, and WS-Security. We are also developing Janus wrappers for other application domains such as network supervision.

Availability: The source code of z2z is available at http://www.labri.fr/perso/reveille/projects/z2z/. The source code for Janus is available on request.

References

1. Almonaies, A.A., Cordy, J.R., Dean, T.R.: Legacy system evolution towards service-oriented architecture. In: SOAME 2010: International Workshop on SOA Migration and Evolution, Madrid, Spain, pp. 53–62 (March 2010)
2. Bromberg, Y.D., Réveillère, L., Lawall, J.L., Muller, G.: Automatic generation of network protocol gateways. In: Bacon, J.M., Cooper, B.F. (eds.) Middleware 2009. LNCS, vol. 5896, pp. 21–41. Springer, Heidelberg (2009)
3. Canfora, G., Fasolino, A., Frattolillo, G., Tramontana, P.: Migrating interactive legacy systems to Web services. In: 10th European Conference on Software Maintenance and Reengineering, pp. 10–36 (March 2006)
4. Canfora, G., Fasolino, A.R., Frattolillo, G., Tramontana, P.: A wrapping approach for migrating legacy system interactive functionalities to Service Oriented Architectures. Journal of Systems and Software 81(4), 463–480 (2008)
5. Cho, E., Chung, S., Zimmerman, D., Muppa, M.: Automatic web services generation. In: HICSS 2009: Proceedings of the 42nd Hawaii International Conference on System Sciences, pp. 1–8 (2009)
6. Chou, W., Li, L., Liu, F.: WIP: Web service initiation protocol for multimedia and voice communication over IP. In: ICWS 2006: Proceedings of the IEEE International Conference on Web Services, Chicago, IL, USA, pp. 515–522 (2006)
7. Feuerlicht, G., Meesathit, S.: Towards software development methodology for web services. In: Proceeding of the 2005 Conference on New Trends in Software Methodologies, Tools and Techniques, Tokyo, Japan, pp. 263–277 (2005)
8. Fielding, R.T.: Architectural Styles and the Design of Network-based Software Architectures. Ph.D. thesis, University of California, Irvine (2000)
9. Han, H., Kotake, Y., Tokuda, T.: An efficient method for quick construction of web services. In: Proceeding of the 2009 Conference on Information Modelling and Knowledge Bases XX, Amsterdam, The Netherlands, pp. 180–193 (2009)
10. Kelly, P.M., Coddington, P.D., Wendelborn, A.L.: A simplified approach to web service development. In: ACSW Frontiers 2006: Proceedings of the 2006 Australasian Workshops on Grid Computing and e-research, Darlinghurst, Australia, pp. 79–88 (2006)

11. Lewis, G., Morris, E., Smith, D., O'Brien, L.: Service-oriented migration and reuse technique (SMART). In: STEP 2005: Proceedings of the 13th IEEE International Workshop on Software Technology and Engineering Practice, Budapest, Hungary, pp. 222–229 (2005)
12. Liu, F., Chou, W., Li, L., Li, J.: WSIP - web service SIP endpoint for converged multimedia/multimodal communication over IP. In: ICWS 2004: Proceedings of the IEEE International Conference on Web Services, San Diego, CA, USA, p. 690 (2004)
13. Lu, Y.H., Hong, Y., Varia, J., Lee, D.: Pollock: automatic generation of virtual web services from web sites. In: SAC 2005: Proceedings of the 2005 ACM Symposium on Applied Computing, Santa Fe, NM, USA, pp. 1650–1655 (2005)
14. Lux, K.D., Michael, J.M., Bhattad, N.L., Gunter, C.A.: WSEmail: Secure internet messaging based on Web services. In: ICWS 2005: Proceedings of the IEEE International Conference on Web Services, Orlando, FL, USA, pp. 75–82 (2005)
15. OASIS: Web Services Reliable Messaging TC. WS-Reliability 1.1 (November 2004)
16. OASIS: Web Services Business Process Execution Language Version 2.0 (April 2007)
17. OASIS: SOAP-over-UDP version 1.1 (July 2009)
18. Papazoglou, M.P., Heuvel, W.J.: Service oriented architectures: approaches, technologies and research issues. The VLDB Journal 16(3), 389–415 (2007)
19. Pautasso, C., Zimmermann, O., Leymann, F.: RESTful Web Services vs. "Big" Web Wervices: Making the Right Architectural Decision. In: Proceedings of the 17th International World Wide Web Conference, Beijing, China, pp. 805–814 (2008)
20. Sneed, H.M.: Wrapping legacy COBOL programs behind an XML-interface. In: WCRE 2001: Proceedings of the Eighth Working Conference on Reverse Engineering (WCRE 2001), Stuttgart, Germany, p. 189 (2001)
21. Sneed, H.M.: Integrating legacy software into a service oriented architecture. In: CSMR 2006: Proceedings of the Conference on Software Maintenance and Reengineering, Bari, Italy, pp. 3–14 (2006)
22. W3C: Web Services Addressing (WS-Addressing) - W3C submission (August 2004)
23. W3C: Web Services Choreography Description Language Version 1.0 (November 2005)
24. Walsh, A.E. (ed.): UDDI, SOAP, and WSDL: The Web Services Specification Reference Book (2002)
25. Zhang, Z., Yang, H.: Incubating services in legacy systems for architectural migration. In: APSEC 2004: Proceedings of the 11th Asia-Pacific Software Engineering Conference, Busan, Korea, pp. 196–203 (2004)

Enforcing End-to-End Application Security in the Cloud
(Big Ideas Paper)

Jean Bacon[1], David Evans[1], David M. Eyers[1], Matteo Migliavacca[2],
Peter Pietzuch[2], and Brian Shand[3]

[1] University of Cambridge
{firstname.lastname}@cl.cam.ac.uk
[2] Imperial College London
{migliava,prp}@doc.ic.ac.uk
[3] CBCU/ECRIC, National Health Serivice
brian.shand@cbcu.nhs.uk

Abstract. Security engineering must be integrated with all stages of application specification and development to be effective. Doing this properly is increasingly critical as organisations rush to offload their software services to cloud providers. Service-level agreements (SLAs) with these providers currently focus on performance-oriented parameters, which runs the risk of exacerbating an impedance mismatch with the security middleware. Not only do we want cloud providers to isolate each of their clients from others, we also want to have means to isolate components and users within each client's application.

We propose a principled approach to designing and deploying end-to-end secure, distributed software by means of thorough, relentless tagging of the security meaning of data, analogous to what is already done for data types. The aim is to guarantee that—above a small trusted code base—data cannot be leaked by buggy or malicious software components. This is crucial for cloud infrastructures, in which the stored data and hosted services all have different owners whose interests are not aligned (and may even be in competition). We have developed data tagging schemes and enforcement techniques that can help form the aforementioned trusted code base. Our big idea—cloud-hosted services that have end-to-end information flow control—preempts worries about security and privacy violations retarding the evolution of large-scale cloud computing.

Keywords: application-level virtualisation, information flow control, publish/subscribe, policy, cloud computing.

1 Introduction

Complex systems are far from bug-free and distributed systems are inherently complex. This is not only because of the fundamental properties of distribution but also because they blur traditional boundaries of data ownership and administrative responsibility. Current approaches to achieving secure, large-scale, distributed systems are not holistic; often, existing abstractions are imperfectly extended (as is the case, for example, for communication of data across networks [1]). Security is an increasingly critical problem as organisations rush to offload their software services to cloud providers. SLAs with these providers currently focus on performance-oriented parameters, which runs the risk of exacerbating security failures.

Fears about security can come from a lack of isolation. It is understood that cloud providers must isolate each of their clients from others. Traditional server and operating system level virtualisation can help, ensuring isolation as appropriate within a data centre. However, each cloud client provides one or more services, each of which in turn may have a multitude of users. We want to ensure that such a service can guarantee that its users' data remains private, even when managed by threads sharing a service's address space.

To see why this is necessary, consider healthcare data. These may be sensitive for a human lifetime or longer and approaches to security that involve only encryption are insufficient; over long timescales, keys may be compromised or become more easy to break. Additionally, we want a way to control, at a fine granularity and in an end-to-end manner, precisely where information is allowed to flow according to policy.

Our vision is that security in the cloud should be incorporated from the start and achieved end-to-end, even when software components may be buggy or malicious. Only thus can cloud clients guarantee that their users' data is safe from cross-contamination or leakage to unauthorised recipients. Cloud service providers therefore need to offer their clients strong but usable isolation support. In effect we want to start with high-level information flow policies that describe how a cloud client manages the data under its control and transform these policies into mechanisms of data isolation enforcement by the cloud infrastructure. We call this *application-level virtualisation*, emphasising that the goal is to provide the illusion of isolated application instances whose interactions are defined by information flow policies.

As a specific example of where this type of isolation is necessary, consider Cancer Registries within the United Kingdom. They compute aggregate statistics about cancer incidence in different parts of the country. Moving these computations into the cloud has the potential benefit of homogenising the processing involved and the data structures used, ensuring that all Cancer Registries operate in the same way. However, there would be a strong need to isolate processing *within this application*—ideally as if there were separate physical resources devoted to each of the sets of data that should not mix. This would match the physical isolation of the data sets between each Cancer Registry that occurs today.

The isolation provided by application-based virtualisation can also be used to protect commercial interests. Suppose that a city runs a service, hosted by a cloud provider, whereby sensors detecting phenomena about the city can be connected with applications that display, process, or store the readings. A company that owns pollution sensors might sell the readings from those sensors to specific customers. The customers, whose applications run in the cloud, should be prevented from sharing the raw sensor data and be permitted to disclose derived data solely based on their agreements with the sensor owner.

For application-level virtualisation to have useful authority, it must express *all* paths that data may follow in any particular system, including messages transferred over networks, data sent within a machine, and information that is written to disk. To realise this, components of the distributed applications that run in the cloud need to specify their communications with others in terms of not only the structure of the data exchanged (as is commonplace with middleware that supports type systems) but their meaning in terms of legal and other obligations. In other words, we argue that software should make explicit the policy context; the attendant information flows describe both security and privacy concerns. Such policy specification must be separate from application code and the correctness of policy enforcement, provided as part of the infrastructure, should be backed up by proofs made against a formal model.

Alongside support for isolation, these explicit security declarations mean that application-level virtualisation allows the cloud infrastructure to do several desirable things:

1. Data flow may be monitored for the sake of audit. Components' description of messages' meaning and relevance to policy mean that the infrastructure is in the position to gather information that not only describes what happened in the course of an interaction but what the components intended to do.

2. The infrastructure may exercise monitoring of compliance with and enforcement of policies. These can codify the types of data that the components will send and are willing to receive.

3. Negotiation facilities for these policies can be provided by the infrastructure.

Overall this means that the details of information flow control and the monitoring of its integrity can be removed from application logic, being placed within the cloud infrastructure for all clients to share. This allows providers to permit clients only the interactions that the clients specify. Ensuring that all communication between components is done using messages annotated with security concerns, the cloud provider can enable end-to-end security that matches the policy requirements set out by the components that make up the clients' systems. This can eliminate disconnects between policies that specify where data may travel and the software paths that are eventually used.

We expect large-scale systems (and those that are based in the cloud are no exception) to span multiple administrative domains, so anything providing application-level virtualisation will have to operate in this environment. A domain is the starting point for naming and authentication of principals, roles, and communication endpoints. Within a domain, it can be assumed that entities are mutually well-known and accountability and trust are relatively high. A domain anchors the expression and enforcement of policy on the rights, obligations, and expectations of principals, although certain policies may be imposed externally by law or as a result of national agreement. A domain must recognise and fulfil its responsibilities for safeguarding data, including the control of data flowing into and out of it.

When a domain is part of a public service, such as in healthcare or policing, public policy can be brought to bear on data protection. With the advent of cloud computing, the protection of the data entrusted to services has not yet been addressed. Indeed, the owners of the services are most likely not the owners of the systems on which the services run. If a major leakage of data occurs, who should be held responsible? Even when there is commonality between stakeholders, such as with the UK Government's cloud computing initiative [2], the scale of aggregation would require inter-departmental responsibilities for data management and security to be made clear.

Paper outline: in section 2, we introduce the key supporting technologies required for our vision: cloud infrastructure, asynchronous messaging and data labelling, information flow control, role-based access control (RBAC), and expression and trusted enforcement of security policy. Section 3 shows how information flow control should be augmented by RBAC and policy to realise application-level virtualisation. We have experimented with this methodology in a number of domains, from healthcare and co-located financial services to social networking, as discussed in section 4. Section 5 continues with an analysis of the major questions still to be answered and provides some proposals for addressing them. Section 6 concludes: we believe that our "Big Idea" could lead to a new standard model for cloud computing, meeting developers' needs for seamless data integration and usability without compromising security.

2 Background

Our plan for application-level virtualisation rests on several pre-existing technologies. In section 2.1, we first describe the infrastructure that cloud providers offer for hosting applications and providing communication between them. For robustness, cloud applications that are large-scale, distributed systems are most easily built using asynchronous messaging (section 2.2). Information Flow Control (IFC) (section 2.3) can sit atop asynchronous communication to curtail leaks of sensitive information and also to prevent inappropriate trust of outside data. Alongside this, parametrised Role-Based Access Control (RBAC) provides a scalable framework for structuring permissions and interactions in large systems (section 2.4). Finally, the security policy must be expressed in a format suitable to the application and requires enforcement by an independent infrastructure, such as a trusted policy module (section 2.5), using IFC to prevent application security breaches.

2.1 Cloud Infrastructure

Cloud services may provide clients with operation at multiple levels of system abstraction and their interfaces come in a consequent variety of shapes and sizes. Some common types of cloud services, and large-scale examples of them, are summarised in this section.

Infrastructure. In this model, clients of the cloud service rent entire computing nodes, such as virtual machines. Although particular operating system templates may be available, the client is responsible for maintaining the operating system and the software that is to run above it. Examples of this model include Amazon's EC2, Rackspace, and Nimbus.

Platform. This model presents a level of abstraction where clients develop their software using a restricted set of programming languages against a particular set of services provided by the cloud. Some platforms may include cloud-hosted incarnations of traditional software such as relational databases but others may provide less familiar functionality such as custom document stores—required when there is necessary coupling between the service and properties of the cloud infrastructure. Google's App Engine and Microsoft's Azure are examples of the platform model.

Application. At the highest level of abstraction, the cloud provides application hosting where clients configure the application on offer but do not have programming-level involvement. Salesforce has been employing the application level of abstraction.

Our focus is on addressing security at the "platform" level. Clients have to redevelop their software against cloud services in any event, and we believe that the additional effort to provide security policy alongside the code would be unproblematic.

2.2 Asynchronous Communication and Data Labelling

Any non-trivial application hosted in a cloud is a large-scale distributed system. To build these, and to provide links between applications, an asynchronous communication model is needed, allowing participants to interact without requiring them to be simultaneously online. Even for cloud services that are stateless (with respect to the cloud servers), message passing is useful for achieving robustness in the face of service reconfiguration and other downtime.

Synchronous communication interfaces can be superimposed on this asynchronous model. At the same time, asynchrony provides a much more accurate view of the realities of distributed operation, with unpredictable failures and delays, distributed multicast used to optimise content delivery, and partial local information. Furthermore, a truly synchronous interface is undesirable because it can act as a covert channel—imagine a message encoded using communication response times.

In our approach, we treat all communicated messages as multi-part structures [3] in which each part has its own data and security label. This allows effective distributed processing because services can annotate the data as needed without altering the security labels attached to the unchanged fields. For example, suppose a pathology laboratory processes a healthcare record and annotates it with diagnostic information. This annotation (a new part) would be of high confidentiality because producing it required access to patient data. However, other parts of the message, such as the identity of the originating pathology laboratory, could remain at their original, lower confidentiality levels and remain accessible to subsequent processors.

2.3 Information Flow Control (IFC)

Information Flow Control (IFC) uses the data labelling within messages to enforce where data may go. Consequently, it is a security technique that guarantees strong protection of data confidentiality and integrity [4].

In IFC, all data are tagged with *security labels* that limit where the information can flow. Each label consists of a set of *confidentiality* tags, describing the "secrecy" of the data, and a set of *integrity* tags that attest to the data's provenance. Data can only flow to processes with compatible labels and data released by a process must be compatible with the process's label. Normally, information can only increase in confidentiality and decrease in integrity as it is processed, unless special *declassification* or *endorsement* privileges are exercised. For example, if a "top-secret" label is more confidential than "secret", then information labelled "secret" can be handled by processes with "top-secret" clearance but not vice versa. "Top-secret" data is therefore confined and can only be declassified to "secret" by trusted processes with the right declassification privilege. A static set of labels is clearly not enough for large distributed systems. *Decentralised information flow control* (DIFC) [5] addresses this, by permitting applications to create their own tags on the fly and allowing privileges over these tags to be assigned dynamically.

Many application domains have shown the value of IFC and DIFC, including military multi-level security [6], operating system process isolation [7], and our own work on event-based distributed systems [8].

2.4 Role-Based Access Control (RBAC)

Distributed applications in general, and effective use of IFC in particular, require allocation, maintenance, and checking of privileges. Role-based access control (RBAC) has been demonstrated as an effective technology for the large scale [9]. RBAC is now in common use across a wide variety of infrastructures, including operating systems, databases, and web-based software. Specific definitions of RBAC are provided by the American National Standards Institute (ANSI) [10], although many software systems implement a simpler version of the RBAC concept. In all interpretations of RBAC, the notion of a *role* is introduced in between principals (e.g., users and processes) and privileges (e.g., method calls and filesystem access requests). Used in this way, roles are essentially a form of grouping. Database and operating system infrastructures often employ this form of RBAC.

The simplest ANSI standard is $RBAC_0$. In addition to the grouping function of a role, the concept of a *session* is included in the model. Sessions are designed to collect a set of active roles that pertain to a given work task. This focuses security management on related sets of roles that are being used, as opposed to having to consider all of a user's potential roles whenever an access control decision needs to be made. This mirrors the way access control tends to work with human principals in a workplace; either functional or organisational roles are activated in appropriate contexts. The activation and deactivation of roles leaves an audit trail as to the intentions of the user over the duration of their session.

For scalable, fine-grained access control, these RBAC approaches are not manageable due to the need for large numbers of roles and the static, simple method of policy specification. The ANSI $RBAC_2$ standard makes steps in the right direction by allowing the specification of additional constraints over the role activation relationships. However, it does not go far enough to effect large-scale, distributed RBAC because its specification of constraints is not sufficiently fine-grained.

Parametrised RBAC mitigates this problem by allowing the connection of dynamically-assigned attributes to roles. The RBAC infrastructure becomes more complex, however, as there is now the need for some inference system to bind the values of parameters during the evaluation of access control rules. Having said this, we have demonstrated that fairly straightforward parametrised RBAC rule specifications with Horn clause form and simple inference semantics are useful and sufficient [11].

2.5 Policy Expression and Enforcement

The techniques of IFC and RBAC are tools that can be used to build a security infrastructure but details of their integration may be below the level at which applications are developed. To solve this mismatch, we need to decouple security specification from the concerns that it protects. What we need is a means of expressing high-level information flow policies and transforming those into appropriate roles and IFC labels. There is usually a trade-off between processing speed and the ability to make sense of the security policy being applied. Policy enforcement requires control flow to cross into specific access control software subsystems, which can add latency on the critical path of some software operations.

Increasingly, software systems are looking to concentrate security management into a focused part of the infrastructure, rather than having security logic scattered throughout the code-base. SELinux and AppArmor provide this sort of policy expression and enforcement at an operating-system kernel level, while the desire to work in environments such as user web-browsers led to the design of Java's system of access control.

One notable policy language that is gaining acceptance is XACML [12]. For application-level concerns, as opposed to operating system or language-level security, XACML has the advantage of security engines having been implemented in a number of programming languages, accompanied by a standardised, expressive policy language.

Regardless of the particular policy languages employed, scaling up the reach of policy requires addressing concerns that cross multiple administrative domains and needs distributed policy enforcement mechanisms; the need to handle cooperating but distinct organisations is common in healthcare scenarios [13].

Small-scale distributed enforcement mechanisms include Kerberos [14], and the widely-deployed Microsoft derivatives of it. At larger scale, short-lived certificates can be used to help distributed enforcement [15], although certificate-based techniques have unavoidably inelegant problems when privilege should be revoked before the certificate expires.

The surge of Web 2.0 applications is starting to beget technology that can effectively manage security in dynamic, heterogeneous environments. The Security Assertion Markup Language (SAML) [16] aims to simplify trust establishment between sites for the sake of user convenience features such as single-sign-on. A related authentication technology is OpenID [17], which provides an approach to managing distributed naming for user identification. Recently, OAuth [18] has emerged as a protocol for evaluating distributed authorisation of privilege.

Many of the above technologies are closely suited to, or even tightly coupled with, specific domains (e.g., web-based authentication or privilege management within a LAN environment). Our aim is to provide security tools for the use of client software, to embed the client software within our security framework, but presume as little as possible about the application's environment.

3 Towards End-to-End Security

Recall that we achieve security by requiring that *all data and communication be protected with Information Flow Control (IFC) constraints.* If these constraints are enforced consistently, the security context is indelibly linked to the data—the security labels can change only when trusted software components deliberately exercise special privileges.

3.1 IFC Compared to Boundary Security

Adding IFC labels to all data allows end-to-end tracking and protection. In contrast, traditional boundary security restricts information only as it enters or leaves a systemic boundary such as a domain. Figures 1 and 2 illustrate the distinction between security controls at the boundaries of a distributed system and continuous, end-to-end security tracking with IFC. In both figures, we see two different events move across two domains. The paths of Event A and Event B are shown as solid and dashed lines, respectively. In figure 1, explicit boundary access control checks prevent Event A from reaching an unauthorised recipient. In figure 2, it is the IFC labels that cause Event A to be blocked before it reaches the unauthorised recipient; Event B is allowed. Even if the recipient republishes data derived from Event B as Event C, the same security restrictions are still enforced.

Figure 2 also shows an anonymiser module, which has additional trust in the form of declassification privileges. It uses these to publish an anonymised event

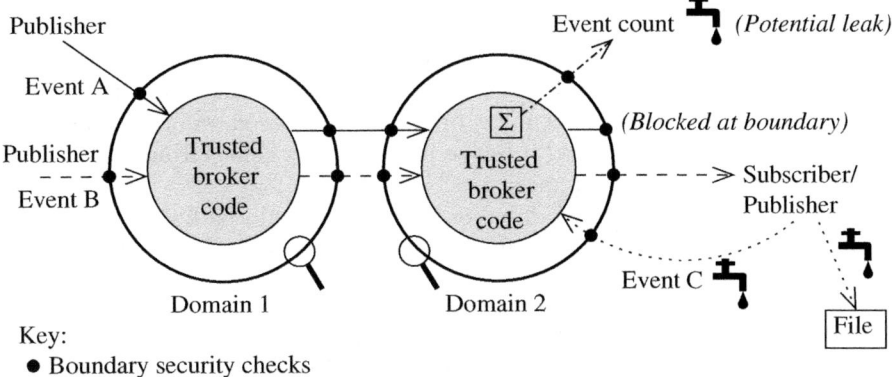

Fig. 1. Boundary security between event publishers, brokers, and subscribers

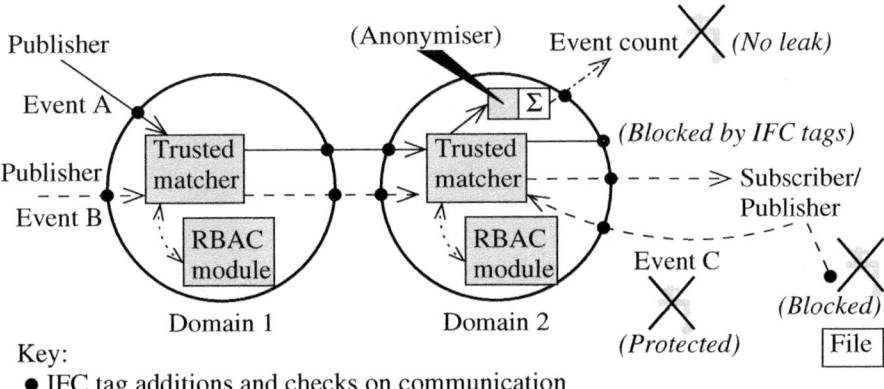

Fig. 2. End-to-end security with Information Flow Control

count. Other portions of the infrastructure, such as the RBAC module, operate entirely within the IFC framework—all of their communications and data are subject to its restrictions. In contrast, the boundary access controls in figure 1 are insufficient to prevent the event counting component (Σ) from potentially accumulating identified data.

This approach provides an end-to-end model of data security that is the precise definition of *application-level virtualisation*. In effect, each user of an application is isolated from every other user except where trusted code explicitly bridges the boundaries. Here, examples of a "user" could be (1) a single service request, (2) healthcare data related to a single patient, or (3) stock trades executed for a single trader in an investment bank on behalf of a third-party client.

This whole scheme hinges on effective use of IFC. The challenge, therefore, is to make IFC-based systems practical and flexible to use in building complex, large, real-world computer systems. IFC is most straightforward in relatively static, strictly hierarchical environments [6]. As systems become more complex and include interconnections between organisations and departments, themselves constantly in flux, the management of IFC security labels becomes an increasing burden. At some point, the meaning of the IFC-enforced security rules is lost and the code is simply tweaked to make it work. This comes from undisciplined label allocation and use strategies.

Instead, we believe that IFC label enforcement should be linked to organisational security policy, expressed using Role-Based Access Control. This has three major advantages:

Simplified management. Policy can be changed without modifying the deployed code and services can be re-engineered without changing the policy. Furthermore, policy analysis tools can be used to validate the overall application structure at a high level.

Appropriate security. Security policy can be represented using concepts of organisational importance—this is useful for both technical and legal reasons. Technically, this ensures that policy operates at the correct granularity and can consistently follow changes in organisational structures. A large organisation can enforce overall security policy, while allowing additional policy refinements by departments. Legally, it means that data security is linked to concepts important to the organisation; thus data security can feature in SLAs and organisational agreements, and data that leaves the secure processing environment (by being printed, say) can be protected by other legal means such as employment contracts.

Independent enforcement. Policy is translated into IFC labels by a small trusted computing base. Bugs in application code cannot violate the policy.

3.2 Programmer-Friendly, Domain-Specific IFC

Programmers need to be given straightforward ways to develop software that uses application-level virtualisation. We have shown that this can be achieved with simple modifications to a standard Java runtime, enforcing IFC restrictions at the communications API and associating IFC labels with each process's local state [8]. This approach lets programmers write code as usual, with the programming and computational overheads of label checking being systematically localised to the communication boundaries. Furthermore, programmers need only write code in terms of policy, not in terms of individual IFC labels. This simplifies programming, providing a higher-level interface to label management—the RBAC module translates policy expressions to IFC tags, and grants appropriate privileges to the receiving processes. Our experience of this approach is summarised in section 4.

This IFC/RBAC model is well suited to a multi-domain architecture. In IFC terms, all data originating from an organisation has one or more confidentiality and integrity labels by default. Thus, data is always embedded within a security context unless explicitly made public by privileged code.

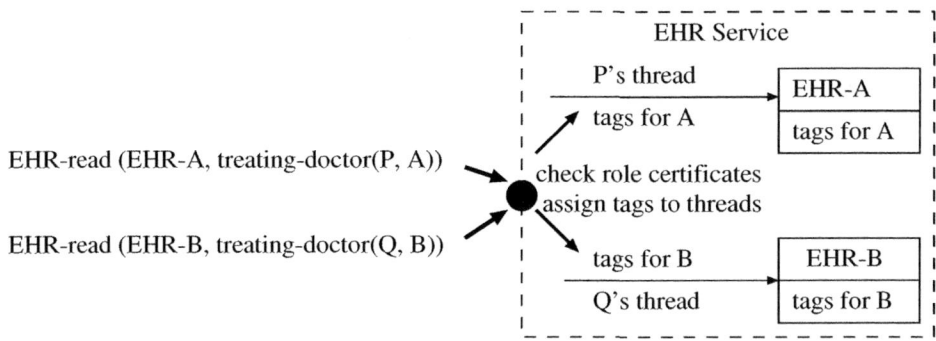

Fig. 3. Isolated threads can access different data

In the cloud, this protection not only insulates co-hosted organisational applications from each other but it isolates users of shared services because the users can employ disjoint sets of security labels. For example, the security policy can use parametrised RBAC to effectively manage separate IFC labels for each user or role set as in the following policy snippet [11]. Avoiding discussion of the denotational semantics, this policy basically states that being able to acquire the role of a "treating doctor" of a particular patient, involves the role acquirer being a "doctor" that has an active ward-round on the ward that contains that patient. This example demonstrates the relevance of fine-grained management of roles: simply being a qualified doctor is not enough to justify interactions with any patient. It is difficult to use non-parameterised RBAC to encode this policy.

$$\text{duty-doctor}(\textit{doctor-ID, hospital-ward-ID}),$$
$$\text{current-inpatient}(\textit{patient-ID, hospital-ward-ID})$$
$$\vdash \text{treating-doctor}(\textit{doctor-ID, patient-ID})$$

Figure 3 shows a component that provides controlled access to Electronic Health Records (EHRs). Each EHR is assumed to have associated IFC security labels, with each label being a set of tags. Doctor P requests to read the EHR of Patient A; Doctor Q requests that of Patient B. The doctors hold treating-doctor roles with doctor and patient identifiers as parameters. On a read invocation, the service checks the validity and applicability of the requester's active roles. If they are satisfactory, the service assigns labels that allow access to the patient's EHR to the thread that executes the service for that doctor. This means that the threads are isolated—they have no access to data having incompatible labels.

To complete our model of end-to-end security, we need secure persistence and storage for data—real world applications do not maintain their state entirely within events. IFC and RBAC support the integration of database access.

3.3 Integration of RBAC and IFC for Database Access

Databases need to offer fine-grained isolation of information in order to support application-level virtualisation. Otherwise they trivially become channels for unauthorised cross-contamination of data. We express database access restrictions using role-based security policy, using the same policy expression as we apply to asynchronous messaging. This has two main advantages: (1) database security is expressed in common terms with operational data security and (2) roles provide long-lasting security labels that naturally are independent of security policy changes. This provides strong protection for persistent data that may be sensitive for decades. In effect, roles act as bridges, allowing IFC-based information security restrictions to provide end-to-end security both in the cloud and for associated long-term data storage.

This approach extends our earlier work on linking database access control with publish/subscribe systems [19]. By protecting the data in this way, rather than exposing encrypted data to application code, we can provide long-term protection while minimising the risks of key loss or cracking of encryption schemes. Furthermore, it is possible to store data using trusted hardware, preventing disclosure even to superusers and system administrators.

3.4 Current Cloud Offerings

Current cloud offerings do not provide facilities for application-level virtualisation, be it by use of of IFC and RBAC as we have advocated or using other techniques. Here we describe the security mechanisms in Amazon's Elastic Compute Cloud (EC2), and the associated S3 storage service, and Google's App Engine as a representative sample of what is currently available.

Amazon EC2 and S3. Amazon's EC2 is a cloud infrastructure as defined in Section 2.1; it provides facilities to create and destroy virtual machines (VMs) with ease. All of the VMs under the control of one EC2 user (what we have called the "cloud provider client") are linked to that user's Amazon ID and great care is taken to ensure that there is no cross-contamination of data, via memory or disk, between VMs owned by different users. Communication between VMs is constrained using a network firewall. No mechanism is provided to control data flow within a VM.

The storage system associated with EC2, Amazon S3, offers more sophistication. It is a key/value store, where each object has a value that is an arbitrary byte stream. A *bucket* is the container for one or more objects; each object resides in precisely one bucket. Again, Amazon IDs are used as principals, though they are augmented by patterns such as "anonymous" and "any authenticated user."

Access Control Lists (ACLs), which are a subset of simple RBAC as outlined in Section 2.4, may be attached to buckets or individual objects [20, chapter covering access control]. More expressive are *bucket policies*, which are used to specify access rules for all objects in a given bucket. Such a policy is a set of statements, each of which describes a permission in the form of "A is/isn't allowed to do B to C where D applies" [20, appendix]. A is a principal, B is an S3 operation (such as "put object"), C is a bucket identifier, and D is a set of conditions. These conditions are composed using a simple language combining the expected operators (`NumericNotEquals`, `StringEqualsIgnoreCase`, and so on) with attributes of the request (the time, the source IP address, etc.), content of the request (such as HTTP Referrer), and properties of the target bucket.

This approach is expressive enough for an implementation that uses static IFC labels. For example, these labels could be translated into Amazon users who could then be incorporated into bucket policies. However, this is unsuitable for a dynamic environment because it is awkward to create and delete users frequently. Furthermore, ACLs are low-level constructs and bucket policies may not be modified but only replaced. This means that an intermediate infrastructure would be needed to add and remove security concerns from policies. It is doubtful that constant replacement of policies, and creation of new buckets when a unique policy was required within the application, would provide high performance or be scalable.

Google App Engine. Google's App Engine [21] provides a platform (in the terminology of Section 2.1) that allows execution of Java[1] and Python programmes within a limited environment. As with Amazon EC2, care is taken to ensure, through effective sandboxing, that one programme does not interact with another, even if those programmes are associated with the same cloud client. Again no facilities are provided to limit the flow of data within each sandbox. Furthermore, the data store provided does not appear to support any access control, permitting the account owning the database complete access to all data.

Based on the above, in its current form App Engine is not suitable for providing application-level virtualisation. In fact, its sandboxing and hence bespoke Java Virtual Machine (JVM) and Java libraries mean that the analysis of the Java libraries that we have done as part of building the DEFCON prototype [8] would not be applicable without further examination.

4 Application Case Studies: Progress to Date

We have demonstrated application-level virtualisation in a number of application domains [22], including health record transfer, cooperative co-location of algorithmic trading systems, social networking, and IFC-enforced policy specification. Here we summarise these experiences to illustrate that (a) application-level virtualisation is feasible and (b) we have identified the necessary prerequisite technologies.

Health records. When health records are exchanged, long-term data security is critical—for a lifetime or more. We have adapted distributed event-based systems to this challenge, by tightly integrating RBAC with publish/subscribe messaging [13,23] along the lines suggested in section 3. Organisational security policy dictates which data flows are allowed; we assume that each domain has at least one trusted event broker node for secure exchange of events, and

---

[1] Technically, App Engine supports the Java Virtual Machine, so any language having that as the target execution environment can be made to work.

uses point-to-point communication between domains. This particular application does not demand high throughput, and health record exchange must follow agreed protocols, so content-based event routing is not required with its sharing of communication paths.

Application-level virtualisation builds on this work and allows a natural deployment of the system in the cloud: using IFC for strong end-to-end security allows security policy to govern not only data exchange but also data processing. Furthermore, enforcing policy with IFC reduces the footprint of trusted code in the messaging middleware and leads to better performance: new IFC tags are needed only when roles are activated to gain privileges, so IFC tags effectively cache policy evaluation.

Stock trading and pairing. We used application-level virtualisation to develop a stock trading application, as part of a high performance event processing platform prototype called DEFCON [8]. Financial applications have stringent performance requirements in terms of throughput and latency. Co-locating clients with investors and sharing facilities among investors is extremely useful for server consolidation in heavily-demanded hosting facilities, and trading systems aim to be co-located with stock exchanges to minimise latency [24,25]. At the same time financial applications are subject to important security policy requirements, including:

1. flow integrity of market data information;
2. strict control of information flows between investment strategies of different clients of a bank and between client and bank investors;
3. confidentiality of orders in Dark Pool trading, used to move large quantities of equities without revealing the trader's identity; and
4. auditing by regulatory authorities on completed transactions.

To satisfy these requirements, we first made the ideas presented in section 2.3 concrete by developing an IFC label model suitable for event-based processing. The model is inspired by OS-level IFC approaches, which provide IFC security among processes in separate address spaces [7]. We applied IFC to processing components that run in the same address space and saw a significant improvement in performance.

An important requirement for financial scenarios is the usability of the target language. We chose Java since it supports high throughput and low latency processing with a tunable garbage collector. Unfortunately, achieving application-level virtualisation is difficult in Java; its security model was designed for isolation between application code and the host system, but does not provide good support for isolation between sections of application code. Crucially, we provided an isolation methodology that can easily be maintained in the face of the continuous evolution of the language runtime.

Our experimental results show that the overhead of checking labels is low: in common applications, labels are quite small and can be checked efficiently without imposing global locking overhead. In comparison, the overhead of using separate Java Virtual Machines to isolate users, both in terms of processing latency and resource consumption, is unacceptable even when the number of users is small.

Social networking. Social networking applications have challenging security requirements: they need to protect their users' individual privacy while still allowing information exchange between these users. As an example, we used IFC tags to protect a Twitter-like microblogging application [26]. Examples of policies that could be enforced are:

1. subscribers to a message topic are guaranteed to have their identities hidden from each other;
2. publications are received only by authorised subscribers and only the publisher of a topic can see the corresponding subscription requests; or
3. publications are received only by authorised subscribers and subscribers' identities are hidden from the publisher.

Our implementation achieves isolation between requests using Erlang's inexpensive process model, with IFC-based policy checks added to Erlang's built-in message passing mechanism. We use IFC restrictions to enforce partitioning of subscription state per subscriber in the message dispatcher. Even in a lightweight application such as this, having essentially no processing overhead, the cost of IFC enforcement is reasonable, being approximately 0.2 ms (of 0.7 ms) per message delivered in an underloaded system. In a distributed deployment, this is small compared to the expected communication delays and computation times.

This example demonstrates two important results: (a) IFC can offer effective privacy protection for users of shared services without preventing appropriate data exchange; in other words, IFC restrictions are usable in practice and are not simply a secure sink for data; and (b) IFC restrictions are compatible with the securing of publish/subscribe communication systems for which the publisher and subscriber sets change dynamically—with microblogging as the special case of one publisher per topic. Whilst we do not expect cloud providers to adopt Erlang, our results show that IFC functionality layered atop an asynchronous message passing facility is sufficient to provide the communication necessary for application-level virtualisation.

Policy specification and compliance monitoring. As we argued in sections 2.4 and 2.5, effective expression of roles and policy is crucial for application-level virtualisation. As a consequence, access control policy for large systems needs to reflect organisational structure, allowing the blending of high-level organisational policy with local policy-based restrictions. Our work has used parametrised RBAC to allow fine-grained enforcement and compact specification [11]; we have shown that this approach can support large and complex organisations, such as the UK National Health Service (NHS). The resulting separation of policy specification and enforcement/compliance monitoring is well suited to cloud computing infrastructure because the deployment platform only needs to enforce policy faithfully but plays no part in its authoring.

In our latest work [22], we explore a flow control policy language in which policy authors explicitly chart how information can flow through IFC-enforcing distributed environments; these span multiple hosting organisations, ranging from corporate intranets to cloud providers. The language uses parametrised flow specifications to link privileges to deployed units of code.

For example, the following is a rule that allows a patient's treating doctor to send the patient's data to a pathology laboratory, which may then process it and send the results back. The pathology lab may also send the data on to a cancer registry for further research studies:

```
NHS.patient-data[doctor-ID, patient-ID]: {
  -> treating-doctor(doctor-ID, patient-ID) ->, NHS.pathlab,
  NHS.cancerregistry ->
}.
```

The effect of this policy is to establish an IFC-protected domain with its own confidentiality and integrity tags. The integrity tags prevent untrusted outside data from being passed off as patient data; the confidentiality tags prevent patient data from being released except as authorised through the policy.

Linking the policy to RBAC privileges has two advantages: (a) privileges can change over time without any change to policy and (b) security policy can be linked to physical security, starting with IFC labels themselves [27,28] and moving towards roles. For example, one can ensure that patient data is released only to a doctor or only displayed on terminals in a physically secure location. This bridge between security policy and physical security allows end-to-end data security to extend beyond electronic data into the real world.

In these flow policy specifications, structured naming is used. For example, NHS.cancerregistry could refer to all cancer registries in the NHS, while NHS.cancerregistry.ecric could refer to a specific cancer registry and NHS.cancerregistry.ecric.dropbox could refer to ECRIC's dropbox service for secure incoming data. This allows high-level organisational policy and low-level operational policy to be specified in the same terms. Multiple policy specifications are automatically combined to determine which flows are allowed; in the above example, the high-level NHS.patient-data rule would allow ECRIC's dropbox to receive patient data. Additional low level rules attached to the dropbox could prevent it from releasing the data to third parties, either by specifying additional flow types or by further restricting NHS.patient-data.

We are still exploring how best to support policy authoring. At the simplest level, we have established rules to detect clashes between policy entries but further work is needed to provide policy visualisation tools, to establish common policy idioms for organisational data exchange, and to verify policy compliance in large, distributed environments that encompass both cloud providers and corporate intranets.

5 Future Work: Open Research Challenges

Our experiences show that application-level virtualisation is a viable design strategy for providing end-to-end security. Our work to date has illustrated the efficacy of necessary pieces of infrastructure. Moving towards a complete, principled methodology that is usable for building cloud-hosted services will require that the research community address the following issues.

Expression of security concerns. So far we have used labelling of data to convey meaning in terms of security. When operating across multiple administrative domains, we have suggested that the tags within labels be interpreted in the context of the data use agreements between participating organisations [27]. However, it is unclear that this is an ideal mechanism. Tagging of data may feel unnatural to the developer and if data are incorrectly identified, enforcement of security will be incorrect. We need mechanisms, for example, integrated into programming languages, whereby security tags about data can be defined and used as naturally as the declarations of the structure of those data.

Roles as macros for policy. We have argued that many of the tags should be constructed based on role definitions. We must define how this can be done in terms of the desirable RBAC primitives and, potentially, provide a "role toolkit" that developers can use to effect end-to-end security quickly. Furthermore, if we are to map tags to data use agreements expressed using deontic logic [29], we must be comfortable with the advice that we give concerning how to write those agreements. To date, we have begun to provide the mechanism to do this [30], and we have started the process of constructing these agreements based on real-world concerns [28].

Secure mechanisms. How should tags and labels be made secure throughout a distributed system, ensuring that they are not altered and are bound permanently to data as appropriate? How can we be certain that data use always respects tags? So far we have assumed that a small and secure trusted code base exists on each host. Is this realistic and, if not, what are the viable alternatives? What are the implications when high performance is needed for large numbers of clients of a shared service with low latency requirements? How much can be achieved by static checks at the language level?

An alternative is to use a single secure host per domain rather than having a trusted component on each host. We have done this for OASIS [11]. This has the advantage of concentrating domain-knowledge of policies and issuing of tags and labels (such as for role activation or on role use) and, as we have argued, is a natural fit with inter-organisation IFC [27].

Confidentiality of tags and labels. So far we have considered tags and labels to be essentially public in that the receiver of an event may look at the security concerns of the data contained, even if the data themselves are hidden. However, what should be done if tags and labels themselves should be secret? If they are protected using encryption, how should one manage key distribution? How would this key distribution affect efficient event dissemination, for example using content-based routing? Whilst checking back with the issuer of tags raises immediate fears about scalability, are there application areas where it is acceptable because correctness is vastly more important than performance? For parametrised label systems, it may be possible to adopt a hybrid approach, for example by identifying to the receiver that events carry `patient-data` parts without revealing the `patient-id` parameter value.

Policy quality. IFC is only as useful as the policy used to define it. If you specify bad policy, you can release your data. We need a disciplined approach to (a) review policy to check for correctness, and (b) formalisms so that high-level policy can restrict the scope for local policy errors.

Performance. We do not as yet have a comprehensive understanding of the performance penalty that must be paid for end-to-end security in a widely-distributed system. However, our results so far [8] indicate that IFC schemes on a single host can be built into an existing language runtime moderately easily and need not incur a significant performance penalty (particularly not given that network costs are likely to dominate IFC checks). We need to confirm that negotiation of policy concerns between hosts can be done off the critical path used for IFC enforcement.

Special requirements of the cloud. Remember that our primary goal in this paper is to highlight techniques that cloud providers can use to effect end-to-end security. Whilst doing so, we must not lose sight of the additional challenges of deployment within cloud environments. For example, design decisions that focus on a particular operating system or hardware, or require a globally-administered naming system, are unlikely to be applicable to cloud infrastructures.

6 Conclusions

Security in the cloud must be included from the start. This demands a new approach to end-to-end security that supports strong isolation of data, even when business processes are outsourced into the cloud. Cloud processing needs isolation between users of shared services, as well as isolation between services. Our vision of *application-level virtualisation* provides this, by integrating (a) event-based communication for robust service interconnection; (b) strong end-to-end security with Information Flow Control; (c) role-based policy specification that bridges data processing, persistent storage, and physical security; and (d) trusted policy enforcement.

Our research to date has demonstrated the feasibility of this approach in the context of large-scale distributed systems. However, more work is needed to extend this into a standard model for cloud computing that can meet developers' requirements for seamless integration and usability without compromising security.

Our big idea—cloud-hosted services that have end-to-end information flow control—preempts concerns about security and data use violations that are holding back the evolution of large-scale cloud computing. With this, we can reassure cloud users who are worried about cross-contamination within their applications and, at the same time, are reluctant to share a system with other companies and therefore refuse, at the moment, to entrust sensitive data to a cloud.

Acknowledgments

This work was supported by grants EP/C547632, EP/F042469, and EP/F044216 from the UK Engineering and Physical Sciences Research Council (EPSRC).

References

1. Dierks, T., Allen, C.: The TLS protocol version 1.0. RFC 2246 (January 1999)
2. Smith, A.: Open source, open standards and re-use: Government action plan (2009), http://www.cabinetoffice.gov.uk/media/318020/open_source.pdf
3. Pietzuch, P., Eyers, D., Kounev, S., Shand, B.: Towards a Common API for Publish/Subscribe. In: Proceedings of the Inaugural Conference on Distributed Event-Based Systems (DEBS 2007), pp. 152–157. ACM Press, New York (June 2007) (short paper)
4. Bell, D.E., La Padula, L.J.: Secure computer systems: Mathematical foundations and model. Technical Report M74-244, The MITRE Corp., Bedford MA (May 1973)
5. Myers, A., Liskov, B.: Protecting privacy using the decentralized label model. ACM Transactions on Software Engineering and Methodology 9(4), 410–442 (2000)
6. Department of Defense: Trusted computer system evaluation criteria, orange book (1983)
7. Krohn, M., Yip, A., Brodsky, M., et al.: Information flow control for standard OS abstractions. In: SOSP 2007, pp. 321–334. ACM, New York (2007)
8. Migliavacca, M., Papagiannis, I., Eyers, D., Shand, B., Bacon, J., Pietzuch, P.: High-performance event processing with information security. In: USENIX Annual Technical Conference, Boston, MA, USA, pp. 1–15 (2010)
9. NHS Connecting For Health: RBAC Statement of Principles, NPfIT Access Control (Registration) Programme (July 2006)
10. American National Standard for Information Technology: Role-based access control. ANSI INCITS 359-2004 (2004)
11. Bacon, J., Moody, K., Yao, W.: A model of OASIS role-based access control and its support for active security. ACM Transactions on Information and System Security (TISSEC) 5(4), 492–540 (2002)
12. OASIS eXtensible Access Control Markup Language (XACML) Technical Committee: eXtensible Access Control Markup Language (XACML) v2.0 (2005), http://www.oasis-open.org/committees/tc_home.php?wg_abbrev=xacml
13. Singh, J., Vargas, L., Bacon, J.: A model for controlling data flow in distributed healthcare environments. In: Proceedings of Pervasive Health 2008: 2nd International Conference on Pervasive Computing Technologies for Healthcare, Tampere, Finland, vol. 30, pp. 188–191 (2008)

14. Neuman, C., Yu, T., Hartman, S., Raeburn, K.: RFC 4120: The Kerberos network authentication service (V5). Technical report, USC-ISI and MIT (2005)
15. Chadwick, D., Zhao, G., Otenko, S., Laborde, R., Su, L., Nguyen, T.A.: PERMIS: a modular authorization infrastructure. Concurrency and Computation: Practice and Experience 20(11), 1341–1357 (2008)
16. OASIS Security Services TC: Security assertion markup language (SAML) V2.0 technical overview. Committee Draft 02 (March 2008)
17. OpenID Foundation: OpenID authentication 2.0 (December 2007)
18. Hammer-Lahav, E.: RFC 5849: The OAuth 1.0 protocol. Technical report, Internet Engineering Task Force (April 2010)
19. Singh, J., Eyers, D.M., Bacon, J.: Controlling historical information dissemination in publish/subscribe. In: MidSec 2008: Proceedings of the 2008 Workshop on Middleware Security, pp. 34–39. ACM, New York (2008)
20. Amazon: Amazon Simple Storage Service developer guide (API version 2006-03-01), http://docs.amazonwebservices.com/AmazonS3/latest/dev/ (retrieved August 25, 2010)
21. Google: App Engine Java overview, http://code.google.com/appengine/docs/java/overview.html (retrieved August 25, 2010)
22. Migliavacca, M., Papagiannis, I., Eyers, D.M., Shand, B., Bacon, J., Pietzuch, P.: Distributed middleware enforcement of event flow security policy. In: Gupta, I., Mascolo, C. (eds.) Middleware 2010. LNCS, vol. 6452, pp. 334–354. Springer, Heidelberg (2010)
23. Bacon, J., Eyers, D.M., Singh, J., Shand, B., Migliavacca, M., Pietzuch, P.: Security in multi-domain event-based systems. it - Information Technology 51(5), 277–284 (2009), doi:10.1524/itit.2009.0552
24. Duhigg, C.: Stock traders find speed pays, in milliseconds. The New York Times (2009)
25. London Stock Exchange: Exchange hosting, http://www.londonstockexchange.com/traders-and-brokers/products-services/connectivity/hosting/hosting.htm (retrieved May 23, 2010)
26. Papagiannis, I., Migliavacca, M., Eyers, D.M., Shand, B., Bacon, J., Pietzuch, P.: Enforcing user privacy in web applications using Erlang. In: Web 2.0 Security and Privacy (W2SP), Oakland, CA, USA (May 2010)
27. Evans, D., Eyers, D.M.: Efficient policy checking across administrative domains. In: Proceedings of the IEEE International Symposium on Policies for Distributed Systems and Networks, Fairfax, VA, USA (July 2010)
28. Evans, D., Eyers, D.M., Bacon, J.: Linking policies to the spatial environment. In: Proceedings of the IEEE International Symposium on Policies for Distributed Systems and Networks, Fairfax, VA, USA (July 2010)
29. Meyer, J.J., Wieringa, R.J.: Deontic Logic in Computer Science. John Wiley & Sons Ltd., Chichester (1993)
30. Evans, D., Eyers, D.M.: Deontic logic for modelling data flow and use compliance. In: MPAC 2008: Proceedings of the 6th international workshop on middleware for pervasive and ad-hoc computing, pp. 19–24. ACM, New York (2008)

LiFTinG: Lightweight Freerider-Tracking in Gossip[*]

Rachid Guerraoui[1], Kévin Huguenin[2], Anne-Marie Kermarrec[3], Maxime Monod[1], and Swagatika Prusty[4]

[1] Ecole Polytechnique Fédérale de Lausanne
[2] IRISA / Université of Rennes 1
[3] INRIA Rennes-Bretagne Atlantique
[4] IIT Guwahati

Abstract. This paper presents LiFTinG, the first protocol to detect freeriders, including colluding ones, in gossip-based content dissemination systems with asymmetric data exchanges. LiFTinG relies on nodes tracking abnormal behaviors by cross-checking the history of their previous interactions, and exploits the fact that nodes pick neighbors at random to prevent colluding nodes from covering up each others' bad actions.

We present a methodology to set the parameters of LiFTinG based on a theoretical analysis. In addition to simulations, we report on the deployment of LiFTinG on PlanetLab. In a 300-node system, where a stream of 674 kbps is broadcast, LiFTinG incurs a maximum overhead of only 8% while providing good results: for instance, with 10% of freeriders decreasing their contribution by 30%, LiFTinG detects 86% of the freeriders after only 30 seconds and wrongfully expels only a few honest nodes.

1 Introduction

Gossip protocols have recently been successfully applied to decentralize large-scale high-bandwidth content dissemination [5, 7]. Such systems are *asymmetric*: nodes propose packet identifiers to a dynamically changing random subset of other nodes. These, in turn, request packets of interest, which are subsequently pushed by the proposer. In such a three-phase protocol, gossip is used to disseminate content location whereas the content itself is explicitly requested and served. These protocols are commonly used for high-bandwidth content dissemination with gossip, e.g., [5, 7, 8, 21] (a similar scheme is also present in mesh-based systems, e.g., [20, 25, 26]).

The efficiency of such protocols highly relies on the willingness of participants to collaborate, i.e., to devote a fraction of their resources, namely their upload bandwidth, to the system. Yet, some of these participants might be tempted to *freeride* [19], i.e., not contribute their fair share of work, especially if they can still

---
[*] This work has been partially supported by the ERC Starting Grant GOSSPLE number 204742.

benefit from the system. Freeriding is common in large-scale systems deployed in the public domain [1] and may significantly degrade the overall performance in bandwidth-demanding applications. In addition, freeriders may collude, i.e., collaborate to decrease their individual contribution and the contribution of the coalition and cover up each other's misbehaviors to circumvent detection mechanisms.

By using the Tit-for-Tat (TfT) incentives (inspired from file-sharing systems [4]), content dissemination solutions (e.g., [21]) force nodes to contribute as much as they benefit by means of balanced *symmetric* exchanges. As we review in related work (Section 7), those systems do not perform as well as *asymmetric* systems in terms of efficiency and scalability.

In practice, many proposals (e.g., [5, 20, 25, 26]) consider instead asymmetric exchanges where nodes are supposed to altruistically serve content to other nodes, i.e., without asking anything in return, where the benefit of a node is not directly correlated to its contribution but rather to the global *health* of the system. The correlation between the benefit and the contribution is not immediate. However, such correlation can be artificially established, in a coercive way, by means of verification mechanisms ensuring that nodes which do not contribute their fair share do no longer benefit from the system. Freeriders are then defined as nodes that decrease their contribution as much as possible while keeping the probability of being expelled low.

We consider a generic three-phase gossip protocol where data is disseminated following an asymmetric push scheme. In this context, we propose LiFTinG, a lightweight mechanism to track freeriders. To the best of our knowledge, LiFTinG is the first protocol to secure asymmetric gossip protocols against possibly colluding freeriders.

At the core of LiFTinG lies a set of deterministic and statistical distributed verification procedures based on *accountability* (i.e., each node maintains a digest of its past interactions). Deterministic procedures check that the content received by a node is further propagated following the protocol (i.e., to the right number of nodes within a short delay) by cross-checking nodes' logs. Statistical procedures check that the interactions of a node are evenly distributed in the system using statistical techniques. Interestingly enough, the high dynamic and strong randomness of gossip protocols, that may be considered as a barrier at first glance, happens to help tracking freeriders. Effectively, LiFTinG exploits the very fact that nodes pick neighbors at random to circumvent collusion: since a node interacts with a large subset of the nodes, chosen at random, this drastically limits its opportunity to freeride without being detected, as it prevents it from deterministically choosing colluding partners that would cover it up.

LiFTinG is lightweight as it does not rely on heavyweight cryptography and incurs only a very low overhead in terms of bandwidth. In addition, LiFTinG is fully decentralized as nodes are in charge of verifying each others' actions. Finally, LiFTinG provides a good probability of detecting freeriders while keeping the probability of false positive, i.e., inaccurately classifying a correct node as a freerider, low.

We give analytical results backed up with simulations, providing means to set the parameters of LiFTinG in a real environment. Additionally, we deployed LiFTinG over PlanetLab, where a stream of 674 kbps is broadcast to 300 PlanetLab nodes having their upload bandwidth capped to 1000 kbps for the sake of realism. In the presence of freeriders, the health of the system (i.e., the proportion of nodes able to receive the stream in function of the stream lag) degrades significantly compared to a system where all nodes follow the protocol. Figure 1 shows a clear drop between the plain line (no freeriders) and the dashed line (25% of freeriders). With LiFTinG and assuming that freeriders keep their probability of being expelled lower than 50%, the performance is close to the baseline.

In this context, LiFTinG incurs a maximum network overhead of only 8%. When freeriders decrease their contribution by 30%, LiFTinG detects 86% of the freeriders and wrongly expels 12% of honest nodes, after only 30 seconds. Most of wrongly expelled nodes deserve it, in a sense, as their actual contribution is smaller than required. However, this is due to poor capabilities, as opposed to freeriders that deliberately decrease their contribution.

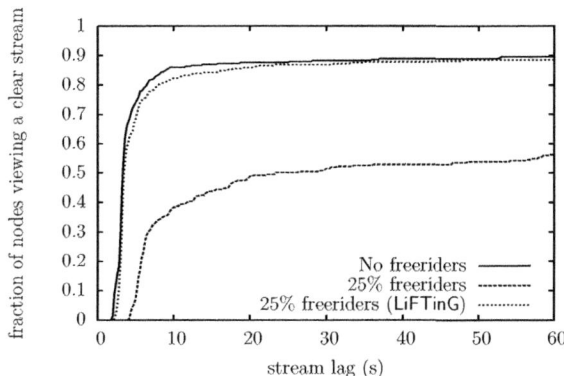

Fig. 1. System efficiency in the presence of freeriders

Gossip protocols are almost not impacted by crashes [6, 16]. However, high-bandwidth content dissemination with gossip clearly suffers more from freeriders than from crashes. When content is pushed in a single phase, a freerider is equivalent to a crashed node. In three-phase protocols, crashed nodes do not provide upload bandwidth anymore but they do not consume any bandwidth either, as they do not request content from proposers after they crash. On the contrary, freeriders decrease their contribution, yet keep requesting content.

The rest of the paper is organized as follows. Section 2 describes our illustrative gossip protocol and Section 3 lists and classifies the opportunities for nodes to freeride. Section 4 presents LiFTinG and Section 5 formally analyzes its performance backed up by extensive simulations. Section 6 reports on the deployment of LiFTinG over the PlanetLab testbed. Section 7 reviews related work. Section 8 concludes the paper.

2 Three-Phase Gossip Protocol

We consider a system of n nodes that communicate over lossy links (e.g., UDP) and can receive incoming data from any other node in the system (i.e., the nodes are not guarded/firewalled, or there exists a means to circumvent such protections [17]). In addition we assume that nodes can pick uniformly at random a set of nodes in the system. This is usually achieved using full membership or a random peer sampling protocol [14, 18]. Such sampling protocols can be made robust to Byzantine attacks using techniques such as Brahms [3].

A source broadcasts a stream to all nodes using a three-phase gossip protocol [5, 7]. The content is split into multiple chunks uniquely identified by ids. In short, each node periodically proposes a set of chunks it received to a set of random nodes. Upon reception of a proposal, a node requests the chunks it needs and the sender then serves them. All messages are sent over UDP. The three phases are illustrated in Figure 2b.

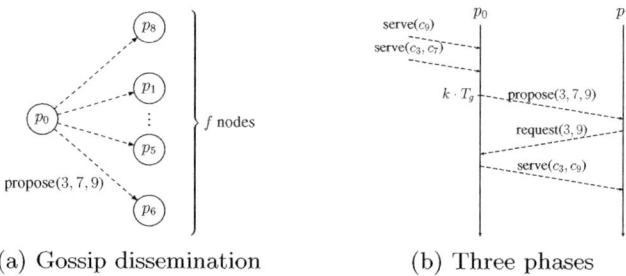

(a) Gossip dissemination (b) Three phases

Fig. 2. Three-phase generic gossip

Propose phase. A node periodically, i.e., at every gossip period T_g, picks uniformly at random a set of f nodes and proposes to them (as depicted in Figure 2a) the set $\mathcal{P}$ of chunks it received since its last propose phase. The size f of the node set, namely the *fanout*, is the same for all nodes and kept constant over time (the fanout is typically slightly larger than $\ln(n)$ [16], that is $f = 12$ for a 10,000-node system). Such a gossip protocol follows an *infect-and-die* process as once a node proposed a chunk to a set of nodes, it does not propose it anymore.

Request phase. Upon reception of a proposal of a set $\mathcal{P}$ of chunks, a node determines the subset of chunks $\mathcal{R}$ it needs and requests these chunks.

Serving phase. When a proposing node receives a request corresponding to a proposal, it serves the chunks requested. If a request does not correspond to a proposal, it is ignored. Similarly, nodes only serve chunks that were effectively proposed, i.e., chunks in $\mathcal{P} \cap \mathcal{R}$.

3 Freeriding

Nodes are either honest or freeriders. Honest nodes strictly follow the protocol, including the verifications of LiFTinG. Freeriders allow themselves to deviate from the protocol in order to minimize their contribution while maximizing their benefit. In addition, freeriders may adopt any behavior not to be expelled, including lying to verifications, or covering up colluding freeriders' bad actions. Note that under this model, freeriders do not wrongfully accuse honest nodes. Effectively, making honest nodes expelled *(i)* does not increase the benefit of freeriders, *(ii)* does not prevent them from being detected, i.e., detection is based solely on the suspected node's behavior regardless of other nodes' behaviors (details in Section 5.1), and finally *(iii)* leads to an increased proportion of freeriders, degrading the benefit of all nodes. This phenomenon is known as the *tragedy of the commons* [12]. We denote by m the number of freeriders.

Freeriders may deviate from the gossip protocol in the following ways: *(i)* decrease the number of partners to communicate with, *(ii)* bias the partner selection, *(iii)* drop messages they are supposed to send, or *(iv)* modify the content of the messages they send. In the sequel, we exhaustively list all possible attacks in each phase of the protocol, discuss their motivations and impacts, and then extract and classify those that may increase the individual interest of a freerider or the common interest of colluding freeriders. In the sequel, attacks that require or profit to colluding nodes are denoted with a '$\star$'.

3.1 Propose Phase

During the first phase, a freerider may *(i)* communicate with less than f nodes, *(ii)* propose less chunks than it should, *(iii)* select as communication partners only a specific subset of nodes, or *(iv)* reduce its proposing rate.

- *(i)* **Decreasing fanout.** By proposing chunks to $\hat{f} < f$ nodes per gossip period, the freerider trivially reduces the potential number of requests, and thus the probability of serving chunks. Therefore, its contribution in terms of the amount of data uploaded is decreased.
- *(ii)* **Invalid proposal.** A proposal is valid if it contains every chunk received in the last gossip period. Proposing only a subset of the chunks received in the last period obviously decreases the potential number of requested chunks. However, a freerider has no interest in proposing chunks it does not have since, contrarily to TfT-based protocols, uploading chunks to a node does not imply that the latter sends chunks in return. In other words, proposing more (and possibly fake) chunks does not increase the benefit of a node and does thus not need to be considered.
- *(iii)* **Biasing the partners selection ($\star$).** Considering a group of colluding nodes, a freerider may want to bias the random selection of nodes to favor its colluding partners, so that the group's benefit increases.
- *(iv)* **Increasing the gossip period.** A freerider may increase its gossip period, leading to less frequent proposals advertising more, but "older", chunks per proposal. This implies a decreased interest of the requesting nodes and thus a decreased contribution for the sender. This is due to the fact that an old chunk has a lower probability of being of interest as it becomes more replicated over time.

3.2 Pull Request Phase

Nodes are expected to request only chunks that they have been proposed. A freerider would increase its benefit by opportunistically requesting extra chunks (even from nodes that did not propose these chunks). The dissemination protocol itself prevents this misbehaving by automatically dropping such requests.

3.3 Serving Phase

In the serving phase, freeriders may *(i)* send only a subset of what was requested or *(ii)* send junk. The first obviously decreases the freeriders' contribution as they serve fewer chunks than they are supposed to. However, as we mentioned above, in the considered asymmetric protocol, a freerider has no interest in sending junk data, since it does not receive anything in return.

3.4 Summary

Analyzing the basic gossip protocol in details allowed to identify the possible attacks. Interestingly enough, these attacks share similar aspects and can thus be gathered into three classes that dictate the rationale along which our verification procedures are designed.

The first is *quantitative correctness* that characterizes the fact that a node effectively proposes to the correct number of nodes (f) at the correct rate ($1/T_g$). Assuming this first aspect is verified, two more aspects must be further considered: *causality* that reflects the correctness of the deterministic part of the protocol, i.e., received chunks must be proposed in the next gossip period as depicted in Figure 2b, and *statistical validity* that evaluates the fairness (with respect to the distribution specified by the protocol) in the random selection of communication partners.

4 Lightweight Freerider-Tracking in Gossip

LiFTinG is a Lightweight protocol for Freerider-Tracking in Gossip that encourages nodes, in a coercive way, to contribute their fair share to the system, by means of distributed verifications. LiFTinG consists of *(i) direct* verifications and *(ii) a posteriori* verifications. Verifications, that require more information than what is available at the verifying node and the inspected node, are referred to as *cross-checking*. In order to control the overhead of LiFTinG, the frequency at which such verifications are triggered is controlled by a parameter p_{cc}, as described in Section 4.2. Verifications can either lead to the emission of *blames* or to *expulsion*, depending on the gravity of the misbehavior.

Direct verifications are performed regularly while the protocol is running: the nodes' actions are directly checked. They aim at checking that all chunks requested are served and that all chunks served are further proposed to a correct number of nodes, i.e, they check the *quantitative correctness* and *causality*. Direct verifications are composed of *(i)* direct checking and *(ii)* direct cross-checking.

A posteriori verifications are run sporadically. They require each node to maintain a log of its past interactions, namely a *history*. In practice, a node stores a trace of the events that occurred in the last h seconds, i.e., corresponding to the last $n_h = h/T_g$ gossip periods. The history is audited to check the statistical validity of the random choices made when selecting communication partners, namely *entropic check*. The veracity of the history is verified by cross-checking the involved nodes, namely a posteriori cross-checking.

We present the blaming architecture in Section 4.1 and present direct verifications in Section 4.2. Since freeriders can collude not to be detected, we expose how they can cover up each other's misbehaviors in Section 4.3 and address this in Section 4.4. The different attacks and corresponding verifications are summarized in Table 1.

Table 1. Summary of attacks and associated verifications

Attack	Type	Detection
fanout decrease ($\hat{f} < f$)	quantitative	direct cross-check
partial propose ($\mathcal{P}$)	causality	direct cross-check
partial serve ($|\mathcal{S}| < |\mathcal{R}|$)	quantitative	direct check
bias partners selection ($\star$)	entropy	entropic check, *a posteriori* cross-check

4.1 Blaming Architecture

In LiFTinG, the detection of freeriders is achieved by means of a score assigned to each node. When a node detects that some other node freerides, it emits a blame message containing a *blame value* against the suspected node. Summing up the blame values of a node results in a score. For scores to be meaningful, blames emitted by different verifications should be comparable and homogeneous. In order to collect blames targeting a given node and maintain its score, each node is monitored by a set of other nodes named *managers*, distributed among the participants. Blame messages towards a node are sent to its managers. When a manager detects that the score of a node p it monitors drops beyond a *fixed* threshold (the design choice of using a fixed threshold is explained in Section 5.1), it spreads – through gossip – a revocation message against p making the nodes of the system progressively remove p from their membership. A general overview of the architecture of LiFTinG is given in Figure 3.

The blaming architecture of LiFTinG is built on top of the AVMON [23] monitoring overlay. In AVMON, nodes are assigned a *fixed-size* set of M *random* managers *consistent* over time which make it very appealing in our setting, namely a dynamic peer-to-peer environment subject to churn with possibly colluding nodes. The fact that the number M of managers is constant makes the protocol scalable as the monitoring load at each node is independent of the system size. Randomness prevents colluding freeriders from covering each other up and consistency enables long-term blame history at the managers. The monitoring relationship is based on a hash function and can be advertised in a gossip-fashion

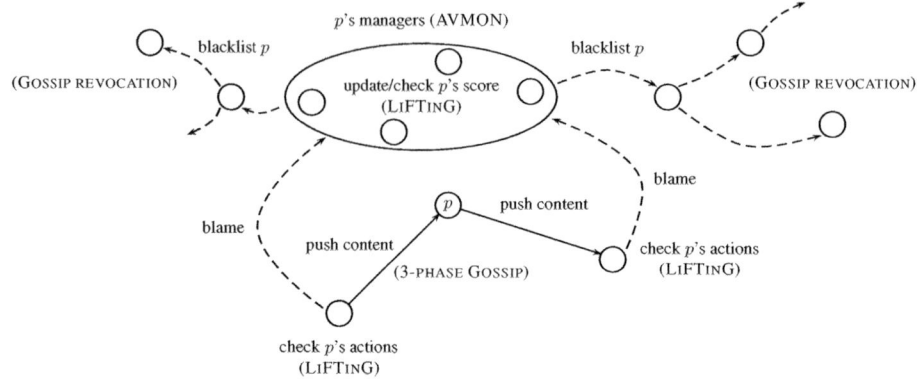

Fig. 3. Overview of LiFTinG

by piggybacking node's monitors in the view maintenance messages (e.g., exchanges of local views in the distributed peer-sampling service). Doing so, nodes quickly discover other nodes' managers – and are therefore able to blame them if necessary – even in the presence of churn. In addition, nodes can locally verify (i.e., without the need for extra communication) whether the mapping, node to managers, is correct by hashing the nodes' ip addresses, preventing freeriders from forging fake or colluding managers. In case a manager does not map correctly to a node, a revocation against the concerned node is sent.

4.2 Direct Verifications

In LiFTinG, two direct verifications are used. The first aims to ensure that every requested chunk is served, namely a *direct check*. Detection can be done locally and it is therefore always performed. If some requested chunks are missing, the requesting node blames the proposing node by $f/|\mathcal{R}|$ (where $\mathcal{R}$ is the set of requested chunks) for each chunk that has not been delivered.

The second verification checks that received chunks are further proposed to f nodes within the next gossip period. This is achieved by a *cross-checking* procedure that works as follows: a node p_1 that received a chunk c_i from p_0 acknowledges to p_0 that it proposed c_i to a set of f nodes. Then, p_0 sends confirm requests (with probability p_{cc}) to the set of f nodes to check whether they effectively received a propose message from p_1 containing c_i. The f witnesses reply to p_0 with answer messages confirming or not p_1's ack sent to p_0.

Figure 4 depicts the message sequence composing a direct cross-checking verification (with a fanout of 2 for the sake of readability). The blaming mechanism works as follows: *(i)* if the ack message is not received, the verifier p_0 blames the verified node p_1 by f, and *(ii)* for each missing or negative answer message, p_0 blames p_1 by 1.

Since the verification messages (i.e., ack, confirm and confirm responses) for the direct cross-checking are small and in order to limit the subsequent overhead

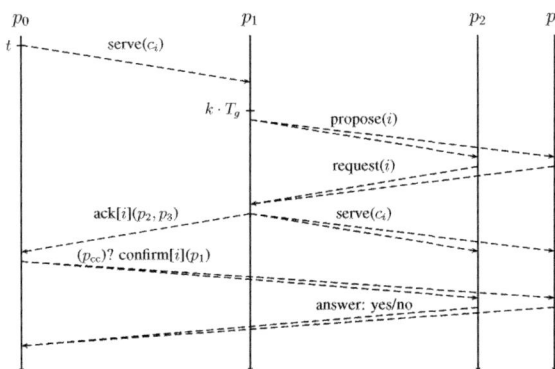

Fig. 4. Cross-checking protocol

Table 2. Summary of attacks and associated blame values

Attacks	Blame values
fanout decrease ($\hat{f} < f$)	$f - \hat{f}$ from each verifier
partial propose	1 (per invalid proposal) from each verifier
partial serve ($|\mathcal{S}| < |\mathcal{R}|$)	$f \cdot (|\mathcal{R}| - |\mathcal{S}|)/|\mathcal{R}|$ from each requester

of LiFTinG, direct cross-checking is done exclusively with UDP. The blames corresponding to the different attacks are summarized in Table 2.

Blames emitted by the direct verification procedures of LiFTinG are summed into a score reflecting the nodes' behaviors. For this reason, blame values must be comparable and homogeneous. This means that two misbehaviors that reduce a freerider's contribution by the same amount should lead to the same value of blame, regardless of the misbehaviors and the verification.

We consider a freerider p_f that received c chunks and wants to reduce its contribution by a factor δ ($0 \leq \delta \leq 1$). To achieve this goal, p_f can: *(i)* propose the c received chunks to only $\hat{f} = (1-\delta) \cdot f$ nodes, *(ii)* propose only a proportion $(1-\delta)$ of the chunks it received, or *(iii)* serve only $(1-\delta) \cdot |\mathcal{R}|$ of the $|\mathcal{R}|$ chunks it was requested. For the sake of simplicity, we assume that $\hat{f}, c \cdot \delta, c/f$ and $\delta \cdot |R|$ are all integers. The number of verifiers, that is, the number of nodes that served the c chunks to p_f is called the *fanin* (f_{in}). On average, we have $f_{in} \simeq f$ and each node serves c/f chunks [9].

We now derive, for each of the three aforementioned misbehaviors, the blame value emitted by the direct verifications.

(i) Fanout decrease (direct cross-check): If p_f proposes all the c chunks to only $\hat{f}$ nodes, it is blamed by 1 by each of the f_{in} verifiers, for each of the $f - \hat{f}$ missing "propose target". This results in a blame value of $f_{in} \cdot (f - \hat{f}) = f_{in} \cdot \delta \cdot f \simeq \delta f^2$.

(ii) Partial propose (direct cross-check): If p_f proposes only $(1-\delta) \cdot c$ chunks to f nodes, it is blamed by f by each of the nodes that provided at least

one of the missing chunks. A freerider has therefore interest in removing from its proposal chunks originating from the smallest subset of nodes. In this case, its proposal is invalid from the standpoint of $\delta \cdot f_{in}$ verifiers. This results in a blame value of $\delta \cdot f_{in} \cdot f \simeq \delta \cdot f^2$.

(iii) *Partial serve (direct check):* If p_f serves only $(1-\delta) \cdot |\mathcal{R}|$ chunks, it is blamed by $f/|\mathcal{R}|$ for each of the $\delta \cdot |\mathcal{R}|$ missing chunks by each of the f requesting nodes. This again results in a blame value of $f \cdot (f/|\mathcal{R}|) \cdot \delta \cdot |\mathcal{R}| = \delta \cdot f^2$.

All misbehaviors lead to the same amount of blame for a given degree of freeriding δ. Therefore, the blame values emitted by the different direct verifications are homogeneous and comparable on average. Thus, they result in a consistent and meaningful score when summed up.

4.3 Fooling the Direct Cross-Check (⋆)

Considering a set of colluding nodes, nodes may lie to verifications to cover each other up. Consider the situation depicted in Figure 5a, where p_1 is a freerider. If p_0 colludes with p_1, then it will not blame p_1, regardless of p_2's answer. Similarly, if p_2 colludes with p_1, then it will answer to p_0 that p_1 sent a valid proposal, regardless of what p_1 sent. Even when neither p_0 nor p_2 collude with p_1, p_1 can still fool the direct cross-checking thanks to a colluding third party by implementing a *man-in-the-middle attack* as depicted in Figure 5b. Indeed, if a node p_7 colludes with p_1, then p_1 can tell p_0 it sent a proposal to p_7 and tell p_2 that the chunk originated from p_7. Doing this, both p_0 and p_2 will not detect that p_1 sent an invalid proposal. The *a posteriori verifications* presented in the next section address this issue.

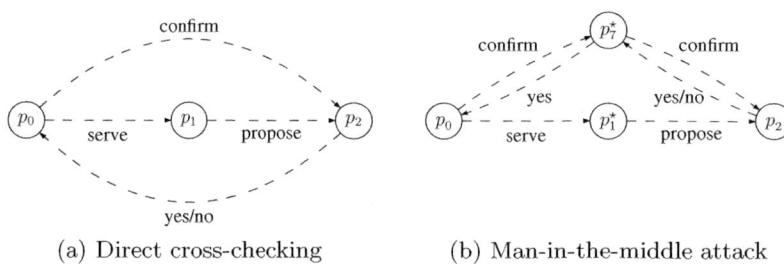

(a) Direct cross-checking (b) Man-in-the-middle attack

Fig. 5. Direct cross-checking and attack. Colluding nodes are denoted with a '⋆'.

4.4 A Posteriori Verifications

As stated in the analysis of the gossip protocol, the random choices made in the partners selection must be checked. In addition, the example described in the previous section, where freeriders collude to circumvent direct cross-checking, highlights the need for statistical verification of a node's past communication partners.

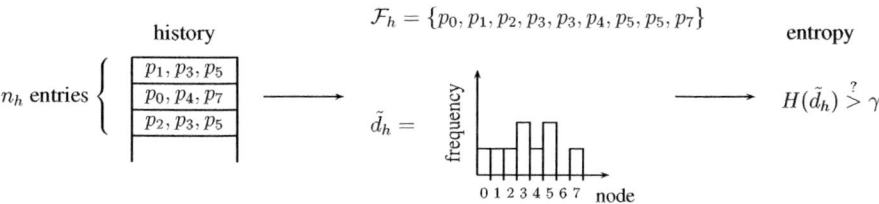

Fig. 6. Entropic check on proposals ($f = 3$)

The history of a node that biased its partner selection contains a relatively large proportion of colluding nodes. If only a small fraction of colluding nodes is present in the system, they will appear more frequently than honest nodes in each other's histories and can therefore be detected. Based on this remark, we propose an *entropic check* to detect the bias induced by freeriders on the history of nodes, illustrated in Figure 6.

Every h seconds, each node picks a random node and verifies its local history. When inspecting the history of p, the verifier computes the number of occurrences of each node in the set of proposals sent by p during the last h seconds. Defining $\mathcal{F}_h$ as the multiset of nodes to whom p sent a proposal during this period (a node may indeed appear more than once in $\mathcal{F}_h$), the distribution $\tilde{d}_h$ of nodes in $\mathcal{F}_h$ characterizes the randomness of the partners selection. We denote by $\tilde{d}_{h,i}$ the number of occurrences of node i ($i \in \{1, \ldots, n\}$) in $\mathcal{F}_h$ normalized by the size of $\mathcal{F}_h$. Assessing the uniformity of the distribution $\tilde{d}$ of p_1's history is achieved by comparing its Shannon entropy to a threshold γ ($0 \leq \gamma \leq \log_2(n_h f)$).

$$H(\tilde{d}_h) = -\sum_i \tilde{d}_{h,i} \log_2(\tilde{d}_{h,i}) \qquad (1)$$

The entropy is maximum when every node of the system appears at most once in $\mathcal{F}_h$ (assuming $n > |\mathcal{F}_h| = n_h f$). In that case, it is equal to $\log_2(n_h f)$. Since the peer selection service may not be perfect, the threshold γ must be tolerant to small deviation with respect to the uniform distribution to avoid *false positives* (i.e., honest nodes being blamed). Details on how to dimension γ are given in Section 5.2.

An entropic check must be coupled with an *a posteriori* cross-checking verification procedure to guarantee the validity of the inspected node's history. Cross-checking is achieved by polling all or a subset of the nodes mentioned in the history for an acknowledgment. The inspected node is blamed by 1 for each proposal in its history that is not acknowledged by the alleged receiver. Therefore, an inspected freerider replacing colluding nodes by honest nodes in its history in order to pass the entropic check will not be covered by the honest nodes and will thus be blamed accordingly.

To cope with potential man-in-the middle attack presented in Section 4.2, a complementary entropic check is performed on the multi-set of nodes $\mathcal{F}'_h$ that asked the nodes in $\mathcal{F}_h$ for a confirmation, i.e., direct cross-checking. On the one hand, for an honest node p_0, $\mathcal{F}'_h$ is composed of the nodes that sent chunks to

p_0 – namely its *fanin*. On the other hand, for a freerider $p_0^\star$ that implemented the man-in-the-middle attack, the set $\mathcal{F}'_h$ of $p_0^\star$ contains a large proportion of colluding nodes – the nodes that covered it up for the direct cross-checking – and thus fail the entropic check. If the history of the inspected node does not pass the entropic checks (i.e, fanin and fanout), the node is expelled from the system.

5 Parametrizing LiFTinG

This section provides a methodology to set LiFTinG's parameters. With this aim, the performance of LiFTinG with respect to detection is analyzed theoretically. Closed form expressions of the detection and false positive probabilities function of the system parameters are given. Theoretical results allow the system designer to set the system parameters, e.g., detection thresholds. Theoretical results are obtained by simulations.

This section is split in two. First, the design of the score-based detection mechanism is presented and analyzed taking into account message losses. Second, the entropy-based detection mechanism is analyzed taking into account the underlying peer-sampling service. Both depend on the degree of freeriding and on the favoring factor, i.e., how freeriders favor colluding partners.

5.1 Score-Based Detection

Due to message losses, a node may be wrongfully blamed, i.e., blamed even though it follows the protocol. Freeriders are additionally blamed for their misbehaviors. Therefore, the score distribution among the nodes is expected to be a mixture of two components corresponding respectively to those of honest nodes and freeriders. In this setting, likelihood maximization algorithms are traditionally used to decide whether a node is a freerider or not. Such algorithms are based on the relative score of the nodes and are thus not sensitive to wrongful blames. Effectively, wrongful blames have the same impact on honest nodes and freeriders.

However, in the presence of freeriders, two problems arise when using relative score-based detection: *(i)* freeriders are able to decrease the probability of being detected by wrongfully blaming honest nodes, and *(ii)* the score of a node joining the system is not comparable to those of the nodes already in the system. For these reasons, in LiFTinG, the impact of wrongful blames, due to message losses, is automatically compensated. Detection thus consists in comparing the nodes' compensated scores to a fixed threshold η. In short, when the compensated score of a node drops below η, the managers of that node broadcast a revocation message expelling the node from the system using gossip.

Considering message losses independently drawn from a Bernoulli distribution of parameter p_l (we denote by $p_r = 1 - p_l$ the probability of reception), we derive a closed-form expression for the expected value of the blames applied to honest nodes by direct verifications during a given timespan. Periodically increasing all scores accordingly leads to an average score of 0 for honest nodes. This way, the fixed threshold η can be used to distinguish between honest nodes and freeriders. To this end, we analyze, for each verification, the situations where message losses can cause wrongful blames and evaluate their average impact. For the sake of the analysis, we assume that *(i)* a node receives at least one chunk during every gossip period (and therefore it will send proposals during the next gossip period), and *(ii)* each node requests a constant number $|\mathcal{R}|$ of chunks for each proposal it receives. We consider the case where cross-checking is always performed, i.e., $p_{cc} = 1$.

Direct check (dc). For each requested chunk that has not been served, the node is blamed by $f/|\mathcal{R}|$. If the proposal is received but the request is lost (i.e., $p_r(1-p_r)$), the node is blamed by f ((a) in Equation 2). Otherwise, when both the proposal and the request message are received (i.e., p_r^2), the node is blamed by $f/|R|$ for each of the chunks lost (i.e., $(1-p_r)|R|$) ((b) in Equation 2). The expected blame applied to an honest node (by its f partners), during one gossip period, due to message losses is therefore:

$$\tilde{b}_{dc} = f \cdot \left[\overbrace{p_r(1-p_r) \cdot f}^{(a)} + \overbrace{p_r^2 \cdot (1-p_r)|\mathcal{R}| \cdot \frac{f}{|\mathcal{R}|}}^{(b)} \right] = p_r(1-p_r^2) \cdot f^2 \quad (2)$$

Direct cross-checking (dcc). On average, a node receives f proposals during each gossip period. Therefore a node is subject to f direct cross-checking verifications and each verifier asks for a confirmation to the f partners of the inspected node. Let p_1 be the inspected node and p_0 a verifier. First, note that p_0 verifies p_1 only if it served chunks to p_1, which requires that its proposal and the associated request have been received (i.e., p_r^2). If at least one chunk served by p_0 or the ack has been lost (i.e., $1 - p_r^{|\mathcal{R}|+1}$), p_0 will blame p_1 by f regardless of what happens next, since all the f proposals sent by p_1 are invalid from the standpoint of p_0 ((a) in Equation 3). Otherwise, that is, if all the chunks served and the ack have been received (i.e., $p_r^{|\mathcal{R}|+1}$), p_0 blames p_1 by 1 for each negative or missing answer from the f partners of p_1. This situation occurs when the proposal sent by p_1 to a partner, the confirm message or the answer is lost (i.e., $1 - p_r^3$) ((b) in Equation 3).

$$\tilde{b}_{cc} = f \cdot p_r^2 \left[\overbrace{(1-p_r^{|R|+1}) \cdot f}^{(a)} + \overbrace{f \cdot p_r^{|\mathcal{R}|+1}(1-p_r^3)}^{(b)} \right] = p_r^2(1-p_r^{|\mathcal{R}|+4}) \cdot f^2 \quad (3)$$

From the previous analysis, we obtain a closed-form expression for the expected value of the blame b applied to an honest node by direct verifications due to message losses:

$$\tilde{b} = \tilde{b}_{dc} + \tilde{b}_{cc} = p_r(1 + p_r - p_r^2 - p_r^{|\mathcal{R}|+5}) \cdot f^2 \quad . \quad (4)$$

The blame value b' applied to a freerider by direct verifications depends on its *degree of freeriding* Δ that characterizes its deviation to the protocol. Formally, we define the degree of freeriding as a 3-uple $\Delta = (\delta_1, \delta_2, \delta_3)$, $0 \leq \delta_1, \delta_2, \delta_3 \leq 1$, so that a freerider contacts only $(1 - \delta_1) \cdot f$ nodes per gossip period, proposes the chunks received from a proportion $(1 - \delta_2)$ of the nodes that served it in the previous gossip period, and serves $(1 - \delta_3) \cdot |\mathcal{R}|$ chunks to each requesting node. With the same methodology as for $\tilde{b}$, we get:

$$\tilde{b}'(\Delta) = (1 - \delta_1) \cdot p_r \left(1 - p_r^2(1 - \delta_3)\right) \cdot f^2 + \delta_2 \cdot f^2 + \qquad (5)$$
$$(1 - \delta_2) \cdot p_r^2 \cdot \left[p_r^{|\mathcal{R}|+1}(1 - p_r^3(1 - \delta_1)) + (1 - p_r^{|\mathcal{R}|+1})\right] \cdot f^2$$

Note that the gain in terms of the upload bandwidth saved by a freerider is $1 - (1 - \delta_1)(1 - \delta_2)(1 - \delta_3)$. Following the same line of reasoning, a closed-form expression of the standard deviation $\sigma(b)$ (resp. $\sigma(b'(\Delta))$) of b (resp. $b'(\Delta)$) can be derived.

Figure 7 depicts the distribution of compensated and normalized scores (see Formula 6) in the presence of $1,000$ freeriders of degree $\delta = \delta_1 = \delta_2 = \delta_3 = 0.1$ in a $10,000$-node system after $r = 50$ gossip periods. The message loss rate is set to 7%, the fanout f to 12 and $|\mathcal{R}| = 4$. The scores of the nodes have been increased by $-\tilde{b} = 72.95$, according to Formula (4). We plot separately the distribution of scores among honest nodes and freeriders. As expected, the probability density function (Figure 7a) is split into two disjoint modes separated by a gap: the lowest (i.e., left most) mode corresponds to freeriders and the highest one to honest nodes. We observe that the average score (dotted line) is close to zero (<0.01) which means that the wrongful blames have been successfully compensated.

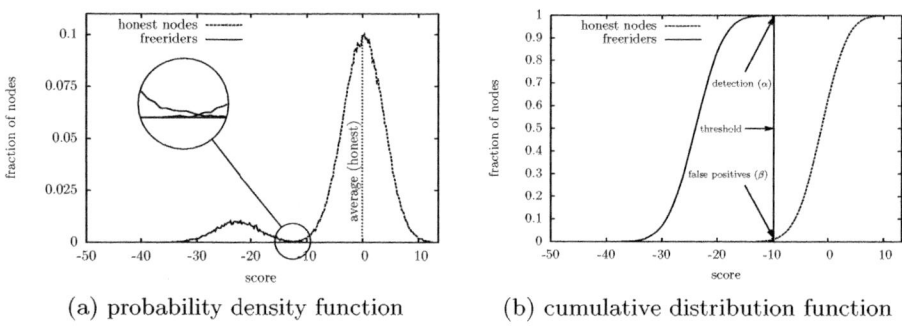

(a) probability density function   (b) cumulative distribution function

Fig. 7. Distribution of normalized scores in the presence of freeriders ($\delta = 0.1$)

We now evaluate the ability of LiFTinG to detect freeriders (probability of detection α) and the proportion of honest nodes wrongfully expelled from the system (probability of false positives β). Figure 7b depicts the cumulative distribution function of scores and illustrates the notion of detection and false positives for a given value of the detection threshold.

In order to enable the use of a fixed threshold η, the scores are compensated with respect to message losses and normalized by the number of gossip periods

r the node spent in the system. At the t-th gossip period, the score of a node writes:

$$s = -\frac{1}{r}\sum_{i=0}^{r}(b_{t-i} - \tilde{b}), \quad (6)$$

where b_i is the value of the blames applied to the node during the i-th gossip period. From the previous analysis, we get the expectation and the standard deviation of the blames applied to honest nodes at each round due to message losses, therefore, assuming that the b_i are independent and identically distributed (i.i.d.), we get $\mathbb{E}[s] = 0$ and $\sigma(s) = \sigma(b)/\sqrt{r}$. Using Bienaymé-Tchebychev's inequality we get:

$$\beta = P(s < \eta) \leq \frac{\sigma(b)^2}{r \cdot \eta^2} \quad \text{and} \quad \alpha \geq 1 - \frac{\sigma(b'(\Delta))^2}{r \cdot (\tilde{b}'(\Delta) - \eta)^2} \quad (7)$$

We set the detection threshold η to -9.75 so that the probability of false positive is lower than 1%, we assume that freeriders perform all possible attacks with degree δ and we observe the proportion of freeriders detected by LiFTinG for several values of δ. Figure 8 plots α function of δ. We observe that a node freeriding by 5% is detected with probability 0.65. Beyond 10% of freeriding, a node is detected over 99% of the time. It is commonly assumed that users are willing to use a modified version of the client application only if it increases significantly their benefit (resp. decreases their contribution). In FlightPath [21], this threshold is assumed to be around 10%. With LiFTinG, a freerider achieves a gain of 10% for $\delta = 0.035$ which corresponds to a probability of being detected of 50% (Figure 8).

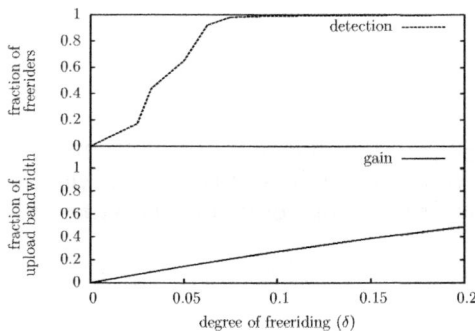

Fig. 8. Proportion of freeriders detected by LiFTinG

5.2 Entropy-Based Detection

For the sake of fairness and in order to prevent colluding nodes from covering each other up, LiFTinG includes an entropic check assessing the statistical validity of the partner selection. To this end, the entropy H of the distribution of the

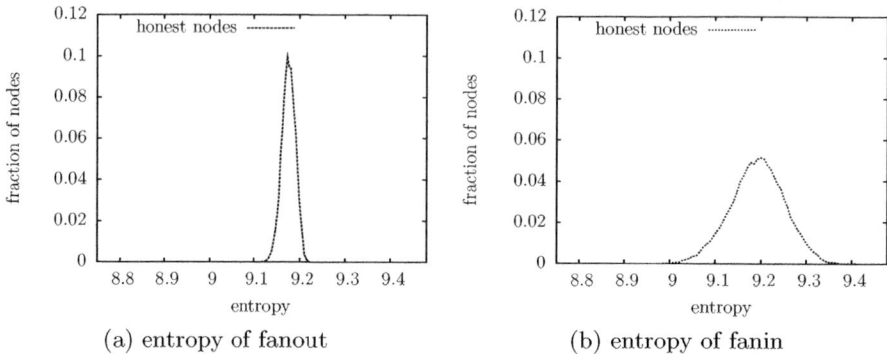

Fig. 9. Entropy distribution of the nodes' histories using a full membership

inspected node's former partners is compared to a threshold γ. The distribution of the entropy of honest nodes' histories depends on the peer sampling algorithm used and the random numbers generator. It can be estimated by simulations. Figure 9a depicts the distribution of entropy for a history of $n_h f = 600$ partners ($n_h = 50$ and $f = 12$) of a 10,000-node system using a full membership-based partner selection. The observed entropy ranges from 9.11 to 9.21 for a maximum reachable value of $\log_2(n_h f) = 9.23$. Similarly, the entropy of the fanin multiset $\mathcal{F}'_h$, i.e., nodes that selected the inspected node as partner, is depicted in Figure 9b. The observed entropy ranges from 8.98 to 9.34.

With $\gamma = 8.95$ the probability of wrongfully expelling a node during local auditing is negligible.

We now analytically determine to what extent a freerider can bias its partner selection without being detected by local auditing, given a threshold γ and a number of colluding nodes m'. Consider a freerider that biases partner selection in order to favor colluding freeriders by picking a freerider as partner with probability p_m and an honest node with probability $1 - p_m$. We seek the maximum value of p_m a freerider can use without being detected, function of γ and m'.

It can be proved [10] that, to maximize the entropy of its history, a freerider must choose uniformly at random its partners in the chosen class, i.e., honest or colluding. In that case, the entropy of its history writes (for $m' < n_h f$):

$$H(\mathcal{F}_h) = -p_m \log_2\left(\frac{p_m}{m'}\right) - (1 - p_m)\log_2\left(\frac{1}{n_h \cdot f}\right) \quad (8)$$

Inverting numerically Formula (8), we deduce that for $\gamma = 8.95$ a freerider colluding with 25 other nodes can serve its colluding partners up to 15% of the time, without being detected.

6 Evaluation and Experimental Results

We now evaluate LiFTinG on top of the gossip-based streaming protocol described in [7], over the PlanetLab testbed. We describe the experimental setup in

Section 6.1. We evaluate the performance of LiFTinG showing its small overhead in Section 6.2 and its precision and speed at detecting freeriders in Section 6.3.

6.1 Experimental Setup

We have deployed and executed LiFTinG on a 300 PlanetLab node testbed, broadcasting a stream of 674 kbps in the presence of 10% of freeriders. The freeriders *(i)* contact only $\hat{f} = 6$ random partners ($\delta_1 = 1/7$), *(ii)* propose only 90% of what they receive ($\delta_2 = 0.1$) and finally *(iii)* serve only 90% of what they are requested ($\delta_3 = 0.1$). The fanout of all nodes is set to 7 and the gossip period is set to 500 ms. The blaming architecture uses $M = 25$ managers for each node.

6.2 Practical Cost

We report on the overhead measurements of direct and *a posteriori* verifications (including blame messages sent to the managers) for different stream rates.

Direct verifications. Table 3 gives the bandwidth overhead of the direct verifications of LiFTinG for three values of p_{cc}. Note that the overhead is not null when $p_{cc} = 0$ since ack messages are always sent. Yet, we observe that the overhead is negligible when $p_{cc} = 0$ (i.e., when the system is healthy) and remains reasonable when $p_{cc} = 1$ (i.e., when the system needs to be purged from freeriders).

Table 3. Practical overhead

	direct verifications			a posteriori verifications
	$p_{cc} = 0$	$p_{cc} = 0.5$	$p_{cc} = 1$	
674 kbps stream	1.07%	4.53%	8.01%	3.60%
1082 kbps stream	0.69%	3.51%	5.04%	2.89%
2036 kbps stream	0.38%	2.80%	2.76%	1.74%

A posteriori verifications. A history message contains n_h entries. Each entry consists of f nodes identifiers and the chunk ids that were proposed. Both the fanout and fanin histories are sent upon a posteriori verification.

Besides the entropic checks, *a posteriori* cross-checking is performed on a subset of the fanout or fanin entries. We measured the maximum overhead, that is when the whole fanout and fanin histories are cross-checked. The overhead incurred by *a posteriori* verifications in our experimental setup (i.e., a history size $n_h = 50$, a gossip period of 500 milliseconds, a fanout of $f = 7$ and a *posteriori* verification period of $h = 25$ seconds) is given in Table 3.

6.3 Experimental Results

We have executed LiFTinG with $p_{cc} = 1$ and $p_{cc} = 0.5$. Figure 10 depicts the scores obtained after 25, 30 and 35 seconds when running direct verifications and cross-checking. The scores have been compensated as explained in the analysis, assuming a loss rate of 4% (average value for UDP packets observed on PlanetLab).

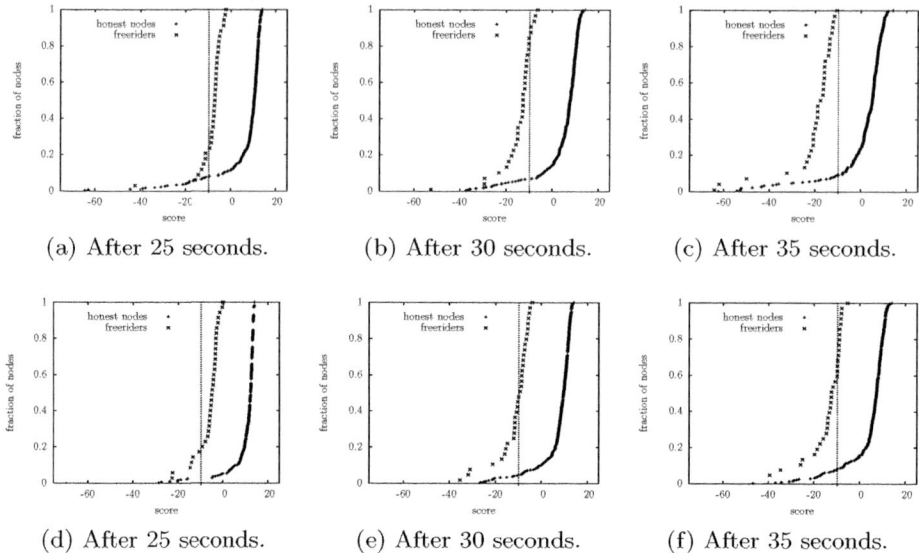

Fig. 10. Scores CDF with $p_{cc} = 1$ (above) and $p_{cc} = 0.5$ (below)

The two cumulative distribution functions for honest nodes and freeriders are clearly separated. The threshold for expelling freeriders is set to -9.75 (as specified in the analysis). In Figure 10b ($p_{cc} = 1$, after 30 s) the detection mechanism expels 86% of the freeriders and 12% of the honest nodes. In other words, after 30 seconds, 14% of freeriders are not yet detected and 12% represent false positives, mainly corresponding to honest nodes that suffer from very poor connection (e.g., limited connectivity, message losses and bandwidth limitation). These nodes do not deliberately freeride, but their connection does not allow them to contribute their fair share. This is acceptable as such nodes should not have been allowed to join the system in the first place. As expected, with p_{cc} set to 0.5 the detection is slower but not twice as slow. Effectively, with nodes freeriding with $\delta_3 > 0$ (i.e., partial serves) the direct checking blames freeriders without the need for any cross-check. This explains why the detection after only 35 seconds with $p_{cc} = 0.5$ (Figure 10f) is comparable to the detection after 30 seconds with $p_{cc} = 1$ (Figure 10b).

As stated in the analysis, we observe that the gap between the two cumulative distribution functions widens over time. However, the variance of the score does not decrease over time (for both honest nodes and freeriders). This is due to the fact that we considered in the analysis that the blames applied to a given node during distinct gossip periods were independent and identically distributed (i.i.d.). In practice however, successive gossip periods are correlated. Effectively, a node with a poor connection is usually blamed more than nodes with high capabilities, and this remains true over the whole experiment.

7 Related Work

TfT distributed incentives have been broadly used to deal with freeriders in file sharing systems based on symmetric exchanges, such as BitTorrent [4]. However, there is a number of attacks, mainly targeting the opportunistic unchoking mechanism (i.e., asymmetric push), allowing freeriders to download contents with no or a very small contribution [22, 24].

FlightPath (built on top of BAR Gossip) [21] is a gossip-based streaming application that fights against freeriding using verifications on partner selection and chunk exchanges. FlightPath operates in a gossip fashion for partner selection and is composed of opportunistic pushes performed by altruistic nodes (essential for the efficiency of the protocol) and balanced pairwise exchanges secured by TfT. Randomness of partner selection is verified by means of a pseudo-random number generator with signed seeds, and symmetric exchanges are made robust using cryptographic primitives. FlightPath prevents attacks on opportunistic pushes by turning them into symmetric exchanges: each peer must reciprocate with junk chunks when opportunistically unchoked. This results in a non-negligible waste of bandwidth. It is further demonstrated in [13] that BAR Gossip presents scalability issues, not to mention the overhead of cryptography.

PeerReview [11] deals with malicious nodes following an accountability approach. Peers maintain signed logs of their actions that can be checked using a reference implementation running in addition to the application. When combined with CSAR [2], PeerReview can be applied to non-deterministic protocols. However, the intensive use of cryptography and the sizes of the logs maintained and exchanged drastically reduce the scalability of this solution. In addition, the validity of PeerReview relies on the fact that messages are always received which is not the case over the Internet.

The two approaches that relate the most to LiFTinG are the distributed auditing protocol proposed in [13] and the passive monitoring protocol proposed in [15]. In the first protocol, freeriders are detected by cross-checking their neighbors' reports. The latter focuses on gossip-based search in the Gnutella network. The peers monitor the way their neighbors forward/answer queries in order to detect freeriders and query droppers. Yet, contrarily to LiFTinG – which is based on random peer selection – in both protocols the peers's neighborhoods are static, forming a fixed mesh overlay. These techniques thus cannot be applied to gossip protocols. In addition, the situation where colluding peers cover each other up (not addressed in the papers) makes such monitoring protocols vain.

8 Conclusion

We presented LiFTinG, a protocol for tracking freeriders in gossip-based asymmetric data dissemination systems. Beyond the fact that LiFTinG deals with the randomness of the protocol, LiFTinG precisely relies on this randomness to robustify its verification mechanisms against colluding freeriders with a very low overhead. We provided a theoretical analysis of LiFTinG that allows system designers to set its parameters to their optimal values and characterizes its performance backed up by extensive simulations. We reported on our experimentations on PlanetLab which prove the practicability and efficiency of LiFTinG.

We believe that, beyond gossip protocols, LiFTinG can be used to secure the asymmetric component of TfT-based protocols, namely *opportunistic unchoking*, which is considered to constitute their Achilles heel [22, 24].

References

1. Adar, E., Huberman, B.: Free riding on Gnutella. First Monday 5 (2000)
2. Backes, M., Druschel, P., Haeberlen, A., Unruh, D.: CSAR: A Practical and Provable Technique to Make Randomized Systems Accountable. In: NDSS (2009)
3. Bortnikov, E., Gurevich, M., Keidar, I., Kliot, G., Shraer, A.: Brahms: Byzantine Resilient Random Membership Sampling. Computer Networks 53, 2340–2359 (2009)
4. Cohen, B.: Incentives Build Robustness in BitTorrent. In: P2P Econ. (2003)
5. Deshpande, M., Xing, B., Lazardis, I., Hore, B., Venkatasubramanian, N., Mehrotra, S.: CREW: A Gossip-based Flash-Dissemination System. In: ICDCS (2006)
6. Eugster, P.T., Guerraoui, R., Handurukande, S.B., Kouznetsov, P., Kermarrec, A.-M.: Lightweight Probabilistic Broadcast. TOCS 21, 341–374 (2003)
7. Frey, D., Guerraoui, R., Kermarrec, A.-M., Monod, M., Quéma, V.: Stretching Gossip with Live Streaming. In: DSN (2009)
8. Frey, D., Guerraoui, R., Koldehofe, B., Kermarrec, A.-M., Mogensen, M., Monod, M., Quéma, V.: Heterogeneous gossip. In: Bacon, J.M., Cooper, B.F. (eds.) Middleware 2009. LNCS, vol. 5896, pp. 42–61. Springer, Heidelberg (2009)
9. Ganesh, A., Kermarrec, A.-M., Massoulié, L.: SCAMP: Peer-to-peer Lightweight Membership Service for Large-scale Group Communication. In: Crowcroft, J., Hofmann, M. (eds.) NGC 2001. LNCS, vol. 2233, p. 44. Springer, Heidelberg (2001)
10. Guerraoui, R., Huguenin, K., Kermarrec, A.-M., Monod, M.: LiFT: Lightweight Freerider-Tracking Protocol. Research Report RR-6913, INRIA (2009)
11. Haeberlen, A., Kouznetsov, P., Druschel, P.: PeerReview: Practical Accountability for Distributed Systems. In: SOSP (2007)
12. Hardin, G.: The Tragedy of the Commons. Science 162, 1243–1248 (1968)
13. Haridasan, M., Jansch-Porto, I., Van Renesse, R.: Enforcing Fairness in a Live-Streaming System. In: MMCN (2008)
14. Jelasity, M., Voulgaris, S., Guerraoui, R., Kermarrec, A.-M., van Steen, M.: Gossip-based Peer Sampling. TOCS 25, 1–36 (2007)
15. Karakaya, M., Körpeoğlu, I., Ulusoy, O.: Counteracting Free-riding in Peer-to-Peer Networks. Computer Networks 52, 675–694 (2008)
16. Kermarrec, A.-M., Massoulié, L., Ganesh, A.: Probabilistic Reliable Dissemination in Large-Scale Systems. TPDS 14, 248–258 (2003)
17. Kermarrec, A.-M., Pace, A., Quéma, V., Schiavoni, V.: NAT-resilient Gossip Peer Sampling. In: ICDCS (2009)
18. King, V., Saia, J.: Choosing a Random Peer. In: PODC (2004)
19. Krishnan, R., Smith, M., Tang, Z., Telang, R.: The Impact of Free-Riding on Peer-to-Peer Networks. In: HICSS (2004)

20. Li, B., Qu, Y., Keung, Y., Xie, S., Lin, C., Liu, J., Zhang, X.: Inside the New Coolstreaming: Principles, Measurements and Performance Implications. In: INFOCOM (2008)
21. Li, H., Clement, A., Marchetti, M., Kapritsos, M., Robinson, L., Alvisi, L., Dahlin, M.: FlightPath: Obedience vs Choice in Cooperative Services. In: OSDI (2008)
22. Locher, T., Moor, P., Schmid, S., Wattenhofer, R.: Free Riding in BitTorrent is Cheap. In: HotNets (2006)
23. Morales, R., Gupta, I.: AVMON: Optimal and Scalable Discovery of Consistent Availability Monitoring Overlays for Distributed Systems. TPDS 20, 446–459 (2009)
24. Sirivianos, M., Park, J., Chen, R., Yang, X.: Free-riding in BitTorrent with the Large View Exploit. In: IPTPS (2007)
25. Venkataraman, V., Yoshida, K., Francis, P.: Chunkyspread: Heterogeneous Unstructured Tree-Based Peer-to-Peer Multicast. In: ICNP (2006)
26. Zhang, M., Zhang, Q., Sun, L., Yang, S.: Understanding the Power of Pull-Based Streaming Protocol: Can We Do Better? JSAC 25, 1678–1694 (2007)

Distributed Middleware Enforcement of Event Flow Security Policy

Matteo Migliavacca[1], Ioannis Papagiannis[1], David M. Eyers[2], Brian Shand[3], Jean Bacon[2], and Peter Pietzuch[1]

[1] Imperial College London
{migliava,ip108,prp}@doc.ic.ac.uk
[2] University of Cambridge
{firstname.lastname}@cl.cam.ac.uk
[3] CBCU/ECRIC, National Health Service
brian.shand@cbcu.nhs.uk

Abstract. Distributed, event-driven applications that process sensitive user data and involve multiple organisational domains must comply with complex security requirements. Ideally, developers want to express security policy for such applications in data-centric terms, controlling the flow of information throughout the system. Current middleware does not support the specification of such end-to-end security policy and lacks uniform mechanisms for enforcement.

We describe DEFCON-POLICY, a middleware that enforces security policy in multi-domain, event-driven applications. Event flow policy is expressed in a high-level language that specifies permitted flows between distributed software components. The middleware limits the interaction of components based on the policy and the data that components have observed. It achieves this by labelling data and assigning privileges to components. We evaluate DEFCON-POLICY in a realistic medical scenario and demonstrate that it can provide global security guarantees without burdening application developers.

Keywords: multi-domain distributed applications, security policy, information flow control, event-based middleware.

1 Introduction

Distributed systems that span multiple organisational or administrative domains are increasingly common in many areas, yet the associated security challenges remain largely unsolved. In the public sector from healthcare to public security, the integration of separate agencies and departments into federations enables the free flow of information and promises better services for citizens. Global companies are moving away from monolithic organisations towards a more dynamic business ecosystem that is reflected in the distributed nature of their software infrastructures. To achieve the necessary degree of integration between software components in such applications, they are often implemented as *event-driven architectures* [1], in which components, potentially belonging to different domains, process and exchange data in the form of event messages.

Multi-domain, event-driven applications process and exchange personal, often sensitive, data belonging to different users. As a result, organisations have to abide by information handling policies, frequently stemming from data protection laws. Such policies often refer to the *flow of sensitive data* within the system. For example, the Department of Health in the UK stipulates that any access to a patient's electronic health record must be controlled by strict protocols.[1] *An open problem is how to encode and enforce such flow-based security policies in the context of multi-domain event-driven applications.* In particular, there is an impedance mismatch between high-level policies governing the handling of confidential data and low-level technical enforcement mechanisms.

Enforcing security policies in multi-domain, event-driven applications is challenging for several reasons: (1) due to the complexity and scale of applications, there is a risk that software faults may render policy checks ineffective. A single component that omits an access control check may reveal a confidential patient record to the outside world; (2) the integration of third-party components and libraries, often without source code auditing, may mean that necessary policy checks are omitted altogether. For example, a third-party developer may have a different interpretation of a security policy and decide incorrectly that revealing a patient record to an insurance provider is acceptable; (3) application deployments across multiple administrative domains introduce issues of trust and legal responsibility when enforcing security policies. For example, a hospital domain may trust an insurance provider with billing-related data but not with a complete patient health history. All these factors put the managed data at risk—security violations of organisations' private data may be disastrous; violations of third-party user data may make them liable to lawsuits.

Traditional event-based and message-oriented middleware[2] leaves the task of enforcing security policy to application developers. They have to include appropriate *policy enforcement points* (PEPs) in application components that carry out checks before executing sensitive operations. The middleware may provide support for the implementation of PEPs in the form of access control models such as access control lists and capabilities. However, these are low-level mechanisms that require the configuration of permissions at the granularity of individual operations. This makes it hard to realise a high-level security policy correctly, in particular, in distributed, multi-domain environments with different levels of trust between organisations.

To address the above security concerns, we argue that it should be possible to express high-level security policy as *constraints on permitted data flows* throughout a distributed, event-driven application. It should be the responsibility of the middleware to enforce such security policy uniformly across domains by taking a *data-centric view*—policy enforcement should occur automatically when data flows cross boundaries between components and domains, instead of carrying out access control checks over individual operations.

---

[1] See http://www.nigb.nhs.uk/guarantee/2009-nhs-crg.pdf
[2] For example, IBM's WebSphere MQ product: http://www.ibm.com/webspheremq

In this paper, we describe DEFCON-POLICY, an event-based middleware that enforces event flow security policy in distributed, multi-domain applications. Flow policy is expressed in the DEFCON *Policy Language* (DPL) as high-level constraints on permitted data flows between components. The middleware takes a DPL specification and translates it into an equivalent assignment of *security labels*, which are associated with data flows, and *privileges*, which enable components to send and receive labelled data. To prevent event flows that would violate the security policy, DEFCON-POLICY *sandboxes* components after they have received sensitive data controlled by the policy.

This approach makes policy enforcement transparent to application developers and does not add complexity to the application implementation. We evaluate DEFCON-POLICY with a case study of a healthcare scenario with multiple distributed domains. Our results show that DEFCON-POLICY can realise a complex, realistic security policy and enforce it with an acceptable runtime overhead.

In summary, the paper makes the following main contributions:

- a high-level event flow policy language for expressing constraints on distributed event flows in multi-domain, event-driven applications;
- the design and implementation of a middleware that can enforce event flow policy by monitoring event flows between application components and restricting them to ensure policy compliance;
- the evaluation of this approach as applied to security policy enforcement in the context of a realistic medical scenario.

The rest of the paper is organised as follows. In §2, we explore security problems in multi-domain, event-driven applications. We present DPL, our event flow policy language, in §3. In §4, we describe how the DEFCON-POLICY middleware enforces event flow policy in a distributed setting by controlling the flow of events between distributed components. Evaluation results are presented in §5. The paper finishes with related work (§6) and future work and conclusions (§7).

2 Security in Multi-domain, Event-Driven Applications

In this section, we describe the problem of providing security guarantees in distributed systems that involve multiple organisational domains. We introduce a sample healthcare workflow and show how event-based middleware can naturally support it but struggles to cover security challenges. Based on this analysis, we propose to enforce high-level security policy by the middleware.

Figure 1 gives an example of a data processing workflow in a healthcare scenario with multiple domains. It is representative of the types of workflows found in the UK National Health Service (NHS). The figure shows domains (dashed regions) and software components within those domains. In this scenario, a patient is worried about a lump on his arm, and visits his general practitioner (GP) for a consultation. The GP takes a skin biopsy, which she sends, together with an electronic biopsy request containing information about the patient, to an NHS pathology laboratory for testing (edge e_1). There, a pathologist analyses the

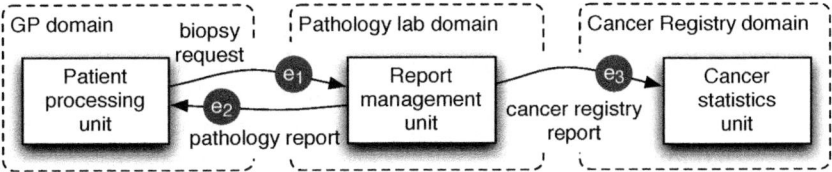

Fig. 1. Multi-domain healthcare scenario. Events are exchanged between processing units belonging to multiple domains.

sample and produces an electronic pathology report. The lab sends this pathology report back to the GP (edge e_2), and also sends a copy to the regional cancer registry (edge e_3), but only if there is any evidence of cancer.

2.1 Event-Based Middleware

A software system that supports the above workflow can be effectively realised as an *event-driven architecture* [1]. In this architectural model, data is presented as structured event messages or **events**. The software components of an application are implemented as a set of event processing **units** that receive, process and emit events. Events are usually transformed by a sequence of units. Units are hosted on physical machines and belong to a given organisational or administrative **domain**. An *event-based middleware* dispatches events between units, either locally or involving network communication between machines.

In the above scenario, the GP, the pathology lab and the cancer registry each form a domain. There are three types of events flowing between them: the biopsy request event e_1, the pathology report event e_2 and the cancer registry report event e_3. These events are exchanged between units belonging to the different domains: a patient processing unit in the GP domain, a report management unit in the pathology lab domain and a cancer statistics unit in the cancer registry.

2.2 Information Security

The above workflow has events that contain confidential patient data, which makes information security important. Their propagation between the different parts of the system is regulated by corresponding data protection legislation.[3] It states that the following security guarantees must be maintained at all times:

1. Pathology reports may be sent only to the requesting GP or a cancer registry.
2. Cancer registries may only receive cancer-related pathology reports.
3. Only doctors in the pathology lab may view sensitive patient data.

In general, the security goals in such scenarios are to prevent *leakage of data* to unauthorised units or third-parties and to ensure the *integrity of data* that

---

[3] http://www.nhs.uk/choiceintheNHS/Rightsandpledges/NHSConstitution/Documents/COI_NHSConstitutionWEB2010.pdf

units use for input. For example, the pathology report event should not be sent to any other units outside of the GP and Cancer Registry domains. In addition, the GP domain should only accept genuine pathology reports as input.

In terms of a threat model, information security can be violated in a number of ways: software bugs in the implementation of units can leak sensitive events or make units accept bogus input data; malicious developers can include back-doors in unit implementations to obtain unauthorised access to data; and units operating in different domains may handle security policy differently due to inconsistent interpretations at implementation time. All of these problems are enabled by the fact that security concerns are distributed across the implementation of many units and are disconnected from the global security requirements. Any unit in the system can potentially violate information security.

Security policy. To ensure that a multi-domain, event-based application guarantees information security, we argue that a policy administrator should first express security concerns in a high-level policy language. By separating security policy from unit implementations, the policy administrator can focus on the high-level security goals of a multi-domain application, without being overwhelmed by implementation details.

A key observation when expressing security policy is that the required security guarantees, as the ones described above, usually pertain to the event data and, more specifically, focus on the flow of events through the system. An *event flow security policy* should therefore control the propagation of event flows through the system. This is in contrast to fine-grained security policy found in access control systems that usually governs permitted operations. For example, when the biopsy request event is received by the report management unit, it is trusted to manage the data appropriately. Any operations carried out by the report management unit internally do not need to be checked, as long as interactions of the unit with other units are controlled.

Policy enforcement. Current implementations of multi-domain, event-driven applications leave the overall enforcement of security policy to the developers of units. A frequent approach is to introduce an access control layer around units, which carries out ad hoc policy checks at the input and output of events. This is not only error-prone but also makes it challenging to enforce security properties that rely on the behaviour of a sequence of event processing units.

In contrast, we want to enforce event flow policy by the middleware itself, independently of the implementation of processing units. For this, the middleware must track the flow of events between components in order to provide end-to-end security guarantees that do not depend on the correct implementation of each individual unit. This assumes that the middleware implementation is correct and can be trusted to enforce event flow policy. In practice, this is a reasonable assumption because only a small part of the middleware implementation is involved with policy enforcement.

Information flow control. Since event flow policy expresses limitations on the flows of events throughout the system, the middleware must be able to prevent invalid flows. This idea of *information flow control* has been successfully applied in different domains for achieving security guarantees, including operating systems [2,3], programming languages [4], web applications [5,6] and high-performance event processing [7].

In previous work, we proposed a Decentralised Event Flow Control (DEFC) model [7] for controlling the flow of events in event-driven applications. DEFC associates events with **labels**, that "contaminate" units that receive them: data output by a contaminated unit must include the labels of the events that contaminated it. As detailed in §4.2, this mechanism is key for implementing mandatory tracking of security properties for data processed in the system. Units may bypass constraints imposed by labels associated with events only when they possess **privileges** over them. As we show in §4, the DEFC model provides an appropriate low-level enforcement mechanism for event flow policy. However, it must be extended to support multiple domains that may enforce policies differently.

3 Event Flow Policy

In this section, we introduce the DEFCON Policy Language (DPL), our language for event flow policy specification. Based on the previous analysis of security in multi-domain, event-based applications, the design of DPL aims to satisfy the following set of requirements:

- Security policies should take a data-centric view, providing end-to-end guarantees for confidentiality and integrity of event flows in the system.
- Security policies should be independent of the functional implementation of processing units and be supported across legacy processing units.
- Security policies should be separate from the details of the enforcement mechanism at the middleware level.
- Security policies should be enforceable efficiently, without resulting in an unacceptable degradation of event processing performance.

We describe DPL with reference to a financial scenario, as illustrated in Figure 2. Within the processing system of a bank, several functions exist: from investment activities to accounting on behalf of clients to internal risk assessment. Flows of

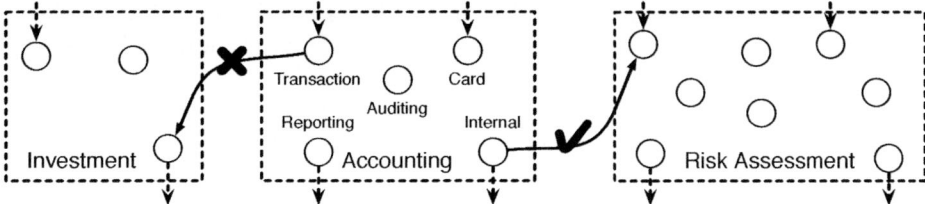

Fig. 2. Protection of flow categories within a bank. Flow categories define boundaries around data and specify which units can pass data over those boundaries. Transaction, as an input unit, cannot send data to the investment flow, while Internal, an output unit, can extract data from the flow.

information are exchanged within each function and among different functions. We consider the case of a bank that wants to improve the security of the software component that processes customer account information. The goal is to ensure that account information cannot be corrupted or leaked by software faults or malicious behaviour of components.

The events in this scenario can be divided into *event flow categories*. An event flow category, such as `accounting_flow`, is used to identify events with distinct security requirements, for example, by pertaining to data containing customers' account details. Alternatively, a flow category could group all data belonging to a single user.

3.1 Event Flow Constraints

Our event flow policy provides security guarantees through the definition of *event flow constraints* on flow categories. We focus on two ways that policy specification can distinguish flows of information by applying flow constraints and we name them *vertical* and *horizontal* flow separation. Vertical separation relates to flow constraints that should hold across the end-to-end processing of events, from input to output. Horizontal separation is used to isolate the processing at one stage from the processing being done in another, and is typically used to achieve security guarantees related to functional transformations such as data cleaning, auditing and anonymisation.

In DPL, event flows constraints have the following syntax:

flow_constraint ::= ⟨*flow_name*⟩ ':' '{' flow_part (',' flow_part)* '}' '.'
    flow_part ::= ['->'] ⟨*processing_context*⟩ ['->']

As an example, the following DPL specification encodes the flow constraints in the above banking scenario:

```
accounting_flow: {
  -> transaction, -> card,
  auditing,
  reporting ->, internal -> }.
```

All flow constraints must name an event flow category (i.e. `accounting_flow` above), and state whether the *flow parts* (i.e. `card`, `transaction`, etc.) can receive or produce events within the flow. Flow parts indicate the processing context, which can be a unit that sees and alters the event flow.[4] The inclusion of a unit as a flow part, without any further annotation, means that the unit is *sandboxed* within the context of the specified event flow. In other words, such units are isolated so that they can only input and output events from and to other units within that event flow.

Parts of event flows contain annotations to indicate that they are able to cause events to flow in or out of the event flow. Input units, preceded by a -> prefix, such as `transaction` and `card` are constrained to output events only within the

---
[4] To simplify discussion, we assume for now that a processing context is a single unit; we relax this assumption in §3.2, when we address the general case.

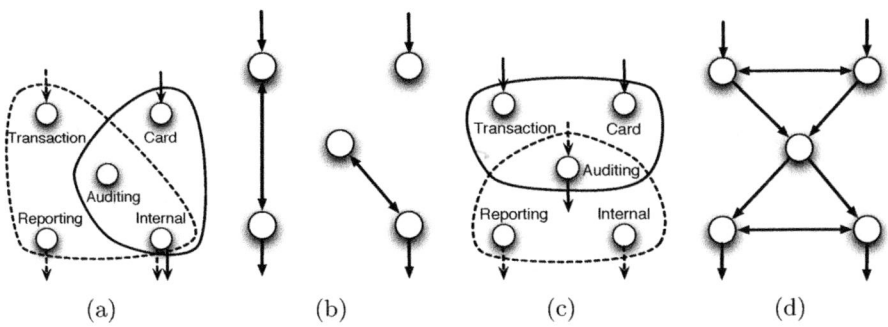

Fig. 3. Vertical and horizontal separation. In 3(a), two constraints are defined to separate the data of the transaction from the details of the credit card; flows permitted by both constraints are shown in 3(b). In 3(c), horizontal separation is used to force events to pass through an Auditing unit as shown in 3(d).

flow, but can receive events from the outside of the flow. Units with a -> suffix, such as reporting can, in addition to sending events into the flow, take events from the flow and let them leave the protected environment created by the flow constraint. Units can also both input and output events to and from a flow. Note that input and output units have a certain degree of freedom in their actions: input units can choose to receive input events from "inside" the flow, "outside" the flow or both; similarly output units can specify where to send new produced events with respect to the flow constraint.

Specification of flow constraints protects both the confidentiality and the integrity of event flows. For example, a policy administrator can ensure that a flow prevents units written by third parties from tampering with accounting data (integrity), or even receiving it in the first place (confidentiality). A sand-boxed unit cannot leak events, or allow unauthorised modifications. As a consequence, the amount of code to be trusted is limited for integrity to the units that are flow inputs and for confidentiality to the units that are flow outputs.

Vertical flow separation. Flow categories isolate and control the diffusion of events with different security requirements. For example, the accounting data above may contain credit card information that should be prevented from reaching the reporting unit. In DPL, this can be expressed by defining two constraints:

```
transaction_flow:                  card_flow:
  { -> transaction,                  { -> card,
    auditing,                          auditing,
    reporting ->, internal -> }.       internal -> }.
```

The personal transaction flow and the credit card flow intersect as part of the auditing and internal units. When two flows intersect, we have some events that are part of only the first flow, some events that are only part of the second flow and some events that are part of both flows. A unit that is present in both flows (e.g. the auditing unit in our example) can only receive events that are accepted in both flows by their respective flow constraints. This means that events in the intersection of the two flows can be created only by units that act as inputs for both flows, or units in one flow that are also inputs for the other flow. As this never happens for personal and card flows, the two units in the intersection are effectively isolated from input events. This can be illustrated using the possible interactions between units shown in 3(b). DPL specifications can be checked for such inconsistencies by the middleware, alerting the policy administrator to such problems.

There are two ways of fixing the above issue. The first is to restructure the system to split a unit into two units e.g. in the auditing case, one unit to monitor for suspicious card numbers, the other for suspicious transactions above a given threshold. An alternative solution is to add `auditing` and `internal` as input units to `card_flow` and `transaction_flow`. This is acceptable as card data entering from the `card` unit would still be constrained to flow only to the `internal` unit. The weakening of the flow constraints would simply allow `auditing` and `internal` to receive additional events as input.

Horizontal flow separation. So far, we have explored the case, in which flows are defined to protect data of a given security category from other categories (vertical separation). There is, however, another use for flow constraints: to constrain the processing within a specific flow (horizontal separation). For example, in our accounting flow, the policy administrator may want to ensure that all transactions and card usage are audited. We can enforce this by separating the auditing flow horizontally into two subflows:

```
unaudited_flow: {                     audited_flow: {
   -> transaction, -> card,              -> auditing,
   auditing -> }.                        reporting ->, internal -> }.
```

The two flows intersect each other again (see Figure 3(c)): the `auditing` unit is common to both event flows. However, the intersection does not cause problems for these two flows (see Figure 3(d)). The case when outputs of one flow are inputs for the other is actually beneficial: `auditing` is an output of the "top stage" of Figure 3(c), it can thus only receive events from the top stage. In general, it could output without constraint, except that being an input to the bottom stage means that it can only present its events to the bottom event flow. Thus, a protected data transfer is forced from one flow category to the next.

Parameterisation. Some policies require separation vertically of many flow categories with the same structure, e.g. to protect data individually by client or patient. To support such constraints, DPL allows *parameterisation* of flow constraints, supporting the inclusion of parameters that appear both in flow categories and in processing units. For example, the above `transaction_flow` can be parameterised by client to prevent transactions from one client to affect a report for another client:

```
transaction_flow[client]: {
   -> transaction[client],
   auditing[client],
   reporting[client] ->, internal[client] -> }.
```

3.2 Abstracting Processing Context

So far, we illustrated the use of DPL in small-scale contexts. We assumed that policy administrators had global knowledge of all processing units that participate in event flows. In such scenarios, it is possible to link policy fragments in the form of flow constraints directly to the units that are constrained by these fragments. However, such an approach is not feasible in larger deployments where the policy spans multiple domains and no domain has control over the details of event processing in other domains. For example in our accounting scenario, including units from a third party would tie in the policy with the units' design: changes to the design would require changes to the event flow specification.

To apply event flow control in a large distributed setting, it is therefore necessary to abstract the relationship between flow policies and units. We achieve this by introducing hierarchical names that correspond to *event processing contexts*. The hierarchical nature of processing contexts facilitates support for multi-domain use of event flow policy: we can map the organisational structure of domains to the hierarchical structure of processing contexts. Also, by using a federated naming service analogous to the domain name system (DNS), the control over subcontexts can be delegated to the domains themselves.

Processing context names provide a common, consistent naming structure to correlate processing units and policies belonging to different organisations. Flow constraints can refer to processing context names, which then map to actual event processing units. This relaxes the previous assumption in §3.1 that each unit maps to exactly one processing context. When a flow constraint states a processing context, the constraint applies to all units that are directly part of the context and to all units that are part of any sub-contexts.

We illustrate processing contexts with two examples. As the first example, we refine the flows that are internal to the previously introduced `reporting` context from Figure 2 by specifying the following flow constraint:

```
anon_reporting_flow: {
    -> reporting.anonymiser,
    reporting.stats -> }.
```

This flow names two sub-contexts of `reporting`: an `anonymiser` and `stats`. The `stats` context is reachable only through the `anonymiser`. All units assigned to `reporting.stats` can only receive data from `reporting.anonymiser`, while units in `anonymiser` or directly in `reporting` are still constrained by any flow constraint mentioning the `reporting` context. As a multi-domain example, we can consider the following version of the `accounting_flow`:

```
policy uk.co.ebank
accounting_flow: {
    -> transaction, -> .uk.co.curr_quotes.ebank,
    local_processing,
    internal ->, .uk.gov.soca.auditing.ebank -> }.
```

In this policy, processing contexts not starting with a dot are treated as relative to the domain specified in the policy header, while fully-qualified names can

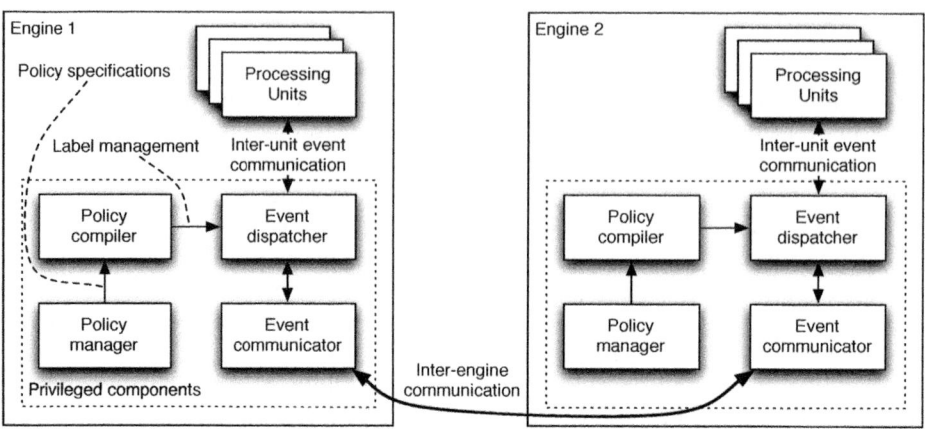

Fig. 4. DEFCon-Policy architecture. Multiple engines house processing units that communicate using message passing while information flow is tracked using labels.

refer to arbitrary contexts. This example has an external provider of quotes for foreign currencies and the UK Serious Organised Crime Agency (SOCA) as an output context. The two organisations with control over these processing context names define processing units operating in these domains, and authorise foreign organisation (`ebank` in this case) to define policies relating to these contexts.

4 Distributed Event Flow Middleware

Given a set of policies described in DPL, we enforce them using the DEFCon-Policy middleware. It implements distributed DPL policies by translating them into local communication constraints on processing contexts and enforces them as units execute. The architecture of the DEFCon-Policy middleware is shown in Figure 4 and consists of the following parts:

Engines. Engines are responsible for policy enforcement in one or more processing contexts. Each engine hosts processing units and isolates them from each other to be able to sandbox units. Engines also control communication channels to and from other engines and outside systems. Engines manage the internal flow of events using the DEFC security model (cf. §4.2).

Event dispatcher. The event dispatcher supports asynchronous communication between units in the form of *publish/subscribe* communication. Publish/subscribe allows units to express their interest in events that match a subscription filter. Events are dispatched in compliance with security labels.

Policy manager. As part of each engine, a policy manager is responsible for locally checking and authorising DPL policies constraining processing contexts local to that engine. In a small-scale deployment, policies can be checked and deployed manually; in more complex deployments, the policy managers of different engines coordinate to set-up policies (cf. §4.1).

Policy compiler. The policy compiler translates DPL policies into security labels and privileges in the DEFC model used for enforcement (cf. §4.1).

Event communicator. In each engine, the event communicator is responsible for securely propagating protected events between engines. It guarantees that events are labelled correctly in each engine trusted by the policy when they are exported and imported over the network (cf. §4.2).

4.1 Distributed Policy Management

To support large multi-domain deployments, DEFCON-POLICY needs to handle many processing contexts deployed in many engines. In such a scenario, policy set-up and management needs support from the middleware. To set up a policy, before enforcement can begin, DEFCON-POLICY performs a series of steps:

1. Context to engine resolution. After a new DPL policy has been submitted, the DEFCON-POLICY middleware first resolves engines responsible for processing contexts mentioned in the policy, thus locating the deployed units to constrain. The resolution from processing contexts to engines is performed through a distributed directory system. Such a directory service can be federated so that each organisation owns a part of the namespace and can delegate subparts to other organisations.

2. Engine trust verification. Engines have to verify that remote engines involved in a policy can be trusted to enforce event flow constraints defined in the policy. This is important because remote engines may belong to independent administrative domains. For example `uk.co.ebank.transactions` from §3.2 might map to a local engine `defcon.ebank.co.uk`, while `uk.co.curr_quotes.ebank` might map to engine `defcon.curr_quotes.co.uk` externally hosted.

In the most general case, each domain, such as `ebank`, can specify the set of DEFCON-POLICY engines that it trusts for enforcement of its policies. These can be specified per organisation, per policy or per flow. We assume that units are deployed on engines with sufficient trust, such as the local engine, to support their execution. Referring to processing contexts by a fully-qualified name is an assertion of trust in the remote policy enforcement of that domain.

3. Policy deployment and authorisation. Once engines are verified, the policy is deployed on all relevant engines. The policy managers on each engine check if the deployed policy is authorised with respect to the contexts involved. Such authorisation may be implemented by using PKI infrastructure[5] for example. Digitally signed policies, and information about the signing certificates, can be integrated with the directory service exploited in step 1.

4. Policy checking. Before a policy is enforced, DEFCON-POLICY checks that the new policy is not inconsistent (cf. vertical separation example in §3). An inconsistent policy may violate liveness properties by leading to units that are unable to receive or send any events because of policy constraints.

---

[5] SPKI would meet our needs: http://www.ietf.org/rfc/rfc2693.txt

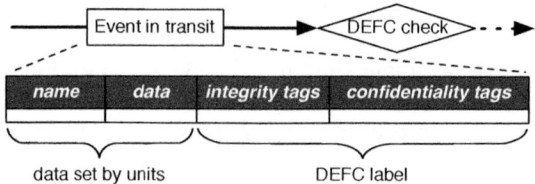

Fig. 5. An event with a DEFC label. DEFC labels are not controlled by units, but are used to enforce event flows.

To check the policy, the policy manager recursively retrieves policies related to the processing contexts specified in the new policy. It then performs a graph traversal to check if, for all units, there exists at least one event flow path from the external world to their input (reachability) and at least one path from their output to the external world (observability).

This policy checking algorithm can be formalised as follows. Let P be the set of all possible processing contexts. The goal of the algorithm is to check the compatibility of a set of flow constraints F where $F \subseteq 2^P \times 2^P \times 2^P$. We can first compute whether two units can send an event to each other according to F:

$$\text{canSendTo}(x, y) \Leftrightarrow \forall (F_{\text{in}}, F_{\text{sand}}, F_{\text{out}}) \in F : F_{\text{all}} = F_{\text{in}} \cup F_{\text{sand}} \cup F_{\text{out}}$$
$$\left(x \in (F_{\text{in}} \cup F_{\text{sand}}) \Rightarrow y \in (F_{\text{sand}} \cup F_{\text{out}}) \right) \wedge$$
$$\left((x \in F_{\text{out}} \vee x \notin F_{\text{all}}) \Rightarrow (y \in F_{\text{in}} \vee y \notin F_{\text{all}}) \right)$$

and based on that, infer reachability via multiple hops:

$$\text{canReach}(x, y) \Leftrightarrow \exists n > 0, \forall i \in [1, \ldots, 2n], z_i \in P$$
$$\wedge (z_1 = x \wedge z_{2n} = y) \wedge \text{canSendTo}(z_i, z_{i+1})$$

Then we consider a unit that is external to all flow constraints of F, i.e. operates in an unconstrained context, modelling the external world ϕ. Given $\phi \in P : \forall (F_{\text{in}}, F_{\text{sand}}, F_{\text{out}}) \in F, \phi \notin F_{\text{in}} \cup F_{\text{sand}} \cup F_{\text{out}}$, the following definitions hold:

$$\text{isObservable}(x) \Leftrightarrow \text{canReach}(x, \phi)$$
$$\text{isReachable}(x) \Leftrightarrow \text{canReach}(\phi, x)$$

The check succeeds if and only if, given F,

$$\forall x \in P : \text{isObservable}(x) \wedge \text{isReachable}(x)$$

at which point the policy is ready for enforcement.

4.2 Enforcement of Event Flow Constraints

After policies have been distributed to engines, the DEFCON-POLICY middleware sets up runtime enforcement within an engine and between engines.

DEFC model. Event flow constraints specified in DPL are enforced at runtime according to the Decentralised Event Flow Control (DEFC) model [7]. In this model, as shown in Figure 5, events are structured messages that consist of (1) a named *data* part that units can manipulate and (2) a *DEFC label*. The data part contains the payload of the event whereas the DEFC label restricts its flow.[6]

A DEFC label (S, I) is composed of a *confidentiality label* (S) and an *integrity label* (I). Labels are sets of *tags*, each representing a concern over confidentiality or integrity of the event. A tag is implemented as a unique bit sequence.

Processing units are also assigned a label L_p that represents the confidentiality and integrity of information contained in their state. Units can create events or process events that they receive, provided that their label can flow to the labels of the events. Intuitively, a unit cannot read data that is "more confidential" than its label, or write data that has "higher integrity" than itself. More precisely, an event flow is only allowed if the source label L_s and the destination labels L_d satisfy a partial order *can-flow-to* relation $\preceq$:

$$L_s = (S_s, I_s) \preceq L_d = (S_d, I_d) \iff S_s \subseteq S_d \land I_s \supseteq I_d.$$

Units possess *privileges* that allow them to change labels. Adding a tag t to a label requires the t^+ privilege, which for integrity is called an "endorsement privilege"—it endorses the unit's state, allowing it to produce higher integrity data. Removing t from a confidentiality label requires the t^- privilege, called a "declassification privilege"—it declassifies the unit's state allowing it to produce unclassified data. Privileges held by units also determine if a unit can communicate externally. Only a unit that holds endorsement privileges t^+ for all tags in I and declassification privileges t^- for all tags in S can freely exchange events with the outside world.

DEFC also controls the *delegation* of privileges between units. Only if a unit possess the *privilege-granting* privileges t^+_{auth} and t^-_{auth}, it is permitted to delegate its endorsement and declassification privileges t^+ and t^- to other units.

Policy translation to DEFC. The DEFC model is used to enforce event flow constraints specified in DPL policy specifications. Each flow constraint f is associated with a tag pair (c_f, i_f) to protect flow confidentiality and integrity. Tags and privileges are assigned to units in the following way:

(1) *Sandboxed and output units* have i_f in their integrity label, constraining them to receive only events that also contain i_f. (2) *Sandboxed and input* units also have c_f in their confidentiality label, thus being constrained to have their output contain c_f. (3) *Input units* are given i_f^+ and therefore can produce events with i_f, even if they do not have i_f in their label. This means that they can receive events form "outside of the flow". (4) *Output units* are given c_f^- to produce data without c_f in their label, even if their confidentiality label contains c_f to be able to receive data from the flow. When a unit is mentioned in multiple flow constraints, its label is the conjunction of all listed constraints.

In the multi-domain example from §3.2, the policy manager on the engine defcon.ebank.co.uk, responsible for the transactions, local_processing and internal subdomains of uk.co.ebank, would create i, c tags to represent the

---

[6] We ignore multiple data parts here; see [7] for more detail on the DEFC model.

flow uk.co.ebank.account_flow. The manager would then instantiate the processing unit parts of those contexts with a label $L = (\{c\}, \{i\})$, it would also bestow i^+ in transactions, and c^- in internal, keeping i^+_{auth} and c^-_{auth} for itself. These privileges can be used by the policy manager in case of a policy change that would require a reconfiguration of privileges.

Inter-engine communication. Tags and privileges that are allocated by policy managers in engines have local meaning. Engines use these to restrict communication between units in the local engine. However, units that are able to process data of a given flow should be able to exchange events even if they are located on different engines. This requires the exchange of events between two engines over the network. It cannot be achieved by just giving units endorsement or declassification privileges because this would enable them to communicate with units outside of the flow, without event flow control.

To address this problem, DEFCON-POLICY provides a trusted proxy unit, called an *event communicator*. The event communicator is delegated endorsement and declassification privileges for a given event flow and can then transfer events to the event communicator in another engine. As part of this process, the tags associated with events are translated at the receiver's engine by the event communicator to equivalent tags for local enforcement. This mapping between tags on different engines is set up on demand, on the basis of the policy specifications shared between the engines during policy deployment (§4.1).

We illustrate inter-engine communication in the context of the example above. The policy manager on the engine defcon.curr_quotes.co.uk, which is responsible for the uk.co.curr_quotes.ebank context, can allocate tags i, c to represent the uk.co.ebank.account_flow flow. It initialises units in the context to $L = (\{c\}, \{i\})$, granting the i^+ privilege to them. The units from the uk.co.curr_quotes.ebank context cannot communicate directly with units in uk.co.ebank.local_processing, which are sandboxed in the accounting flow.

Each policy manager instantiates an event communicator, granting it the i^+ and c^- privileges. When a unit in the uk.co.curr_quotes.ebank context sends an event to uk.co.ebank.local_processing, the event is received by the communicator, which exports it from the accounting flow by exercising its declassification privilege. The event is then transmitted securely, for example, using an encrypted transport-level connection, to the other event communicator. The second event communicator possesses the i^+ privilege, which enables it to insert the received event in the accounting flow in the other engine.

5 Evaluation

We evaluate the effectiveness of DPL and DEFCON-POLICY with respect to specifying and enforcing security policy in a multi-domain, event-driven application. We focus on the ease-of-use from a software developer's standpoint and also experimentally evaluate the performance impact of the middleware.

```
1  policy uk.nhs
2  sensitive[gp]: { -> GP[gp].sensitive ->, -> lab.doc[gp] ->,
3    lab.sensitive[gp], cancer_registry.sensitive -> }. {...}
4
5  policy uk.nhs.GP[gp]
6  patient_data_flow: { -> sensitive.patient_data,
7    sensitive.patient_data.anonymiser ->,
8    sensitive.pathology.patient_data ->,
9    -> sensitive.pathology.incoming_reports }.
10 anonymised_data: { -> sensitive.patient_data.anonymiser,
11   statistics.anonymised_data -> ,
12   performance.anonymised_data -> }.
13 path_request: { -> sensitive.pathology.test_requests,
14   -> sensitive.pathology.patient_data,
15   .uk.nhs.lab.doc[gp].pathology.request ->,
16   .uk.nhs.lab.sensitive[gp].pathology.patient_data -> }. {...}
17
18 policy uk.nhs.lab
19 path_report[gp]: { -> doc[gp].pathology.report,
20   -> sensitive[gp].pathology.patient_data,
21   sensitive[gp].pathology.cancer_registry_reporting ->,
22   .uk.nhs.GP[gp].sensitive.pathology.incoming_reports -> }.
23 tumour_report: { -> sensitive[gp].pathology.cancer_registry_reporting,
24   .uk.nhs.cancer_registry.sensitive.pathology.incoming -> }. {...}
```

Fig. 6. Extract of the healthcare policy scenario in DPL. Constraints not related to managemet of sensitive medical data are omitted.

5.1 Healthcare Case Study

In our case study, we examined an NHS policy involving GPs, Pathology Laboratories, a Primary Care Trust (PCT), the UK Office of National Statistics (ONS) and a Cancer Registry. Figure 6 shows an extract of the policy that enforces the guarantees introduced in §2.

An overarching NHS policy (lines 1–3) specifies a high-level constraint that sensitive data are controlled and partitioned by GPs. Partitioning is enforced by the use of a constraint parametrised by gp. Data processing in the laboratory is also partitioned by GP and only doctors within the lab can see and contribute to confidential information (lines 2–3). Finally, Cancer Registries can receive sensitive information for computing statistics about tumours (line 3).

GPs specify their own local policy (lines 5–16) to refine and extend the global policy. In this example, all GPs have the same policy: patient data can be transformed by an anonymiser into anonymised data (line 7), which in turn can be used for computing statistics by the ONS and measuring performance by the PCT (lines 10–12). Alternatively, patient data can be used to generate pathology requests that are to be sent to a lab (lines 8 and 13–16), while reports received from the lab can be combined with patient data (line 9). The lab pathology reports can either be sent back to the same GP (line 22) or included in tumour reports (lines 23–24) by specific reporting units (line 21).

Policy enforcement in DEFC. After the policy is specified in DPL, it is compiled into tags that are used for DEFC enforcement. We now show how the resulting tag assignment enforces the guarantees presented in §2. Each flow constraint is enforced by a tag pair, which we represent symbolically as (i_x, c_x) where x is the line at which the constraint is defined in Figure 6. Pathology reports are produced within the lab.doc[gp].pathology.report context, specific to each *GP*, that is tainted by c_{19}^{gp}. The declassification privilege for this tag, c_{19}^{gp+}, is held by the corresponding GP[gp].sensitive.pathology.incoming_report context and not by any other context under a different GP. The only other context with declassification privilege for the report tag is lab.sensitive[gp].pathology.cancer_registry_reporting. It is, however, tainted by tag c_{23}, which can be removed only by cancer_registry.pathology.incoming. This completes the enforcement of the first guarantee protecting sensitive pathology reports.

As the cancer_registry.pathology.incoming context is tainted by i_{23}, lab.sensitive[gp].pathology.cancer_registry_reporting, holding the i_{23}^+ privilege, is the only context that can send data to it. Furthermore, as units in this context drop reports not classified as cancerous, the second guarantee on Cancer Registry input is enforced.

To enforce the third guarantee, the GP[gp].sensitive.patient_data context is protected by c_2^{gp} and c_6^{gp}. Only units under lab.doc[gp].pathology.request can reveal sensitive data to authenticated doctors within the lab because, as a sub-context of GP[gp], they have the c_2^{gp-} privilege. While these units do not hold privileges for c_6^{gp}, units in GP[gp].sensitive.pathology.patient_data can exchange c_6^{gp} with c_{13}^{gp} for which units in lab.doc[gp].pathology.request have the c_{13}^{gp-} privilege.

The policy fragment consists of 24 lines. It generates $10n + 2$ tags and distributes $37n + 1$ privileges where n is the total number of GPs in the system. Assuming that one unit is instantiated in every context, at least $14n + 2$ units must be initialised with correct taints. To provide this initial set-up manually, a programmer would have to call the low level DEFC API at least $24n + 4$ times. Instead, these calls, the creation of tags and the distribution of privileges are automatically carried out by DEFCON-POLICY.

5.2 Performance Overhead

In this section, we present an experimental evaluation of the performance impact of enforcing event flow policy using DEFCON-POLICY. We measure overhead as a micro-benchmark in terms of (1) the end-to-end event propagation latency between a set of units and (2) the throughput of event processing. For these experiments, we deploy the following simple security policy:

```
policy secure_Policy
sensitive_data: { -> context_a ->, context_b }
```

Table 1. Performance overhead of DEFCON-POLICY middleware

Configuration			Throughput	Penalty	Latency	Penalty
Engines	TLS	Policy	(Events/sec)		(ms)	
1	n/a	✗	99,723	–	0.028	–
1	n/a	✓	82,334	17.4%	0.030	7.1%
2	✗	✗	62,215	–	0.268	–
2	✓	✗	42,344	31.9%	0.283	5.6%
2	✓	✓	37,500	39.7%	0.294	9.7%

This policy specifies that only units in context_a can cause events to flow in or out of the sensitive_data flow. Units in context_b can perceive and process such events without the ability to disclose them. A single unit A and a single unit B are instantiated in each context, respectively. We compare processing latency and throughput while varying the following parameters:

1. **Number of engines.** The units/contexts are deployed in a single engine or in two different engines.
2. **Network encryption.** When network communication is involved, Transport Layer Security (TLS) can be used to encrypt data.
3. **Policy enforcement.** The engines enforce that events are propagated according to secure_policy.

Our experiments are conducted on two Intel Core 2 Duo E6850 3 GHz machines with a maximum of 1 GiB of heap memory allocated per engine. We use Sun's unmodified JVM 1.6.0.06 on Ubuntu 8.04. The average network round trip-time between the machines is 0.18 ms. Each event contains a single integer.

Table 1 shows the average throughput and the 95th percentile of latency for events sent from unit A to unit B and back to A. As this experiment does not involve actual event processing, it mainly stresses the event dispatching mechanism. In the single-engine configurations, DEFCON-POLICY enforcement introduces an overhead of 17.4% for throughput and 7.1% for latency. This is the result of storing, propagating and checking tags at runtime.

The overall lower performance achieved in the two-engine configurations is a consequence of the work carried out by the event communicators. Throughput is reduced by 31.9% due to network encryption. On top of this, DEFCON-POLICY enforcement introduces a further relative overhead of only 11.4% for throughput and 3.9% for latency. We believe that the overhead of policy enforcement becomes even more marginal for realistic applications with more costly processing.[7]

6 Related Work

Middleware. Messaging middleware, and event-based middleware in particular, such as Sun JMS or IBM WebSphere support efficient exchange of information

---
[7] Note that Sun's JVM does not fully enforce unit isolation; the overhead imposed to achieve such isolation was the focus of previous research [7].

in large-scale distributed systems. Security in these systems usually focuses on access control at the boundary of the middleware API rather than end-to-end tracking of information. Any component with access to multiple channels can transfer information between them. As such each component needs to be trusted to comply with integrity and confidentiality requirements of messages.

Policy. Most approaches to policy specification focus on actions (i.e. privileges) rather than data, e.g. access control lists and role-based access control. Higher level firewall policy languages [8] facilitate the definition of rules for "allow/deny" actions, but such policies are only enforced locally. To achieve end-to-end security, policies need to be attached to data (i.e. "sticky policies" [9]). A survey and taxonomy of enforcement of sticky policies through distributed systems is provided in [10]. In contrast, our work is a contribution regarding the use of a high-level policy language with a view to translation into distributed, low-level enforcement with security labels.

Information flow control (IFC) originated in the military domain in the setting of Multi-Level Security (MLS) systems, and in that context used a limited number of centrally-defined security labels. Declassification of information was dealt with outside of the model. Myers and Liskov [4] extended IFC to decentralised enforcement allowing unprivileged principals to define and share labels and privilege over those new labels dynamically. More recently OS-level DIFC proposals [2,3,11] protect OS processes and resources by using dynamic labels that can be created at runtime. DEFC [7] brings tag-based security to event processing systems, by allowing the labelling of event parts and assigning labels to processing components.

In the past, decentralised IFC has mainly been applied to processes within a single machine. An exception is DStar [12], which automates translation between tags in remote enforcement engines. However, DStar aims to scale to a limited number of machines, e.g. multi-tiered web applications. In contrast, the focus of our work are large-scale distributed applications that contain engines under control of independent administrative domains.

Creating a policy language for decentralised IFC has been explored in Asbestos [13]. They compute tag configurations from pairwise communication patterns between sets of processes. In contrast, DPL supports policies independently authored by multiple policy administrators in the context of multi-domain distributed applications and explicitly addresses policy compatibility checking, policy authorisation and distributed enforcement.

7 Conclusions

Our research is motivated with reference to use cases in complex, multi-domain scenarios found in electronic healthcare and financial services. We have presented DEFCON-POLICY, a middleware that achieves end-to-end enforcement of distributed event flow control based on high-level policy. The benefits of strict, mandatory access control are coupled with the expressiveness and independence required by policy specification within multi-domain, distributed systems. We provide details of DPL, our event flow policy language, and sketch its formal semantics. We detail the way in which event flow policies are compiled down to be enforced using a distributed event flow control model. The evaluation of our prototype demonstrates that in both single node and distributed cases, an acceptably low overhead is incurred, while benefitting from the end-to-end, event-based security features.

In future work, we want to explore the interaction of programming languages and flow-based policy enforcement. By integrating flow constraints with programming paradigms, we can make it more natural for programmers to remain compliant with flow constraints. In addition, we want to determine the potential for interconnection of our policy and enforcement systems with existing parameterised, role-based access control infrastructures. Finally, we will acquire further experience of using DEFCON-POLICY in real-world policy environments. This will allow us to judge better the proportion of common policy requirements that are covered by DEFCON-POLICY.

Acknowledgements

This work was supported by grants EP/F042469 and EP/F044216 ("SmartFlow: Extendable Event-Based Middleware") from the UK Engineering and Physical Sciences Research Council (EPSRC).

References

1. Luckham, D.: The Power of Events: An Introduction to Complex Event Processing in Distributed Enterprise Systems. Addison-Wesley, Reading (2002)
2. Efstathopoulos, P., Krohn, M., VanDeBogart, S., et al.: Labels and event processes in the Asbestos Operating System. In: SOSP 2005, pp. 17–30. ACM, New York (2005)
3. Zeldovich, N., Kohler, E., et al.: Making information flow explicit in HiStar. In: OSDI 2006, Berkeley, CA, USA, pp. 263–278 (2006)
4. Myers, A., Liskov, B.: Protecting privacy using the decentralized label model. ACM Transactions on Software Engineering and Methodology 9(4), 410–442 (2000)
5. Chong, S., Vikram, K., Myers, A.: SIF: Enforcing confidentiality and integrity in web applications. In: USENIX Security Symposium, Berkeley, CA, pp. 1–16 (2007)
6. Papagiannis, I., Migliavacca, M., Eyers, D.M., Shand, B., Bacon, J., Pietzuch, P.: Enforcing user privacy in web applications using Erlang. In: Web 2.0 Security and Privacy (W2SP), Oakland, CA, USA. IEEE, Los Alamitos (2010)
7. Miglivacca, M., Papagiannis, I., Eyers, D., Shand, B., Bacon, J., Pietzuch, P.: High-performance event processing with information security. In: USENIX Annual Technical Conference, Boston, MA, USA, pp. 1–15 (2010)
8. Bandara, A., Kakas, A., Lupu, E., Russo, A.: Using argumentation logic for firewall policy specification and analysis. In: Distributed Systems: Operations and Management (DSOM), Dublin, Ireland, pp. 185–196 (2006)

9. Mont, M.C., Pearson, S., Bramhall, P.: Towards accountable management of identity and privacy: Sticky policies and enforceable tracing services. In: Mařík, V., Štěpánková, O., Retschitzegger, W. (eds.) DEXA 2003. LNCS, vol. 2736, pp. 377–382. Springer, Heidelberg (2003)
10. Chadwick, D.W., Lievens, S.F.: Enforcing "sticky" security policies throughout a distributed application. In: Middleware Security (MidSec), pp. 1–6. ACM, New York (2008)
11. Krohn, M., Yip, A., Brodsky, M., et al.: Information flow control for standard OS abstractions. In: SOSP 2007, pp. 321–334. ACM, New York (2007)
12. Zeldovich, N., Boyd-Wickizer, S., Mazières, D.: Securing distributed systems with information flow control. In: NSDI 2008, Berkeley, CA, USA, pp. 293–308 (2008)
13. Efstathopoulos, P., Kohler, E.: Manageable fine-grained information flow. In: EuroSys European Conference on Computer Systems, pp. 301–313. ACM, New York (2008)

Automatically Generating Symbolic Prefetches for Distributed Transactional Memories

Alokika Dash and Brian Demsky

University of California, Irvine

Abstract. Developing efficient distributed applications while managing complexity can be challenging. Managing network latency is a key challenge for distributed applications. We propose a new approach to prefetching, symbolic prefetching, that can prefetch remote objects before their addresses are known. Our approach was designed to hide the latency of accessing remote objects in distributed transactional memory and a wide range of distributed object middleware frameworks. We present a static compiler analysis for the automatic generation of symbolic prefetches — symbolic prefetches allow objects whose addresses are unknown to be prefetched.

We evaluate this prefetching mechanism in the context of a middleware framework for distributed transactional memory. Our evaluation includes microbenchmarks, scientific benchmarks, and distributed benchmarks. Our results show that symbolic prefetching combined with caching can eliminate an average of 87% of remote reads. We measured speedups due to prefetching of up to 13.31× for accessing arrays and 4.54× for accessing linked lists.

1 Introduction

Developing efficient distributed applications while managing complexity can be challenging. Recently, several researchers have developed distributed transactional memory systems that adapt ideas from work on software transactional memory for use in distributed systems [1,2,3,4,5,6,7,8]. These systems use the transaction mechanism to simplify managing concurrent access to data structures in distributed systems while eliminating possibility of distributed deadlocks. Moreover, these techniques can be adapted to provide memory transactions that guarantee durability, atomicity, and isolation even in the presence of failures [1]. An additional benefit of distributed transactional memory is that it batches communications to achieve consistency and allows safe speculation. This approach amortizes communication overhead and therefore reduces the overhead of coherency. Distributed transactional memory middleware frameworks provide powerful constructs and sophisticated optimizations to greatly simplify the process of developing distributed applications.

A key challenge in designing distributed software applications is managing the latency of accessing remote data. Traditional prefetching approaches have had limited success in hiding the latency of remote object accesses because they require programs to compute or predict objects' addresses before issuing prefetches. We propose a novel prefetching mechanism, *symbolic prefetches*, as an optimization for distributed object middleware frameworks including distributed transactional memory.

Symbolic prefetches specify a start point in a program's heap and a set of fields or array indices that define a path through the heap. Symbolic prefetches allow an application to prefetch a chain of objects (some of whose addresses are unknown) in a single round trip message exchange instead of the multiple round trips that are currently necessary. Therefore, symbolic prefetches have the potential to hide much of latency of accessing remote objects. To our knowledge, this is the first prefetching approach to specify objects in terms of paths through the heap. While we have only evaluated symbolic prefetching in the context of a distributed transactional memory middleware framework, we expect the technique to be applicable to a wide range of distributed object middleware frameworks ranging from distributed object stores [9,10,11] to mobile object frameworks.

This paper presents a novel static compiler analysis that can automatically generate symbolic prefetches for distributed applications. It combines this static analysis with a dynamic optimization that turns off symbolic prefetching during execution phases when it does not yield performance benefits. This paper makes the following contributions:

- **Prefetch Analysis:** It presents a prefetch analysis that automatically generates symbolic prefetches: a symbolic prefetch specifies the first object to be prefetched followed by a list of fields or array indices that define a path through the heap.
- **Dynamic Optimizations:** It presents several novel dynamic optimizations that lower runtime overheads.
- **Evaluation:** We have evaluated our implementation on several parallel and distributed benchmarks and found that our system works well and that prefetching improves the performance of our benchmarks and can hide a significant percentage of the network latency.

The remainder of the paper is structured as follows. Section 2 presents an example that we use to illustrate our approach. Section 3 presents an overview of the system. Section 4 presents programming model. Section 5 presents the prefetching analysis. Section 6 presents dynamic optimizations. Section 7 presents our evaluation of the approach on several benchmark applications. Section 8 discusses related work; we conclude in Section 9.

2 Example

Figure 1 presents a distributed matrix multiplication example. The example takes as input the matrices a and btrans and computes the product matrix c. The shared keyword that appears in the allocation statement in the Matrix constructor indicates that the allocated array is shared and can be accessed by remote machines. The parallelmult method partitions the matrix multiplication into several subcomputations. Each MatrixMultiply object represents one such subcomputation and its x0 and x1 fields define the block of the product matrix that it computes.

2.1 Program Execution

We next describe the execution of a MatrixMultiply thread. A MatrixMultiply thread starts when the program invokes the start method on the MatrixMultiply object's *object identifier*. An object identifier uniquely identifies a shared object. The start method takes as input the *machine identifier* for the machine that should execute the thread. The start method causes the runtime to start a thread on the given machine to execute the object's run method.

The atomic keyword in line 17 causes the code from lines 18 through 26 to execute with transactional semantics. Transactional semantics means that the reads and writes that a transaction performs are consistent with some total ordering of the transactions. Upon entering this transaction, the thread executes compiler-inserted code that converts the object identifier stored in the this variable into a reference to a *transaction local copy* of the object. A transaction local copy of an object is made the first time the transaction accesses an object and it contains any changes the transaction has made to the object. This code first checks if the transaction has already accessed the object and therefore contains a transaction local copy of the object. If not the code checks for a

```
1   public class Matrix {
2     double[][] m;
3     public Matrix(int M, int N) {
4       m = shared new double[M][N];
5     }
6   }
7   public class MatrixMultiply extends Thread {
8     public MatrixMultiply(int x0, int x1, Matrix a, Matrix btrans, Matrix c) {
9       this.a=a;
10      this.btrans=btrans;
11      this.c=c;
12      this.x0=x0;
13      this.x1=x1;
14    }
15    Matrix a, btrans, c; int x0, x1;
16    public void run() {
17      atomic {
18        for(int i=x0; i<x1; i++) {
19          for(int j=0; j<c.m[i].length; j++) {
20            double prod=0;
21            for(int k=0; k< a.m[i].length; k++)
22              prod+= a.m[i][k]*btrans.m[j][k];
23            c.m[i][j]=prod;
24          }
25        }
26      }
27    }
28    public static void parallelmult(int numthreads, ...) {
29      Wrapper thread[]=new Wrapper[numthreads];
30      atomic {
31        Matrix a=shared new Matrix(L,M);
32        Matrix btrans=shared new Matrix(N,M);
33        Matrix c=shared new Matrix(L,N);
34        for(int i=0;i<numthreads;i++) {
35          int low=i*(L/numthreads);
36          int high=(i==numthreads-1)?L:(i+1)*(L/numthreads);
37          thread[i]=new Wrapper(shared new MatrixMultiply(low, high, a, btrans, c));
38        }
39      }
40      for(int i=0;i<numthreads;i++)
41        thread[i].wrap.start(machine[i]);
42      ...
43    }
44  }
```

Fig. 1. MatrixMultiply Example

cached copy on the local machine. Our implementation caches objects to avoid communication overhead. If the cache does not contain the object, then the code contacts the machine that holds the *authoritative copy* of the object. The authoritative copy contains all the committed changes and is stored on the machine that allocated the object.

In line 22, the run method accesses Matrix objects through the a and btrans fields. To implement these field accesses, the generated code reads the object identifier from the m field, locates the corresponding object, makes a transaction local copy, and points a temporary at the copy. Our compiler maintains the invariant that if a transaction uses a variable and that variable references a shared object, the variable points to the transaction local copy for the duration of the transaction.

When the transaction completes, the run method calls the runtime to commit the transaction. A secondary benefit of transactions in our system is that accessing remote objects inside of transactions is cheaper than accessing them outside of transactions because the transactions enable our system to safely speculatively prefetch and cache objects without violating memory coherency.

2.2 Object Prefetching

The example accesses array objects that are unlikely to be available on the local machine. Our system uses symbolic prefetching to hide the latency of such accesses. Consider the expression a.m[i][k] in line 22 of Figure 1. The traditional approach to prefetching this expression would use three consecutive round trips over the network to prefetch a, then a.m, and finally a.m[i]. Symbolic prefetches instead bundle a starting object identifier along with a symbolic expression for a path through the heap into a single message to the remote machine. For the example expression, our approach would generate a single symbolic prefetch expression a.m[i] that begins with the object identifier stored in a and then specifies the path defined by the offset of field m and the ith array element. When the symbolic prefetch a.m[i] is executed, the system sends a message containing the object identifier stored in a along with the symbolic expression .m[i] to the remote machine. If the remote machine contains all three objects it sends all of them at once, and therefore all three objects can be prefetched in a single round trip communication.

Prefetch Analysis. The prefetch analysis computes at each program point a set of symbolic prefetch expressions that contain (1) a heap path to specify the objects to prefetch and (2) an estimation of the probability that the program will access these objects. The prefetch compiler analysis is structured as a standard backwards fixed-point computation over the control flow graph. At program statements that access a field, the analysis creates a prefetch expression for the field access and associates an initial probability of 100% with it. For example, in line 22 the analysis would generate the prefetch expression btrans.m[j] (and a.m[i]) with a 100% probability because the statement reads those expressions. Note that k does not appear in the prefetch expression because b.m[j][k] does not refer to an object.

When the prefetch analysis propagates this prefetch expression backwards it hits the for loop on line 21. To propagate the prefetch expression beyond this loop the analysis uses a 90% loop conditional branch probability. As the expression propagates the analysis calculates new probabilities by multiplying the old probabilities with the loop condition probability. As a result, the analysis computes the prefetch expression b.m[j] with a 90% probability after line 20. When the analysis propagates the btrans.m[j] expression to line 19, the variable increment j++ along with the conditional branch for the loop causes the analysis to rewrite the expression btrans.m[j] into the expression btrans.m[j+1] with an 81% probability at line 24. The analysis computes an 81% probability for the prefetch expression btrans.m[j+1] because the analysis propagates it through the two loop conditions at lines 19 and 21 (each with a 90% probability). The fixed-point computation continues until it satisfies the convergence criteria described in Section 5.2.

Prefetch Placement. After the prefetch analysis computes prefetch expressions for all program points, the compiler computes where to generate code for the symbolic prefetches. In general, we want to place prefetches as early as possible while ensuring that there is a high probability that the prefetches will fetch useful objects. The analysis places prefetches on control flow edges where the prefetch probabilities cross a threshold. By default we set this threshold at 30%. For example, the compiler might place a prefetch for the analysis-generated expression btrans.m[j+10] after line 19 as its probability will drop below 30% if it propagates across the loop body again; and would place prefetches for analysis-generated expressions btrans.m[0], btrans.m[1], btrans.m[2], btrans.m[3], ..., and btrans.m[9] before line 18 as this is the first statement of the transaction.

3 System Overview

Our distributed transactional memory is object-based — data is accessed and committed at the granularity of objects. Our system uses a partitioned global address space (PGAS) programming model [12] with two classes of objects: local and shared objects. Shared objects are assigned a globally unique object identifier when they are allocated. The object identifier is then used to reference the object.

Each shared object has an *authoritative copy* that contains the most recent committed version and resides on the machine that allocated the object. When a transaction accesses a shared object, it makes a transaction local copy of the object. The transaction then performs all updates to the transaction local copy.

Each shared object has a version number, which is incremented when a transaction commits an update to the object. Our system uses the version numbers to check if the transaction local copies of objects are up to date when committing. We use a standard two phase transaction commit protocol [13] with commit-time locking and validation.

Each machine contains an object cache that can cache recently accessed objects. There is no guarantee that these objects are up to date. However, a best effort invalidation approach ensures with high probability that stale object copies are removed from the cache. The commit procedure ensures that committed transaction always access the latest versions of objects.

We use an optimistic approach to commit transactions. It is possible for some transactions to end up aborting repeatedly with prefetched objects that could be more likely to be stale with eager prefetching. Our system can admit such zombie transactions (transactions that have accessed stale objects). As our system is type safe and its distributed nature increases the cost of guaranteeing that a transaction always operates on consistent snapshots, we use a sandboxing approach that validates a transaction's read set periodically or upon runtime errors.

4 Programming Model

Our system extends Java with several language constructs designed to support distributed transactional memory. We add the atomic keyword for declaring that a block of code should have transactional semantics. This keyword can be applied to either (1) a method declaration to declare that the method should be executed inside a transaction or (2) a block of code enclosed by a pair of braces. The shared memory extensions are similar to those present in Titanium [12].

The shared keyword can be used as a modifier to the new allocation statement to declare that an object should be allocated in the shared heap. Object fields in shared objects can only reference other shared objects. Local objects can reference both shared and local objects. However, the developer must declare that a field in a local object references a shared object by using the shared keyword in that field's declaration.

In general, methods are polymorphic in whether their parameters are shared. The developer may desire that method has different behavior depending on whether its parameters are shared. Our compiler supports creating different method versions for shared and local objects — the shared version is designed by the shared keyword and the local version by the local keyword. The compiler uses a flow-sensitive, data-flow analysis to infer for each program point whether a variable references a shared object or a local object. The compiler uses the analysis results to generate specialized versions of methods for each calling context.

5 Prefetching

Traditional address-based prefetching approaches were largely designed to hide the latency of the local memory system — addressed-based prefetching incurs large latencies when accessing remote linked data structures because the computation must compute an object's address before prefetching it. In effect this requires waiting for a round trip over the network for each object to be accessed in the linked data structure.

Our prefetching approach eliminates the need to know an object's address prior to prefetching it. Symbolic prefetches describe paths through the heap that traverse the objects to be prefetched. Symbolic prefetches have the form:

symbolic prefetch := *base object identifier*(*.field* | [*integer*])*

The base object identifier component of the symbolic prefetch holds the object identifier of the first object to be prefetched. The list of fields and array indices define a path through the heap from the first object. We combine the runtime technique with a compiler analysis that automatically generates prefetches for arbitrary structures and arrays. Symbolic prefetches allow our system to prefetch multiple objects along a chain of references with a single round-trip network communication. Consider the following code:

```
1    LinkedList search(int key) {
2      for(LinkedList ptr=head;ptr!=null&&ptr.key!=key)
3        ptr=ptr.next;
4      return ptr;
5    }
```

Without prefetching, traversing a remote linked list of length n requires n consecutive round-trip communications. If we add a prefetch for ptr.next.next.next.next.next between lines 2 and 3, the runtime will have prefetch requests in flight for the next linked list node and the subsequent four nodes that follow that node[1]. The example prefetch enables the search method to potentially execute five times faster. Longer symbolic prefetches can further increase the potential speedup. Note that while prefetching objects for five loop iterations ahead may not be sufficient to hide all of the latency of accessing remote objects, the latency of the single round trip communication is now divided over the five objects that have prefetch requests in flight. In this example the symbolic prefetch effectively decreases the latency of accessing the remote objects by 80%.

5.1 Prefetch Analysis

We have developed an unsound, intraprocedural static analysis in our compiler that uses a simple probabilistic model to generate prefetches for the objects that the program may access and to estimate the probabilities that the objects represented by the prefetch expressions will be accessed. The probabilistic model is naïve and makes assumptions of independence that are not true in general. However, the object access frequencies need not be precise and simply provide an approximation of the program's data access patterns. It is safe for the analysis to be unsound because prefetches do not affect the program's correctness.

The analysis is a backwards program analysis that computes a set of prefetch tuples $\mathcal{P} \subseteq \Phi \times \mathbb{R}$ containing a symbolic prefetch expression $\phi \in \Phi$ and a corresponding probability $d \in \mathbb{R}$ for each program point. Each symbolic prefetch expression $\phi = \mathcal{V}\mathcal{I}_0\mathcal{I}_1...\mathcal{I}_{n-1} \in \Phi$ is comprised of a variable $\mathcal{V}$ and a sequence of field offsets or array indices $\mathcal{I} = .\textit{offset} \mid [\textit{index}]$. Each array index $\textit{index} = tmp_0 + ... + tmp_{m-1} + c$ is a sum of m temporary variables represented by the terms tmp_i and a constant offset c.

The analysis initializes the set of tuples for each program point to the empty set. The ordering relation for the set of prefetch tuples at each program point is $\mathcal{P}_1 \sqsubseteq \mathcal{P}_2$ iff $\forall \langle \phi, d_1 \rangle \in \mathcal{P}_1, \exists d_2 > d_1$ such that $\langle \phi, d_2 \rangle \in \mathcal{P}_2$.

Figure 2 presents the transfer functions for the analysis. The transfer functions for statements that read an object reference from a field or an array element generate new symbolic prefetches with an associated probability of 100% and rewrite any symbolic prefetches that contain the destination variable. The transfer functions for statements that make assignments, write to fields, or write to array elements rewrite symbolic prefetches that begin with the same variable and field or array index. Figure 3 presents the REPLACE function that rewrites the symbolic prefetch. The REPLACE($\phi_1, \phi_2, \mathcal{P}$) function takes all prefetch tuples in $\mathcal{P}$ that contain a symbolic prefetch expression with the prefix ϕ_1 and replace that prefix with ϕ_2. The REPLACE function simply copies the

---

[1] The prefetch look-ahead distance is not fixed. Instead it depends on the analysis's estimation of how likely the prefetched values are to be used.

st	$[\![st]\!](\mathcal{P})$
x = y.f	$(\text{REPLACE}(\text{x}, \text{y.f}, \mathcal{P}) - \langle \text{y.f}, * \rangle) \cup \langle \text{y.f}, 1 \rangle$
x = y[t]	$(\text{REPLACE}(\text{x}, \text{y[t]}, \mathcal{P}) - \langle \text{y[t]}, * \rangle) \cup \langle \text{y[t]}, 1 \rangle$
x = y	$\text{REPLACE}(\text{x}, \text{y}, \mathcal{P})$
x.f = y	$\text{REPLACE}(\text{x.f}, \text{y}, \mathcal{P})$
x[t] = y	$\text{REPLACE}(\text{x[t]}, \text{y}, \mathcal{P})$
t = t_1+t_2	$\text{REPLACE}(\text{t}, t_1 + t_2, \mathcal{P})$
t = c	$\text{REPLACE}(\text{t}, \text{c}, \mathcal{P})$
other assignments to x	$\mathcal{P} - \langle \text{x}, * \rangle$

Fig. 2. Transfer Functions

$$\text{REPLACE}(\phi_1, \phi_2, \mathcal{P}) = \text{COMBINE}(\text{REWRITE}(\phi_1, \phi_2, \mathcal{P}))$$
$$\text{REWRITE}(\phi_1, \phi_2, \mathcal{P}) = \{\langle \pi(\phi, \phi_1, \phi_2), d \rangle \mid \langle \phi, d \rangle \in \mathcal{P}\}$$
$$\text{COMBINE}(\mathcal{P}) = \{\langle \phi, d \rangle \mid \{d_0, d_1, ..., d_{n-1}\} = \mathcal{P}(\phi),$$
$$d = 1 - (1 - d_0)(1 - d_1)...(1 - d_{n-1})\}$$
$$\pi(\phi, \phi_1, \phi_2) = \begin{cases} \phi_2 \mathcal{I}_0...\mathcal{I}_n & \text{if } \phi = \phi_1 \mathcal{I}_0...\mathcal{I}_n \\ \phi & \text{otherwise} \end{cases}$$

Fig. 3. Equation for the REPLACE Function

prefetch tuples with symbolic prefetch expressions whose prefixes do not match. One potential issue is that a rewritten symbolic prefetch may match an existing symbolic prefetch. The COMBINE function computes the new probability making the assumption that the probabilities for the symbolic prefetches are independent. We have omitted the REPLACE functions for index variables for space reasons.

Our analysis associates a probability with each conditional branch. By default, we assume that loops continue with a 90% probability and other conditional branches take the true branch with a 50% probability. The prefetch tuples for a given exit edge of a conditional branch are weighted by the branch probability for that exit. The two sets of symbolic tuples are merged and if two symbolic tuples have identical symbolic prefetch expressions they are replaced with a new symbolic tuple with a probability equal to the sum of their probabilities. We note it is straightforward to extend the analysis to use branch statistics collected from profiling.

5.2 Termination of Prefetch Analysis

While the transfer functions are monotonic, the partial order on $\mathcal{P}$ is not a lattice because there is no top element. Therefore, the standard termination arguments for dataflow analysis do not apply. We extend our prefetch analysis to ensure termination. One issue is that the analysis can generate symbolic prefetch expressions of unbounded length. We address this issue by introducing a minimum symbolic prefetch probability μ. If a prefetch tuple has a probability less than μ at a program point, the analysis drops that prefetch tuple. A second issue is that the analysis can converge slowly as the analysis makes increasingly smaller increments to the symbolic prefetch probabilities. We introduce a minimum change threshold δ. If the probability changes by less than δ, the fixed-point algorithm considers the probability to be the same.

5.3 Prefetch Placement

There is a trade-off between placing prefetches early to minimize the time that the application waits for data and waiting long enough to make sure that the program is likely to use the prefetched data. This trade-off can depend on the specific architecture of the machine and the application — bandwidth constraints can be satisfied by delaying prefetches, while latency constraints can be satisfied by moving prefetches earlier. Our implementation, therefore, allows the developer to specify a probability threshold σ. Our compiler places symbolic prefetches at the program point that the probability for a prefetch expression crosses this threshold. By default we selected σ to be 30%.

We instrument the prefetch analysis to record the mapping $\gamma(\phi, E) \to \phi'$ which maps the symbolic prefetch ϕ at the source of the edge E to the corresponding symbolic prefetch ϕ' at the target of the edge E. Prefetches are placed on edges where the probability of using the objects specified by a symbolic prefetch crosses the developer specified threshold. Formally, we state this criterion by defining the function τ below to check if a prefetch crosses the probability threshold at the an edge E:

$$\tau(\phi, E) = (\mathcal{P}_{dst(E)}(\phi) > \sigma) \wedge (\mathcal{P}_{src(E)}(\gamma(\phi, E)) < \sigma)$$

Simply using this threshold-crossing criteria to generate prefetch calls can place redundant prefetch calls. We therefore extend our static analysis to check whether the symbolic prefetch is redundant. We define the set S_N at each program point to be the set of symbolic prefetches that have been prefetched when the program executes the statement at node N. This set is the intersection of the set of prefetched symbolic prefetches along each incoming edge E to node N. We split the prefetched symbolic prefetches into two components: $\mathcal{S}_E$ is the set of symbolic prefetches that have been prefetched before the source node of E has been executed and δ_E is the set of prefetches inserted at E. The equations for each set follow:

$$S_N = \bigcap_{E=\text{incoming edges to } N} (\mathcal{S}_E \cup \delta_E)$$
$$\mathcal{S}_E = \{\gamma(\phi, E) \mid \phi \in S_{src(E)}\}$$
$$\delta_E = \{\phi \mid \exists d, \langle \phi, d \rangle \in \mathcal{P}_{src(E)}, \tau(\phi, E)\}$$

We use a fixed point algorithm to compute these sets for all program points. At each edge E, our prefetch placement algorithm places prefetches for the symbolic prefetches in $\delta_E - \mathcal{S}_E$, the set of symbolic prefetches that cross the threshold but have not already been prefetched.

5.4 Prefetch Runtime Mechanism

Our analysis generates prefetch calls at each prefetch site. A prefetch call takes as input the site identifier of the prefetch call, the number of prefetches, an array of base object identifiers for each prefetch, an array of lengths of each prefetch, and an array of unsigned shorts that stores the sequence of field offsets and array indices for every prefetch at that site. The runtime system differentiates between fields and array indices based on the type of the previous object in the path.

Processing a prefetch starts by locally looking up the base object identifier component of the prefetch request in both the local distributed heap and the object cache — in many cases some of the objects in the request are available locally. If the object is found locally, the local runtime uses the field offset (or array index) to look up the object identifier of the next object in the path and removes the first offset value from the symbolic prefetch. The runtime repeats this procedure to process the components of the prefetch request that are available locally. The runtime then prunes the local component from the prefetch request to generate a new prefetch request with the first non-locally available object as its base object identifier.

The runtime groups the prefetch requests by the machine that is authoritative for the base object identifier. The local machine next sends the prefetch requests to the remote machines. Each request contains the machine identifier that should receive the response. Note that it may become apparent at runtime that a prefetch request is redundant. Consider the two prefetch requests a.f.g and b.f.g.h. If at runtime both the expressions a and b reference the same object, the set of objects described by the prefetch request a.f.g is a subset of the set of objects described by the prefetch request b.f.g.h. If one request subsumes another request, the runtime drops the subsumed request.

When the remote machine receives a prefetch request it begins by looking up the base object identifier in its local distributed heap and then (optionally) if necessary in its object cache. Once it finds the object, it looks up the next object identifier by using the field offset or array index from the symbolic prefetch. It repeats this process until it has served the complete request. As it serves the request it sends the copies of the objects to the machine that initiated the prefetch request. When the local machine receives objects it adds the objects to its object cache.

If the remote machine does not have an object specified by the symbolic prefetch, it forwards the remainder of the prefetch request along with the machine identifier of the machine that originated the request to the machine that holds the authoritative copy of the object. Forwarding is necessary because a single machine may not have all the objects for the symbolic prefetch.

Our prefetching implementation includes a heuristic optimization for frequently updated objects. Consider for example a shared hash table data structure. The hash table's array may be frequently updated and reference objects on different machines, and therefore will likely introduce an extra forwarding step in processing the prefetch. If the local machine does not contain a valid copy of the object, our implementation checks whether the local machine contains an invalid copy of an object. The intuition is that while invalid objects cannot safely be used to execute transactions, their fields or elements often contain the correct reference. If an invalid object is present locally, the runtime uses the invalid object copy to skip forwarding while processing the prefetch. This heuristic avoids the network latency that would be incurred if the request has to be forwarded and is safe because the actual transaction never accesses the invalidated objects.

6 Dynamic Prefetching Optimizations

In some applications, transactions repeatedly access the same objects. For example, matrix multiplication accesses some of the same objects in different iterations of the outermost loop. In this case, a prefetch call will repeatedly prefetch the same objects. Processing repeated prefetches introduces overhead and yields no performance benefits as the objects are already cached.

We observe that in many benchmarks, the execution transitions between phases in which it accesses new objects and phases in which it accesses the same objects. We therefore support a mechanism that dynamically shuts down prefetch sites when they stop providing benefits. This mechanism allows the application to benefit from prefetching while minimizing the overhead.

Each time a prefetch is generated for objects that are already in the local cache, the runtime increments a count associated with the prefetch site. When the prefetch site generates a prefetch request that is not locally available, the runtime resets this count. Once this count hits a threshold, the runtime sets a flag that shuts down this prefetch site. Our implementation continues to monitor the prefetch site by occasionally retrying prefetches after a shutdown. If the prefetch retry request prefetches a non-cached object, the runtime turns the prefetch site back on.

7 Evaluation

We ran our benchmarks on a cluster of eight 3.06 GHz Intel Xeon servers running Linux and connected through gigabit Ethernet. Our implementation contains over 120,000 lines of code and is available for download along with all benchmarks at http://demsky.eecs.uci.edu/compiler.php. To evaluate our Java compilation, we have performed experiments to compare the code outputted by our compiler with hand-developed C code and have found the performance to be similar. We present results for several microbenchmarks, five scientific benchmarks, and two distributed benchmarks. We report results for: Base, versions without caching or prefetching, and Prefetch, versions with both caching and prefetching. For the scientific benchmarks, we report results for 1J, single-threaded reference Java implementations compiled into C code. For the distributed benchmarks, we also report results for Caching, versions with only caching enabled. We average execution times over ten executions.

We performed all of the experiments on a LAN-based test bed system. The relative benefits of eliminating message exchanges through symbolic prefetches increase as the round trip message latency between machines increases. Therefore, we expect that symbolic prefetches will yield much larger benefits for wide area networks because they have significantly larger latencies than our LAN-based test bed system.

7.1 Microbenchmarks

The microbenchmarks are intended to quantify the benefits of prefetching. We present results from a three-dimensional array traversal microbenchmark to measure the performance gains from prefetching objects for regular access patterns. The array microbenchmark sums all of the elements in a 10×32,000×4 array of integers that is located on a remote machine. Prefetching improves the performance of this microbenchmark by a factor of 13.31×. The linked list microbenchmark traverses a remote linked list with 1,000,000 nodes. Prefetching improves the performance of this benchmark by 4.54×. The speedup of the linked list microbenchmarks is limited because each prefetch must traverse many linked-list nodes to prefetch one new linked list node.

7.2 Distributed SpamFilter

The distributed spam filter benchmark is a collaborative spam filter that identifies spam using user feedback. It is based on the Spamato spam filter project and contains 2,457 lines of code [14]. In the original version, a collection of spam filters communicates information to a centralized server. Our implementation replaces the centralized server with distributed data structures.

When the spam filter receives an email, it calculates a set of MD5-hash based signatures for that message. It generates Ephemeral hash-based signatures for the text parts of a message and Whiplash URL-based signatures for the URLs in the message. It then looks up those signatures in a distributed hash table that maps a signature to the associated spam statistics. The spam statistics are generated from collaborative user feedback. The spam filter uses those statistics to estimate whether an email is spam. If the user corrects the spam filter's categorization of an email, it updates the spam statistics for all of the signatures in that email.

Figure 4 presents the results for the distributed spam filter benchmark. Our workload presents each spam filter client with 1,000 emails. Note that our workload holds the work constant per client machine. Therefore, the total amount of work increases as we add more clients. The observed increase in execution time has two primary causes: (1) the hash table is more likely to contain the hash signature and therefore lookups access more objects and (2) a larger percentage of the objects are remote. We show the results for caching to quantify the benefits of caching versus prefetching. Prefetching provides speedups up to 4.54× relative to the base version and 1.49× relative to the caching version. Prefetching and caching hide up to 98% of remote reads relative to the base version and prefetching hides up to 87% of remote reads relative to the caching version. Figure 5 presents the abort rate for transactions running on multiple clients for this benchmark. Up to 9% of transactions abort due to conflicts. We omit Java comparisons because we do not have a Java version of this benchmark.

7.3 Distributed Multiplayer Game

In the multiplayer game benchmark clients play the roles of tree planters and lumberjacks. The benchmark contains 1,420 lines of code. The game is played on a map by planters and lumberjacks — planters plant trees while lumberjacks cut trees. Both the planters and lumberjacks choose a location in the map to either plant a tree or cut one down and take the shortest path to the destination. The clients use the A* graph search algorithm to plan routes. The clients introduce contention in this benchmark when they attempt to plant or remove trees in the same region of the map. If a client accessed the part of the map updated by another client, the transactional version aborts the transaction surrounding that move. The Java version is optimized to only recompute a client's move if another client's move makes client's original move illegal.

SpamFilter	Base	Caching	Prefetch
1	1.50s	—	—
2	13.41s	4.39s	2.95s
4	17.12s	5.17s	3.83s
8	20.97s	6.40s	5.32s

Fig. 4. SpamFilter Results

	SpamFilter		Game		SOR	
Thds	Base	Prefetch	Base	Prefetch	Base	Prefetch
2	4.2%	5.8%	0.2%	0.2%	0.0%	0.2%
4	6.1%	8.3%	1.0%	0.2%	0.2%	0.5%
8	8.1%	9.0%	2.5%	1.0%	0.7%	1.2%

Fig. 5. Abort rate

Figure 6 presents results for the multiplayer gaming benchmark. The game is played on a map of size 400×100 for 512 rounds. We held the work constant per client machine and therefore the total amount of work increases as we add more clients. For this benchmark, perfect scaling occurs when the execution time holds constant as the number of machines increases. This benchmark accesses the same data in different transactions and therefore caching provides a benefit. Prefetching and caching provided speedups of up to 26%. Prefetching and caching hide up to 77% of remote reads relative to the base version and prefetching hides up to 26% of remote reads relative to the caching version.

Game	Java	Base	Caching	Prefetch
1	46.78s	8.06s	—	—
2	51.99s	10.22s	9.99s	9.76s
4	71.54s	12.75s	11.35s	10.93s
8	97.22s	16.73s	13.69s	12.34s

Fig. 6. Multiplayer Game Results

The base version is faster than the Java version because of the way the A* algorithm accesses the map. In the Java version, the server transfers the map at the beginning of each round to make the code manageable. The transactional version only transfers the parts of the map that are needed. We see a $7.87\times$ speedup for the 8 threaded prefetching version relative to the 8 threaded Java version.

Figure 5 presents the abort rate for transactions in this benchmark.

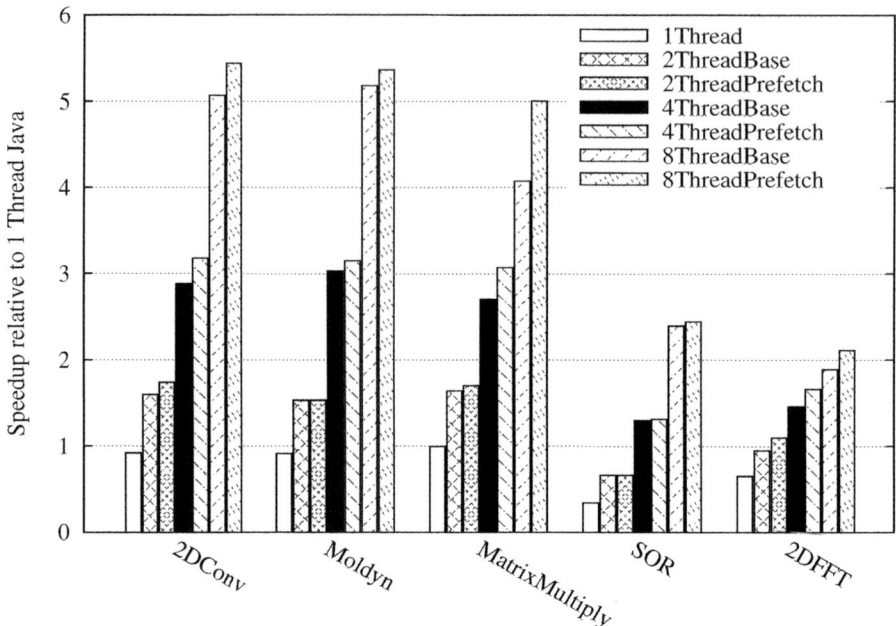

Fig. 7. Scientific Benchmark Speedups (Higher is Better)

7.4 Scientific Benchmarks

We next present results from five scientific benchmarks: 2DConv, Moldyn, MatrixMultiply, SOR, and 2DFFT. These benchmarks do not access the same versions of objects in multiple transactions and therefore caching adds no benefit beyond the base version. We therefore omit caching results for the scientific benchmarks and only report results for the base and the prefetching versions. Figure 7 presents the speedups for all scientific benchmarks relative to single-threaded Java version and Figure 8 presents the absolute execution times.

2DConv. The 2D Convolution benchmark computes the application of a mask to a 2D image. Each machine computes a region of the output image in parallel. The base version contains 1,015 lines of code. The output and input matrices are shared objects in our experiment with dimensions $10,000 \times 1,000$ with a convolution mask of 13×13. Figure 8 presents results for the 2DConv benchmark. The 8 threaded prefetching version provides a speedup of $5.44\times$ over the single-threaded Java version. Prefetching hides nearly 100% of remote reads and provides speedups of up to 9%.

Molecular Dynamics. Moldyn is from the Java Grande benchmark suite [15]. The base version contains 1,172 lines of code. Moldyn models the interaction of molecular particles. We used 8,788 particles and 50 iterations. The 8 threaded prefetching version provides a speedup of 5.35× over the single-threaded Java version. This benchmark accesses a small number of remote objects and therefore we observe speedups of up to 4% from prefetching even though prefetching hides up to 79% of remote reads.

	2DConv		MolDyn		Matrix Multiply		SOR		2DFFT	
	Base	Prefetch	Base	Prefetch	Base	Prefetch	Base	Prefetch	Base	Prefetch
1J	34.20s	—	103.10s	—	96.00s	—	239.05s	—	16.29s	—
1	37.11s	—	113.92s	—	96.48s	—	646.86s	—	25.09s	—
2	21.32s	19.71s	67.57s	67.46s	58.62s	56.31s	362.29s	360.98s	17.08s	14.81s
4	11.86s	10.75s	34.02s	32.72s	35.53s	31.28s	183.66s	183.13s	11.15s	9.79s
8	6.74s	6.29s	19.91s	19.26s	23.61s	19.19s	100.17s	98.00s	8.61s	7.69s

Fig. 8. Scientific Benchmark Results

Matrix Multiply. The matrix multiplication benchmark implements the standard matrix multiplication algorithm for matrix A and matrix B to get the product matrix C. This version computes fifty 650×650 product matrices. All matrices are shared objects. The computation of each product matrix is partitioned over multiple machines. The 8 threaded prefetching version provides a speedup of 5.00× over the single-threaded Java version and prefetching improves performance by 19%. Prefetching hides up to 88% of remote reads for this benchmark.

SOR. The SOR benchmark is from the Java Grande benchmark suite [15]. SOR contains 737 lines of code. It performs 200 iterations of an over-relaxation algorithm on a $8,000 \times 8,000$ grid. The 8 threaded prefetching version provides a speedup of 2.43× over the single-threaded Java version. The one machine distributed transactional version is slower than the single-threaded Java version because each machine must locally copy many large array objects to implement transactions. This overhead means that although the benchmark scales extremely well, the 8-threaded version is only a little over two times faster than the single-threaded Java version, Figure 5 presents the abort rate for transactions running on multiple machines. Prefetching only improves the performance up to 2% even though prefetching hides up to 83% of remote reads because this benchmark accesses a small number of remote objects.

2DFFT. The 2DFFT benchmark is a two-dimensional fast Fourier transform. The base version contains 889 lines of code. The algorithm was taken from *Digital Signal Processing* by Lyon and Rao. We set the matrix dimensions to $1,500 \times 1,500$ and we compute the FFT for five matrices. The FFT of each matrix is parallalized across all machines. The computation performs 1D FFT in parallel, a serial transpose, and then 1D FFT in parallel. The 8 threaded prefetching version provides a speedup of 2.11× over the single-threaded Java version. The speedup was limited as the transpose operation is performed serially and the benchmark requires moving a large amount of data across the network relative to the amount of computation that is performed. Prefetching improves performance up to 13% and hides up to 99% of remote reads.

7.5 Prefetching Effectiveness

Figure 9 presents the hit percentage in the cache for the prefetching versions. We hit in the cache 87% of the time on average eliminating the majority of requests over the network. Figure 10 presents the total numbers of remote reads averaged over all machines participating in the running the transactions per benchmark. The Base version shows the number of remote reads without prefetching, the Cache version shows the number of remote reads with caching alone, and the Prefetch version shows the number of remote reads with prefetching. We omit results for the Cache version of the scientific benchmarks as they never access the same object in two transactions and therefore the Cache versions perform exactly the same number of remote reads as the Base versions. Note that reducing remote reads eliminates the latency from an equivalent number of round trips.

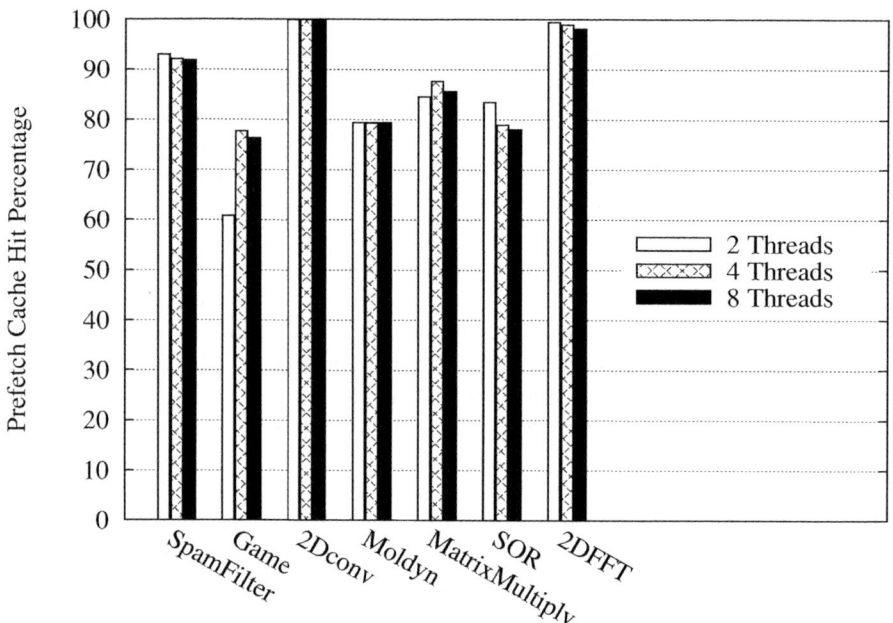

Fig. 9. Prefetching Hit Percentage

Thds	SpamFilter			Game			2DConv		MolDyn		Matrix Multiply		SOR		2DFFT	
	Base	Cache	P	Base	Cache	P	Base	P	Base	P	Base	P	Base	P	Base	P
2	94037	18059	2197	10335	4312	4049	10018	2	1740	359	32736	5059	1205	201	15029	85
4	104303	21118	3907	11791	3632	2699	5018	1	1740	359	36936	4541	1276	269	7529	82
8	109220	22929	5525	13115	4398	3194	2518	2	1740	359	35816	5136	1301	289	3780	71

Fig. 10. Remote Read Results - Scientific Benchmarks (P = Prefetch)

7.6 Tunable Parameters

We studied the sensitivity of the benchmarks' performance to the tunable parameters for the loop conditional branch probability and the probability threshold σ. For the first experiment we executed all of the benchmarks for several different branch probabilities in the range between 50% and 96%. We found that all benchmarks achieved maximum performance for probabilities larger than 90% and that in this range performance was relatively insensitive to the exact value. We conducted a similar experiment for the user defined probability threshold σ. We varied the threshold between 50% for less aggressive prefetching and 5% for more aggressive prefetching. We found that we achieved maximum performance for thresholds near 30% and that near this value performance was relatively insensitive to the exact value.

8 Related Work

We survey related work in prefetching, distributed shared memory systems, and distributed transactional memory systems.

8.1 Distributed Transactional Memory Systems

We next survey the large body of existing research on distributed transactional memory. Symbolic prefetching is applicable to most of these systems and would greatly improve their performance by hiding much of their latency to access remote objects.

Researchers have explored distributed transactional memory [16,17] systems as a mechanism for providing stronger consistency properties. Bodorik et al. developed a hardware-assisted lock-based approach, in which transactions must hold a lock on a memory location before accessing location [18]. Hastings extended Camelot distributed system to support transactions through a lock-based approach [19]. Ahn et al. developed a lock-based distributed shared memory with support for transactions [20]. LOTEC is another lock-based transactional distributed shared memory [21]. All of these implementations incur round trip network latencies whenever the application accesses a remote object because the machine must first communicate to acquire a lock.

DiSTM is a distributed transactional memory system [5]. Its commit process checks whether any running transactions conflict with the current transaction and therefore may not scale well. Anaconda is a distributed transactional memory system that uses a distributed commit algorithm [3]. It uses a three phase commit protocol in which locks are first acquired, the transaction is validated against running transactions on other nodes, and finally it updates the objects.

D^2STM is a fault-tolerant distributed transactional memory system [1]. D^2STM replicates objects to provide fault tolerance. D^2STM is a non-voting based transactional memory approach that uses atomic broadcast to ensure that all nodes see the transaction commit requests in the same order. A transaction's read set is encoded as a bloom filter and is validated against transactions that have committed since the beginning of the committing transaction.

Manassiev et al. introduced a version-based transactional distributed shared memory that replicates all program state on all machines [8]. Sinfonia allows machines to share data in a fault-tolerant and scalable manner using mini-transactions [22].

Bocchino et al. developed a word-based software transaction memory [7]. Herlihy and Sun proposed a distributed transaction memory for metric-space networks [6]. Their design moves objects to the local machine before writing to the object.

8.2 Prefetching

Researchers have developed several techniques for prefetching recursive data structures. Luk and Mowry propose to greedily prefetch object fields, automatically add prefetch pointers to objects that point to objects to prefetch, and linearize recursive data structures when possible [23]. Greedy prefetches require knowing the address of an object. Prefetch pointers do not help with the initial traversal of data structures. Linearizing is only applicable if the creation order is the same as the traversal order. Cahoon and McKinley proposed an analysis for software prefetching [24]. Roth et al. propose a hardware-based approach to prefetching linked data structures that hides the latency of accessing linked data structures in useful work [25]. Wu et al. [26] and Inagaki et al. [27] propose stride prefetching for irregular references. However, in distributed systems the latency of accessing remote memory is likely to be longer than the time that can be filled with useful work.

Researchers have explored communication optimizations for distributed computations. Zhu and Hendren combine multiple reads into a single block [28]. Because their approach requires that the address of objects to be read is known, it incurs a round trip network latency for accessing each object in a linked data structure traversal. Rogers et al. propose thread migration to improve the performance of accessing remote data structures [29]. An issue with thread migration is that it cannot provide efficient simultaneous access to data that spans multiple machines.

Gupta proposes a naming scheme for objects in data structures to enable fast traversals of remote data structures [30]. In this approach many data structure updates require renaming all the objects in a data structure and propagating changes to all machines.

Speight uses a dynamic prediction-based prefetching approach [31]. Joseph and Grunwald use Markov predictors to generate prefetches on a single machine [32]. Ferdman and Falsafi store access sequences and then stream the addresses from these access sequences into a chip's cache [33]. These prefetching approaches typically require object accesses that repeat during execution — as our caches for remote objects can be much larger than CPU caches it is likely that such objects are already in the cache.

8.3 Distributed Systems

Researchers have developed distributed object stores that present a transparent object-oriented view of storage. Such systems are designed to simplify scalable service in cluster environments. TODS [11] is a cluster object storage system. Thor [10] provides a distributed object-oriented database system that supports object navigation and therefore incurs additional message round trips for each commit. Ceph [9] is a scalable object based storage system that uses metadata server (MDS) clusters for managing a distributed file system. We expect that symbolic prefetching along with our prefetch analysis would improve the performance of these distributed object stores.

Distributed shared memories were intended to provide developers with a simple shared memory abstraction on message-passing machines. While earlier systems provide a strict consistent memory model, other sophisticated approaches [34,35,36] achieve higher performance by weakening the memory consistency guarantees and reduce coherence overheads. Developing software for weaker memory models requires the developer to understand complicated consistency properties.

9 Conclusion

Transactional memory provides a powerful new approach to developing distributed applications — it provides information about the granularity of a thread's accesses to distributed data structures and a mechanism to enable speculative optimizations. We have presented an analysis that generates symbolic prefetches for objects. Our prefetch analysis and runtime provides developers with a simple programming model for writing applications in a distributed system. Our benchmark results show that our system provides excellent performance and that prefetching can hide the latency of the majority of remote object accesses.

Acknowledgments. This research was supported by the National Science Foundation under grants CCF-0846195 and CCF-0725350. We would like to thank Brad Chamberlain for feedback on our paper and the anonymous reviewers for their helpful comments.

References

1. Couceiro, M., Romano, P., Carvalho, N., Rodrigues, L.: D2STM: Dependable distributed software transactional memory. In: Proceedings of the 15th IEEE Pacific Rim International Symposium on Dependable Computing (2009)
2. Carvalho, N., Cachopo, J., Rodrigues, L., Silva, A.R.: Versioned transactional shared memory for the FénixEDU web application. In: Proceedings of the 2nd Workshop on Dependable Distributed Data Management (2008)
3. Kotselidis, C., Luján, M., Ansari, M., Malakasis, K., Khan, B., Kirkham, C., Watson, I.: Clustering JVMs with software transactional memory support. In: Proceedings of the 24th IEEE International Parallel and Distributed Processing Symposium (2010)
4. Zhang, B., Ravindran, B.: Relay: A cache-coherence protocol for distributed transactional memory. In: Proceedings of the 2009 International Conference on Principles of Distributed Systems (December 2009)
5. Kotselidis, C., Ansari, M., Jarvis, K., Luján, M., Kirkham, C., Watson, I.: DiSTM: A software transactional memory framework for clusters. In: Proceedings of the 2008 37th International Conference on Parallel Processing, Washington, DC, USA, pp. 51–58 (2008)
6. Herlihy, M., Sun, Y.: Distributed transactional memory for metric-space networks. In: Fraigniaud, P. (ed.) DISC 2005. LNCS, vol. 3724, pp. 324–338. Springer, Heidelberg (2005)
7. Bocchino, R.L., Adve, V.S., Chamberlain, B.L.: Software transactional memory for large scale clusters. In: Proceedings of the 13th Symposium on Principles and Practice of Parallel Programming (2008)
8. Manassiev, K., Mihailescu, M., Amza, C.: Exploiting distributed version concurrency in a transactional memory cluster. In: Proceedings of the Eleventh ACM SIGPLAN Symposium on Principles and Practice of Parallel Programming (2006)
9. Weil, S.A., Brandt, S.A., Miller, E.L., Long, D.D.E., Maltzahn, C.: Ceph: A scalable, high-performance distributed file system. In: Proceedings of the 7th Symposium on Operating Systems Design and Implementation, pp. 307–320 (2006)

10. Liskov, B., Castro, M., Shrira, L., Adya, A.: Providing persistent objects in distributed systems. In: Guerraoui, R. (ed.) ECOOP 1999. LNCS, vol. 1628, p. 230. Springer, Heidelberg (1999)
11. Jin, C., Zheng, W., Zhou, F., Wu, Y.: A distributed persistent object store for scalable service. SIGOPS Operating Systems Review 36(4), 36–49 (2002)
12. Yelick, K., Semenzato, L., Pike, G., Miyamoto, C., Liblit, B., Krishnamurthy, A., Hilfinger, P., Ham, S.G., Gay, D., Colella, P., Aiken, A.: Titanium: A high-performance Java dialect. Concurrency: Practice and Experience 10(10-13) (September-November 1998)
13. Gray, J., Reuter, A.: Transaction Processing: Concepts and Techniques. Morgan Kaufmann, San Francisco (1993)
14. Albrecht, K., Burri, N., Wattenhofer, R.: Spamato - an extendable spam filter system. In: 2nd Conference on Email and Anti-Spam (CEAS) (July 2005)
15. Smith, L.A., Bull, J.M., Obdrzalek, J.: A parallel Java Grande benchmark suite. In: Proceedings of SC 2001 (2001)
16. Shavit, N., Touitou, D.: Software transactional memory. In: Proceedings of the 14th ACM Symposium on Principles of Distributed Computing (August 1995)
17. Herlihy, M., Luchangco, V., Moir, M., Scherer, W.: Software transactional memory for dynamic-sized data structures. In: Proceedings of the Twenty-Second Annual ACM SIGACT-SIGOPS Symposium on Principles of Distributed Computing (July 2003)
18. Bodorik, P., Smith, F.I., J-Lewis, D.: Transactions in distributed shared memory systems. In: Proceedings of the Eigthth International Conference on Data Engineering (February 1992)
19. Hastings, A.B.: Distributed lock management in a transaction processing environment. In: Proceedings of the Ninth Symposium on Reliable Distributed Systems (October 1990)
20. Ahn, J.H., Lee, K.W., Kim, H.J.: Architectural issues in adopting distributed shared memory for distributed object management systems. In: Proceedings of the Fifth IEEE Computer Society Workshop on Future Trends of Distributed Computing Systems (August 1995)
21. Graham, P., Sui, Y.: LOTEC: A simple DSM consistency protocol for Nested Object Transactions. In: Proceedings of the 18th Annual ACM Symposium on Principles of Distributed Computing (1999)
22. Aguilera, M.K., Merchant, A., Shah, M., Veitch, A., Karamanolis, C.: Sinfonia: A new paradigm for building scalable distributed systems. In: Proceedings of 21st ACM SIGOPS Symposium on Operating Systems Principles (2007)
23. Luk, C.K., Mowry, T.C.: Automatic compiler-inserted prefetching for pointer-based applications. IEEE Transactions on Computers 48(2), 134–141 (1999)
24. Cahoon, B., McKinley, K.S.: Data flow analysis for software prefetching linked data structures in Java. In: Proceedings of the 10th International Conference on Parallel Architectures and Compilation Techniques (2001)
25. Roth, A., Moshovos, A., Sohi, G.S.: Dependence based prefetching for linked data structures. In: Proceedings of the Eighth International Conference on Architectural Support for Programming Languages and Operating Systems (October 1998)
26. Wu, Y., Serrano, M.J., Krishnaiyer, R., Li, W., Fang, J.: Value-profile guided stride prefetching for irregular code. In: Horspool, R.N. (ed.) CC 2002. LNCS, vol. 2304, pp. 307–324. Springer, Heidelberg (2002)
27. Inagaki, T., Onodera, T., Komatsu, H., Nakatani, T.: Stride prefetching by dynamically inspecting objects. In: Proceedings of the ACM SIGPLAN 2003 Conference on Programming Language Design and Implementation, pp. 269–277 (2003)
28. Zhu, Y., Hendren, L.J.: Communication optimizations for parallel C programs. In: Proceedings of the 1998 Conference on Programming Language Design and Implementation (1998)
29. Rogers, A., Carlisle, M.C., Reppy, J.H., Hendren, L.J.: Supporting dynamic data structures on distributed-memory machines. ACM Transactions on Programming Languages and Systems 17(2), 233–263 (1995)

30. Gupta, R.: SPMD execution of programs with dynamic data structures on distributed memory machines. In: Proceedings of the 1992 International Conference on Computer Languages (April 1992)
31. Speight, E., Burtscher, M.: Delphi: Prediction-based page prefetching to improve the perforrmance of shared virtual memory systems. In: Proceedings of the International Conference on Parallel and Distributed Processing Techniques and Applications (June 2002)
32. Joseph, D., Grunwald, D.: Prefetching using markov predictors. In: Proceedings of the 24th International Symposium on Computer Architecture (1997)
33. Ferdman, M., Falsafi, B.: Last-touch correlated data streaming. In: IEEE International Symposium on Systems and Software (April 2007)
34. Keleher, P., Cox, A.L., Dwarkadas, S., Zwaenepoel, W.: TreadMarks: Distributed shared memory on standard workstations and operating systems. In: Proceedings of the USENIX Winter 1994 Technical Conference (1994)
35. Bershad, B.N., Zekauskas, M.J.: Midway: Shared memory parallel programming with entry consistency for distributed memory multiprocessors. In: Compcon 1993 (1993)
36. Bennett, J.K., Carter, J.B., Zwaenepoel, W.: Munin: Distributed shared memory based on type-specific memory coherence. In: Proceedings of the Second Symposium on Principles and Practice of Parallel Programming, pp. 168–176 (1990)

Asynchronous Lease-Based Replication of Software Transactional Memory[*]

Nuno Carvalho, Paolo Romano, and Luís Rodrigues

INESC-ID/IST
{nonius,romanop}@gsd.inesc-id.pt, ler@ist.utl.pt

Abstract. Software Transactional Memory (STM) systems have emerged as a powerful middleware paradigm for parallel programming. At current date, however, the problem of how to leverage replication to enhance dependability and scalability of STMs is still largely unexplored. In this paper we present Asynchronous Lease Certification (ALC), an innovative STM replication scheme that exploits the notion of *asynchronous lease* to reduce the replica coordination overhead and shelter transactions from repeated abortions due to conflicts originated on remote nodes. These features allow ALC to achieve up to a tenfold reduction of the commit latency phase in scenarios of low contention when compared with state of the art fault-tolerant replication schemes, and to boost the throughput of long-running transactions by a 4x factor in high conflict scenarios.

Keywords: Dependability, Software Transactional Memory, Replication, Leases.

1 Introduction

The advent of multi-core architectures has decreed the end of the free performance gains' era for single-threaded applications. Hereafter, unleashing the full potential of multi-core processors demands a radical shift in the way software is developed, moving parallel programming from the niche of scientific and high performance computing to mainstream application domains. Building on the abstraction of atomic transactions, and freeing the programmer from the complexity of conventional lock-based synchronization schemes, Transactional Memory (TM) allows simplifying the development and verification of concurrent programs, enhancing code reliability and boosting productivity [7]. Over the last years, a wide body of literature has been developed in the area of STMs and, recently, the first real-world, enterprise-class STM-based applications have started to be deployed in production systems [7,33]. One of the key lessons learnt from the development and deployment of these applications [32] is that existing

---
[*] This work has been partially supported by the project "Cloud-TM" (co-financed by the European Commission through the contract no. 257784), the FCT project ARISTOS (PTDC/EIA- EIA/102496/2008) and by FCT (INESC-ID multiannual funding) through the PIDDAC Program Funds.

STM platforms suffer of a significant limitation: the lack of efficient replication schemes capable of fulfilling the scalability and reliability requirements of real-world, service-oriented applications.

Replication of Transactional Memory systems represents a promising new approach for building fault-tolerant distributed systems, providing powerful building blocks that shelter programmers from the complexity of dealing with machine failures and developing lock-based (distributed) synchronization schemes. At current date, only a handful of solutions have been proposed and evaluated [24,5,27,11]. On the other hand, since transactional memory and databases share the common notion of atomic transaction, the large body of literature developed in the area of replicated databases represents a natural source of inspiration for the design of replication schemes for transactional memory. Among the plethora of database replication schemes, recent approaches based on Atomic Broadcast (AB) [18] and distributed certification procedures [31,23,30], appear to be particularly attractive for employment in a TM context. In fact, unlike classic eager replication schemes (based on fine-grained distributed locking and atomic commit), that suffer of large communication overheads and fall prey of distributed deadlocks [15], certification based schemes avoid the costs of replica coordination during the execution phase, running transactions locally in an optimistic fashion. The consistency of replicas (typically, 1-Copy serializability [4]) is ensured at commit-time, via a distributed certification phase that uses AB to enforce agreement on a common transaction serialization order, avoiding distributed deadlocks, and providing non-blocking guarantees in the presence of replicas' failures.

Unfortunately, as previously observed in [11,32] (and confirmed by the experimental results presented later in this paper), the overhead of previously published certification schemes based on AB can be particularly detrimental in STM environments. In fact, unlike in classical database systems, STMs incur neither in disk access latencies nor in the overheads of SQL statement parsing and plan optimization. This makes the execution time of typical STM transactions normally much shorter than in database settings [32], making the cost of inter-replica coordination a major source of overhead. Further, distributed certification schemes are based on an inherently optimistic approach: transactions are only validated at commit time and no bound is provided on the number of times that a transaction will have to be re-executed due to the occurrence of conflicts. This can lead to undesirably high abort rates in high conflict scenarios or with heterogeneous workloads that contain mixes of short and long-running transactions (as it is actually the case for several well-known TM benchmarks [17,2]). In this case, the latter ones may be repeatedly aborted due to the occurrence of (remote) conflicts with a stream of short-lived transactions, leading to fairness violation that might be regarded as unacceptable by the users of interactive applications.

In this paper we tackle the above issues by presenting the Asynchronous Lease Certification (ALC) protocol. In the core of the ALC scheme is the notion of *asynchronous lease*. Analogously to classic lease schemes [13,14], asynchronous leases are used by a replica to establish temporary privileges in the management of a subset of the replicated data-set. Specifically, in ALC, the ownership of an asynchronous lease on a set of data items provides a replica with two key benefits: i) reducing the commit phase latency of the transactions that access those data items and; ii) sheltering transactions by repeated abortions due to remote conflicts.

While the ALC protocol may rely on any STM for locally regulating the concurrent execution of transactions, we chose to integrate the ALC scheme with a multi-versioned STM, namely JVSTM [8]. This allows sheltering read-only transactions from the possibility of aborts (due both to local or remote conflicts), as well as to prevent them from incurring in stalls due to concurrent conflicting accesses. Through an extensive experimental evaluation, based on both synthetic micro-benchmarks, as well as complex STM benchmarks we show that ALC permits to achieve up to a tenfold reduction of the commit latency, and a 4x factor increase of throughput when compared with competing replicated STMs [11].

The rest of this paper is organized as follows. Section 2 discusses related work. A description of the considered system model and of the consistency criteria ensured by ALC is provided in Section 3, which also describes the architecture of an ALC-based system and discusses the issues related to the integration with JVSTM. The ALC scheme is presented in Section 4 and Section 5 presents the results of our experimental evaluation study. Finally, Section 6 concludes the paper.

2 Related Work

The only distributed STM solutions we are aware of are those in [24,5,27,11]. Except for the work in [11], none of these solutions leverages on replication in order to ensure cluster-wide consistency and availability in scenarios of failures. In ALC, on the other hand, dependability is seen as a first class design goal, and the STM performance is optimized through a holistic approach that tightly integrates low level fault-tolerance mechanisms (such as AB) with a novel, highly efficient lease based distributed transaction certification scheme.

In our previous work [11], we introduced D^2STM, which is, to the best of our knowledge, the first and only fault-tolerant distributed STM platform presented up to date. D^2STM adopts an optimistic certification scheme, which avoids any remote synchronization during transaction's execution and relies on a commit-time AB based distributed validation to ensure global consistency. In order to reduce the AB latency, D^2STM uses a Bloom-filter based encoding that minimizes the amount of information to be sent through the AB primitive, at the cost of a small, tunable additional abort rate. ALC provides two significant advantages with respect to D^2STM, as described in the following. Firstly, rather than atomically broadcasting the writeset and the (Bloom filter encoded) readset of a committing transaction, ALC relies on the cheaper Uniform Reliable Broadcast (URB) [18] primitive to disseminate exclusively the writesets. This results in a significant reduction of the inter-replica synchronization overhead. Secondly, the optimistic certification approach used in D^2STM may force transactions to undergo a high (and theoretically unbounded) number of aborts. The lease based certification scheme of ALC, conversely, shelters transactions from repeated aborts due to remote conflicts, which leads to remarkable throughput increases in high conflict scenarios.

The problem of replicating a STM is naturally closely related to the problem of database replication, given that both STMs and DBs share the same key abstraction of atomic transactions. Modern database replication schemes [31,30,9,23] rely on AB to enforce, in a non-blocking manner, a global transaction serialization order without incurring in the scalability problems affecting classical eager replication mechanisms based on distributed locking and atomic commit protocols [15]. Existing database replication schemes based on AB can be coarsely classified in two main categories, depending on whether transactions are executed optimistically [31,23] or conservatively [22]. In the conservative case, which can be seen as an instance of the classical state machine/active replication approach [18], transactions are serialized through AB *prior* to their actual execution and are then deterministically scheduled on each replica in compliance with the resulting total order. This prevents aborts due to concurrent execution of conflicting transactions in different replicas. On the other hand, the need for enforcing deterministic thread scheduling at each replica requires a careful identification of the conflict classes to be accessed by each transaction, prior to its actual execution. Further, as update transactions need to be fully executed by all replicas, these approaches do not scale in presence of write intensive workloads [30]. Optimistic approaches avoid the above problems by relying on a commit-time certification phase but may generate unacceptable abort rates in high conflict scenarios. ALC shares the key benefits of these schemes (no need to determine the data-sets to be accessed by transactions prior to their execution; no need to fully execute update transactions on every replica), but leverages on the notion of asynchronous lease to lower the commit phase latency and shelter transactions from repeated aborts in presence of high conflict workloads.

The large body of literature on distributed shared memory (DSM) is clearly related to our work. Early DSM implementations [26] enforced strong consistency guarantees at the granularity of a single memory access. Those systems have proved hard to implement with good performance. Due to this reason, a significant body of research was devoted to build DSM systems that aim at achieving better performance at the cost of relaxing memory consistency guarantees [21]. Unfortunately, developing software for relaxed DSM's consistency models can be challenging as programmers are required to fully understand sometimes unintuitive consistency models. Conversely, the simplicity of the atomic transaction abstraction, at the core of (distributed) STM platforms, allows to increase programmers' productivity [7] with respect to both locking disciplines and relaxed memory consistency models. Further, the strong consistency guarantees provided by atomic transactions can be supported through efficient algorithms that, like in ALC, incur only in a single synchronization phase per transaction, amortizing the communication overhead across a (possibly large) set of memory accesses.

Atomic transactions play a key role also in the recent Sinfonia [1] platform, where these are referred to as "mini-transactions". However, unlike in conventional STM settings or in D^2STM, Sinfonia assumes transactions to be static, i.e. that their data-sets and operations are known in advance, which limits the generality of the programming paradigm provided by this platform.

The notion of leases has been widely used in the context of replicated systems to simplify and/or optimize the replica consistency mechanisms, e.g. [13,14]. However, traditional leases are time-based contracts, being therefore tightly coupled to the notion of real-time. As a consequence, lease schemes have been traditionally designed and implemented assuming strong, and hence restrictive, synchrony levels (such as bounded communication delay and clock skew across processes). Conversely, the ALC replication scheme is implementable in a partially/eventually synchronous system [18], namely in any system where AB is implementable. The only other lease based solution we are aware of that is designed for employment in an asynchronous system is the one in [6]. There are a number of significant differences between the lease notion defined in [6] with respect to the one leveraged on by the ALC protocol. First, in [6], users are required to pre-declare the number of operations to be executed while holding the lease. In ALC, instead, leases are held by a replica as long as possible, i.e. as long as no conflicting transaction is executed by a different replica. Second, upon crash of a process p that has successfully established a lease, in [6] the remaining processes are forced to block until p recovers and "uses" all the intervals over which it has acquired a lease. Also, the success in the acquisition of an Asynchronous Lease is conditioned to the fact that there are no contending requesters. In our protocol, instead, conflicting leases requests are globally ordered, in a non-blocking fashion, using AB.

3 System Model and Architecture

We consider a classical asynchronous distributed system model [18] consisting of a set of processes $\Pi = \{p_1, \ldots, p_n\}$ that communicate via message passing and can fail according to the fail-stop (crash) model. We assume that a majority of processes is correct and that the system ensures a sufficient synchrony level to permit implementing a View Synchronous Group Communication Service (GCS) [10]. GCS integrates two complementary services: *membership* and *multicast communication*. Informally, the role of the membership service is to provide, each participant in a distributed computation with information about which process is active (or reachable) and which one is failed (or unreachable). Such information is called a *view* of the group of participants. The multicast service allows a member to send a message to the group of participants with different reliability and ordering properties.

We assume that the GCS provides a primary-component group membership service [3], which maintains a single agreed view of the group at any given time and provides processes with information on whether they belong to the primary component. Specifically, the GCS delivers to the application a *viewChange* event to notify the alteration of the (primary component) view, and an *ejected* event to notify the exclusion of the process from the primary component (typically because of a false failure suspicion). We say that a process is v_i-correct in a given view v_i if it does not fail in v_i and if v_{i+1} exists, it transits to it. We assume a GCS ensuring the following properties on the delivered views:

Self-inclusion if process p delivers view v_i, then p belongs to v_i.
Strong virtual synchrony messages are delivered in the same view in which they were sent.
Primary component view the sequences of views delivered are totally ordered and for any two consecutive views v_i, v_{i+1} there always exists a v_i correct process
Non-Triviality when a process fails or it is partitioned from the primary view, it will be eventually excluded from the primary component view
Accuracy a correct process is eventually included in every view delivered by the GCS

The GCS offers two communication services, namely: Optimistic Atomic Broadcast (OAB) [12] and Uniform Reliable Broadcast (URB) [18]. URB is defined by the primitives *UR-broadcast(m)* and *UR-deliver(m)*. Three primitives define OAB: *OA-broadcast(m)*, which is used to broadcast message m; *Opt-deliver(m)*, which delivers message m without providing ordering guarantees; *TO-deliver(m)*, which delivers message m in the final total oder. *Opt-deliver(m)* provides an early estimate of the final order of the corresponding *TO-deliver(m)*; this estimate may be inaccurate without violating the safety of ALC.

The properties of the OAB are as follows:

Validity If a v_i-correct process p *OA-broadcasts* message m in v_i, then p *Opt-delivers* and *TO-delivers* m.
Integrity Any message m is *Opt-delivered* and/or *TO-delivered* by a process p at most once, and only if it had been previously *OA-broadcast*.
Optimistic Order If a node p *TO-delivers* m, then node p has previously *Opt-delivered* m.
Uniform Agreement If process p *TO-delivers* m in view v_i, then any v_i-correct process *TO-delivers* m in view v_i.
Total Order If two processes p and q *TO-deliver* messages m and m', then they do so in the same order.

The properties of the URB are as follows:

Validity If a v_i-correct process p *UR-broadcasts* message m in v_i, then p *UR-delivers* m.
Integrity Any message m is *UR-delivered* by a process p at most once, and only if it had been previously *R-broadcast*.
Uniform Agreement If process p *UR-delivers* m in view v_i, then any v_i-correct process $q \in v_i$ *UR-delivers* m in view v_i.
Causal Order If a process p *UR-delivers* m and m' such that m causally precedes m', according to Lamport's causal order [25] (denoted $m \to m'$), then p *UR-delivers* m before m'.

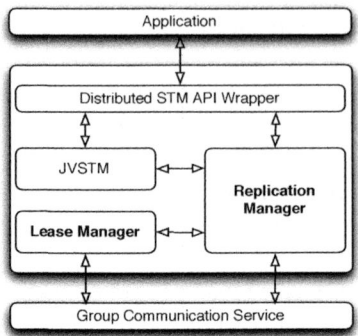

Fig. 1. Middleware architecture of an ALC replica

Note that in addition to the URB properties, OAB ensures total order of the *TO-deliver* events, preceded by a guess of the final order through the *Opt-deliver* event. Providing the total order property is more expensive than causal order in terms of exchanged messages and communication latency.

We now describe the software architecture of the middleware running on each replica, illustrated in Figure 1. The top layer is a wrapper that intercepts the application level calls for transaction demarcation (i.e. to begin, commit or abort transactions), not interfering with the application accesses (read/write) to the transactional data items, which are managed directly by the underlying JVSTM layer. This approach allows for transparently extending the classic STM programming model to a distributed setting.

JVSTM implements a multi-version scheme which is based on the abstraction of a *versioned box* (VBox). A VBox is a container that keeps a tagged sequence of values - the history of the versioned box. Each of the history's values corresponds to a change made to the box by a successfully committed transaction and is tagged with the timestamp of the corresponding transaction. To this end, JVSTM maintains an integer timestamp, *commitTimestamp*, which is incremented whenever a transaction commits. Each transaction stores its timestamp in a local *snapshotID* variable, which is initialized at the time of the transaction activation with the current value of *commitTimestamp*. This information is used both during transaction execution, to identify the appropriate values to be read from the VBoxes, and, at commit time, during the validation phase, to determine the set of concurrent transactions to check against possible conflicts. JVSTM relies on an optimistic approach which buffers transactions' writes and detects conflicts only at commit time, by checking whether any of the VBoxes read by a committing transaction T was updated by some other transaction T' with a larger timestamp value. In this case T is aborted. Otherwise, T's *commitTimestamp* is increased, its *snapshotID* is set to the new value of *commitTimestamp* and the new values of all the VBoxes it wrote are atomically updated. The integration of JVSTM within the ALC replication protocol entailed extending, in a non-intrusive manner, the JVSTM's original API so to allow the Replication Manager to (i) extract information concerning transactions' read-set, write-set, and *snapshotID* timestamp; (ii) explicitly trigger the transaction validation procedure, which detects conflict generated by a transaction T_x with any other (local or remote) transaction that committed after T_x started; and (iii) atomically apply, the write-set WS of a remotely executed transaction (i.e. atomically updating the VBoxes of the local JVSTM with the new values written by a remote transaction) and simultaneously increasing the JVSTM's *commitTimestamp*.

The bottom layer is a Group Communication Service (GCS) [10] which provides the view synchronous membership, OAB and URB services. In our middleware implementation, we use the Appia GCS [29].

The core components of ALC are the Lease Manager (LM) and the Replication Manager (RM). The role of the LM is to ensure that there are never two replicas simultaneously disseminating updates for conflicting transactions. To this end, the LM exposes an interface consisting of two methods, namely GETLEASE() and FINISHEDXACT(), which are used by the RM to acquire/free leases on a set of DataItems. The RM is responsible of managing the transactions' commit phase, implementing a distributed certification scheme which leverages the local JVSTM replica to commit and certify local and remote transactions, as well as the services provided by the LM and the GCS.

Just like JVSTM, which ALC encapsulates, ALC preserves the strong atomicity [28] and opacity [16] properties. The former property avoids conflicts among transactional and non-transactional memory accesses. Opacity [16], on the other hand, can be informally viewed as an extension of the classical database serializability property with the additional requirement that even non-committed transactions are prevented from accessing inconsistent states. Our target consistency criterion for replication is 1-copy serializability [4], which ensures that transaction execution history across the whole set of replicas is equivalent to a serial transaction execution history on a not replicated (JV)STM.

4 The ALC Protocol

For the sake of clarity, we present the ALC protocol in an incremental fashion. We start by presenting a baseline version that relies on a simple, yet quite inefficient, lease establishment scheme. We will initially assume that the set of data items accessed by transactions do not vary across different re-executions of a same transaction and show how to deal with the case of transactions accessing different sets of data items across different executions in Section 4.4. In the Section 4.5 we introduce two optimizations that permit to drastically reduce the communication latency associated with the lease transfer mechanism by achieving full overlapping with the distributed certification phase. Finally, to simplify presentation, we will assume a single threaded execution model. This will allow us to avoid describing in detail the intra-replica synchronization scheme required to ensure consistency in a multi-threaded environment, and to focus on the description of the inter-replica coordination protocol.

Algorithm 1. Replication Manager.

```
boolean commit(Transaction T)
    if (¬JVSTM.validate(T)) then // early validation
        JVSTM.abort(T)
        return false
    LeaseRequestID leaseID=LeaseManager.GETLEASE(JVSTM.getReadAndWriteSet(T))
    if (leaseID=⊥ ∨ ¬JVSTM.validate(T)) then // final validation
        JVSTM.abort(T)
        return false
    else
        trigger UR-broadcast([ApplyWS,T,leaseID,JVSTM.getWriteset(T)])
        wait until (committedXact(T) ∨ ejected)
        if ( ejected ) then
            JVSTM.abort(T)
            return false
        else
            return true

upon event UR-deliver([ApplyWS,T,leaseID,ws]) from p_j do
    if (p_j = p_i) then
        JVSTM.commitLocalXact(T)
        trigger committedXact(T)
        LeaseManager.FINISHEDXACT(leaseID)
    else
        JVSTM.commitRemoteXact(ws)
```

The intuition behind the ALC approach is the following. Analogously to classic certification schemes, transactions are run based on local data, avoiding any inter-replica synchronization till they enter commit phase. At this stage, however, ALC ensures to have established a lease for the accessed data items, prior to proceed with transactions' validation. In case a transaction T is found to have accessed stale data, this is re-executed without releasing the lease. This ensures that, during T's re-execution, no other replica can update any of the data items accessed during the first execution of T, guaranteeing the absence of remote conflicts on the subsequent re-execution of T provided that this deterministically accesses the same set of data items accessed during its first execution.

The ownership of the lease, in fact, ensures that no other replica will be allowed to validate any conflicting transaction, making it unnecessary to enforce distributed agreement on the global transactional serialization order. ALC takes advantage of this by limiting the use of OAB exclusively for establishing the lease ownership. Subsequently, as long as the lease is owned by the replica, transactions can be locally validated and their updates can be disseminated using URB, which can be implemented in a much more efficient manner than OAB.

Unlike classic lease based approaches, where the lease duration is defined at the time of the lease establishment, in ALC leases are said to be asynchronous since the concept of lease is detached from the notion of time. Conversely, once that a replica acquires a lease on a set of data items, it holds the lease as long as it does not require an explicit lease request from another replica. In order to avoid distributed deadlocks during the lease acquisition phase, lease requests are disseminated via OAB, and atomically enqueued at each node in the

TO-delivery order. Fairness is ensured by establishing leases in FIFO order and leases are transferred to a requesting replica as soon as the transactions (in execution at the lease-owner) to which those leases had been granted have committed.

4.1 Replication Manager

As already stated, transactions are executed locally, without any inter-replica synchronization, until the commit phase is reached. At this stage, if the committing transaction did not issue any write operation, it can be locally committed given that the JVSTM multi-versioned concurrency control scheme ensures the serializability of the observed snapshot. On the other hand, if we are not in presence of a read-only transaction, the STM API wrapper invokes the commit method of the Replication Manager, triggering the execution of the ALC protocol.

The pseudo-code describing the behavior of the RM is shown in Algorithm 1. Following an early validation phase, aimed at detecting any conflict developed with (local or remote) transactions already committed since the activation of the committing transaction, the RM requires the LM to acquire the leases corresponding to the set of data-items read and written during the transaction execution. The lease acquisition phase (described in the following) eventually terminates returning either a lease identifier, or the special value $\bot$ notifying the RM about the impossibility to acquire the requested leases. As we will see, the only case in which the LM ever fails to acquire leases is in case the process is excluded from the primary component view (due to a wrong failure suspicion). In such a case, for the RM it is only safe to keep on processing read-only transactions, and will therefore abort the current transaction. On the other hand, in absence of failures or failure suspicions, the lease manager will eventually succeed in acquiring the requested set of leases and return a lease request identifier to the RM. In this case, p_i is guaranteed to have already installed the updates of every remotely (and locally) executed transaction, and can therefore proceed with the validation. If this is successful, the transaction's writeset (and the corresponding lease request identifier) is disseminated using URB.

The properties of URB ensure that if p_i self-delivers the transaction's writeset in the current view, any other v_i-correct process will also deliver it in view v_i (even if p_i is subject to a failure right after the writeset delivery). This allows to safely commit the local transaction. Finally, the RM informs the LM of the successful execution of the transaction by invoking the FINISHEDXACT method specifying, as input parameter, the identifier of the lease request previously returned by the GETLEASE method.

The RM is also responsible of applying the writeset of remotely executed transactions, which are triggered by the corresponding *UR-deliver*. Note that the Causal Order property of the primitive ensures that the sequence of local transactions committed by a process p_i is delivered in FIFO order (i.e. in the same order in which p_i committed them) by any replica that deliver them.

Algorithm 2. Lease Manager at process p_i - Basic Algorithm.

```
FIFOQueue<LeaseRequest> CQ[NumConflictClasses]={⊥,...,⊥}
View currentView={p₁,...,pᵢ,...,pₙ}
boolean inPrimaryComponent=true

LeaseRequestID GETLEASE(Set DataSet)
  if (¬inPrimaryComponent) then return ⊥
  ConflictClass[] CC = getConflictClasses(DataSet)
  if (∃req∈CQ s.t. req.proc=pᵢ ∧ ¬req.blocked ∧ (∀cc∈CC : cc∈req.cc) ) then
    req.activeXacts++
  else
    LeaseRequest req = new LeaseRequest(pᵢ,CC)
    trigger OA-broadcast([LeaseRequest,req])
    wait until isEnabled(req) ∨ ¬inPrimaryComponent
    if (¬inPrimaryComponent) then return ⊥
    else return req.getID()

void FINISHEDTRANSACTION(LeaseRequestID reqID)
  getLeaseReqFromId(reqID).activeXacts--

upon event TO-deliver([LeaseRequest, req]) from pₖ do
  freeLocallyEnabledLeases(roq.cc)
  ∀ cc∈req.cc do CQ[cc].enqueue(req)

upon event UR-deliver([LeaseFreed, reqs]) from pₖ do
  ∀req∈reqs do
    ∀ cc∈req.cc do CQ[cc].dequeue(req)

void freeLocalLeases(LeaseRequest req)
  Set<LeaseRequest> locallyEnabledLeases
  ∀req† ∈CQ s.t. req†.proc=pᵢ∧ (req†.cc∩req.cc)≠∅ do
    req†.blocked=true
    if (req†.isEnabled()) then locallyEnabledLeases=locallyEnabledLeases ∪ req†
  if (locallyEnabledLeases ≠ ∅) then
    wait until ∀req* ∈locallyEnabledLeases : req*.activeXacts=0
    trigger UR-broadcast([LeaseFreed,locallyEnabledLeases)]

boolean isEnabled(LeaseRequest req)
  return ∀cc∈req.cc : CQ[cc].isFirst(req)
```

4.2 Lease Manager

The LM's pseudo-code for process p_i is reported in Algorithm 2 and Algorithm 3. Let us start by analyzing the pseudo-code in Algorithm 2, which represents the core of the lease establishment protocol. As already hinted, in order to establish/relinquish leases, the LM exposes two interfaces, namely the GETLEASE and FINISHEDXACT methods. Leases are associated with data items indirectly, namely through conflict classes. This allows to flexibly control the granularity of the leases abstraction. We abstract over the mapping between a data item and a conflict class (which can in practice be implemented through classic hashing schemes since each transactional object is already uniquely identified) through the getConflictClasses() primitive, taking a set of data items as input parameter and returning a set of conflict classes. The trade-off between coarse and fine lease granularity is in that coarse granularity is prone to false sharing, i.e. lease requests associated with disjoint data items' sets may be mapped to common conflict classes, generating unnecessary lease migrations across replicas. On the other hand, fine granularity schemes may generate larger communication and

Algorithm 3. Lease Manager at process p_i - Dealing with View Changes.

```
upon event ViewChange(View newView) do
    if (¬inPrimaryComponent ∨ p_i is joining the group for the first time) then
        perform state transfer
        inPrimaryComponent=true
    else
        ∀p_j s.t. (p_j ∈currentView ∧ p_j ∉ newView) do
            ∀ req∈CQ s.t. req.proc=p_j do CQ.remove(req)
        currentView = newView

upon event ejected do
    inPrimaryComponent=false
```

processing overhead, since they impose the transmission of larger lease request messages among replicas and the management of larger local data structures for detecting conflicts among lease requests.

The data structures maintained by replicas for regulating the establishment/release of leases are the following: CQ, namely an array of FIFO queues, one per conflict class, that serves as a lock table to keep track of the conflict relations among lease requests; $currView$, namely the set of processes belonging to the current view; $inPrimaryComponent$, a boolean flag which indicates whether p_i is in the primary component or not. A LeaseRequest type is a structure containing the following fields: cc, namely the set of conflict classes associated with the lease request; $activeXacts$, an integer keeping track of the number of active transactions associated with the lease request, which is initialized to 1 when a lease request is created; $blocked$, a boolean variable indicating whether new transactions can be associated with this lease request or not, which is initialized to $false$ when a lease request is created; a unique identifier, which is transparently generated by p_i and is retrievable through the getID() primitive.

When the GETLEASE() method is invoked by the RM to establish a lease on the set of data items accessed by a committing transaction, the LM first checks whether p_i has already been ejected from the primary component. In this case it returns the special value ⊥, notifying the RM that it is currently impossible to establish new leases. Otherwise, it determines, through the getConflictClasses() primitive, the set of conflict classes associated with the data-sets accessed by the transaction. Then it checks whether p_i has already enqueued in CQ a lease request req i) associated with a super-set of the currently requested conflict classes, and ii) which can still be associated with additional transactions (i.e. whose $blocked$ field is set to false). In this case, it is not necessary to issue a new lease request, and the current transaction can simply be associated with req. Otherwise, a new lease request is created and OA-$broadcast$. In both cases, p_i waits either until the corresponding lease request is enabled (this happens when the lease request reaches the first position in all the FIFO queues associated with its conflict classes - see the isEnabled() function), or until p_i is ejected from the primary component. In the latter case, the LM returns the special value ⊥. If the lease request is eventually enabled, on the other hand, its unique identifier is retrieved via the getID() primitive and returned to the RM.

The FINISHEDTRANSACTION() method takes as input parameter a lease request identifier (i.e. the identifier previously returned by the GETLEASE() method when a lease request was associated with the transaction), retrieves the corresponding lease request via the getLeaseReqFromId() primitive, and decrements the number of active transactions associated with the lease request.

Upon a *TO-deliver* event of a lease request *req*, p_i first of all checks whether some of his locally issued lease requests need to be freed or blocked. This is done by invoking the freeLocalLeases procedure which, determines whether there is any of p_i's lease requests (denoted as req† in the pseudo-code) already enqueued in CQ which conflicts with *req* (i.e. whether req and req† have at least a conflict class in common). In this case, it sets the blocked field of these lease requests to true. This is the key mechanism employed to ensure the fairness of the lease rotation scheme: in order to prevent a remote process p_j from starving while waiting for process p_i to relinquish a lease, in fact, p_i is prevented from associating new transactions with existing lease requests as soon as a conflicting lease request from p_j is *TO-delivered* at p_i (as explained while describing the GETLEASE method). Next, the LM waits for the successful completion of every transaction associated with any locally issued conflicting lease request that is also currently enabled (note that this implies that such transactions have been already allowed to proceed with the validation phase). When these transactions have successfully committed, the LM triggers a *UR-broadcast* specifying the set of locally owned lease requests that p_i is freeing. The handling of the *TO-deliver* event terminates by enqueueing the corresponding lease request in every associated conflict class.

The logic associated with *UR-deliver* events is very simple: every lease request specified in the uniformly broadcast message is removed from the corresponding conflict class queues.

View Changes. It remains to discuss the replicas' behavior in the presence of view changes and ejections from the primary component view, which is formalized by the pseudo-code in Algorithm 3. Upon delivery of a new view event, if the replica re-joins the primary component or is joining the group of replicas for the first time, it triggers a state transfer procedure that realigns the content of the local replica of the STM, as well as of the state variables of the ALC protocol. Due to space constraints, we do not detail a description of the state transfer procedure, as, indeed, conventional state transfer mechanisms, such as [20] may be used at this purpose. On the other hand, if upon a view change, some processes are eliminated from the current view (because they have crashed or are partitioned away from the primary component), all of their lease requests are purged from the local CQ. Recall also that, if a process gets disconnected from the primary component, it will fail to deliver any pending lease request. This will cause the failure of the lease acquisition procedure at this replica (see the GETLEASE method). Overall, these two mechanisms (the removal of lease requests issued by processes excluded from the primary component, and the failure of the acquisition of lease requests pending at a process that is ejected from the primary component) guarantee the liveness of the lease management protocol. Note also

Algorithm 4. Lease Manager – Optimistic delivery optimization.

upon event *Opt-deliver(LeaseRequest request)* **from** p_k **do**
    freeLocalLeases(request)

upon event *TO-deliver(LeaseRequest request)* **from** p_k **do**
    foreach $cc \in request.cc$ **do**
        CQ[cc].enqueue($[p_k$,request$]$)

---

that replicas outside of the primary component may still continue processing read-only transactions, which will observe a serializable, albeit possibly obsolete, snapshot of the replicated (JV)STM.

4.3 Correctness Arguments

For space constraints we omit a full proof of correctness, but we still present some informal arguments analyzing why ALC ensures 1-copy serializability. First of all, we note that the enqueuing of lease requests at the various replicas takes place in a common order, namely the one determined by the final delivery of OAB, and that the logic for the advancement of the lease requests in the conflict classes' queues is deterministic. Also, the sequence of ApplyWS and LeaseFreed messages is disseminated via URB, which ensures causally ordered delivery. This guarantees that the stream of writesets associated with transactions accessing non-disjoint data items' sets are all applied in the same order at all replicas. The same applies for the delivery LeaseFreed messages, which implies that the order of dequeuing from the the conflict classes' queues for each pair of conflicting lease request is the same at all replicas. This also implies that every pair of conflicting transactions is validated in the same total order by each replica.

4.4 Non-deterministic Re-executions

The above presented lease management scheme guarantees the absence of remote conflicts during the re-execution of a transaction as it avoids releasing the lease on the conflict classes accessed during the previous execution of the transaction until this is successfully commit. This scheme can deterministically guarantee the absence of remote conflicts only if the set of conflict classes accessed when re-executing the transaction do not vary. While this is not always true in general for real applications, on the other hand it is very likely (as also supported by our experimental evaluation) that two re-executions of the same transaction access a large number of conflict classes in common (especially if lease granularity is moderately coarse). In practical settings, therefore, the presented ALC scheme is still very likely to significantly reduce the transactions' abort rate.

A simple, albeit somewhat extreme, workaround to deterministically bound the number of aborts/re-runs undergone by "problematic" transactions dramatically altering their data access patterns upon re-execution would consist in requesting a lease on the whole set of conflict classes. This would clearly suffice to ensure their successful re-execution, at the price of a temporary, though significant, bridling of concurrency.

Finally, it is important to highlight that the scheme presented in Section 4.2 can suffer of deadlocks in case the conflict classes accessed during transactions' re-execution, say cc', are not a subset of those accessed during a previous execution, say cc. This is due to the fact that the LM won't relinquish the lease on cc granted during the first transaction's execution, and will issue a new lease request on cc'. The latter may block if some other replica is simultaneously retaining the lease on cc' while requesting a lease on cc.

Fortunately, such an issue can be resolved by using simple and lightweight deadlock avoidance or detection schemes. A possible deadlock avoidance scheme is to detect whether $cc' \not\subseteq cc$ as a transaction completes its re-execution, and to piggyback a LeaseFreed message to the lease request OA-broadcast for cc'. An alternative deadlock detection scheme could check for the presence of cycles in the wait-for graph of the lease requests locally enqueued in CQ, and use a deterministic rule for breaking the cycle by aborting one of the involved lease requests. Note that as the state of the CQ is consistently replicated by all replicas, the deadlock detection would not require any additional inter-replica coordination.

4.5 Analysis and Optimizations

Provided that a replica owns a lease on the conflict classes accessed by a transaction, ALC allows committing the transaction using a single URB, which can be implemented incurring in a two communication steps latency [18]. This is in contrast with state of the art distributed certification schemes [31], which incur in the latency of (at least) an AB during the commit phase (whose latency is of at least 3 communication steps latency[1]). On the other hand, in the presented ALC scheme, if a transaction has accessed data items for which its process does not hold a lease, it incurs in the latency associated with lease acquisition phase. As depicted in the Figure 2 (a), this entails one AB to deliver the lease request, plus one URB for delivering the lease granted messages, yielding a total latency of 5 communication steps. Including the final URB for the dissemination of the transactions' writeset, we get 7 communication steps latency.

Two optimizations can be employed to reduce to just 3 communication steps latency the cost required for both committing a transaction and acquiring the corresponding lease. The first optimization, reported in Algorithm 4 and depicted in Figure 2 (b), consists in exploiting the *Opt-deliver* of the lease request (which incurs in a single communication step latency [22]) to immediately trigger the relinquishment of the required leases at a remote node (and the corresponding URB of a LeaseFreed message). This is safe since, even in the case of mismatches between the optimistic and the final delivery of two conflicting lease requests at some node p_i, the net effect would be anyway to trigger the relinquishment of the leases currently owned by p_i. This allows to totally overlap the execution of

---

[1] The only exception being AB protocols such as [34] which, relying on additional system assumptions - such as the existence of a bound Δ on the minimum inter-arrival time of messages at the replicas, achieve a latency of to $2+\Delta$ communication steps.

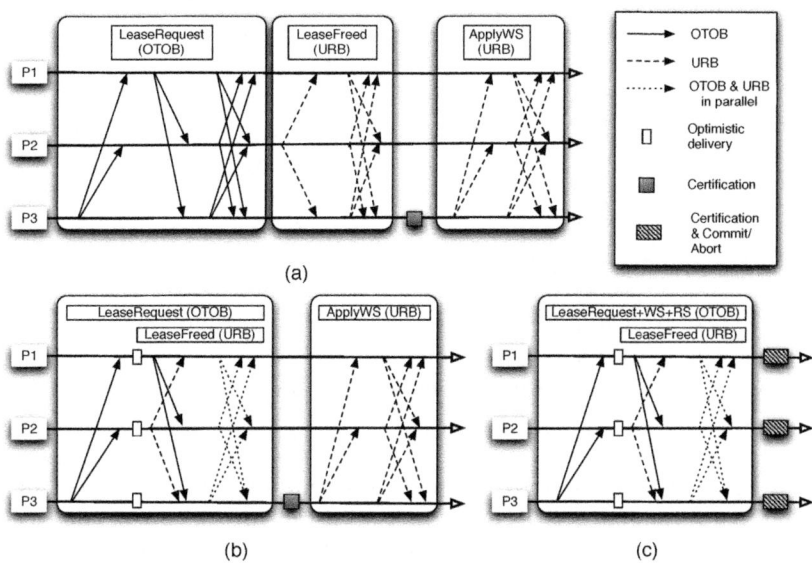

Fig. 2. Message pattern for (a) the baseline ALC protocol, (b) the optimization exploiting optimistic deliveries to free the leases, and (c) the optimization that piggybacks the readset and writeset on the LeaseRequest message (P3 requesting a lease owned by P2)

the OAB for the lease request and the URB for the lease granted, reducing to three communication steps the latency of the lease acquisition phase.

The second optimization consists in OA-broadcasting the set of data items accessed by a transaction T while issuing a lease request, rather than the corresponding conflict classes. This would allow each replica to validate T as soon as the corresponding lease request gets locally established, thus avoiding the *URB* of the transaction's writeset and reducing the latency for committing T to three communication steps (see Figure 2 (c)).

5 Performance Evaluation

In this section we report the results of an experimental study aimed at quantifying the performance gains achievable by the proposed ALC protocol with respect to state of the art transactional replication schemes. We use, as baseline, an atomic broadcast based certification scheme, such as the one in [31], which we refer to as CERT. More specifically, we use D^2STM [11] since it is the only fully replicated STM that uses a certification based scheme that we are aware of. Analogously to ALC, CERT allows replicas to process transactions locally, avoiding any form of synchronization during transaction execution. This protocol permits to achieve better scalability than pessimistic approaches [22] that

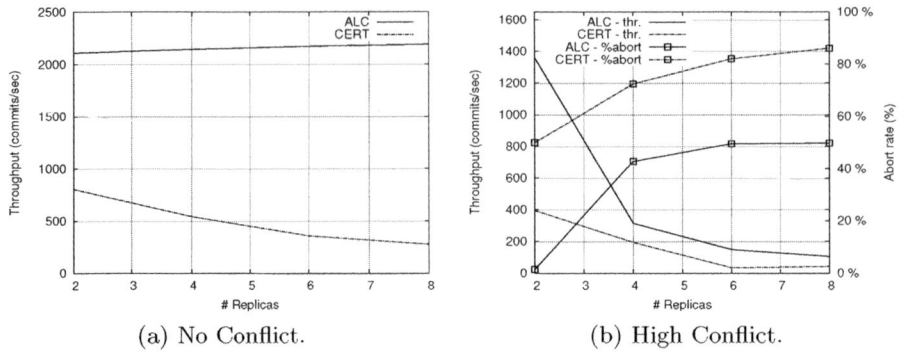

(a) No Conflict. (b) High Conflict.

Fig. 3. Bank Benchmark

force all replicas to process every update transactions, does not rely on a-priori knowledge on transactions' data access patterns and requires a single atomic broadcast to disseminate the readset and writeset of a certifying transaction.

Concerning ALC, we implemented all the optimizations described in Section 4.5. In order to prevent the possibility of incurring in deadlocks in the presence of transactions altering their data access pattern during transaction execution, we implemented the simplest deadlock avoidance scheme among those previously described in Section 4.4: we piggyback a *LeaseFreed* message to the lease request message OA-broadcast during the commit phase of the re-started transaction if the set of conflict classes accessed is not a subset of those accessed during its former execution. All the results reported in the following were obtained by setting the conflict class granularity to coincide with a single data item. We deployed the prototypes of ALC and CERT[2] on a cluster of 8 nodes, each one equipped with an Intel QuadCore Q6600 at 2.40GHz, 8 GB of RAM, running Linux 2.6.27.7 and interconnected via a private Gigabit Ethernet.

We start by considering a synthetic workload (obtained by adapting the Bank Benchmark originally used in [19]) which serves for the purpose of quantifying the performance of the ALC scheme in two extreme scenarios for what concerns conflicts. In detail, we initialize the STM at each replica with an array of *numMachines*·2 items. In the first scenario, each machine reads and updates a distinct fragment of the array, thus never generating conflicts. In the second scenario, all the machines read and update the same data items, thus always conflicting.

Figure 3 shows the throughput (committed transactions per second) and the abort rate as the number of nodes in the system varies. In the scenario with no conflicts (Figure 3(a)), when using ALC, replicas disseminate transactions exclusively via URB (after establishing the lease upon their first transaction). This allows ALC to achieve a throughput from 3 to 10 times higher than CERT, which, requiring one OAB per committed transaction, puts a significantly higher

---

[2] Both prototypes are implemented in Java and are publicly available at the url: http://aristos.gsd.inesc-id.pt

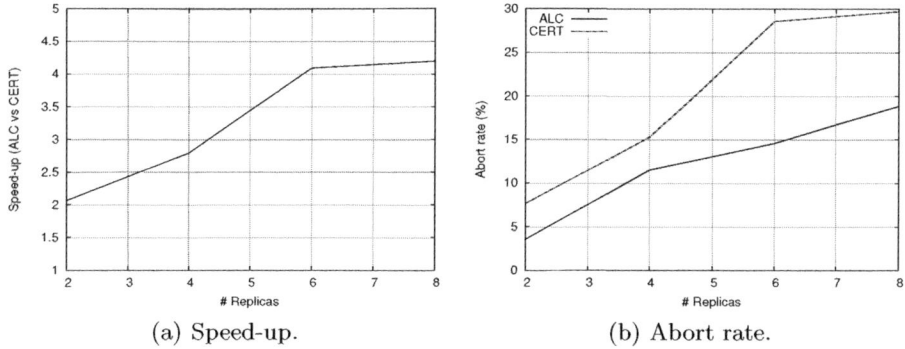

(a) Speed-up. (b) Abort rate.

Fig. 4. Lee Benchmark

load on the GCS (which represents the bottleneck in this benchmark, being the transaction's logic extremely lightweight) especially as the number of replicas increase. The high conflict scenario (Figure 3(b)) represents a worst case scenario for ALC, since leases are constantly rotated across the replicas, and a lease request must be OA-broadcast for each transaction that commits. Nevertheless, ALC's throughput is on average 3 times higher with respect to CERT. This can be explained by observing that, with CERT, the percentage of transactions that abort is significantly larger than with ALC. In the 8 replicas' scenario, for instance, transactions are re-executed on average around 10 times before committing with CERT. On the other hand, ALC ensures that a transaction can be aborted at most once, as also proved by the fact that the abort rate for ALC never grows larger than 50% independently of the degree of concurrency.

We now consider a complex benchmark, namely Lee-TM [2], which is a parallel, STM-based implementation of the Lee algorithm for routing junctions in a circuit. The Lee-TM generates a very heterogeneous workload encompassing a wide range of transactions' duration and length. More in detail, the benchmark starts by routing the shortest junctions in the circuit - generating transactions whose local processing lasts just a few msecs - and then progressively lays junctions of increasing length - generating transactions whose local processing lasts up to a few seconds. Additionally, in Lee-TM, multiple re-runs of a transaction have a non-negligible probability of accessing different data-sets, permitting to evaluate the performance of the ALC's deadlock avoidance mechanisms proposed in Section 4.4. Figure 4(a) reports the speed-up achieved by ALC with respect to CERT computed considering the time required to route the whole set of junctions of the mainboard circuit [2] when using the two protocols. Also in this case, the performance gains achieved by ALC are clear, ranging from around 2x to more than 4x and growing along with the number of replicas in the system. Being the inter-transaction data locality of this benchmark pretty low (i.e. the likelihood to re-use a previously acquired leases when running two different transactions on a same replica was found to be less than 10%), the reason underlying the performance boost achievable by ALC is mainly imputable to its ability to reduce the transaction abort rate (see Figure 4(b)), and, in particular, to shelter long-running transactions from repeated aborts. Despite the lack of deterministic guarantees on the immutability of the data accessed during transactions' re-runs, in fact, ALC guaranteed to execute transactions at-most once in the 98% of the cases. On the other hand, with CERT, long running transactions are very likely to be aborted tens of times before being successfully committed, causing a huge waste of computing resources.

6 Conclusions and Future Work

In this paper we have introduced ALC, a novel STM replication scheme that relies on the notion of asynchronous lease to boost the performance of existing AB-based transaction certification schemes. We have integrated ALC within a middleware that allows STM applications to transparently leverage the computational resources available in commodity clusters and shown the significant performance benefits achievable by ALC (up to 10x reduction of the commit phase latency in low conflict scenarios, and up to 4x speed-ups in high conflict scenarios) via a fully fledged, publicly available prototype.

This work opens several interesting research perspectives that we intend to pursue in our future work. In particular, it would be interesting to identify techniques capable of effectively minimizing the frequency of rotation of leases among the replicas, so to maximize the performance gains achievable through the use of ALC. These include locality aware load balancing strategies, as well as mechanisms capable of adaptively adjusting the lease rotation mechanism based on the actual replicas' (spatial/temporal) locality of reference.

References

1. Aguilera, M.K., Merchant, A., Shah, M., Veitch, A., Karamanolis, C.: Sinfonia: a new paradigm for building scalable distributed systems. In: Proc. of the 21st ACM SIGOPS Symposium on Operating Systems Principles, pp. 159–174. ACM, New York (2007)
2. Ansari, M., Kotselidis, C., Watson, I., Kirkham, C.C., Lujin, M., Jarvis, K.: Lee-tm: A non-trivial benchmark suite for transactional memory. In: Bourgeois, A.G., Zheng, S.Q. (eds.) ICA3PP 2008. LNCS, vol. 5022, pp. 196–207. Springer, Heidelberg (2008)
3. Bartoli, A., Babaoglu, O.: Selecting a "primary partition" in partitionable asynchronous distributed systems. In: IEEE Symp. on Reliable Dist. Systems, p. 138 (1997)
4. Bernstein, P.A., Hadzilacos, V., Goodman, N.: Concurrency Control and Recovery in Database Systems. Addison-Wesley, Reading (1987)
5. Bocchino, R.L., Adve, V.S., Chamberlain, B.L.: Software transactional memory for large scale clusters. In: Proc. of the Symposium on Principles and Practice of Parallel Programming (PPOPP), pp. 247–258. ACM, New York (2008)
6. Boichat, R., Dutta, P., Guerraoui, R.: Asynchronous leasing. In: Proc. of the The International Workshop on Object-Oriented Real-Time Dependable Systems, p. 180. IEEE Computer Society, Washington (2002)

7. Cachopo, J.: Development of Rich Domain Models with Atomic Actions. Ph.D. thesis, Technical University of Lisbon (2007)
8. Cachopo, J., Rito-Silva, A.: Versioned boxes as the basis for memory transactions. Sci. Comput. Program. 63(2), 172–185 (2006)
9. Cecchet, E., Marguerite, J., Zwaenepole, W.: C-JDBC: flexible database clustering middleware. In: Proc. of the USENIX Annual Technical Conference, p. 26. USENIX Association (2004)
10. Chockler, G.V., Keidar, I., Vitenberg, R.: Group communication specifications: a comprehensive study. ACM Comput. Surv. 33(4), 427–469 (2001)
11. Couceiro, M., Romano, P., Carvalho, N., Rodrigues, L.: D^2STM: Dependable Distributed Software Transactional Memory. In: Proc. of the 15th Pacific Rim Int. Symposium on Dependable Computing, PRDC (2009)
12. Defago, X., Schiper, A., Urban, P.: Total order broadcast and multicast algorithms: Taxonomy and survey. ACM Computing Surveys 36(4), 372–421 (2004)
13. Duvvuri, V., Shenoy, P., Tewari, R.: Adaptive leases: A strong consistency mechanism for the world wide web. IEEE Transactions on Knowledge and Data Engineering 15(5), 1266–1276 (2003)
14. Gray, C., Cheriton, D.: Leases: an efficient fault-tolerant mechanism for distributed file cache consistency. In: Proc. of the Symposium on Operating Systems Principles (SOSP), pp. 202–210. ACM, New York (1989)
15. Gray, J., Helland, P., O'Neil, P., Shasha, D.: The dangers of replication and a solution. In: Proc. of the Conference on the Management of Data (SIGMOD), pp. 173–182. ACM, New York (1996)
16. Guerraoui, R., Kapalka, M.: On the correctness of transactional memory. In: PPoPP 2008: Proceedings of the 13th ACM SIGPLAN Symposium on Principles and Practice of Parallel Programming, pp. 175–184. ACM, New York (2008)
17. Guerraoui, R., Kapalka, M., Vitek, J.: STMBench7: a benchmark for software transactional memory. SIGOPS Oper. Syst. Rev. 41(3), 315–324 (2007)
18. Guerraoui, R., Rodrigues, L.: Introduction to Reliable Distributed Programming. Springer, Heidelberg (2006)
19. Herlihy, M., Luchangco, V., Moir, M.: A flexible framework for implementing software transactional memory. SIGPLAN Not. 41(10), 253–262 (2006)
20. Jiménez-Peris, R., Patiño-Martínez, M., Alonso, G.: Non-intrusive, parallel recovery of replicated data. In: Proc. of the 21st IEEE Symp. on Reliable Distributed Systems (SRDS), p. 150. IEEE Computer Society, Washington (2002)
21. Keleher, P., Cox, A.L., Zwaenepoel, W.: Lazy release consistency for software distributed shared memory. In: Proceedings of the 19th Int. Symp. on Computer Architecture (ISCA), pp. 13–21. ACM, New York (1992)
22. Kemme, B., Pedone, F., Alonso, G., Schiper, A.: Processing transactions over optimistic atomic broadcast protocols. In: Proc. of the 19th IEEE International Conference on Distributed Computing Systems, p. 424. IEEE Computer Society, Los Alamitos (1999)
23. Kemme, B., Alonso, G.: A suite of database replication protocols based on group communication primitives. In: Proc. of the International Conference on Distributed Computing Systems (ICDCS), p. 156. IEEE Computer Society, Los Alamitos (1998)
24. Kotselidis, C., Ansari, M., Jarvis, K., Lujan, M., Kirkham, C., Watson, I.: DiSTM: A software transactional memory framework for clusters. In: Proc. of the International Conference on Parallel Processing (ICPP), pp. 51–58 (2008)
25. Lamport, L.: Time, clocks, and the ordering of events in a distributed system. ACM Commun. 21(7), 558–565 (1978)

26. Li, K., Hudak, P.: Memory coherence in shared virtual memory systems. In: Proc. of the Symp. on Principles of Distributed Computing, pp. 229–239. ACM, New York (1986)
27. Manassiev, K., Mihailescu, M., Amza, C.: Exploiting distributed version concurrency in a transactional memory cluster. In: Proc. of the Symposium on Principles and Practice of Parallel Programming (PPOPP), pp. 198–208. ACM, New York (2006)
28. Martin, M., Blundell, C., Lewis, E.: Subtleties of transactional memory atomicity semantics. IEEE Comput. Archit. Lett. 5(2), 17 (2006)
29. Miranda, H., Pinto, A., Rodrigues, L.: Appia, a flexible protocol kernel supporting multiple coordinated channels. In: Proc. International Conference on Distributed Computing Systems (ICDCS), pp. 707–710. IEEE, Los Alamitos (2001)
30. Patino-Martínez, M., Jiménez-Peris, R., Kemme, B., Alonso, G.: Scalable replication in database clusters. In: Herlihy, M.P. (ed.) DISC 2000. LNCS, vol. 1914, pp. 315–329. Springer, Heidelberg (2000)
31. Pedone, F., Guerraoui, R., Schiper, A.: The database state machine approach. Distributed and Parallel Databases 14(1), 71–98 (2003)
32. Romano, P., Carvalho, N., Rodrigues, L.: Towards distributed software transactional memory systems. In: Proc. of the Workshop on Large-Scale Distributed Systems and Middleware, LADIS (2008)
33. Romano, P., Carvalho, N.M.R., Couceiro, M., Rodrigues, L., Cachopo, J.: Towards the integration of distributed transactional memories in application servers' clusters. In: The 3rd Int. Workshop on Advanced Architectures and Algorithms for Internet DElivery and Applications, ICST. Springer, Las Palmas (2009)
34. Vicente, P., Rodrigues, L.: An indulgent uniform total order algorithm with optimistic delivery. In: Proc. of the Symposium on Reliable Distributed Systems (SRDS), pp. 92–101 (2002)

Author Index

Anderson, Paul   212

Bacon, Jean   293, 334
Balmin, Andrey   1
Bertier, Marin   191
Bhagwan, Ranjita   85
Birman, Ken   148
Bissyandé, Tegawendé F.   273
Blackburn, Jeremy   212
Borcea, Cristian   212
Bromberg, Yérom-David   273

Carvalho, Nuno   376
Chaitanya, Shiva   107
Chandra, Ranveer   252
Chaudhary, Amitabh   64

Dasgupta, Gargi   42
Dash, Alokika   355
Demsky, Brian   355
De, Pradipta   42

Eugster, Patrick   128
Evans, David   293
Eyers, David M.   293, 334

Finnis, Joshua   212
Freedman, Daniel A.   148
Frey, Davide   191

Gokhale, Aniruddha   21
Guerraoui, Rachid   191, 313

Hildrum, Kirsten   1
Hoffert, Joe   21
Huang, Qi   148
Huguenin, Kévin   313

Iamnitchi, Adriana   212

Jayalath, Chamikara   128
Jayaram, K.R.   128

Kermarrec, Anne-Marie   191, 313
Khandekar, Rohit   1

Kim, Kyungbaek   169
Kjærgaard, Mikkel B.   232
Kompella, Ramana Rao   252
Kothari, Ravi   42
Kourtellis, Nicolas   212
Kumar, Vibhore   1

Langdal, Jakob   232
Lawall, Julia L.   273
Leroy, Vincent   191
Little, Philip   64

Malik, Tanu   64
Mann, Vijay   42
Mehrotra, Sharad   169
Migliavacca, Matteo   293, 334
Monod, Maxime   313
Muller, Gilles   273

Nayak, Tapan   42

Padmanabhan, Venkata N.   85
Papagiannis, Ioannis   334
Parekh, Sujay   1
Peng, Bo   148
Pietzuch, Peter   293, 334
Prakash, Pawan   252
Prusty, Swagatika   313
Purohit, Amit   42
Puttaswamy, Krishna P.N.   85

Rajan, Deepak   1
Ramasubramanian, Venugopalan   252
Réveillère, Laurent   273
Rodrigues, Luís   376
Romano, Paolo   376

Schmidt, Douglas C.   21
Schougaard, Kari R.   232
Shand, Brian   293, 334
Sivasubramaniam, Anand   107

Thakar, Ani   64
Toftkjær, Thomas   232

Urgaonkar, Bhuvan 107

Venkatasubramanian, Nalini 169
Verma, Akshat 42
Vigfusson, Ymir 148

Vijayakumar, Dharani 107

Wang, Xiaodan 64
Wolf, Joel 1
Wu, Kun-Lung 1

GPSR Compliance

The European Union's (EU) General Product Safety Regulation (GPSR) is a set of rules that requires consumer products to be safe and our obligations to ensure this.

If you have any concerns about our products, you can contact us on ProductSafety@springernature.com

In case Publisher is established outside the EU, the EU authorized representative is:

Springer Nature Customer Service Center GmbH
Europaplatz 3
69115 Heidelberg, Germany

Batch number: 09478804

Printed by Printforce, the Netherlands